Temples with Multiple Garbhagṛhas

An Iconographic Consideration of Selected Indian Monuments

Cataloging in Publication Data — DK

[Courtesy: D.K. Agencies (P) Ltd. docinfo@dkagencies.com]

Bunce, Fredrick W.

Temples with multiple garbhagrhas : an iconographic consideration of selected Indian monuments / Fredrick W. Bunce.

p. cm.

Includes bibliographical references (p. [illegible])

ISBN 13: 9788124607251

1. Hindu shrines — India. 2. Hindu temples — India — Designs and plans. I. Title.

DDC 726.1450954 23

Temples with Multiple Garbhagṛhas

An Iconographic Consideration of Selected Indian Monuments

Fredrick W. Bunce

DK PRINTWORLD
Publishers of Indian Traditions

Cataloging in Publication Data — DK

[Courtesy: D.K. Agencies (P) Ltd. <docinfo@dkagencies.com>]

Bunce, Fredrick W.

Temples with multiple garbhagr̥has : an iconographic consideration of selected Indian monuments / Fredrick W. Bunce.

p. cm.

Includes bibliographical references (p.).

ISBN 13: 9788124607251

1. Hindu shrines — India. 2. Hindu temples — India — Designs and plans. I. Title.

DDC 726.1450954 23

ISBN 13: 978-81-246-0725-1 **ISBN** 10: 81-246-0725-7

First published in India, 2014

Printed and published by:
D.K. Printworld (P) Ltd.
Regd. office : *"Vedaśrī,"* F-395, Sudarshan Park
(Metro Station: Ramesh Nagar)
New Delhi - 110 015
Phones : (011) 2545 3975, 2546 6019; *Fax* : (011) 2546 5926
e-mail : indology@dkprintworld.com
Web : www.dkprintworld.com

Preface

A NUMBER of years ago my interest in iconography began to focus on plans, specifically plans of the temples of India and the Indianized states. Over a period of time, I encountered temples which had more than one shrine or *garbhagṛha*. I was first attracted to the Paya-Thon-Zu in Pagan, Burma, and then found a number of others.

Recently, I became aware that there were few studies, if any, that focused on temples with multiple *garbhagṛha*s, so I undertook to gather together as many plans as possible revolving around this type of temple. I was able to identify well over one-hundred temples labelled as: *dvikūṭa, trikūṭa, catuṣkūṭa, pañcakūṭa, navakūṭa* and *cauṅsaṭh* temples. Yet, there was a surprising dearth of plans published.

The majority of my endeavours revolve around the consideration of published plans. Many plans display a small component, a multi-sanctum shrine as a part of a larger complex. In this case, the redrawing of the plan — i.e. employing PageMaker 6.0 — posed some problems, particularly in the indication of specific details of the plan. Indeed, some studies even feature temples or shrines with multiple *garbhagṛha*s which are clear, and to scale.[1] Most of the sources were exact. There were, unfortunately, exceptions.[2]

The two studies of Suresh presented scores of plans and attendant descriptions. In this sense, these studies were a veritable gold mine of plans with multiple *garbhagṛha*s, even though there were obvious errors. The descriptions were thorough and were greatly appreciated, however, there were numerous errors throughout. These were noted in the footnotes of this consideration. More importantly, the sections displaying the various plans presented a number of plans which simply did not follow the descriptions, or vice versa. They were not to scale! For example the description of the Durgā Temple, KMS, p. 55, states "The *garbhagṛha* is square . . . ." However, the plan of that temple found on p. 139, indicates a clearly rectangular *garbhagṛha*, approximately 1:1.5, and columns of the *sabhā-maṇḍapa* that are also rectangular. Immediately, I realized that the plans and elevations that Suresh had provided the publisher had been "widened" or distorted, obviously to conform

---

1 The reprint editions of Henry Cousens, *The Chalukyan Architecture of the Kanarese Districts* (Archaeological Survey of India, vol. XLII, Imperial Series), repr., New Delhi: 1996 (1926); and *Bijapur and Its Archaitectural Remains: With an Historical Outline of the 'Adil Shahi Dynasty* (Archaeological Survey of India, vol. XXXVIII, Imperial Series), repr., Delhi: 1996 (1916) both exhibit clear, to scale plans.

2 The two studies of K.M. Suresh (KMS), *Temples of Hampī and Its Environs*, Delhi: 2003; and K.M. Suresh (KMS II), *Temples of Karnataka: Ground Plans and Elevations*, 2 vols., Delhi: 2003.

more readily to the format of the page. This strange protraction of the height and elongation of the width appears on nearly everyone of the pages 135-74. One particularly odd, even amusing plan is found on p. 150, KMS, in which the "Bala Krishna temple complex" is "squashed" down to two-thirds of its normal east–west configuration. The same holds true in KMS II. The plans on pages 321-490, of the second volume, are also distorted in the same manner. If it weren't for the thorough descriptions, the redrawing of the plans would have been impossible with any accuracy. For two such important books, this is an inexcusable error! With reference to the latter, every effort was made to translate these mutated plans to ones which were to scale, considering the obstacle. Any deviation herein from the scale of the original plans of these temples was unavoidable and any ensuing, inadvertent errors are admitted by this researcher.

Therefore, this consideration concentrates on temples which exhibit either *dvikūṭa*, or *trikūṭa*, or *catuṣkūṭa*, or *pañcakūṭa*, or *navakūṭa*, or *cauṅsaṭh* types of plans.

Selected temples are considered in detail — i.e. their historical milieu, their iconography and the application of *maṇḍala*(s) to the plan(s) are provided. In addition, there also appears those multiple *garbhagṛha* temples which are initially found to be flawed in both KMS and KMS II. They are included with a brief description, but their *raison d'être* is to provide a relatively precise scale rendering of those temples and in a size and format commensurate with their importance.

It is hoped that the representation of these mutated plans in proper scale will be of benefit.

Fredrick W. Bunce

Contents

Contents (Continued)

Contents (Continued)

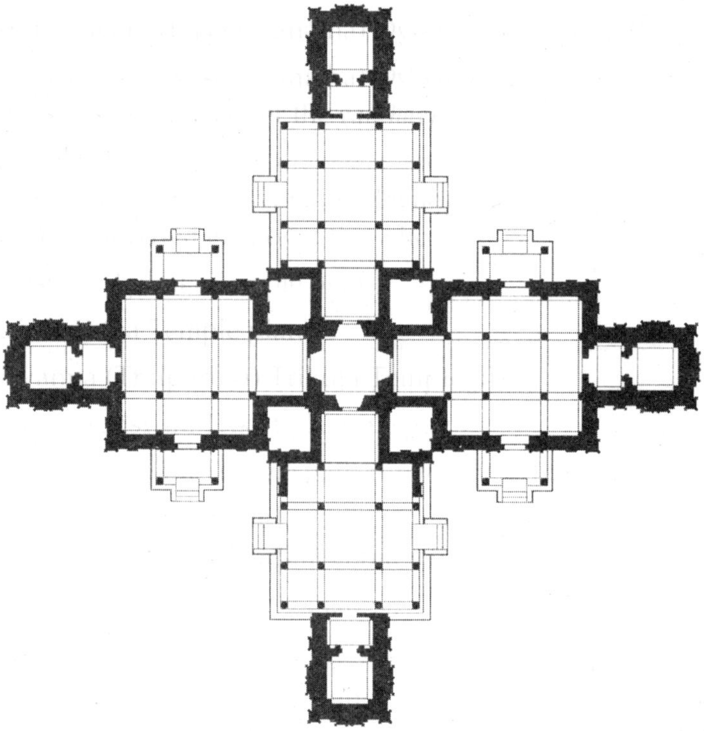

List of Plates

List of Plates (Continued)

List of Plates (Continued)

List of Plates (Continued)

List of Plates (Continued)

Appendix C

List of Figures

List of Figures (Continued)

Figure **Page**

List of Figures (Continued)

Conclusions and Observations

Abbreviations

The following are identifying initial abbreviations which appear within the text, and/or within the "Notes". Full bibliographic information is to be found in the Bibliography.

AB	Alice Boner and Sadasiva Rathsarma, *Śilpa Prakāśa: Medieval Orissan Sanskrit Text on Temple Architecture.*
AD	Anna Dallapiccola et al., *The Rāmacandra Temple at Vijayanagara.*
AK	Amar Nath Khanna, *Archaeology of India.*
CT	Christopher Tadgell, *The History of Architecture in India.*
DD	Devangana Desai, *Khajuraho: Monumental Legacy.*
FWB	Fredrick W. Bunce, *Monuments of India and the Indianized States.*
FWB II	Fredrick W. Bunce, *Numbers: Their Iconographic Consideration in Buddhist and Hindu Practices.*
FWB III	Fredrick W. Bunce, *The Iconography of Plans: A Study of the Influence of Buddhism and Hinduism on Architectural Plans of South and Southeast Asia.*
FWB IV	Fredrick W. Bunce, *An Encyclopaedia of Hindu Deities, Demi-Gods, Godlings, Demons and Heroes: With Special Focus on Iconographic Attributes.*
GF	Gerard Foekema, *A Complete Guide to Hoysala Temples.*
HC	Henry Cousens, *The Chalukyan Architecture of the Kanarese Districts.*
HC II	Henry Cousens, *Bijapur and Its Architectural Remains: With an Extensive Outline of the 'Adil Shahi Dynasty.*
HS	Henri Stierlin, ed., *Architecture of the World: India.*
HS II	Henri Stierlin, *Hindu India: From Khajuraho to the Temple City of Madurai.*
HSa	H. Sarkar, *An Architectural Survey of the Temples of Kerala.*
JF	J.M. Fritz, G. Michell et al., *New Light on Hampī: Recent Research at Vijayanagara.*
KD	Krishna Deva, *Temples of India*, 2 vols.
KMS	K.M. Suresh, *Temples of Hampī and Its Environs.*
KMS II	K.M. Suresh, *Temples of Karnataka: Ground Plans and Elevations*, 2 vols.
SG	Satish Grover, *Masterpieces of Traditional Indian Architecture.*
SK	Stella Kramrisch, *The Hindu Temple.*

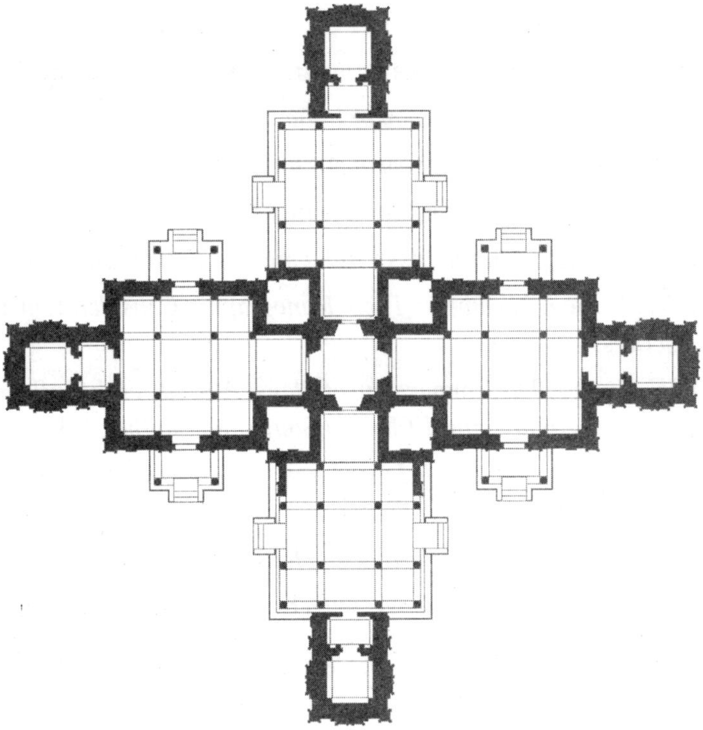

Introduction

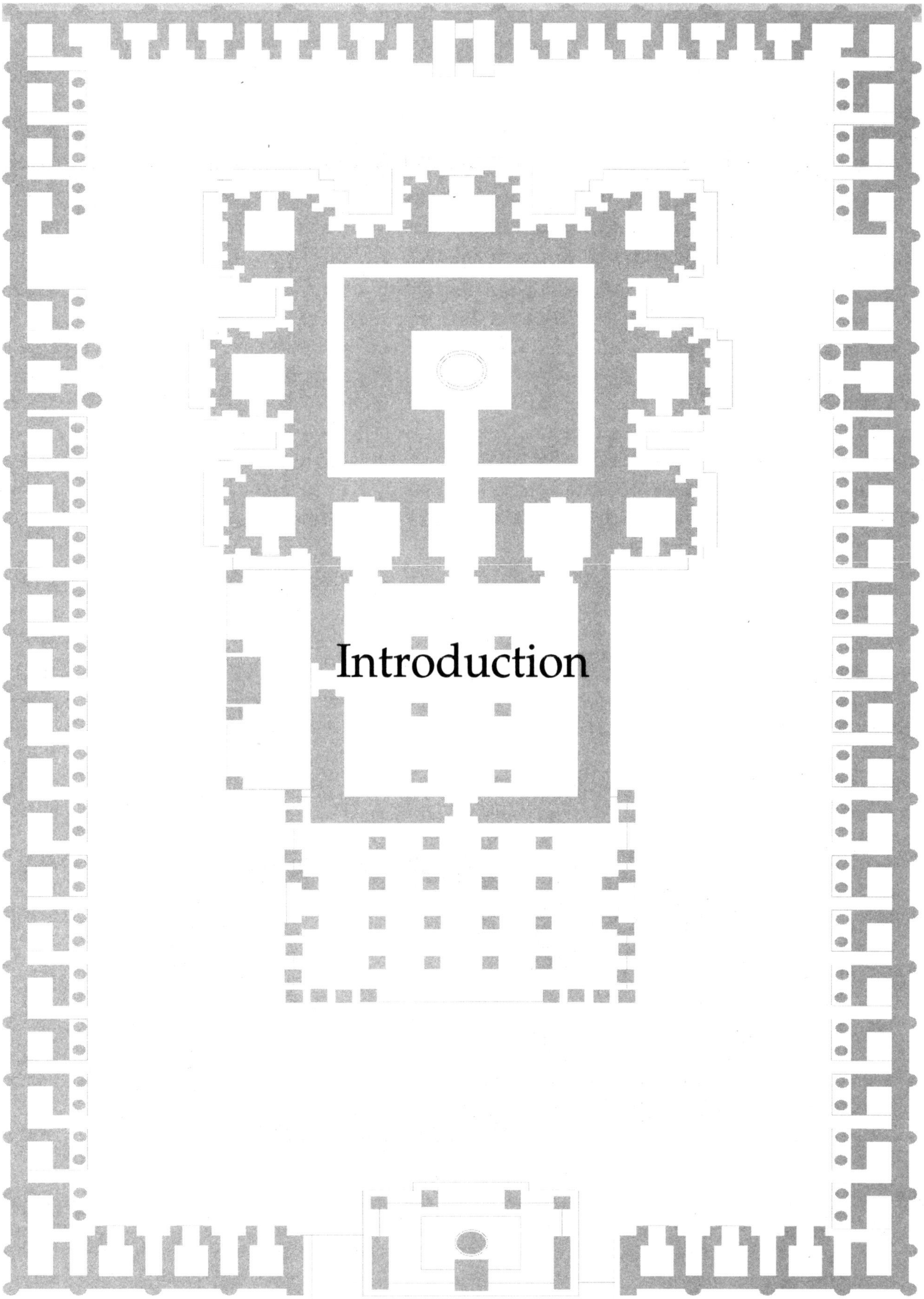

Introduction

THE Roman statesman Marcus Vispanius Agrippa had assumed the cost of building a temple called the Pantheon on the site where the present structure of the same name stands. It was destroyed by fire in CE 80. Forty-five years later the Emperor Publius Aelius Traianus Hadrianus[1] (r. CE 117-38) raised the present monument and retained the name Pantheon.

The Pantheon represents a type of ecumenism that was practised by the Roman State at that period. So as not to offend any of the major deities commonly worshipped at the time, it was dedicated to seven major Roman deities — i.e. the seven planets: Saturn, Jupiter, Mars, Venus, Mercury, Diana (moon) and Apollo (sun). Their shrines were so placed as none had pride of place (**Appendix A, Plate 67**). Although, one might feel that the shrine opposite the entrance would assume major importance. The modern major religions — i.e. Christianity and Islam — were not faced with this dilemma since they were essentially monotheistic. Yet, the Christians flirted with the circular form on more than one occasion (**Appendix A, Plates 68, 70**) and not always with great success as tradition always placed the altar in the east. The Pantheon was, by virtue of its polytheistic character, a more successful solution, at least to the circle.

Whether *vimāna*[2] or *prāsāda* or *stūpa* or *vihāra*, Buddhists, Hindus and Jainas raised monuments to the deities. They were constructed to acknowledge the deity. They were constructed to enshrine images of the deity. They were constructed so that the devotees might honour and worship the deity.

Compared to the numerous Roman deities, the Hindu pantheon is vast! This enormous array of divinities is spread over three major sects — i.e. Vaiṣṇava, Śaiva and Śākta. They are essentially disparate entities with little common ground other than they fall under the umbrella known as Hinduism and derive from Vedic beliefs. Whether Vaiṣṇava, Śaiva or Śākta, the vast majority of Indian Hindu temples are exclusively dedicated to a single deity with a solitary sanctum (*garbhagṛha*) — i.e. *ekakūṭa* (**Figure 1**). Even the trinity — lords Brahmā, Viṣṇu and Śiva — are more often than not worshipped as separate

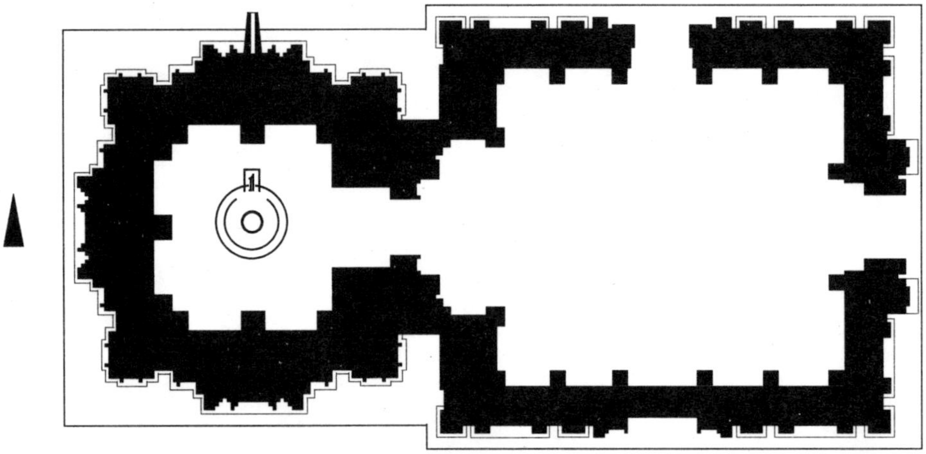

Figure 1: Śiśireśvara Temple, Bhubaneswar

1 The Emperor Hadrianus is among the "Five Good Emperors" of the Nervan-Antonian Dynasty and distantly related to his predecessor, the Emperor Marcus Ulpius Nerva Traianus (Trajan). After the disastrous Julio-Claudian Dynasty, Rome saw a series of able administrators/emperors. Hadrianus was not the least of these.

2 Herein, the term *vimāna* will be employed as it applies to the structure which surrounds the *garbhagṛha* and the *pradakṣiṇāpatha*.

entities within their own temples. The forms (*mūrti*) of Lord Śiva, the *avatāra* of the Lord Viṣṇu or the forms of the lady Devī are frequently worshipped within numerous single sanctum temples. The standard is a temple that often consists of a *garbhagṛha*, *antarāla* and *maṇḍapa*. Jainá temples tend to vary somewhat from the Hindu standard, but their relationship to the Hindu faith is apparent. Within the Brāhmanic faith, the design of a temple, the construction of a temple that might serve a number of deities on an essentially equal basis is anathema even within the individual sects. Yet there are a number of temples which display more than one sanctum where the cultic image is enshrined.

But, early in the development of Hindu temple architecture there appears the *pañcāyatana* plan, a complex in which the central temple is surrounded by four other shrines, frequently at the intercardinal point of the compass (**Appendix A, Plate 71**). Both the Dasāvathara Temple (Gupta Temple) at Deogaṛh and the Avantisvāmi Temple of Avantipur indicate a quincunx (**Figure 5B**) arrangement. However, the quincunx arrangement clearly separates the four cardinal point shrines, *en plan*, from the central shrine (**Appendix A, Plates 72-73**). The Indianized Khmer state at Angkor conceived of a quincunx in which the main difference was that the central shrine was raised higher than the other four (**Appendix A, Plates 74-75**). The traditional Indian *pañcāyatana* plan develops in such a way that the central shrine is clearly larger than the diminutive intercardinal shrines (**Appendix A, Plates 76-78**).

The Buddhists wrestled with the concept of equals amongst many, particularly the *pañca-buddha*s — i.e. the Buddha Akṣobhya, Buddha Amitābha, Buddha Amoghasiddhi, Buddha Ratnasambhava and Buddha Vairocana. It was solved in the unique *stūpa dhamma-yazika* at Pagan in a most novel manner and to a lesser degree in the Pentagonal Temple (Pañca-Buddhas) also of Pagan (**Appendix A, Plates 79-80**). In these two monuments the central position is implied and remains the realm of The Absolute, the Ādi-Buddha — i.e. in the case of *stūpa,* it is the soaring spire and in the Pentagonal Temple (Pañca-Buddhas) *śikhara.*

Although, as noted above, in the Hindu faith there was no elemental theological need or requirement to present a number of the pantheon on an equal footing. All deities were manifestations of Brahmā–Sarasvatī or Viṣṇu–Lakṣmī or Śiva–Pārvatī and they were manifestations of the Absolute One, *Brahman.*[3] The *trimūrti* of Hinduism did not suffer the same interpretational or presentational problems as the Christian Trinity!

Multiple Sanctums

Dvikūṭa: However, there were instances in which temples were constructed in which two sanctuaries, two sanctums, two *garbhagṛha*s are to be found — i.e. a *dvikūṭa* temple. The simplest solution would seem to be to place the two *garbhagṛha*s on the same axis (**Figure 2A**). This particular resolution is encountered in a number of temples and although the temple is named for one deity, two are honoured — e.g. the Kallappa-Mallappa (Harihara) Dvikūṭa Temple at Devaragennur (**Plate 15**). Herein, this will be identified as an **A**-type *dvikūṭa* temple. A second solution is seen in which the second *garbhagṛha* is not placed on the same axis, but on an axis that is 90°, perpendicular axis (**Figure 2B**). This solution to the *dvikūṭa* temple is seen in the Dvikūṭa Shrine of the Rāmacandra Temple Complex at Vijayanagara

[3] *Brahman* is neuter and not the same as the Lord Brahmā, who is masculine.

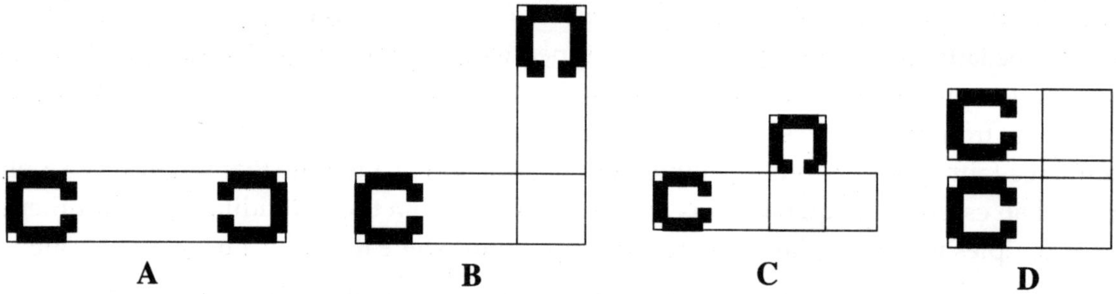

Figure 2: Arrangement of a *dvikūṭa* temple

(**Plate 54**). Herein, this will be identified as a **B**-type *dvikūṭa* temple. The **B**-type solution presents a temple that is essentially asymmetrical. Symmetry was not an absolute requirement for either the Buddhists or the Hindus. But, generally speaking, it was a design element that was highly sought and desired. There were a number of requirements that dealt with alignment of a temple to a point of the compass.[4] These considerations may have entered into the asymmetrical alignment shown in **Figure 2B**. Further, there may be inferred a "pride-of-place" in either alignment. Generally, alignment towards the west is preferred, but not an absolute requirement, and alignment towards the north is preferred to the south. A third variation is the **C**-type which is also asymmetrical and is related to the **B**-type except the secondary *garbhagṛha* does not possess an *antarāla* (**Figure 2C**). The last of the *dvikūṭa* temple types is the **D**-type seen when two *garbhagṛhas* are set side by side often sharing a common *maṇḍapa*. This solution to the *dvikūṭa* temple may be seen in the Śaiva Dvikūṭa Temple at Chaudaḍampur (**Plate 12**). Herein, this will be identified as a **D**-type *dvikūṭa* temple (**Figure 2D**).

Trikūṭa: When a third sanctum — i.e. a *trikūṭa* temple — enters the equation, three solutions appear inevitable — i.e. one in which two *garbhagṛhas* are at right angles to the third and generally equidistant from the crossing (**Figure 3A**). Herein, this will be identified as an **A**-type *trikūṭa* temple. The Kedāreśvara Trikūṭa Temple (**Plate 23**) of Balagamve is representative of this — i.e. an **A**-type *trikūṭa* temple. There are a number of temples, particularly in the south, in which this solution is put into practice with pleasing results. A second variation is the **B**-type which is related to the **A**-type except the secondary *garbhagṛhas* do not possess an *antarāla* (**Figure 3B**). The third solution is similar to the **A**-type — i.e. two sanctums are on the same axis and the third is 90° to that axis and not equidistant to the crossing (**Figure 3C**). Herein, this will be identified as a **C**-type *trikūṭa* temple. An example of the **C**-type *trikūṭa* temple is encountered in the Trikūṭeśvara Temple at Gaḍag (**Plate 20**). And, the

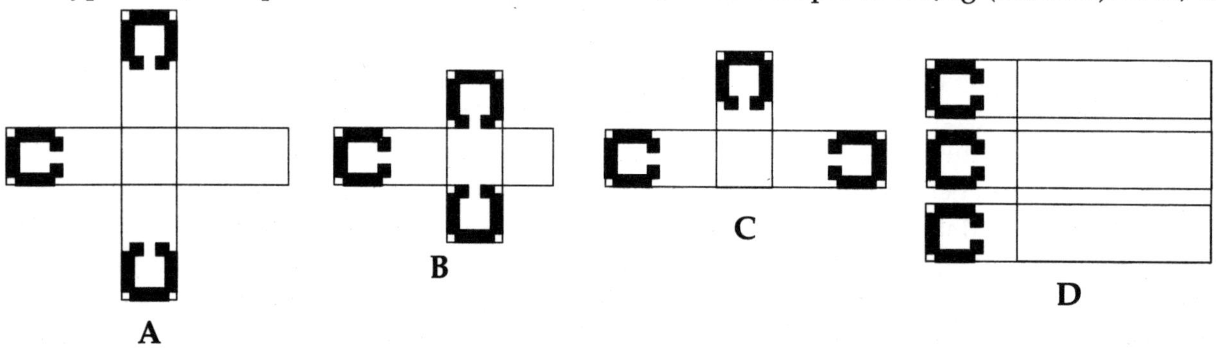

Figure 3: Arrangement of a *trikūṭa* temple

[4] F.W. Bunce, *The Iconogrphy of Architectural Plans*, pp. 3-19.

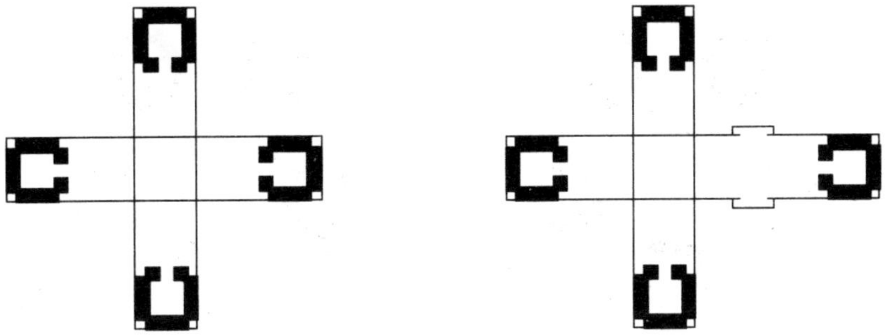

A B

Figure 4: Arrangement of a *catuṣkūṭa* temple (left) and indicating entrance (right)

last variation is seen when the sanctums are ranked, facing the same direction and generally sharing a *maṇḍapa* (**Figure 3D**). Herein, this will be identified as a **D**-type *trikūṭa* temple. An example of the **D**-type *trikūṭa* temple is seen in the Ananataśayana Trikūṭa Temple at Navali (**Plate 48**) (**Appendix C, Plate 129**).

Catuṣkūṭa: The addition of a fourth sanctum creating a *catuṣkūṭa* temple is also a simple solution as seen in **Figure 4A**. In this solution, the four sanctums all face inward, towards the crossing and are equidistant from that crossing. Herein, this will be identified as an **A**-type *catuṣkūṭa* temple. The only design problem in the *catuṣkūṭa* temple plan, **A**-type, is where is the entrance to be? Generally, it is placed beyond the crossing towards one of the sanctums. In so doing, that "arm" is generally extended to accommodate the entrance (**Figure 4B**). Herein, this will be identified as a **B**-type *catuṣkūṭa* temple. There are no examples of type **A**, for obvious reasons. However, an example of a type **B** *catuṣkūṭa* temple is seen in the Lakṣmī-Devī Catuṣkūṭa Temple of Dodda Gadduvalli (**Plate 42**).

Pañcakūṭa: The addition of another, a fifth sanctuary — i.e. *pañcakūṭa* — creates certain problems. A simple solution is to place a sanctum in the centre and two sanctums on either side and two more at 90°. The four sanctums are equidistant from the centre shrine. Herein, this will be identified as an **A**-type *pañcakūṭa* temple (**Figure 5A**). This unique solution is found in the Siddhaliṅgeśvara Pañcakūṭa Temple of Siruvala (**Plate 58**). A second solution is similar, but the four surrounding shrines are rotated 45°, on axis from the central sanctum. Herein, this will be identified as an **A**-type *pañcakūṭa* temple (**Figure 5B**). This solution is frequently encountered in the *pañcāyatana* plan noted above. However, the

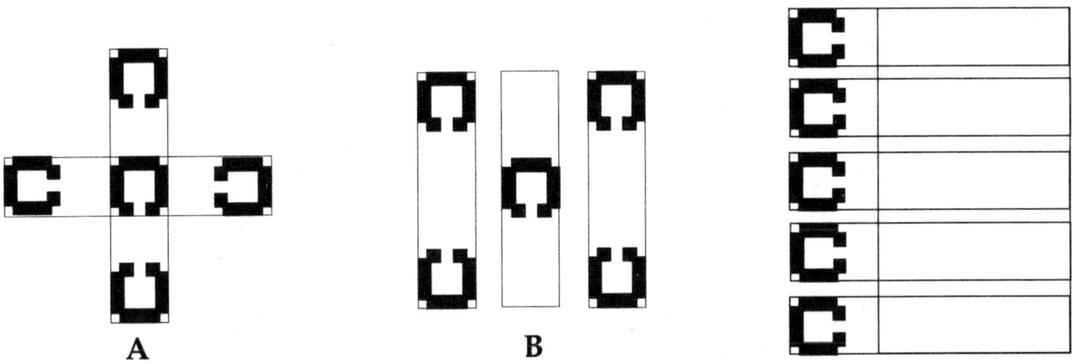

A B C

Figure 5: Arrangement of five sanctums, Khmer quincunx (**A**), *pañcāyatana* (**B**), and Pañcaliṅgeśvara Temple (**C**)

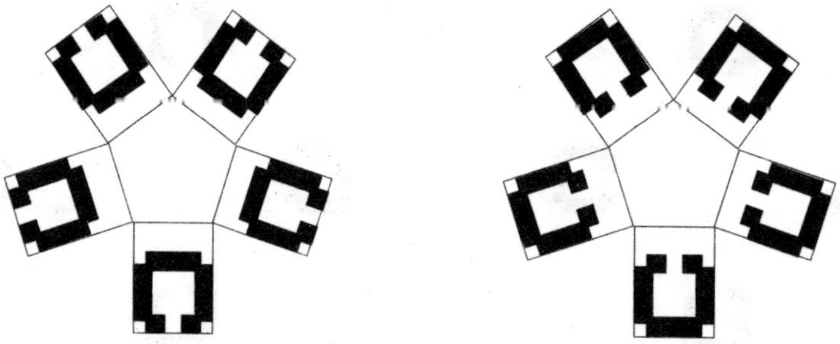

Figure 6: Arrangement of five sanctums, the Pagan solution

central shrine almost always predominates due to its larger size and generally is not considered to be a true *pañcakūṭa* temple (Lakṣmaṇa Temple Ensemble, Khajurāho; **Appendix C, Plate 126**). However, this solution presents a problem. If the construction of a *pañcakūṭa* is undertaken in order to give all five deities an equal status, then the shrine in the centre, by pride of place, assumes prominence, and, therefore, less than satisfactory. The Khmer, in their quincunx design (**Figure 5B**), clearly gave precedent to the central shrine, not only because of its location, but also due to the fact that this shrine was frequently elevated above the other four (**Appendix A, Plates 122-123**). The Theravādists of Pagan, as mentioned, solved this problem in a most unique way. They constructed five shrines, the centre axis of each was shifted 72° one from the other (**Figure 6** [left]). The Dhamma-Yazika with its five shrines and the towering *cedi* is a proper solution.[5] However, the Pentagonal Temple (Pañca-Buddhas), Pagan (a. CE 1175) (**Figure 6** [left]) is less satisfactory due to its crude execution, but the same solution, none the less (**Appendix A, Plates 127-128**). A third solution, unique to the subcontinent, is where the temples are placed in a row — i.e. side by side (**Figure 5C**). Herein, this will be identified as a **C**-type *pañcakūṭa* temple. An example of the **C**-type *pañcakūṭa* temple is seen in the Pañcaliṅgeśvara Pañcakūṭa Temple at Govindanahalli (**Plate 90**).

Ṣaṣkūṭa: A temple with six shrines or sanctums — i.e. *ṣaṣkūṭa* — could have at least two design solutions regarding the arrangement, although there are no examples in the subcontinent. One in which the shrines or sanctums are aligned to the cardinal points of the compass, much in the same way as the *pañcāyatana* plan (**Figure 7** [left]). A second possible solution which is related to the Pagan solution, indicated above, is that in which the axis of each temple is rotated 60° (**Figure 7** [right]).

Saptakūṭa: Seven shrines or sanctums — i.e. *saptakūṭa* — offer a much different solution. The Kailāsanātha Temple (**Plate 5**) of Kāñcīpuram in Tamil Nadu, offers one possible solution. There, six

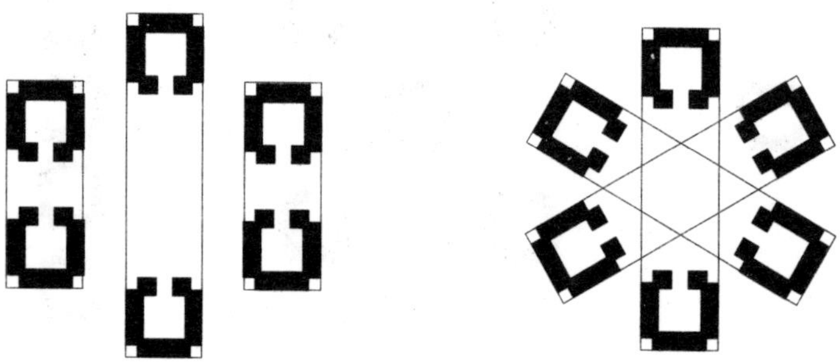

Figure 7: Solutions for the arrangement of six shrines

[5] This solution will be noted, herein, as the "Pagan solution".

of the seven exterior shrines are aligned along the northern and southern sides of the *vimāna*, three on each side, the seventh is centred on the western side (**Figure 8** [left]). A solution is derived from the Hindu *pañcāyatana* plan (**Figure 8** [centre]). Another solution is possible in which the axis of each of the temples is rotated 51.428° (**Figure 8** [right]), an adaptation of the Pagan solution noted above. However, the Kailāsanātha Temple may not be seen as a true *saptakūṭa* temple. One temple remains, the Kalleśvara Saptakūṭa Temple of Bennikallur. The solution encountered here is so eccentric, so erratic as to be seen as a temple in which the chapels or sanctums were added haphazardly over a period of time and can only be called *saptakūṭa* due to the number of chapels.

Examples of an *ekakūṭa*, *dvikūṭa* and *trikūṭa* temples abound in the subcontinent. *Catuṣkūṭa*, *pañcakūṭa* as well as *saptakūṭa* and *navakūṭa* temples find examples, although, far less frequently solutions to the design of a temple with eight shrines or sanctums — i.e. *aṣṭakūṭa* — could be seen to be adaptations to either the Pagan solution (**Figure 9** [right]) or the Hindu *pañcāyatana* plan (**Figure 9** [left]). It must be

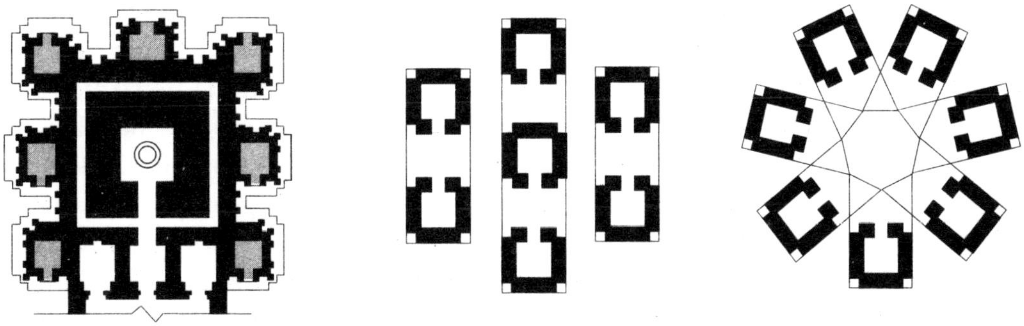

Figure 8: Arrangement of seven shrines, Kailāsanātha Temple (left) solution and two other solutions

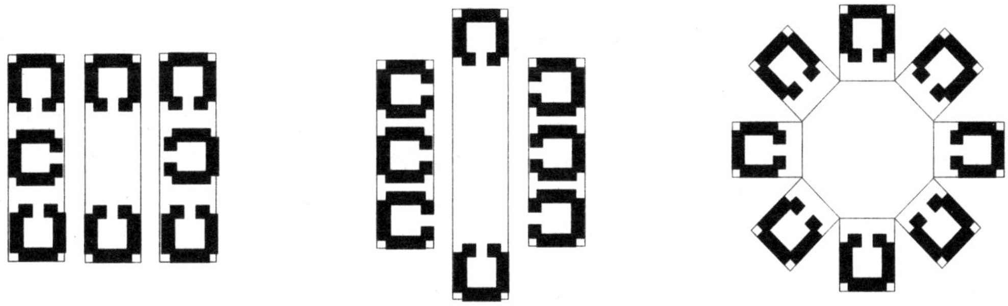

Figure 9: Solutions for the arrangement of eight shrines

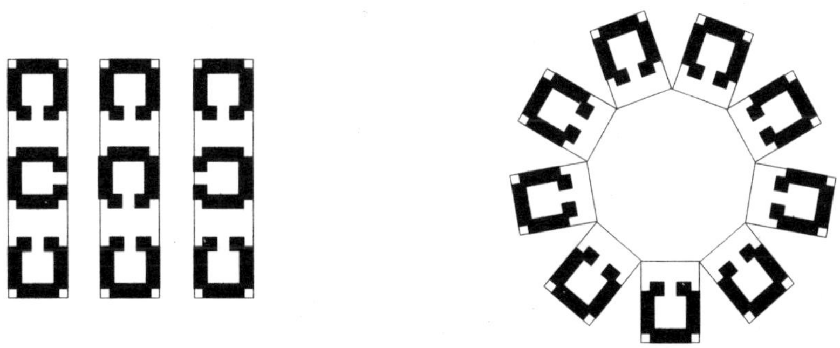

Figure 10: Hindu *pañcāyatana*-related and Pagan-related solutions for the arrangement of nine shrines

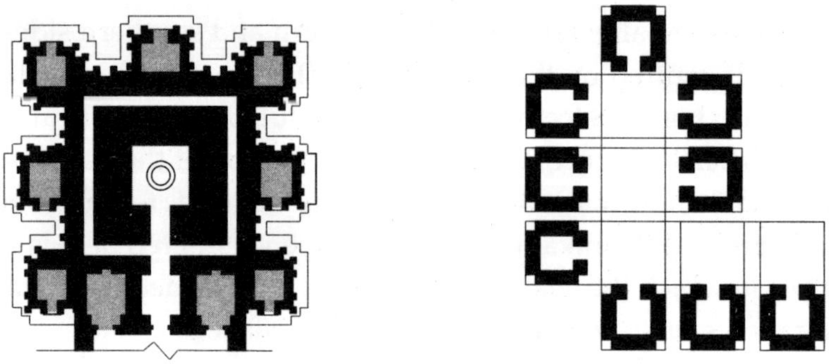

Figure 11: Alternative arrangements of nine sanctums, Kailāsanātha Temple (left) and Navaliṅga Navakūṭa Temple (right)

noted, however, that although the inclusion of eight sanctums is a possibility, there are no examples to be found in India.

Navakūṭa: A temple of nine shrines or sanctums — i.e. *navakūṭa* — might well follow similar possible solutions — i.e. an adaptation of the Hindu *pañcāyatana* plan (**Figure 10** [left]) or the Pagan solution (**Figure 10** [right]). One may assert that the Kailāsanātha Temple (**Figure 11** [left]) may also be seen to be *navakūṭa* as there are nine shrines — i.e. seven exterior and two interior shrines. This arrangement presents a fairly workable solution. However, the Navaliṅga Navakūṭa Temple of Kukkanur, Karnataka, presents a truly eccentric plan (**Figure 11** [right, **Plate 69**). There, it appears that a variation of Hindu *pañcāyatana* plan (**Figure 11**) is subverted. One shrine — i.e. the lower right shrine (**Figure 10** [left] [lower right shrine]) is removed and two additional shrines are inserted (**Figure 11**). This solution doubtless was achieved, not during a single construction process, but, over a number of years in which it was deemed meritorious by some devotee to add a shrine to the complex. If nothing else, the solution of the Navaliṅga Navakūṭa Temple is interesting although a bit unusual, maybe even haphazard!

The above enumeration, particularly the *dvikūṭa, trikuta, catuṣkūṭa, pañcakūṭa, saptakūṭa* and *navakūṭa* find examples more or less throughout India. There is one further temple type which exhibits multiple sanctums or chapels and that is the Causaṭh (Cauṅsaṭh) Yoginī Temples — i.e. a temple with sixty-four shrines (**Figure 12**). These circular, hypaethral temples are found in the west central region of the subcontinent. They are dedicated to the sixty-four *yoginī*s and in some cases the Sapta-Mātr̥kās are added. The Cauṅsaṭh Yoginī Mandir of Bherāghāṭ (**Plate 38**) possesses eighty-one chapels and

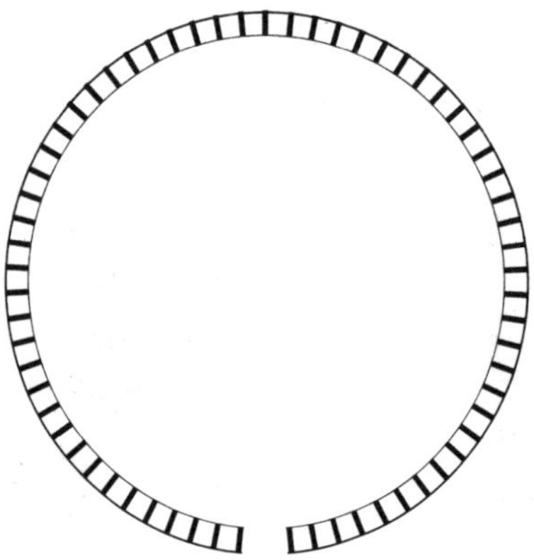

Figure 12: After Cauṅsaṭh Yoginī Temple solution for the arrangement of sixty-four shrines

the Cauṅsaṭh Yoginī Temple of Hīrāpur (**Plate 3**) and the Cauṅsaṭh Yoginī Temple of Rānīpur-Jharial (**Appendix C, Plate 131**) both have sixty-four shrines. In addition, there exists a little known temple in Mitāoli, Madhya Pradesh, known as the Ekottaso Mahādeva Mandir or the Cauṅsaṭh Yoginī Mandir.[6] Rather than dedicated to the *yoginī*, it is dedicated to the Lord Śiva and displays sixty-four *liṅga*s in shallow shrines with a large Śivaliṅga in a central shrine (**Appendix C, Plate 132**).

Ekakūṭa, dvikūṭa, trikūṭa, catuṣkūṭa and *pañcakūṭa* all may be considered orthodox, *en plan. Navakūṭa* and *cauṅsaṭh-kūṭa*, because of their rarity, may appear to be somewhat heterodox, particularly the Navaliṅga Navakūṭa Temple.

Maṇḍalas

*Maṇḍala*s are a vitally important design basis for every temple in India. The standard *maṇḍala* is square, *en form*, and provides the elemental standard for temples as outlined in the Śilpa-Śāstra. Normally,

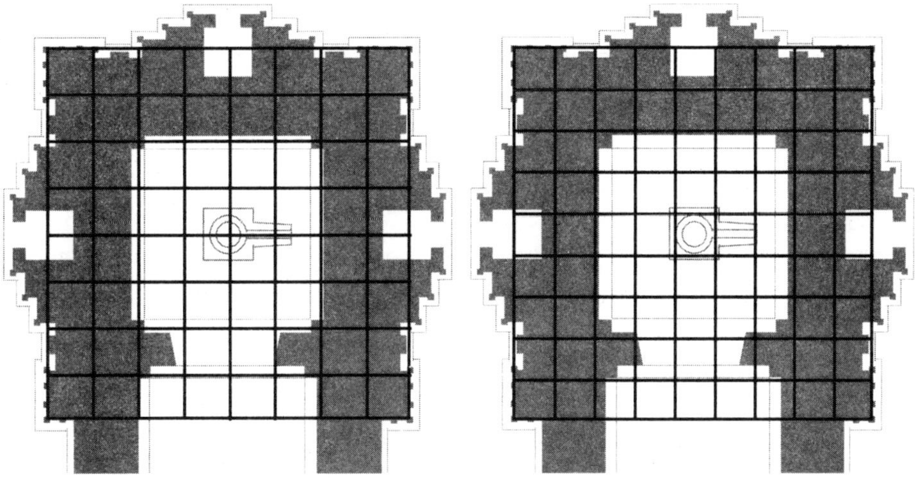

Figure 13: *Maṇḍūka maṇḍala* (left) and *paramaśāyika maṇḍala* (right) applied to Bhīmeśvara Catuṣkūṭa Temple

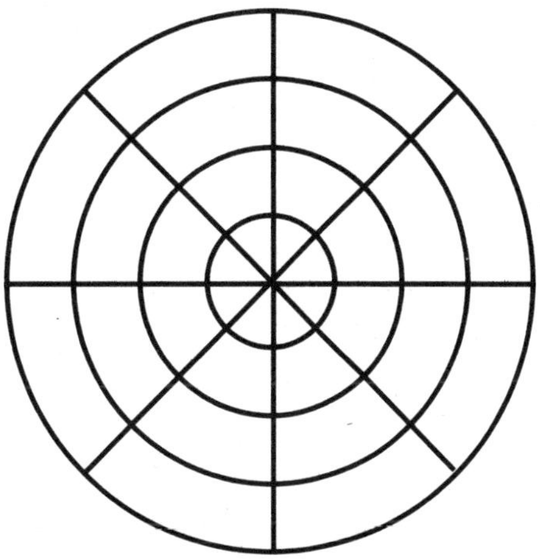

Figure 14: Circular *maṇḍūka maṇḍala*

6 It is erroneously called Cauṅsaṭh Yoginī Mandir. Sixty-four *liṅga*s are displayed here, not sixty-four *yoginī*s.

the square *maṇḍala*, either *maṇḍūka maṇḍala* or *paramaśāyika maṇḍala* (**Figure 13**), is applicable to the sanctum (*vimāna*) of most temples, whether Hindu, Buddhist or Jaina. However, there are examples in which one is hard-pressed to apply the square e.g. the Telī-kā-mandir Temple of Gwalior and the Mahā-Vihāra Dharmapāla at Pahāṛpur in Bangladesh (**Appendix C, Plates 130, 133**). On the other hand, a circular *maṇḍūka maṇḍala* (**Figure 14**) may be applicable. Another circular *maṇḍala*, the *vāstu-puruṣa maṇḍala* (**Figure 15**), is based upon a circular *maṇḍūka maṇḍala* which was initially employed in the design of the perfect city. In this form, the circle is divided into eight segments that fall within four circles placed equidistant one from the other. The lines, created by this segmentation, were seen to be the main thoroughfares of the city. Rather than creating sixty-four *padas*, the circular *maṇḍūka maṇḍala* creates thirty-two segments, half of sixty-four. Thirty-two is considered by some to be a perfect number as it is the result of four times eight (4 x 8 = 32). Both four and eight were highly auspicious in Hindu numerology. The circular *vāstu-puruṣa maṇḍala*, on the other hand, is segmented into twenty-four parts. The numeral twenty-four is also highly propitious. It is seen as representing totality and the combination of opposites. Further, the number twenty-four may be arrived at in a number of ways: 1 x 2 x 3 x 4 = 24, 6 x 4 = 24, 8 x 3 = 24, 2 + 4 = 6 x 4 = 24 and 12 + 12 = 24. These twenty-four segments are divided by four circles as is seen in the circular *maṇḍūka maṇḍala*. Further, sixteen segments are presented without the second ring — i.e. four each in the direction of the cardinal points. The segments within the second ring — i.e. those shaded in **Figure 15** — may be seen to represent the arms and legs of the *vāstu-puruṣa*.

A magic circle/*maṇḍala* (**Figure 16**), based on the cardinal and intercardinal points, resembles closely the circular *maṇḍūka maṇḍala* (**Figure 14**) and appears to be a viable source for circular *maṇḍalas*. The magic circle/*maṇḍala* centres on the complete, mystic number nine (9). The numerical sequence

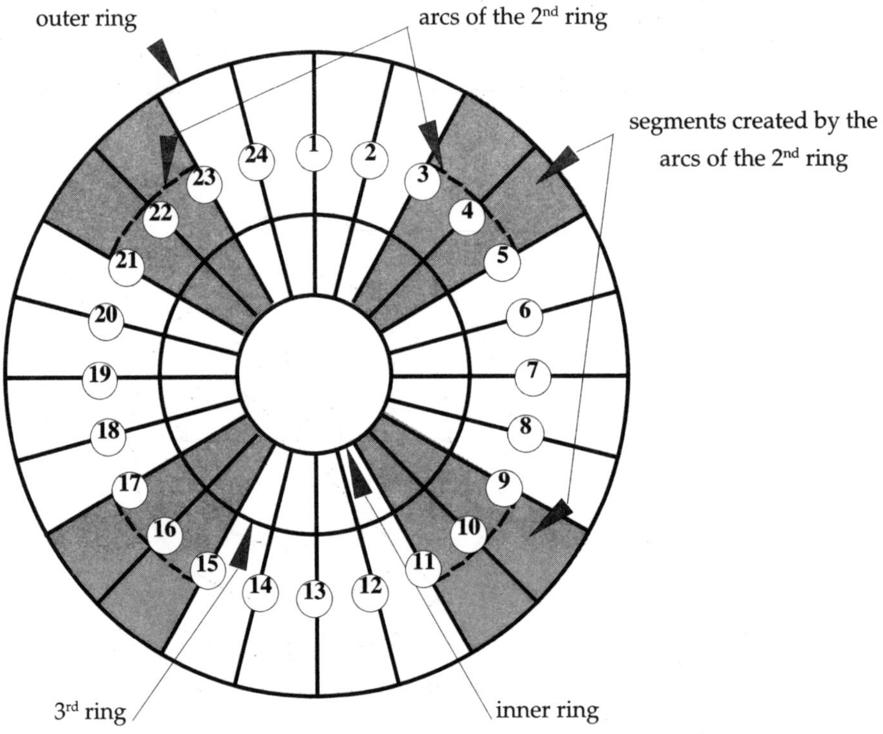

Figure 15: Circular *vāstu-puruṣa maṇḍala* and its elements

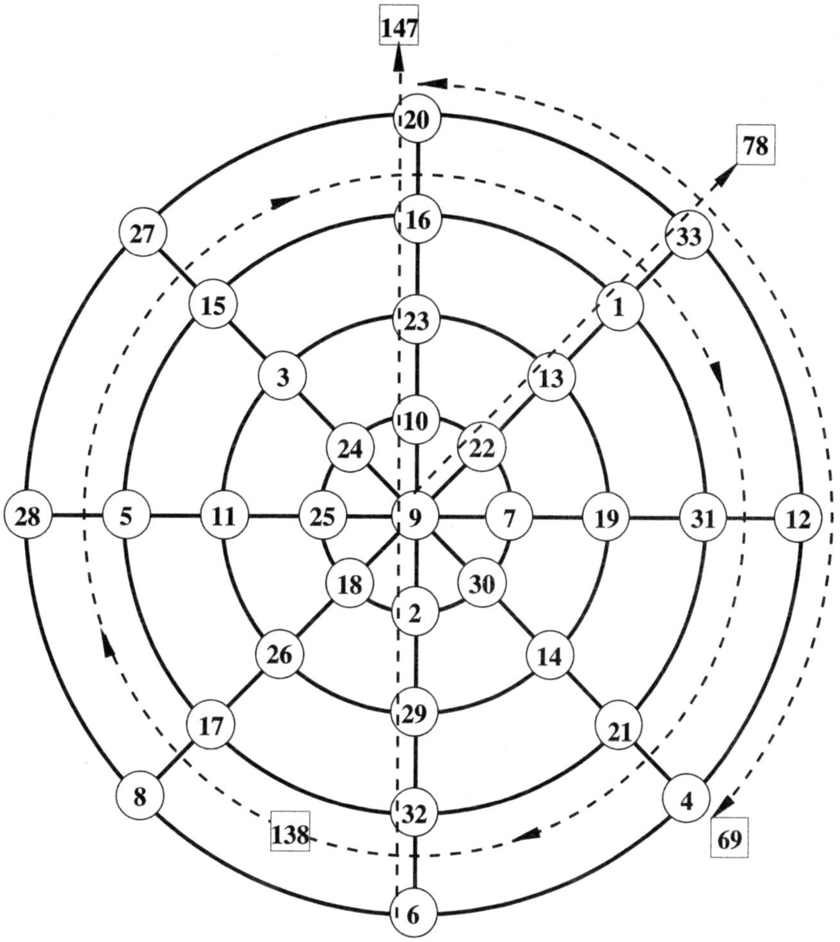

Figure 16: Magic circle based on the circular *maṇḍūka maṇḍala*

of this magic circle/*maṇḍala* is one through thirty-three, and the sum of each arm from the centre nine out — i.e. five numbers — equals seventy-eight or 147 across in any direction (**Figure 16**). In addition, each circle of numbers amounts to 138. There is a further phenomenon in that if one chooses any circle and begins with either the top (north) or bottom (south) numeral and follow clockwise — e.g. N, NE, E and SE, or S, SW, W and NW — the sum is the same, sixty-nine. Both the sequence of five numbers — i.e. from the centre out — with the sum of seventy-eight and the sequence of the half circle with the sum of sixty-nine when reduced produces the macrocosmic and spiritual number, six. Similarly when the sum of the nine integers in any direction — i.e. 147 — and the sum of any complete circle of numbers — i.e. 138 — are reduced, the resultant numeral is the perfect three. The use of numbers in a symbolic manner as an application to architecture, in a very real sense, gives concrete form to abstract concepts.[7]

The application of a circular *maṇḍala* to the plans of a square or rectilinear Hindu temple is not normally done. However, this researcher found efficacy in so doing while dealing with the Wat Phra Chetuphon Wimonmangkhalaram of Bangkok.[8] The *vāstu-puruṣa maṇḍala* is related to the magic circle/

[7] This paragraph is taken, nearly verbatim from: FWB III, pp. 36-38.

[8] Ibid., pp. 338-43.

maṇḍala and for this reason, it is employed herein. It finds numerous applications in temples, particularly when they stray from the usual square format — e.g. the Bhīmeśvara Catuṣkūṭa Temple (**Plate 16**).

Further, there may be some connection between multiple *garbhagṛhas* and numerology.[9] This connection does not mean to imply that the significance of a number would have be the prime force in the design and construction of a temple or shrine. But, the significance of a number — e.g. two, three, four, five, etc. — may have been used as a justification after the fact. Certainly, sixty-four, as in the temples dedicated to the Causaṭh (Chauṅsaṭh) Yoginī, is a number of considerable importance and connotes eternal blessedness and *karma*. Sixty-four is associated with the eight attendants of the Aṣṭa-Mātṛkās. Further, it represents the number of *padas* in the *maṇḍūka maṇḍala* and is a number whose √ is the auspicious number eight. Likewise, the eighty-one chapels of the Cauṅsaṭh Yoginī Mandir at Bherāghāt, is represented in the number of *padas* in the *paramaśāyika maṇḍala* and is a number whose √ is the highly mystical number nine.

In a number of temples contemplated within this consideration, it appeared to this researcher that *maṇḍalas* were imminently applicable to the whole — i.e. the *maṇḍūka maṇḍala*,[10] as well as the circular *maṇḍūka maṇḍala*,[11] the circular *vāstu-puruṣa maṇḍala*[12] and the *paramaśāyika maṇḍala*.[13] Certainly, a *maṇḍala* was the basis for the sanctuaries of all the temples, but their total design, also appeared in many cases to be *maṇḍala* derived. These are considered where they seem applicable.

Terms

Herein, the consideration of multiple *garbhagṛhas* (shrines) — i.e. *dvikūṭa*, *trikūṭa*, etc. — revolves around sanctums, the *garbhagṛhas* which are separate from another but under a single, contiguous roof. There are temples, more specifically, temple complexes for which a number of researchers label as *trikūṭa* — e.g. the Kalleśvara Temple, Hirehadagali, Karnataka — or as *pañcakūṭa* — e.g. the Pañcakūṭa Bastī, Kambadahalli, Karnataka — which indicate (1) a *dvikūṭa* structure plus a separate shrine/sanctum, or (2) a *trikūṭa* with a separate *dvikūṭa* temple/shrine. For the purposes of this study, they will be considered as separate architectural entities, rather than combines.

As noted above, the term *vimāna* is employed in this consideration to include the *garbhagṛha* and where applicable the attached *antarāla*. This is done for the sake of simplicity.

Suresh employs throughout his two studies the term *sabhā-maṇḍapa*.[14] Other applicable terms which are variously employed are: *maṇḍapa*, *godha-maṇḍapa*, *jagamohana*, *kalyāṇa-maṇḍapa*, *mandira*, *mukhaśalā*, *navaraṅga* and *nṛtta-maṇḍapa* (**Appendix A, Glossary**). The term *sabhā-maṇḍapa* is herein employed and is seen as applicable since *sabhā* means "gathering" and the space is indeed a place of gathering.

---

9 FWB II, for the specific number considered, and FWB, pp. 3-63, for the consideration of architectural iconography and its application.

10 FWB III, p. 42.

11 Ibid., p. 46.

12 Ibid.

13 Ibid., p. 44.

14 KMS, KMS II.

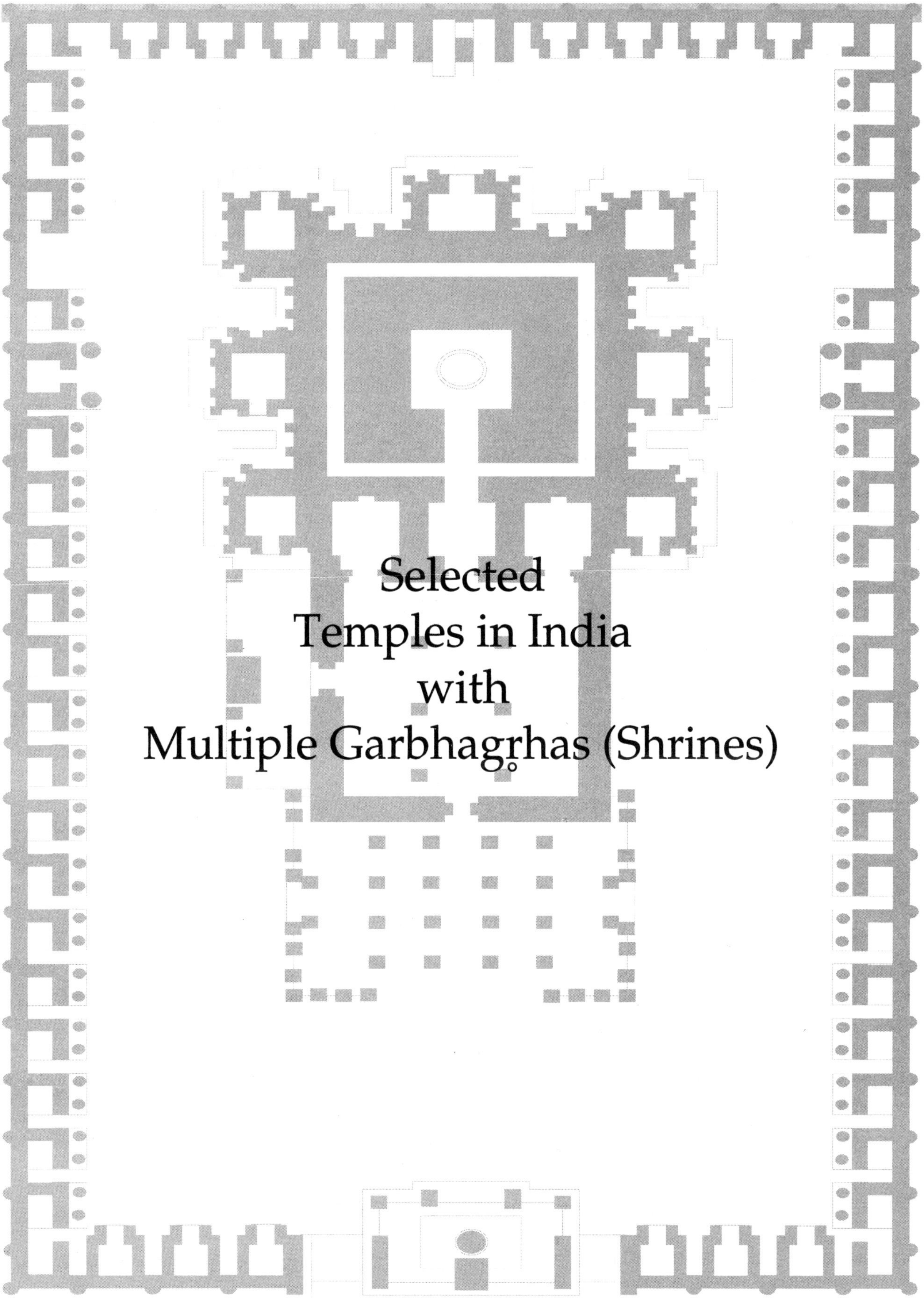

Selected Temples in India with Multiple Garbhagṛhas (Shrines)

Raciguḍi Trikūṭa Temple, Aihoḷe, Karnataka (seventh century CE)[1]

One of numerous temples constructed in south India which is dedicated to the deity Śiva, the Raciguḍi Trikūṭa Temple,[2] at the famed site of Aihoḷe, is an **A**-type *trikūṭa* plan (**Figure 3**), constructed during the dynasty of the Early Cāḷukyas of Bādāmī (CE 543–757) (**Appendix D**). Aihoḷe, near Hunugunda, contains a plethora of notable monuments raised by the Cāḷukyas despite the incursions of the Pallavas. The area is often referred to as the cradle of ancient Indian architecture and the Raciguḍi Trikūṭa Temple is not the least of these exemplars.

The temple consists of three *garbhagṛha*s. The northern and western sanctuaries are of similar design, while the eastern is larger and more ornate, *en plan*. The three *garbhagṛha*s exhibit a square interior space, and *antarāla*s which are essentially rectilinear. The three *vimāna* share in common an enclosed *sabhā-maṇḍapa* with four pillars on a raised platform. A portal from the enclosed *sabhā-maṇḍapa* gives way to a larger, open *sabhā-maṇḍapa* on the south. *En plan*, it exhibits sixteen columns placed in the usual manner — i.e. four free-standing columns in the centre raised on a square platform and twelve additional columns, four of which are engaged to the southern wall of the enclosed *sabhā-maṇḍapa*, which forms nine *aṅkana*s. A railing (*kakṣāsana*) with eight pillars frames the south, east and west sides. Centred in these three sides are stepped entrances which lead into this large, open *sabhā-maṇḍapa*.

---

1 KMS I, p. 211, states that the temple is "assignable to the seventh century CE", and adds, p. 121, that the eastern *vimāna* is a "later addition". Other sources assign the temple to the eleventh century. The northern and western *vimāna*s clearly indicate that they were constructed far earlier than the eleventh century.

2 Redrawn using PageMaker 6.0 from: KMS II, p. 439, description pp. 211-12. See also **Preface**.

Plate 1: Raciguḍi Trikūṭa Temple plan

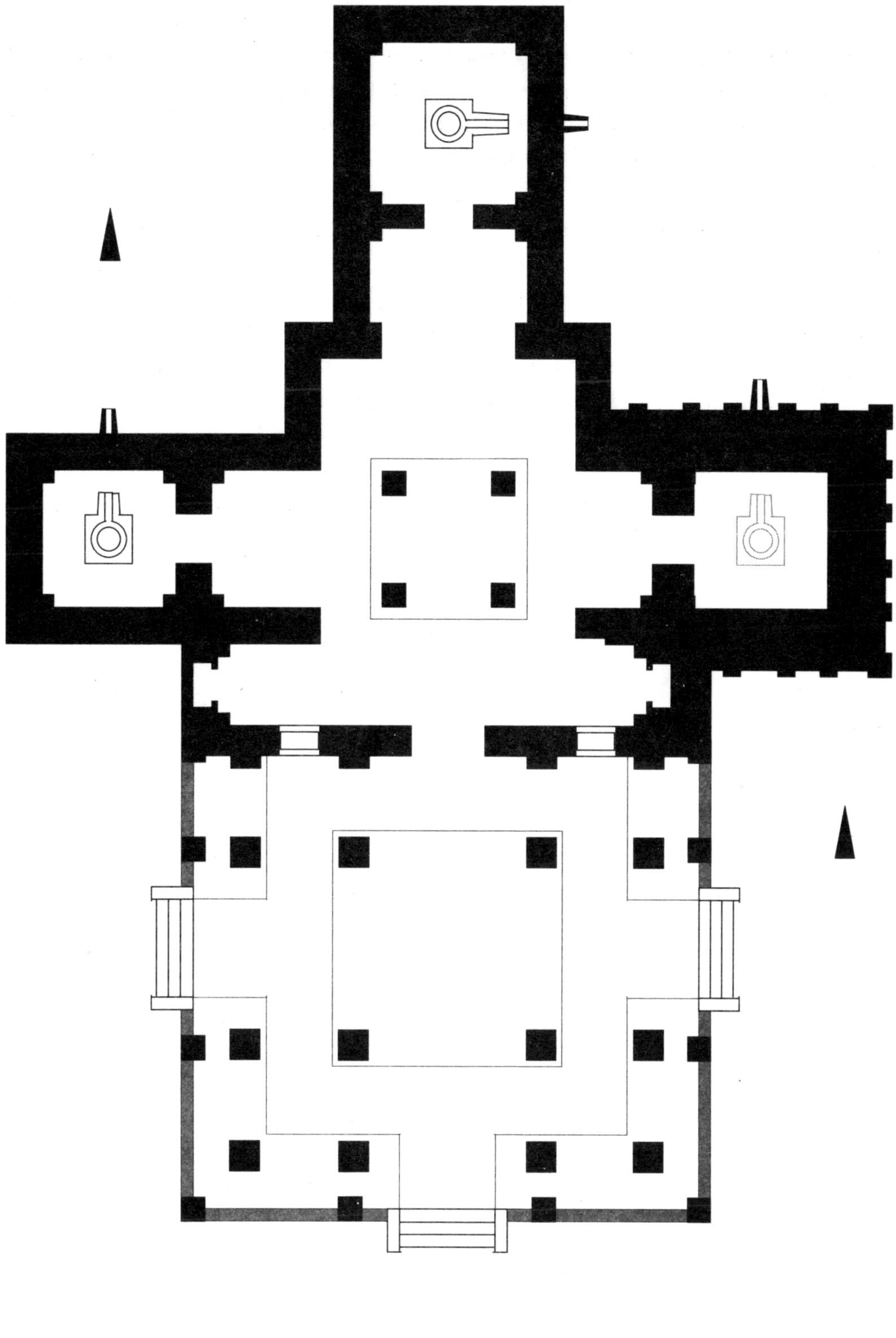

Jambuliṅgeśvara Trikūṭa Shrine, Bādāmī (seventh century CE)

The Cāḷukyas, natives of Karnataka, were one of the most vibrant kingdoms which grew and flourished in much of the south-west and central India from the Malabar to the Coromandal Coasts and as far north as Navsari. The early Cāḷukyas were centred, primarily around Bādāmī where numerous examples of their monuments are encountered. The Jambuliṅgeśvara Trikūṭa Shrine[3] of Bādāmī is somewhat closer to the temple plan norm than the Raciguḍi Trikūṭa Temple (**Plate 1**). It exhibits an **A**-type *trikūṭa* plan (**Figure 3**).

The temple consists of three *garbhagṛhas*, which exhibit a square interior space, but without *antarālas*. The northern and western sanctuaries are of similar design — i.e. extreme simple with little or no ornamentation. The western *garbhagṛha* is of similar size and a bit more ornate, *en plan*. The three *vimānas* share in common an enclosed, rectangular *sabhā-maṇḍapa* with eight pillars arranged in two ranks of four, and twelve engaged pillars. It is of note that the number and arrangement of the pillars of the *sabhā-maṇḍapa* do not follow the normal arrangement — i.e. there are no engaged pillars in the corners. To the east of the *sabhā-maṇḍapa* is a rectangular *mukha-maṇḍapa*, aligned east to west, the roof of which is supported by sixteen pillars. At the eastern edge of the *sabhā-maṇḍapa* is a set of stairs, descending to the north and south from a common landing.

3 Redrawn using PageMaker 6.0 from: KMS II, p. 440, description on p. 212. See also **Preface**.

Plate 2: Jambuliṅgeśvara Trikūṭa Shrine plan

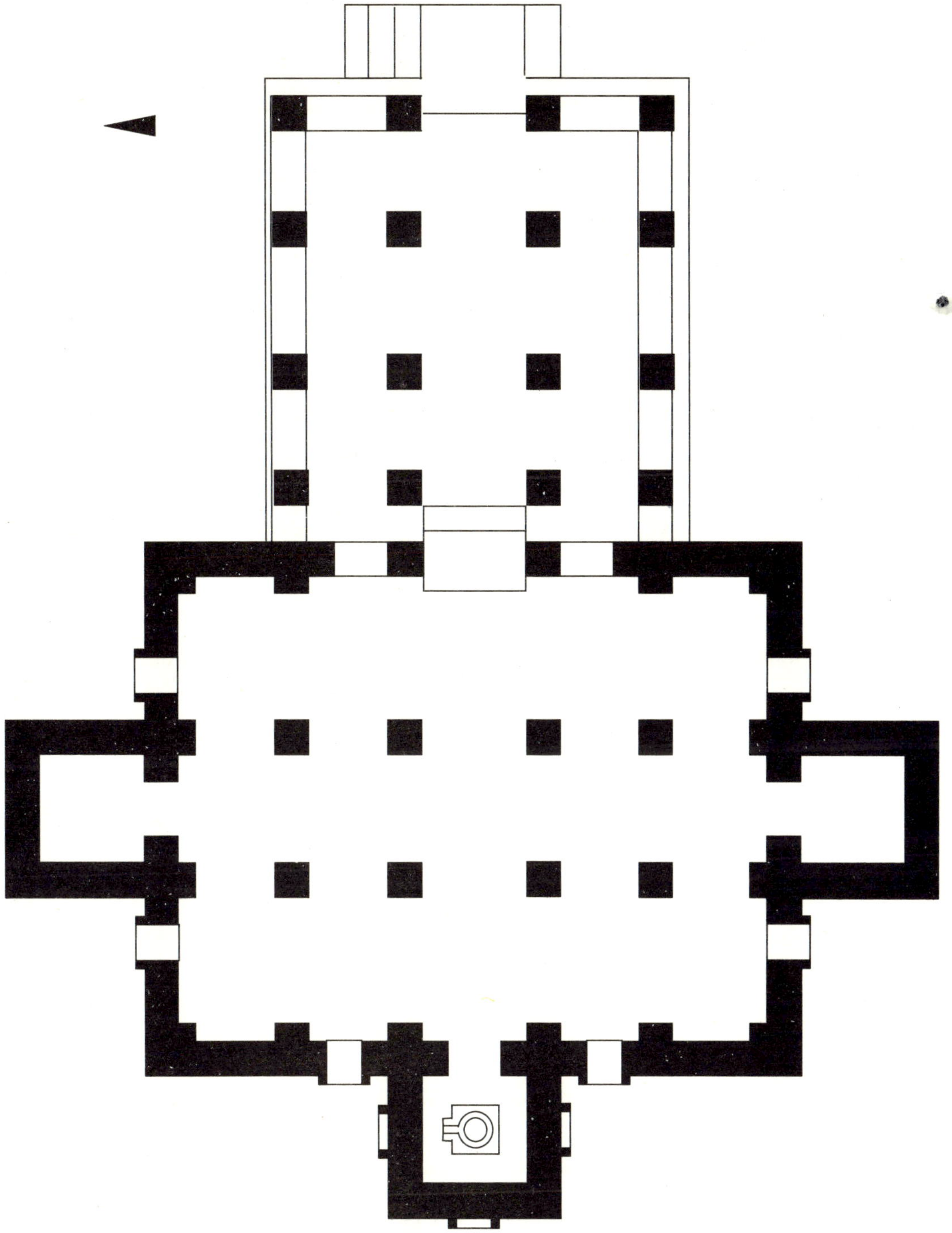

Cauṅsaṭh Yoginī Temple, Hīrāpur (ninth century CE)

Orissa, under the aegis of the Bhaumakara and Somavaṁśī dynasties (**Appendix D**), produced a number of notable monuments. In addition, certain philosophics also flowered in the region. During this time, often referred to as the Medieval Period, occult practices flourished in the guise of tāntric Hinduism in which the acquisition of extraordinary powers are sought. In part, it espouses the *vāmācāra* form of tāntric worship in which the female plays a dominant role. Orthodox practices of mainstream Hinduism are suspended, especially as women are concerned — i.e. marriage only within a woman's caste, allowing her to speak to whom she wishes and participate in certain intimate practices with whom she chooses. Tāntric Hinduism exists outside the orthodox Brāhmanical tradition, but it was not widely practised throughout the rest of India.

The Cauṅsaṭh Yoginī Temple[4] is a tāntric temple dedicated to Kālī or Durgā and the tāntric mother goddess Kāmākhyā.[5] Within India, there are four Cauṅsaṭh Yoginī temples, the other three being the Cauṅsaṭh Yoginī sanctuary at Khajurāho (**Plate 13**), the Cauṅsaṭh Yoginī Temple in Rānīpur-Jharial (**Plate 132**) and the Cauṅsaṭh Yoginī Mandir in Bherāghāṭ (near Jabalpur) (**Plate 38**).[6] All are hypaethral, circular, *en plan*, except the rectilinear Khajurāho example. The Cauṅsaṭh Yoginī Temple of Hīrāpur is the smallest — i.e. 30 ft in diameter and the outer wall is almost 8 ft tall. The circular Cauṅsaṭh Yoginī Temple consists of an entrance porch, facing east. Projecting from the outer wall are nine niches which hold wrathful Kātyāyanīs. On the interior of the temple are sixty-four niches. The number sixty-four is a feminine number and as a compound number it is associated astronomically with the planet Venus (Śukra) (6) and the planet Rāhu (the ascending node of the moon) (4). The shallow niches, each holds one of the *yoginīs*,[7] here are portrayed as voluptuous maidens in various poses. In the centre of the circular court is free-standing, square, open shrine which holds an image of Lord Śiva embracing his consort Pārvatī.

---

4 Redrawn using PageMaker 6.0.

5 Kālī and/or Durgā are the fierce forms of Pārvatī, the consort of Lord Śiva. She is the Lady Devī, the centre of the Śākta cult.

6 A fifth hypaethral temple is found in Mitāoli, Madhya Pradesh, called Ekottaso Mahādeva Mandir (Cauṅsaṭh Yoginī Mandir). It too is circular but rather than dedicated to the Cauṅsaṭh Yoginī, it is dedicated to Lord Śiva and contains sixty-four niches each with a Śivaliṅga (**Appendix C, Plate 132**).

7 The sixty-four *yoginīs* (*ḍākinīs*) are: Chāyā, Māyā, Nārāyaṇī, Brahmāyaṇī, Bhairavī, Māheśvarī, Rudrāyaṇī, Baseli, Tripurā, Ugratārā, Carcikā, Tāriṇī, Ambikā, Kumārī, Bhagavatī, Nīlā, Kamalā, Śānti, Kānti, Ghaṭabarī, Cāmuṇḍā, Candrakānti, Mādhavī, Kīcakeśvarī, Analā Rūpā, Vārāhī, Nāgarī, Khecarī, Bhūcarī, Betāli, Kālīñjarī, Śaṅkhā, Rudrakālī, Kalāvatī, Kaṅkālī, Bukuchai, Bali, Dohinī, Dvāriṇī, Sohinī, Saṅkaṭa Tāriṇī, Kotalai, Anuchāyā, Kecamukhī Samūha, Ullakā, Samaśilā, Mūḍha, Dakhinai, Gopāli, Mohinī, Kāmasenā, Kapālī, Uttarāyaṇī, Trailokya Byāpinī, Trilocanā, Nimai, Dakṣeśvarī, Kamalā, Ramāyaṇī, Anādi Śaktī, Bālakṣatrāyaṇī, Brāhmaṇī, Dhāraṇī, and Mātaṅgī.

Plate 3: Cauṅsaṭh Yoginī Temple plan

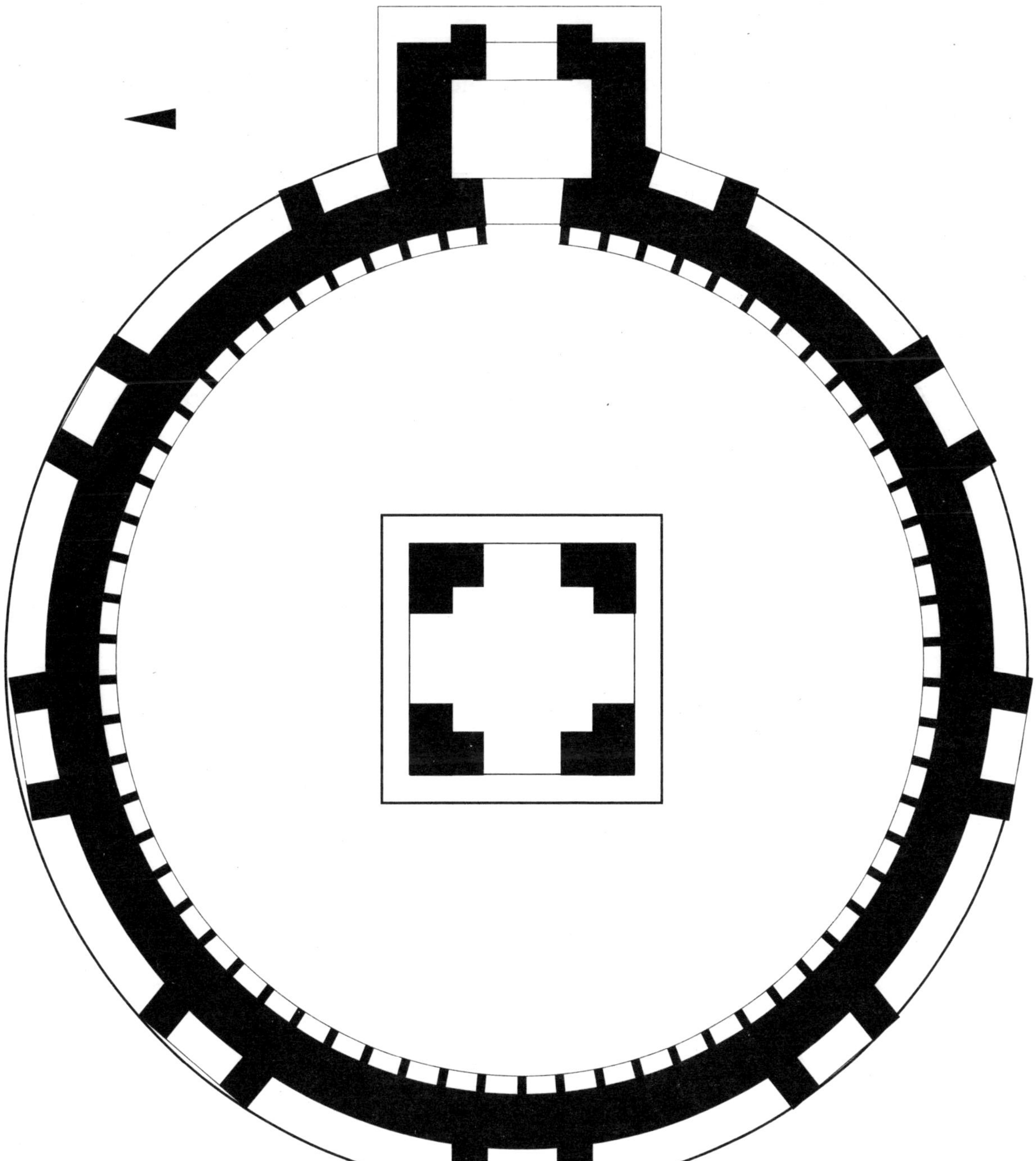

Candragupta Trikūṭa Basadī, Śravaṇabeḷagoḷa (eighth century CE)

Believed to have been constructed in the eighth century, during the reign of the Gaṅga monarch Śivamāra II (r. CE 788–817) (**Appendix D**), the Candragupta Trikūṭa Basadī[8] at Śravaṇabeḷagoḷa is a simplified example of Jaina sanctuary. Śravaṇabeḷagoḷa is known to contain a number of Jaina sanctuaries both large and small.

The Candragupta Trikūṭa Basadī's plan is based upon a rectangle, aligned south to north and exhibits a **C**-type *trikūṭa* plan (**Figure 3**). Along the northern wall are three rectilinear *garbhagr̥has* with narrow entrances into a common *mukha-maṇḍapa*. The central *garbhagr̥ha* is the larger of the three and houses the image of Pārśvanātha. In the northern, exterior wall, directly behind the image of Pārśvanātha is a small niche/shrine in the thickness of the wall. The eastern *garbhagr̥ha* exhibits Padmavati, while the western sanctum is occupied by Kūṣmāṇḍinī Yakṣī. The *mukha-maṇḍapa* is long and narrow, fronting the three *garbhagr̥has*. The southern wall of the temple consists of a central entrance and an elaborate *jālī*. Along the external north, east and western walls are elaborate engaged columns which are more decorative than supportive.

[8] Redrawn using PageMaker 6.0 from: KMS II, p. 441, description pp. 212-13. See also **Preface**.

Plate 4: Candragupta Trikūṭa Basadī plan

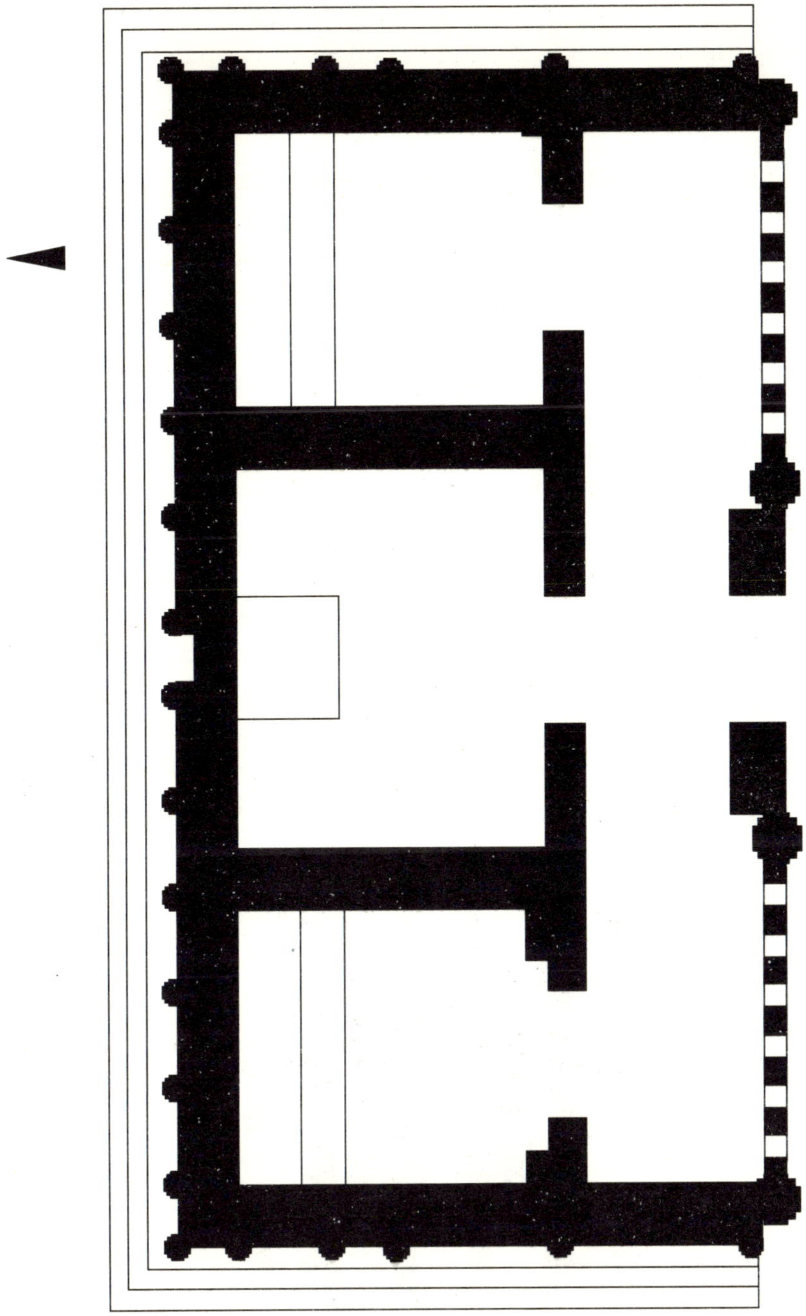

Kailāsanātha Temple, Kāñcīpuram (*c.* CE 700-28)

The famed Kailāsanātha Temple[9] at Kāñcīpuram, dedicated to Lord Śiva, was built during the reigns of Narasiṁhavarman II Rājasimha (r. CE 680–720) and Parameśvaravarman II (r. CE 720-31) of the vibrant Pallava Dynasty (**Appendix D**). An additive monument of surprisingly durable sandstone, the temple stands as a benchmark for many future temple complexes.

Although not a temple with a number of *garbhagṛhas*, the Kailāsanātha Temple does seem to indicate nine chapels, prominently placed around the *vimāna* (**Figure 17**) — i.e. seven exterior and two interior shrines. These are referred to by some as *parivāra*-shrines.[10] It is not unusual for the *parivāra* of a deity to be included in the plan of his/her temple. However, frequently these members of the deity's retinue are enshrined within the *pradakṣiṇāpatha* of the *vimāna*. Generally, *parivāras* are not as conspicuously enshrined as seen here. The Kailāsanātha Temple prominently provides a number of substantial shrines on the outer perimeter, and against the girdle wall. Deva states that these nine shrines surrounding *garbhagṛha* are dedicated to "Śiva, Viṣṇu, Gaṇeśa, Dikpālas, Chanddeśa and Mātṛkās".[11] But this does not account for all the chapels/shrines.

The seven, small, *triratha* chapels give the impression that they are emerging from, or are being enveloped by the large *vimāna*. Chapels/shrines 2, 3, 7 and 8 are aligned towards the east, as is the temple proper; while chapels/shrines 4, 5 and 6 face towards the west. Chapel/shrine 5 is somewhat larger than the other exterior chapel/shrines, giving it some precedence (**Figure 17**). The two interior chapels/shrines are oriented towards the east. As the nine chapels/shrines are arranged, they would appear to be related to the "Pagan solution" as noted in the "Introduction" of this study.[12] This unique arrangement, this design, finds certain parallels in the antecedent Gupta Temple at Deogaṛh (*c.* CE 500-25) and the later Avantisvāmi Temple of Avantipur (*c.* CE 850-60) (**Appendix C, Plates 120-121**).

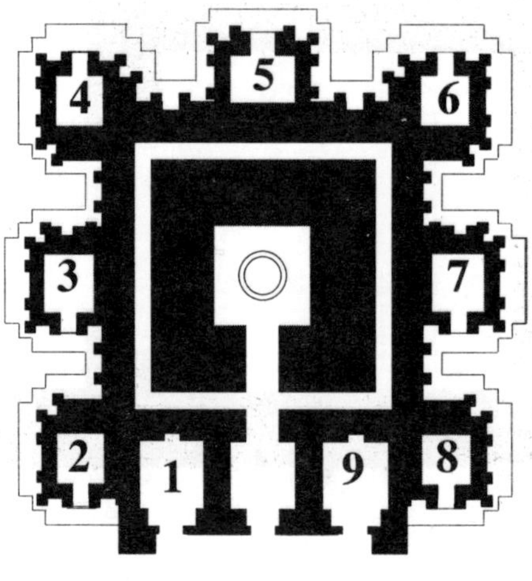

Figure 17: Kailāsanātha Temple, chapels surrounding the *vimāna*

9 Redrawn using PageMaker 6.0 from: HS II, p. 41.

10 KD, pp. 237-38, states "... From its (*vimāna*) outer wall project eight *parivāra*-shrines..." This is an error. There are seven chapels/shrines projecting from the *vimāna*'s outer wall.

11 Ibid., p. 238.

12 See "Introduction", p. 3.

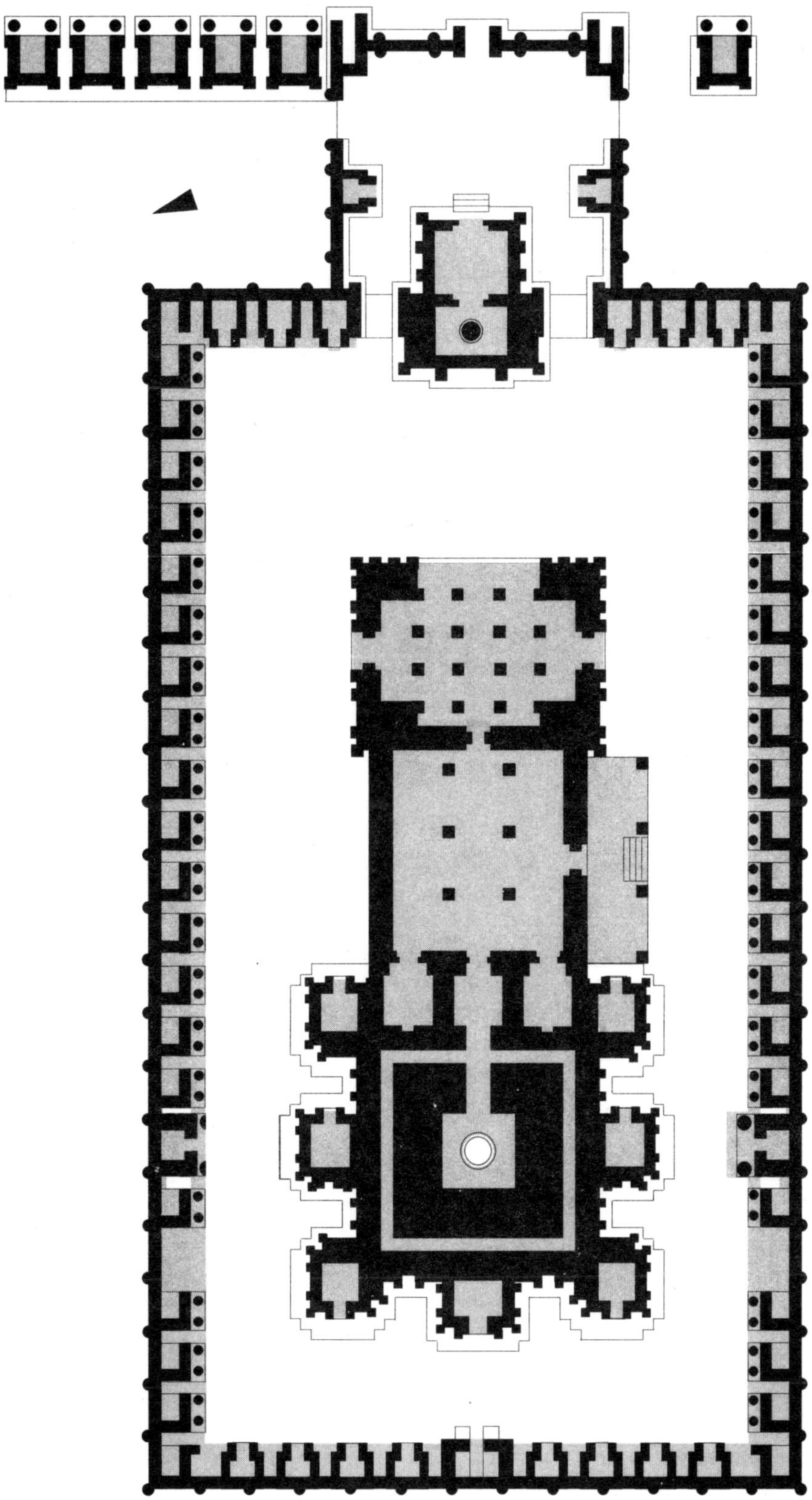

Kailāsanātha Temple

The application of a *maṇḍala* to the *vimāna* of the Kailāsanātha Temple, in this case a *paramaśāyika maṇḍala*, produces the expected results (**Figure 18**). The Śilpa-Śastras[13] were the benchmarks by which a temple was designed and the *maṇḍalas* were the key. Little has been researched regarding the basis of the design for the other parts of the temple or temple complex, *en toto*.

Of particular interest with the Kailāsanātha Temple is the design basis for the *vimāna* and the nine surrounding chapels/shrines. In a quest for this underpinning, two *maṇḍalas* are applied to the *vimāna*–chapel ensemble — i.e. a *paramaśāyika maṇḍala*[14] (**Plate 6** [top]) and a circular *vāstu-puruṣa maṇḍala* (**Plate 6** [bottom]). In both cases there are a number of interesting conjunctions. Regarding the *paramaśāyika maṇḍala*, the seven exterior chapels/shrines fall neatly within the nine *pada* divisions (**Appendix C, Plate 134**) — i.e. chapels/shrines "2" through "8". The same chapels/shrines rest within segments: **x–a, c–d, f–g, i–j, o–p, r–s** and **u–v** (**Appendix C, Plate 135**) of the circular *vāstu-puruṣa maṇḍala*. The two interior chapels — i.e. 1 and 9 do not fit conveniently within the various confines of either the *paramaśāyika maṇḍala* or the *vāstu-puruṣa maṇḍala*.

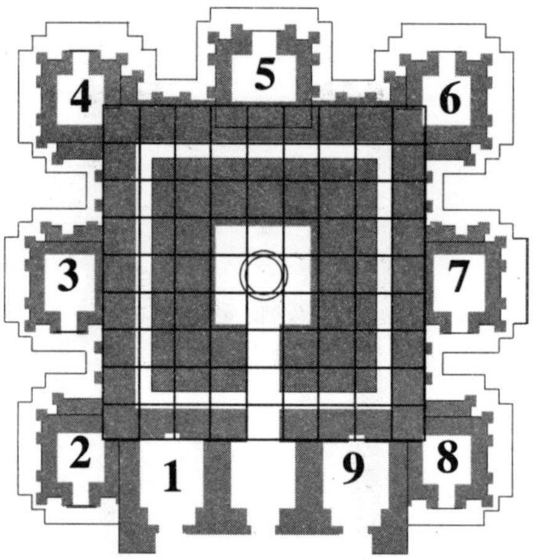

Figure 18: Kailāsanātha Temple with *paramaśāyika maṇḍala* applied to the *vimāna*

[13] Over the centuries various Śilpa-Śastras were formulated. Among them are: *Mānasāra, Mayamatam, Vāstuvidyā*, the *Manuṣyālaya-Candrikā, Tantrasamuccya* and *Śilparatna*.

[14] Each *paramaśāyika maṇḍala* is subdivided into nine *padas* (**Appendix C, Plate 134**).

Plate 6: Kailāsanātha Temple, *vimāna* with *paramaśāyika maṇḍala* (top) and circular *vāstu-puruṣa maṇḍala* (bottom)

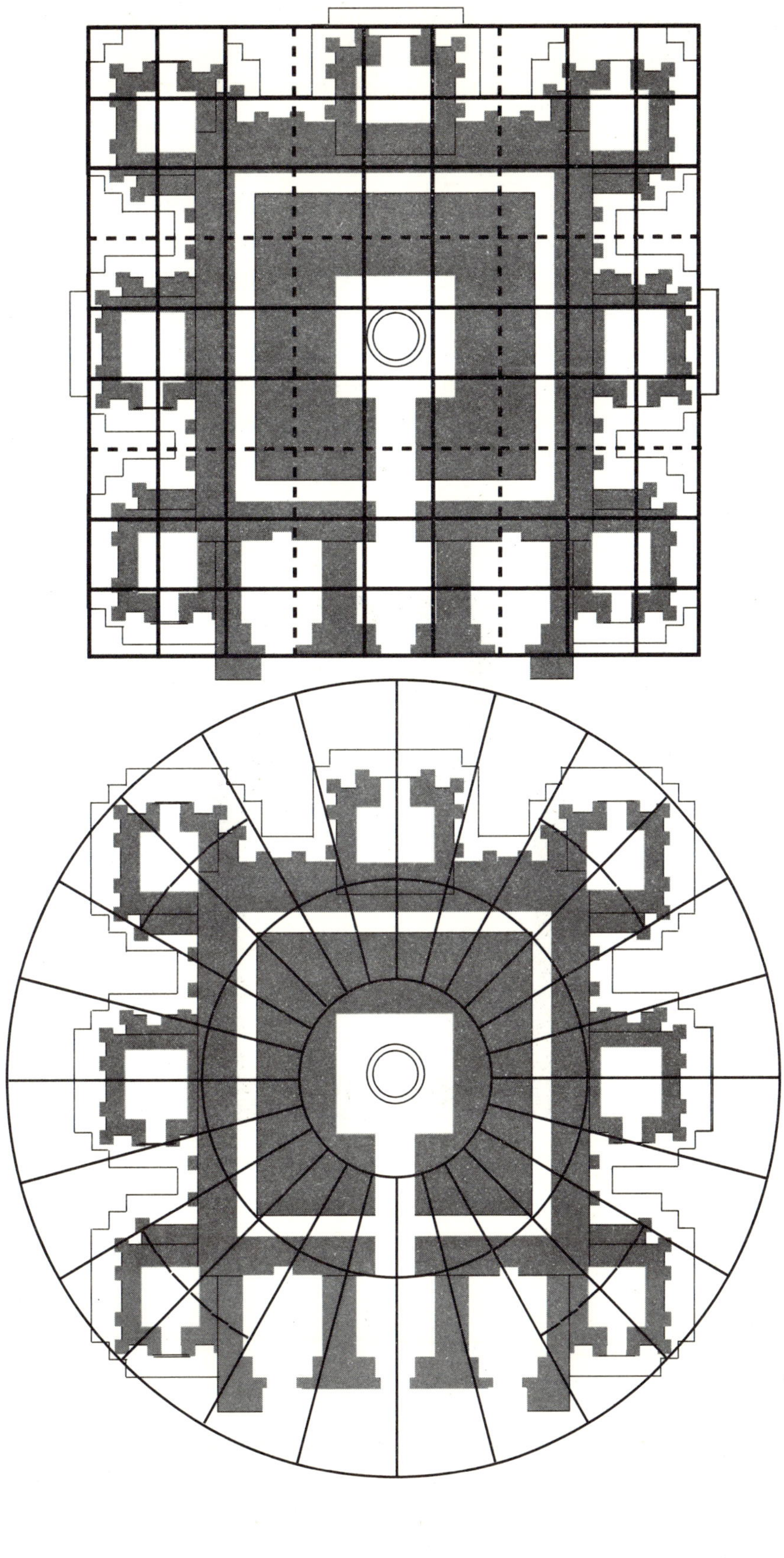

Siddheśvara Dvikūṭa Temple, Aḷgoḍu, Karnataka (a. 725 during the second quarter of the eighth century CE)

The Siddheśvara Dvikūṭa Temple[15] at Aḷgoḍu is believed to have been constructed during the second quarter of the eighth century CE. This would have placed the raising of the temple during the reign of the Western Gaṅga Dynasty when it was ruled by the King Śrī Puruṣa (r. CE 725-88) (**Appendix D**). The rise of the Western Gaṅga Dynasty came at the expense of the tottering Pallava Dynasty and Śrī Puruṣa allied his kingdom with the Cāḷukyas to overthrow the imperial yoke of the Pallavas.

The Siddheśvara Dvikūṭa Temple is a small, granite temple with an interesting, even unusual plan — i.e. a **C**-type *dvikūṭa* plan (**Figure 2**). It is oriented towards the south and consists of a square *sabhā-maṇḍapa* with four central columns on a platform and twelve engaged columns arranged in a traditional manner. In the southern wall is the doorway leading to the interior and the only source of light for the interior. To the north of the *sabhā-maṇḍapa* are doorways leading to two *garbhagṛhas* of differing size. The larger of the two is the shrine dedicated to Siddheśvara, while the smaller *garbhagṛha,* to the east, enshrines Devī. Although it is not noted, nor does the ruined state of the temple clearly indicate that the Devī shrine may have been a later addition (**Figure 19**). However, *en plan,* the possibility appears to be a cogent supposition.

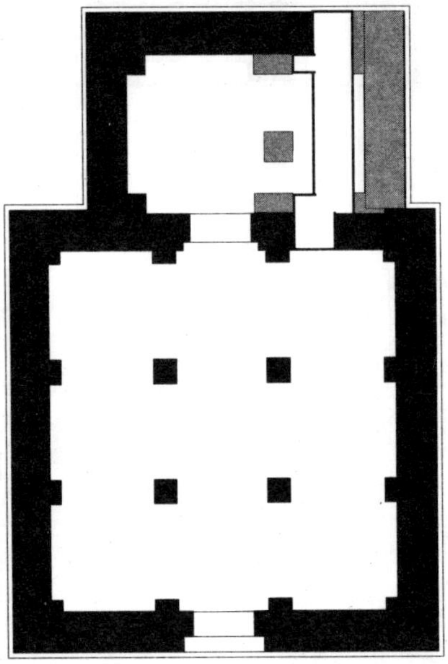

Figure 19: Siddheśvara Dvikūṭa Temple as an *ekakūṭa* type

[15] Redrawn using PageMaker 6.0 from: KMS II, p. 419, description on pp. 189-90. See also **Preface**.

Plate 7: Siddheśvara Dvikūṭa Temple plan

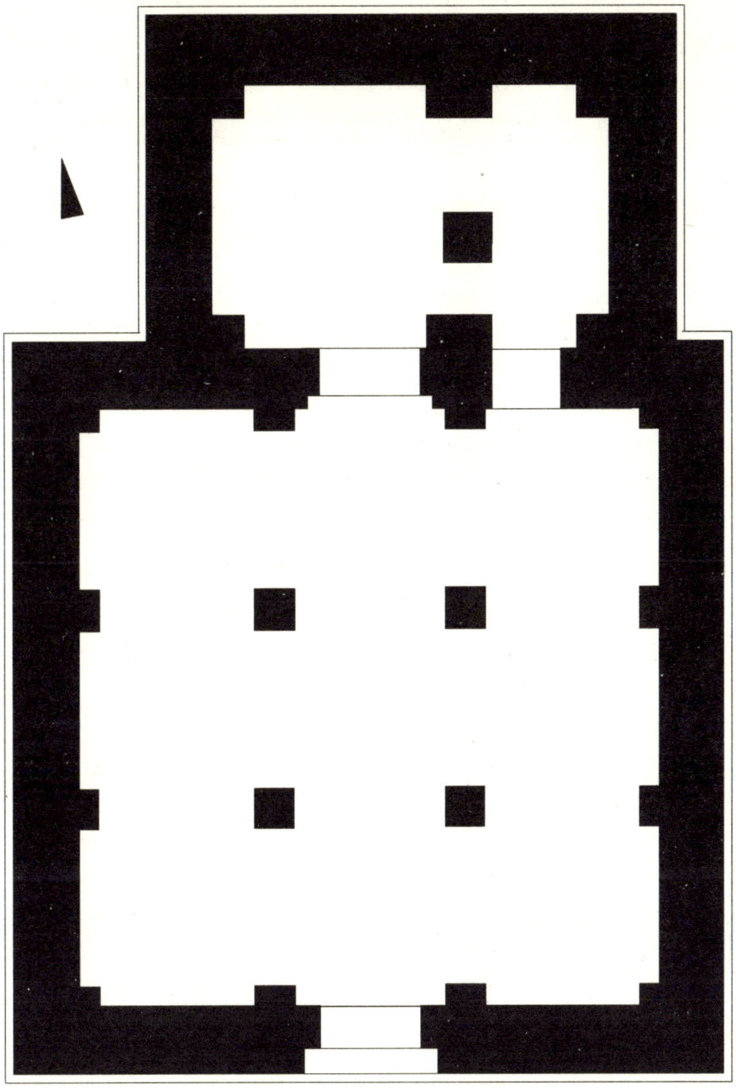

Jaina (Trikūṭa) Basadī No. 15, Deogaṛh , Rajasthan (*c.* CE 775)

Constructed during the Gujarātī Pratihāra Dynasty, possibly during the reign of King Vatsarāya (r. CE 772-94) (**Appendix E**), the Jaina (Trikūṭa) Basadī No. 15[16] at Deogaṛh , indicates a mirror symmetry in temple design which is related to an **A**-type *trikūṭa* plan (**Figure 3**). Its plan is nearly in the form of a Greek Cross.

The Jaina (Trikūṭa) Basadī No. 15 is aligned towards the west with a rectangular *mukha-maṇḍapa* or *ardha-maṇḍapa* fronted with two columns with a doorway leading to a square *sabhā-maṇḍapa* with four central pillars and twelve engaged pillars arranged in a traditional manner. The engaged pillars on the north, south and east walls frame doorways that leads to a shallow, rectilinear shrine or *grabhagṛha.* These three shrines/*garbhagṛhas* are further untraditional in that they do not possess an *antarāla. En plan*, these three shrines are identical. These internal shrines find their counterpart on the exterior walls of the *sabhā-maṇḍapa* — i.e. the shrines extend outwards and a shallow, identical shrine/niche is found in each. As with most temples the only interior light is via the western door, creating rather low internal ambient illumination.

The Jaina (Trikūṭa) Basadī No. 15 is covered by a single roof which technically does not create a *trikūṭa* temple as indicated in **Figure 3**. None the less the three interior shrines of the *basadī* exist in independent, identical, internal isolation, suggesting an **A**-type *trikūṭa* plan.

---

16 The plan is redrawn using Adobe PageMaker 6.0, from KD, p. 103.

Plate 8: Jaina (Trikūṭa) Basadī No. 15 plan

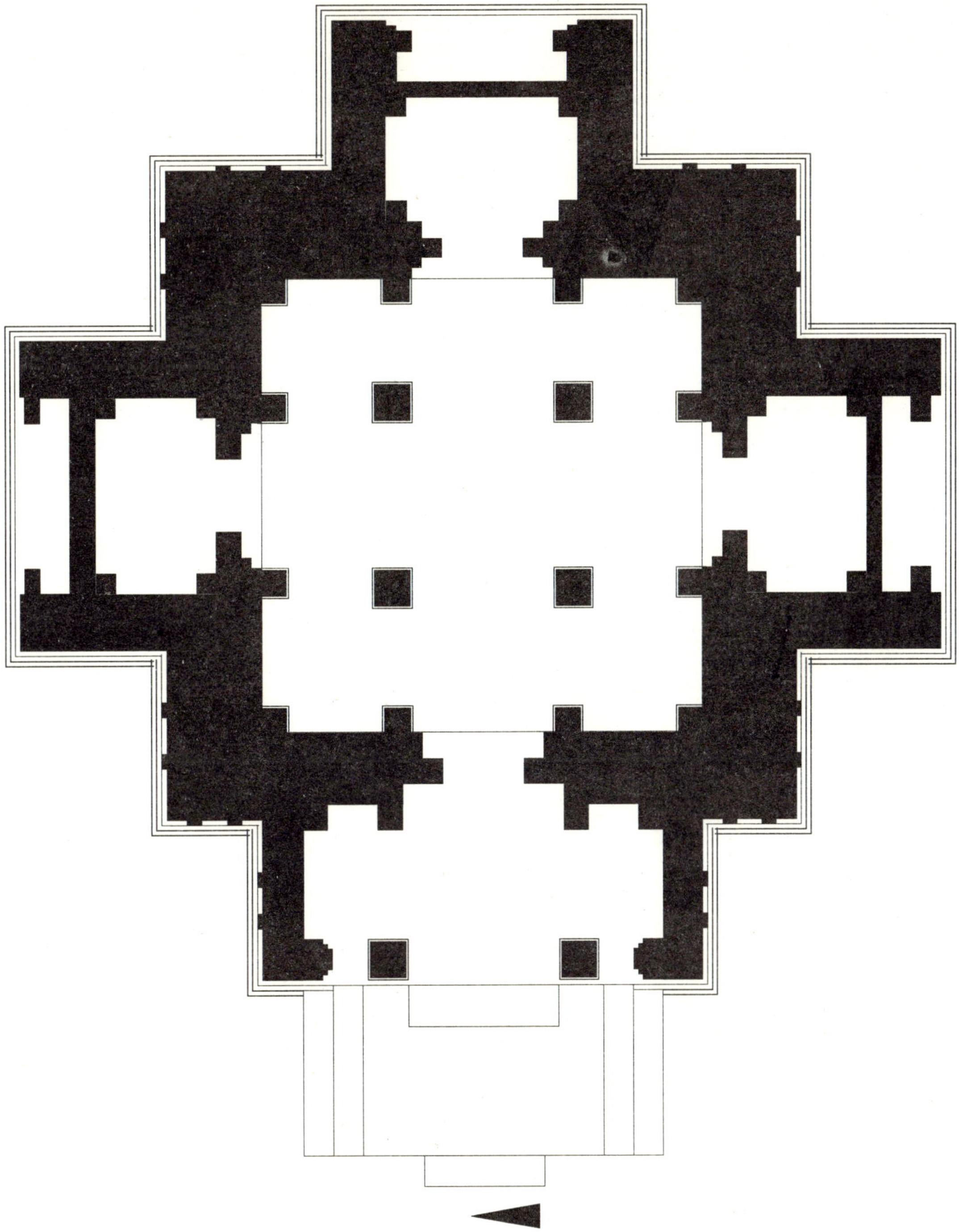

Jaina (Trikūṭa) Basadī No. 15

The Jaina (Trikūṭa) Basadī No. 15 which is essentially cruciform, *en plan,* does not readily conform in its entirety to a square *maṇḍala*. A *paramaśāyika maṇḍala* is applicable to the *vimāna*, proper (**Figure 20**).

The overlaying of a *paramaśāyika maṇḍala* on the whole plan creates a certain viability (**Plate 9** [top]), but it is not entirely applicable as part of the *mukha-maṇḍapa* appears to extend beyond the *maṇḍala*. As is seen, each of the interior–exterior shrines falls within one of the nine divisions — i.e. division **2, 4** and **6** (**Appendix C, Plate 134**).

When a circular *vāstu-puruṣa maṇḍala* is applied, a number of conjunctions appear (see arrows **Plate 9** [bottom]). A number of these conjunctions may appear fortuitous considering the mirror axiality and cruciform quality of the design of the Jaina (Trikūṭa) Basadī No. 15. However, there does appear certain conjunctions that are more than merely accidental. Each of the interior–exterior shrines and the *mukha-maṇḍapa* fall within the open cardinal segments of the *maṇḍala* — i.e. **x–a, f–g, l–m** and **r–s** (**Appendix C, Plate 135**).

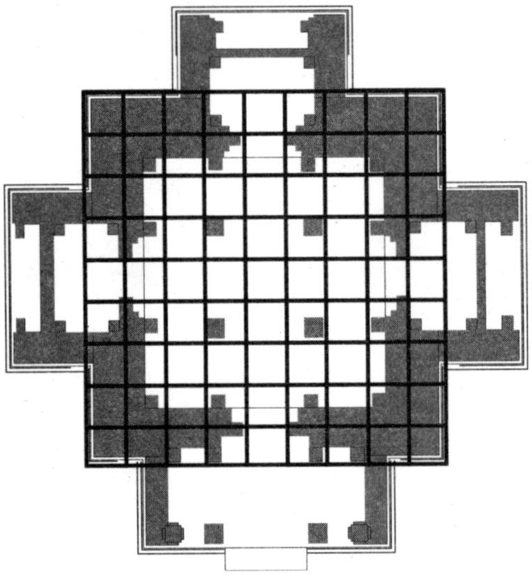

Figure 20: Jaina (Trikūṭa) Basadī No. 15 with *paramaśāyika maṇḍala* applied to the *vimāna*

Plate 9: Jaina (Trikūṭa) Basadī No. 15 with *paramaśāyika maṇḍala* (top) and circular *vāstu-puruṣa maṇḍala* (bottom)

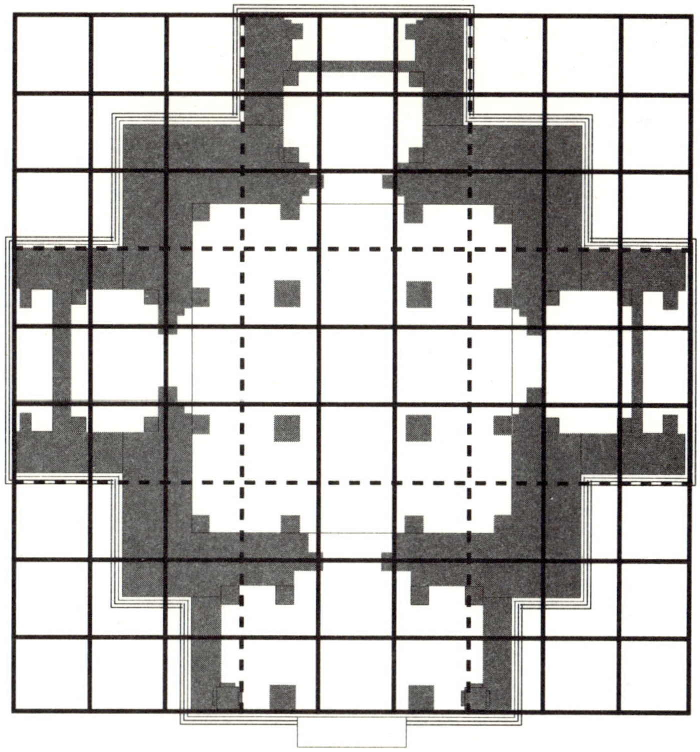

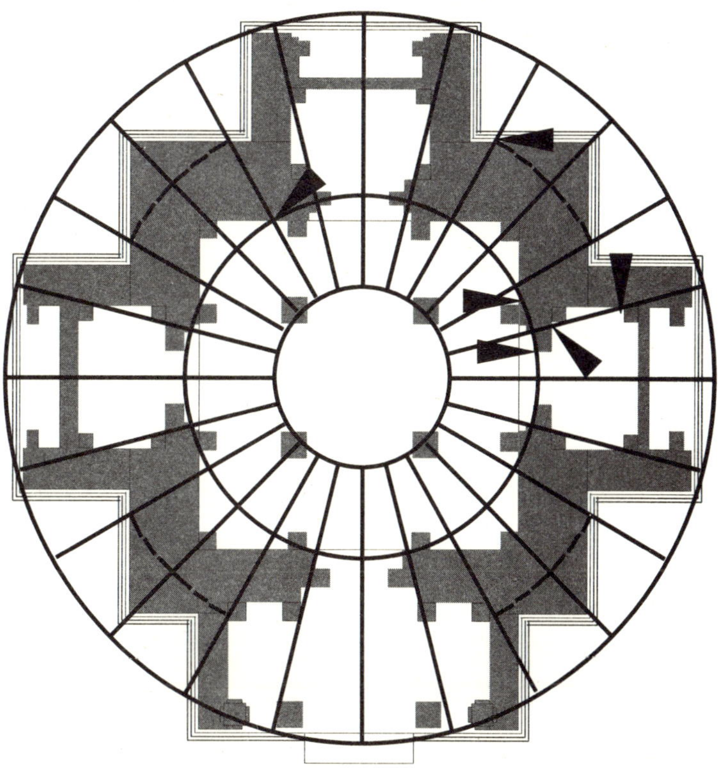

Vaidyanātheśvara Dvikūṭa Temple, Vaidyanāthapura, Karnataka (a. CE 775)

As with the Candragupta Trikūṭa Basadī at Śravaṇabeḷagoḷa (**Plate 4**), the Śaiva Vaidyanātheśvara Dvikūṭa Temple[17] is believed to have been constructed during the reign of the Gaṅga king Śivamāra II (r. CE 788–817) (**Appendix D**) and exhibits a **B**-type *dvikūṭa* temple plan (**Figure 2**).

The temple is aligned east to west. The western *garbhagṛha* is square and houses a Śivaliṅga. To the east is an *antarāla* which opens onto a square, enclosed *sabhā-maṇḍapa*. The *sabhā-maṇḍapa* has sixteen columns in a normal configuration — i.e. four in the centre and twelve engaged columns, four of which are quarter columns, on the walls of the *sabhā-maṇḍapa* — which form nine *aṅkana*s. Centred in the eastern wall of the *sabha-maṇḍapa* is a door leading to a larger, rectangular *mahā-maṇḍapa*. There are twelve columns in three ranks in the centre and twenty engaged columns attached to the inner walls. However, it is interesting to note that the engaged columns do not correspond to the twelve central columns, a curious anomaly. To the north of the *mahā-maṇḍapa*, but not centred is a second *garbhagṛha*, simple *en plan*. Opposite this *garbhagṛha* is an entrance with a porch. There is a second entrance to the *mahā-maṇḍapa*, centred in the eastern wall, but without porch.

17 Redrawn using PageMaker 6.0 from: KMS II, p. 418, description on p. 189. See also **Preface**.

Plate 10: Vaidyanātheśvara Dvikūṭa Temple plan

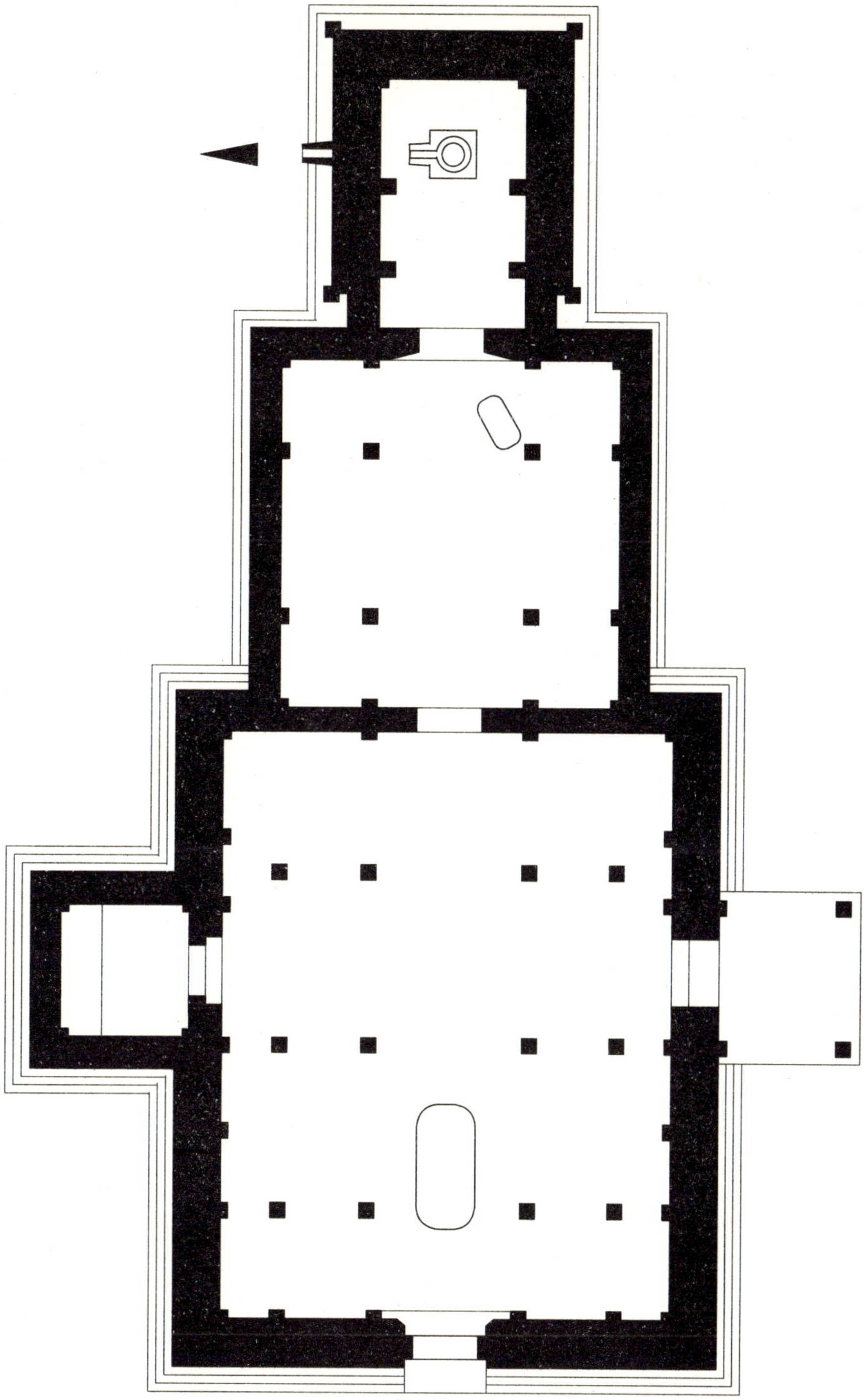

Gaṅgādhareśvara Dvikūṭa Temple, Doḍḍaiśvara, Karnataka (a. CE 775)

As with the Candragupta Trikūṭa Basadī at Śravaṇabeḷagoḷa (**Plate 4**) and the Śaiva Vaidyanātheśvara Dvikūṭa Temple of Vaidyanāthapura (**Plate 10**), the Gaṅgādhareśvara Dvikūṭa Temple[18] of Doḍḍaiśvara is the product of the Gaṅga Dynasty. It is believed to have been constructed in the late eighth century during the reigns of the Gaṅga king Śrī Puruṣa II (r. CE 725-88) or Śivamāra II (r. CE 788–817)[19] (**Appendix D**) and exhibits an **A**-type *dvikūṭa* temple plan (**Figure 2**).

The Gaṅgādhareśvara Dvikūṭa Temple's *vimānas* are vastly different in size. The eastern[20] *garbhagṛha* is nearly twice the size of the western counterpart and holds a Śivaliṅga. Both open onto a rectangular *antarāla*, and thence into a square, enclosed *sabhā-maṇḍapa*. Whereas, the eastern *garbhagṛha* holds a Śivaliṅga, the western *garbhagṛha* is devoid of an image at this time. The roof of the *sabhā-maṇḍapa* is supported by four centred columns, while to the south is a simple entrance to this temple.

18 Redrawn using PageMaker 6.0 from: KMS II, p. 418, description on pp. 188-89. See also **Preface**.

19 KHMS II, p. 188, states that the temple is "assignable to the fourth quarter of the eighth century CE of Mārasiṁha I . . . who ruled between CE 796-99". However, Mārasiṁha I is not listed in the standard genealogies of the Gaṅgas. But, Mārasiṁha II Satyavākya's reign is normally listed as CE 963-75. During the years CE 796-99, Śivamāra I (r. CE 679–726) was the monarch.

20 Ibid., KMS seems to have misidentified the locations of the *garbhagṛhas* as his description does not match the plan on p. 418. Since there are a number of errors in the Suresh study, it is possible that the plan on p. 418 is "flipped". **Plate 11** displays the plan as seen on page 418.

Plate 11: Gaṅgādhareśvara Dvikūṭa Temple plan

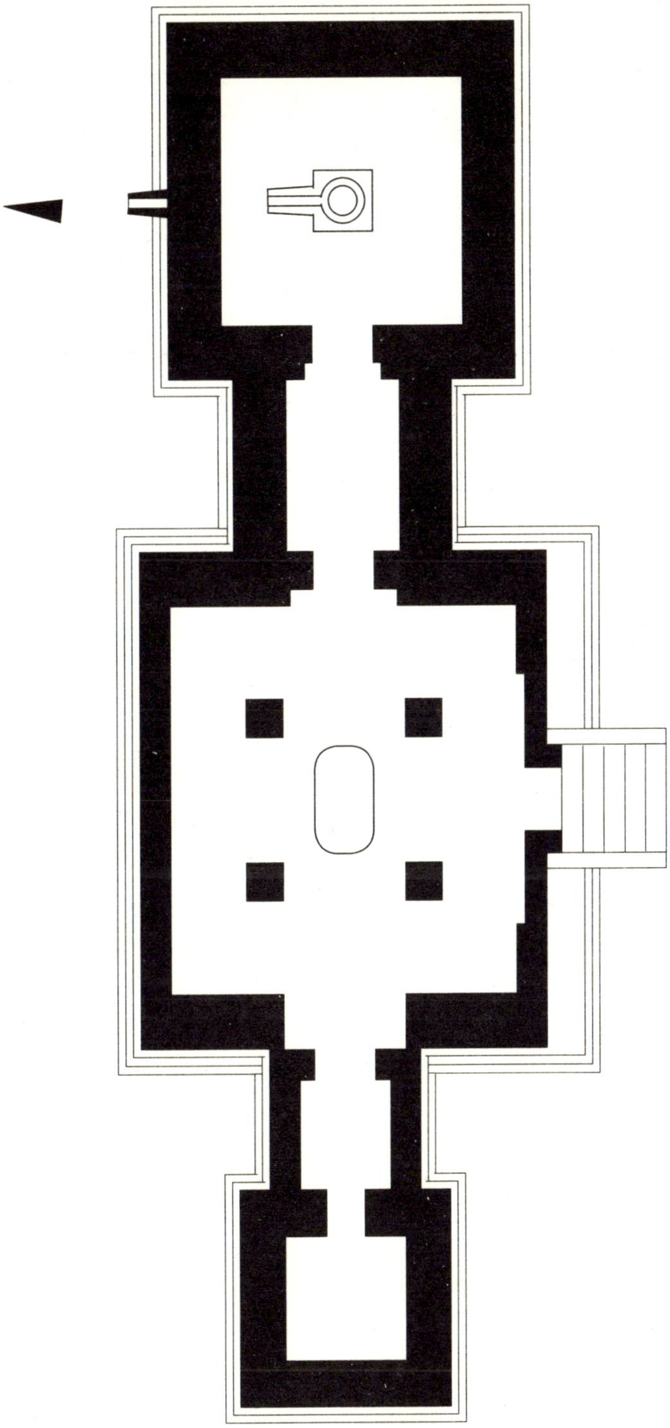

Śaiva Dvikūṭa Temple Chauḍadampur, Karnataka (a. CE 899)

Chauḍadampur is a small village on the banks of the Tuṅgabhadrā River in the Dhārwāṛ district. This village is unremarkable except for a small complex of partially ruined temples and shrines, the most prominent of which is the Mukteśvara Temple. It is suggested that this complex was constructed after the Western Cāḷukyas (Kalyāṇa) assumed dominance over the Rāṣṭrakūṭas (**Appendix E**). Southeast of the Mukteśvara Temple, which is the largest temple of this complex, stands the Śaiva Dvikūṭa Temple.[21]

Oriented towards the west, this *dvikūṭa* temple is somewhat unique. It consists of two, virtually identical, conjoined elements set side by side and resting upon a substantial platform (**Figure 21**). Each of the elements is composed of a *pañcaratha vimāna* with a square *garbhagṛha* fronted by an enclosed, square *maṇḍapa* without columns. To the south of these *maṇḍapa*s are appended two rectangular, simple, enclosed shrines with an image against the back (eastern) wall each — i.e. the *garbhagṛha-maṇḍapa*s and the simple shrines — have entrances towards the west.

India provides many unique variations from the standard, *en plan*. The Śaiva Dvikūṭa Temple, although diminutive, is entirely unique in its plan and duplication.

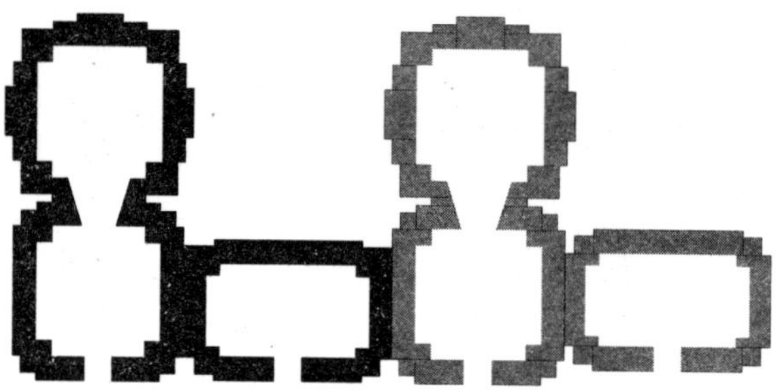

Figure 21: Śaiva Dvikūṭa Temple (S-E of Mukteśvara Temple) indicating duplication

---

21 Redrawn using PageMaker 6.0 from: HC, **Plate LXXVIII**.

Plate 12: Śaiva Dvikūṭa Temple plan

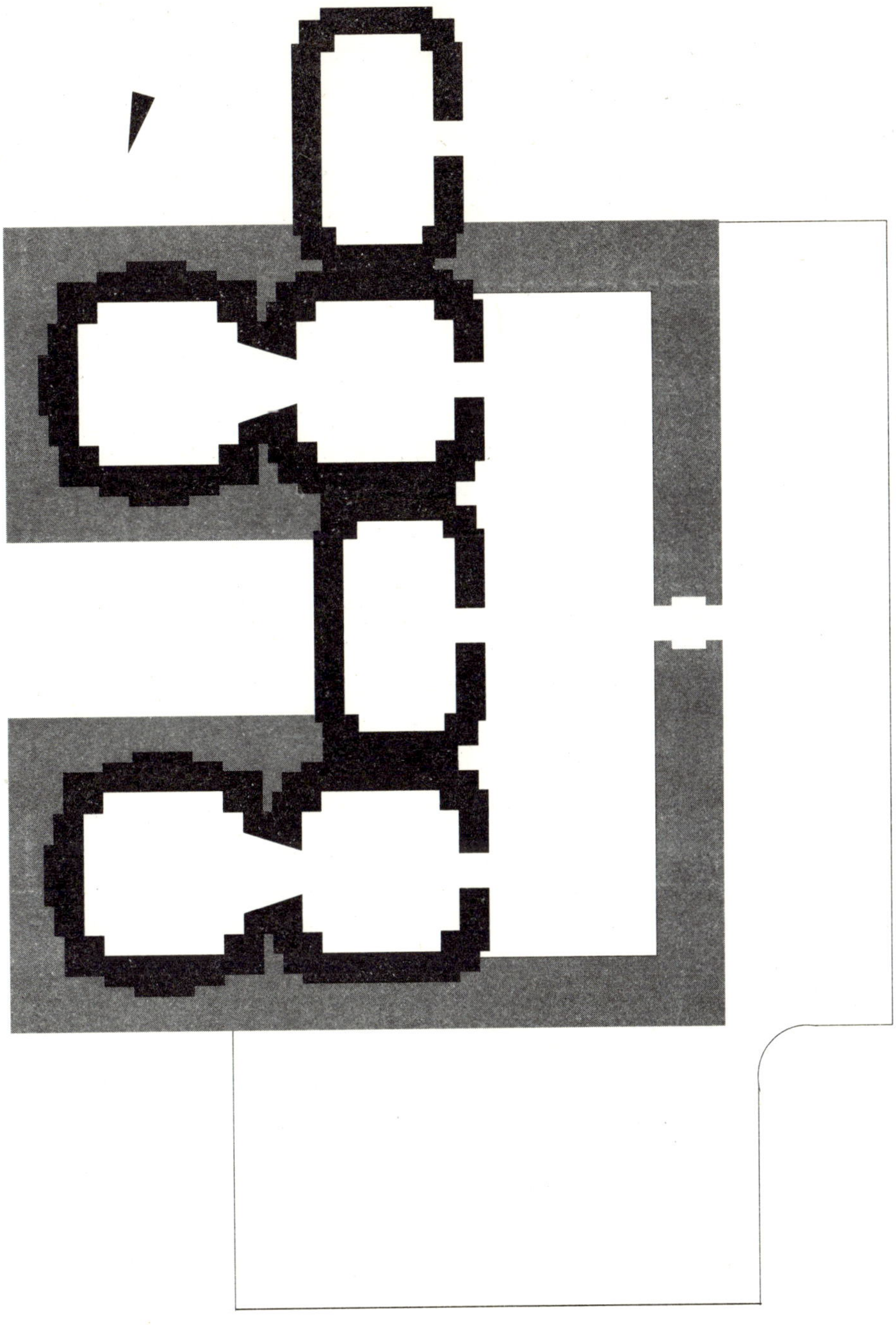

Cauṅsaṭh Yoginī Sanctuary, Khajurāho (a. CE 850)

Early in the ninth century a vigorous Rājpūt clan advanced to the Bundelkhaṇḍ, found a commodious locale and established a vibrant kingdom, the Candella Dynasty. There, at Khajurāho they constructed a series of truly magnificent and imposing monuments. One of the oldest of these temples at this famed site is the Cauṅsaṭh Yoginī Sanctuary.[22] It is dedicated to the Goddess Kālī in the forms of Durgā-Mahiṣāsuramardinī.[23] Only about half of this large monument remains standing today. Unlike the other temples of the Khajurāho group, the sanctuary is constructed of hard, durable granite. The three-dimensional, exuberance found in the other Candella temples of Khajurāho is lacking here, in the Cauṅsaṭh Yoginī Sanctuary, due, undoubtedly, to the employment of the hard, unyielding granite.

The Cauṅsaṭh Yoginī Sanctuary is a hypaethral temple in the form of a rectilinear trapezium, or irregular quadrilateral. It is unlike the other three hypaethral temples in India dedicated to the sixty-four *yoginīs* which are circular, *en plan* — i.e. the Cauṅsaṭh Yoginī Temple near Hīrāpur (**Plate 3**), the Cauṅsaṭh Yoginī Temple in Rānīpur-Jharial (**Plate 132**) and the Cauṅsaṭh Yoginī Mandir in Bherāghāṭ (near Jabalpur) (**Plate 38**). The Sanctuary faces north-east and consists of twenty-two shrines along the southern wall, facing northwards, and complimentary twenty-two additional shrines along the northern wall, facing southwards. Ten shrines face westward on the eastern, entrance wall. In the western wall are another ten shrines, separated by a larger central shrine which contains the image of Durgā-Mahiṣāsuramardinī. These face the entrance across a vast, unroofed courtyard. Each of the sixty-four shrines is topped by a rectilinear, truncated tower. The interior space of the shrines is small, hardly enough space for a single individual and each holds an image of a *yoginī*. The whole rests upon a rough, battered platform.

One may question the arrangement of the shrines in this rectilinear format. As with most of Buddhist and Hindu traditions, particularly in India, numerology[24] often plays an important role. Twenty-two is a number that is related to Candra, or Soma, or Rāhu. These moon-related deities are auspicious. The northern and southern shrines are divided into fives. Five is the sum of the first masculine number and the first feminine number, and therefore, is seen as a union which is magical, mystical and revolutionary. It is noteworthy that the southern rank of ten shrines and the larger, central shrine is broken between the eastern five shrines and the western five to which the sanctuary is attached. If they were a continuous rank, they would have amounted to eleven. Eleven is one of the most inauspicious numbers in Buddhist/Hindu numerology and is assiduously avoided as it is seen to be abstinent, illusive and transgressive.

---

22 Redrawn using Adobe "InDesign" CS3 from: CT I, p. 115. This rectilinear complex is not orthogonal, but a trapezium as seen in DD, p. 67. Liberties were taken — i.e. simplified — and presented as shown in Plate 13. The number of shrines is correct and their relative size and form conform to the existing monument.

23 DD, op. cit., pp. 64-65.

24 FWB II, see specific numbers.

Plate 13: Cauṅsaṭh Yoginī Sanctuary plan (simplified)

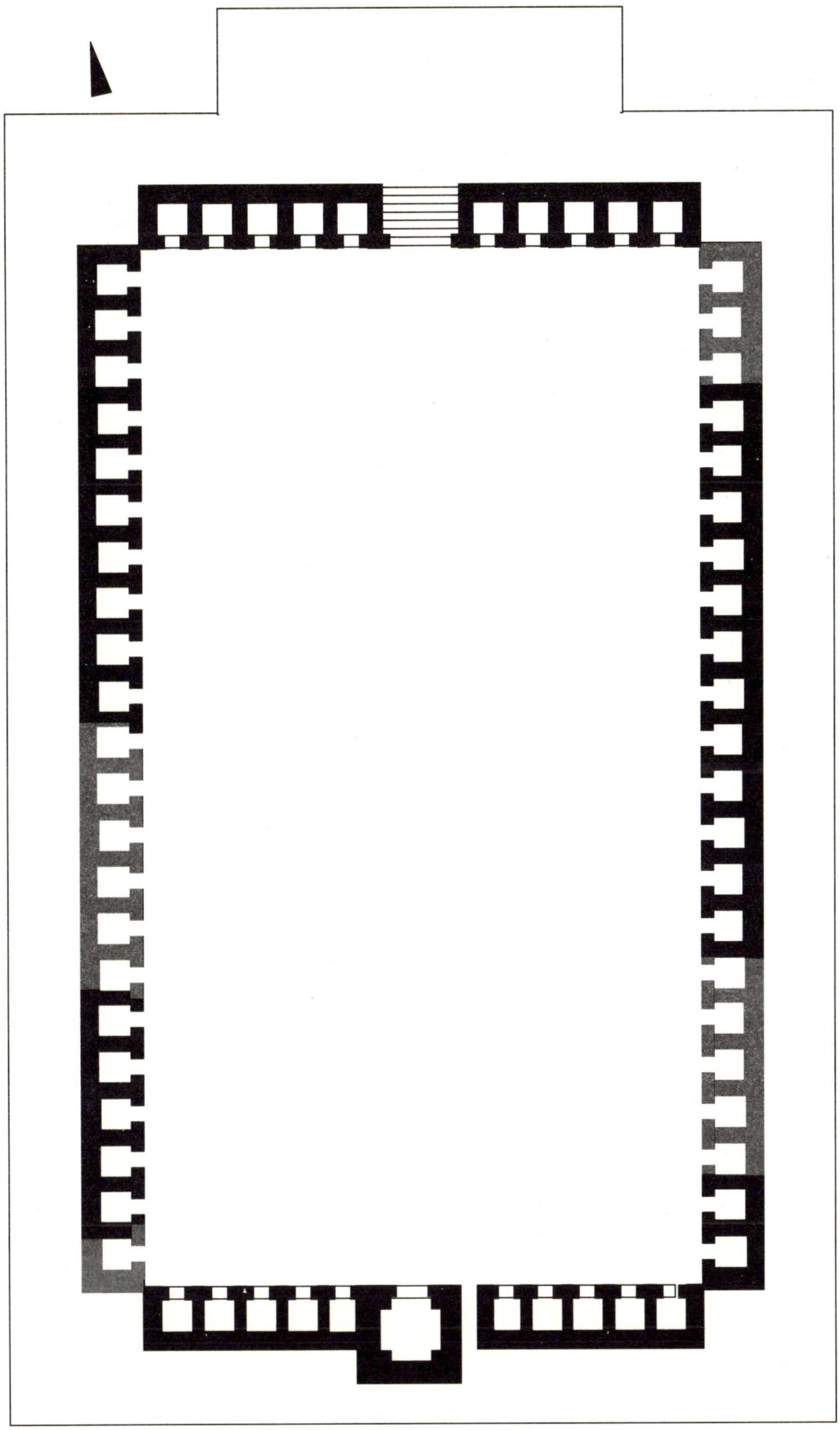

Kalleśvara Dvikūṭa Temple, Bagali, Karnataka (*c.* CE 987–1062)

The initial construction at the beginning of the Western Cāḷukya Dynasty (Kalyāṇa) by the king Taila Āhavamalla or Tailapa II (CE 973-95) and later construction occurred during the reign of King Someśvara I (aka Trailokyamalla or Āhavamalladeva) (r. CE 1043-68) (**Appendix D**). The Western Cāḷukya Dynasty (Kalyāṇa) came to power nearly two centuries after the fall of the Cāḷukyas of Bādāmī when they threw off the yoke of the Rāṣṭrakūṭa Dynasty. Their reign in the region is considered by some to be the golden age.

The plan of the Kalleśvara Temple[25] represents a **B**-type *dvikūṭa* plan and places the main *garbhagṛha* in the west with a rectilinear *antarāla* opening to an enclosed *sabhā-maṇḍapa* which exhibits sixteen columns placed in the usual manner — i.e. four free-standing columns in the centre raised on a square platform and twelve additional columns which are engaged. *En plan*, the western *vimāna* is considerably more elaborate than the smaller northern counterpart. This *sabhā-maṇḍapa* has an entrance to the south and its main entrance is to the east where it gives way to a large and complex *mahā-maṇḍapa*. *En plan*, the *mahā-maṇḍapa* is essentially a square consisting of six pillars on each side. To this square has been added an extension of four pillars per side giving the whole a stepped appearance. Fifty-two pillars support the roof the *mahā-maṇḍapa*. To the north is the second *garbhagṛha* of this temple dedicated to Narasiṁha. It is because of the essentially different character of the two *vimāna*s that the assignment of the different periods is indicated.

To the east of the larger *vimāna* and physically separated from the *mahā-maṇḍapa* is a small temple dedicated to Sūrya which is aligned towards the west. It would appear that because of the close proximity of the Sūrya Temple to the *mahā-maṇḍapa*, Suresh lists the Kalleśvara Temple among the *trikūṭa* temples in his study. Because it is physically separated and not architecturally attached to the *mahā-maṇḍapa* this author identifies it as a *dvikūṭa* temple type.

[25] Redrawn using PageMaker 6.0 from: KMS II, p. 442, description on pp. 214-15. See also **Preface**.

Plate 14: Kalleśvara Temple plan

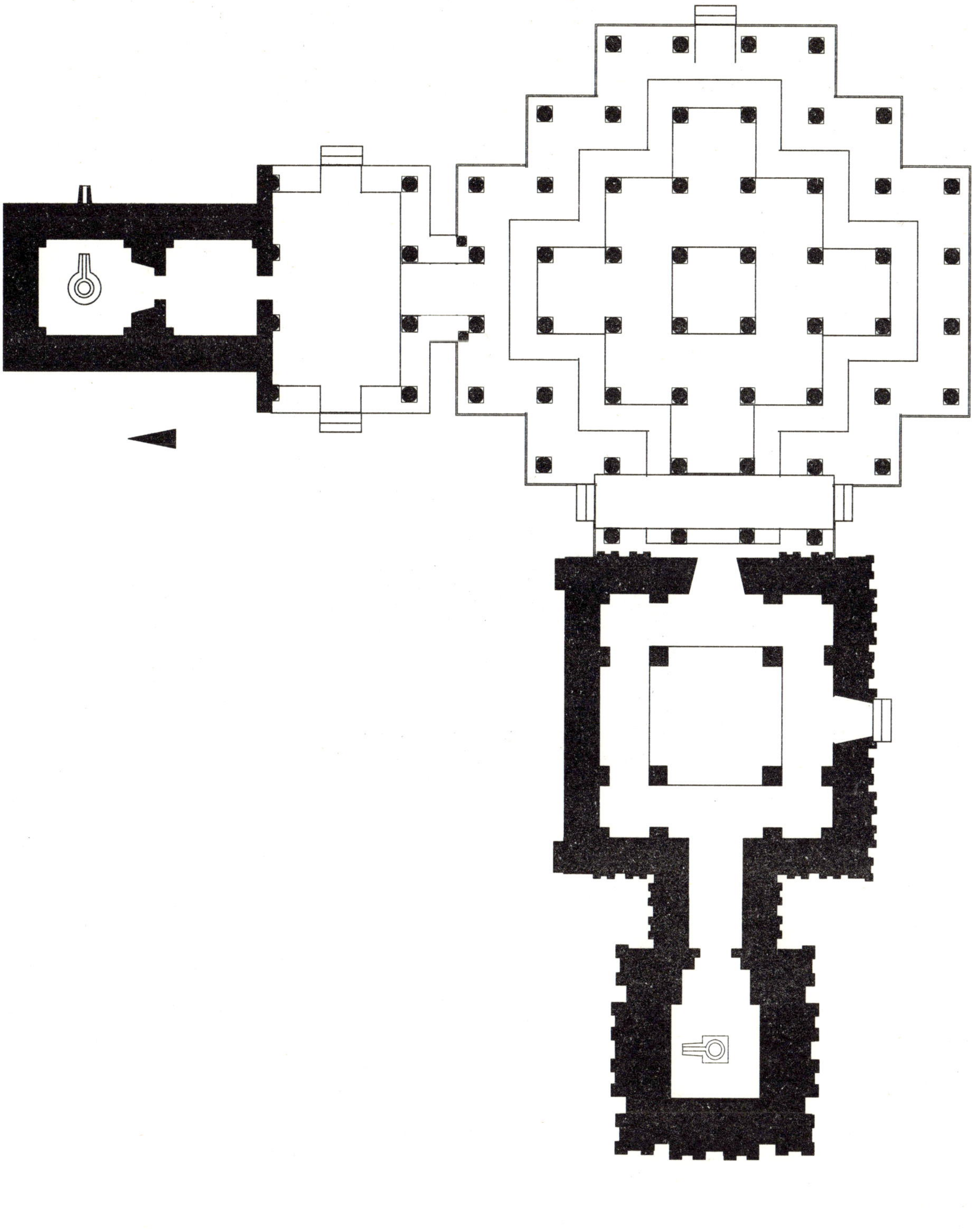

Jaina Tīrthaṅkara Trikūṭa Basadī, Arasibedi, Karnataka (a. CE 1025)

The Jaina Tīrthaṅkara Trikūṭa Basadī[26] at Arasibedi was constructed during the reign of Someśvara I (aka Trailokyamalla or Āhavamalladeva) (r. CE 1043-68) (**Appendix D**), king of the Western Cāḷukya (Kalyāṇa). This **A**-type *trikūṭa* temple plan (**Figure 3**) is aligned east to west. The *vimāna* of the *basadī* is dedicated to the Jaina *Tīrthaṅkara*.

Three identical elements (**Figure 22**) to the north, south and west, consist of a square *garbhagṛha* attached to a square *antarāla*, make up this plan. These elements are attached to a square *sabhā-maṇḍapa* with sixteen columns arranged in the traditional manner — i.e. four columns on a platform in the centre and twelve engaged columns, four of which are quarter columns in the corners — creating nine *aṅkanas*. The western *vimāna* contains a mutilated Jaina *Tīrthaṅkara's* image. To the east of the *sabhā-maṇḍapa* is an open *mahā-maṇḍapa* with four central pillars set upon a raised platform and twelve smaller columns surrounding the four. Four of these smaller pillars are engaged to the eastern, outer wall of the *sabhā-maṇḍapa*. Again, to the east is a *mukha-maṇḍapa*, the roof of which is supported by two columns. There are two means of ingress — to the east and to the south of the *sabhā-maṇḍapa*.

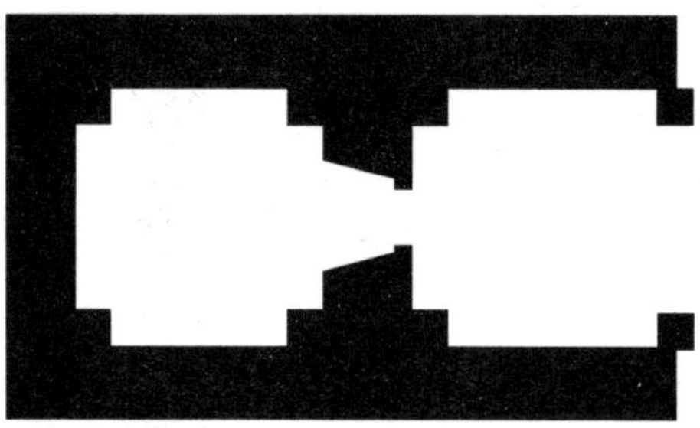

Figure 22: Jaina Tīrthaṅkara Trikūṭa Basadī *vimāna* element

[26] Redrawn using PageMaker 6.0 from: KMS II, p. 444, description on pp. 216-17. See also **Preface**.

Plate 15: Jaina Tīrthaṅkara Trikūṭa Basadī plan

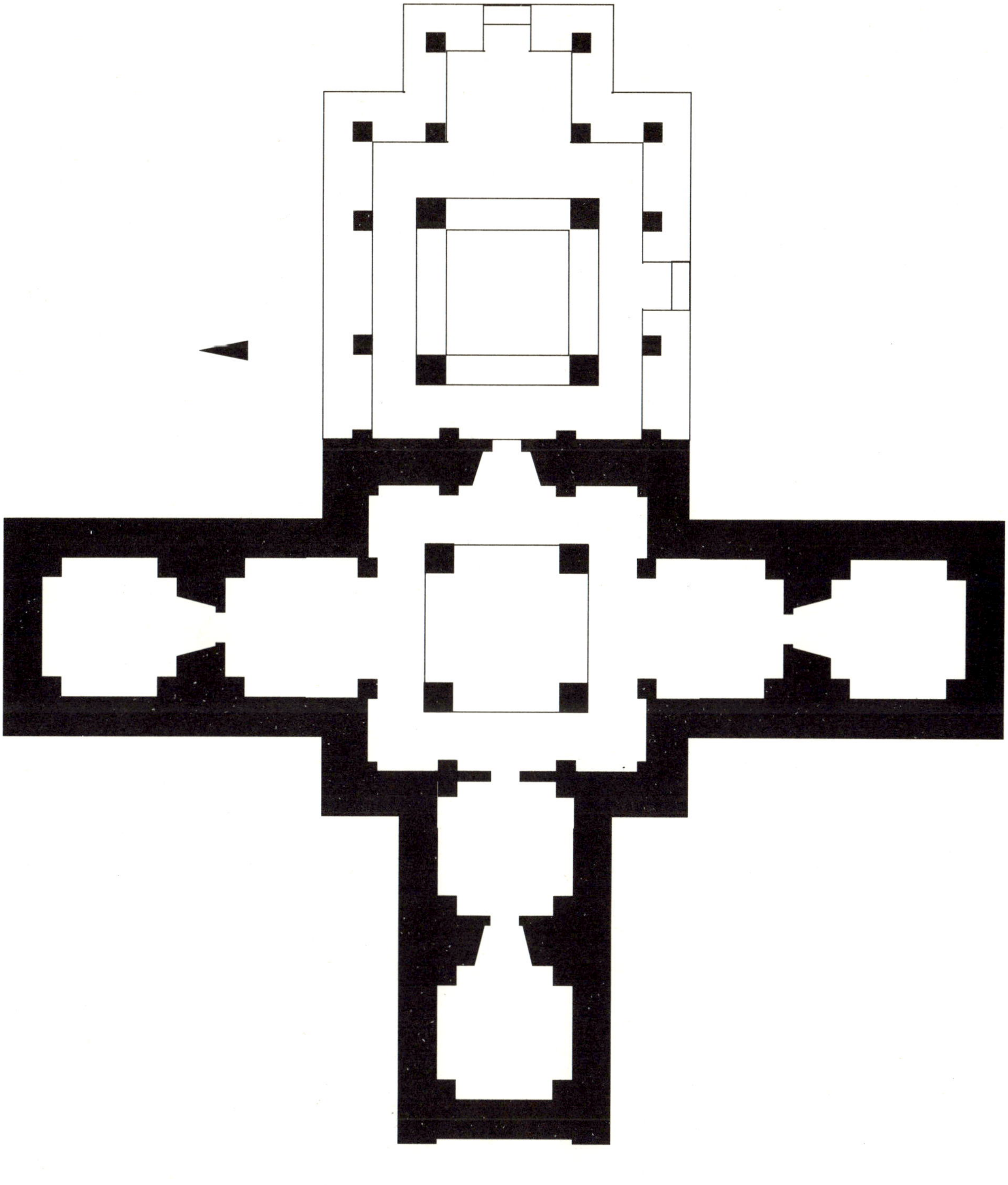

Bhīmeśvara Catuṣkūṭa Temple, Nīlaguṇḍa (a. CE 1050)

The Bhīmeśvara Catuṣkūṭa Temple[27] at Nīlaguṇḍa is generally dated in the third quarter of the eleventh century, a time of some unrest in the Karnataka region. This date would place the construction somewhere within the reigns of the Western Cāḷukya (Kalyāṇa) kings Someśvara I (Trailokyamalla or Āhavamalladeva) (r. CE 1043-68) and/or Someśvara II (r. CE 1068-76) or the Hoysaḷa king Vinayāditа (r. CE 1047-98) who co-reigned with Ereyaṅga (r. CE 1063–1100). Inscriptions which refer to both the Cāḷukyas and the Hoysaḷas appear within the temple.

The Bhīmeśvara Catuṣkūṭa Temple is aligned towards the east and is composed of four *garbhagṛhas* in the manner of a **B**-type *catuṣkūṭa* plan (**Figure 4**). The western sanctum is larger and more elaborate, *en plan*, than the other three which are essentially identical and relatively restrained in comparison. The western sanctum exhibits three external deep shrines on the north, south and west façades. The western *garbhagṛha* is square, as are those of the other three, and holds a Śivaliṅga. A enclosed, rectangular *antarāla* leads from the main sanctum to a large *sabhā-maṇḍapa*. This columned *sabhā-maṇḍapa* unites the eastern three *vimānas*. The northern *garbhagṛha* is dedicated to Keśava and the southern *vimāna* to Lord Brahmā.[28] Both possess an *antarāla*, but in these cases they are completely open onto the *sabhā-maṇḍapa* (**Figure 23**). In the north-western and south-western corners of the *sabhā-maṇḍapa* are niches/ shrines. The eastern portion of this hall is disturbingly plain. The *sabhā-maṇḍapa*, in turn, leads to an open, columned *mukha-maṇḍapa* with stairs descending to the north and south. Attached to this *mukha-maṇḍapa* is the fourth, west-facing sanctum with its *garbhagṛha*, but minus an *antarāla* (**Figure 23**). This *vimāna* is dedicated to Sūrya.

The application of a *maṇḍala*(s) over the whole of the Bhīmeśvara Catuṣkūṭa Temple presents certain problems (**Plates 17-18**). With a *paramaśāyika maṇḍala* placed over the whole (**Plate 17** [top]), the four *vimānas* rest within the middle nine *padas* of each side — i.e. squares **2, 4, 6** and **8** (**Appendix C, Plate 134**). A *maṇḍūka maṇḍala* appears applicable when it is used in grid form (**Plate 17** [bottom]).

When a circular *vāstu-puruṣa maṇḍala* is employed and centred on the *sabhā-maṇḍapa*, the four *vimānas* rest with in two sections on either side of the cardinal directions — i.e. within **x–a, f–g, m–l**, and **r–s** (**Appendix C, Plate 135**) — and the *sabhā-maṇḍapa* is bounded by the second ring from the centre (**Plate 18**).

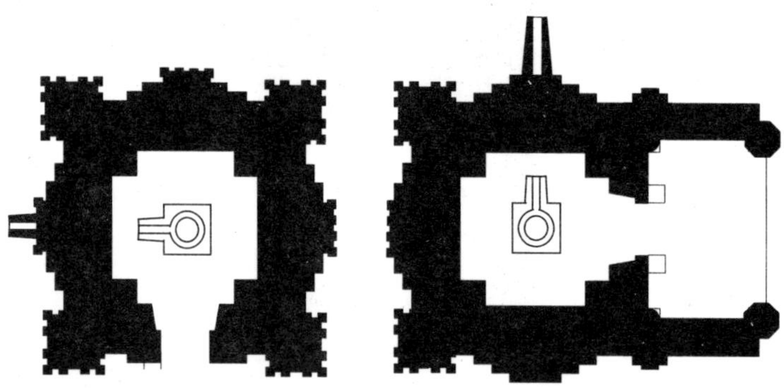

Figure 23: Bhīmeśvara Catuṣkūṭa Temple *vimāna* elements (left: east *vimāna*; right: north and south *vimānas*)

---

[27] Redrawn using PageMaker 6.0 from: CT, p. 2330; and KMS II, p. 476, description on pp. 264-66. See also **Preface**.

[28] KMS II, p. 265. The inclusion of Lord Brahmā is extraordinary.

Plate 16: Bhīmeśvara Catuṣkūṭa Temple plan

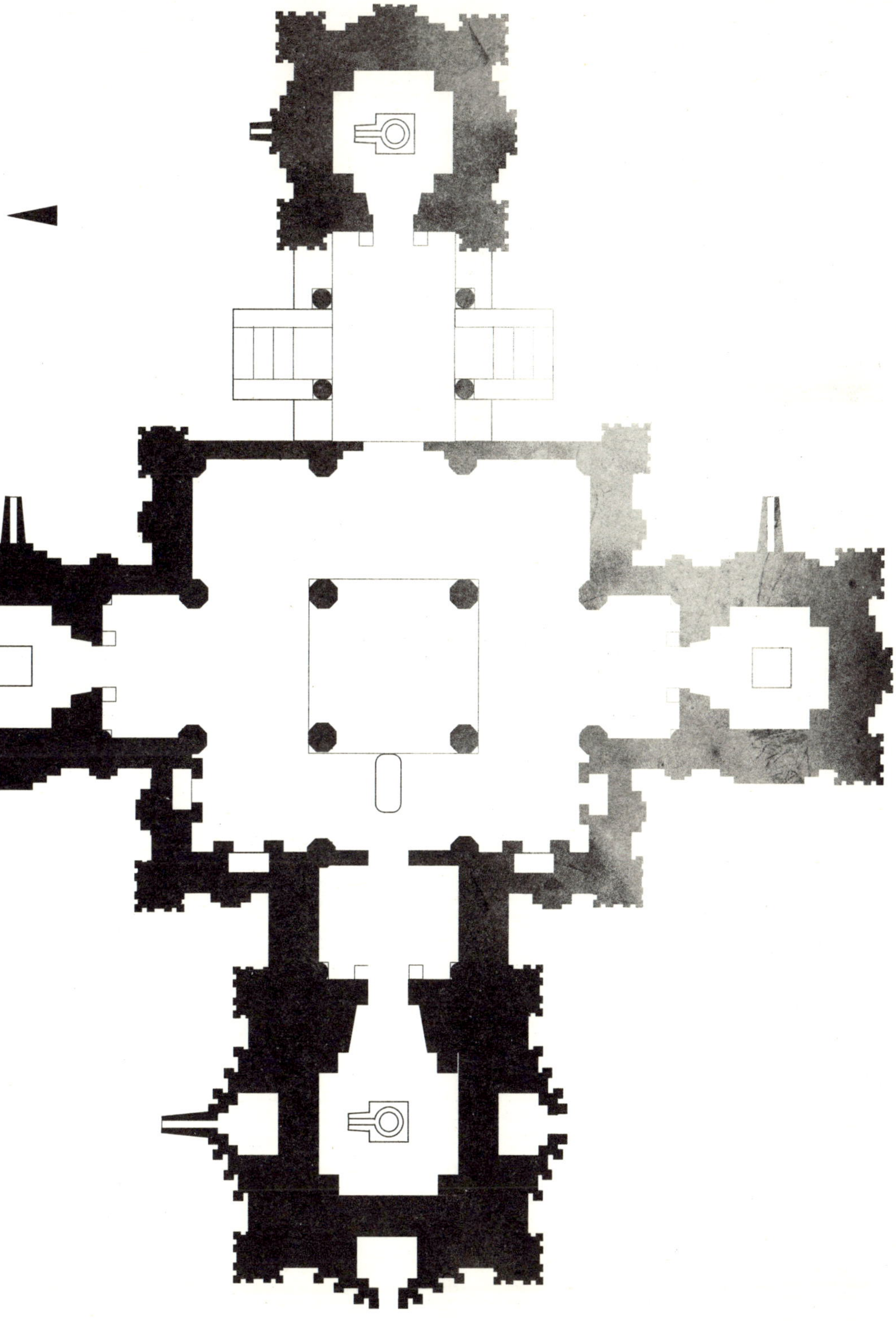

Plate 17: Bhīmeśvara Catuṣkūṭa Temple with *paramaśāyika maṇḍala* (top) and *maṇḍūka maṇḍala*-based grid (bottom)

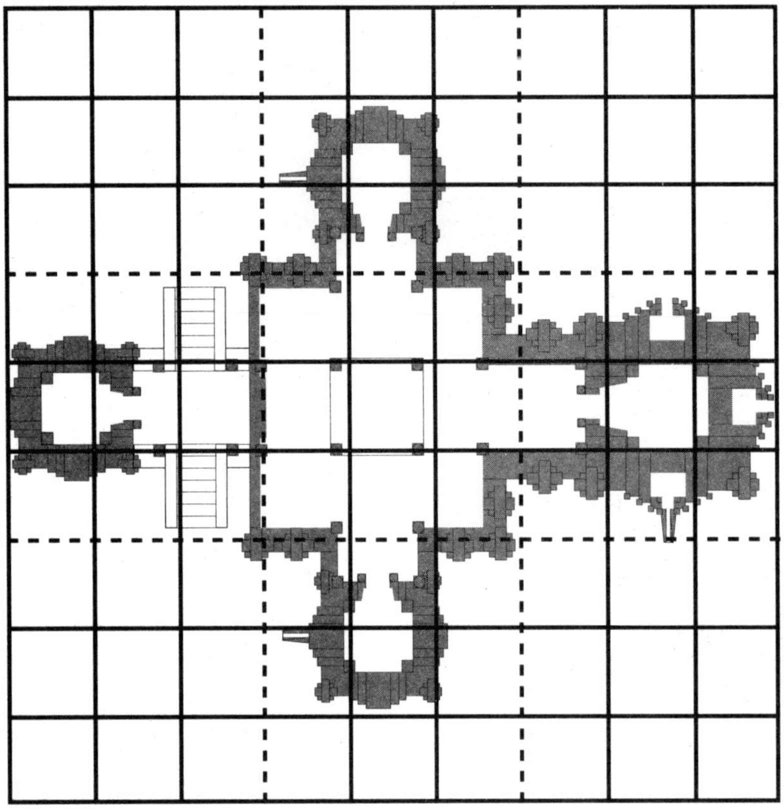

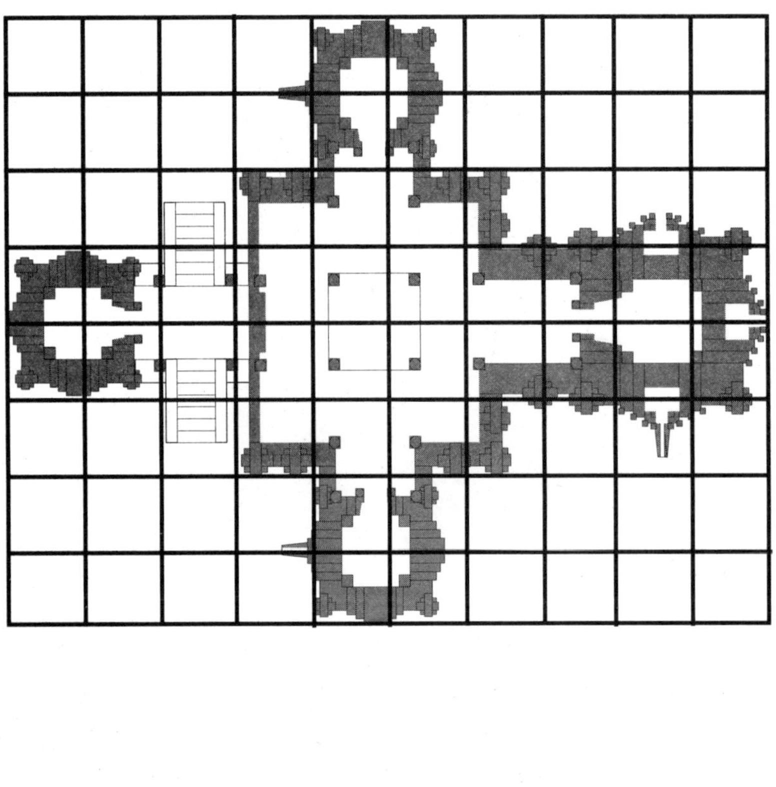

Plate 18: Bhīmeśvara Catuṣkūṭa Temple with circular *vāstu-puruṣa maṇḍala* centred over the *maṇḍapa*

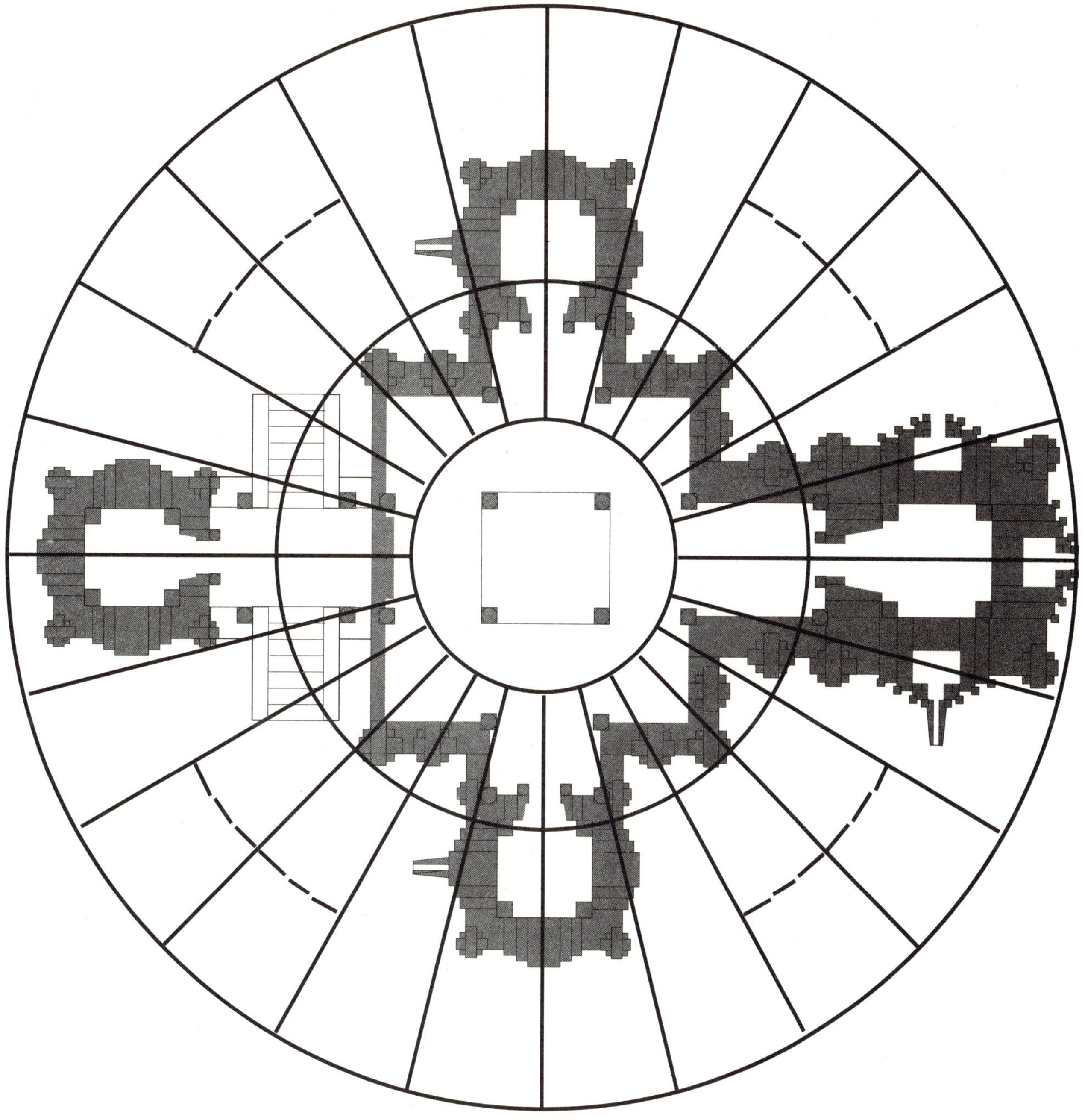

Mahādeva Trikūṭa Temple, Benakoṭagi, Karnataka (c. CE 1050)

Exhibiting an A-type *trikūṭa* plan (**Figure 3**) the Mahādeva Trikūṭa Temple[29] of Benakoṭagi was constructed sometime during the reigns of Jayasiṁha I Jagadekamalla (r. CE 1015 43) or Someśvara I (Trailokyamalla or Āhavamalladeva) (r. CE 1043-68) (**Appendix D**) of the Western Cāḷukya (Kalyāṇa) Dynasty. It is dedicated to the Lord Śiva and oriented east to west.

The plan is composed of three identical *vimāna* elements (**Figure 24**) with the *garbhagṛha*'s outer walls in *pañcaratha*. The *garbhagṛhas* are square as are the *antarālas*. In addition to the engaged columns at the entrance of the *antarālas* to the *sabhā-maṇḍapa*, there are two columns forming the entrance into the *vimāna*. The main *vimāna* is aligned towards the east, while the other two are oriented towards the north and south. The three *vimānas* front a common, enclosed *sabhā-maṇḍapa* if sixteen columns arranged in a traditional manner — i.e. four columns in the centre on a raised platform and twelve engaged columns, four of which are quarter, corner columns. Nine *aṅkanas* are formed by these columns. Centred in the eastern façade is the doorway to the interior and a short flight of steps. This door provides the only source of light to the interior.

Suresh posits, not without reason, that the western *garbhagṛha* was dedicated to Bhairava, while the northern sanctum holds a Śivaliṅga, and the southern was probably dedicated to Bhairavī.[30]

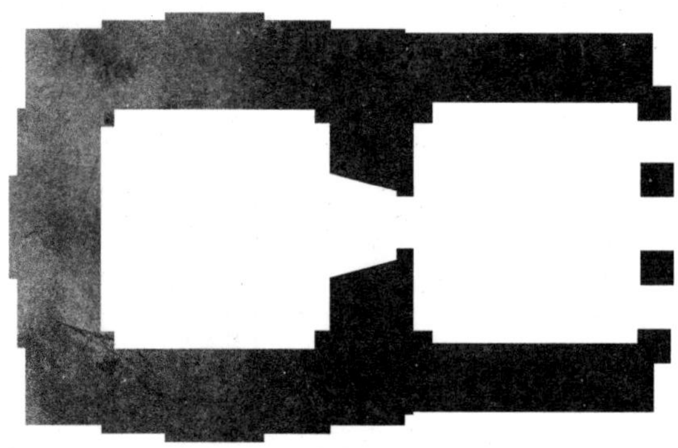

Figure 24: Mahādeva Trikūṭa Temple *vimāna* element

[29] Redrawn using PageMaker 6.0 from: KMS II, p. 443, description on pp. 215-16. See **Preface**.

[30] Loc. cit., p. 216.

Plate 19: Mahādeva Trikūṭa Temple plan

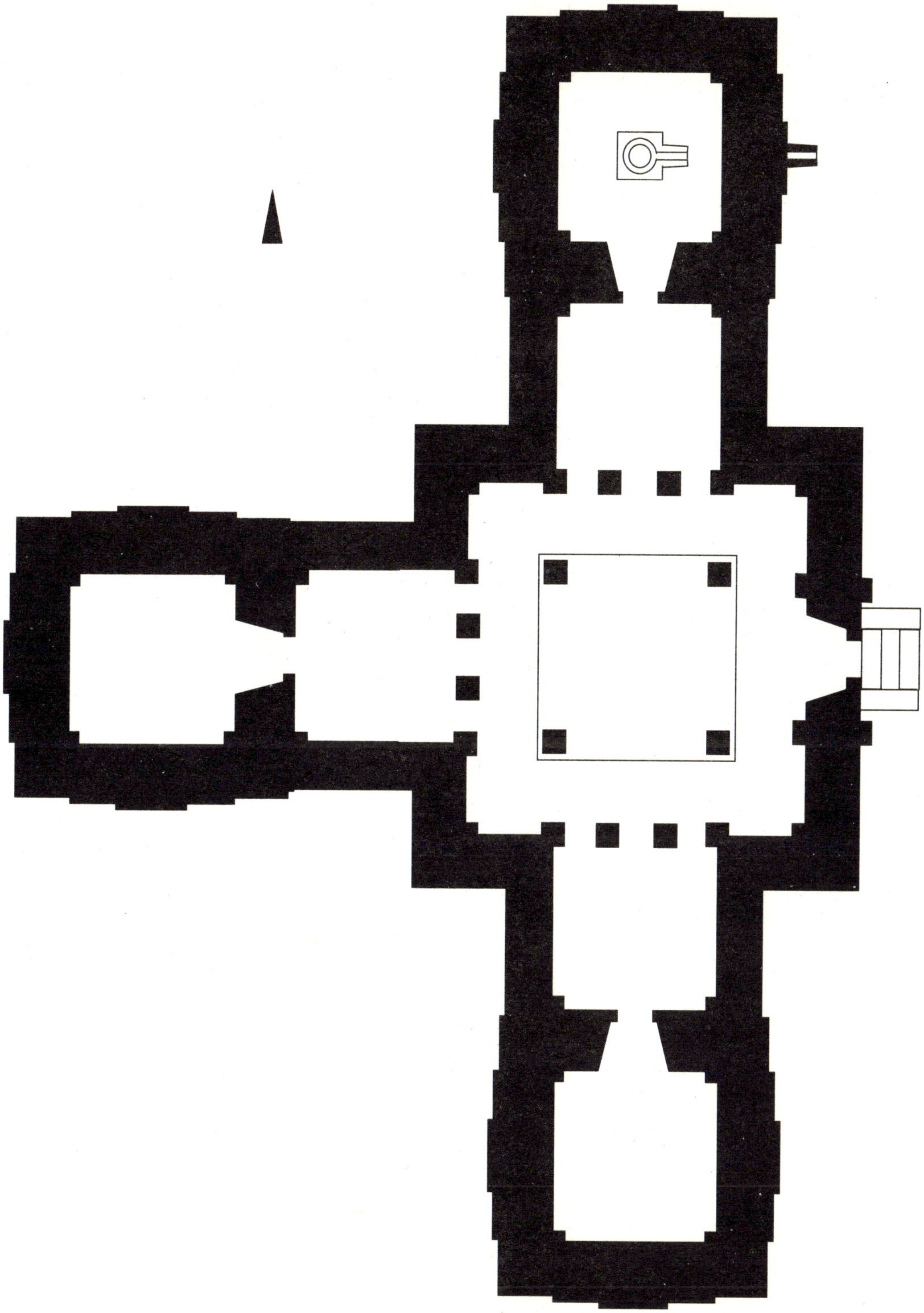

Trikūṭeśvara Temple, Gaḍag, Karnataka (*c*. CE 1062)

The Cāḷukya Trikūṭeśvara Temple,[31] found in the small town of Gaḍag, was initially constructed around the time of the monarchs Someśvara I (Trailokyamalla or Āhavamalladeva) (r. CE 1043-68)[32] and Someśvara II (r. CE 1068-76)[33] (**Appendix E**). Certainly Someśvara I was the more important of the two and was instrumental in establishing Cāḷukyan dominance in the region. Later evidence lists the date as CE 1101, within the range of Vikramāditya II (VI) CE 1076–1127), while a third inscription, apparently Hoysaḷa, is dated 1193, well within the reign of the Hoysaḷa king Ballāla III (r. CE 1291–1342). Gaḍag is a small town, but holds additional temples of note, especially the Sarasvatī Temple and the Someśvara Temple.

The Trikūṭeśvara Temple is a **B**-type *trikūṭa* temple (**Figure 3**) of vastly unequal proportions. Aligned towards the east, the pre-eminent sanctum — i.e. the western *vimāna* — contains a *garbhagṛha* with a triple Śivaliṅga. It is larger than the eastern *vimāna* and considerably larger than the diminutive northern sanctum. This, the western *vimāna*, exhibits a *pradakṣiṇāpatha* separating the sanctum from the thick outer wall. When one compares the size of the western sanctum with that of the east, it is apparent that they both are, *en plan*, of similar size and design. Cousens asserts that this temple was originally a *dvikūṭa* temple to which the western *vimāna* was enclosed, creating a *pradakṣiṇāpatha* and the northern sanctum was later added (**Figure 25**). These two assertions seem quite plausible, especially the enlarging of the western *vimāna*. To this element a relatively small, traditionally arranged *sabhā-maṇḍapa* is attached with an entrance to the south and one to the east. This eastern entrance leads to a large, multi-pillared, open, *mukha-maṇḍapa* with thirty-two columns. The *mukha-maṇḍapa* exhibits two, centred, stepped entrances — one to the north and the other to the south.

None the less, the Trikūṭeśvara Temple may be seen to be composed, *en plan*, of three combined elements — i.e. the western sanctum made up of a *garbhagṛha* and *aṇtarāla* enclosed by a larger structure creating a *pardakṣiṇāpatha* attached to a columned *sabhā-maṇḍapa*. This leads to a large, open *mukha-maṇḍapa*. This *mukha-maṇḍapa* leads to a smaller *vimāna* composed of a *garbhagṛha* with a rectangular *antarāla*. To these three elements has been appended a dominative *garbhagṛha* to the north.

Due to the erratic nature of this plan, the application of a *maṇḍala* is difficult. However a *paramaśāyika maṇḍala* is applicable to both the western *vimāna* and then pillared *mukha-maṇḍapa* (**Plate 21**). In addition a grid based on a *paramaśāyika maṇḍala* is applicable to the whole, minus the northern *garbhagṛha* (**Plate 22**). It is interesting to note that three-and-one-third grids are required — i.e. thirty *pada*s in length.

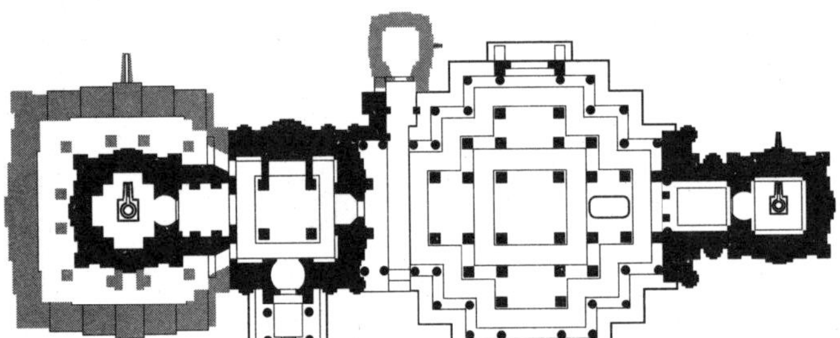

Figure 25: Trikūṭeśvara Temple as *dvikūṭa*

31 Redrawn using PageMaker 6.0 from: HC, Plate CXX.

32 HC, p. 112, states there "among the inscriptions . . . in the time of the Western Cāḷukyan king Āhavamalladeva II . . ." etc. However, on pp. 5-8 he lists the genealogy of the "Rulers of the Cāḷukyan Territories" and there is no mention of King Āhavamalladeva.

33 Ibid., p. 107.

Plate 20: Trikūṭeśvara Temple plan

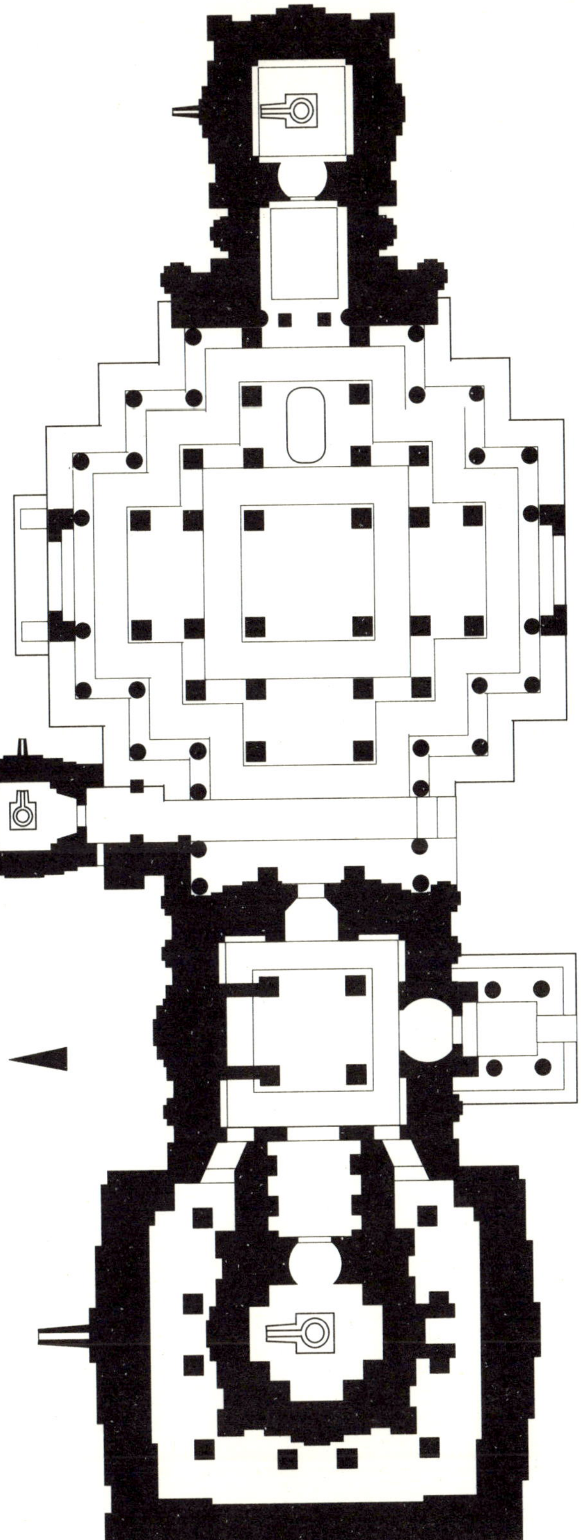

Plate 21: Trikūṭeśvara Temple with *paramaśāyika maṇḍala* over *vimāna* and *mukha-maṇḍapa*

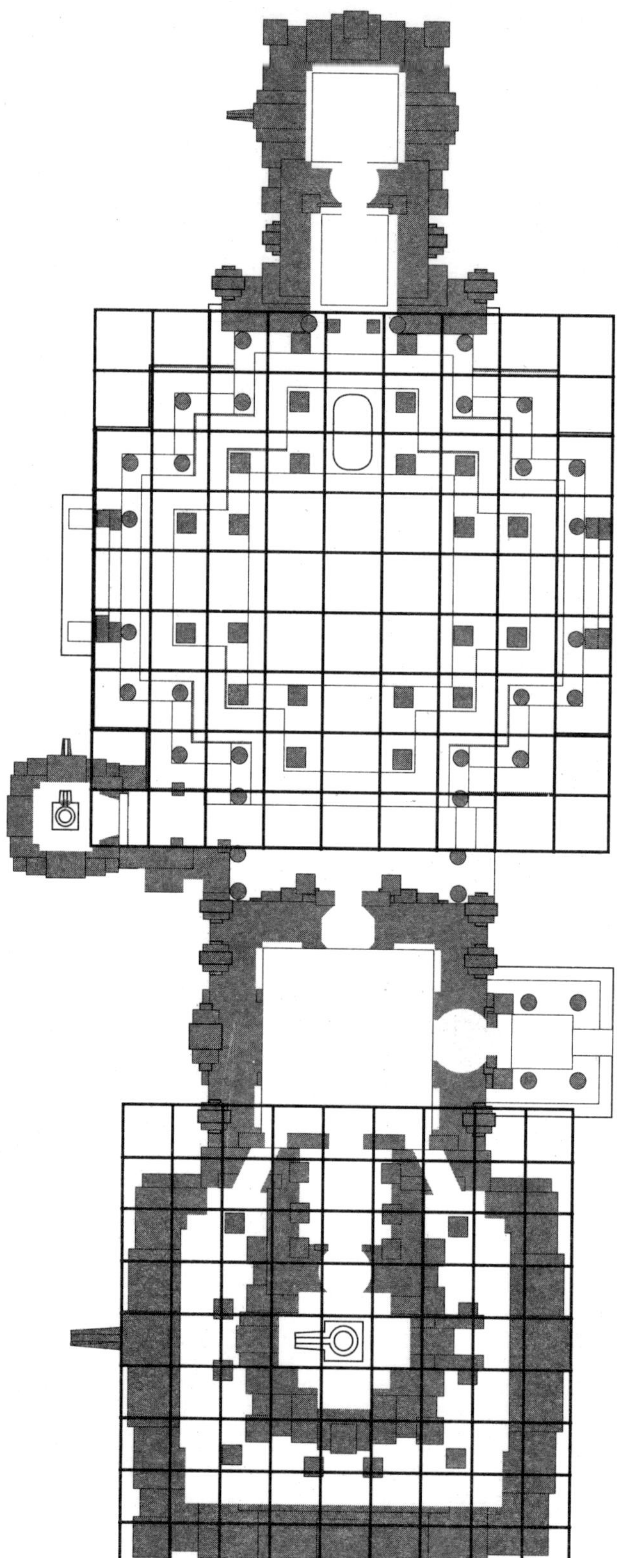

Plate 22: Trikūṭeśvara Temple plan with *paramaśāyika maṇḍala*-based grid over the whole except the northern *garbhagṛha*

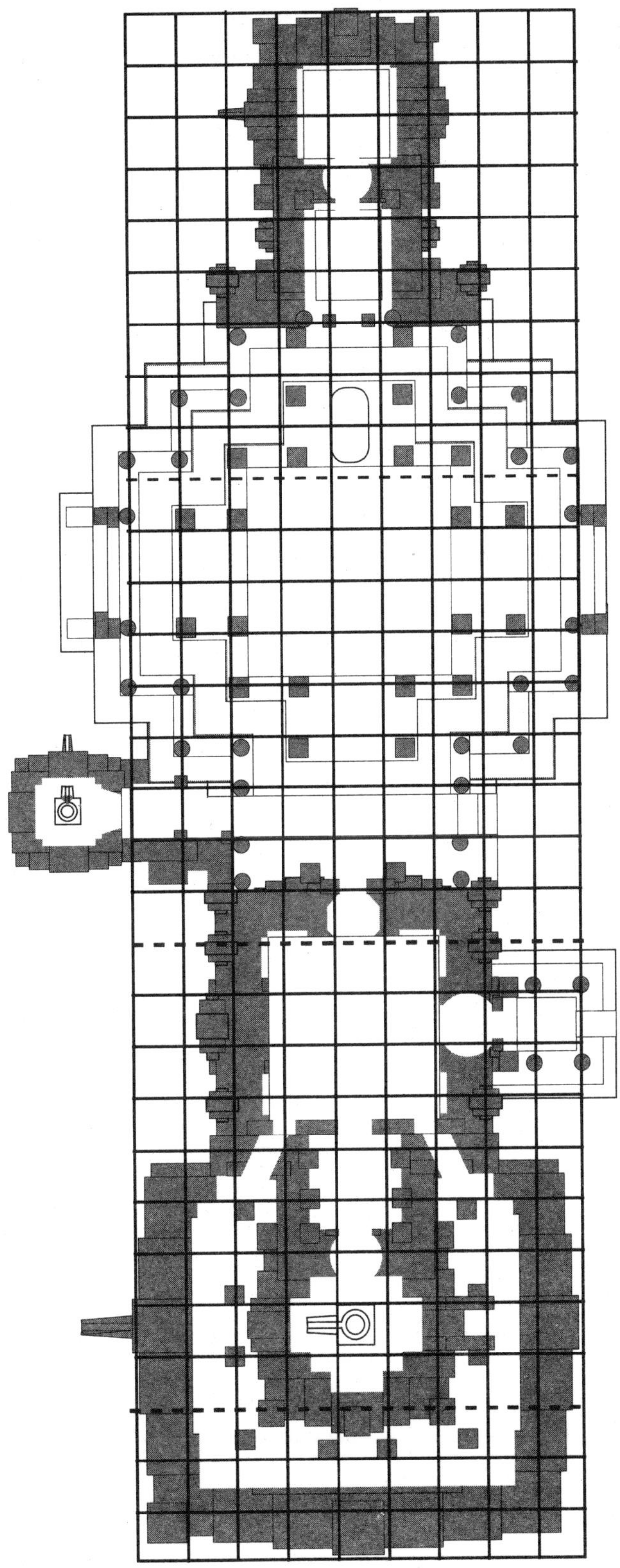

Kedāreśvara Trikūṭa Temple, Balagamve (*c.* CE 1060)

During the high point of Hoysaḷa power, Balagamve (aka Belligavi, Belligavmi or Dakṣiṇa Kedāra) was a city of no mean importance. It is believed that Kedāreśvara Trikūṭa Temple[34] was built under the auspices and patronage of a Hoysaḷa queen (c. CE 1060). Constructed sometime during the co-reigns of kings Vinayāditya (r. CE 1047-98) and Ereyaṅga (r. CE 1063–1100) (**Appendix E**), the Śaiva Trikūṭa Temple exists as a benchmark of Cāḷukya–Hoysaḷa transitional temple design of that period. Although there are a number of **A**-type *trikūṭa* temples (**Figure 3**) in the region, few exhibit the development of plan as seen in the Kedāreśvara Trikūṭa Temple.[35] Also of interest is that there is a similar temple — i.e. the Kadambeśvara Temple — at Rattehalli which appears to be a twin of this Balagamve temple.

The Kedāreśvara Trikūṭa Temple of Balagamve is smaller in scale when compared to other temples of the period and region. It is, none the less, noteworthy for its developed design. This *trikūṭa* temple consists of three nearly identical *vimāna*s, the principle one — i.e. the western *vimāna* — is somewhat more ornate than the northern and southern sanctums, and is attached to a rectangular the *antarāla*. The *vimāna*s of the north and south exhibit merely vestigial *antarāla*s. All three sanctums are entered via a pillared *mukha-maṇḍapa*, which, in turn, leads to a larger *sabhā-maṇḍapa*, cruciform, *en plan*. The two subsidiary *vimāna*s and the porches of the *sabhā-maṇḍapa* on the north and south along with the main east–west axis of the whole, create a plan resembling the Cross of Lorraine (**Figure 26**). The disposition of the three *garbhagṛha*s is such that there is an absolute minimum of ambient lighting filtering into the sanctums. The *mukha-maṇḍapa* receives sufficient light from the attached *sabhā-maṇḍapa*. The latter is composed of a floating roof, a short surrounding balustrade and forty-two pillars providing the interior with abundant diffuse light while shading the interior from direct sunlight.

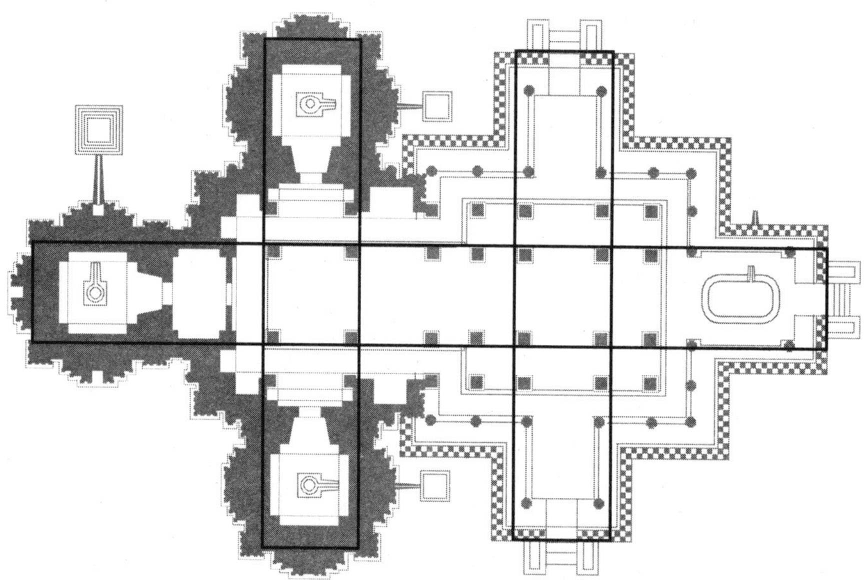

Figure 26: Kedāreśvara Trikūṭa Temple resembling the Cross of Lorraine

[34] Redrawn using PageMaker 6.0 from: HC, Plate CXI.

[35] The exceptions are: Mallikārjuna Temple, Basaralu; Keśava Temple, Somanāthapura; Sūryanārāyaṇa Temple, Magala; and Nārāyaṇa Temple, Anekannambadi.

Plate 23: Kedāreśvara Trikūṭa Temple plan

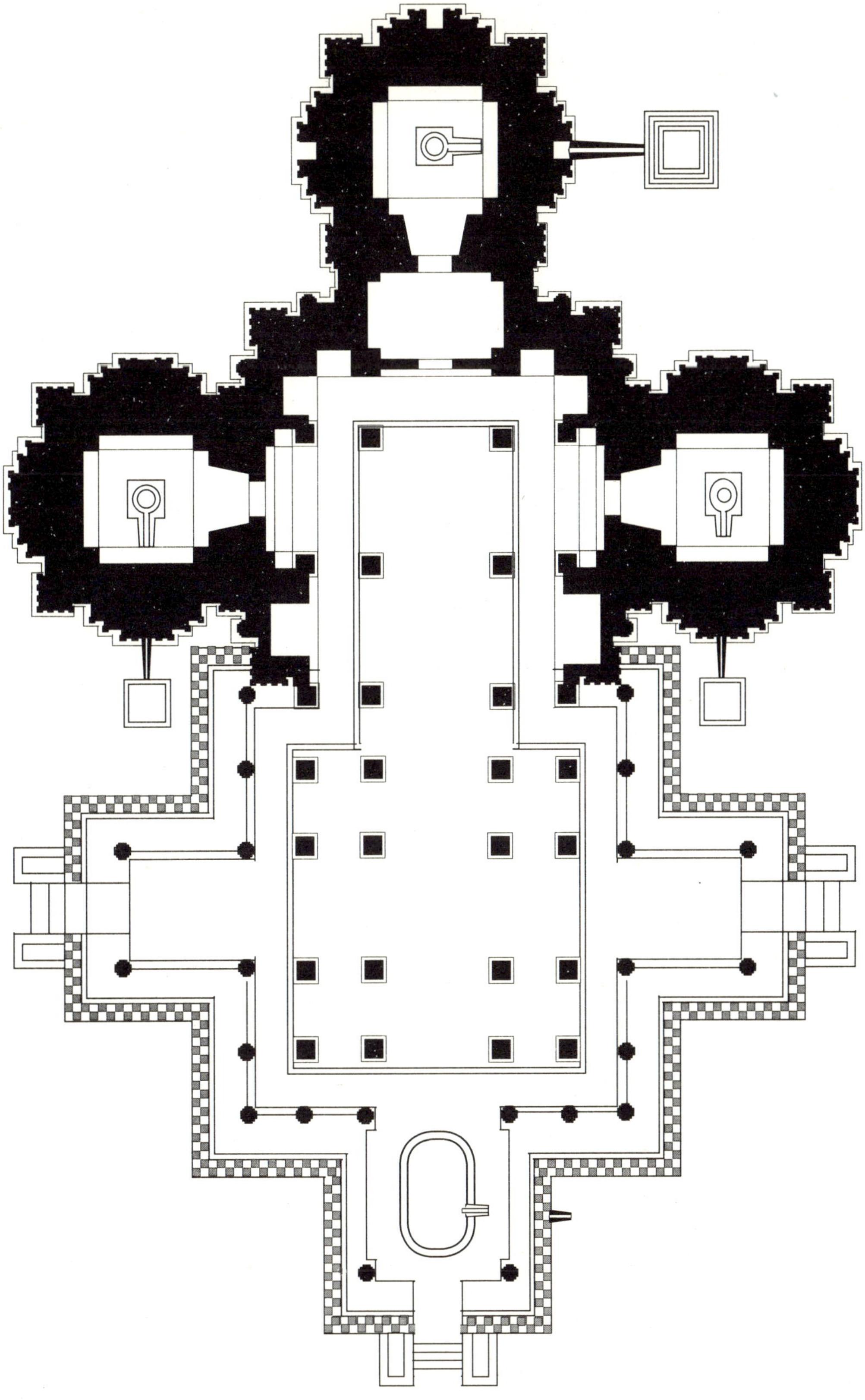

Kedāreśvara Temple

The application of a *maṇḍala* to the whole of the Kedāreśvara Trikūṭa Temple is problematic. A circular *vāstu-puruṣa maṇḍala* centred on the *mukha-mandapa* placed the three *vimānas* within segments **x–a, l–m** and **r–s** (**Appendix C, Plate 135**), and the whole of the *mukha-maṇḍapa* within the second ring from the centre. In addition, a number of interesting conjunctions occur (**Plate 24** [top]). A *paramaśāyika maṇḍala,* centred on the *mukha-maṇḍapa,* places the three *vimānas* with the nine *padas* group as indicated in **Appendix C, Plate 134** — i.e. **2, 4** and **8**. The extension of that *maṇḍala* — i.e. four *padas* — encloses the whole (**Plate 24** [bottom]).

Plate 24: Kedāreśvara Temple with circular *vāstu-puruṣa maṇḍala* (top) and *paramaśāyika maṇḍala*-based grid (bottom)

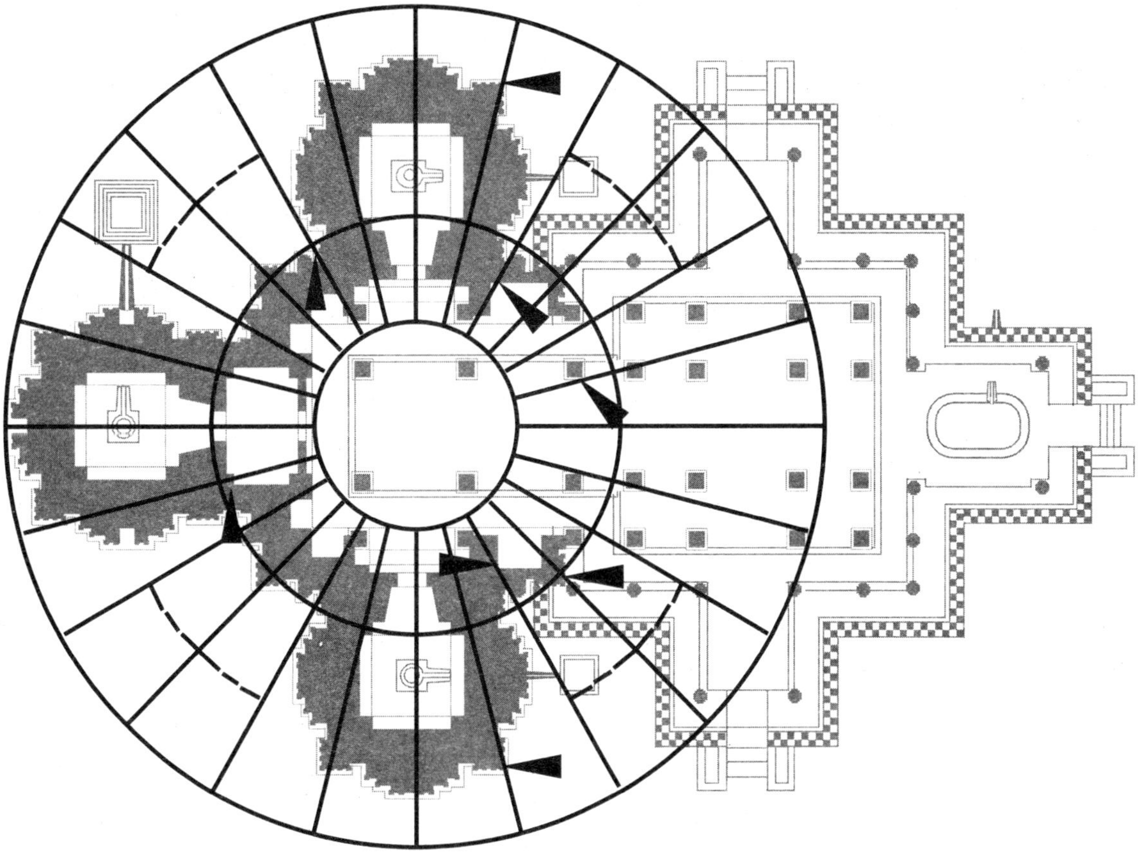

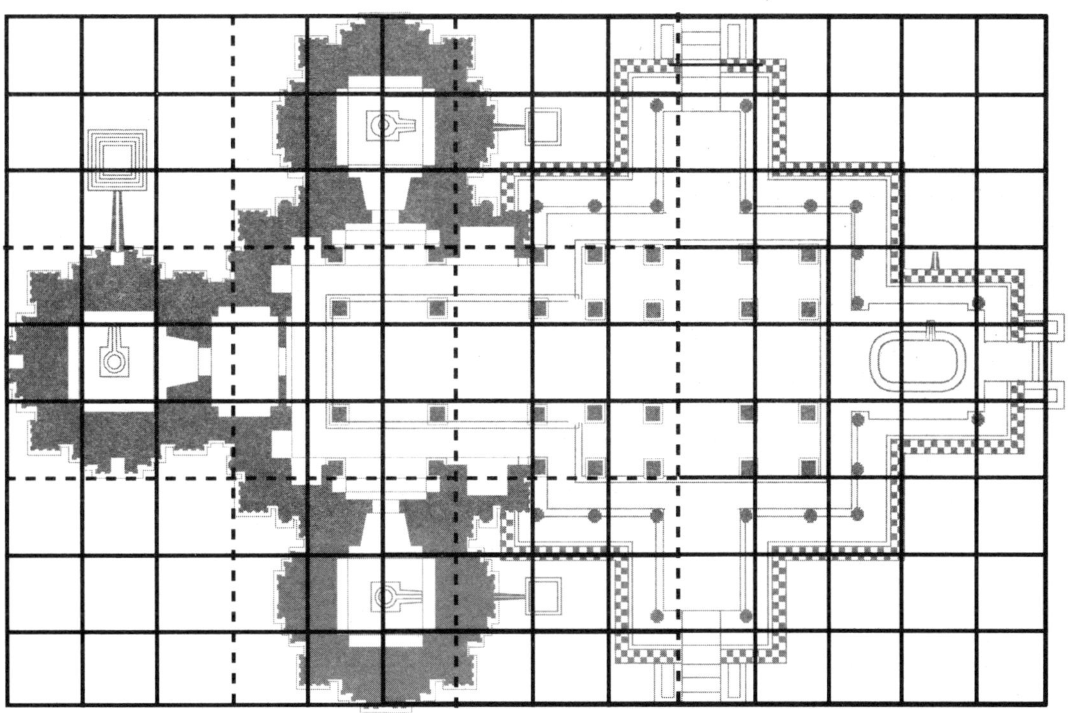

Kallappa-Mallappa (Harihara) Dvikūṭa Temple, Devaragennur, Karnataka (a. CE 1088)

Constructed in the last quarter of the eleventh century (i.e. CE 1088) during the reign of the Cāḷukya monarch Vikramāditya II (r. CE 1076–1127) (**Appendix E**), the temple is dedicated to Harihara and Keśava. The Kallappa-Mallappa (Harihara) Dvikūṭa Temple[36] is an example of an **A**-type *dvikūṭa* temple (**Figure 2**).

Aligned on an east–west axis, the temple possesses a square *sabhā-maṇḍapa* with a stepped entrance towards the south, mirror axial, *en plan* (**Figure 27**), based on the east–west axis, the Kallappa-Mallappa (Harihara) Dvikūṭa Temple exhibits twin *garbhagṛhas* with duplicate square *antarālas* opening onto the *sabhā-maṇḍapa*. The square *sabhā-maṇḍapa* is made up of sixteen supporting columns traditionally arranged — i.e. four columns in the centre set upon a raised platform and twelve engaged columns, four of which are quarter, corner columns. The eastern *garbhagṛha*, dedicated to Harihara, holds a Śivaliṅga, while the western *garbhagṛha* had once held an image of Keśava. It is stated that within the *sabhā-maṇḍapa* is to be found a "couchant Nandī"[37] but the location is not noted. The southern façade of the *sabhā-maṇḍapa* indicates a developed gate-like structure with the centred doorway. Similarly, the same form is found on the northern façade, but without an opening or indention.

The proportion of the whole appears to be nearly 3 : 1. This proportion does not strictly apply to the whole. However, there is an interesting relationship between the dimensions of the east and west *vimānas* and the dimensions of the interior of the *sabhā-maṇḍapa* (**Figure 27**).

The application of a *maṇḍala*, in particular a *paramaśāyika maṇḍala*, over the individual parts produces the expected results (**Plate 26**). The same *maṇḍala* is extended to produce a grid over the whole. In this instance several interesting and fortuitous results are achieved (**Plate 27**).

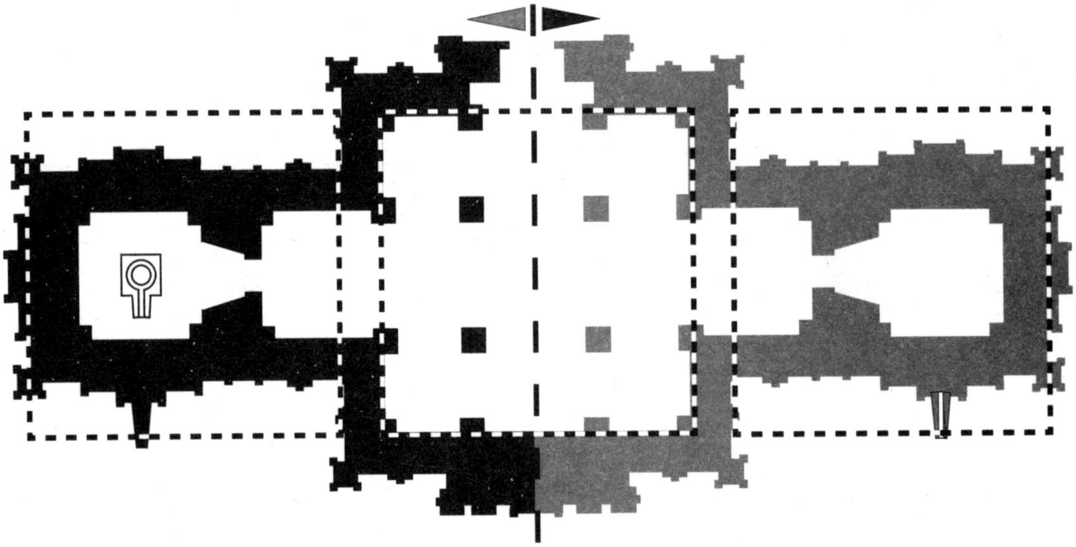

Figure 27: Kallappa-Mallappa (Harihara) Dvikūṭa Temple indicating relationship of *sabhā-maṇḍapa* dimension and mirror axiality

36 Redrawn using PageMaker 6.0 from: KMS II, p. 419, description on p. 191. See also **Preface**.

37 Ibid., p. 191.

Plate 25: Kallappa-Mallappa (Harihara) Dvikūṭa Temple plan

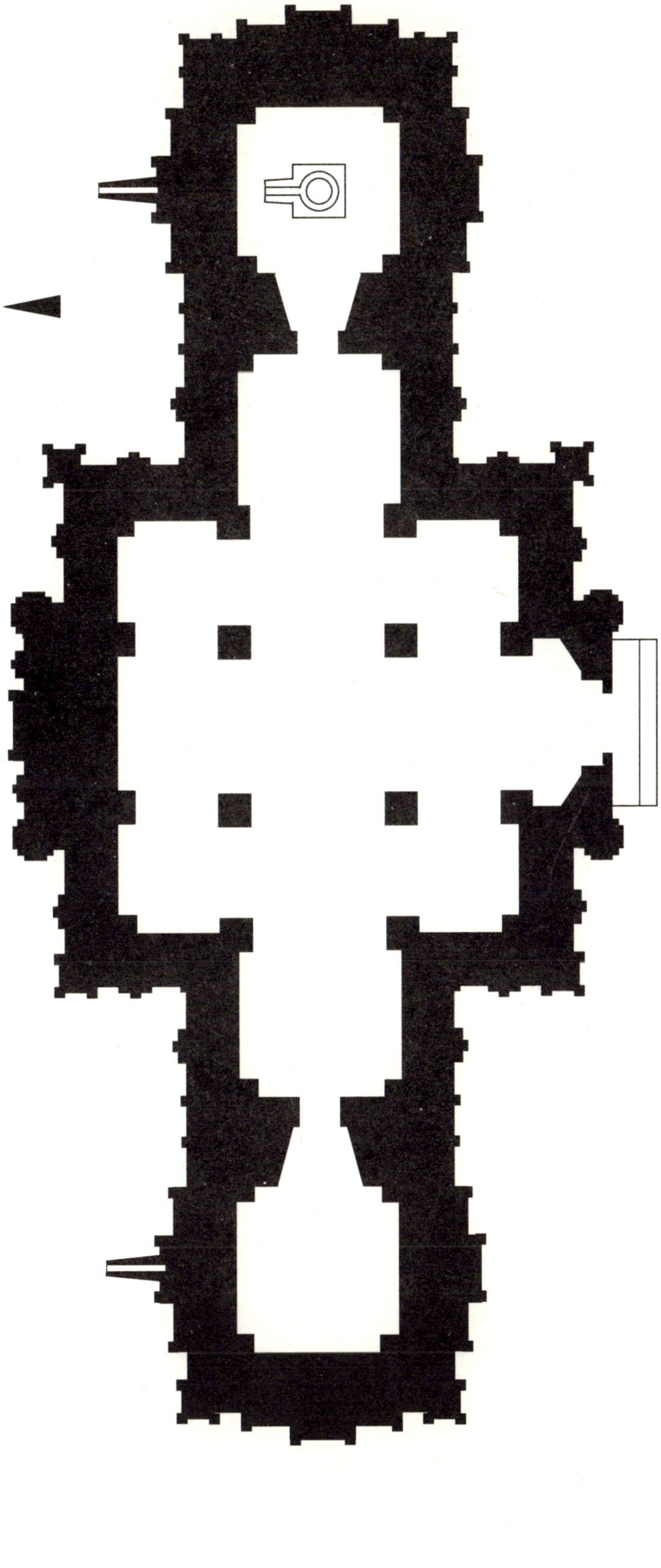

Plate 26: Kallappa-Mallappa (Harihara) Dvikūṭa Temple with *paramaśāyika maṇḍala* over *vimāna* and *sabhā-maṇḍapa*

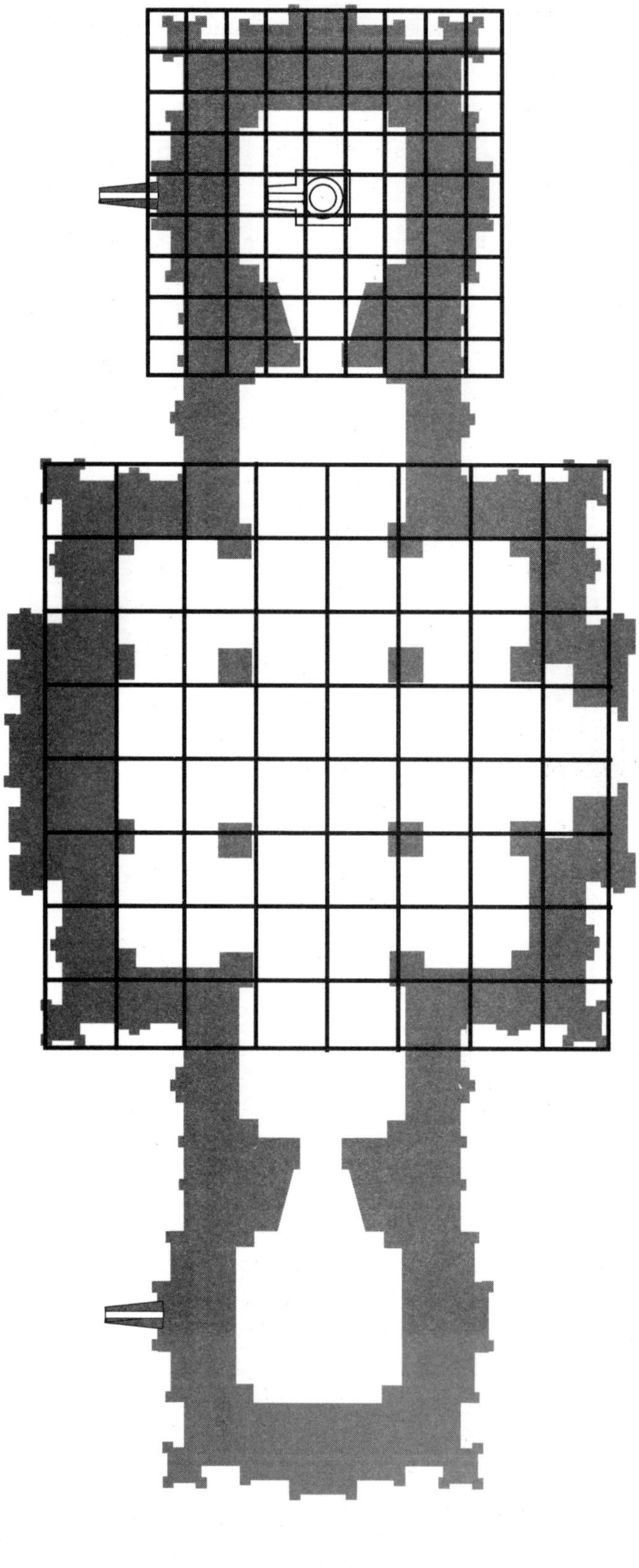

Plate 27: Kallappa-Mallappa (Harihara) Dvikūṭa Temple with grid, based on a *paramaśāyika maṇḍala* over the whole

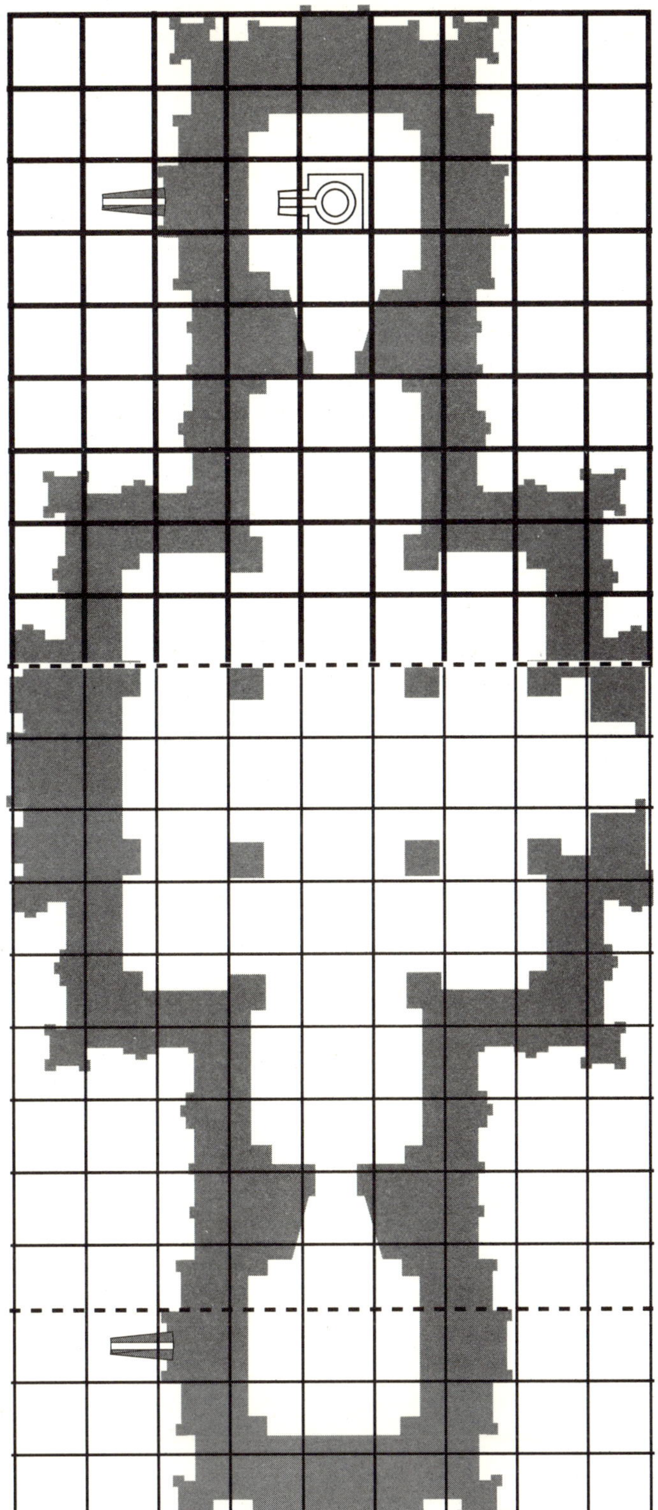

Kāśīviśveśvara (Kāśīviśvanātha) Dvikūṭa Temple, Lakkuṇḍī, Karnataka (*c.* CE 1075)

It was sometime around CE 1075 when the Western Cāḷukyas had reached a level of power and renown that the Kāśīviśveśvara (Kāśīviśvanātha) Dvikūṭa Temple[38] at Lakkuṇḍī was initially raised — i.e. during the reigns of the kings Someśvara II (r. CE 1068-76) and Vikramāditya II (VI) (r. CE 1076–1127). The main, western *vimāna* is dedicated to Lord Śiva, while the smaller, eastern *vimāna* is the realm of Sūrya-Nārāyaṇa.

The Kāśīviśveśvara (Kāśīviśvanātha) Dvikūṭa Temple consists of an elaborate *vimāna* to the west with deep niches in the north, south and west *raha-rathas*. An *antarāla* leads to a large, square *sabhā-maṇḍapa* with the usual sixteen columns arranged in the traditional manner — i.e. four columns in the centre set upon a raised platform and twelve engaged columns, four of which are quarter, corner columns. This arrangement of columns creates nine *aṅkanas*. The second *vimāna*,[39] simpler, *en plan*, is reached via an open *mukha-maṇḍapa*. The rectangular *antarāla* gives way to the second, square *garbhagṛha* dedicated to Sūrya-Nārāyaṇa. As with the western *vimāna*, this too has three niches, shallower than their counterparts and found on the north, south and east façades. The whole rests on an elevated plinth.

The application of a *maṇḍala* to the whole is fruitless. However when a *paramaśāyika maṇḍala* is applied to either the western *vimāna* and/or the *sabhā-maṇḍapa*, the appropriate results are eminently apparent (**Plate 29**). Also, when a grid, based on a *paramaśāyika maṇḍala* is overlaid on the whole, salutary results appear (**Plate 30**) — i.e. there are three *paramaśāyika maṇḍalas* from east to west and three additional rows of nine *padas* each, amounting to thirty *padas*. This same arrangement — i.e. a grid of thirty *padas* along the length — is also found in the Trikūṭeśvara Temple (**Plate 22**), and the Kallappa-Mallappa (Harihara) Dvikūṭa Temple (**Plate 27**). Three, of course, is a holy number in Hindu numerology, and thirty is auspicious and psychic.

[38] Redrawn using PageMaker 6.0 from: CT, p. 130.

[39] Ibid., p. 191.

Plate 28: Kāśīviśveśvara (Kāśīviśvanātha) Dvikūṭa Temple plan

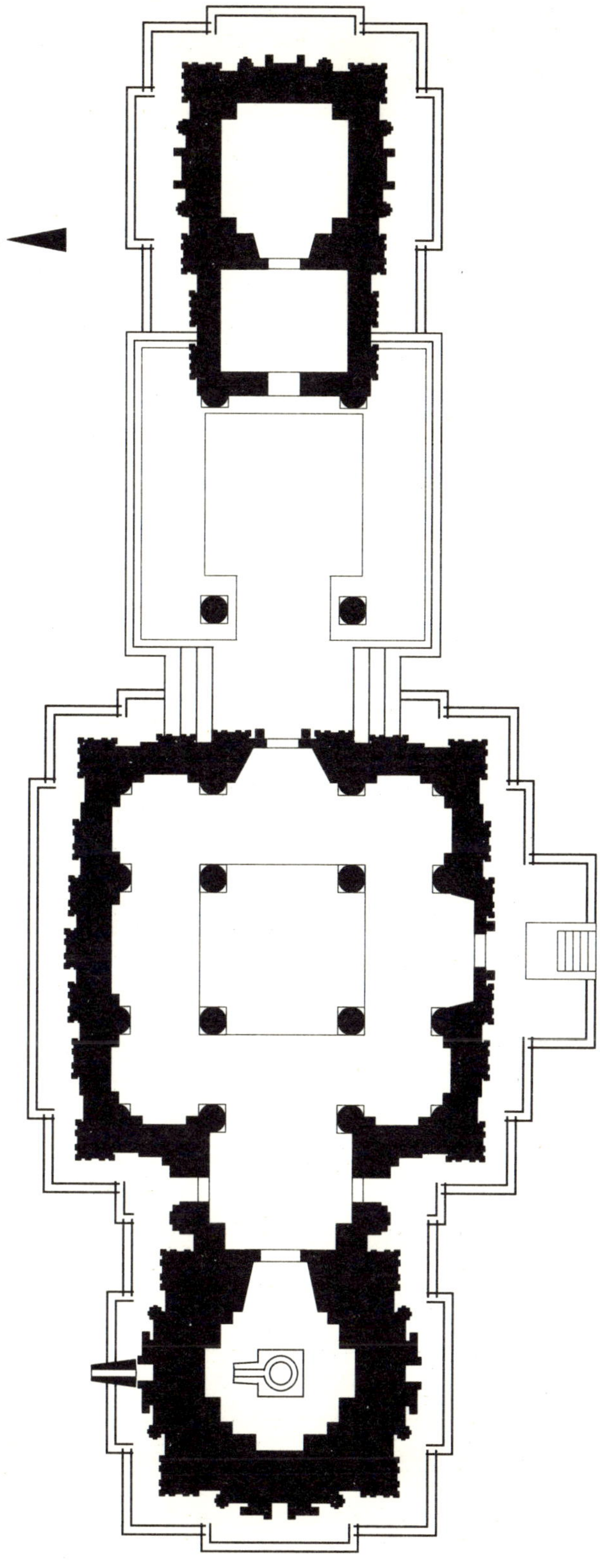

Plate 29: Kāśīviśveśvara (Kāśīviśvanātha) Dvikūṭa Temple with *paramaśāyika maṇḍala* over the *garbhagṛha* and *sabhā-maṇḍapa*

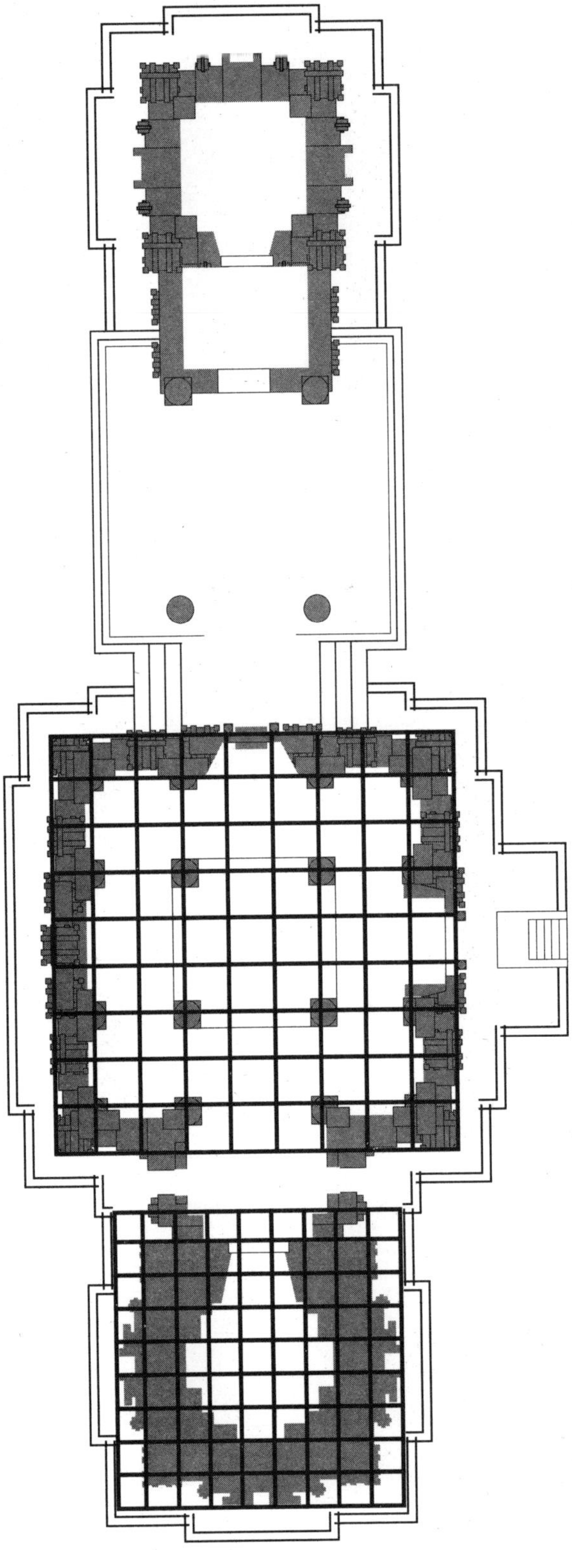

Plate 30: Kāśīviśveśvara (Kāśīviśvanātha) Dvikūṭa Temple with *paramaśāyika*-based grid over the whole

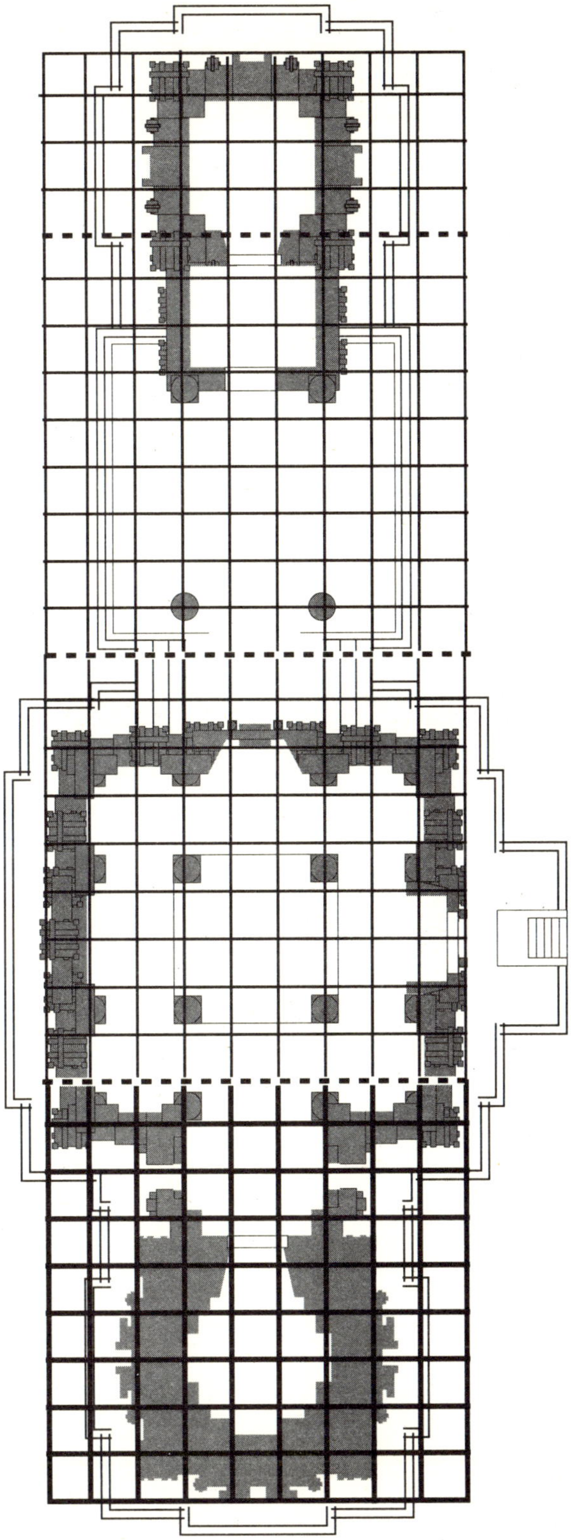

Rāmeśvara Trikūṭa Temple, Yaragal, Karnataka (a. CE 1094)

Dedicated to Lord Śiva, the Rāmeśvara Trikūṭa Temple[40] at Yaragal was constructed during the reign of the Western Cāḷukya (Kalyāṇa) King Vikramāditya II (VI) (r. CE 1076–1127). It is an **A**-type *trikūṭa* plan and similar to the preceding temples — i.e. Jaina Tīrthaṅkara Trikūṭa Basadī (**Plate 15**) and the Mahādeva Trikūṭa Temple (**Plate 19**) — and a number of temples that follow.

The Rāmeśvara Trikūṭa Temple consists of a major *vimāna* aligned towards the north and two additional, identical sanctums at the east and the west. All three *vimānas* are of similar design and plan (**Figure 28**). These three sanctums, each with a Śivaliṅga, open onto a common, square *sabhā-maṇḍapa*. The *sabhā-maṇḍapa* exhibits sixteen columns arranged in a traditional manner — i.e. four columns in the centre set upon a raised platform and twelve engaged columns, four of which are quarter, corner columns. This arrangement of columns creates nine *aṅkanas*. To the north of the *sabhā-maṇḍapa* is a diminutive *sabhā-maṇḍapa* with four supporting columns, two of which are engaged, and a narrow stairway leading to the main level.

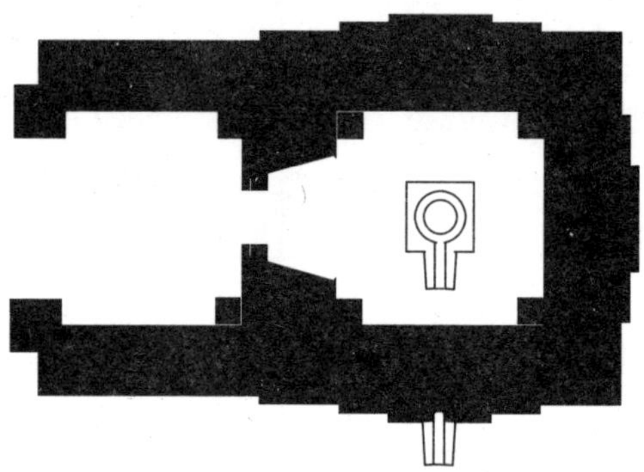

Figure 28: Rāmeśvara Trikūṭa Temple *vimāna* element

40 Redrawn using PageMaker 6.0 from: KMS II, p. 445; description on pp. 217-18. See also **Preface**.

Plate 31: Rāmeśvara Trikūṭa Temple plan

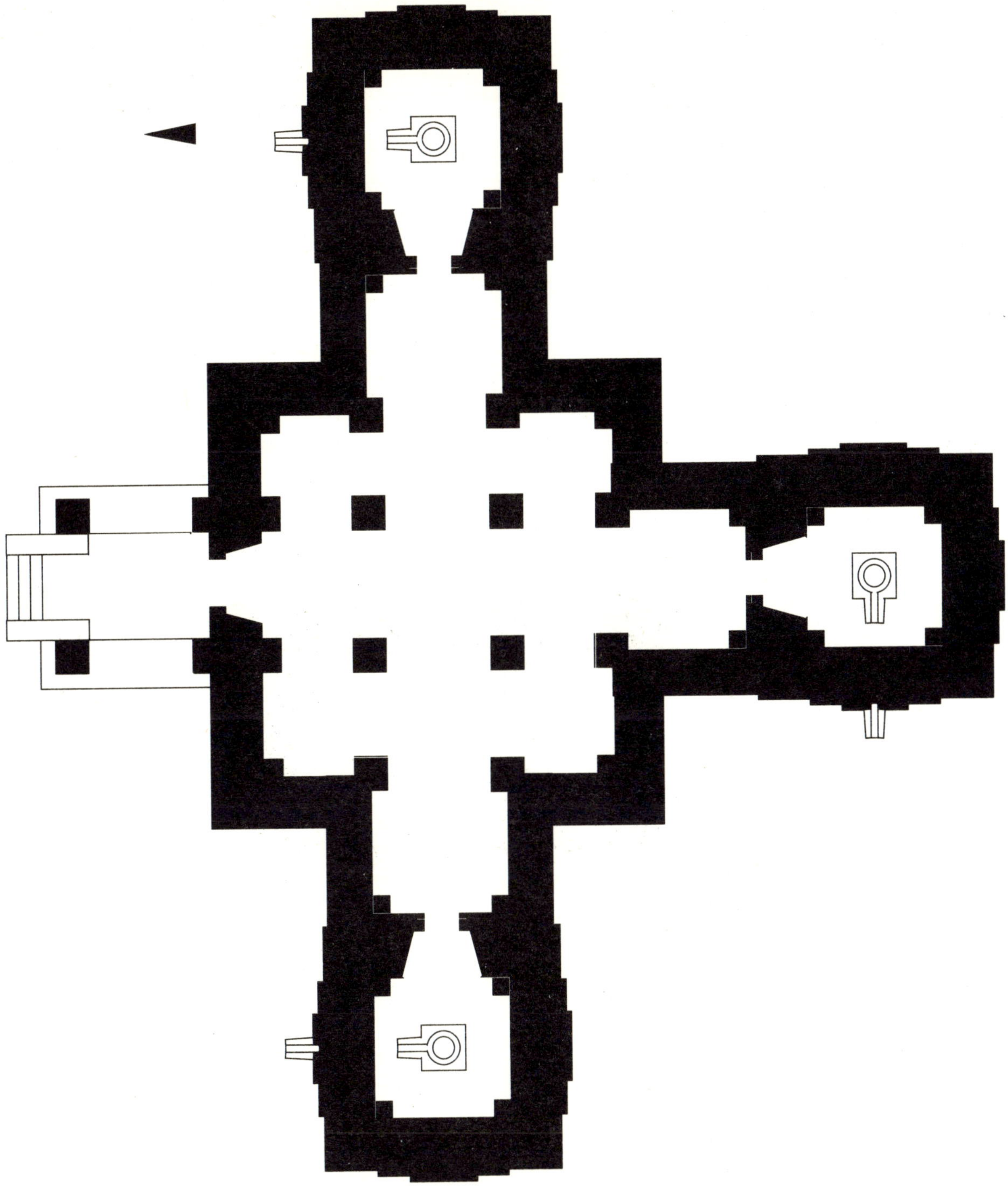

Īśvara Trikūṭa Temple, Basarakoḍu, Karnataka (a. CE 1100)

The construction of sacred monuments by the Western Cāḷukyas (Kalyāṇa) Dynasty continued well into the twelfth century. Near the village of Basarakoḍra is found the Īśvara Trikūṭa Temple.[41] It was constructed during the first quarter of that century, and during the reigns of either King Vikramāditya II (VI) (r. CE 1076–1127) or Someśvara III (r. CE 1127-35) (**Appendix D**), and dedicated to Lord Śiva.

Essentially, it is similar, *en plan*, to the preceding temple, the Rāmeśvara Trikūṭa Temple (**Plate 31**) being an **A**-type *trikūṭa* plan (**Figure 3**). The dedicatory *vimāna* of the elaborately designed Īśvara Trikūṭa Temple holds a Śivaliṅga. The eastern and western *vimānas* are identical, *en plan*, and only *pīṭhas* remain (**Figure 29**). These sanctums were possibly dedicated to Sūrya and Keśava. The western sanctum is a variation on the other two, in that there are small shrines inserted into the *raha-ratha* of the north, south and west façades. The three *vimānas* lead to a square *sabhā-maṇḍapa* which is open to the north. The *sabhā-maṇḍapa* holds sixteen columns, traditionally arranged, forming nine *aṅkanas* — i.e. four columns in the centre resting on a square platform, two columns to the north at the open side of the *sabhā-maṇḍapa* and ten engaged columns, four of which are quarter, corner columns. The open northern façade of the *sabhā-maṇḍapa* leads to a small, pillared *mukha-maṇḍapa* and a flight of steps.

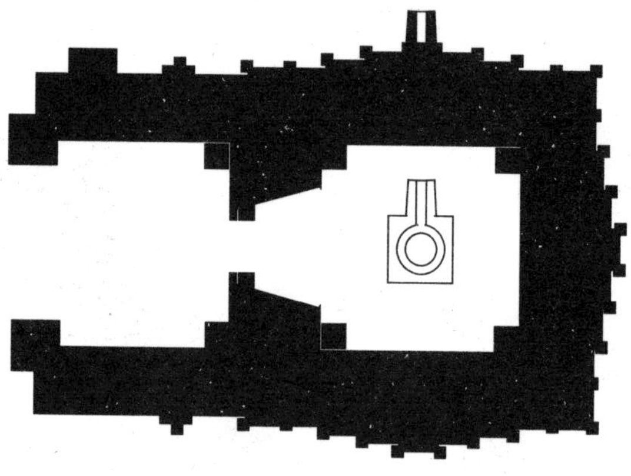

Figure 29: Īśvara Trikūṭa Temple *vimāna* element

[41] Redrawn using PageMaker 6.0 from: KMS II, p. 467; description on pp. 256-57. See also **Preface**.

Plate 32: Īśvara Trikūṭa Temple plan

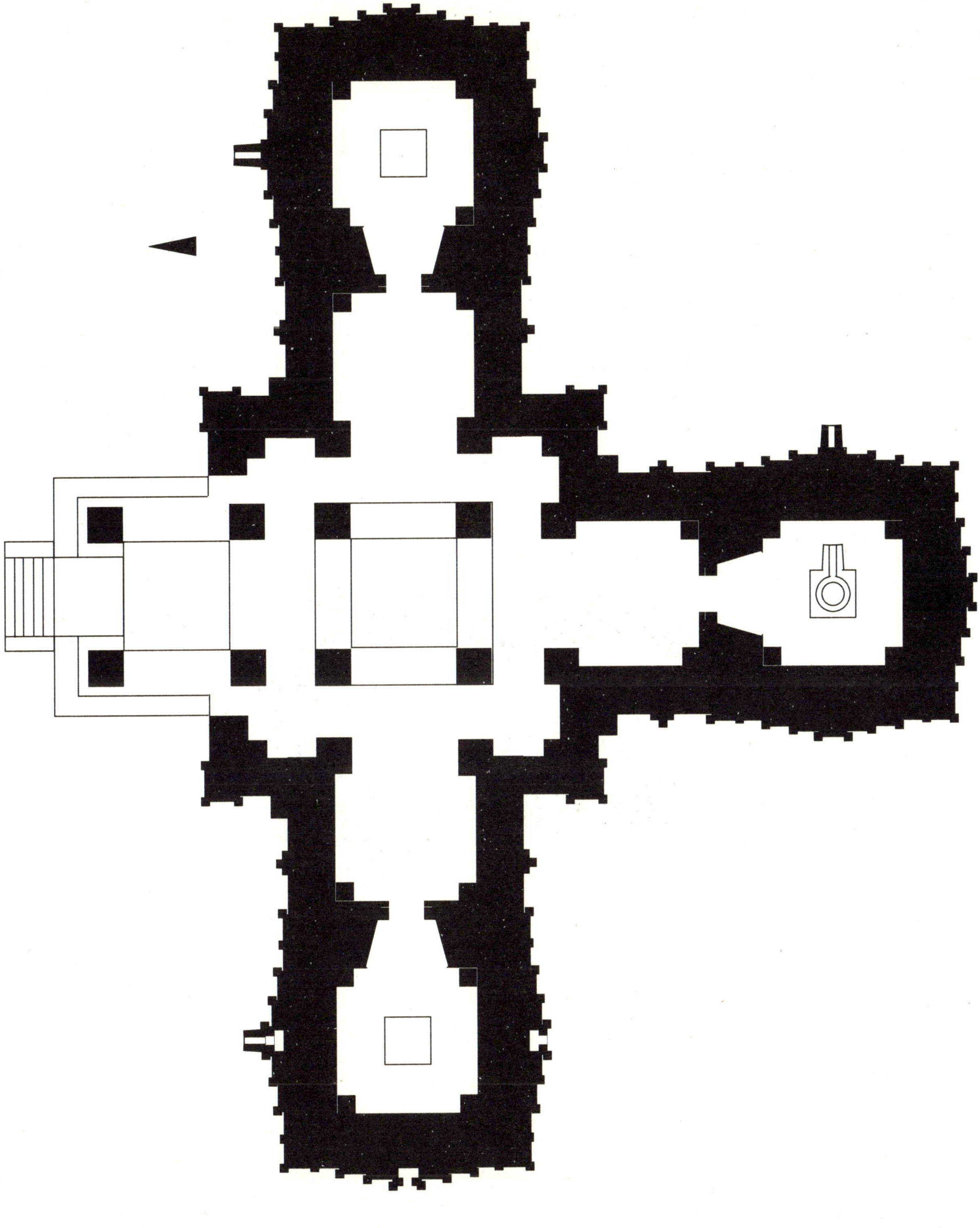

Basavaṇṇa (Traipuruṣa) Trikūṭa Temple, Malghana, Karnataka (a. CE 1100)

One of a number of minor sacred monuments constructed by the Western Cāḷukyas (Kalyāṇa) Dynasty is the Basavanna (Traipurusa) Trikūṭa Temple[42] at Malghana. This temple follows an **A**-type *trikūṭa* temple plan (**Figure 3**). It was raised in the first quarter of the twelfth century, during the reign of King Vikramāditya II (VI) (r. CE 1076–1127) (**Appendix D**). The Basavaṇṇa (Traipuruṣa) Trikūṭa Temple was dedicated to Lord Viṣṇu in the form of Keśava, Sūrya and Lord Śiva (Mahādeva).

Like the Mahādeva Trikūṭa Temple of Benakoṭagi (**Plate 19**), the Rāmeśvara Trikūṭa Temple at Yaragal (**Plate 31**) and the Īśvara Trikūṭa Temple of Basarakoḍu (**Plate 32**), the Basavaṇṇa (Traipuruṣa) Trikūṭa Temple is composed of three, nearly identical *vimānas* (**Figure 30**). The main, southern sanctum holds the image of Keśava in its *garbhagṛha*. A Śivaliṅga occupies the western *vimāna* and an image of Sūrya (Ādityadeva) is housed in the eastern sanctum. The three *vimānas* share a common *sabhā-maṇḍapa*. Like the *sabhā-maṇḍapa* of the Īśvara Trikūṭa Temple, it is open to the north and exhibits sixteen columns, traditionally arranged forming nine *aṅkanas* — i.e. four columns in the centre resting on a square platform, two columns to the north at the open side of the *sabhā-maṇḍapa* and ten engaged columns, four of which are quarter, corner columns. Nine *aṅkanas* are formed by these columns and a short flight of steps leads out towards the north.

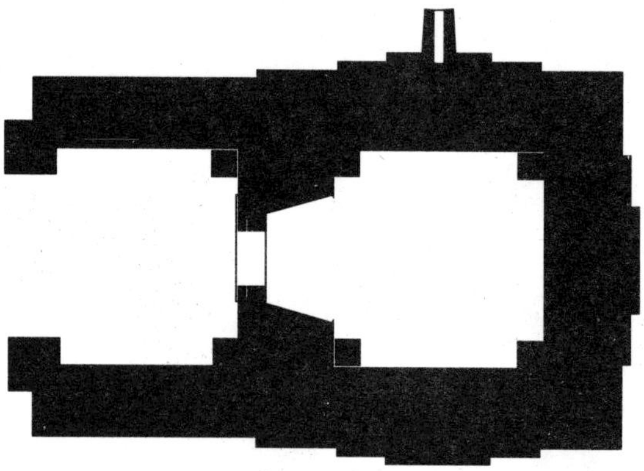

Figure 30: Basavaṇṇa Trikūṭa Temple *vimāna* element

[42] Redrawn using PageMaker 6.0 from: KMS II, p. 456; descripti on pp. 223-24. See: slso **Preface**.

Plate 33: Basavaṇṇa (Traipuruṣa) Trikūṭa Temple plan

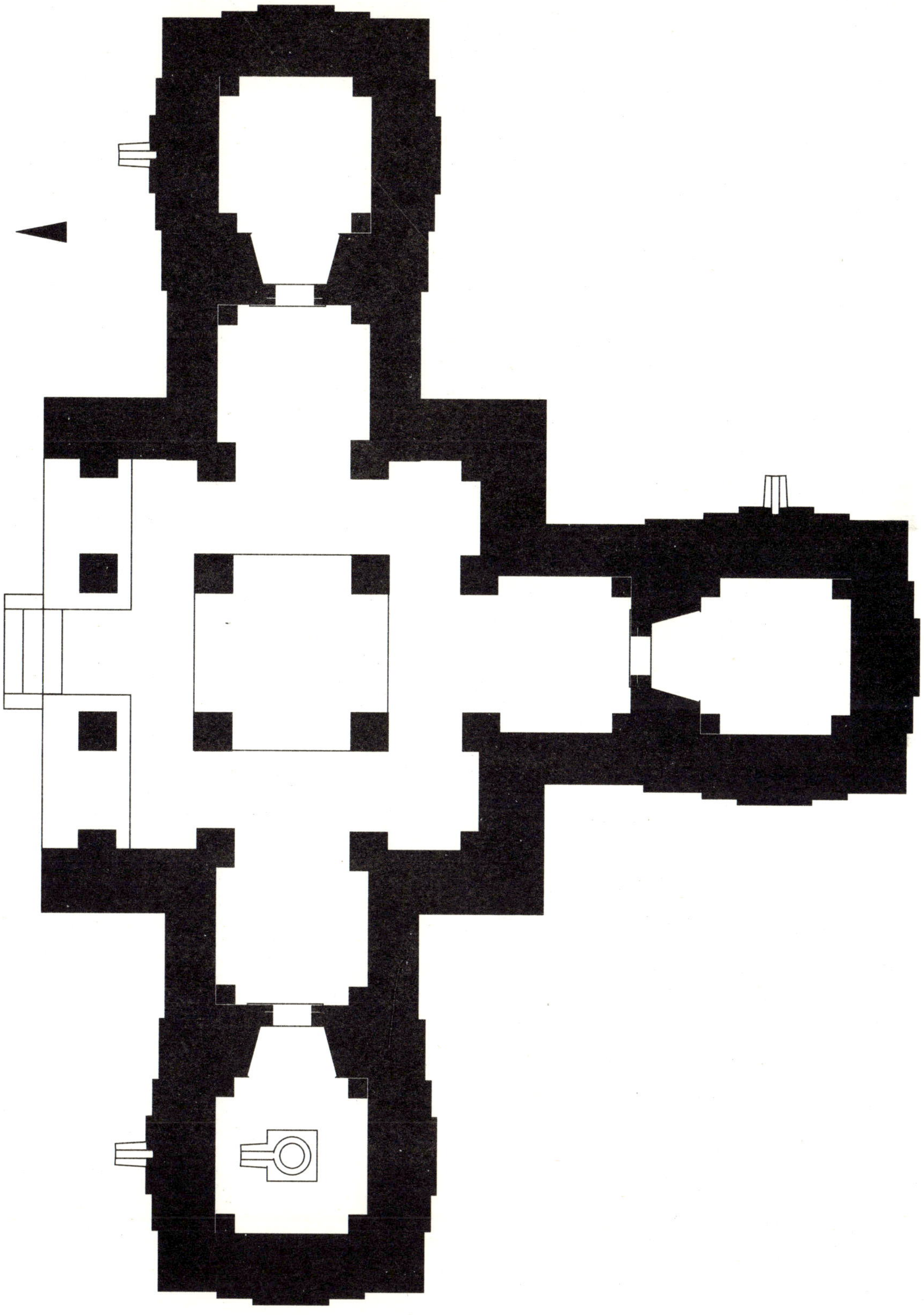

Candramaulīśvara Temple, Unkal, Karnataka (a. CE 1100)

Built during the reign of the Western Cāḷukya (Kalyāṇa) King Vikramāditya II (VI) (r. CE 1076–1127) the Śaiva Candramaulīśvara Temple[43] at Unkal, has been turned, by force, into what appears to be a multi-sanctum temple. It is assumed that at some later period the temple had been appropriated by the Liṅgāyats. Candramaulīśvara refers to the "crystal *liṅga*" which is a powerful icon for Lord Śiva.

The temple consists of a central, open shrine surrounded by a *pradakṣiṇāpatha* with four *sukhanis* which resemble open *garbhagṛhas* with shallow *antarālas*, which give the appearance of separate shrines. *En plan*, the Candramaulīśvara Temple resembles that of the principal shrine atop Angkor's Ta Keo (**Figure 31**) both of which conform to one of the models proposed by Gerard Foekema.[44] It is also not too dissimilar, *en plan*, to the Jaina (Trikūṭa) Basadī No. 15 (**Plate 8**).

Cousens posits, and rightly so, that this temple which now enshrines a Śivaliṅga was most probably dedicated originally to Lord Brahmā. There is the head of an image placed on a low plinth in the western chamber with four faces. The local inhabitants refer to that head as the Pañcānana even though there are clearly four faces, not five. Temples dedicated to Lord Brahmā are not unheard of, but they are, to be sure few in number. Furthermore, it is also not unheard of for a temple to have been raised honouring one deity only to be "reconditioned" as the abode of another.

The application of a *paramaśāyika maṇḍala* (**Plate 35**) onto the whole appears quite viable. The four *sukhanis* fall within the middle nine *padas* on each side — i.e. squares **2, 4, 6** and **8** (**Appendix C, Plate 134**). When a *circular vāstu-puruṣa maṇḍala* is applied (**Plate 36**) a number of conjunctions appear — i.e. the four *sukhanis* fall within segments **x–a, f–g, l–m** and **r–s** (**Appendix C, Plate 135**); the inner ring encloses the *garbhagṛha*, the second ring nearly matches the *pradakṣiṇāpatha*, and the third circle encloses the *vimāna*.

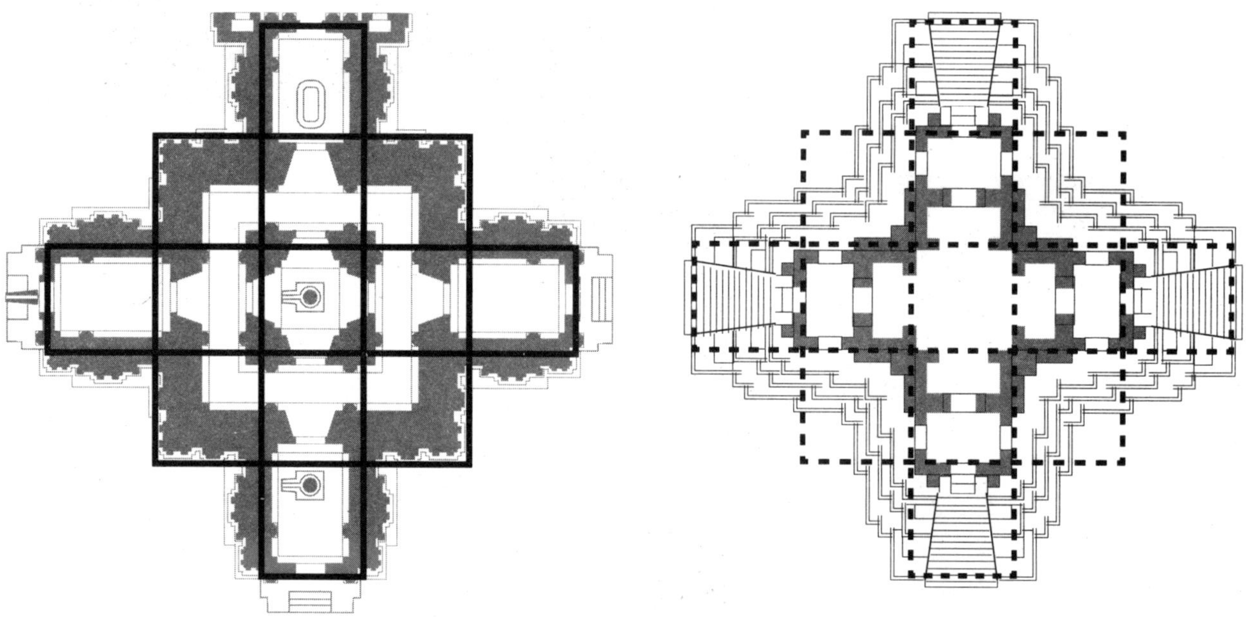

Figure 31: Candramaulīśvara Temple (left) and Ta Keo, Angkor, principal shrine, applying the Foekema model

[43] Redrawn using PageMaker 6.0 from: HC, Plate CXXV.

[44] GF, p. 23.

Plate 34: Candramaulīśvara Trikūṭa Temple plan

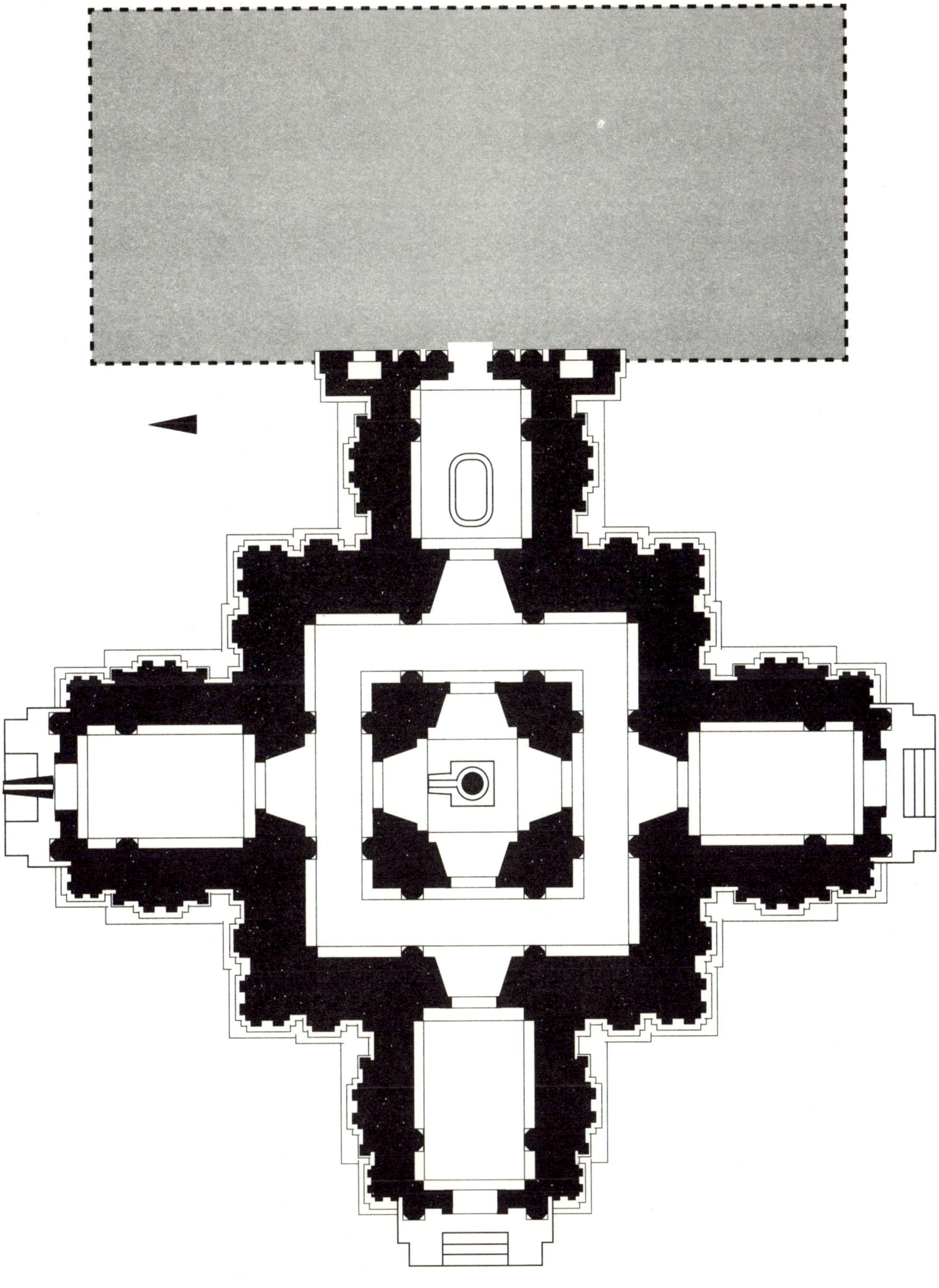

Plate 35: Candramaulīśvara Temple with *paramaśāyika maṇḍala* details

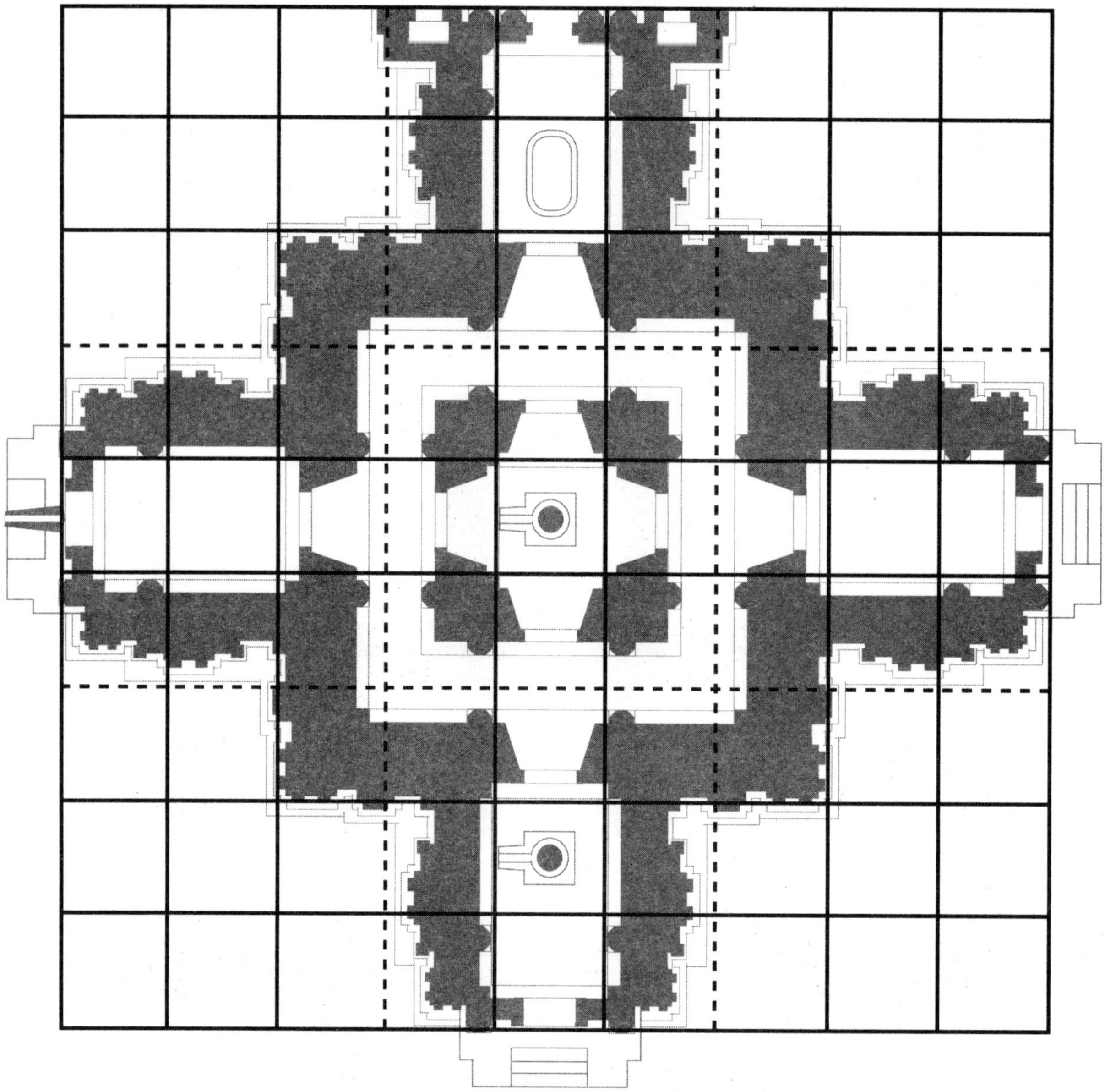

Plate 36: Candramaulīśvara Temple with circular *vāstu-puruṣa maṇḍala* indicating important conjunctions

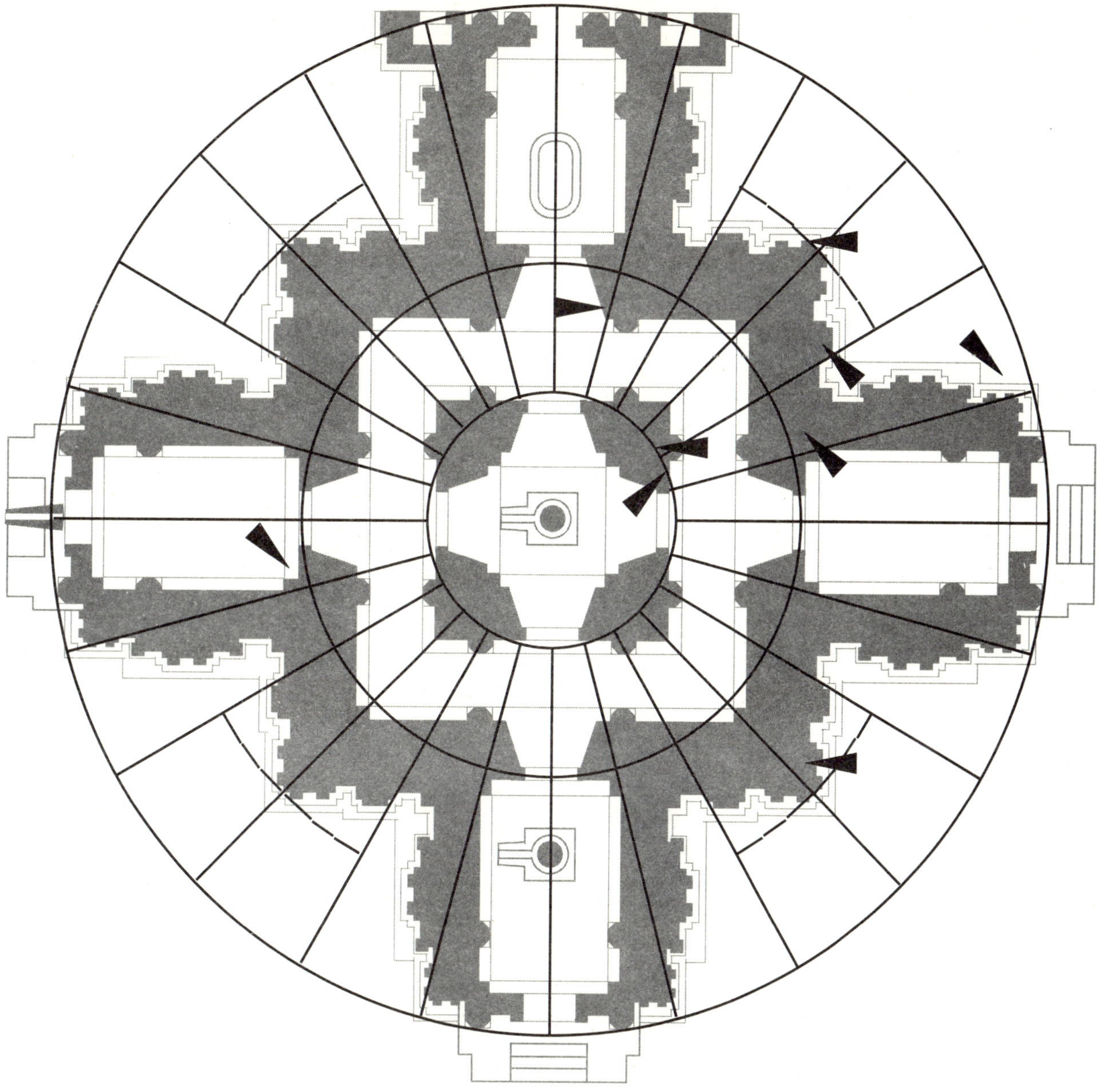

Someśvara Trikūṭa Temple, Kabali, Karnataka (a. CE 1100)

Regardless of the threats from the Pāṇḍyas to the south and the Yādavas to the north the Hoysaḷas were able to focus a portion of the energy into the design and construction of numerous outstanding temple monuments. Sometime after CE 1100, during the reign of either King Ballāla I (r. CE 1100-10) or his successor King Bittiga Viṣṇuvardhana (r. CE 1110-52) the Someśvara Trikūṭa Temple[45] at the small village of Kabali (Kabbali or Kabli) to the west and north of Bangalore was raised.

Related, *en plan*, to the **A**-type *trikūṭa* temple plans already considered (**Plates 31-33**), the **B**-type plan of Someśvara Trikūṭa Temple is eccentric in relation. It is aligned towards the east, but the major shrine with its Śivaliṅga and *antarāla* is in the south, and that *vimāna* is more developed than either the northern or western sanctums.[46] The southern *garbhagṛha*, dedicated to Lord Śiva, is square and it flows into a square *antarāla* which, in turn, opens onto a common *sabhā-maṇḍapa*. Both the western sanctum, dedicated to Sūrya, and northern sanctum, enshrining Keśava, are identical (**Figure 32**), *en plan*, and consist of a square *garbhagṛha* without *antarāla* and open onto the *sabhā-maṇḍapa*. The *sabhā-maṇḍapa* holds sixteen columns, traditionally arranged forming nine *aṅkanas* — i.e. four columns in the centre resting on a square, raised platform, twelve engaged columns, four of which are quarter, corner columns.

As noted above, the *garbhagṛhas* are dedicated to Lord Śiva (Śivaliṅga), Keśava (Lord Viṣṇu) and Sūrya. This dedicatory form is similar to a number of other temples, particularly the Basavaṇṇa (Traipuruṣa) Trikūṭa Temple (**Plate 33**).

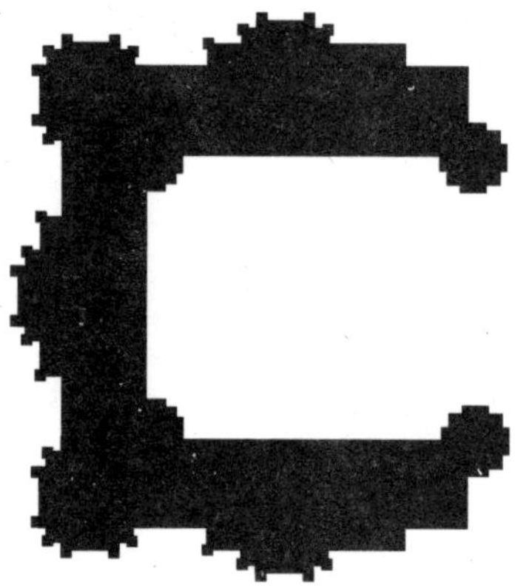

Figure 32: Someśvara Trikūṭa Temple north and west *vimāna* elements

45 Redrawn using PageMaker 6.0 from: KMS II, p. 464, description on p. 254. See also **Preface**.

46 There is some confusion between the description (KMS I, p. 254) and the plan of the Someśvara Trikūṭa Temple (KMS II, p. 464). The plan with a clearly delineated "north marker" indicates that the entrance is aligned to the east. And, "the main western *garbhagṛha* facing east" is, in fact, facing north.

Plate 37: Someśvara Trikūṭa Temple plan

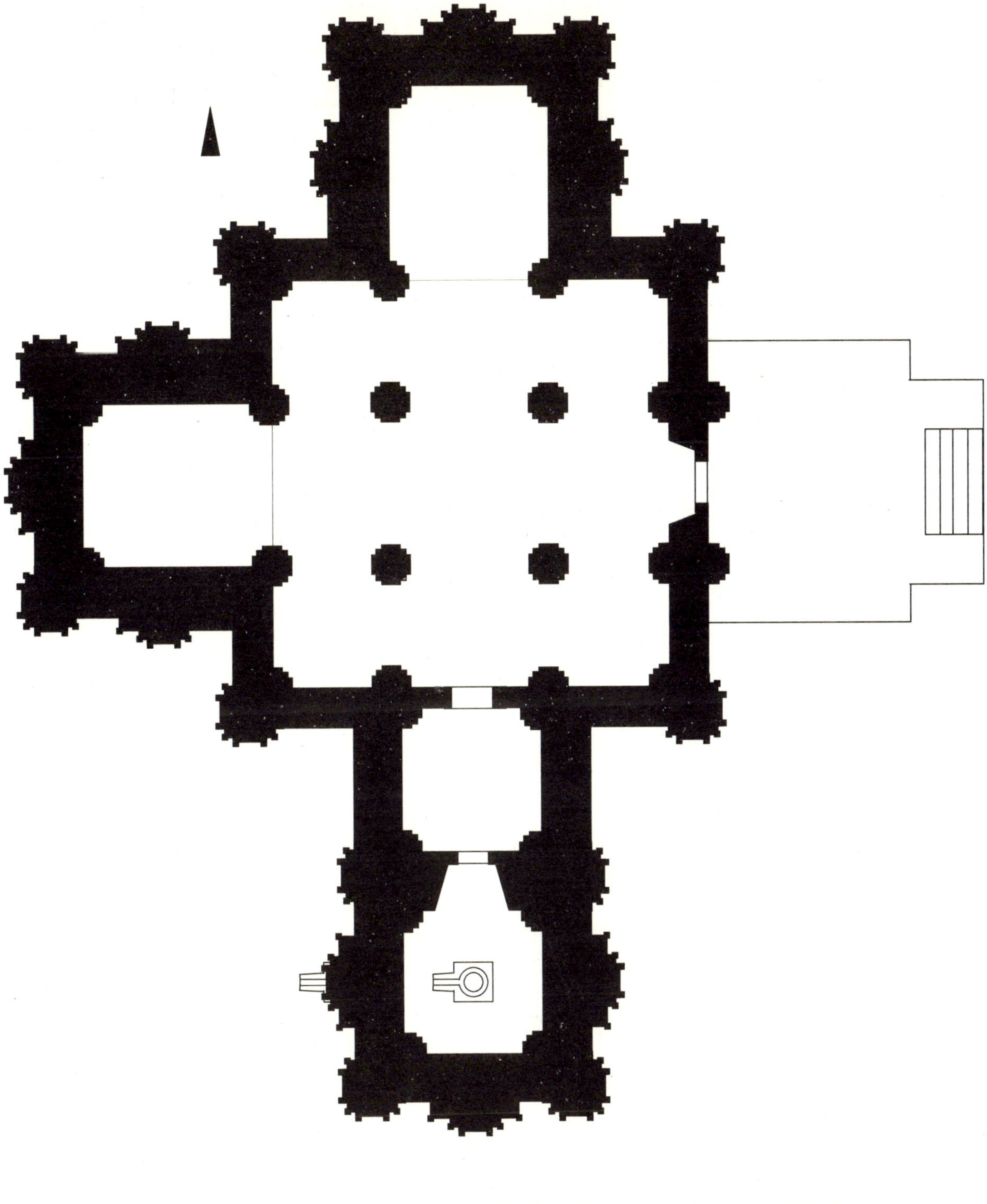

Cauṅsaṭh Yoginī Mandir and Gaurī Śaṅkara Temple, Bherāghāṭ (tenth century & a. CE 1100)

The Cauṅsaṭh Yoginī Mandir[47] (aka Madanpur Temple) at Bherāghāṭ or Bhedāghāṭ[48] near Jabalpur is one of the most interesting temples, *en plan*, in India. The Causaṭh (Cauṅsaṭh) Yoginī Mandir is dedicated to the Śakti sect — i.e. the sixty-four *yoginī*s and the Sapta-Mātṛkās. The *yoginī*s fierce demi-goddesses who attend the Goddess Durgā. The Sapta-Mātṛkās, the "Divine Mothers", were early mother goddesses who were auspicious and powerful, and later were elevated to embody the fruitful forces of nature. In the case of the *yoginī*s and the Sapta-Mātṛkās, no one goddess was dominant, therefore, the circular design was most practical.

It is suggested that the construction of the Cauṅsaṭh Yoginī Mandir was in two phases. The first phase was raised during the reign of the Northern Kaḷacuri Dynasty's King Yuvarājadeva I Keyūravarṣa (r. CE 915-45) (**Appendix D**). This first phase, doubtlessly was the construction of the circular hypaethral temple. The Gaurī-Śaṅkara Temple was a later addition.

Unlike the other temples dedicated to the *yoginī*s — i.e. Cauṅsaṭh Yoginī Temple (**Plate 3**), the Cauṅsaṭh Yoginī Sanctuary at Khajurāho (**Plate 13**) and the Cauṅsaṭh Yoginī Temple in Rānīpur-Jharial (**Plate 132**) — the Cauṅsaṭh Yoginī Mandir at Bherāghāṭ possesses a number of additional chapels/niches. These open niches (**Figure 33**) number not sixty-four but eighty-one — i.e. sixty-four dedicated to the *Yoginī*s plus seven to the Sapta-Mātṛkās and ten additional.[49] The eighty-one chapels/niches are arranged in the following manner: counting clockwise from the southern entrance there are forty-four chapels/niches; and from the north-eastern entrance there are an additional thirty-seven chapels/niches completing the circle. Each space between the chapels/niches is punctuated by a square pillar and that is mirrored by another pillar set outward forming a narrow, covered cloister-like *patha*.

It is interesting to note the numerological iconography associated with sixty-four — i.e. the Cauṅsaṭh Yoginī is related to the *maṇḍūka maṇḍala* of sixty-four *padas*. Here, in the Cauṅsaṭh Yoginī Mandir, the eighty-one shrines appear to be related to the *paramaśāyika maṇḍala* of eighty-one *padas*.[50]

Later in the twelfth century the Śakti temple, dedicated to Gaurī-Śaṅkara, was added and placed in the most unusual alignment when considering the whole. Its location is inexplicable and destroys the symmetry of the Cauṅsaṭh Yoginī Mandir.

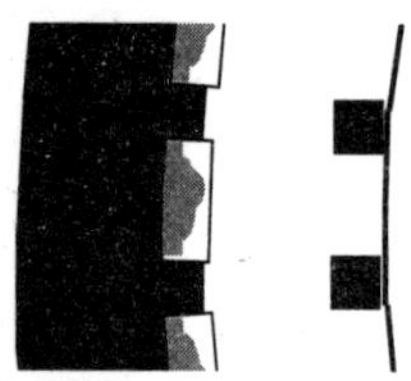

Figure 32: Cauṅsaṭh Yoginī Mandir (details) indicating niche with image

[47] Redrawn using PageMaker 6.0 from: FWB, p. 106.

[48] Before Bherāghāṭ or Bhedāghāt, the town was earlier called Bhairavi-ghāṭ after the fierce form of Durgā.

[49] The eighty-one images include sixty-four *yoginī*s (*chauṅsaṭ yoginī*) (fifty-seven intact, seven missing); eight Śaktis, also called *aṣṭa-śakti* (including the Sapta-Mātṛkās); three River goddesses (Gaṅgā, Yamunā and Sarasvatī); four dancing goddesses including Kālī; and Śiva and Gaṇeśa.

[50] FWB II, see: specific number entry.

Plate 38: Cauṅsaṭh Yoginī Mandir and Gaurī-Śaṅkara Temples plan

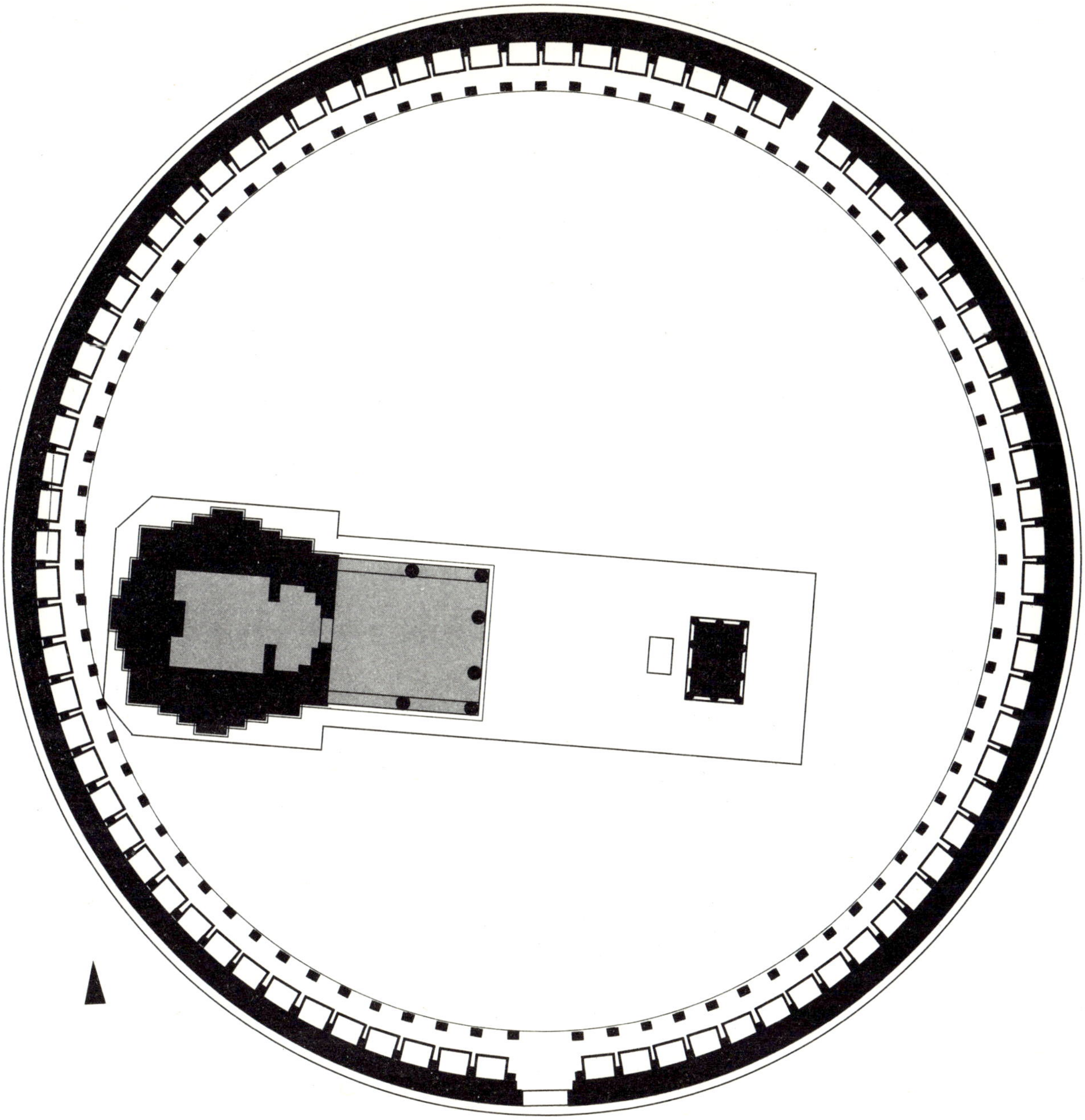

Someśvara Trikūṭa Temple, Haralhaḷḷi, Karnataka (a. CE 1100)

During the reign of King Vikramāditya II (VI) (r. CE 1076–1127) (**Appendix D**), the Śaiva Someśvara Trikūṭa Temple[51] of Haralhaḷḷi was designed and constructed. Like many temples of the Western Cāḷukya (Kalyāṇa) period, the Someśvara Trikūṭa Temple presents a complete and developed plan for an **A**-style *trikūṭa* temple.

The temple is oriented towards the east. The western *vimāna*, which is duplicated in the north and south, exhibits a square *garbhagṛha* with a Śivaliṅga which leads to a square *antarāla* (**Figure 34**). The *antarāla* opens to a common *sabhā-maṇḍapa* with a traditional arrangement of columns — i.e. four columns in the centre set upon a raised platform and twelve engaged columns, four of which are quarter, corner columns — forming nine *aṅkana*s. The north and south *vimāna*s are identical, *en plan*, to the western sanctum with its Śivaliṅga and *antarāla*. Upon the raised platform and towards the eastern edge is a Nandī couchant. To the east of the *sabhā-maṇḍapa* is an open, rectilinear *mukha-maṇḍapa* supported by two columns which leads to a short flight of steps. The eastern entrance of the Someśvara Trikūṭa Temple is the only source of light into the recesses of the temple.

The application of a *maṇḍala* to the Someśvara Trikūṭa Temple finds its preference in the form of a *paramaśāyika maṇḍala* (**Plate 41**). The three *vimāna*s and the *mukha-maṇḍapa* are found with the nine *pada* segments **2, 6, 8** and **4**, while the *sabhā-maṇḍapa* rests within segment **5** (**Plate 134**). The application of the circular *vāstu-puruṣa maṇḍala* (**Plate 40**), likewise, provides certain interesting conjunctions — e.g. the three *garbhagṛha*s lay within segments **x–a, m–l** and **r–s** (**Plates 134-135**).

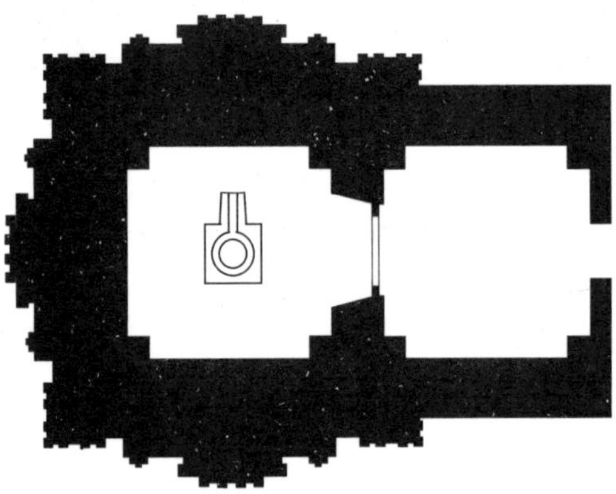

Figure 34: Someśvara Trikūṭa Temple *vimāna* element

[51] Redrawn using PageMaker 6.0 from: KMS II, p. 457, description on pp. 234-35. See also **Preface**.

Plate 39: Someśvara Trikūṭa Temple plan

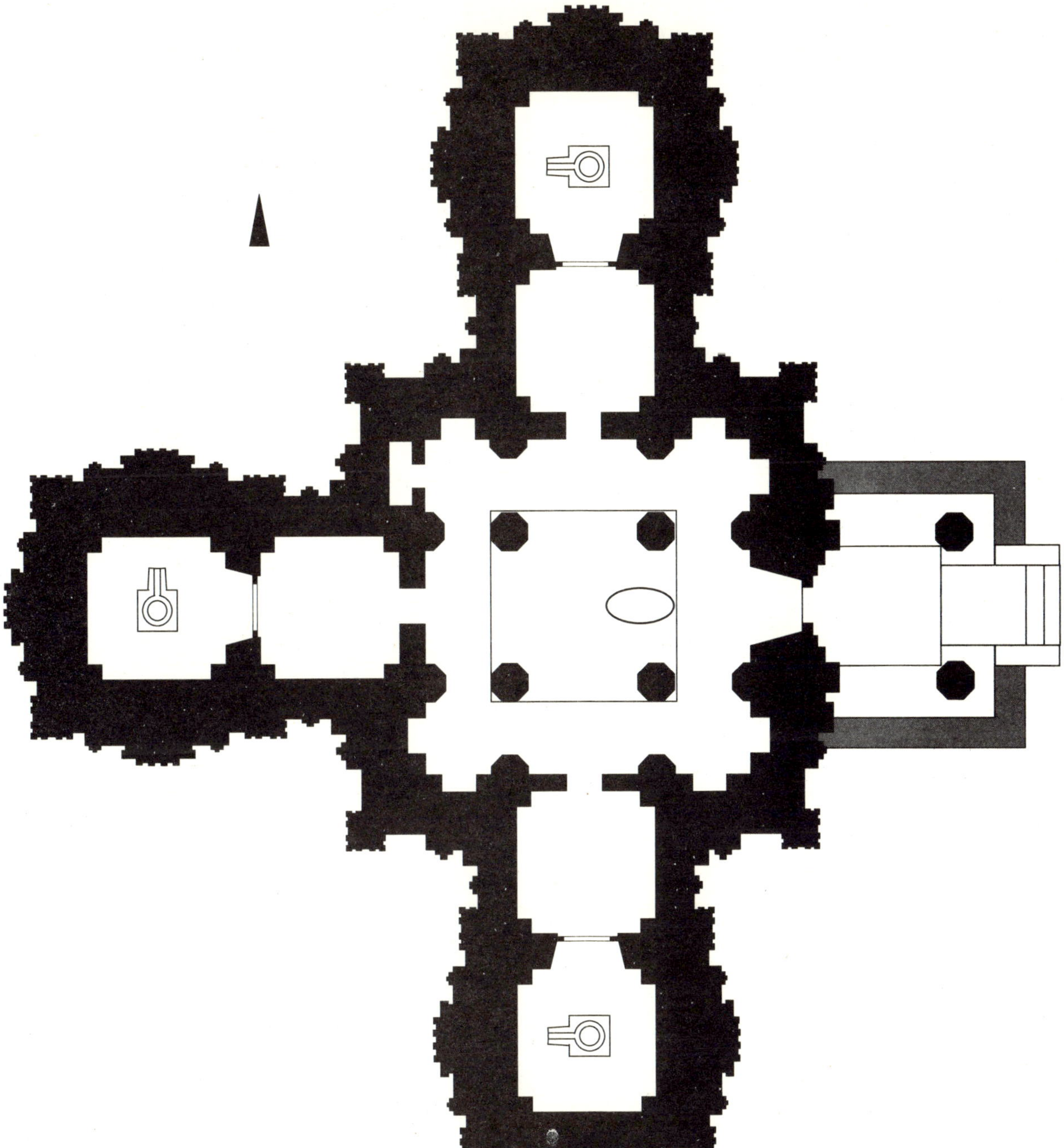

Plate 40: Someśvara Trikūṭa Temple with circular *vāstu-puruṣa maṇḍala*

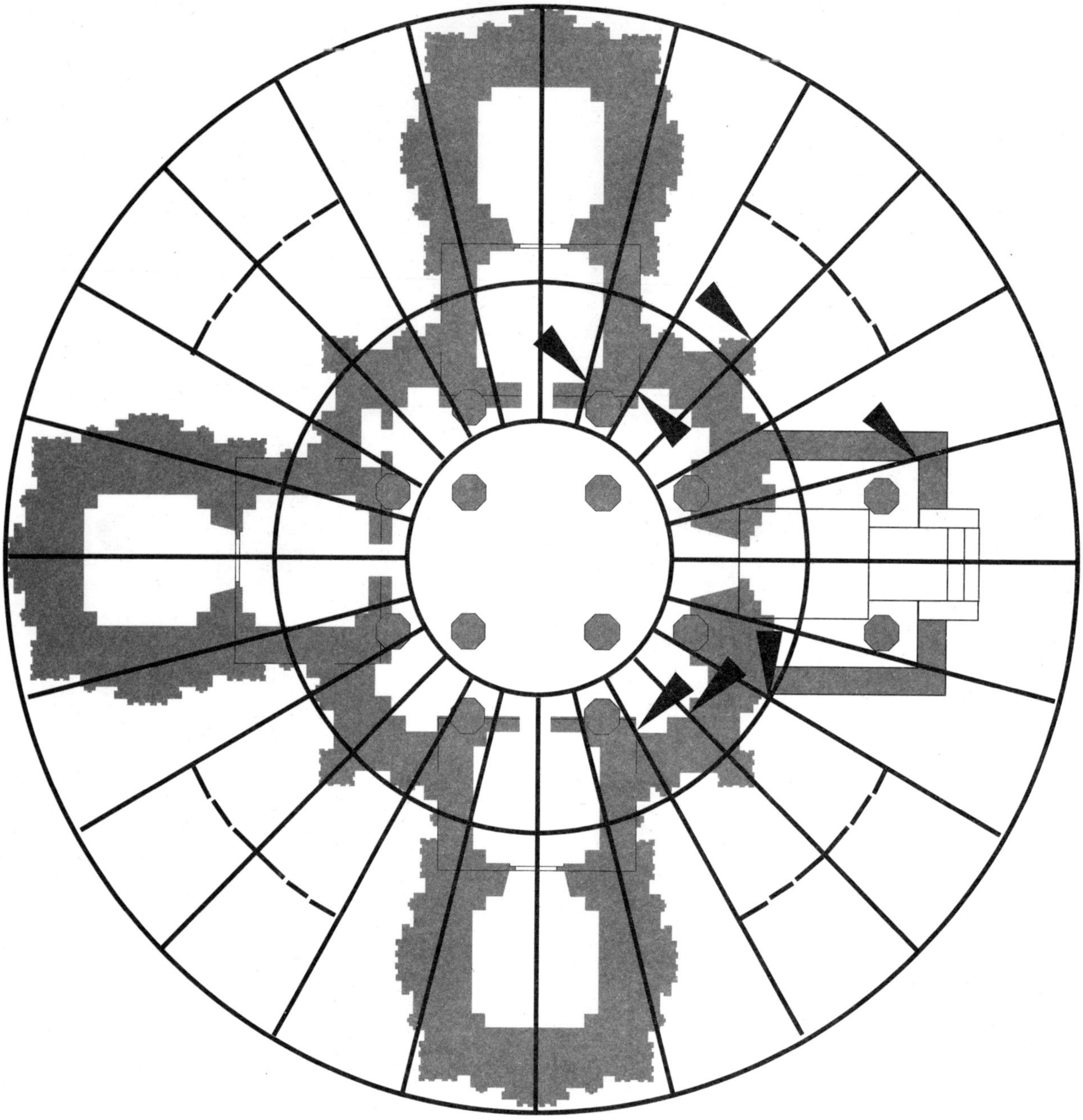

Plate 41: Someśvara Trikūṭa Temple with circular *paramaśāyika maṇḍala*

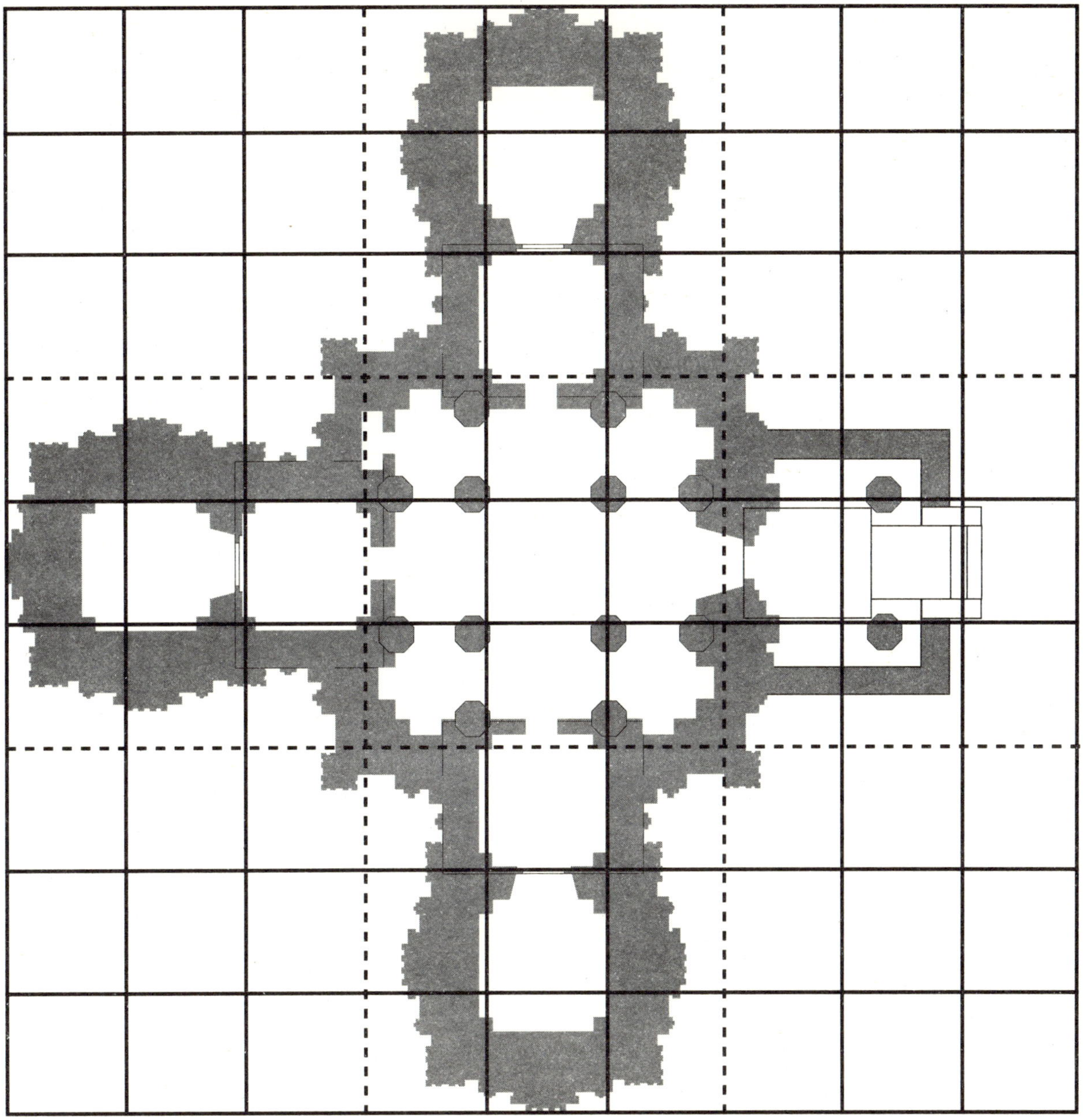

Lakṣmī-Devī Catuṣkūṭa Temple, Doḍḍa Gaḍḍuvalli, Karnataka (*c.* CE 1113)

The Lakṣmī-Devī Catuṣkūṭa Temple[52] theoretically approaches as close to the iconic standard of the Roman Pantheon as any of the temples of India — i.e. housing four deities from the three major sects — i.e. Vaiṣṇava, Śaiva and Śakti. Constructed during the forty two year reign of the Hoysaḷa King Viṣṇuvardhana (aka Bittiga Viṣṇuvardhana) (r. CE 1110-52) (**Appendix E**) who was arguably the greatest of the dynasty's monarchs. He was instrumental in throwing off the yoke of the Western Cāḷukyas (Kalyāṇa). It is believed that he was born and raised a Jaina and was possibly converted, none the less, he caused to be constructed this important Hindu temple as well as others within his vibrant realm.

The Lakṣmī-Devī Catuṣkūṭa Temple is a **B**-type *catuṣkūṭa* temple (**Figure 4**). As such, its plan is relatively unusual. Its uniqueness also rests in the fact that the temple contains two *garbhagṛhas* dedicated to Vaiṣṇava/Śakti deities and two consecrated to Śaiva/Śakti deities. The eastern *garbhagṛha* is dedicated to Lakṣmī (**Plate 2C**) and the southern to Keśava (**Plate 2D**); while the northern sanctum is dedicated to Kālī (**Plate 2A**), the western contains the Śivaliṅga (**Plate 2B**).

The Lakṣmī-Devī Catuṣkūṭa Temple consists of three identical *vimānas* with square *antarālas* — i.e. one to the east, one to the west and the third to the south. The fourth *vimāna* — i.e. the northern sanctum dedicated to Kālī — is of the same size and plan as the other three, but without the square *antarāla* that the others possess. This plan is similar to one of the models proposed by Foekema[53] (**Figure 35**). The southern three share a common *sabhā-maṇḍapa*. The *sabhā-maṇḍapa* is made up of sixteen columns, four of which are engaged to the *antarālas* of the east–west *vimānas*. To the north of this *sabhā-maṇḍapa* is an extention containing the entrances — i.e. one to the east and the other to the west. The whole assumes the conformation associated with either the Latin Cross or the Cross of St. Peter.

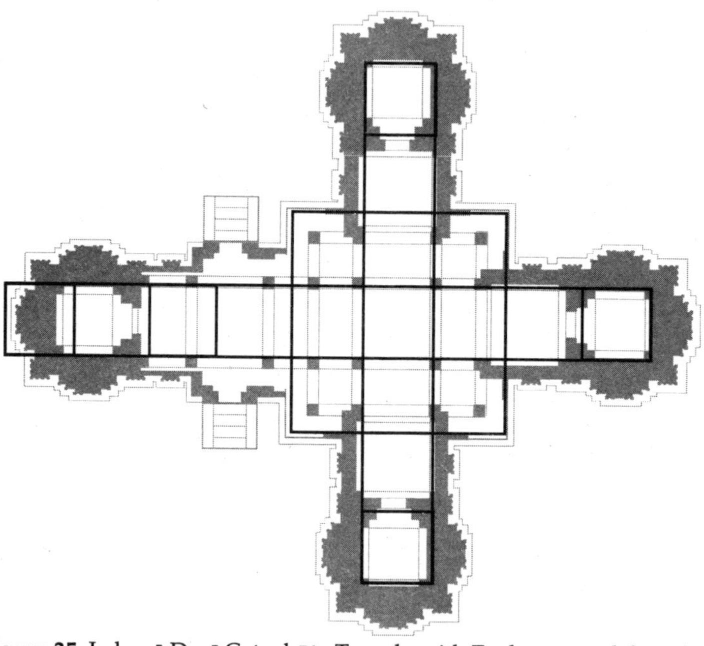

Figure 35: Lakṣmī-Devī Catuṣkūṭa Temple with Foekema model applied

[52] The plan is redrawn using Adobe PageMaker 6.0, from: KMS II, p. 477. See also "Introduction", p. xx, n. 6.

[53] GF, p. 43.

Plate 42: Lakṣmī-Devī Catuṣkūṭa Temple plan

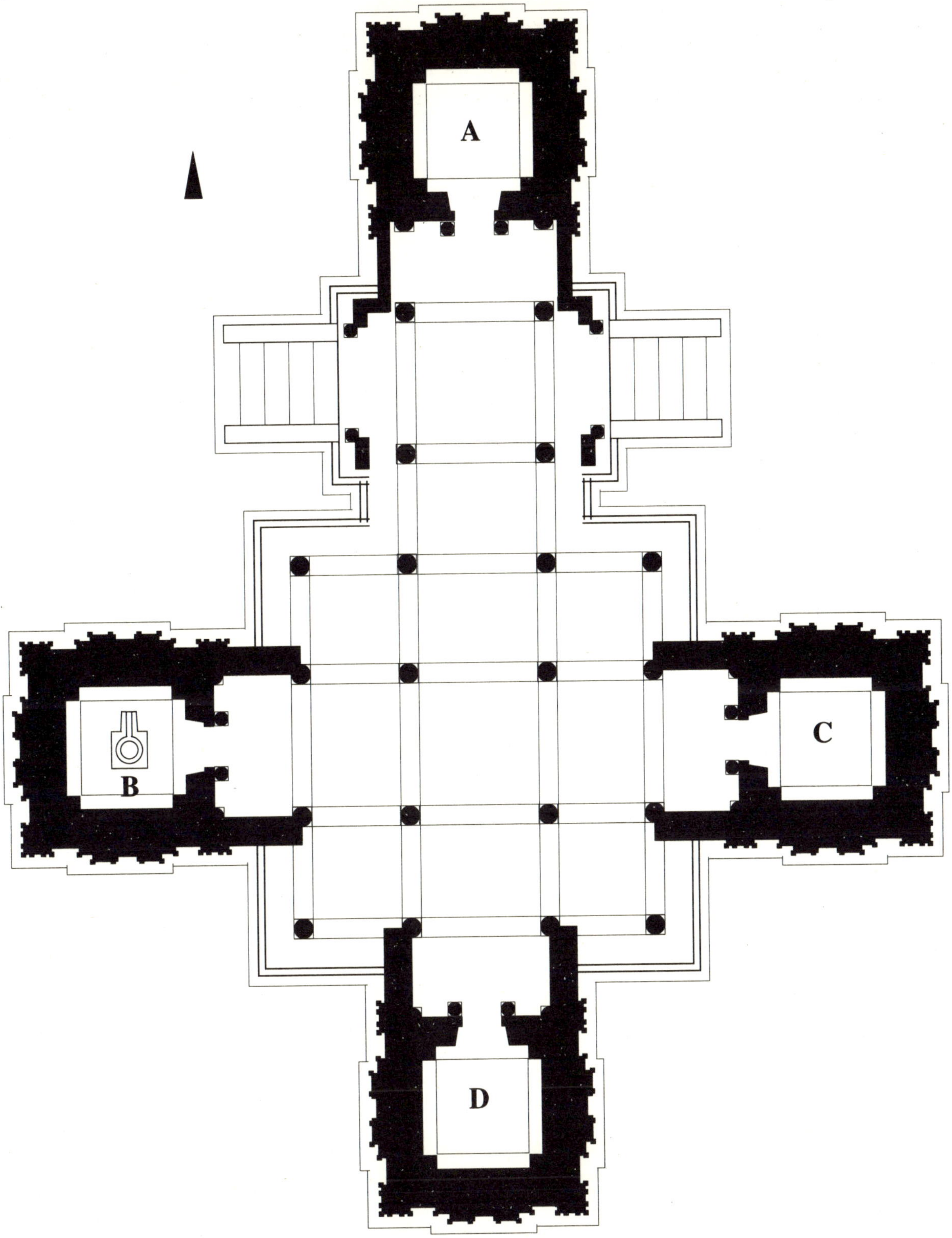

Lakṣmī-Devī Catuṣkūṭa Temple

The application of a *maṇḍala* indicates several interesting conjunctions. A *paramaśāyika maṇḍala* (**Plate 43** [top]) finds that the four *garbhagṛhas* fall within the middle nine *padas* of each side — i.e. **2, 4, 6** and **8** (**Appendix C, Plate 134**). Similarly, in the application of a circular *vāstu-puruṣa maṇḍala* (**Plate 44** [bottom]) centred on the *sabhā-maṇḍapa*, the *vimāna* fall within the segments bordering the cardinal points as would be expected.

Plate 43: Lakṣmī-Devī Catuṣkūṭa Temple with *paramaśāyika maṇḍala* over whole (top) and circular *vāstu-puruṣa maṇḍala* centred on *maṇḍapa* (bottom)

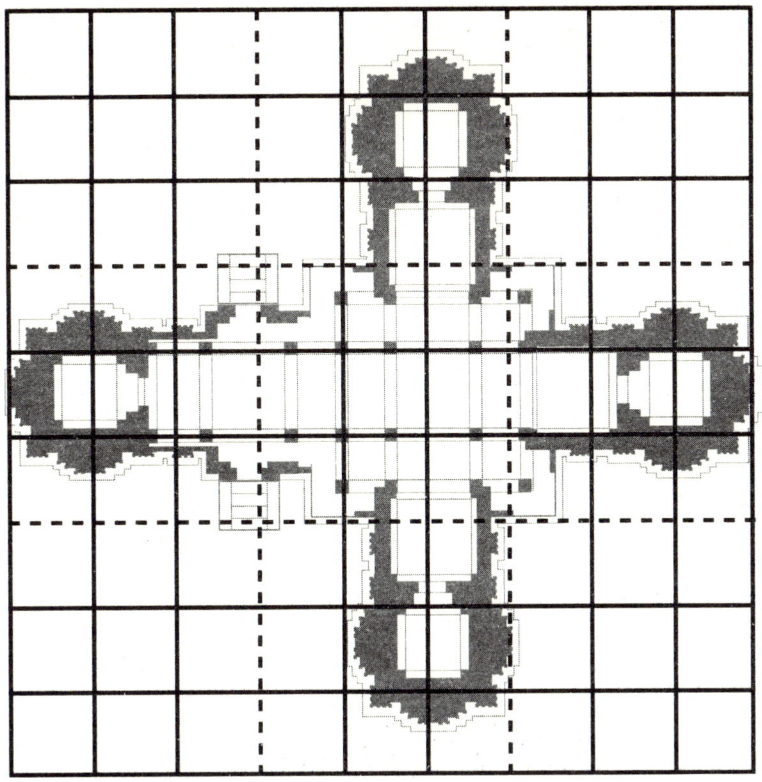

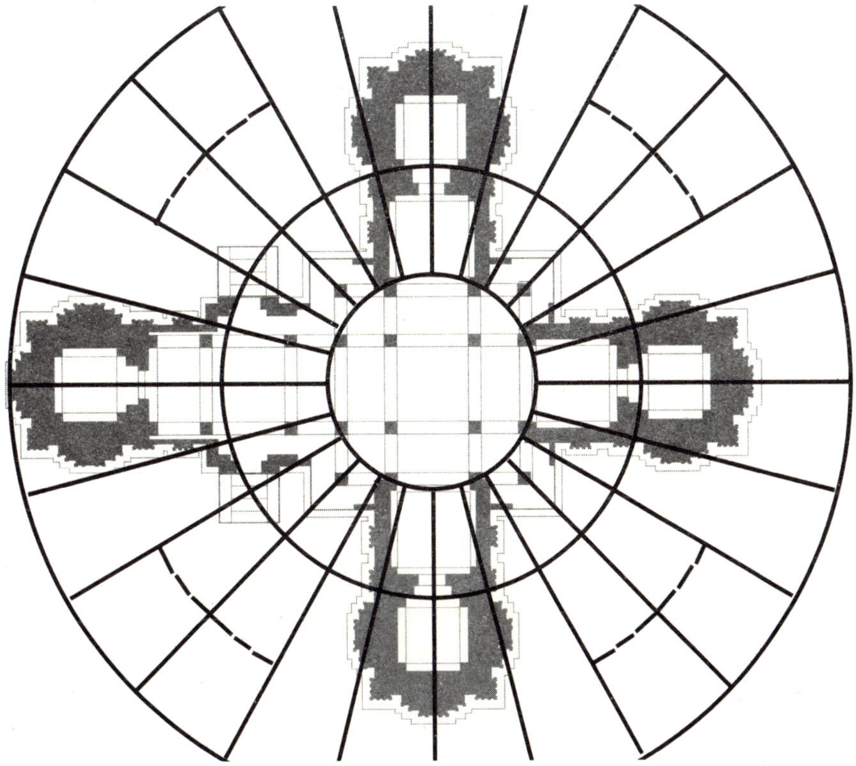

Trikūṭeśvara Trikūṭa Temple, Gorur, Karnataka (*c.* CE 1116)

During the reign of the famed Hoysaḷa king Viṣṇuvardhana (aka Bittiga Viṣṇuvardhana) (r. CE 1110-52) (**Appendix E**) the Śaiva Trikūṭeśvara Trikūṭa Temple[54] at Gorur was constructed. Like many temples of the Western Cāḷukya (Kalyāṇa) and the Hoysaḷa periods, the Trikūṭeśvara Trikūṭa Temple presents an **A**-style *trikūṭa* temple.

En plan, the Trikūṭeśvara Trikūṭa Temple is nearly a duplicate of the elaborately designed Someśvara Trikūṭa Temple (**Plate 39**). However there is a difference. The difference is obvious — the exterior of the *vimānas* of the Trikūṭeśvara Trikūṭa Temple are rather plain — i.e. they are essentially square with shallow pilasters attached to the outer façade breaking up what would have been an unrelenting cube. Square *garbhagṛhas* open via a narrow doorway onto equally square *antarālas*. The northern and western *garbhagṛhas* exhibit Śivaliṅgas. The entrance from the *antarālas* into the common *sabhā-maṇḍapa* is nearly as wide as the *antarāla* itself. The *sabhā-maṇḍapa* is traditional, *en forme* — i.e. consisting of four pillars on a raised platform and twelve engaged pillars, the corner pillars being quarter pillars. This arrangement creates nine *aṅkanas*. In the eastern wall of the *sabhā-maṇḍapa* is a doorway leading to a small, pillared, open *mukha-maṇḍapa* and the outside. Any ambient light filtering into the *sabhā-maṇḍapa* and the sanctums is minimal, plunging the *garbhagṛhas* into near darkness.

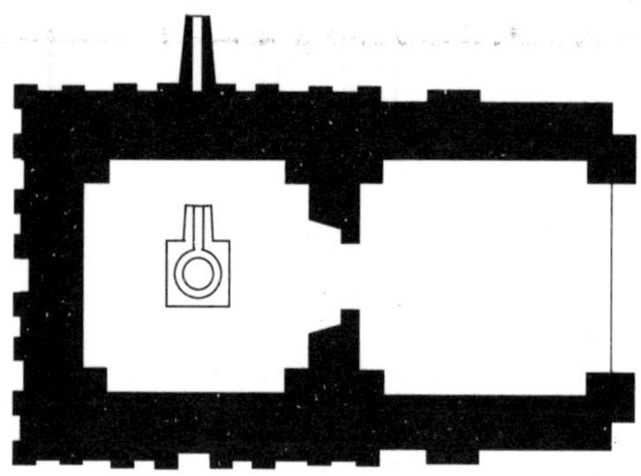

Figure 36: Trikūṭeśvara Trikūṭa Temple *vimāna* element

[54] The plan is redrawn using Adobe PageMaker 6.0, from: KMS II, p. 458; description on pp. 235-36. See also **Preface.**

Plate 44: Trikūṭeśvara Trikūṭa Temple plan

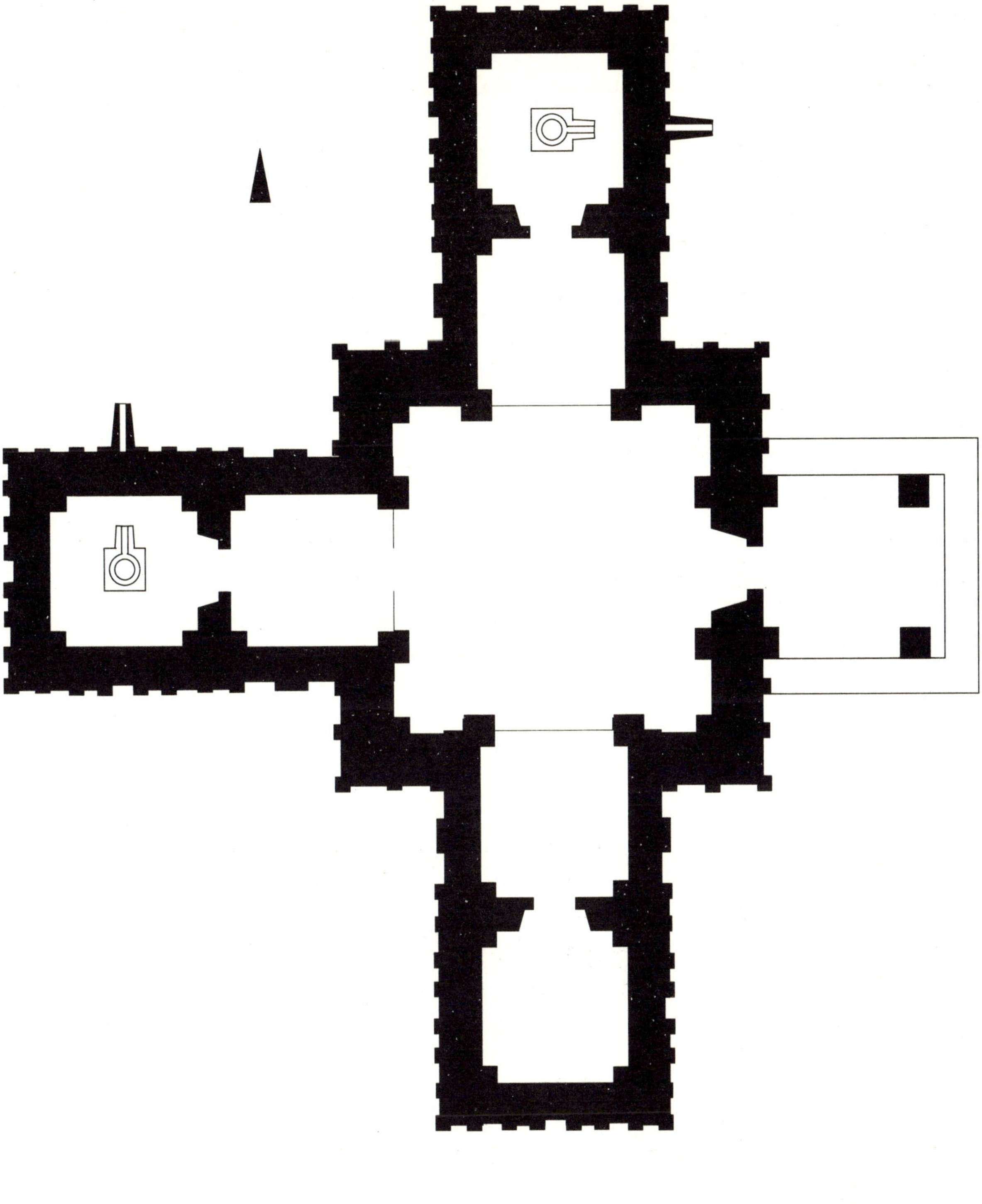

Cennakeśava Temple, Beḷūr, Karnataka (*c.* CE 1117)

The Hoysaḷa realm was relatively small, at first, being sandwiched between the larger Coḷa of Thañjāvūr and the Cāḷukya of Kalyāṇa. Around the year CE 1117, the Cennakeśava Temple[55] at Beḷūr was consecrated. It was built by King Viṣṇuvardhana (aka Bittiga Viṣṇuvardhana) (r. CE 1110-52), a Hoysaḷa monarch, in part, as a celebration of his defeat of the Coḷa and the annexation of Talakad the year before. The Cennakeśava Temple, the second of important temples built by the King Viṣṇuvardhana (first being Lakṣmī-Devī Catuṣkūṭa Temple) is one of the famous temples of south India and an important Vaiṣṇava pilgrimage site as well.

Strictly speaking, the Cennakeśava Temple is an *ekakūṭa*-type temple. However, it is included, herein, because of the fact that the *vimāna* includes three, developed, exterior shrines facing towards the north, south and west (**Figure 37**). *En plan*, the *vimāna* is unusual, being based on a sixteen-point star (**Plate 46**) and the shrines occupy three of the four cardinal points of the star. In addition, the walls of the *vimāna* are unusually thick; supporting a *śikhara* that no longer exists. There are numerous temples throughout India with attached, exterior shrines — e.g. the Kāmeśvara Temple of Auwa (a. CE 899), the Baśeśar Mahādeva Temple at Bajaurā (*c.* CE 850) and the Javari Temple at Khajurāho (a. CE 1075). The three exterior, attached shrines of the Cennakeśava Temple *vimāna* are more prominent and more developed than most.

Finally, the Cennakeśava Temple is placed upon a broad plinth or terrace that mimics the shape of the whole, thereby creating a wide, exterior *pradakṣiṇāpatha*. This *pradakṣiṇāpatha* would offer sufficient and focused attention on the three shrines.

The application of a *maṇḍala* indicates a number of interesting conjunctions, particularly when a circular *vāstu-puruṣa maṇḍala* is employed (**Plate 47**). As would be expected the three external shrines fall within the cardinal segments — i.e. **r–s**, **x–a** and **f–g** (**Appendix C, Plate 135**). In addition, the three external shrines rest on the exterior portion of the second circle from the centre (**Plate 47,** see arrows).

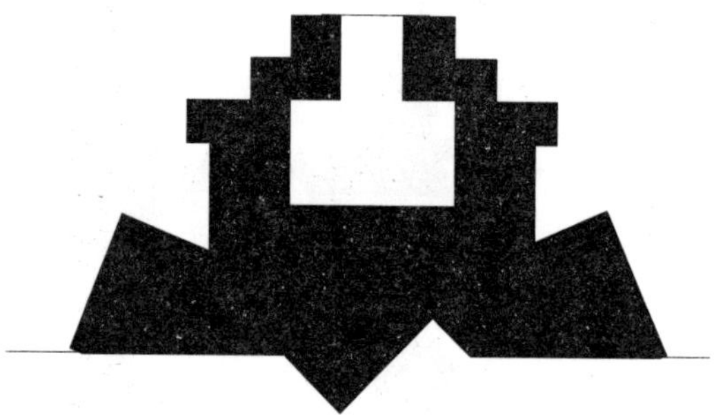

Figure 37: Cennakeśava Temple, detail of exterior chapels

[55] The plan is redrawn using Adobe PageMaker 6.0, from: HS II, p. 173.

Plate 45: Cennakeśava Temple plan

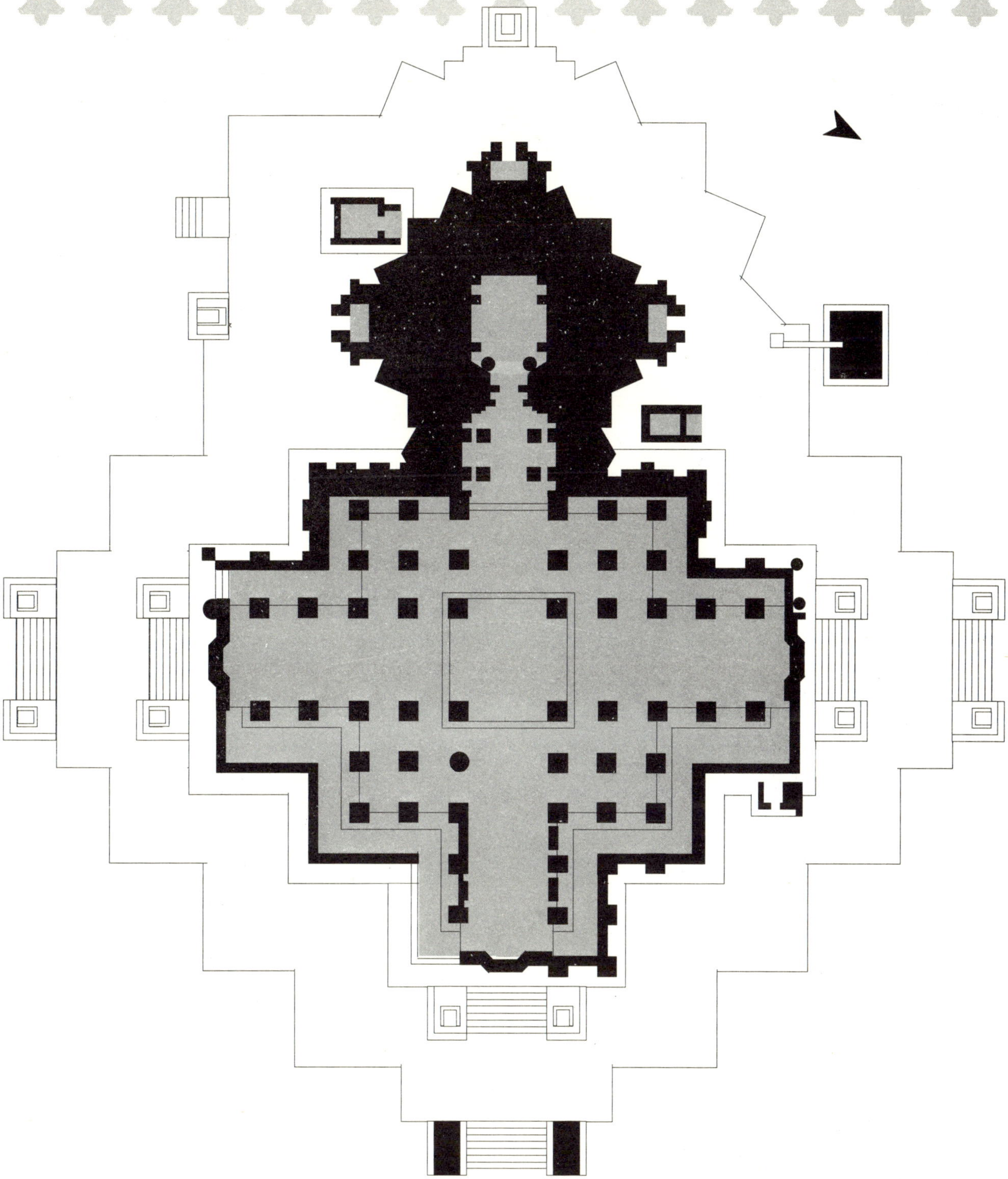

Plate 46: Cennakeśava Temple *vimāna* with a sixteen-point star

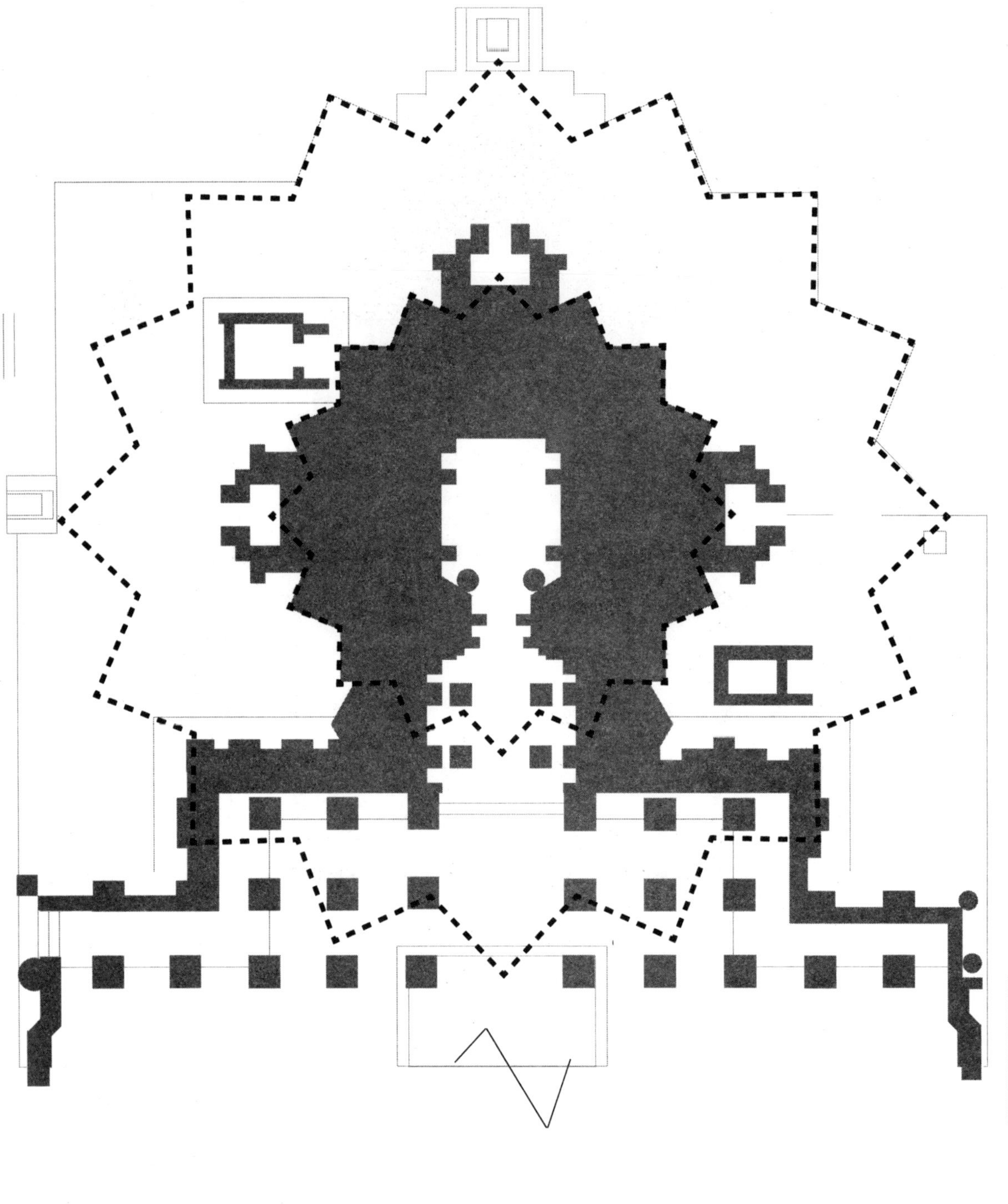

Plate 47: Cennakeśava Temple *vimāna* with circular *vāstu-puruṣa maṇḍala*

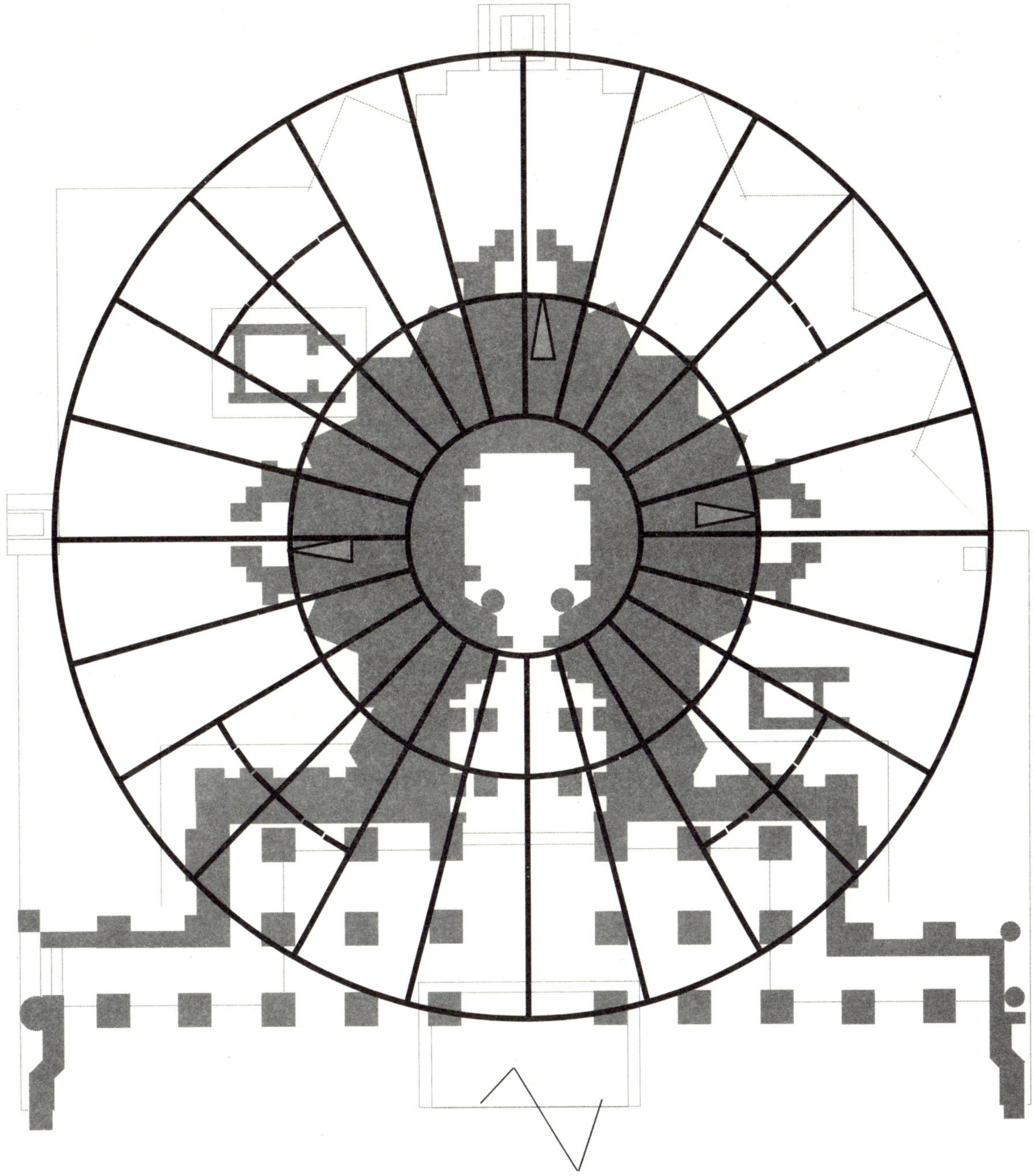

Anantaśayana Trikūṭa Temple, Navali, Karnataka (a. CE 1119)

The Cāḷukyas of Kalyāṇa or the Western Cāḷukyas had long established their domain in the present-day region centred in Karnataka. The Cāḷukya king Vikramāditya II (VI)[56] (r. CE 1076–1127) of Kalyāṇa was not a pre-eminent member of this western dynasty, nor was he particularly deleterious. Near the small village of Navali, the Anantaśayana Trikūṭa Temple[57] was erected during his reign. It is neither an important temple nor a noteworthy design. None the less, the plan of the temple is interesting.

The Anantaśayana Trikūṭa Temple is essentially rectangular, *en plan*. It is composed of three sanctums, in line, along the western side of the whole, creating a variation on the **C**-type *trikūṭa* plan (**Figure 3**). The northern and southern *garbhagṛhas* are square, while the central sanctum is rectangular. It is within this middle *garbhagṛha* that the image of Lord Viṣṇu-Anantaśayana (Viṣṇu reclining on the serpent Ananta) is found. The *sabhā-maṇḍapa* is square and contains sixteen standing and twenty engaged columns. Between each of the engaged columns on the north and south sides are small windows. A doorway is found in the centre of the eastern façade as well as two additional windows. The windows allow for sufficient ambient light into the interior of the *sabhā-maṇḍapa*, but the *garbhagṛhas* are into near darkness.

As noted, this design is highly unusual and it is difficult to find architectural precedents for its employment. The truly noteworthy element of this temple is the large *sabhā-maṇḍapa* and the number of windows which penetrate the outer wall.

56 Vikramāditya was the first of the Cāḷukya of Kalyāṇa and the sixth of the Cāḷukya as a whole.

57 The plan is redrawn using Adobe PageMaker 6.0, from: KMS II, p. 446. See also "Introduction", p. xx, n. 6.

Plate 48: Anantaśayana Trikūṭa Temple plan

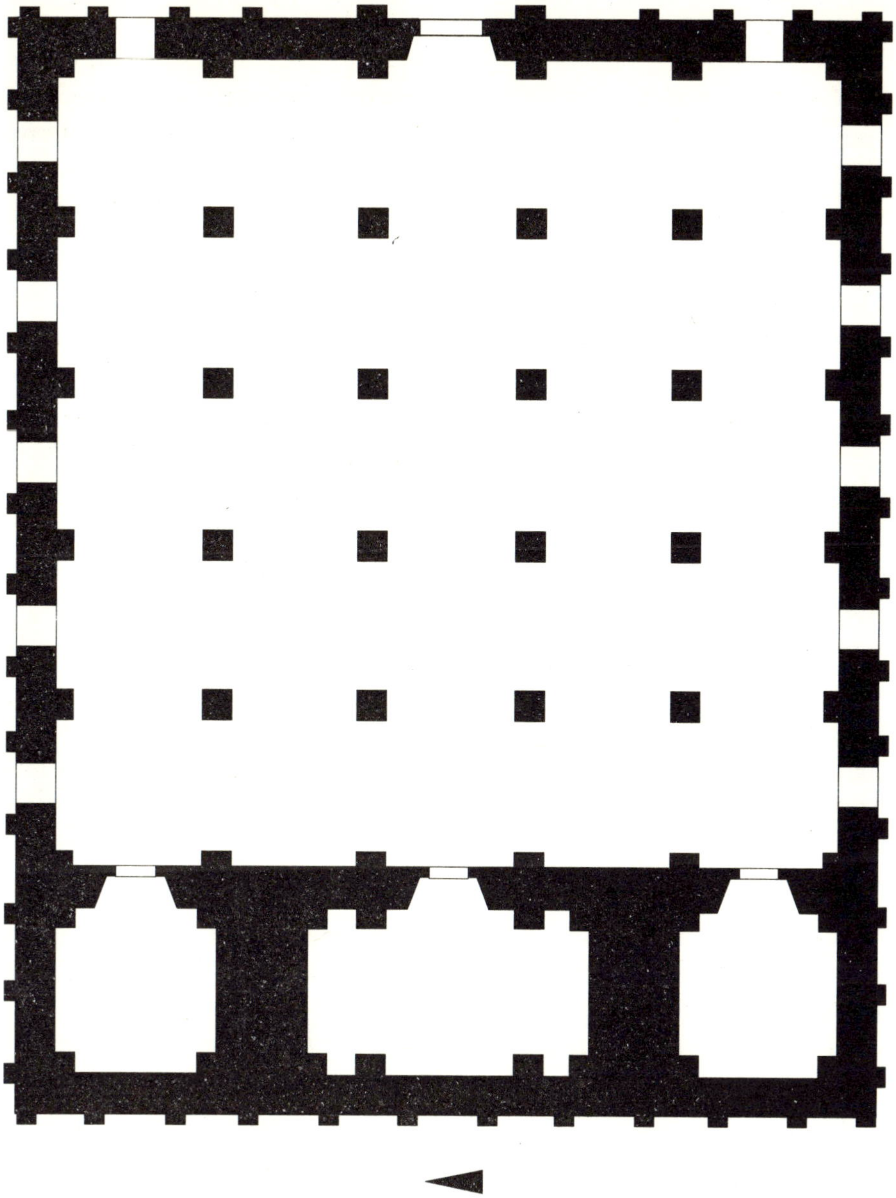

Hoysaḷeśvara Dvikūṭa Temple, Halebiḍ, Karnataka (a. CE 1120)

Related to the Cennakeśava Temple (**Plate 45**) at Beḷūr, the Hoysaḷeśvara Dvikūṭa Temple[58] of Halebiḍ is dedicated to the "Lord of the Hoysaḷas" (Hoysaḷeśvara) — i.e. Naṭarāja. This Siamese twin temple was also built by King Viṣṇuvardhana (aka Biṭṭiga Viṣṇuvardhana) (r. CE 1110-52) (**Appendix D**), a truly gifted and powerful monarch responsible for the construction of a number of important temples. The Hoysaḷeśvara Dvikūṭa Temple is seen by Stierlin[59] to be a dynastic temple which is an interesting assertion since two of the three most important Hoysaḷa temples are Vaiṣṇava — i.e. the Cennakeśava Temple and the Keśava Trikūṭa Temple of Somanāthapur (**Plate 97**).

En plan, the temple consists of two *garbhagṛhas* nestled within sixteen-point star *vimānas* (**Plate 50** [top]). As with the Cennakeśava Temple, each of these two *vimānas* also contains three deep-set, secondary shrines; one to the north, one to the south and one to the west. However, unlike the Beḷūr Temple, these shrines are much deeper and more developed (**Figure 38**). Each of the two *garbhagṛhas* is fronted by a rectangular *antarāla* which leads to an open *sabhā-maṇḍapa*. The *sabhā-maṇḍapa* exhibits a number of small shrines set within the thick western wall — i.e. four to the south and four to the north of each entrance into the *antarāla*. Each of the *sabhā-maṇḍapas* has four columns in the centre of the space supporting the roof and ten towards the east which are stepped to conform with the larger plan. Beyond these columns to the east is the exterior wall which is made up of *jālī*. These screens and the entrances are the only means by which light enters these spacious *sabhā-maṇḍapas*. In the connecting space between the two *sabhā-maṇḍapas* are two smaller shrines — i.e. one to the east which is *pañca-ratha, en plan*, and a simpler one to the west which is *triratha, en plan*. To the east of the main entrance of the *sabhā-maṇḍapas*, and on the same spacious platform are two *namaskāra-maṇḍapas* dedicated to Nandī. The one to the south is nearly twice the size of the one to the north and the southern *maṇḍapa* also possesses a small rectilinear shrine to the east. The southern *namaskāra-maṇḍapa* consists of twenty-four columns supporting the roof, while, its northern counterpart has only sixteen. The capacious platform upon which the whole ensemble rests is wide enough to allow for *pradakṣiṇā*.

The application of a *maṇḍala* to the whole is highly problematical due to the nature of the plan. However, a grid based on a *karṇāṣṭaka maṇḍala* does indicate some interesting conjunctions (**Plate 50** [bottom]). The *karṇāṣṭaka maṇḍala* is related to the *paramaśāyika maṇḍala*, having eighteen *padas* in a rank, twice that of the *paramaśāyika maṇḍala*. In addition when either a *paramaśāyika maṇḍala* (**Plate 51** [top]) or a circular *vāstu-puruṣa maṇḍala* (**Plate 51** [bottom]) are overlaid on the *vimāna*, either appears applicable. In either case the number of significant conjunctions is interesting.

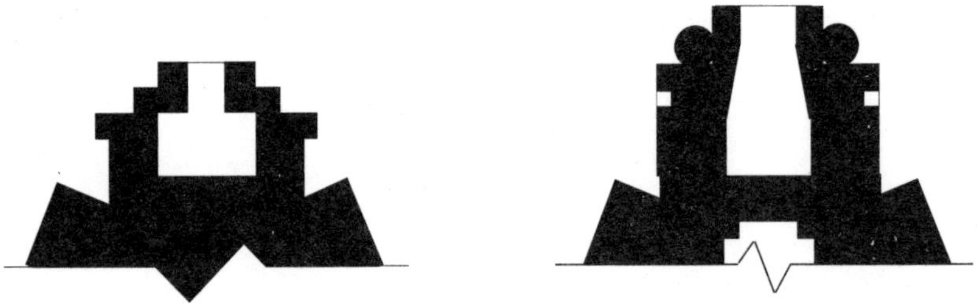

Figure 38: Detail of exterior chapels: Cennakeśava Temple (left) and Hoysaḷeśvara Temple (right)

[58] The plan is redrawn using Adobe PageMaker 6.0, from: HS II, p. 174.

[59] Ibid., p. 169.

Plate 49: Hoysaḷeśvara Dvikūṭa Temple plan

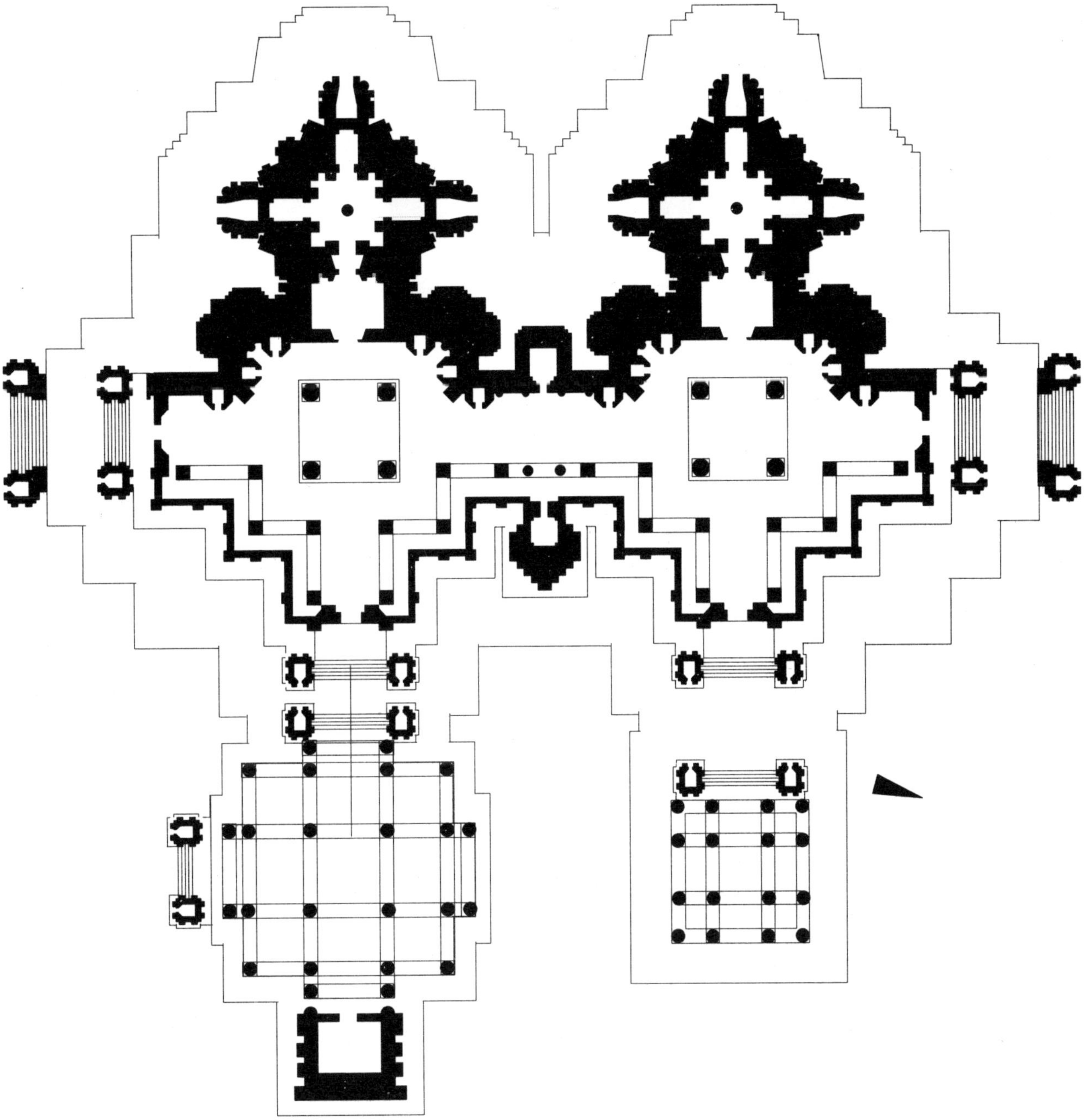

Plate 50: Hoysaḷeśvara Temple detail with sixteen-point star (top) and grid based on *karṇāṣṭaka maṇḍala* (bottom)

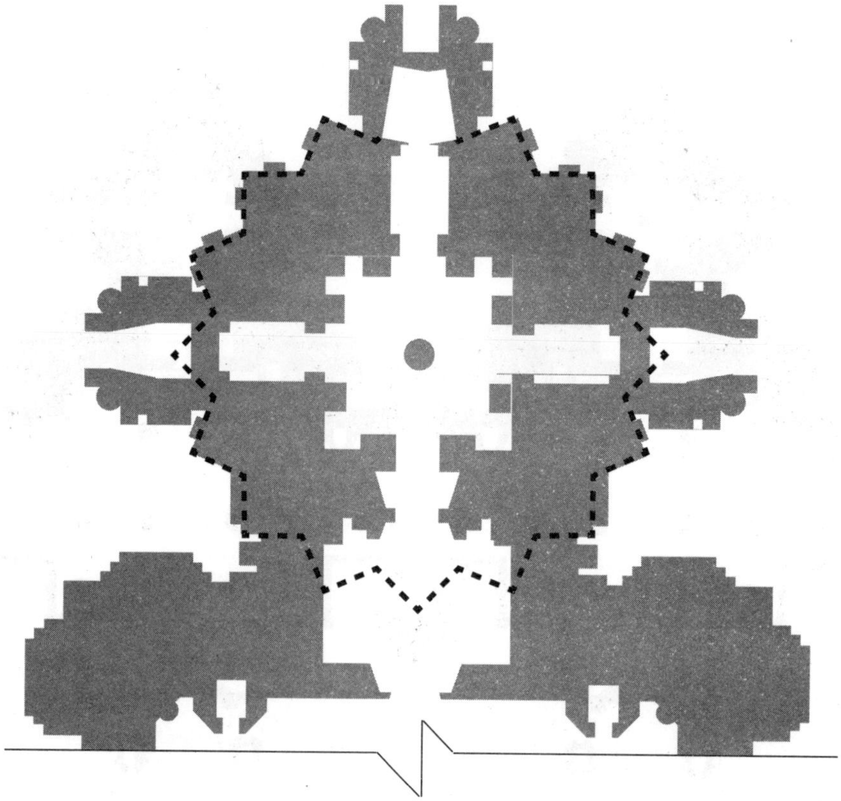

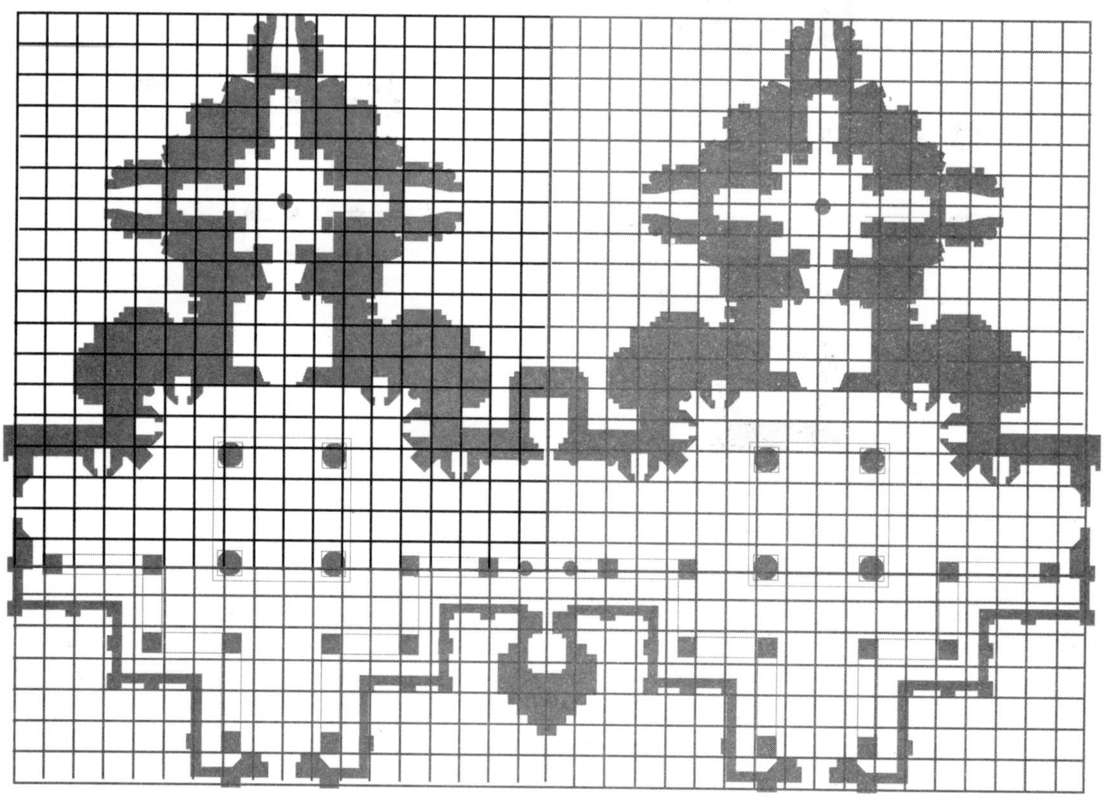

Plate 51: Hoysaḷeśvara Temple detail with *paramaśāyika maṇḍala* (top) and circular *vāstu-puruṣa maṇḍala* (bottom)

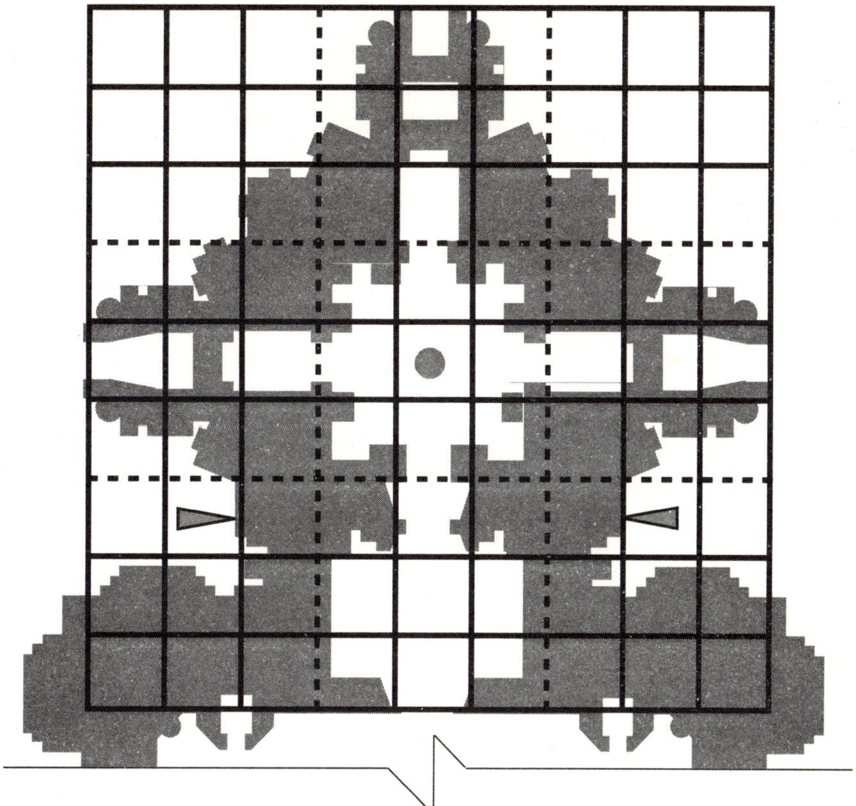

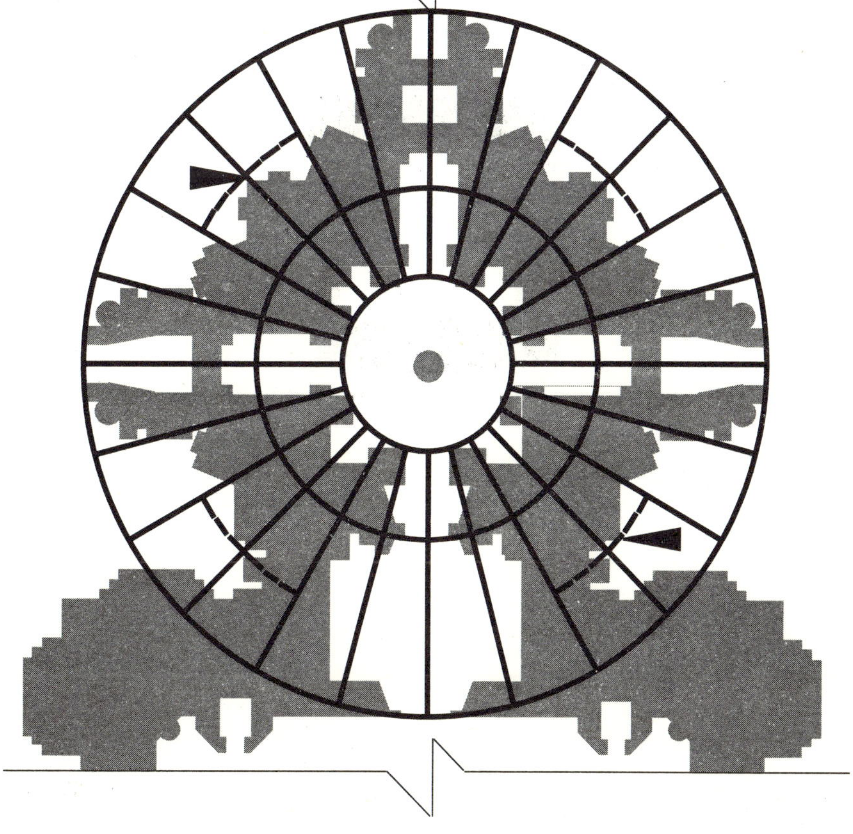

Mallikārjuna Trikūṭa Temple, Hirebevinuru, Karnataka (*c.* CE 1124)

Constructed during the reigns of the Western Cāḷukya (Kalyāṇa) monarchs Vikramāditya II (VI) (r. CE 1076–1127) and Someśvara III (r. CE 1127-35) (**Appendix D**), Mallikārjuna Trikūṭa Temple[60] possesses a **B**-type Trikūṭa plan (**Figure 3**). It differs in proportion from a number of other **B**-type Trikūṭa plans in that the northern and southern *vimāna* are without *antarāla* and appear truncated (**Figure 39**). The Mallikārjuna Trikūṭa Temple is a Śaiva temple and the three sanctums are locally assigned to Mallikārjuna, Revasiddha and Siddharāmeśvara.

The temple's main *pañcaratha vimāna* is in the west and consists of a square *garbhagṛha* with Śivaliṅga and square *antarāla*. They are separated from the *sabhā-maṇḍapa* by a wall considerably less thick than either the walls of the *vimāna* or *sabhā-maṇḍapa*. On either side of the entrance into this sanctum are two niches. The two other *pañcaratha vimāna*s with Śivaliṅga are identical, one to the north and the other to the south. They are without *antarāla*s and open directly onto the *sabhā-maṇḍapa* with the same narrow wall as seen in the western *vimāna*. It is this transitional element — i.e. the narrow wall — that gives the Mallikārjuna Trikūṭa Temple its unusual, truncated appearance, *en plan*. The three *vimāna* shares a common square *sabhā-maṇḍapa* which, like most, is supported by sixteen traditionally arranged columns — i.e. four free-standing columns in the centre raised on a square platform and twelve engaged columns, four of which are quarter, corner columns — which form nine *aṅkana*s. To the east is a porch, a *mukha-maṇḍapa* supported by four pillars. Two are free-standing and two are engaged and frame the doorway. A short flight of stairs lead to the north.

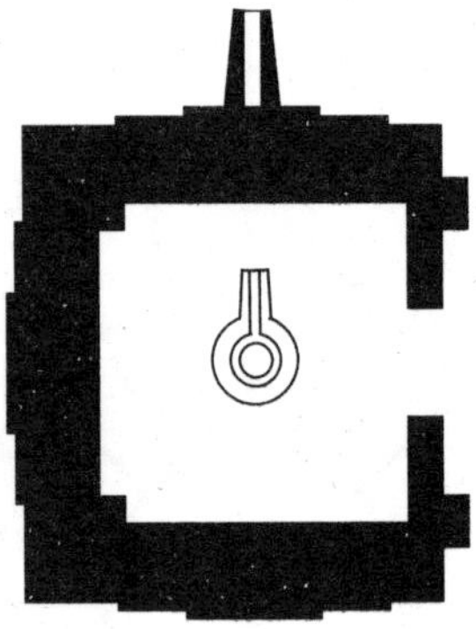

Figure 39: Mallikārjuna Trikūṭa Temple north and south *vimāna* elements

60 Redrawn using PageMaker 6.0 from: KMS II, p. 473, description on pp. 260-61. See also **Preface**.

Plate 52: Mallikārjuna Trikūṭa Temple plan

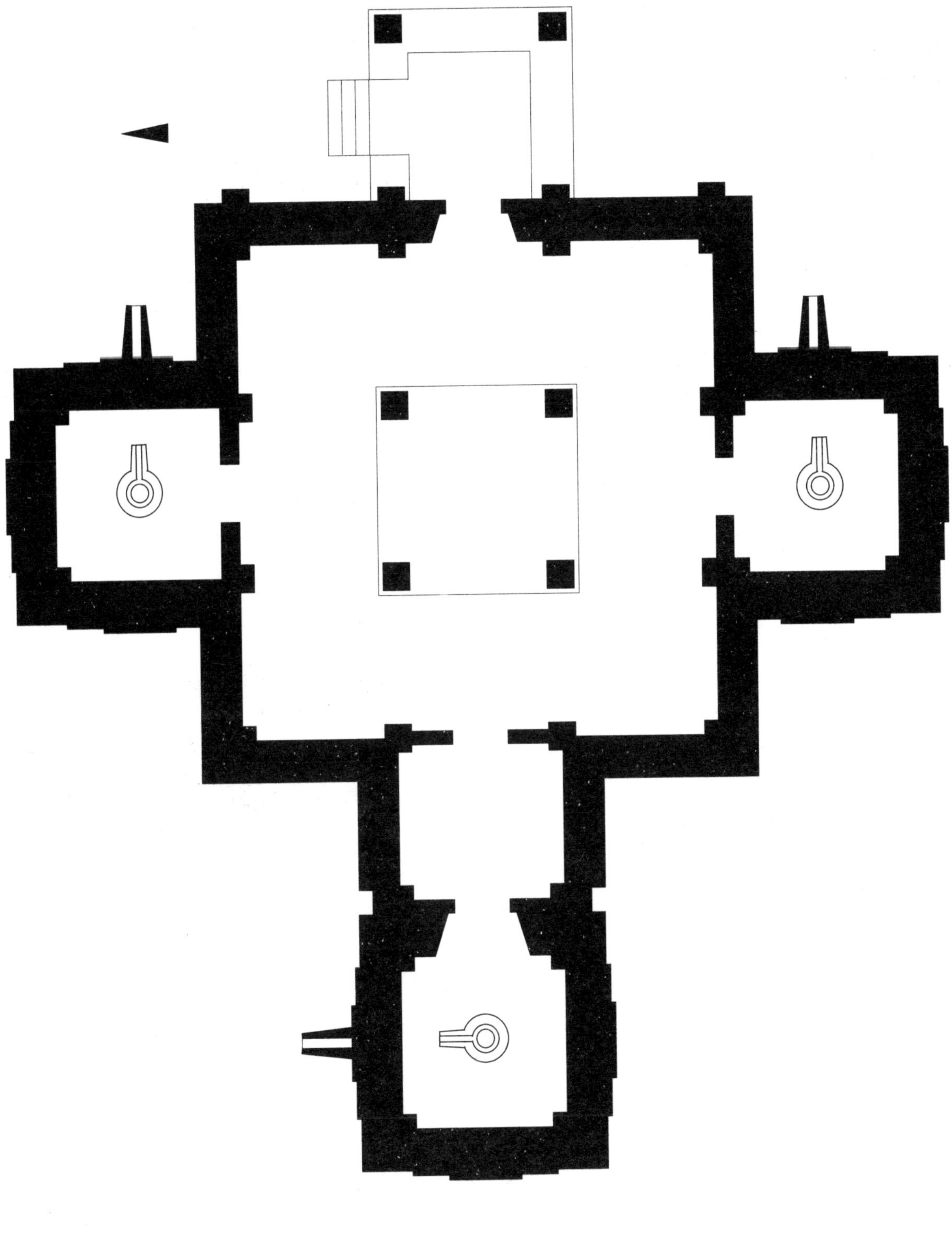

Rāmeśvara Dvikūṭa Temple, Yaragal, Karnataka (a. CE 1125)

The date of the Rāmeśvara Dvikūṭa Temple[61] at Yaragal is assigned to the second quarter of the twelfth century CE. It was constructed, probably during the reign of the Western Cāḷukya (Kalyāṇa) king Someśvara III (r. CE 1127-35) (**Appendix D**). The Rāmeśvara Dvikuṭa Temple is an **A**-type *dvikuṭa* plan (**Figure 2**).

Essentially, mirror axial (**Figure 40**), the temple consists of two identical *pañcaratha garbhagṛhas* with square *antarālas*. It is similar in its mirror axiality to the Kallappa-Mallappa (Harihara) Dvikūṭa Temple (**Plate 25**). The western *garbhagṛha* of the Rāmeśvara Dvikūṭa Temple holds a Śivaliṅga, while the eastern *garbhagṛha* is empty. As is seen in the Mallikārjuna Trikūṭa Temple (**Plate 52**), the two *antarālas* are separated from the *sabhā-maṇḍapa* by a wall not as thick as the walls of the *vimāna*. The two *vimānas* share a common, open *sabhā-maṇḍapa* with sixteen columns, traditionally arranged — i.e. four free-standing columns in the centre, four free-standing columns in the north and an additional four to the south, as well as four engaged columns. To the north as well as to the south are *mukha-maṇḍapas* each with two free-standing columns and a short flight of stairs leading to the ground level.

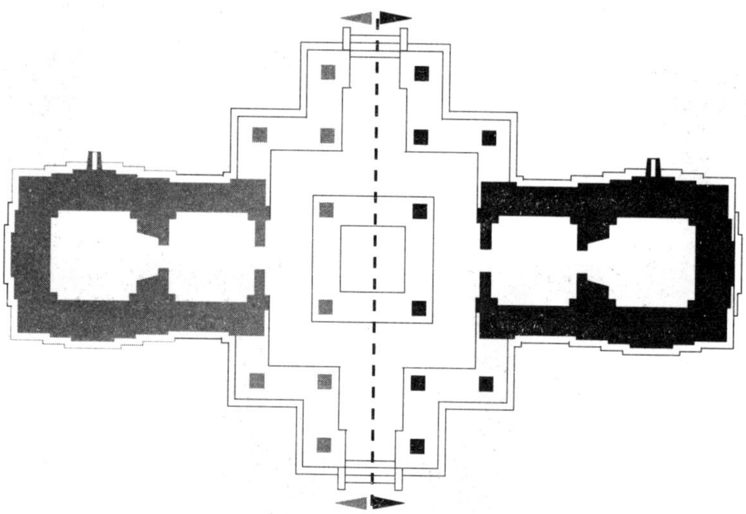

Figure 40: Rāmeśvara Dvikūṭa Temple indicating mirror axiality

[61] Redrawn using PageMaker 6.0 from: KMS II, p. 420, description on pp. 192-93. See also **Preface**.

Plate 53: Rāmeśvara Dvikūṭa Temple plan

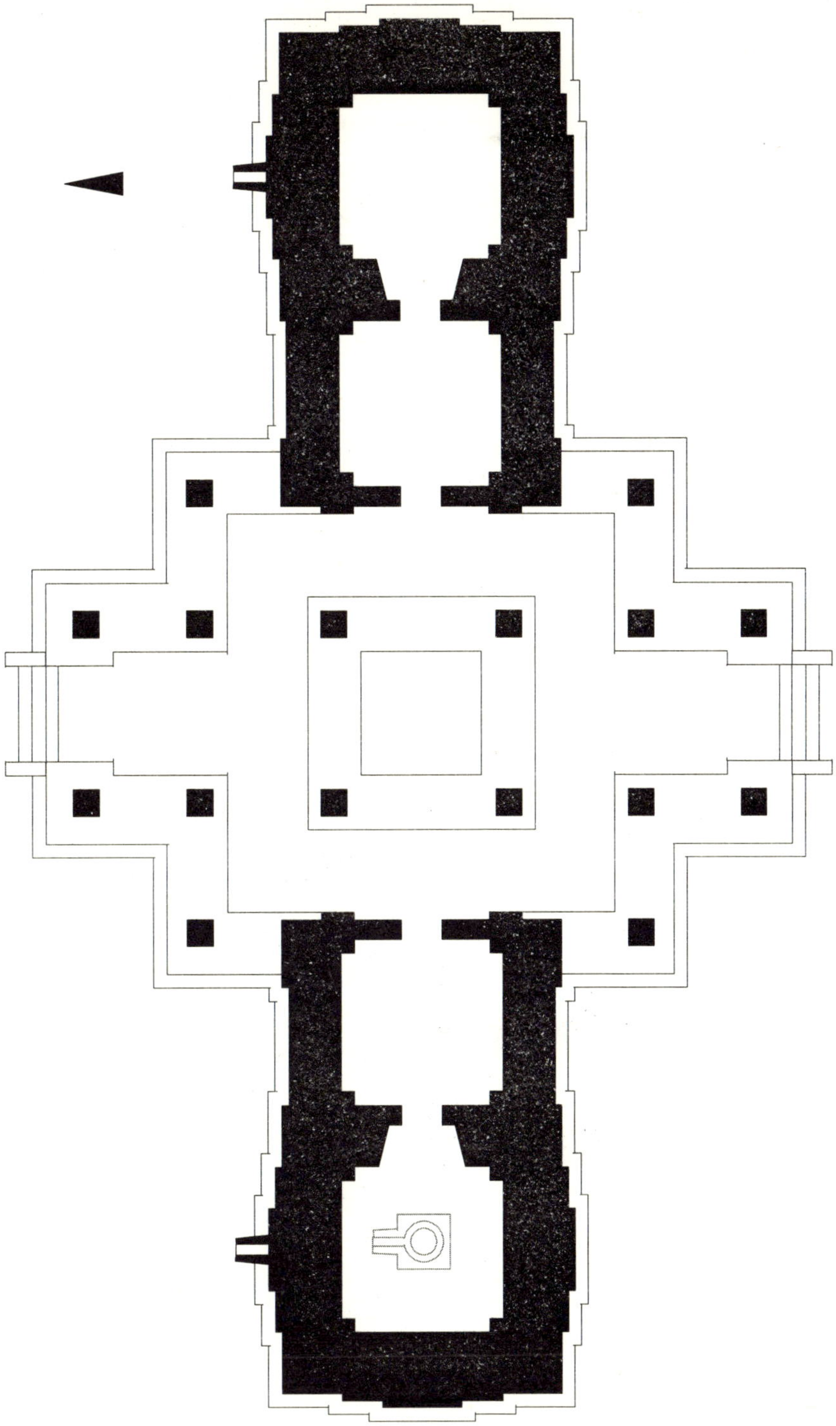

Śaṅkaraliṅga Trikūṭa Temple, Dhulakheḍa, Karnataka (a. CE 1125)

The Western Cāḷukyas (Kalyāṇa Cāḷukyas) had carved out a realm which bordered the Coḷa and their cousins, the Eastern Cāḷukyas (Veṅgī Cāḷukyas), all of which they were in conflict from time to time. None the less, the Western Cāḷukya were still inveterate builders of some remarkable monuments. The Śaiva Śaṅkaraliṅga Trikūṭa Temple[62] is an example of interest, although it is not one of the more remarkable temples of this dynasty. Constructed during the reigns of the kings Jayasiṁha II Jagadekamalla (r. CE 1015-43) and Someśvara I (Trailokyamalla or Āhavamalladeva) (r. CE 1043-68) (**Appendix D**), this temple indicates one of the plan variations that can occur. It is a **B**-type *trikūṭa* temple (**Figure 3**) of rather plain design.

The Śaṅkaraliṅga Trikūṭa Temple consists of the main *garbhagṛha* to the west with a developed, *pañcaratha* design, *en plan*. A square *antarāla* leads to a truncated, rectilinear *sabhā-maṇḍapa*. This *sabhā-maṇḍapa* exhibits twelve columns, eight of which are engaged and four are free-standing columns supporting the roof. Normally, this element would have been square and containing sixteen columns, twelve of which would have been engaged (**Figure 41**). How this strange solution was arrived at is a mystery. To the north and south are two more *vimānas*. However, these *garbhagṛhas* are without an *antarāla* and their eastern façade defines the eastern limits of the plan and frame the open, eastern part of the *sabhā-maṇḍapa*.

The application of a *maṇḍala* is applicable only to the individual elements of the Śaṅkaraliṅga Trikūṭa Temple. A *maṇḍala* over the whole is virtually impossible.

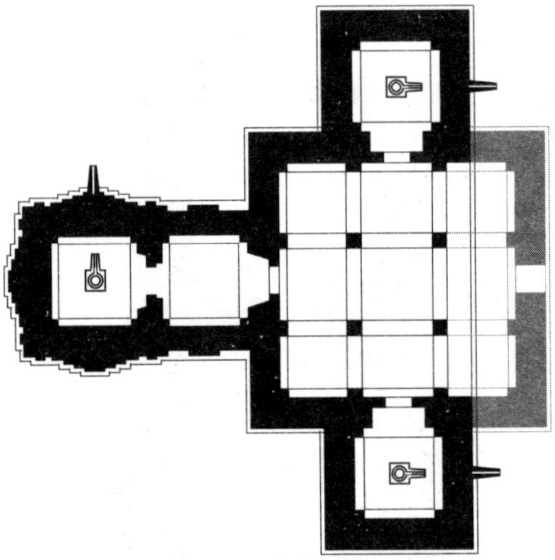

Figure 41: Śaṅkaraliṅga Trikūṭa Temple with developed *sabhā-maṇḍapa* shown

[62] Redrawn using PageMaker 6.0 from: KMS II, p. 468, description on p. 257. See also **Preface**.

Plate 54: Śaṅkaraliṅga Trikūṭa Temple plan

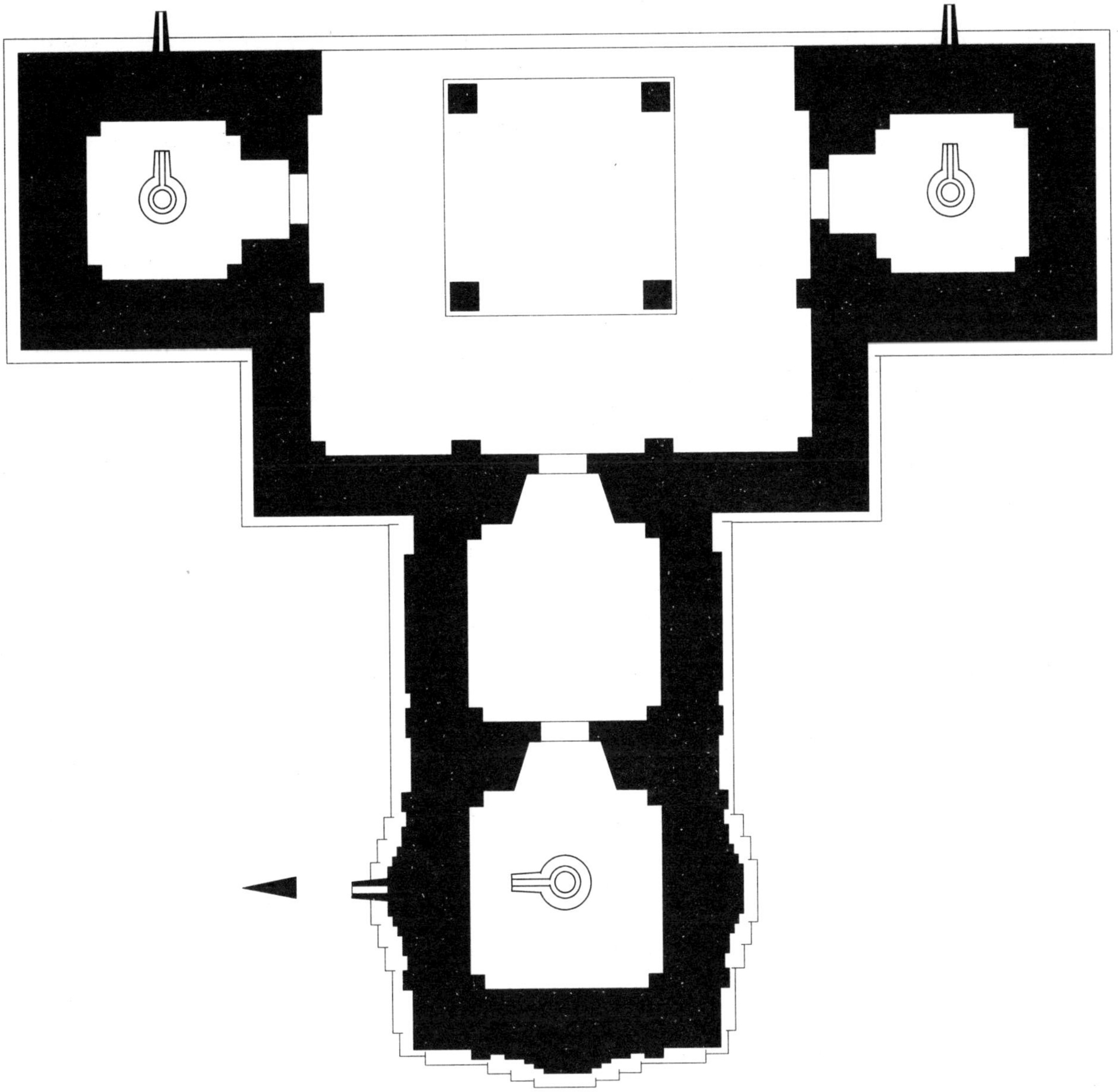

Rāmaliṅga Dvikūṭa Temple, Sirūr, Karnataka (a. CE 1125)

The **A**-type *dvikūṭa* temple (**Figure 2**) at Sirūr, Rāmaliṅga Dvikūṭa Temple,[63] was constructed during the reign of the Western Cāḷukya (Kalyāṇa) king Jagadekamalla II (r. CE 1135-51) (**Appendix D**) and is also associated with the Queen Lakṣmīdevī. This temple differs considerably from the Rāmeśvara Dvikūṭa Temple at Yaragal (**Plate 53**) in that the two *vimānas* are considerably different and the employment of two *sabhā-maṇḍapas*.

The Rāmaliṅga Dvikūṭa Temple is composed of a main and simple *garbhagṛha* with a square *antarāla* in the west and housing a Śivaliṅga. This *vimāna* is opposite the eastern *pañcaratha garbhagṛha* which is without *antarāla* and also housing a Śivaliṅga. The main sanctum with *antarāla* opens onto an enclosed *sabhā-maṇḍapa* with sixteen columns, arranged in the traditional manner — i.e. four free-standing columns in the centre raised on a square platform and twelve engaged columns, four of which are quarter, corner columns — which form nine irregular *aṅkanas*. The eastern *garbhagṛha* opens directly onto an open *sabhā-maṇḍapa* composed of twelve columns — i.e. four free-standing columns in the centre and three free-standing pillars to the north and three to the south as well as two engaged columns on the wall of the enclosed *sabhā-maṇḍapa*.

An **A**-type *dvikūṭa* temple with disparate *vimānas* is not unusual. However, the inclusion of an enclosed and open *sabhā-maṇḍapa* of similar space is unusual. This arrangement would cause one to surmise that the two elements were constructed at different times.

---

[63] Redrawn using PageMaker 6.0 from: KMS II, p. 421, description on p. 193. See also **Preface.**

Plate 55: Rāmaliṅga Dvikūṭa Temple plan

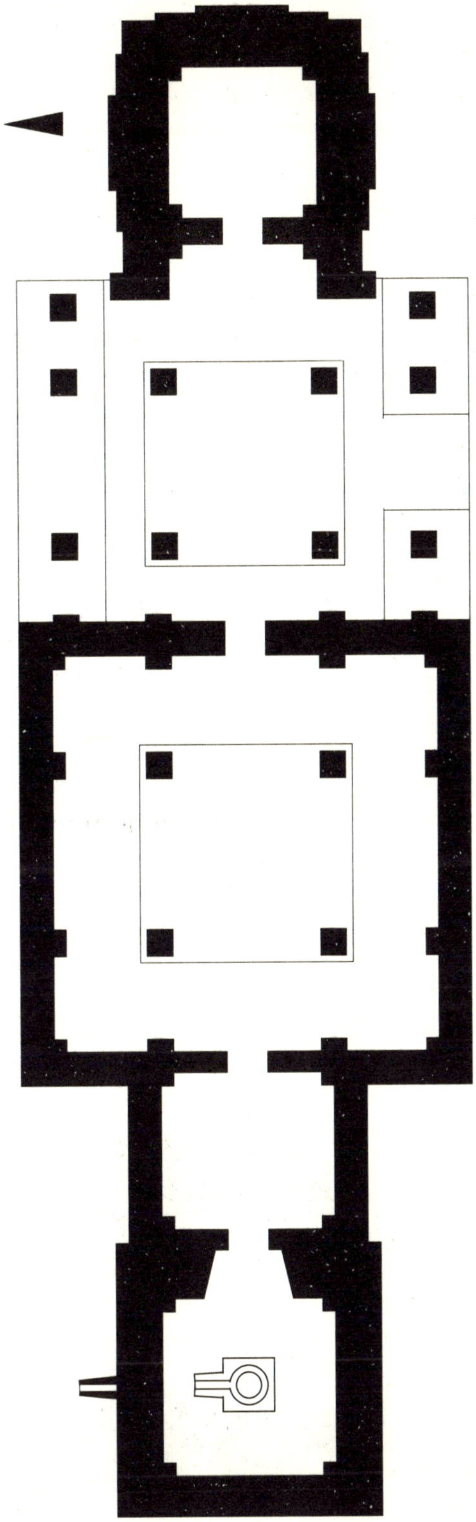

Nārāyaṇa Trikūṭa Temple, Anekannambadi, Karnataka (a. CE 1125)

The Hoysaḷas constructed the Nārāyaṇa Trikūṭa Temple[64] in Anekannambadi. It is a **B**-type *trikūṭa* plan (**Figure 3B**), and as with a number of the temples of the Hoysaḷa, this temple exhibits a rather complex plan. As with the Cennakeśava Temple (**Plate 45**) and the Hoysaḷeśvara Dvikūṭa Temple (**Plate 49**), the Nārāyaṇa Trikūṭa Temple exhibits a sixteen-point star plan for the western *vimāna* (**Figure 42**) and enshrines the deity Keśava. The northern *garbhagṛha* is dedicated to the deity Lakṣmī-Narasiṁha while the southern is the realm of Veṇugopāla.

The complex, exotic, stellate-plan of Nārāyaṇa Trikūṭa Temple's western *vimāna* presents a square *garbhagṛha* and a square *antarāla* which opens onto the *sabhā-maṇḍapa*. The northern and southern *vimānas* are identical to each other but lack *antarālas*. They are essentially *pañcaratha*, but with small subsidiary *ratha*-like forms coupled with elaborate corner piers, *en plan*, creating an equally complex plan (**Figure 43**). The three *vimānas* share a common, square *sabhā-maṇḍapa* with sixteen columns arranged in the usual manner — i.e. four free-standing columns in the centre raised on a square platform and twelve engaged columns, four of which are quarter, corner columns — which form nine irregular *aṅkanas*. As with the western *vimāna* and the twin north and south *vimānas*, the exterior plan of the *sabhā-maṇḍapa* is also elaborate in its detail. To the east is a singular *mukha-maṇḍapa*. It is rectangular and exhibits eight supporting columns at the front arranged in two groups of four. They bracket a broad staircase which leads to the singular Nārāyaṇa Trikūṭa Temple.

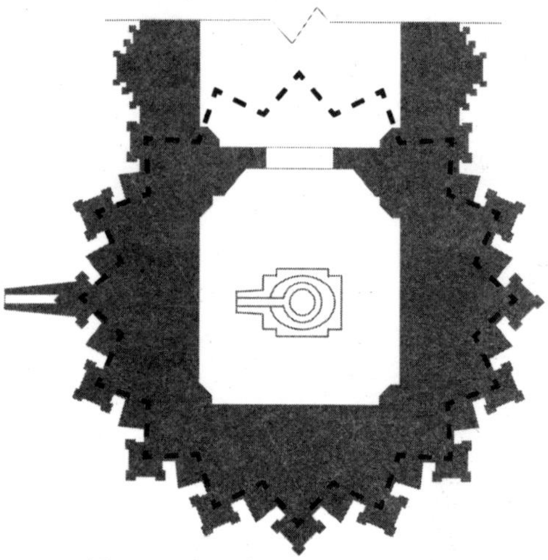

Figure 42: Nārāyaṇa Trikūṭa Temple with a sixteen-point star over western *garbhagṛha*

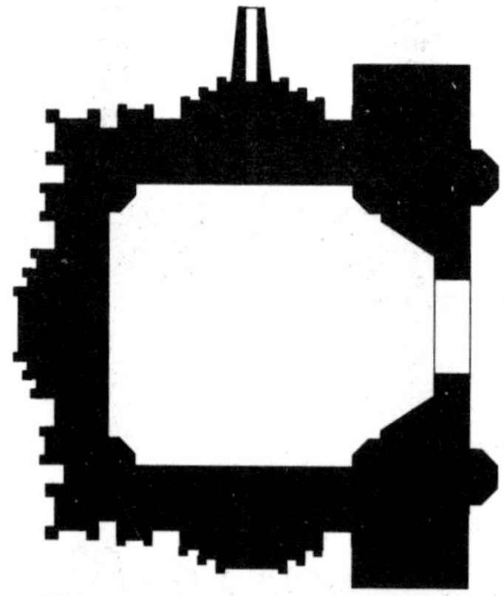

Figure 43: Nārāyaṇa Trikūṭa Temple north and south *vimāna* elements

[64] Redrawn using PageMaker 6.0 from: KMS II, p. 463, description on pp. 252-53. See also **Preface**.

Plate 56: Nārāyaṇa Trikūṭa Temple plan

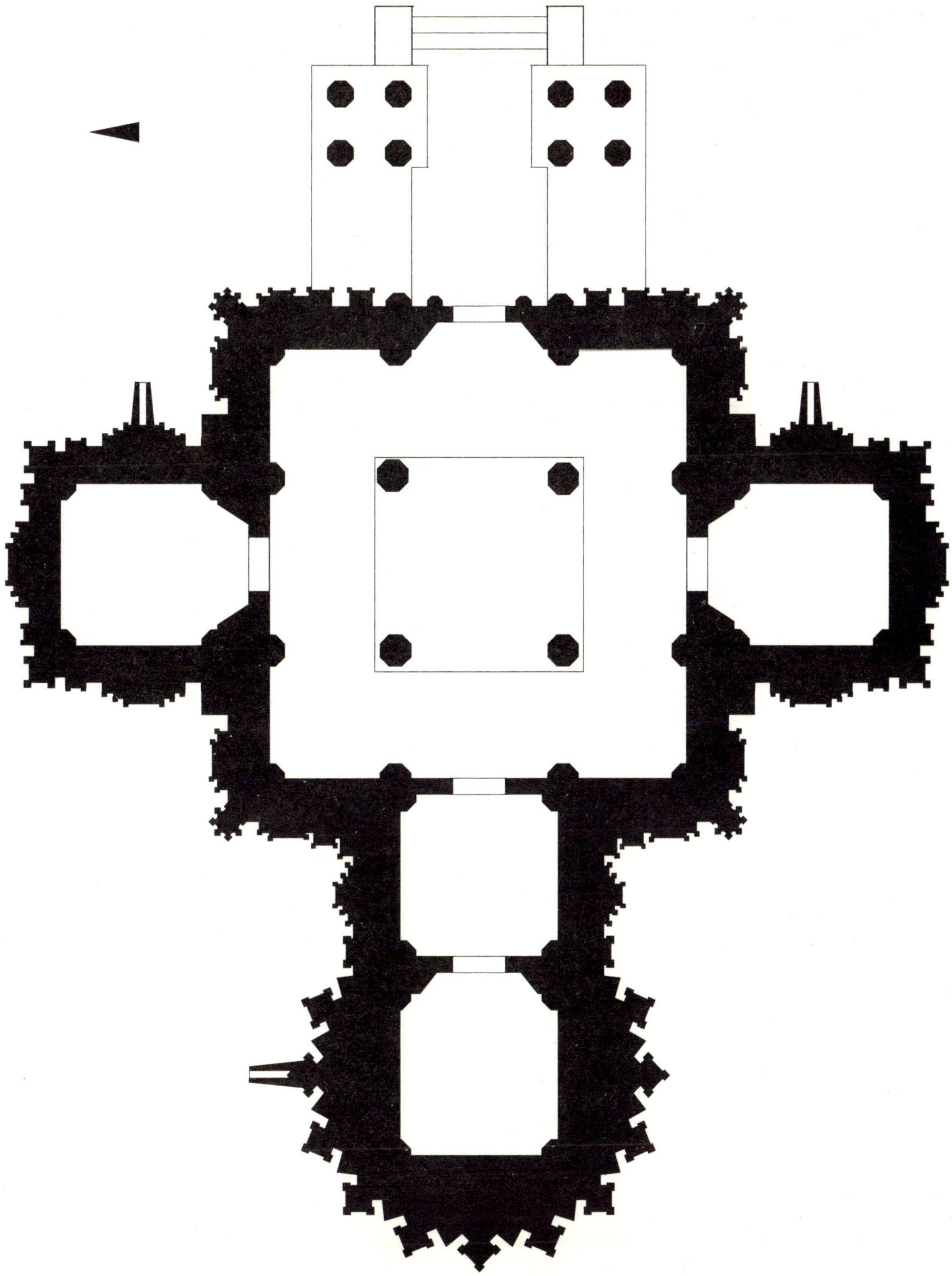

The application of either a *paramaśāyika* or *maṇḍūka maṇḍala* on the plan of the Nārāyaṇa Trikūṭa Temple is fraught with problems (**Figure 44**). However, when a circular *vāstu-puruṣa maṇḍala* is centred on the *sabhā-maṇḍapa* and including the western *vimāna* (**Plate 57**), a number of interesting conjunctions are evident. The same fortuitous condition appears when a circular *maṇḍūka maṇḍala* is overlaid on the western, stellate *garbhagṛha*.

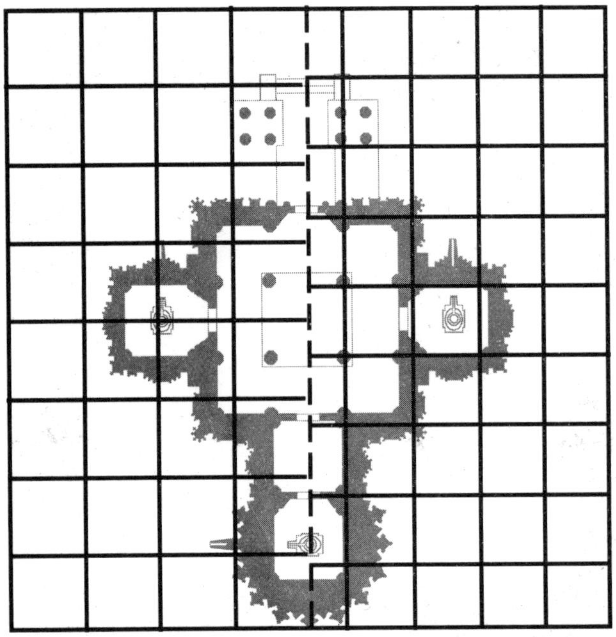

Figure 44: Nārāyaṇa Trikūṭa Temple with *maṇḍūka maṇḍala* (left) and *paramaśāyika maṇḍala* (right)

Plate 57: Nārāyaṇa Trikūṭa Temple plan with *vāstu-puruṣa maṇḍala* centred on the *sabhā-maṇḍapa* and cricular *maṇḍūka maṇḍala* on western *vimāna*

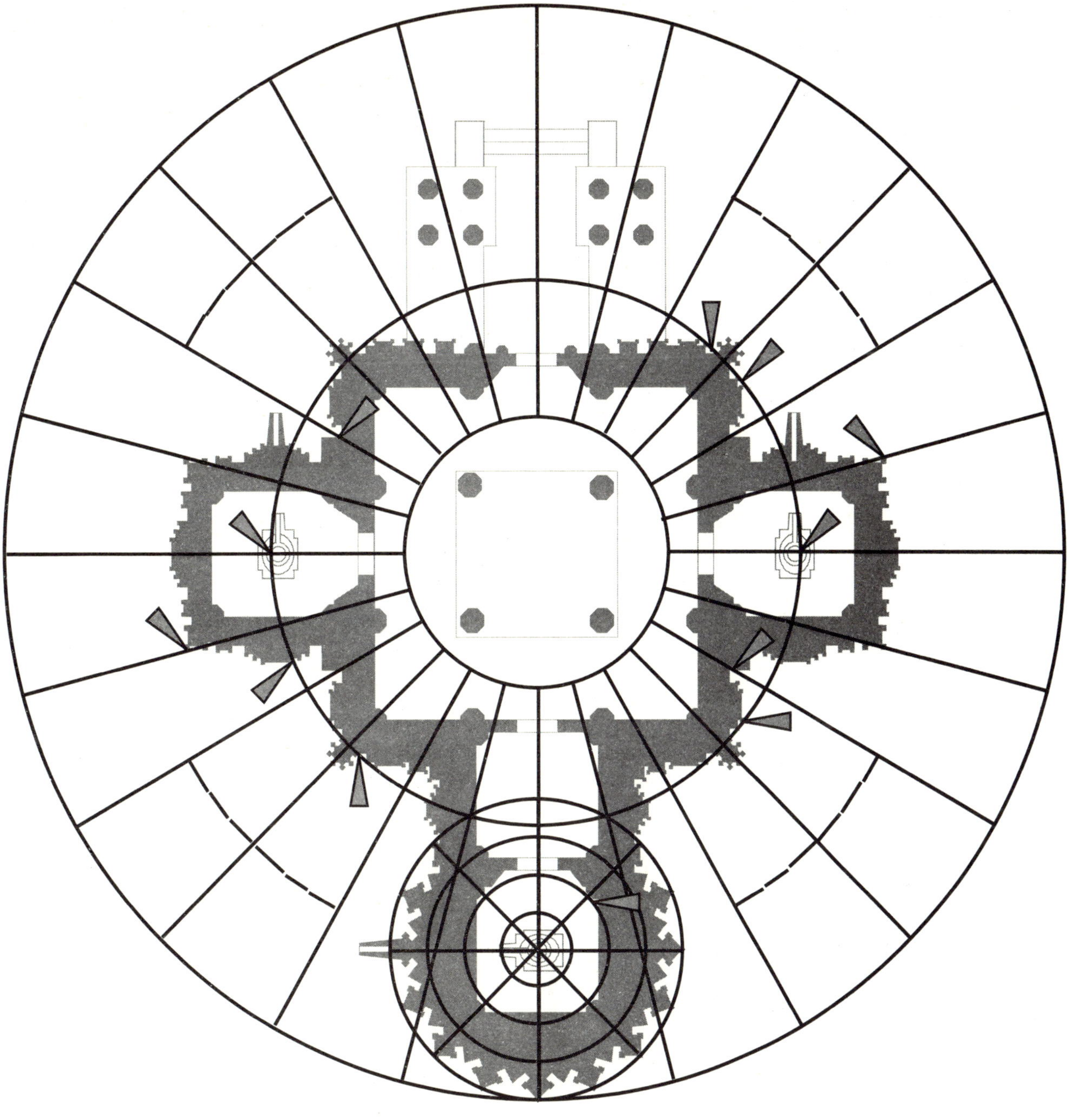

Siddhaliṅgeśvara Pañcakūṭa Temple, Siruvala, Karnataka (c. CE 1138)

The Western Cāḷukyas (Kalyāṇa) were not only responsible for the eccentric Śaṅkaraliṅga Trikūṭa Temple, also, under their auspices was conceived and raised the remarkable Siddhaliṅgeśvara Pañcakūṭa Temple[65] at Siruvala. This temple's construction is associated with the kings Someśvara II (r. CE 1068-76), Someśvara III (r. CE 1127-35), and Jagadekamalla II (r. CE 1135-51) (**Appendix D**). The Siddhaliṅgeśvara Pañcakūṭa Temple is an **A**-type *pañcakūṭa* temple (**Figure 5**), a rare plan, to be sure.

The temple consists of five elements; four are made up of a *vimāna* with square *garbhagṛha* and rectangular *antarāla*. On the north and south, two of these sanctums are attached to an open *sabhā-maṇḍapa* with sixteen, free-standing columns supporting the roof (**Figure 45** [right]). The east and west *vimāna*s exhibit an enclosed *sabhā-maṇḍapa* (**Figure 45** [left]) with sixteen columns — i.e. four free-standing and twelve engaged. All four *sabhā-maṇḍapa*s have two entrances centred perpendicular to their axis with a short flight of steps. The two enclosed *sabhā-maṇḍapa*s on the east–west axis have an additional porch or *mukha-maṇḍapa* with two columns framing the steps. In the centre of the Śaṅkaraliṅga Trikūṭa Temple is a square *garbhagṛha* with entrances at the four cardinal points, the fifth element. The four doorways lead into four square *antarāla*s which, in turn, flow into their four respective *sabhā-maṇḍapa*s described above.

The Siddhaliṅgeśvara Pañcakūṭa Temple is dedicated to Sadāśiva (aka Mahādeva) and displays the five aspects of the Lord Śiva. The four *vimāna*s of the cardinal points are dedicated to Mahādeva or Tatpuruṣa (east), Bhairava or Aghora (south), Ādivaktra or Vāmadeva (west), and Umāvaktra or Sadyojāta (north). Īśāna occupies the central shrine of the temple.

The plan of Siddhaliṅgeśvara Pañcakūṭa Temple is such that either a *paramaśāyika maṇḍala* (**Plate 59**) or a circular *vāstu-puruṣa maṇḍala* (**Plate 60**) is imminently applicable. In **Plate 59**, it is seen that the four cardinal *vimāna*s fall within the middle nine *pada*s of each side — i.e. **2, 4, 6** and **8**; while the central *garbhagṛha* occupies **5** (**Appendix C, Plate 134**). The circular *vāstu-puruṣa maṇḍala* produces a number of important conjunctions as are seen by the arrows in **Plate 60**.

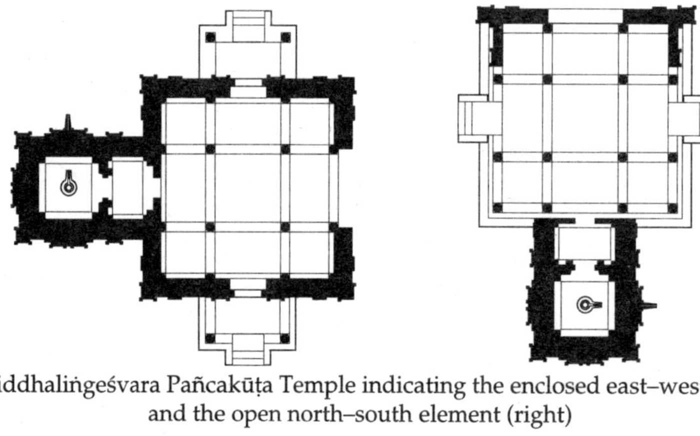

Figure 45: Siddhaliṅgeśvara Pañcakūṭa Temple indicating the enclosed east–west element (left) and the open north–south element (right)

65 The plan is redrawn using Adobe PageMaker 6.0, from: KMS II, p. 484. However, it is distorted. See also "Introduction", p. xxiii, n. 1.

Plate 58: Siddhaliṅgeśvara Pañcakūṭa Temple plan

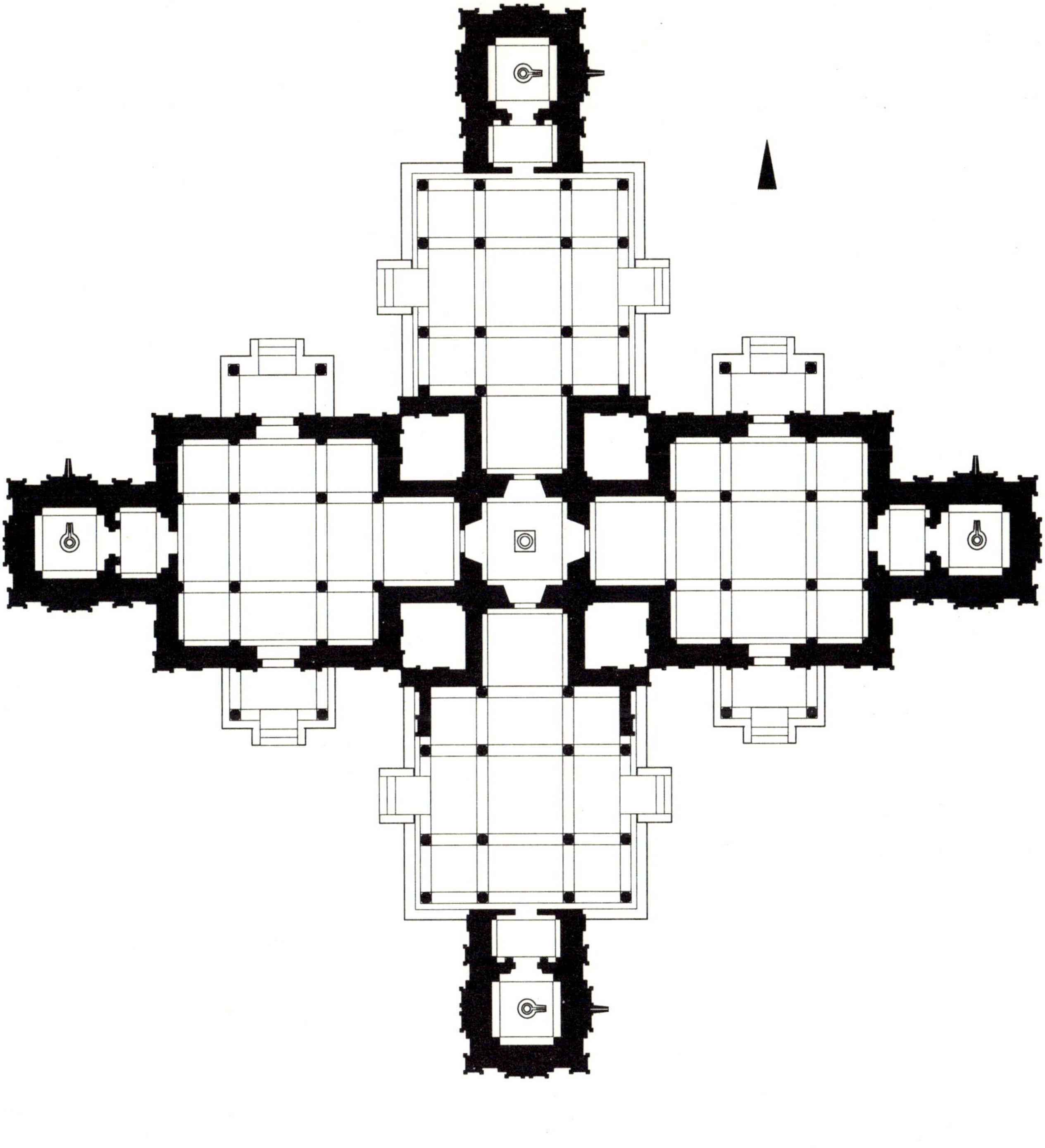

Plate 59: Siddhaliṅgeśvara Pañcakūṭa Temple with *paramaśāyika maṇḍala*

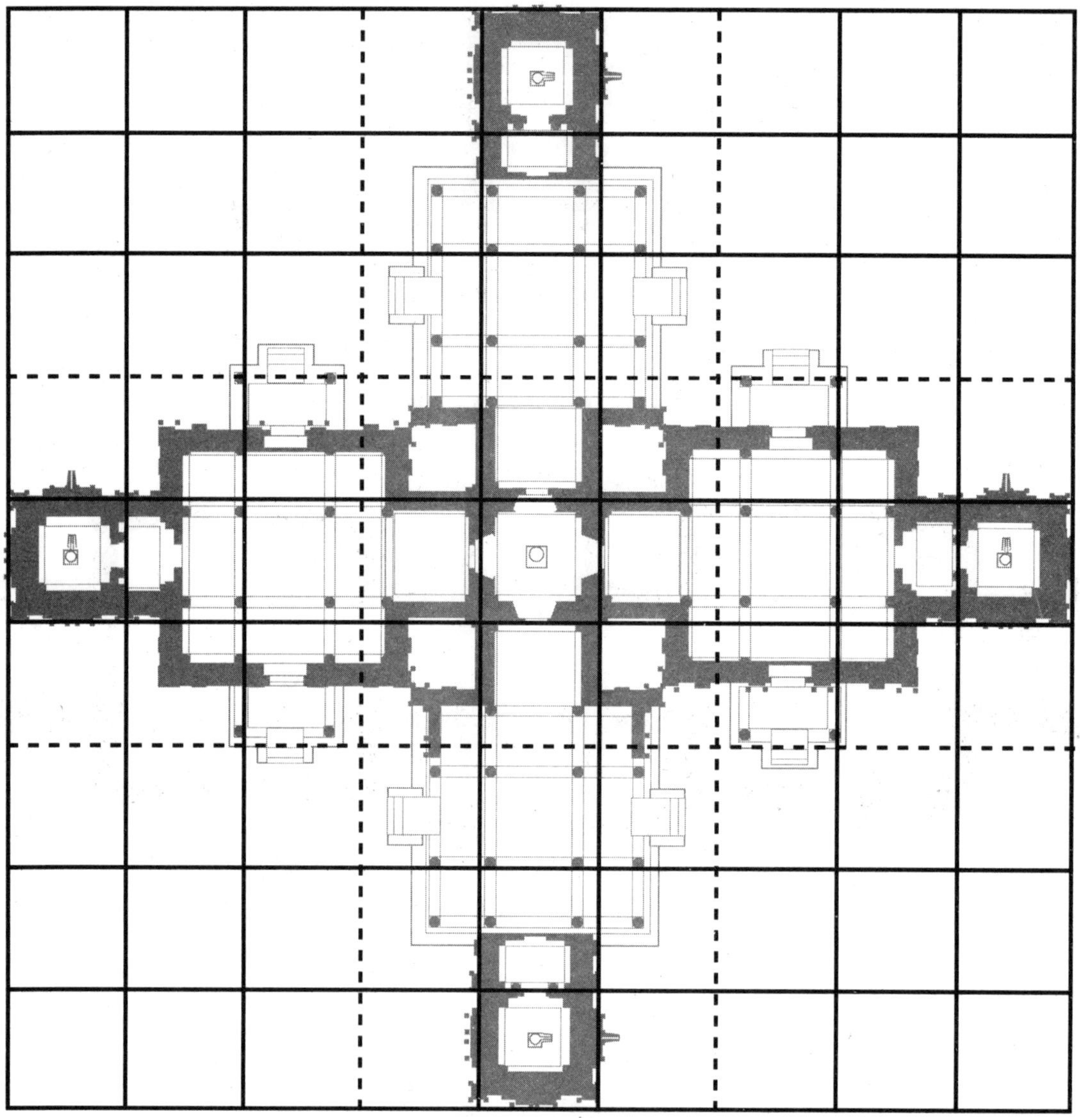

Plate 60: Siddhaliṅgeśvara Pañcakūṭa Temple with circular *vāstu-puruṣa maṇḍala*

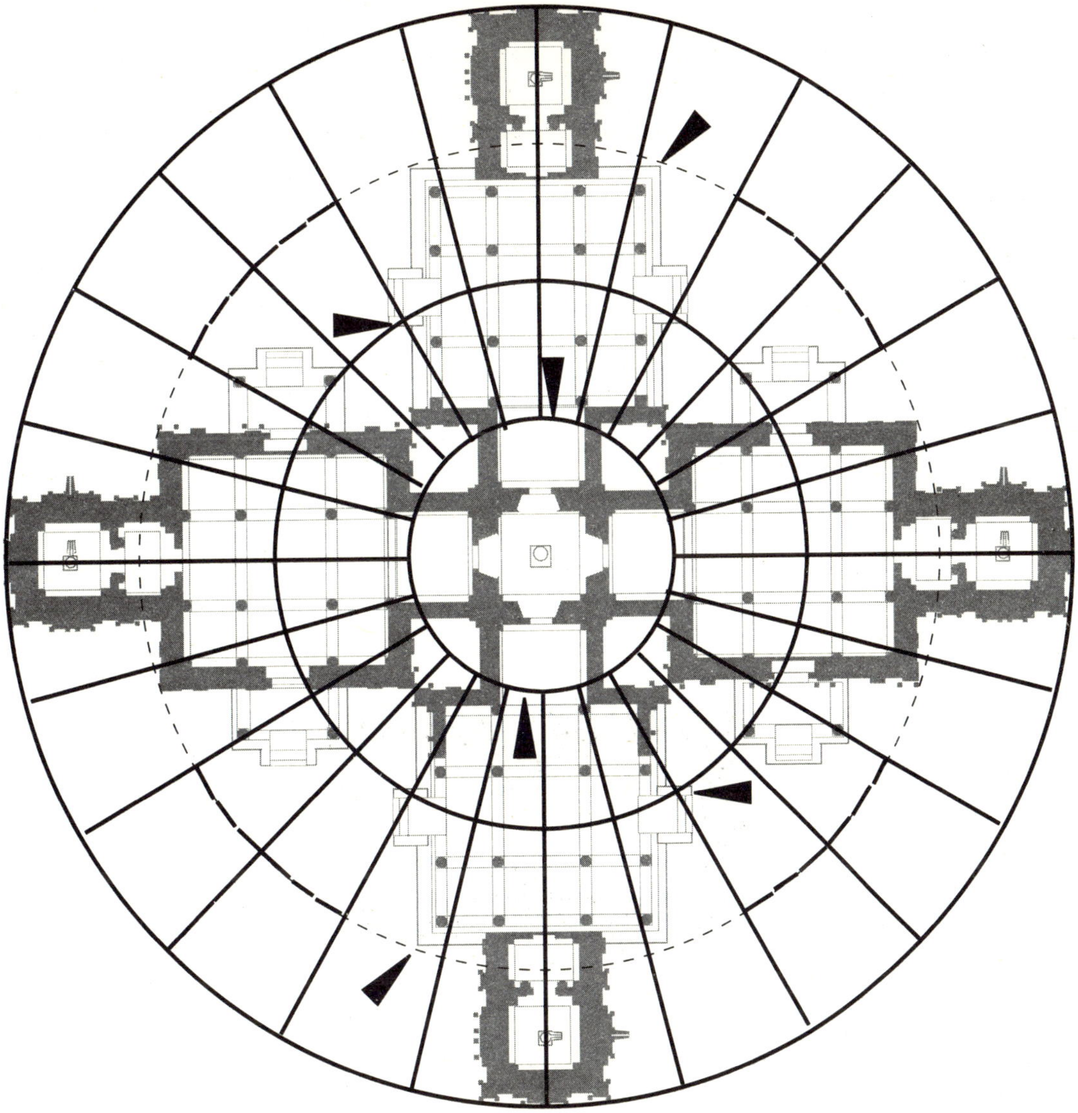

Mallikārjuna Trikūṭa Temple, Katnahaḷḷi, Karnataka (a. CE 1139)

One of a number of temples in the south of India dedicated to the deity Mallikārjuna (**Plates 52, 62 and 93**), the Mallikārjuna Trikūṭa Temple[66] at Katnahaḷḷi is an **A**-type *trikūṭa* plan (**Figure 3**). Constructed during the reign of the Western Cāḷukya (Kalyāṇa) king Jayasiṁha I Jagadekamalla (r. CE 1015-43) (**Appendix D**), rests in the small village that was part of the Cāḷukya domain. In comparison to many of the other temples built during the dominance of the Western Cāḷukyas, the Mallikārjuna Trikūṭa Temple is rather simple, *en plan*.

The temple consists of three *vimānas* of similar design (**Figure 46**). They exhibit a square *garbhagṛha* with attached, square *antarāla*. The outer walls of the *vimāna* are plain and without adornment. The three *vimānas* share a common *sabhā-maṇḍapa*. It is square, *en plan*, and exhibits sixteen columns placed in the usual manner — i.e. four free-standing columns in the centre raised on a square platform and twelve engaged columns, four of which are quarter, corner columns — which forms nine *aṅkanas*. To the south is a *mukha-maṇḍapa* which is supported by two free-standing columns on a broad porch. From there, a flight of stairs leads to ground level.

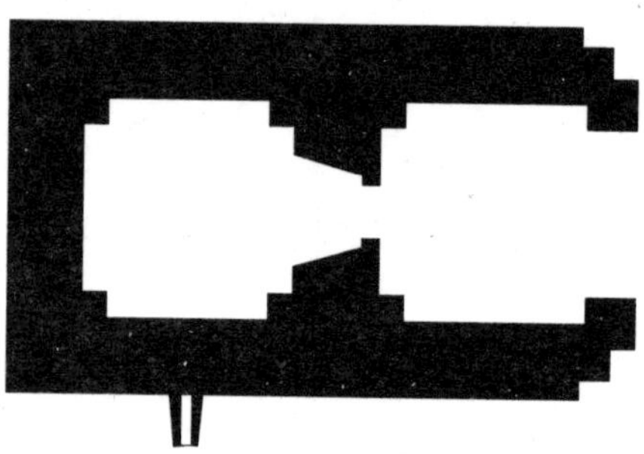

Figure 46: Mallikārjuna Trikūṭa Temple *vimāna* element

[66] Redrawn using PageMaker 6.0 from: KMS II, p. 447, description on pp. 220-21. See also **Preface**.

Plate 61: Mallikārjuna Trikūṭa Temple plan

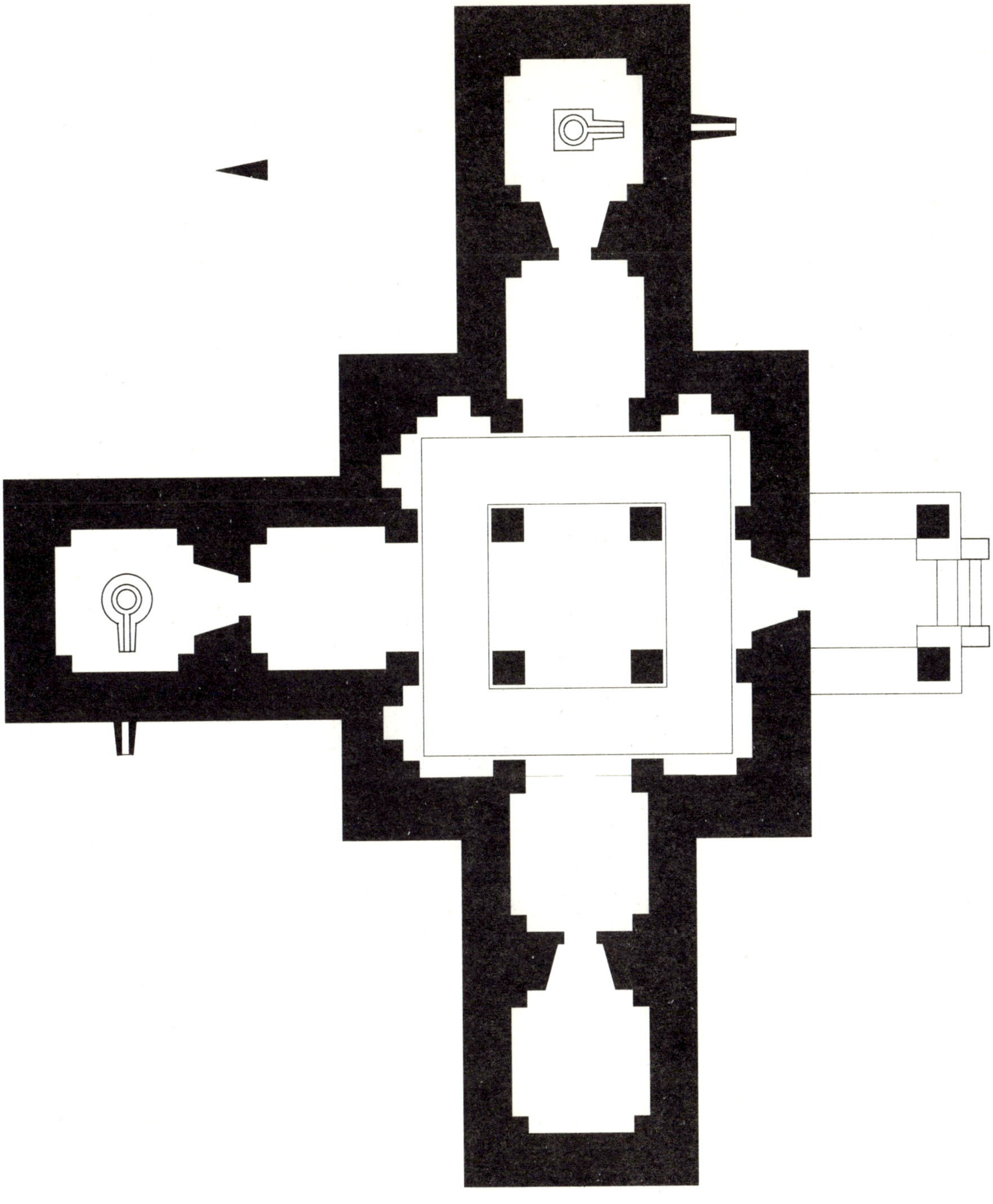

Mallikārjuna Trikūṭa Temple, Devaranavadagi, Hospeṭ, Karnataka (a. CE 1140)

The Mallikārjuna Trikūṭa Temple[67] of Devaranavadagi seems to be the opposite of the Mallikārjuna Trikūṭa Temple at Katnahaḷḷi (**Plate 61**). Whereas, the Katnahaḷḷi Temple is exceedingly plain, the plan of the Devaranavadagi example is quite developed. It, apparently, was constructed during the time of King Jagadekamalla II[68] (r. CE 1135-51) (**Appendix D**) who sat on the Western Cāḷukya (Kalyāṇa) throne. This Mallikārjuna Trikūṭa Temple is an **A**-type *trikūṭa* plan (**Figure 3**).

The temple consists of three identical *vimānas* (**Figure 47**). The *garbhagṛhas* are square as are the attached *antarālas*. The three exposed façades of the *saptaratha garbhagṛhas* exhibit small shrines in the *raha-rathas* and each sanctum hold a Śivaliṅga. In the northern sanctum the Śivaliṅga is on a circular *pīṭha* while the other two are on square *pīṭhas*. The three, thick-walled *vimānas* open directly onto a common, thick-walled square *sabhā-maṇḍapa*. As with many of the other *sabhā-maṇḍapas* of this region, it holds sixteen columns in a conventional alignment — i.e. four free-standing columns in the centre raised on a square platform and twelve engaged columns, four of which are quarter, corner columns — which form nine *aṅkanas*. To the south is a small, square *mukha-maṇḍapa* with four columns. Two of the *mukha-maṇḍapa* columns are free-standing, while the other two are engaged to the wall of the *sabhā-maṇḍapa*. A short flight of steps lead to ground level.

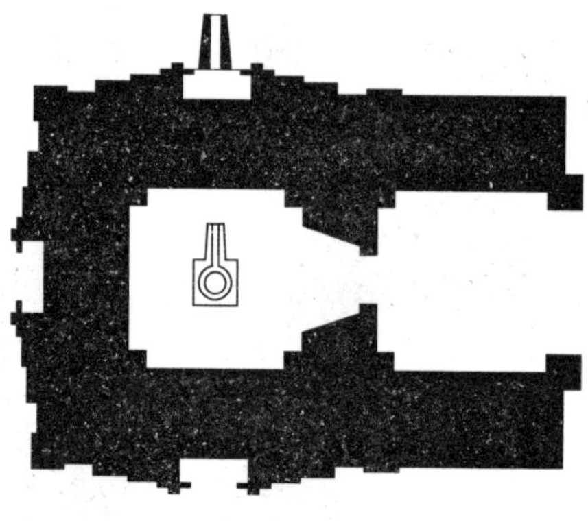

Figure 47: Mallikārjuna Trikūṭa Temple *vimāna* element

[67] Redrawn using PageMaker 6.0 from: KMS II, p. 448, description on p. 221. See also **Preface**.

[68] Ibid., p. 221, states that the temple was built in "1140 CE in the reign of . . . Someśvara III" (r. CE 1127-35). Since accepted dating sees Someśvara II dying in 1135, he could hardly construct the temple in 1140!

Plate 62: Mallikārjuna Trikūṭa Temple plan

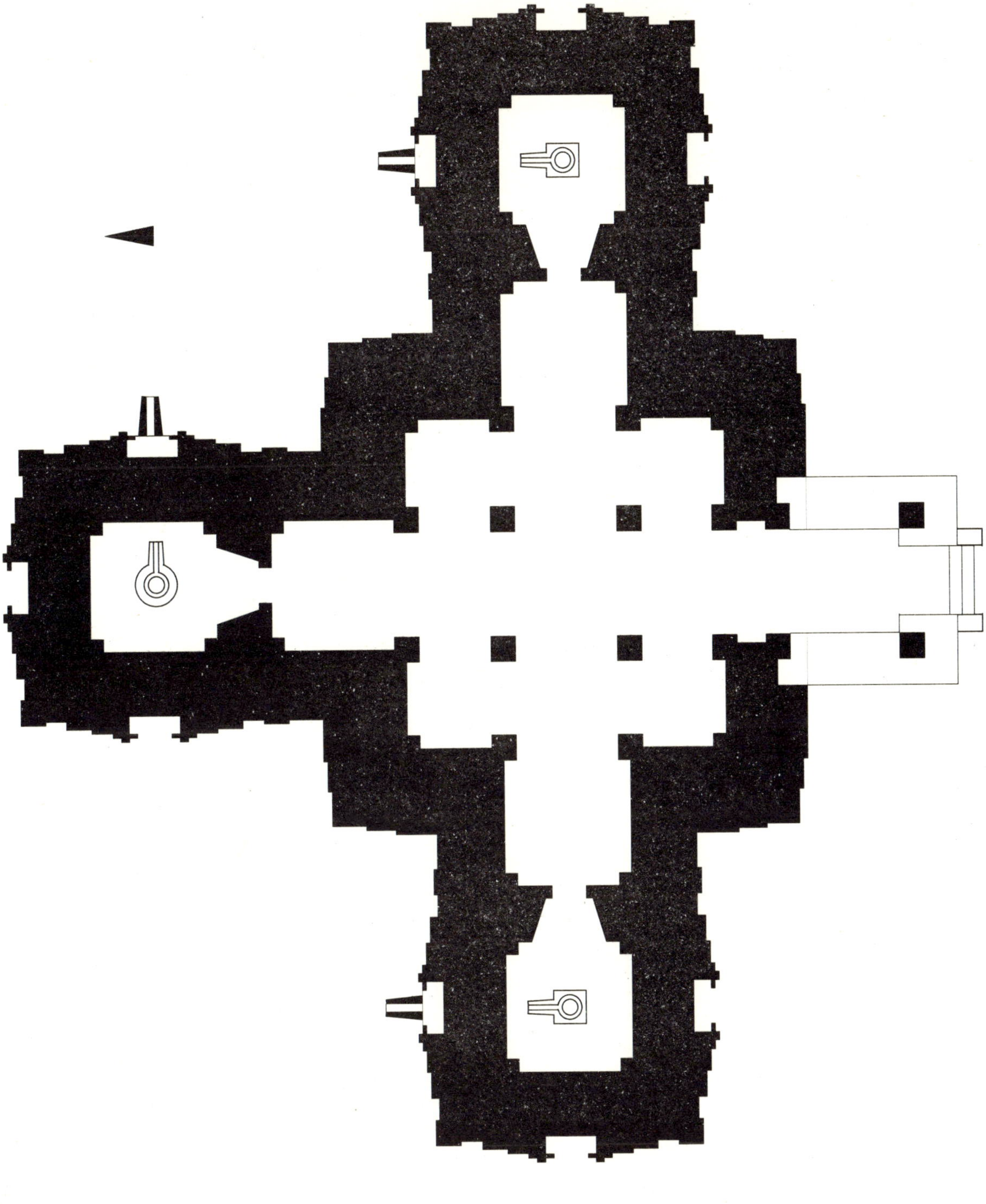

Saṅgameśvara Trikūṭa Temple, Bevura, Karnataka (*c.* CE 1150)

The Saṅgameśvara Trikūṭa Temple[69] came into existence under the auspices of the Cāḷukya king Someśvara I (Trailokyamalla or Āhavamalladeva) (r. CE 1043-68) (**Appendix D**). Constructed in the small village of Bevura, it stands as fine example of the **A**-type *trikūṭa* temple plan (**Figure 3**). Unlike the Śaṅkaraliṅga Trikūṭa Temple, the Saṅgameśvara Trikūṭa Temple is fully developed and more pleasing, *en plan*. The name of the temple, Saṅgameśvara, "Lord of the Confluence", refers to a form of Lord Śiva, whose abode is the western *garbhagṛha*.

The Saṅgameśvara Trikūṭa Temple consists of three identical *vimāna*s (**Figure 48**) with the main *garbhagṛha*, opposite the entrance, facing south and dedicated to Keśava[70] with a square-based Śivaliṅga. This alignment is not usual. Generally, the main *vimāna* faces either east or west and sometimes north, rarely, as here, does it faces south. The western sanctum holds a circular-based Śivaliṅga, while the eastern, unadorned *vimāna* is dedicated to the deity Sūrya. Each of the three *vimāna*s is composed of a square *garbhagṛha* enclosed in a *saptaratha vimāna* with a rectangular *antarāla*. The *antarāla*s are open towards the *sabhā-maṇḍapa*. The *sabhā-maṇḍapa* exhibits the rather standard sixteen columns — i.e. four free-standing columns in the centre raised on a square platform and twelve engaged columns, four of which are quarter, corner columns — which forms nine *aṅkana*s that is found in smaller Cāḷukya temples. The enclosed *sabhā-maṇḍapa* opens towards the south onto an open, small *mukha-maṇḍapa*. The *mukha-maṇḍapa*'s roof is partially supported by two columns to the south.

Initially, the northern *vimāna* once housed an image of the Lord Viṣṇu as Keśava, while the western holds a Śivaliṅga and the eastern *vimāna* is dedicated to Sūrya. The Śivaliṅga, now seen in the northern *garbhagṛha* is obviously a later addition, possibly placed there by the Liṅgāyats who were active in southern India.

Finally, the application of either a *paramaśāyika maṇḍala* (**Plate 64**) or a circular *vāstu-puruṣa maṇḍala* (**Plate 65**) produces viable results in both cases. The three *vimāna*s fall within the middle nine *pada*s of each side — i.e. **2, 4** and **6** (**Appendix C, Plate 134**) of the *paramaśāyika maṇḍala*, and within **r–s, x–a** and **f–g** of the circular *vāstu-puruṣa maṇḍala* (**Appendix C, Plate 135**).

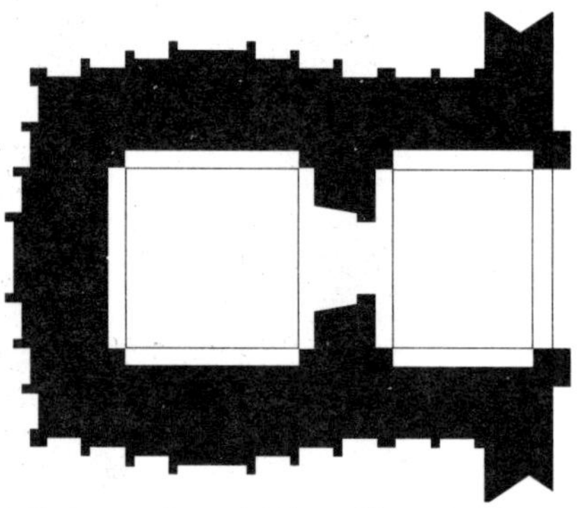

Figure 48: Saṅgameśvara Trikūṭa Temple *vimāna* element

[69] The plan is redrawn using Adobe PageMaker 6.0, from: KMS II, p. 472, with description on pp. 259-60. See also **Preface**.

[70] This placement — i.e. to the north, is most unusual. The name of the temple would seem to indicate that the main *garbhagṛha* is the Saṅgameśvara *garbhagṛha* to the west.

Plate 63: Saṅgameśvara Trikūṭa Temple plan

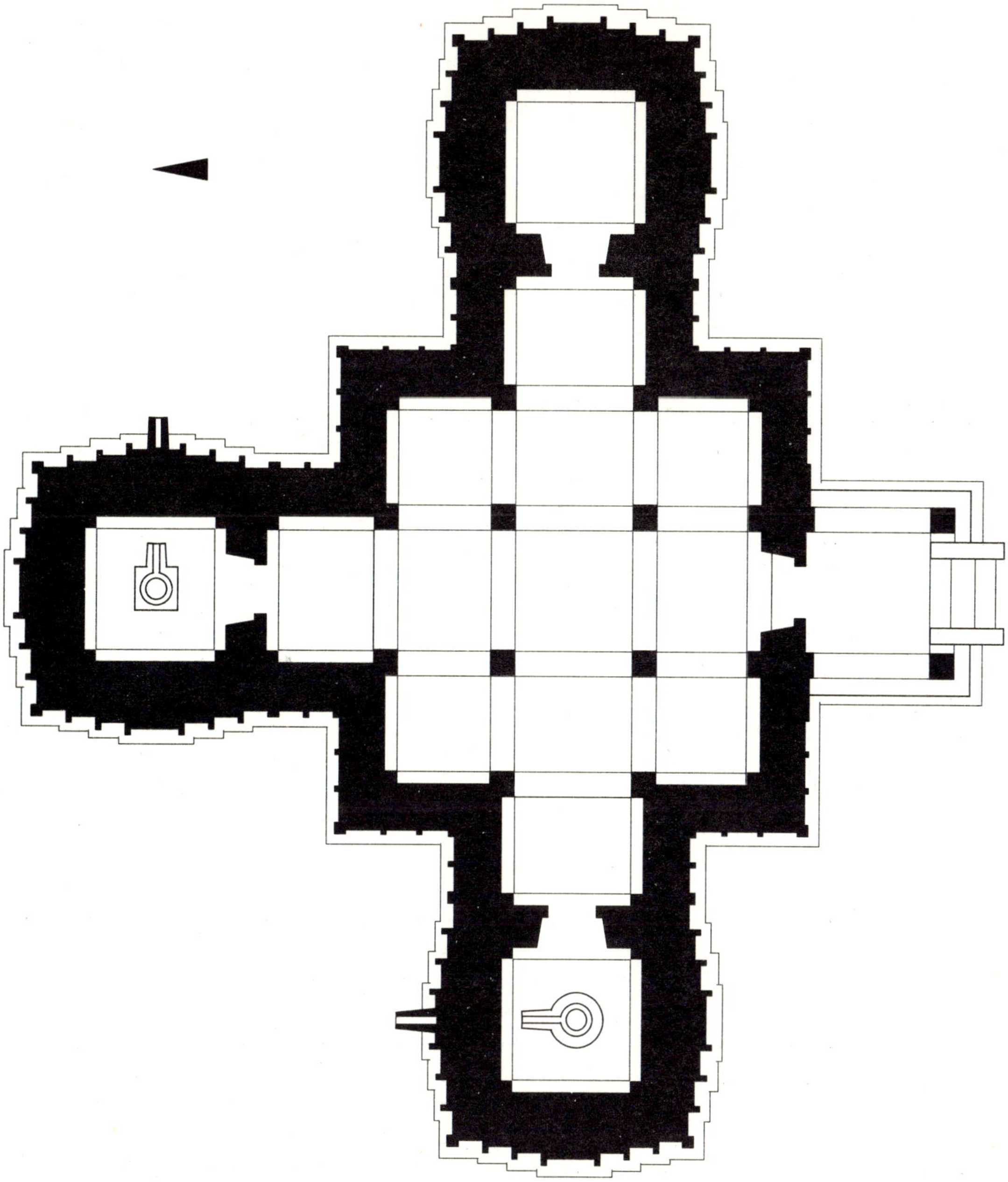

Plate 64: Saṅgameśvara Trikūṭa Temple with *paramaśāyika maṇḍala*

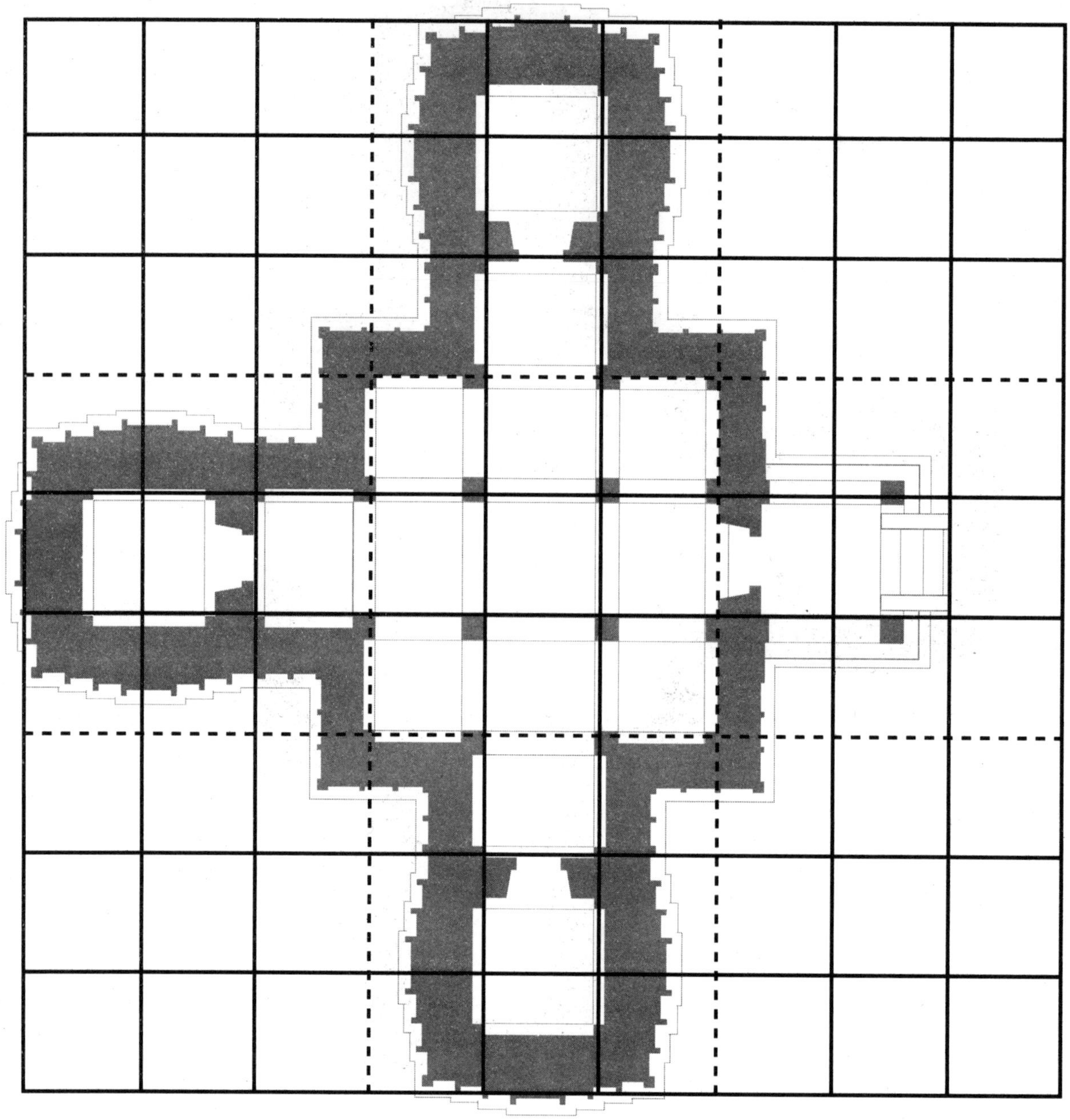

Plate 65: Saṅgameśvara Trikūṭa Temple with circular *vāstu-puruṣa maṇḍala*

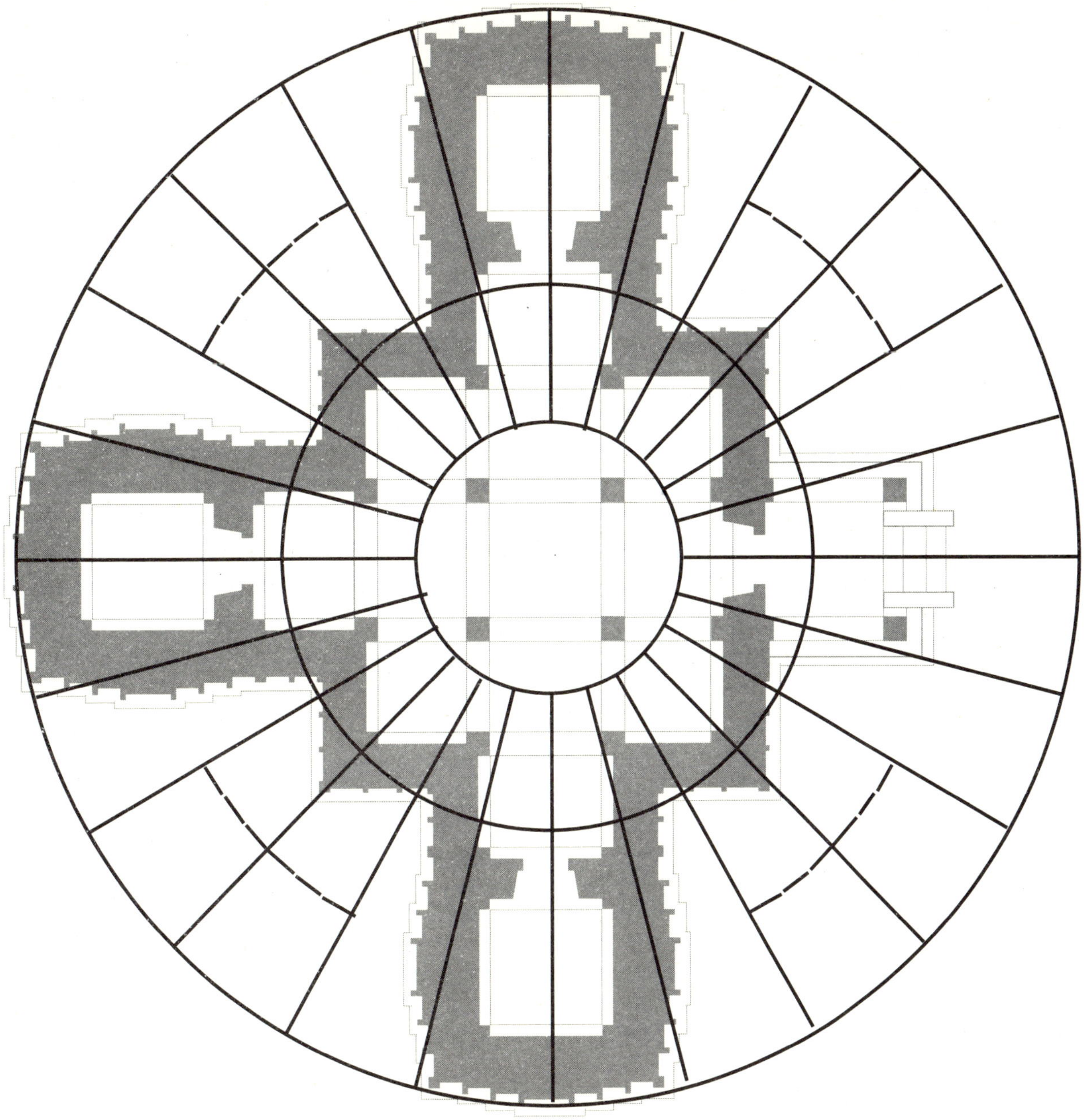

Rāmaliṅga Dvikūṭa Temple, Horti, Karnataka (*c.* CE 1150)

Believed to have been constructed in the middle of the twelfth century by the Western Cāḷukyas (Kalyāṇa) — i.e. sometime during the reigns of Jagadekamalla II (r. CE 1135-51) or Taila III (r. CE 1151-56) — before the dominance of the Kaḷacuri (**Appendix D**). The Rāmaliṅga Dvikūṭa Temple[71] is a **A**-type *dvikūṭa* plan temple (**Figure 2**). It is obvious that there were two separate concepts in operation during the process of the construction of this temple.

The Rāmaliṅga Dvikūṭa Temple consists of a large rather developed western *vimāna* which holds a square *garbhagṛha* with a Śivaliṅga and a square *antarāla*. The *antarāla* opens onto a *sabhā-maṇḍapa* and exhibits two free-standing columns in the transitional entrance to the *sabhā-maṇḍapa*. The walls at the eastern side of the *vimāna* extend north and south and are terminated with two *pañcaratha* projections. This eastern projection of the western *vimāna* extends to the limits established by the columns of the northern and southern *mukha-maṇḍapa*. This "addition" is rather unusual and seems to indicate the possibility that the *sabhā-maṇḍapa* had originally been conceived of as being enclosed. The *sabhā-maṇḍapa* is essentially square, *en plan,* and exhibits sixteen columns arranged in the usual manner — i.e. four free-standing columns in the centre and twelve engaged columns, four of which are quarter, corner columns — which form nine *aṅkana*s. To the north and to the south of the *sabhā-maṇḍapa* are *mukha-maṇḍapa*s with two free-standing columns and a short flight of steps that leads down onto a wide terrace that acts as an external *pradakṣiṇāpatha*. This wide platform has stairs leading to the north and south and in line with the stairs of the *sabhā-maṇḍapa*. Attached to the eastern area of the *sabhā-maṇḍapa* is the second *vimāna*. It is simplicity incarnate and possesses a square *garbhagṛha* and a square *antarāla* which opens without fanfare onto the *sabhā-maṇḍapa*. It appears obvious that this eastern *vimāna* may have been an addition. It also seems obvious that it was added by a person or persons who had limited resources and/or time.

[71] Redrawn using PageMaker 6.0 from: KMS II, p. 424, description on p. 195. See also **Preface**.

Plate 66: Rāmaliṅga Dvikūṭa Temple plan

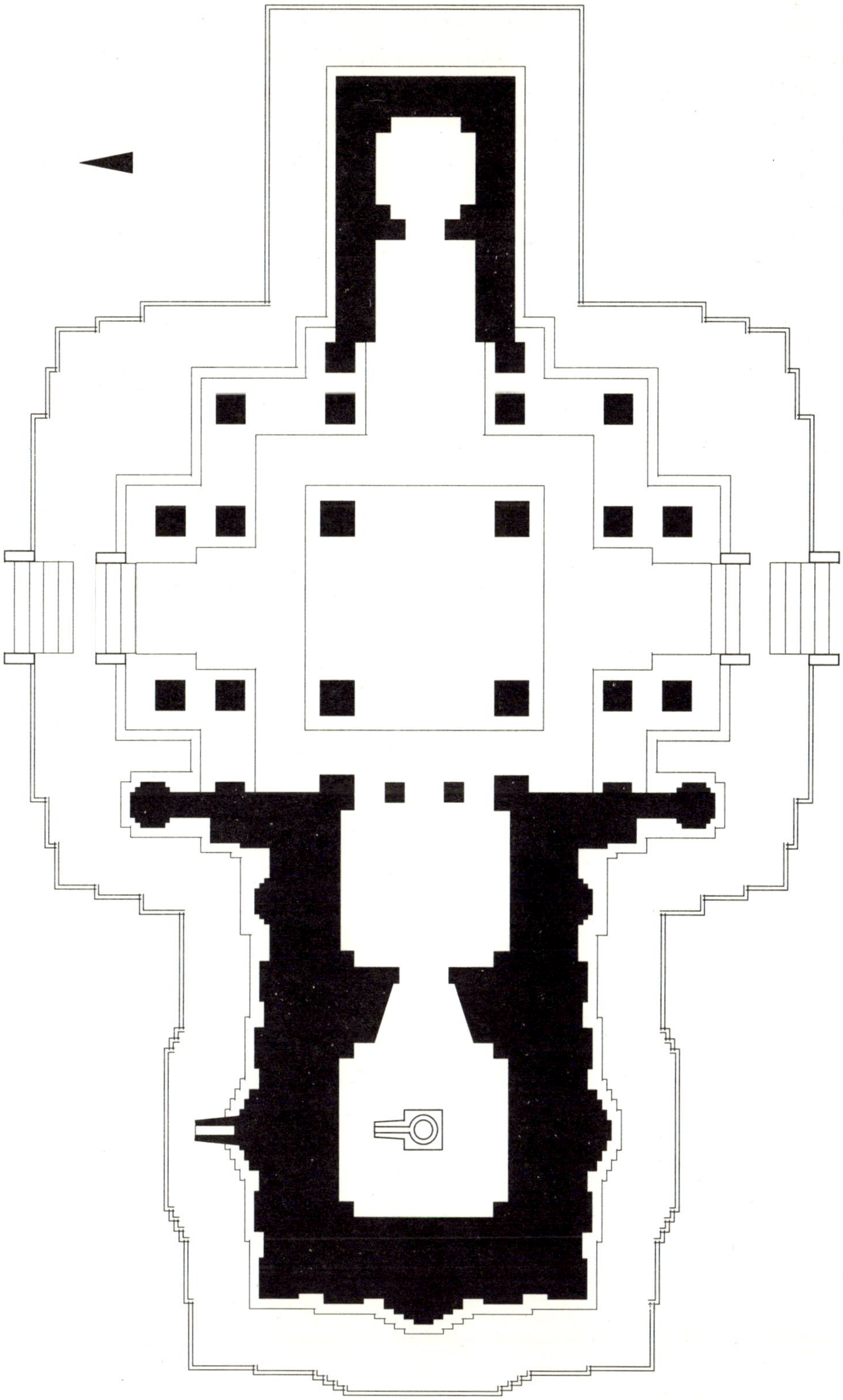

Koṭe Śaṅkaraliṅga Dvikūṭa Temple, Nimbal, Karnataka (*c.* CE 1150)

The Śaiva Koṭe Śaṅkaraliṅga Dvikūṭa Temple[72] at Nimbal is related to the Rāmaliṅga Dvikūṭa Temple of Horti (**Plate 66**) in three ways — first, it is a *dvikūṭa* **A**-type temple plan; second, it exhibits two *vimānas* of vastly different designs and levels of development; and third, it is obvious that the temple was constructed at two different times. The temple was raised at the same time as the Rāmaliṅga Dvikūṭa Temple of Horti, and is attributed to the same dynasty.

The western *vimāna* is the more developed of the two and consists of a square *garbhagṛha* and *antarāla*. The *garbhagṛha* rests within a *pañcaratha* form with shrines in the *raha-rathas*. This elaborate *vimāna* opens onto a square, enclosed *sabhā-maṇḍapa*. It, like most *sabhā-maṇḍapas* of the region, consists of sixteen columns in the usual arrangement — i.e. four free-standing columns in the centre raised on a square platform and twelve engaged columns, four of which are quarter, corner columns — which form nine *aṅkanas*. The enclosed *sabhā-maṇḍapa* has three doorways leading out of its confines — i.e. to the north, south and east. The northern and southern entrances are covered by *mukha-maṇḍapas*, each with two free-standing pillars and steps leading downward. The eastern doorway leads to the open *sabhā-maṇḍapa*. In the east rests the second *vimāna*. Unlike the first it is quite simple, *en plan*. It consists of a square *garbhagṛha* and *antarāla* which open onto an open *sabhā-maṇḍapa*. A wall extends to the limits of the open *sabhā-maṇḍapa*, to the north and to the south of its western border. The open *sabhā-maṇḍapa* is made up of sixteen columns in the traditional arrangement. Here the central eight columns are free-standing and those against the enclosed *sabhā-maṇḍapa* and against the eastern *vimāna* wall are engaged. This open *sabhā-maṇḍapa* possesses but one entrance, leading southward with a short flight of steps.

It is apparent that the western *vimāna* and *sabhā-maṇḍapa* were constructed at a different time than the eastern *vimāna* with its open *sabhā-maṇḍapa*. Different periods of construction are not unusual, nor is the obvious difference in the development of the two components.

[72] Redrawn using PageMaker 6.0 from: KMS II, p. 425, description on pp. 195-96. See also **Preface**.

Plate 67: Koṭe Śaṅkaraliṅga Dvikūṭa Temple plan

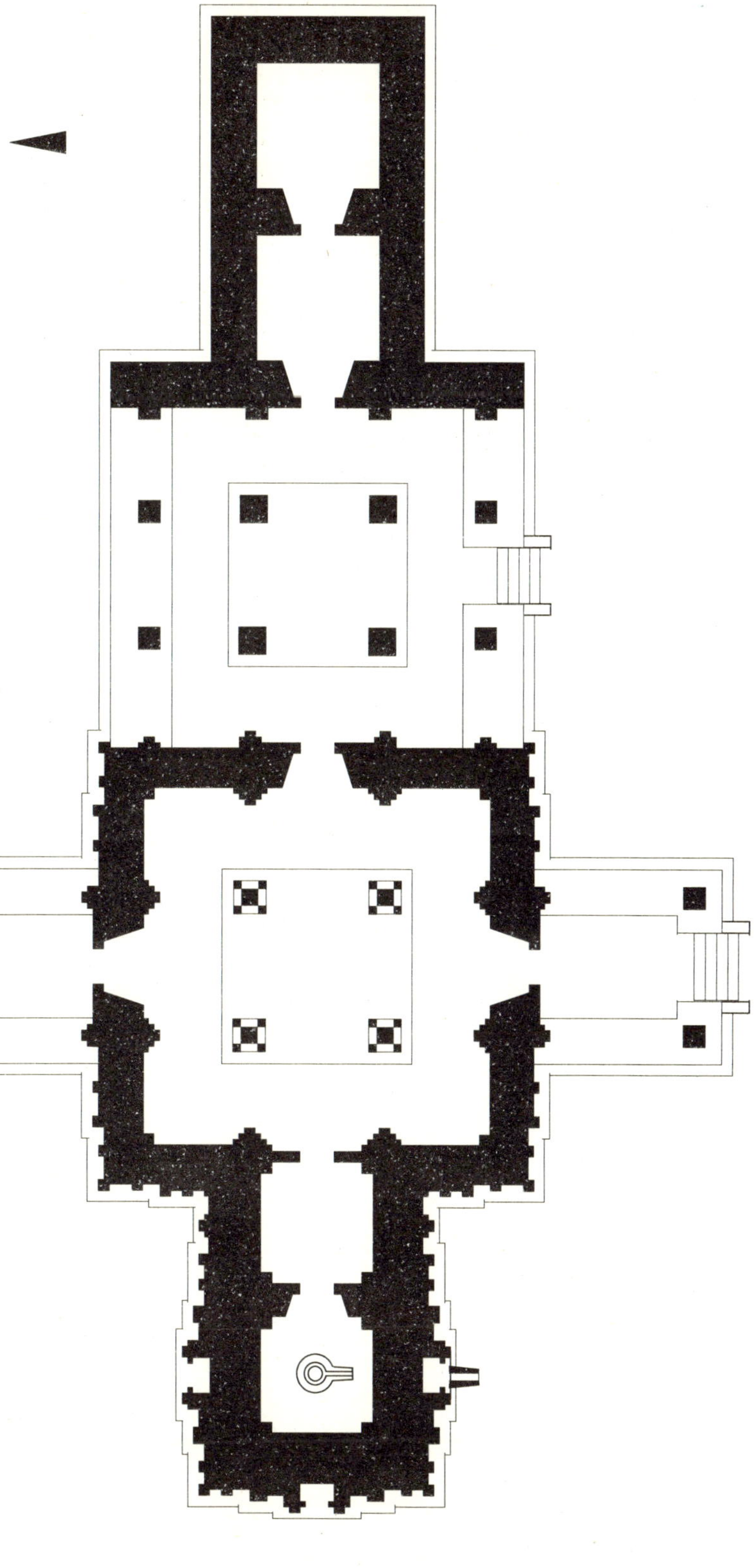

Śambhuliṅga Dvikūṭa Temple, Kakkalameli, Karnataka (*c.* CE 1150)

Raised in mid-twelfth century by the Western Cāḷukyas (Kalyāṇa) and aligned east–west, the Śambhuliṅga Dvikūṭa Temple[73] is an **A**-type *dvikūṭa* plan. Its conception and construction follow the same period and dynasty as the Rāmaliṅga Dvikūṭa Temple (**Plate 66**).

The eastern *vimāna* is the main shrine and holds a square *garbhagṛha* with Śivaliṅga and a square *antarāla* which is open towards the west and the common *sabhā-maṇḍapa*. The *garbhagṛha* is surrounded by walls of a *saptaratha* plan as is that of the western *vimāna*. The *sabhā-maṇḍapa* is supplied with exit doorways to the north and the south. Its interior consists of the usual sixteen columns in the usual alignment — i.e. four free-standing columns in the centre and twelve engaged columns, four of which are quarter, corner columns — which form nine *aṅkana*s. The *mukha-maṇḍapa*s are a bit unusual. They both are made up of four columns, two of which are enfolded by the thick walls of the *sabhā-maṇḍapa* and two stand in the open. A short flight of stairs leads to the ground level. The western *garbhagṛha*, unlike its eastern counterpart, is without an *antarāla* but, with Śivaliṅga and opens onto the *sabhā-maṇḍapa* through a simple doorway. Its plan is slightly different from the *garbhagṛha* to the east.

The placement of the western *garbhagṛha*, without *antarāla*, gives that direction of the plan a blunted appearance. This arrangement of a *dvikūṭa* plan is not the norm, however, it is not terribly unusual.

---

[73] Redrawn using PageMaker 6.0 from: KMS II, p. 428, description on pp. 197-98. See also **Preface**.

Plate 68: Śambhuliṅga Dvikūṭa Temple plan

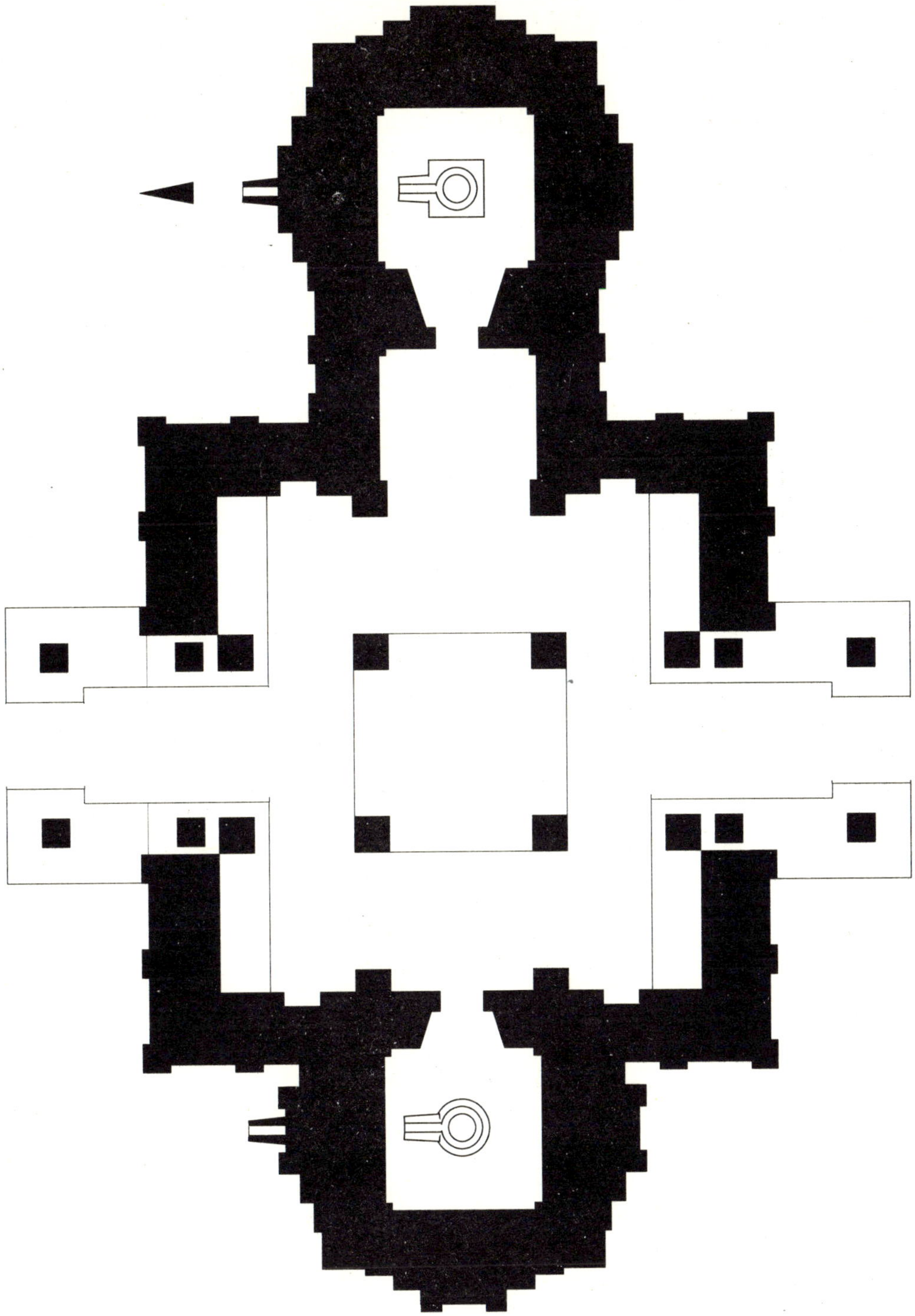

Navaliṅgeśvara Navakūṭa Temple, Kukkanur, Karnataka (ninth century – *c.* CE 1150)

The Navaliṅgeśvara Navakūṭa Temple[74] at Kukkanur is strange, eccentric, erratic, unusual in design. It is singular in its baroque character, *en plan*, within the subcontinent. Dedicated to Lord Śiva, it finds in its number — i.e. nine sanctums — a relationship to the Nava Brahmā temples of Ālampur.[75] These temples are also dedicated to the same deity. However, Cousens suggests that the temple was initially dedicated to a Vaiṣṇava temple cult rather than a Śaiva temple.[76] This assertion is made as the figure of Gaja-Lakṣmī, who is an important Vaiṣṇava/Śakti goddess/consort,[77] is seen over every door. This fact alone adds to the eccentric quality of this ensemble. Pārvatī is the consort of the Lord Śiva, not Lakṣmī, who is the consort of the Lord Viṣṇu. Could this complex fallen to the workings of the active Liṅgāyats in this area?

The *vimāna*s of the east–west and north–south axes all appear to be similar, *en plan* (**Figure 49**), and the whole temple appears to verge on an east–west axiality. The main axis runs from east to west through *garbhagr̥ha*s and *sabhā-maṇḍapa*s. None of the *sabhā-maṇḍapa*s is of similar size or lay-out, although each does have four columns in the centre supporting the ceiling. Adding to the erratic quality of the whole, there are two, additional sanctums in the south-western part of the complex which defy this initial observation of axiality. Stepped entrances are found to the north and south of the second *sabhā-maṇḍapa* — i.e. second from the east. In addition there is a point of ingress in the north-east corner of the easternmost *sabhā-maṇḍapa*. Finally, most of the southern wall of the south-western *sabhā-maṇḍapa* is missing, allowing entrance at this point.

Not only is the plan problematical, but there seems some confusion regarding the dates of construction of the various elements of the Navaliṅgeśvara Navakūṭa Temple at Kukkanur. Suresh states that the complex is "assignable to the eleventh century of the Cāḷukyas of Kalyāṇa".[78] Further on, he asserts that "the central *sabhā-maṇḍapa* (**Plate 70(2)**) with two *garbhagr̥ha*s one on the north and another on (the) south, and the south *sabhā-maṇḍapa* . . . (to the) west (**Plate 70(4)**) with its *garbhagr̥ha* on (the) west are the earliest and datable to (the) ninth century CE".[79] Immediately the problem arises! Which is it? The Cāḷukyas of Kalyāṇa or the Western Cāḷukya Dynasty (Kalyāṇa) did not assert dominance until

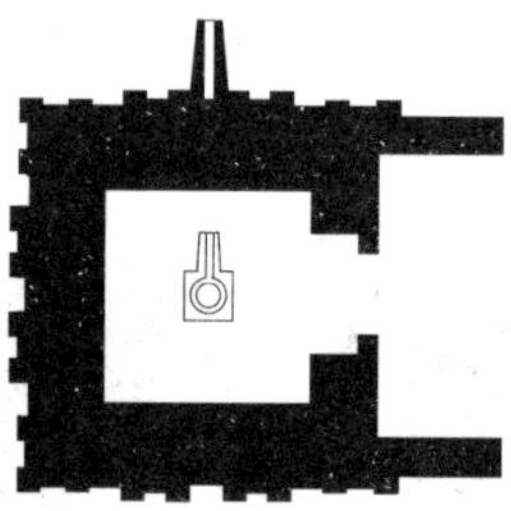

Figure 49: Navaliṅgeśvara Navakūṭa Temple *vimāna* element

[74] The plan is redrawn using Adobe PageMaker 6.0, from: HC, Plate LV; KMS II, p. 490. See also "Introduction", p. xxiii, n. 1.

[75] The nine Brahmās are Tāraka Brahmā, Svarga Brahmā, Padma Brahmā, Bāla Brahmā, Garuḍa Brahmā, Kumāra Brahmā, Arka Brahmā, Vīra Brahmā and Viśva Brahmā.

[76] HC, p. 74.

[77] Gaja-Lakṣmī is one of the Aṣṭa-Lakṣmīs, who are Ādi-Lakṣmī, Dhana-Lakṣmī, Dhānya-Lakṣmī, Gaja-Lakṣmī, Santāna-Lakṣmī, Vīra-Lakṣmī, Vijayā-Lakṣmī and Vidyā-Lakṣmī.

[78] KMS II, vol. I, p. 279.

[79] Ibid.

Plate 69: Navaliṅgeśvara Navakūṭa Temple plan

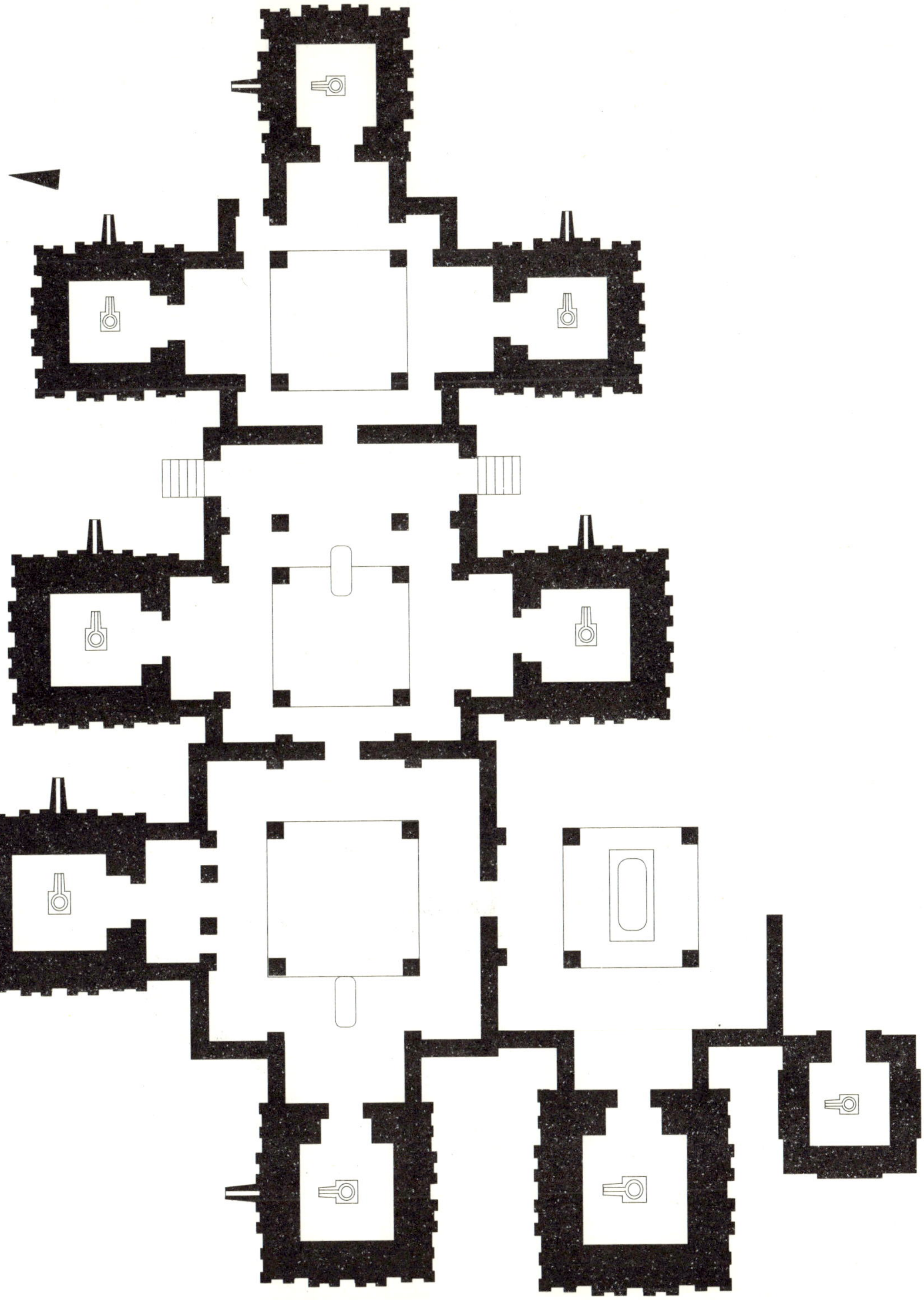

after CE 975 (**Appendix D**). If the *sabhā-maṇḍapas* (**Plate 70(2 and 4)**) with their *garbhagṛhas* were built in the ninth century CE, then that period would have fallen in the Rāṣṭrakūṭa Dynasty who flourished between CE 543 and 982.

Suresh asserts that "the western *sabhā-maṇḍapa* (**Plate 70(3)**), with two *garbhagṛhas* one on (the) north and the other on (the) west, was constructed in CE 1005"[80]. Finally, "the eastern *sabhā-maṇḍapa* (**Plate 70(1)**) with three *garbhagṛhas*, one each on (the) north, east and south, is datable to the first quarter of the eleventh century CE"[81]. No mention is made of the south-western *garbhagṛha*.

Stylistically, the *śikharas* of the *garbhagṛhas* [D], [F] and [H] are similar (**Plate 70[A], [I]**), while those of *garbhagṛhas* [A], [B] and [C] are nearly identical. However, the *śikharas* of *garbhagṛhas* [E], [G] and [I] are each rather different, subtly, one from the other and from the other six.

Finally, the placement of *garbhagṛhas* [H] and [I] are, to this researcher, highly problematical from the standpoint of design and symmetry. First, there appears to be a tenuous symmetry established by *garbhagṛhas* [A] through [G]. Second, the size and scale of *garbhagṛha* [H] are different, bigger, thicker than the *garbhagṛhas* [A] through [G] with the exception of *garbhagṛha* [E] which appears similar to *garbhagṛha* [H]. Third, *garbhagṛha* [I] has little relationship in size or scale to the other eight. It is obvious that the Navaliṅgeśvara Navakūṭa Temple was built in stages. However, it seems within the realm of possibility that *garbhagṛhas* [H] and [I] may have been the last two additions and that the temple may have been an *aṣṭakūṭa* design (**Figure 9; Figure 50**).

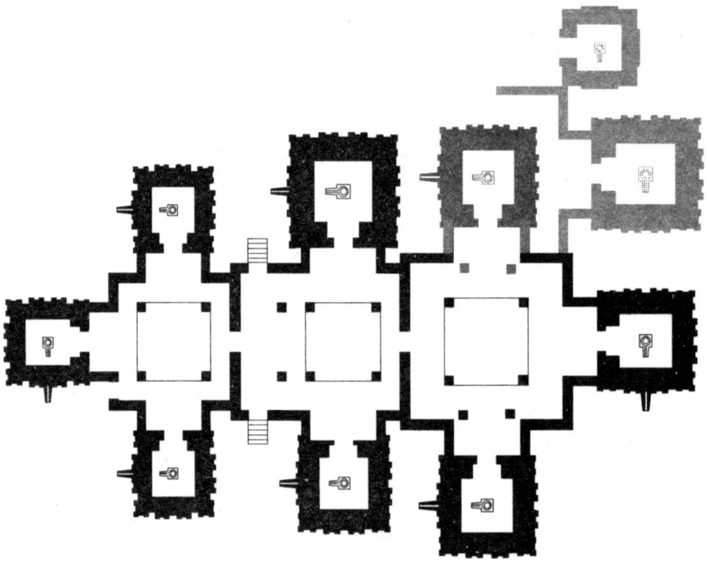

Figure 50: Navaliṅgeśvara Navakūṭa Temple, indicating possible variation

80 KMS II, vol. I, p. 279.

81 Ibid.

Plate 70: Navaliṅgeśvara Navakūṭa Temple (periods of construction)

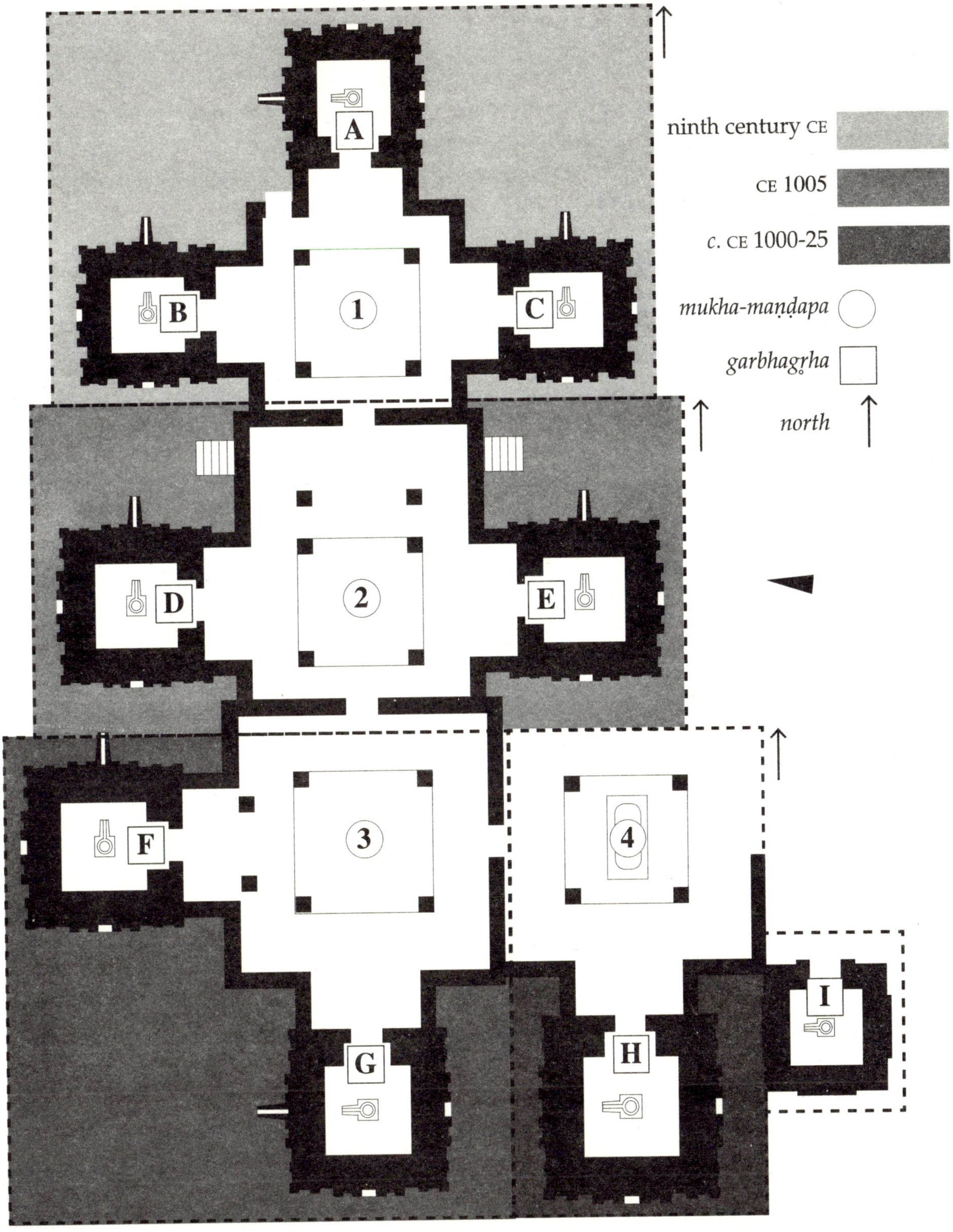

Kalideva Dvikūṭa Temple, Kummsi, Karnataka (*c.* CE 1150)

The middle of the twelfth century was a time of nearly unprecedented temple construction in the southern part of India. In part, this plethora of temple buildings was due to the Western Cāḷukyas (Kalyāṇa). Probably raised during the reigns of Jagadekamalla II (r. CE 1135-51) or Taila III (r. CE 1151-56) and before the dominance of the Kaḷacuri in that region (**Appendix D**), the Śaiva Kalideva Dvikūṭa Temple[82] at Kummsi is an example of the **B**-type *dvikūṭa* plan (**Figure 2**).

The temple consists of the principal, exceedingly plain *vimāna* with Śivaliṅga aligned towards the north. The *vimāna* consists of a square *garbhagṛha* and an *antarāla* which is open towards the *sabhā-maṇḍapa*. To the west is the second *vimāna* which is a duplicate of the north–south counterpart with Śivaliṅga (**Figure 51**). Both *vimānas* share a common, enclosed *sabhā-maṇḍapa*. The *sabhā-maṇḍapa* of the Kalideva Dvikūṭa Temple possesses sixteen columns in the usual arrangement — i.e. four free-standing columns in the centre raised on a square platform and twelve engaged columns, four of which are quarter, corner columns — which form nine *aṅkanas* — and eight niches — i.e. two on each wall near the corners.[83] A simple doorway, centred in the northern wall, allows egress. The Kalideva Dvikūṭa Temple is without a *mukha-maṇḍapa*, which is in line with the simplicity of the whole.

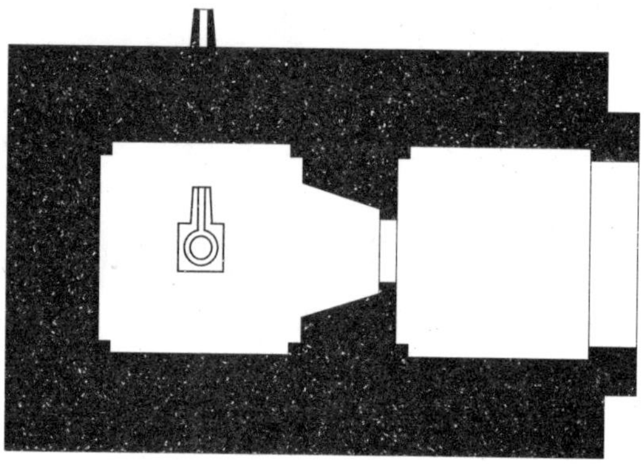

Figure 51: Kalideva Dvikūṭa Temple *vimāna* element

82 Redrawn using PageMaker 6.0 from: KMS II, p. 429, description on pp. 198-99. See also **Preface**.

83 Ibid., p. 199, states: "The *sabhā-maṇḍapa* has eight deep niches . . . ." However, the plan on p. 429 only indicates seven — i.e. only one in the eastern wall. It is the opinion of this researcher that the plan is an error.

Plate 71: Kalideva Dvikūṭa Temple plan

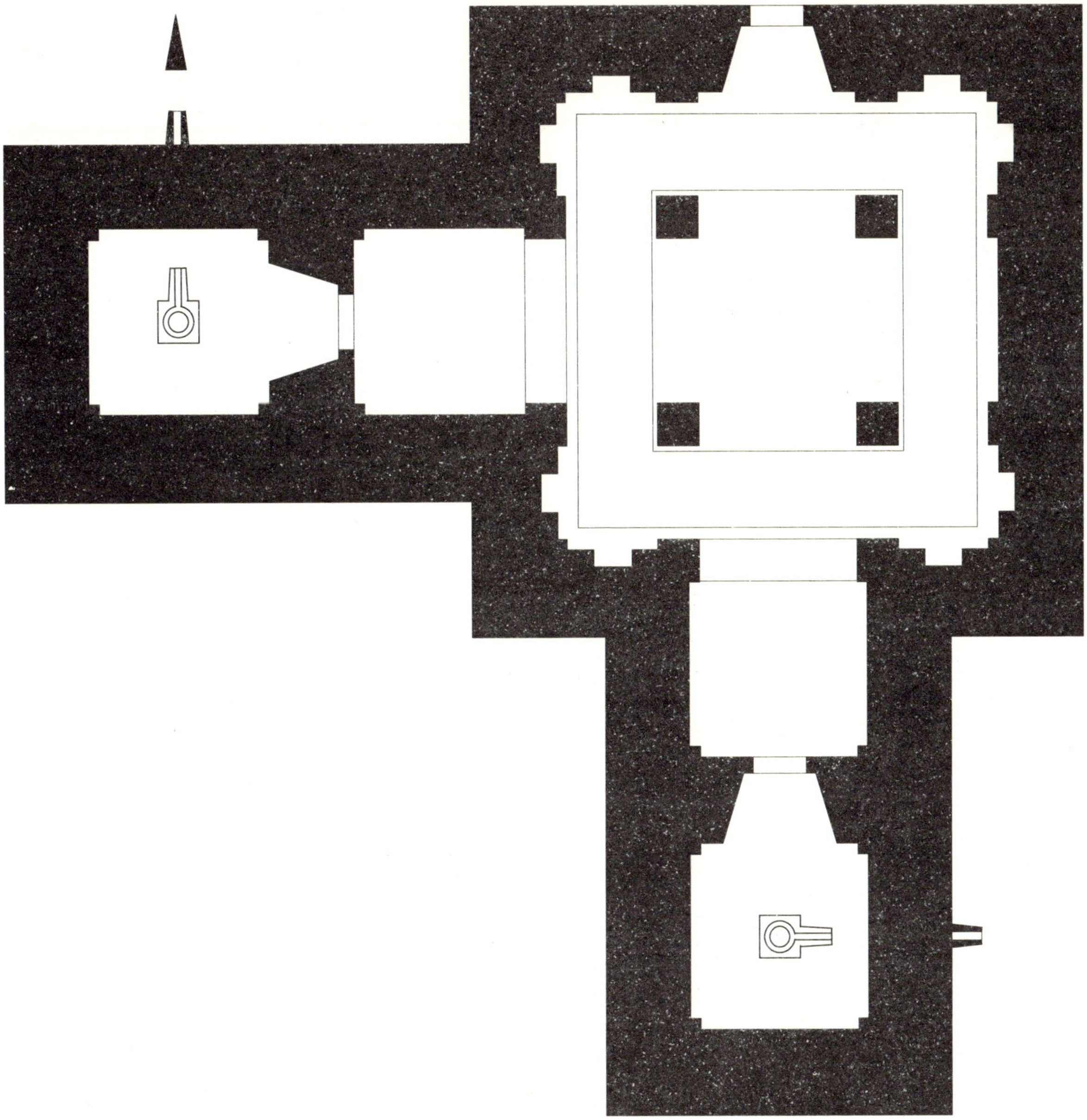

Śaṅkaraliṅga Dvikūṭa Temple, Kalakere, Karnataka (*c*. CE 1150)

The Śaṅkaraliṅga Dvikūṭa Temple[84] at Kalakere, with a **B**-type *dvikūṭa* plan (**Figure 2**), is a temple of some interest. Constructed around the middle of the twelfth century, it is a temple which is dedicated to both Śaiva and Vaiṣṇava deities — i.e. the Lord Śiva in the form of a Śivaliṅga and Nārāyaṇa, a form of the Lord Viṣṇu, the image of which is missing. The disparity in the design of the *vimānas* may cause one to believe that they were constructed at different times.

The western *pañcaratha vimāna,* with a square *garbhagṛha,* a Śivaliṅga and an *antarāla* which open directly onto the *sabhā-maṇḍapa,* is the more developed of the two *vimānas*, and is aligned towards the east. This western *vimāna* possesses three deep, external shrines — i.e. one each to the north, south and west *raha-rathas*. In contrast, the northern *vimāna* is exceedingly simple, possessing a square *garbhagṛha* and *antarāla* which open directly onto the *sabhā-maṇḍapa*. The two *vimānas* share a common, enclosed *sabhā-maṇḍapa* of unusual design. Rather than the usual sixteen columns, this *sabhā-maṇḍapa* exhibits thirty-six columns — i.e. sixteen free-standing columns and twenty engaged columns of which four are quarter columns in the corners; creating twenty-five *aṅkanas* (**Figure 52**). There are doorways leading from the *sabhā-maṇḍapa* to the outside — i.e. one to the east and the other to the south — but they are without *mukha-maṇḍapas*. The other feature is the appearance of windows with *jālī* in the eastern wall and in the north-eastern and south-eastern corners of the *sabhā-maṇḍapa*.

It is the fact that the western *vimāna* presents a far more complicated design than its northern counterpart, and the placement, or orientation of the *jālī* that causes one to feel that the Śaṅkaraliṅga Dvikūṭa Temple had originally been conceived of as an *ekakūṭa* temple, dedicated to Lord Śiva. Certainly the inequality of design and detail, *en plan*, of the Nārāyaṇa *vimāna* would also suggest this possibility, if not probability.

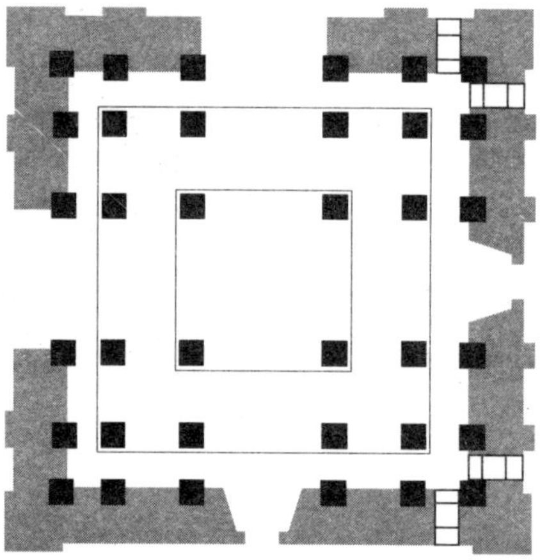

Figure 52: Śaṅkaraliṅga Dvikūṭa Temple arrangement of columns in the *sabhā-maṇḍapa*

[84] Redrawn using PageMaker 6.0 from: KMS II, p. 426, description on pp. 196-97. See also **Preface**. In addition, there is some confusion between the name "Śaṅkaraliṅga Temple" described on pp. 196-97, and the Plan 112, on p. 426, which is entitled "Śāntaliṅga". It is assumed that the title "Śāntaliṅga" is an error.

Plate 72: Śaṅkaraliṅga Dvikūṭa Temple plan

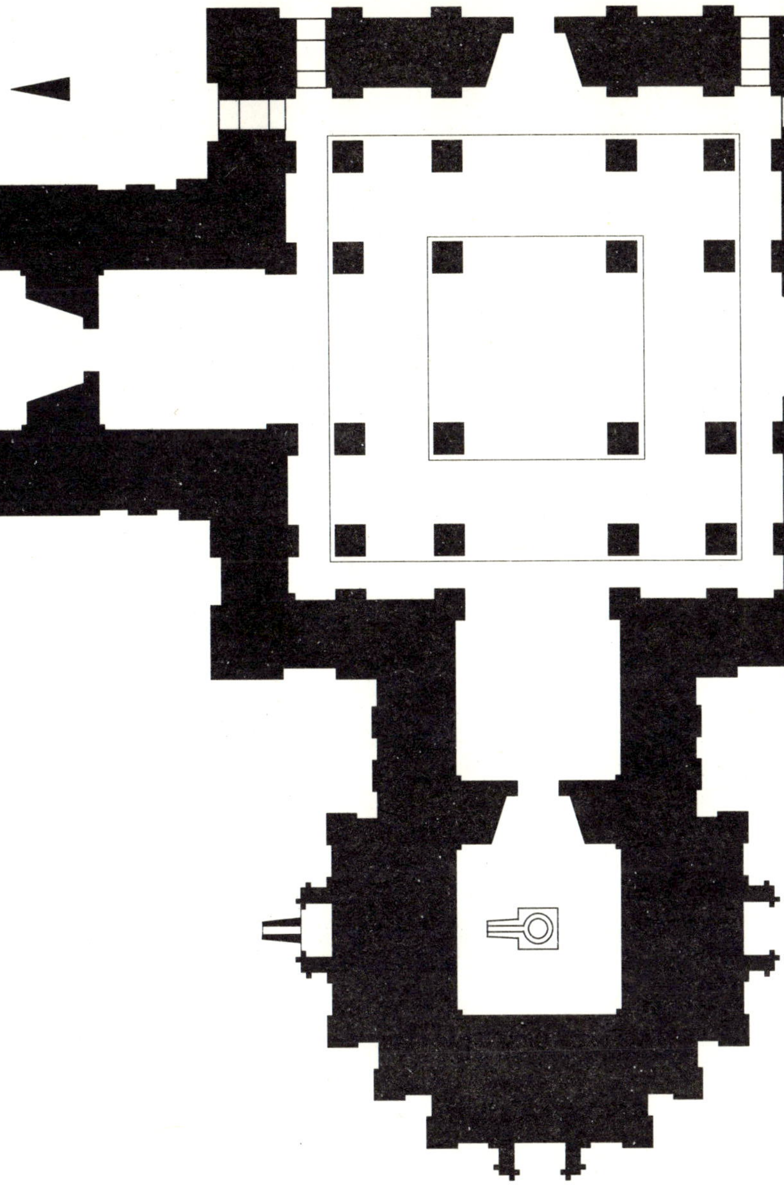

Saṅgameśvara Trikūṭa Temple, Babaleśvara, Karnataka (*c.* CE 1150)

Another of the mid-twelfth-century temples constructed during the waning days of the Western Cāḷukya (Kalyāṇa) dynasty, the Saṅgameśvara Trikūṭa Temple[85] is of an **A**-type *trikūṭa* plan. Unlike a number of other *trikūṭa* temples of this period, it presents a coherent, developed plan.

The Saṅgameśvara Trikūṭa Temple is aligned towards the north. The main, southern sanctum is made up of a square *garbhagṛha* and *antarāla* which opens directly into the *sabhā-maṇḍapa*. The outer walls of the *garbhagṛha*, which holds a Śivaliṅga, present a *navaratha* appearance. The eastern and western *vimāna*s are essentially identical to the southern counterpart except the sanctums are presently bare (**Figure 53**). The three *vimāna*s open onto a common, enclosed, square *sabhā-maṇḍapa* which holds sixteen columns in the traditional arrangement — i.e. four free-standing columns in the centre raised on a square platform and twelve engaged columns, four of which are quarter, corner columns — which forms nine *aṅkana*s. To the north are the scant remains of a *mukha-maṇḍapa* which consisted of two free-standing columns.

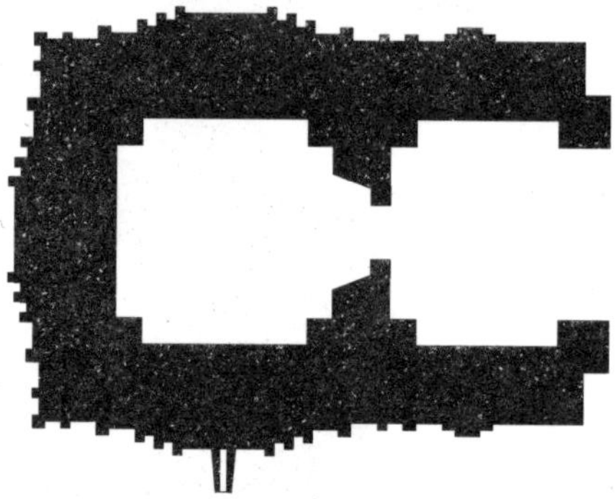

Figure 53: Saṅgameśvara Trikūṭa Temple *vimāna* element

85 Redrawn using PageMaker 6.0 from KMS II, p. 454, description on pp. 232-33. See also **Preface**.

Plate 73: Saṅgameśvara Trikūṭa Temple plan

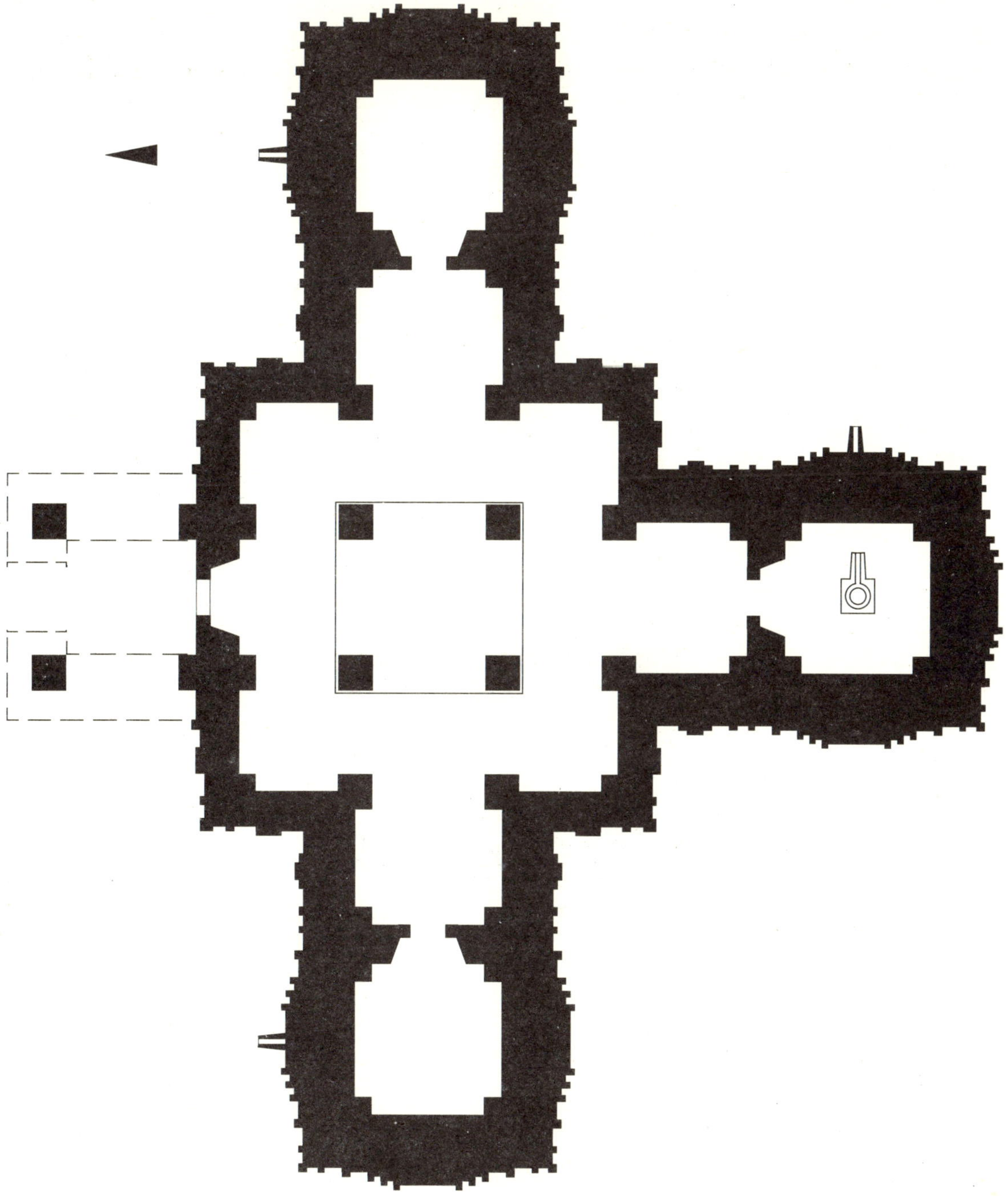

Rāmaliṅga Trikūṭa Temple, Iṭigi, Karnataka (*c.* CE 1150)

Constructed in the mid-twelfth century, this **A**-type *trikūṭa* temple presents a slight conundrum. The Rāmaliṅga Trikūṭa Temple[86] of Iṭigi presents one of the variations that the Western Cāḷukyas (Kalyāṇa) have left to posterity.

The Rāmaliṅga Trikūṭa Temple is aligned towards the east. The three *vimānas* are essentially identical, *en plan* (**Figure 54**). The principal *vimāna* is in the west. Like the other two, it consists of a square *garbhagṛha* with square *antarāla* leading directly into the *sabhā-maṇḍapa* and contains a Śivaliṅga (**Figure 3**). The three *vimānas* open onto a three-quarter enclosed *sabhā-maṇḍapa* (**Appendix A, p. 224**). Unlike the usual enclosed *sabhā-maṇḍapa* with sixteen columns exhibiting four free-standing columns in the centre raised on a square platform and eight engaged columns, two of which are quarter, corner columns forming nine *aṅkanas*; this *sabhā-maṇḍapa* is open towards the east with four free-standing columns making up that part of the ensemble. The Rāmaliṅga Trikūṭa Temple has a rather interesting *mukha-maṇḍapa*, which, in part, shares the four eastern free-standing columns of the *sabhā-maṇḍapa*. From between the middle two columns a short flight of stairs leads down to a wide platform which serves as an external *pradakṣiṇāpatha*.

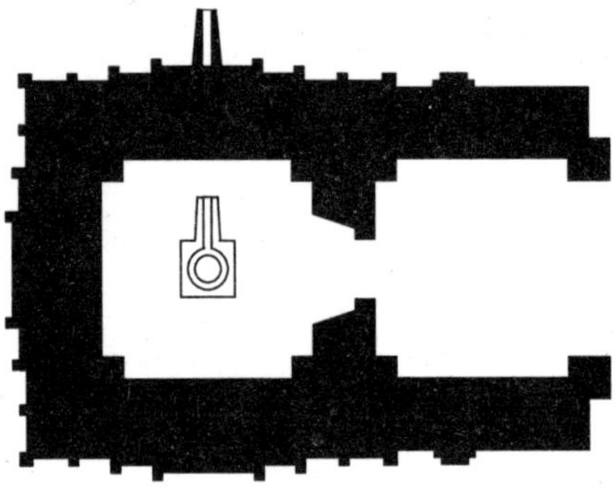

Figure 54: Rāmaliṅga Trikūṭa Temple *vimāna* element

[86] Redrawn using PageMaker 6.0 from KMS II, p. 455, description on p. 233. See also **Preface**.

Plate 74: Rāmaliṅga Trikūṭa Temple plan

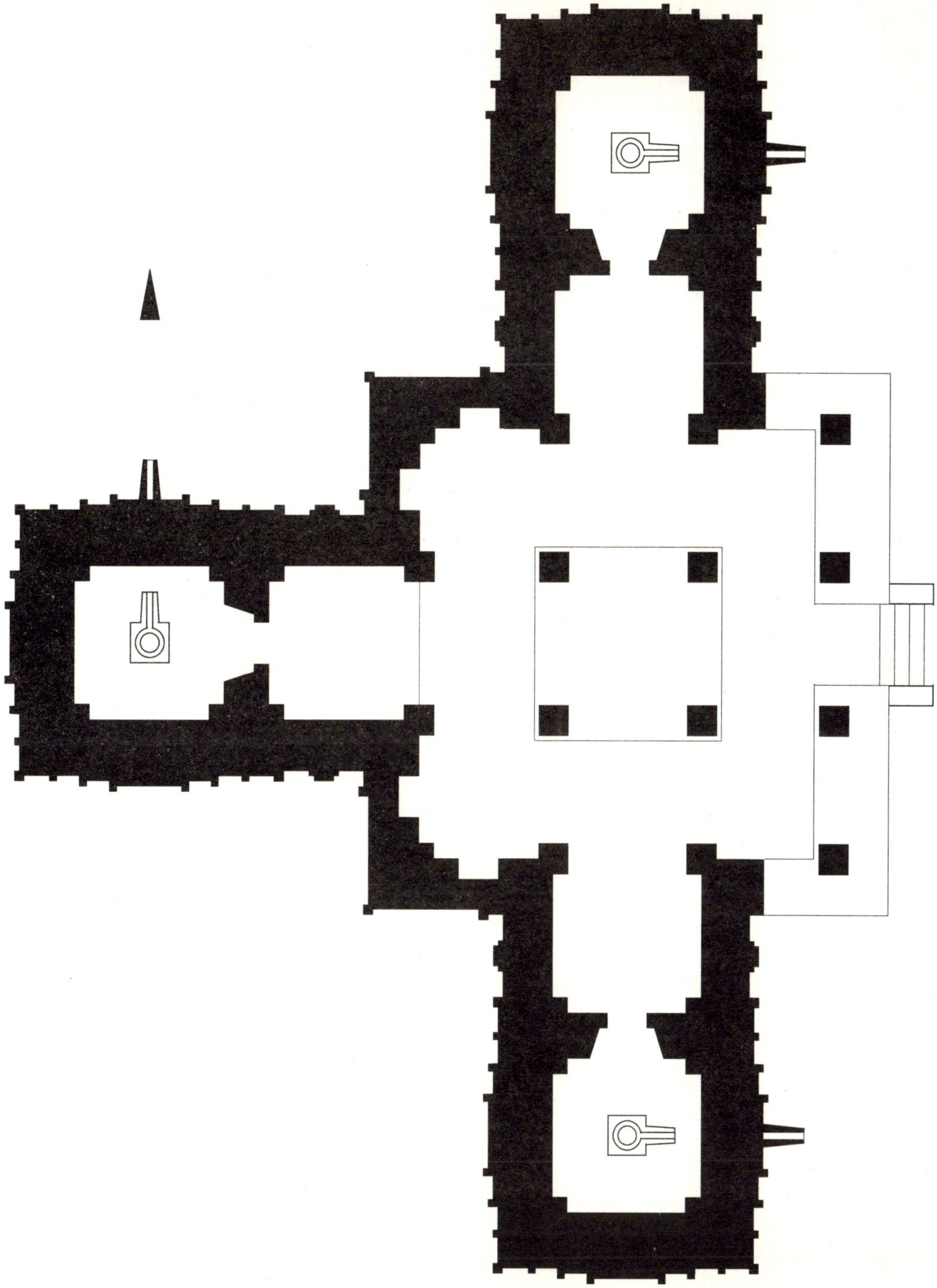

Nārāyaṇa Trikūṭa Temple, Iṅgaleśvara, Karnataka (*c*. CE 1150)

The Nārāyaṇa Trikūṭa Temple[87] at Iṅgaleśvara was one of those numerous temples constructed by the Western Cāḷukyas (Kalyāṇa) in the mid-twelfth century and is an example of an **A**-type *trikūṭa* plan (**Figure 3**). It is one of the few temples of the region dedicated to the three major sects — i.e. Vaiṣṇava, Śaiva and Śakti.

The temple consists of three *vimānas* which are essentially identical, *en plan* (**Figure 55**). Aligned towards the north, the main *vimāna* is dedicated to Nārāyaṇa (Viṣṇu). The eastern sanctum is assigned to Lord Śiva and contains a Śivaliṅga, while the western *vimāna* once contained a Śakti image. The three *vimānas* of the Nārāyaṇa Trikūṭa Temple are *pañcaratha, en plan,* and each indicates a square *antarāla* attached to the *garbhagṛhas*. The three *vimānas* share a common, square, three-quarter enclosed *sabhā-maṇḍapa* which is enclosed on the east, west and south sides. As is normally seen, the *sabhā-maṇḍapa* possesses sixteen columns traditionally arranged — i.e. six free-standing columns, four of which are in the centre and raised on a square platform as well ten engaged columns, two of which are quarter, corner columns — which form nine *aṅkanas*. Two additional engaged columns extend beyond the eastern and western *sabhā-maṇḍapa* wall presenting a rank of six columns and may be seen as part of the *mukha-maṇḍapa*. The Nārāyaṇa Trikūṭa Temple possesses a rather elaborate *mukha-maṇḍapa*. This is created by two ranks of six free-standing columns which are duplicated from the northern six columns of the *sabhā-maṇḍapa* — i.e. four engaged and two free-standing as noted above. Finally, two more free-standing columns to the north complete the plan of the *mukha-maṇḍapa*. Of interest is the fact that the northern six columns of the *sabhā-maṇḍapa* may also be seen to be part of those associated with the *mukha-maṇḍapa* (**Figure 56**).

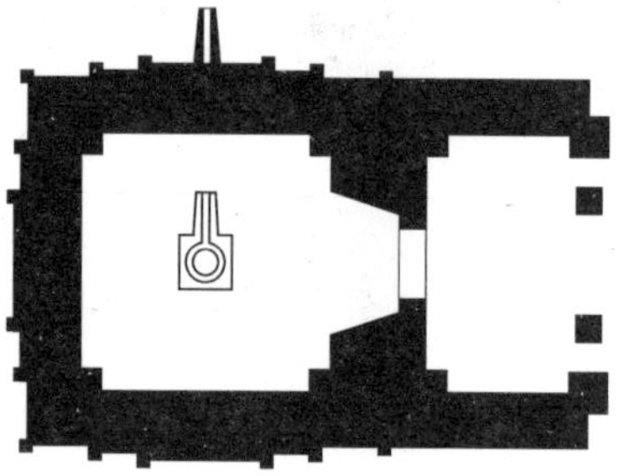

Figure 55: Nārāyaṇa Trikūṭa Temple *vimāna* element

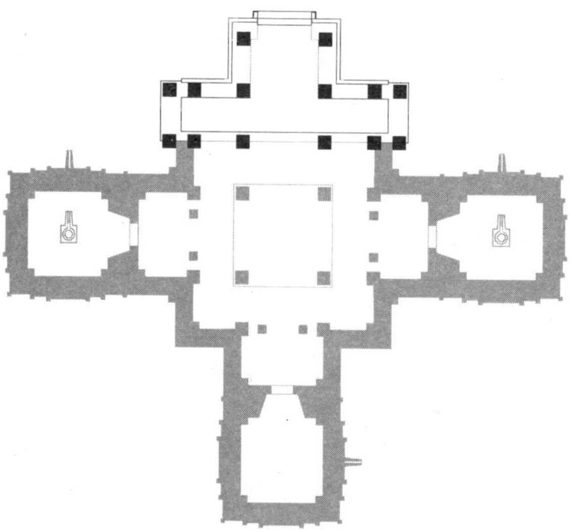

Figure 56: Nārāyaṇa Trikūṭa Temple *mukha-maṇḍapa* variant

[87] Redrawn using PageMaker 6.0 from KMS II, p. 470, description on pp. 258-59. See also **Preface**.

Plate 75: Nārāyaṇa Trikūṭa Temple plan

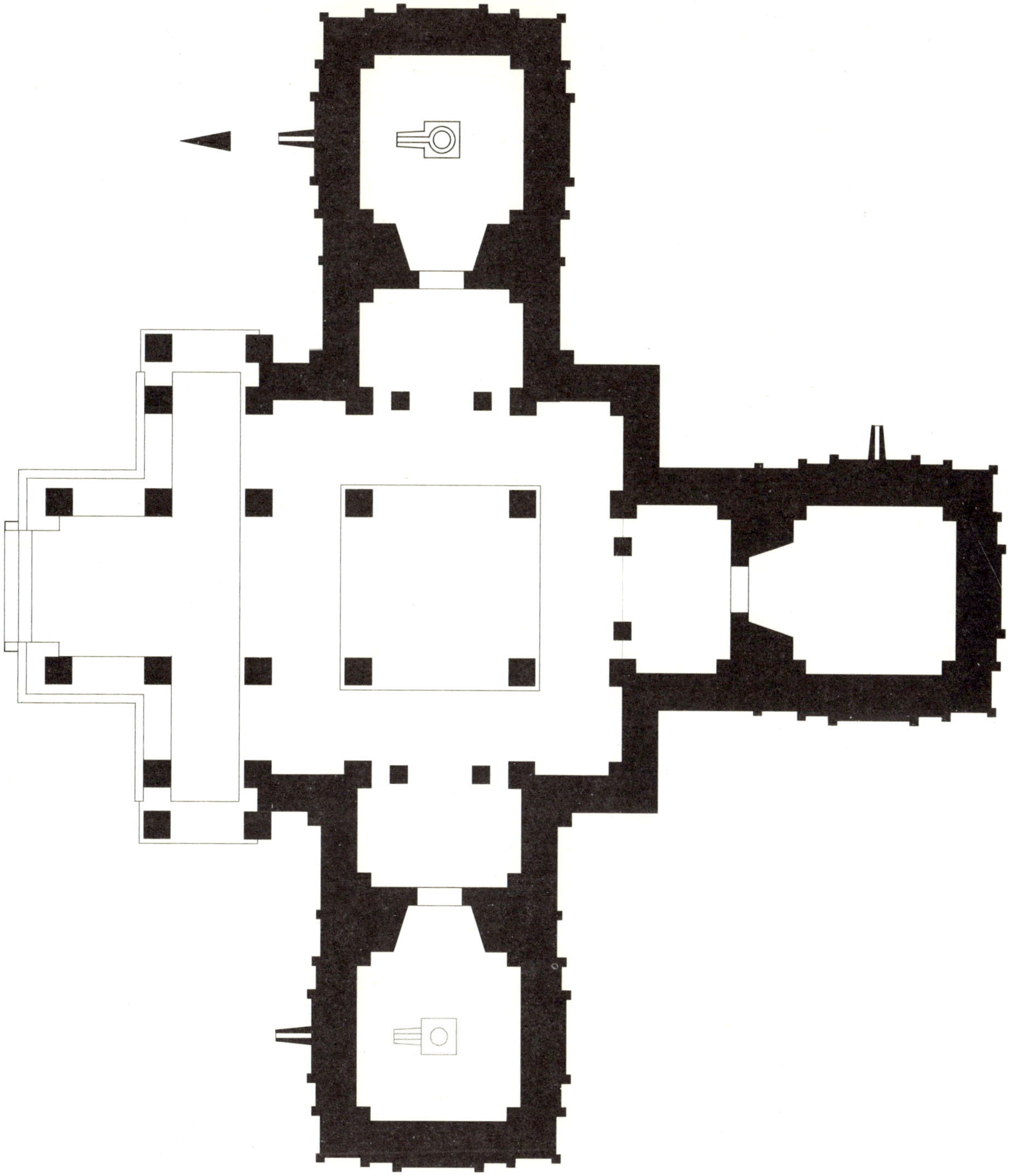

Rāmaliṅgeśvara Trikūṭa Temple, Kundaragi, Karnataka (*c.* CE 1150)

Of the numerous temples constructed by the Western Cāḷukyas (Kalyāṇa) during the mid-twelfth century, the Rāmaliṅgeśvara Trikūṭa Temple[88] of Kundaragi possesses a rather simple exterior, but a developed interior. This Trikūṭa temple, an **A**-type *trikūṭa* plan (**Figure 3**), is not large, but relates in size to the numerous other temples constructed during the same period.

The Rāmaliṅgeśvara Trikūṭa Temple consists, *en plan*, of three nearly identical *vimāna*s each with a Śivaliṅga. These *vimāna*s consist of a square *garbhagṛha* and a square *antarāla*. The *antarāla*s open, via a door onto a common *sabhā-maṇḍapa* (**Figure 57**). The enclosed *sabhā-maṇḍapa* is square and contains sixteen traditionally arranged columns — i.e. four free-standing columns in the centre raised on a square platform and twelve engaged columns, four of which are quarter, corner columns — which form nine *aṅkana*s. The three entrances into the *vimāna*s is augmented by a fourth doorway — i.e. the entrance into the temple proper. On either side of each of these four entrances are deep shrines. The design of theses shrines creates niches with the engaged columns flanking them (**Figure 58**). This creates a rather elaborate, internal design, *en plan*, of the *sabhā-maṇḍapa*. To the east are eight columns — i.e. four free-standing and four engaged — upon a platform. This creates a substantial *mukha-maṇḍapa* for the Rāmaliṅgeśvara Trikūṭa Temple. Between the two, central, free-standing columns is a narrow set of steps leading down to ground level.

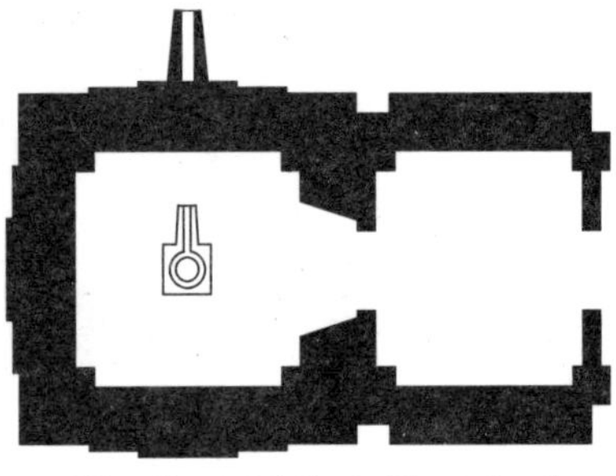

Figure 57: Rāmaliṅgeśvara Trikūṭa Temple *vimāna* element

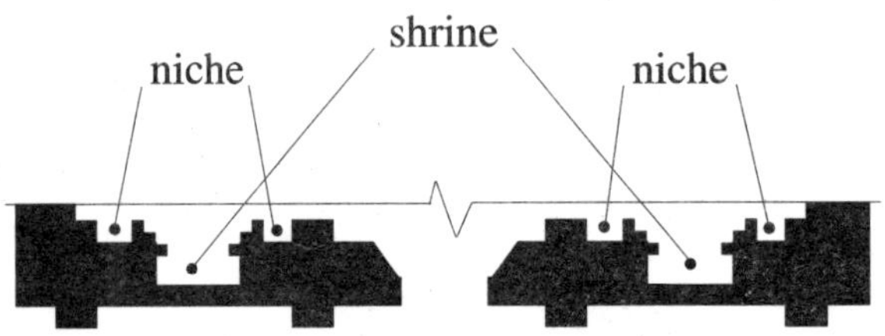

Figure 58: Rāmaliṅgeśvara Trikūṭa Temple shrines with niches

[88] Redrawn using PageMaker 6.0 from KMS II, p. 471, description on p. 259. See also **Preface**.

Plate 76: Rāmaliṅgeśvara Trikūṭa Temple plan

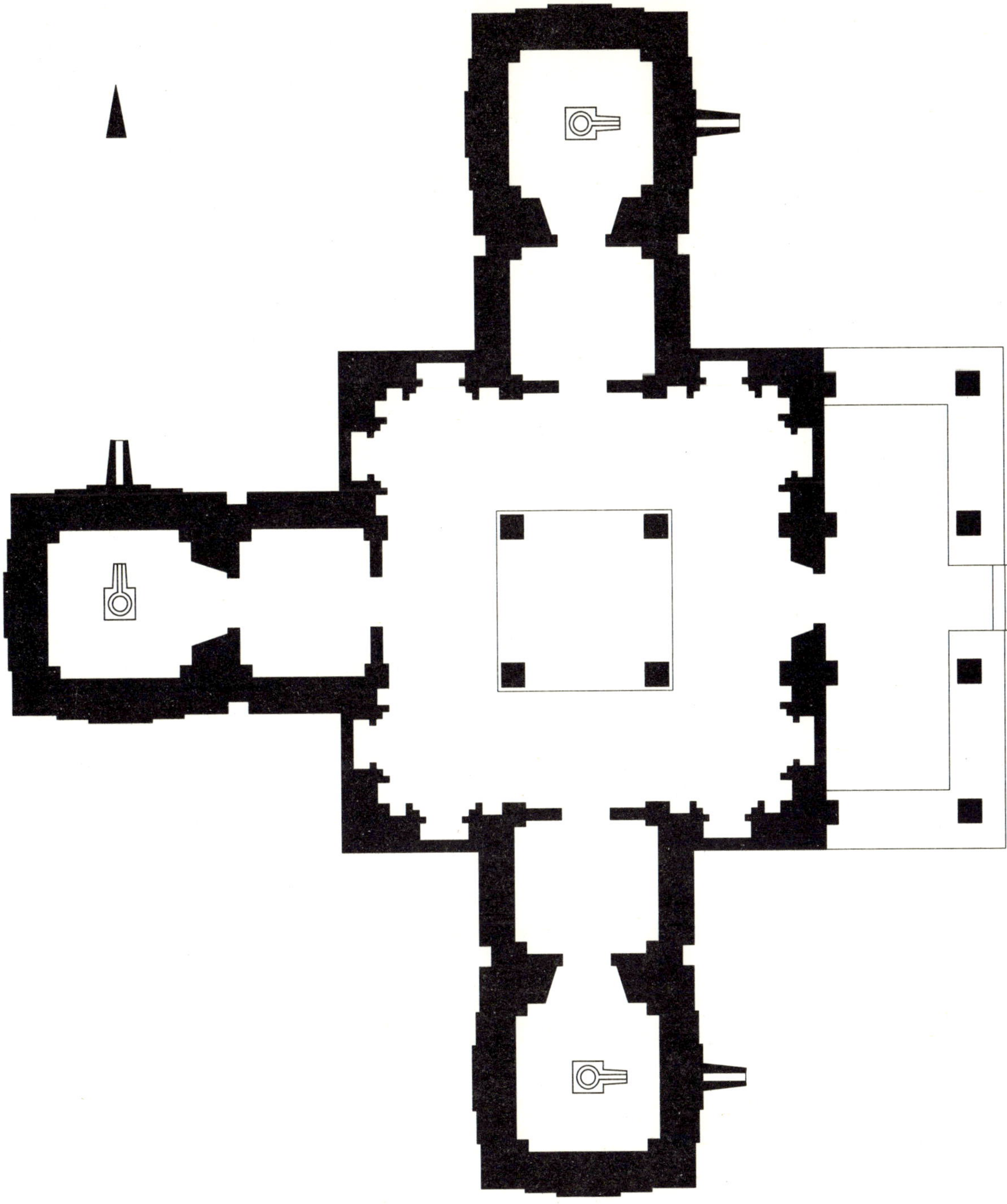

Bucesvara Dvikūṭa Temple, Koravaṅgala, Karnataka (*c.* CE 1173)

With the collapse of the dominance of the Western Cāḷukyas (Kalyāṇa) in the region, the Hoysaḷa during the reigns of Narasiṁha I (r. CE 1152-73) and Ballāla II (Vīraballāla) (r. CE 1173–1220) wrested control from the Cāḷukyas. One of the earliest temples to be raised after their gaining supremacy was the Bucesvara Dvikūṭa Temple[89] at Koravaṅgala. The construction was undertaken not by one of the members of the ruling family, but by an officer of the court. This would seem to indicate that the Hoysaḷas had not only achieved political dominance, but had amassed considerable wealth.

The Bucesvara Dvikūṭa Temple is an **A**-type *dvikūṭa* plan (**Figure 2**). The principle *garbhagṛha* with Śivaliṅga is in the west and is attached to a square *antarāla* which leads directly into an enclosed, square *sabhā-maṇḍapa*. The external walls of the *garbhagṛha* are essentially *saptaratha, en plan*. Six shrines are found in the *sabhā-maṇḍapa* — i.e. two in the western wall and two each in the northern and southern walls. However, the northern and southern shrines appear in the centre of their respective walls and the second ones to the west. This presents a plan which is unusually asymmetrical except when viewed on its east–west axis. The enclosed, square *sabhā-maṇḍapa* possesses sixteen columns in a traditional arrangement — i.e. four free-standing columns in the centre raised on a square platform and twelve engaged columns, four of which are quarter, corner columns — which form nine *aṅkanas*. A door in the east of the enclosed *sabhā-maṇḍapa* leads to an *aṅkana* and thence to an open *sabhā-maṇḍapa*. The open *sabhā-maṇḍapa* exhibits a myriad of columns in a complex arrangement. Suresh describes the arrangement of this open *sabhā-maṇḍapa* as "star-shaped". The *sabhā-maṇḍapa* consists of forty-two columns — i.e. four on a raised platform in the centre, surrounded by twelve (two of which are one-quarter engaged to the eastern *vimāna*), which are, in turn, surrounded by twelve, again, two of which are engaged to the eastern *vimāna*, and six to the north and six to the south (**Figure 59**).[90] Of these forty-two columns last mentioned twelve may be seen to act as a *mukha-maṇḍapa* — i.e. six to the north and six to the south. To the east is the secondary *vimāna* which is composed of a *garbhagṛha* with a Sūrya image and a square *antarāla* opening onto the open *sabhā-maṇḍapa*. The eastern *vimāna* is similar, *en plan*, to the western counterpart. On its east–west axis the Bucesvara Dvikūṭa Temple is mirror axial.

The application of a *paramaśāyika paṇḍala* to both *sabhā-maṇḍapa* (**Plate 78**) produces interesting conjunctions. Similarly of a grid based upon a *paramaśāyika maṇḍala* is overlaid, similar conjunctions appear (**Plate 79**).

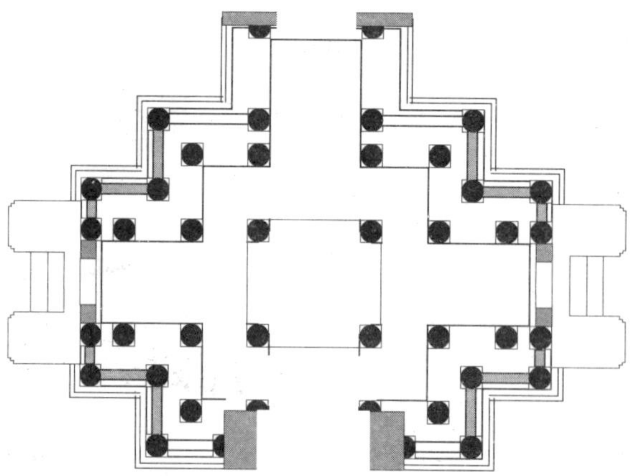

Figure 59: Bucesvara Dvikūṭa Temple shrines with niches

[89] The plan is redrawn using Adobe PageMaker 6.0, from KMS II, p. 431, description on pp. 202-03.

[90] Ibid., p. 203.

Plate 77: Buceśvara Dvikūṭa Temple plan

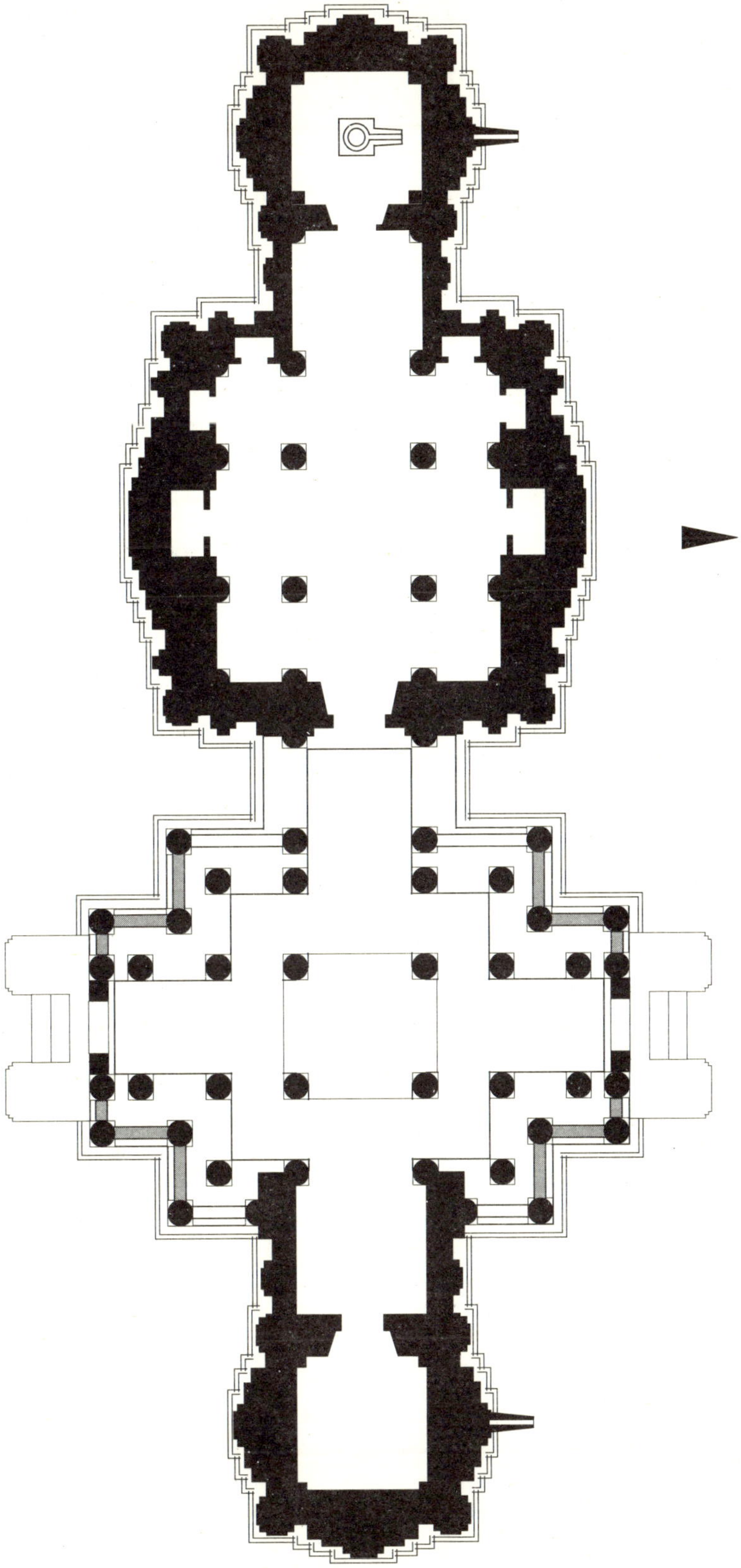

Plate 78: Buceśvara Dvikūṭa Temple with *paramaśāyika maṇḍalas* over *sabhā-maṇḍapas*

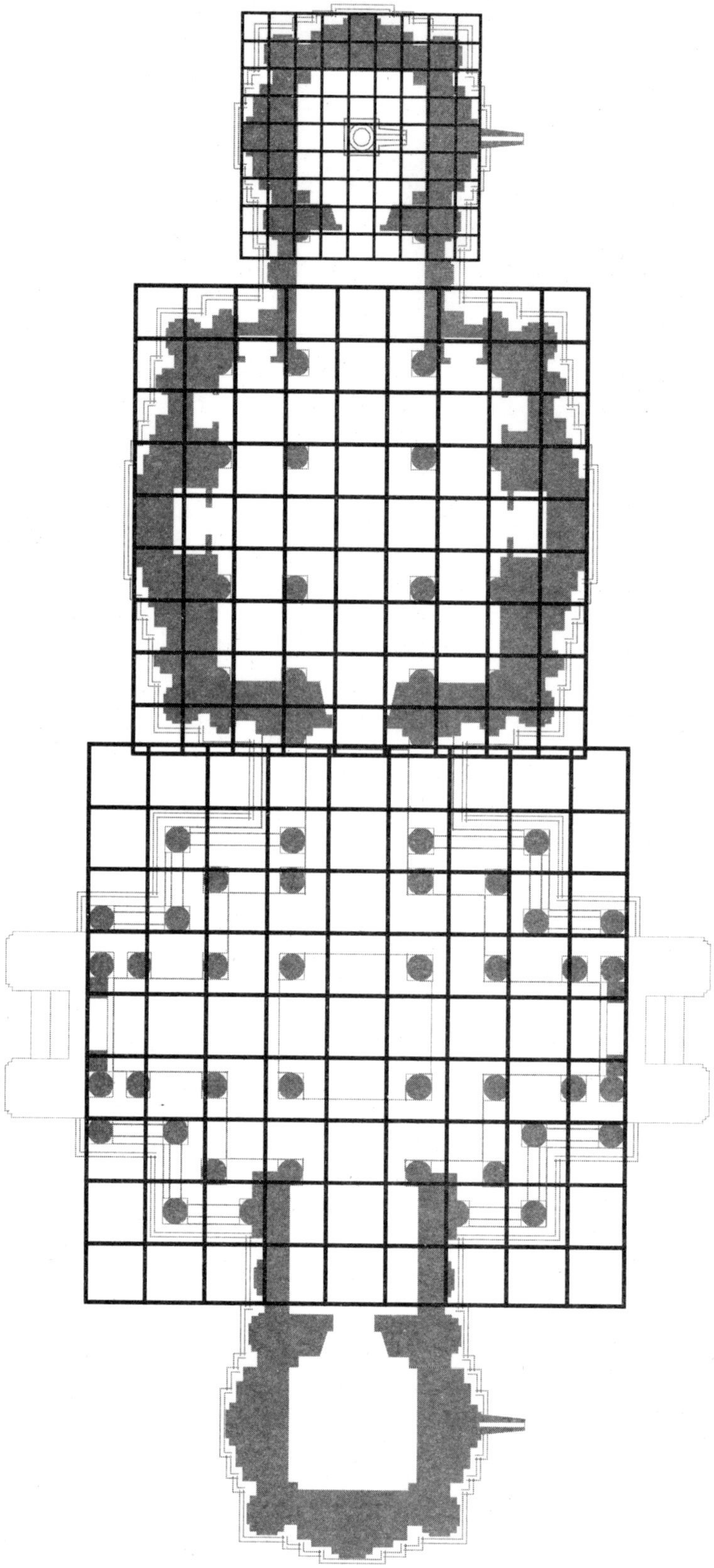

Plate 79: Buceśvara Dvikūṭa Temple with grid based on *paramaśāyika maṇḍala* over whole

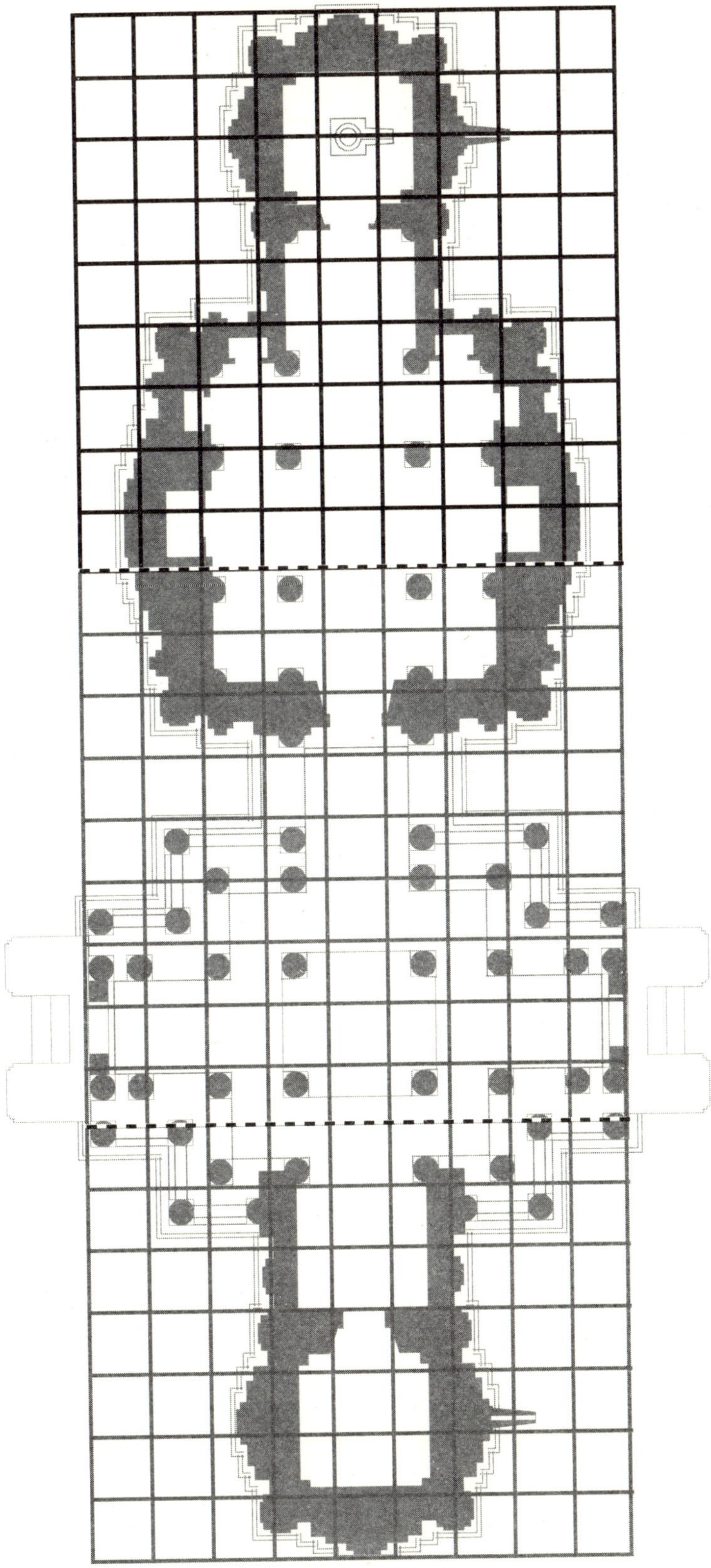

Rāmeśvara Trikūṭa Shrine, Kurugod, Karnataka (a. CE 1175)

Constructed during the short reign of the Southern Kaḷacuri, specifically during the reign of King Saṅkama (Saṅkamavarmadeva) (r. CE 1176-80) (**Appendix D**), the Rāmeśvara Trikūṭa Temple[91] offers a brief and partial glimpse into this minor dynasty. Their independence lasted a mere twenty-two years.

The Rāmeśvara Trikūṭa Temple consists of the principle *vimāna* to the west. It is made up of a square *garbhagṛha* and a square *antarāla* opening directly onto a common *sabhā-maṇḍapa*. This sanctum is dedicated to the deity Gavareśvara in the form of a Śivaliṅga. Two similar *vimāna*s appear: to the north, dedicated to Mallikārjuna in the form of a Śivaliṅga and in a state of complete ruin, and to the south dedicated to Muddeśvara in the form of a Śivaliṅga, partially ruined. The northern *vimāna* is in a state of ruin. The three *vimāna*s shared a common *sabhā-maṇḍapa*. Because of the ruinous state of this part of the temple, it is impossible to tell with certainty its design. However, there are four engaged columns and one quarter engaged column — i.e. in the corner — which would presuppose that the *sabhā-maṇḍapa* was in the traditional columnar design — i.e. four free-standing columns in the centre raised on a square platform and twelve engaged columns, four of which are quarter, corner columns — which form nine *aṅkana*s. Whether this temple possessed a *mukha-maṇḍapa* or not is impossible to tell.

[91] Redrawn using PageMaker 6.0 from KMS II, p. 450, description on pp. 223-24. See also **Preface**.

Plate 80: Rāmeśvara Trikūṭa Shrine proposed plan

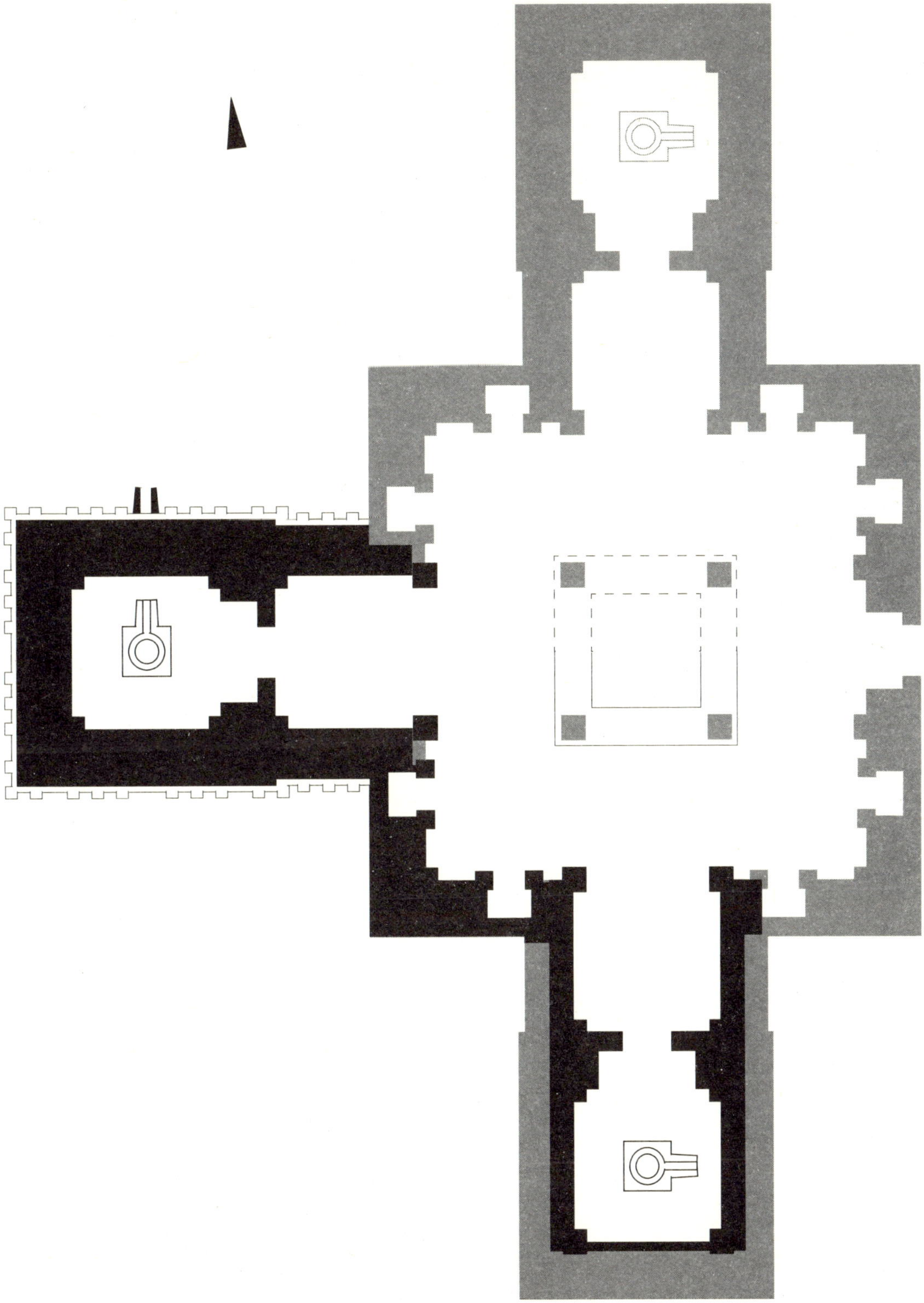

Bastī or Kalla-Guḍi Trikūṭa Temple, Degamve, Karnataka (*c.* CE 1175)

The Bastī or Kalla-Guḍi Trikūṭa Temple[92] at Degamve is a **D**-type *trikūṭa* plan (**Figure 2**). Its history is connected with the Kadamba Dynasty of Goa. It is believed that the temple was built under the auspices of the wife of King Śivacittavīrapermadideva (r. CE 1147-87), one Kamalādevī in CE 1175 (**Appendix D**). Queen Kamalādevī is associated with a number of temples in the region.

The Bastī or Kalla-Guḍi Trikūṭa Temple presents an interesting plan. Cousens comments on the three "shrines".[93] However the central, subsidiary shrine is minuscule compared with the two *vimānas*. The north and south *vimānas* consist of a square *garbhagṛha* and a rectangular *antarāla* which open directly, via steps down, into the *sabhā-maṇḍapa* (**Figure 60**). The southern shrine appears to have been dedicated to Sarasvatī — i.e. the four-arm form — while the northern sanctum has an image of Mahākalī. Between the two *vimānas* and within the common *sabhā-maṇḍapa* is found the smaller shrine with a rectangular *garbhagṛha* and without an *antarāla*. It appears from the lintel that this shrine may also have been dedicated to Sarasvatī. It appears little more than a transitional element for the whole. With the three shrines apparently dedicated to goddesses, it would seem that this temple belongs to the Śakti sect. The *sabhā-maṇḍapa* is rectangular and contains forty columns, sixteen of which are engaged. However, they are so arranged as to indicate three *sabhā-maṇḍapas* — i.e. one for the northern *vimāna*, one for the southern *vimāna* and one for the central, transitional shrine. The latter *sabhā-maṇḍapa* shares columns from the proposed northern and southern *sabhā-maṇḍapas* (**Figure 61**). Across the eastern face of the Bastī or Kalla-Guḍi Trikūṭa Temple are ten free-standing columns which form a *mukha-maṇḍapa*. On the east–west axis of the northern and southern *vimānas* are two entrances to this *trikūṭa* temple.

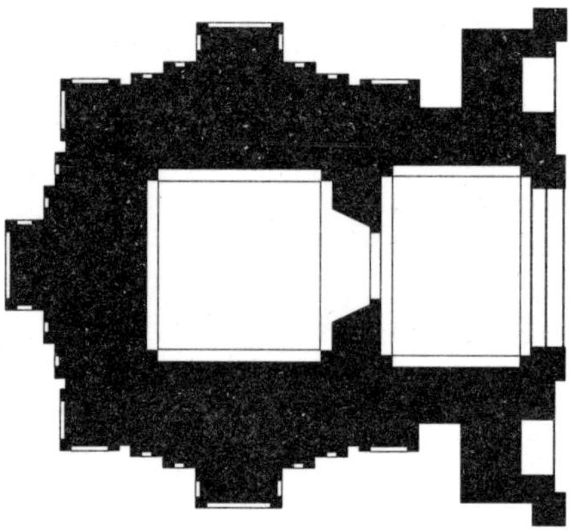

Figure 60: Bastī or Kalla-Guḍi Trikūṭa Temple vimāna element

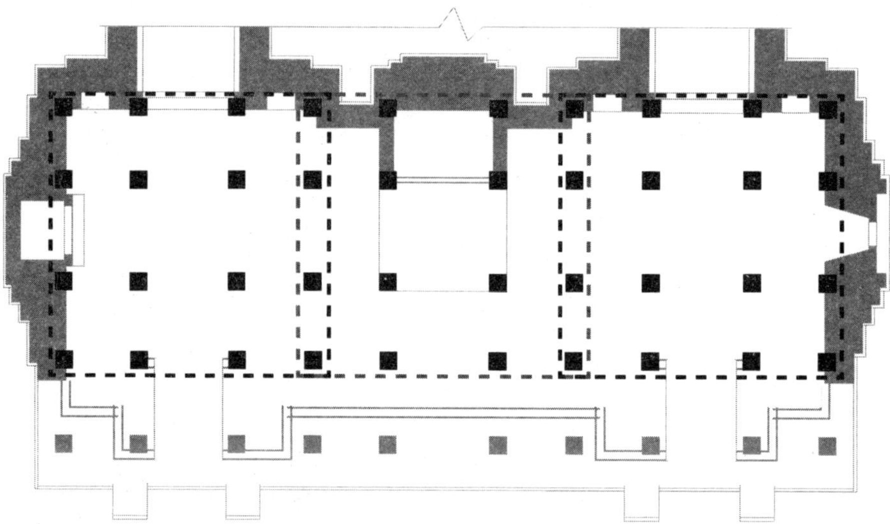

Figure 61: Bastī or Kalla-Guḍi Trikūṭa Temple indicating three *sabhā-maṇḍapa* arrangements

[92] The plan is redrawn using Adobe PageMaker 6.0, from HC, Plate CXXXIII.

[93] Ibid., pp. 119-20.

Plate 81: Bastī or Kalla-Guḍi Trikūṭa Temple plan

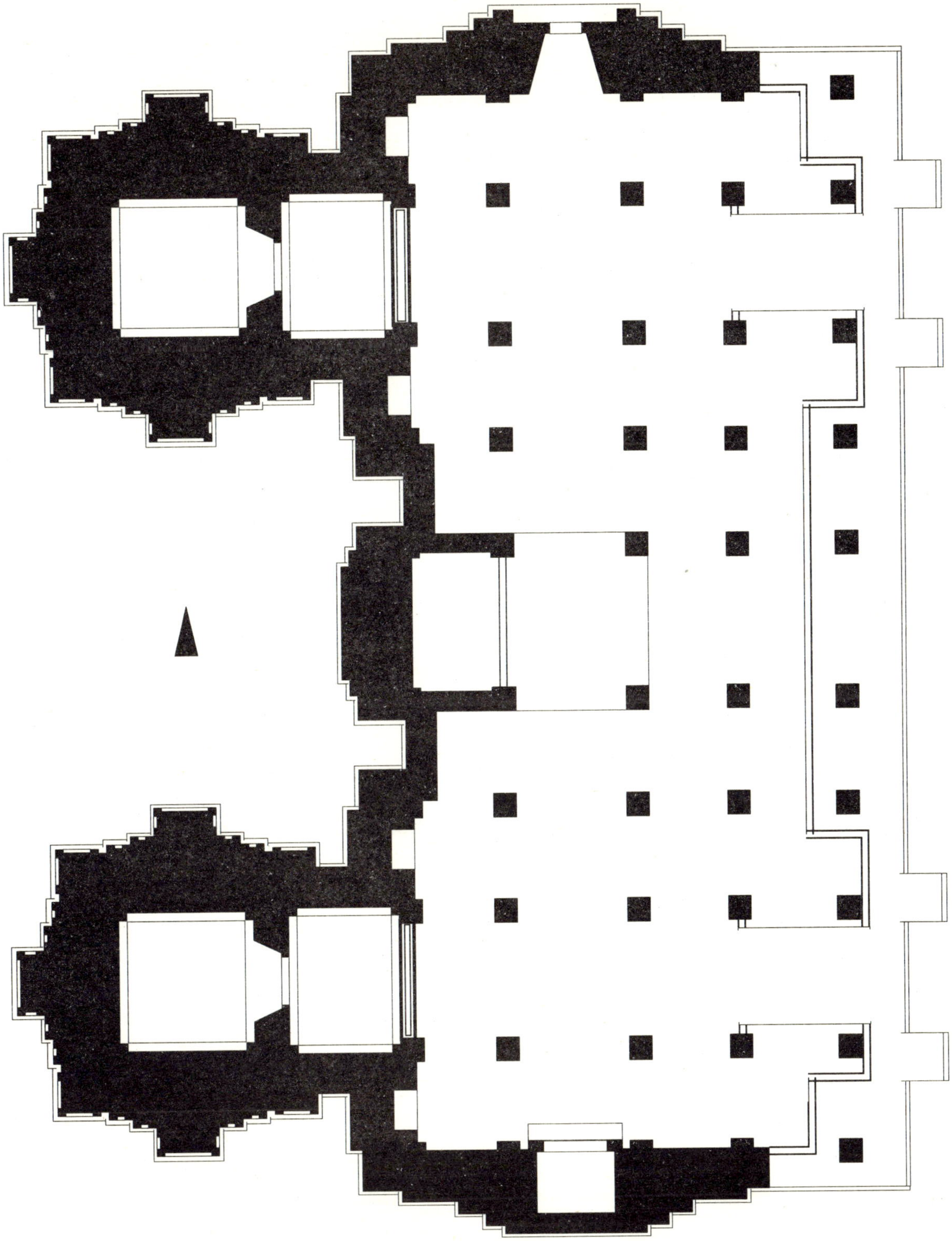

Someśvara Trikūṭa Temple, Iṅgaleśvara, Karnataka (*c.* CE 1176)

The Someśvara Trikūṭa Temple[94] at Iṅgaleśvara was constructed either at the end of the Western Cāḷukya (Kalyāṇa) Dynasty — i.e. during the reigns of Jagadekamalla II (r. CE 1135-51) or Taila III (r. CE 1151-56) — or at the beginning of the Southern Kaḷacuri Dynasty — i.e. during the reign of Sovideva (Someśvara) (r. CE 1167-76). It is an example of an **A**-type *trikūṭa* plan (**Figure 3**). It is believed to have originally been a temple dedicated to the Vaiṣṇava, Śaiva and Śakti deities.

The temple is aligned towards the west and exhibits three, identical *vimānas*. The main, eastern *vimāna* is *pañcaratha, en plan*, and holds a square *garbhagṛha* with a square *antarāla* separated from a common *sabhā-maṇḍapa* by two, free-standing columns. This *garbhagṛha* now holds a Śivaliṅga, but is believed to have originally held an image of the Lord Viṣṇu as Nārāyaṇa.[95] The northern *vimāna* is identical and held a Śivaliṅga, while the similar southern sanctum probably held a Śakti image. The common, square, enclosed *sabhā-maṇḍapa* holds sixteen columns in the normal arrangement — i.e. four free-standing columns in the centre raised on a square platform and twelve engaged columns, four of which are quarter, corner columns — which form nine *aṅkanas*. The *sabhā-maṇḍapa* is simple in form and strictly square — i.e. indicating no *rathas*. In the western wall of the enclosed *sabhā-maṇḍapa* is a door leading to an open *mukha-maṇḍapa* of sixteen columns. To the north, south and east of the *mukha-maṇḍapa* are stairs leading to ground level.

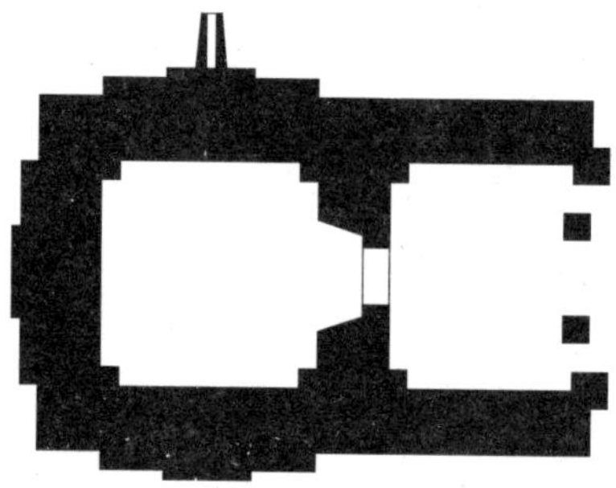

Figure 62: Someśvara Trikūṭa Temple *vimāna* element

[94] Redrawn using PageMaker 6.0 from KMS II, p. 469, description on pp. 257-58. See also **Preface**.

[95] Ibid., p. 258.

Plate 82: Someśvara Trikūṭa Temple plan

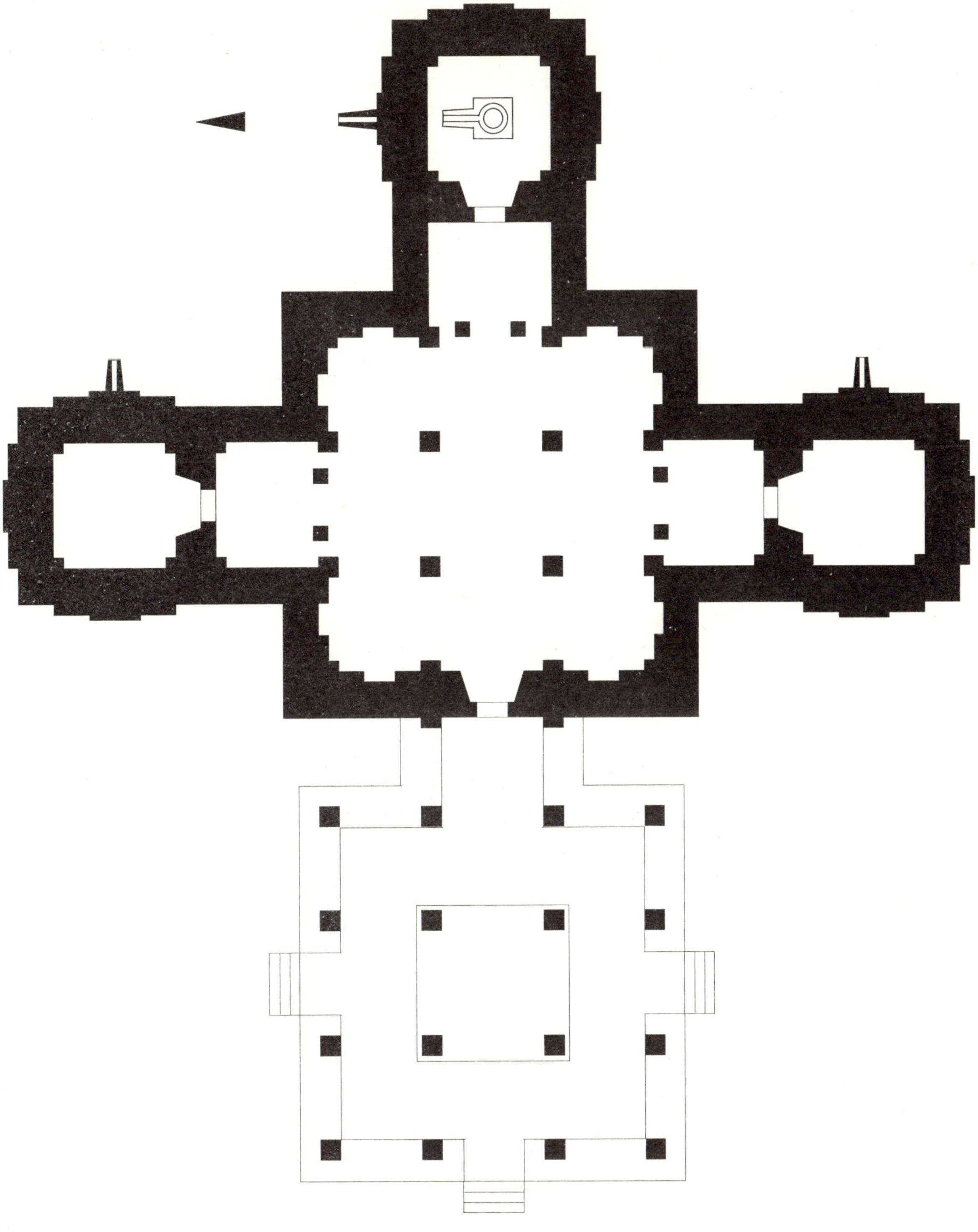

Paramānanda Trikūṭa Temple, Konnur, Karnataka (a. CE 1185)

After the reign of the hapless monarch, Taila III (r. CE 1151-56) (**Appendix D**), the Western Cāḷukyas (Kalyāṇa) succumbed to the Kaḷacuri who then dominated the region. However, the resurgent Western Cāḷukya (Kalyāṇa) King Someśvara IV (r. CE 1183–1200) reigned briefly. It was during this period that the Paramānanda Trikūṭa Temple[96] was constructed at Konnur.

An **A**-type *trikūṭa* plan (**Figure 3**), the exterior Paramānanda Trikūṭa Temple is extremely simple, *en plan*. It consists of the principle, western *vimāna* which contains a square *garbhagṛha*, a Śivaliṅga and square *antarāla* which opens to the common *sabhā-maṇḍapa* (**Figure 63**). The northern sanctum containing an image of Harihara and the southern sanctum which displays Lakṣmī-Nārāyaṇa with their square *antarāla* are identical, *en forme*. The square, enclosed *sabhā-maṇḍapa* holds sixteen columns is the usual arrangement — i.e. four free-standing columns in the centre raised on a square platform and twelve engaged columns, four of which are quarter, corner columns — which forms nine *aṅkanas*. In addition, on either side of the entrances into the *antarāla*s as well as the entrance door in the east are deep niches — i.e. eight, *en toto*. To the east is a narrow entrance with a short flight of stairs. This doorway is the only source of light for the interior of the temple.

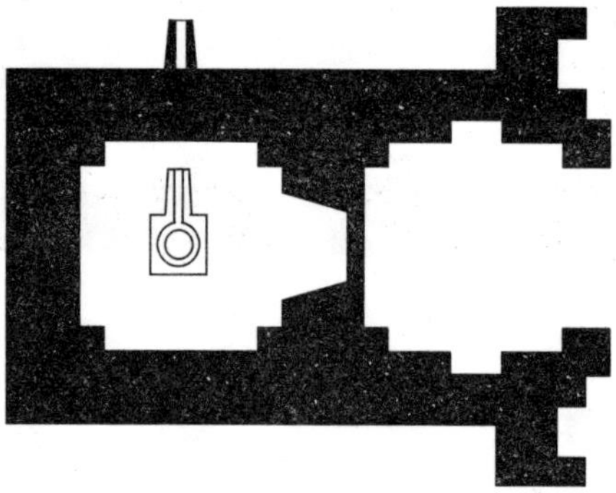

Figure 63: Paramānanda Trikūṭa Temple *vimāna* element

[96] Redrawn using PageMaker 6.0 from KMS II, p. 451, description on pp. 224-25. See also **Preface**.

Plate 83: Paramānanda Trikūṭa Temple plan

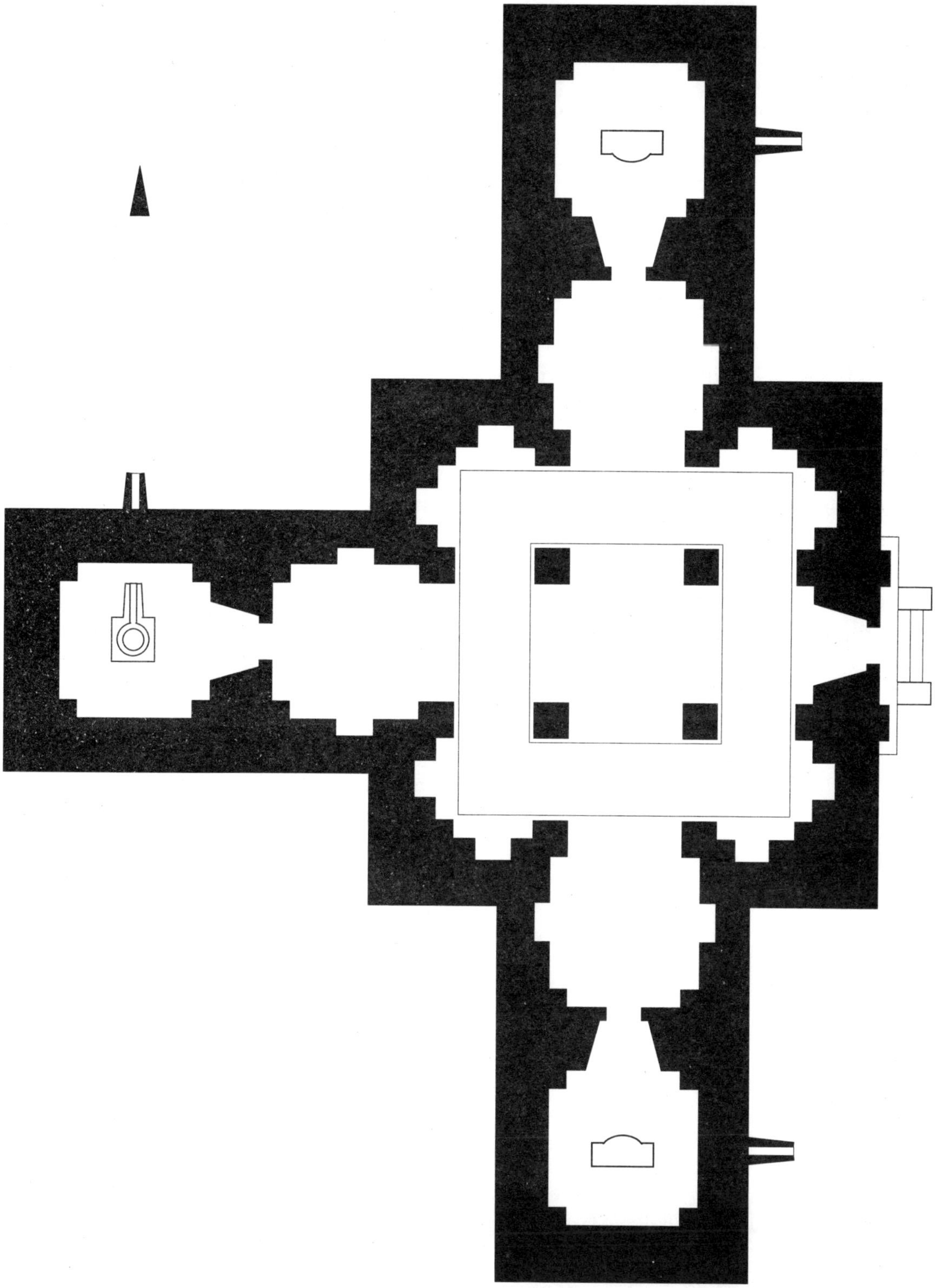

Vīranārāyaṇa Trikūṭa Temple, Belvadi, Karnataka (*c.* CE 1200)

Sometime during the reigns of the Hoysaḷa kings Ballāla II (Vīraballāla) (r. CE 1173–1220) and Narasiṁha II (r. CE 1220-38) (**Appendix E**) was raised one of the most remarkable temples in south India. Belvadi is a small town in Karnataka, but it holds the impressive Vīranārāyaṇa Trikūṭa Temple.[97] There are a number of large temple complexes in Karnataka and Tamil Nadu, but few single temples of this region compete with the Vīranārāyaṇa Trikūṭa Temple in size and complex design. Unlike the Hoysaḷa temples at Beḷūr — i.e. the Cennakeśava Temple (**Plate 45**) — and Halebiḍ — i.e. the Hoysaḷeśvara Temple (**Plate 49**) — this temple is most complete with its three *śikhara* intact. Aligned towards the east, this Vaiṣṇava temple is dedicated to Vīranārāyaṇa who occupies the western sanctum. The southern sanctum houses Kṛṣṇa in the form of Veṇugopāla, while Yoga-Narasiṁha occupies the northern *vimāna*.

The Vīranārāyaṇa Trikūṭa Temple consists of a western, main sanctum with a square *garbhagṛha* and connecting *antarāla*. This *vimāna* is connected to an enclosed, windowless *sabhā-maṇḍapa* of nine bays (*aṅkanas*), which, in turn is attached to an open, staggered-bay *sabhā-maṇḍapa* — i.e. with bays in the following order: one, three, five, three, one, each centred on the previous — of thirteen bays. The temple, thus far, is seen by Foekema and Suresh as being the initial construction — i.e. an *ekakūṭa* temple.[98] This initial temple leads to an anomalous transverse element of five, open *aṅkanas*. The reason for this strange element can only be that a different plan was initially undertaken, but abandoned and the large *mahāmaṇḍapa* with its opposing *vimāna* was added instead. This transverse element is unique to the Vīranārāyaṇa Trikūṭa Temple. From here one enters the large *mahāmaṇḍapa* consisting of thirty-nine bays (**Figure 64**).[99] To the north is a *vimāna*, similar to the western, *en plan*, and to the south is the third sanctum of this *trikūṭa* temple. This is seen as the second stage of construction, creating this temple.

The interesting, but erratic plan of the Vīranārāyaṇa Trikūṭa Temple makes the application of a *maṇḍala* to any but the individual parts, extremely problematical.

				1				
			2	3	4			
		5	6	7	8	9		
	10	11	12	13	14	15	16	
0	17	18	19	20	21	22	23	0
	24	25	26	27	28	29	3	
		31	32	33	34	35		
			36	37	38			
				39				

Figure 64: Numbering of bays (*aṅkanas*) within the large *sabhā-maṇḍapa* of Vīranārāyaṇa Trikūṭa Temple

[97] The plan is redrawn using Adobe PageMaker 6.0, from GF, pp. 52 and Pls. 14-17; KMS II, p. 459. See also "Introduction", p. 9, n. 6.

[98] GF, pp. 53-55; KS, pp. 237-39.

[99] GF, p. 53, states that it is a "hall of fifty-nine bays"; KS, p. 238, states that the "*mahāmaṇḍapa* has thirty-seven *aṅkanas*". Suresh assigns bay #1 (**Figure 63**) and bay #39 as *mukha-maṇḍapas*.

Plate 84: Vīranārāyaṇa Trikūṭa Temple plan

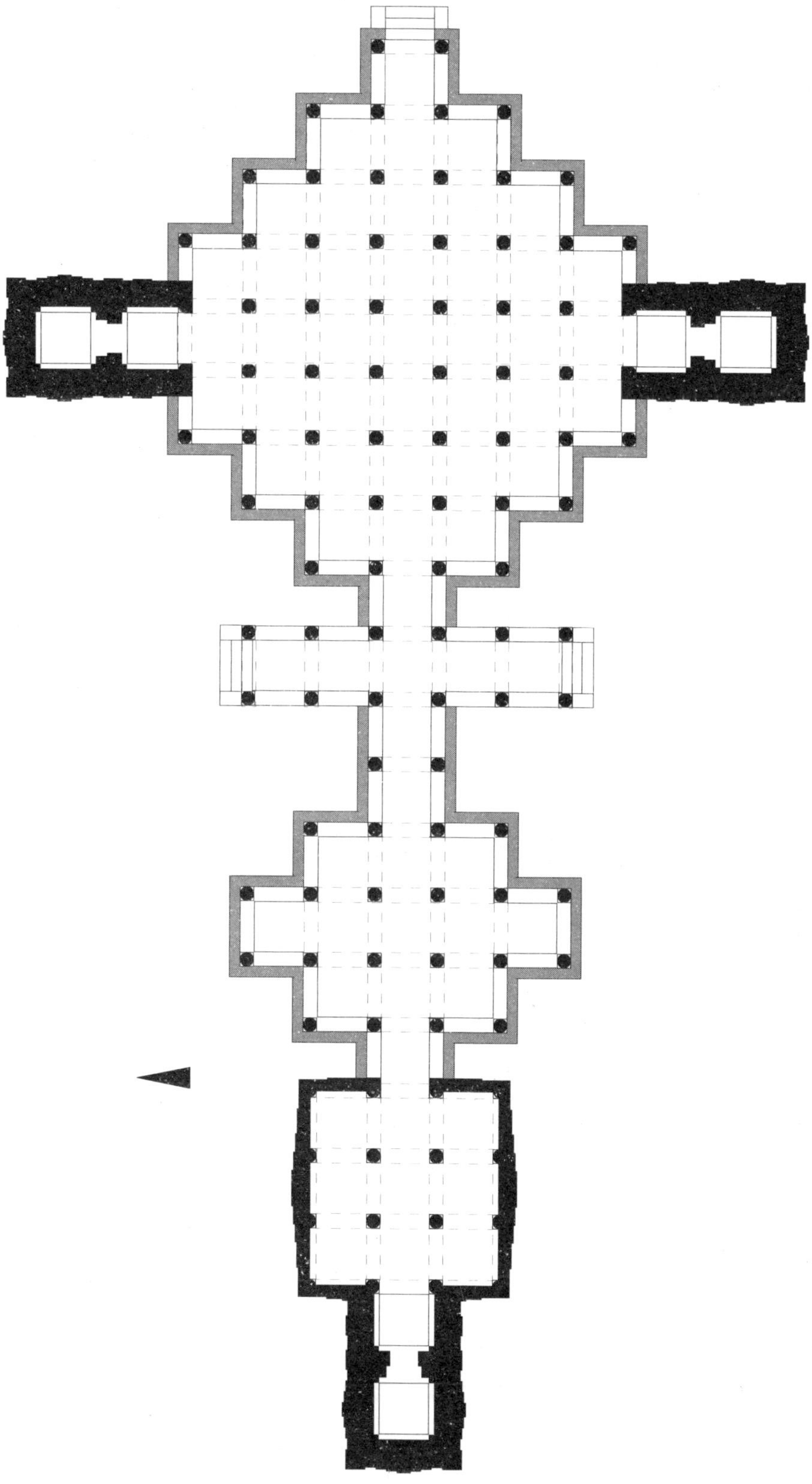

Sūrya-Nārāyaṇa Trikūṭa Temple, Magala, Karnataka (a. CE 1209)

About half way during the long reign of the Hoysaḷa king Ballāla II (Vīraballāla) (r. CE 1173–1220) (**Appendix D**), the Sūrya-Nārāyaṇa Trikūṭa Temple[100] was raised in the small town of Magala. The temple is of the **A**-type *trikūṭa* plan and presents a fully developed, if not complicated plan.

The main *vimāna*, originally dedicated to the Viṣṇu in the form of Keśava, is aligned towards the south and consists of a *pañcaratha* plan with a square *garbhagṛha*. The *garbhagṛha* leads to a square *antarāla* which is separated from the common *sabhā-maṇḍapa* by small engaged columns and narrow *jālī*. In addition, there are three small shrines in the *raha-ratha*s of the *vimāna*s (**Figure 65**). The eastern and western *vimāna*s are identical to the northern, main sanctum. The eastern *garbhagṛha* enshrines an image of Sūrya, while the western *vimāna* is dedicated to the Lord Śiva in the form of a Śivaliṅga. The common, three-quarter enclosed *sabhā-maṇḍapa* is walled on the northern, eastern and western sides and open towards the south. It contains sixteen columns arranged in the traditional manner — i.e. four free-standing columns in the centre raised on a square platform, two free-standing columns to the south and ten engaged columns, two of which are quarter, corner columns — which form nine *aṅkana*s. The *sabhā-maṇḍapa* has four deep niches, two each to the east and two to the west. The *mukha-maṇḍapa* is also semi-enclosed, consisting of a pierced wall enclosing four free-standing columns in line with the columns of the *sabhā-maṇḍapa*. To the east is a doorway with a short flight of steps leading to the ground level.

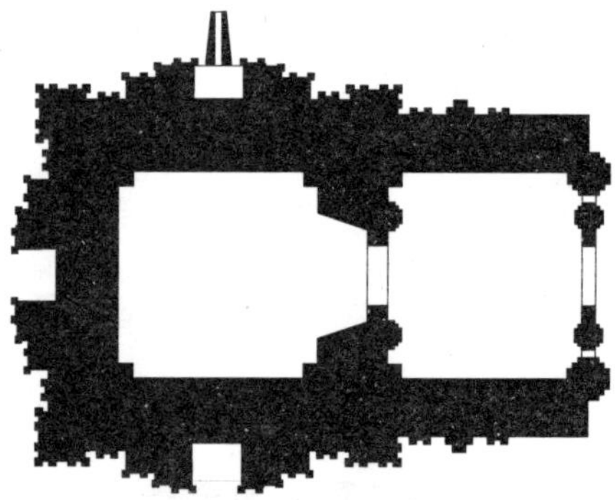

Figure 65: Sūrya-Nārāyaṇa Trikūṭa Temple *vimāna* element

[100] Redrawn using PageMaker 6.0 from KMS II, p. 452, description on pp. 225-27. See also **Preface**.

Plate 85: Sūrya-Nārāyaṇa Trikūṭa Temple plan

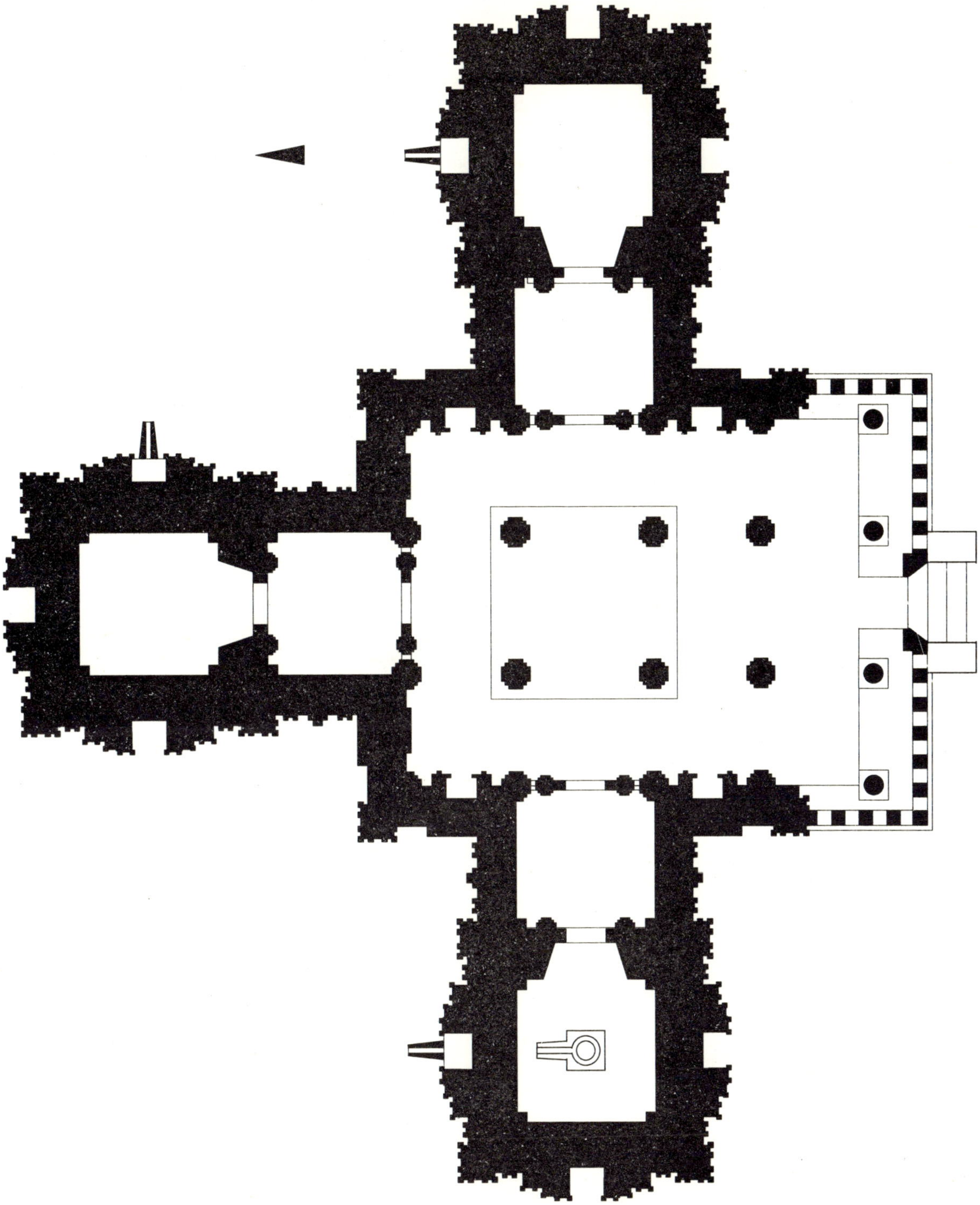

Īśvara Dvikūṭa Temple, Arsikere, Karnataka (*c.* CE 1219)

The reign of the Hoysaḷa king Ballāla II (Vīraballāla) (r. CE 1173–1220), saw the raising of the Īśvara Dvikūṭa Temple[101] at Arsikere. This little known temple exhibits an **A**-type *dvikūṭa* plan (**Figure 2**).

The Īśvara Dvikūṭa Temple consists of two identical *vimāna*s placed side by side towards the west (**Figure 66**). They are made up of square *garbhagṛha*s each with Śivaliṅga, and attached square *antarāla*s. The *antarāla*s open directly onto a common *sabhā-maṇḍapa*. The *sabhā-maṇḍapa* is rectangular, enclosed along its western side and open to the north, south and east. Thirty-two columns support the roof — i.e. twenty-four free-standing columns and eight engaged to the western wall. Either of the *vimāna* and half of the columns in the *sabhā-maṇḍapa* may be seen to make up a traditional arrangement of sanctum and sixteen columns (**Figure 67**). The eastern rank of columns of the *sabhā-maṇḍapa* may be seen to also be part of the two *mukha-maṇḍapa*s — i.e. one towards the north and one towards the south. These entrances to the Īśvara Dvikūṭa Temple consist of two short flights of steps leading up to the level of the *sabhā-maṇḍapa*.

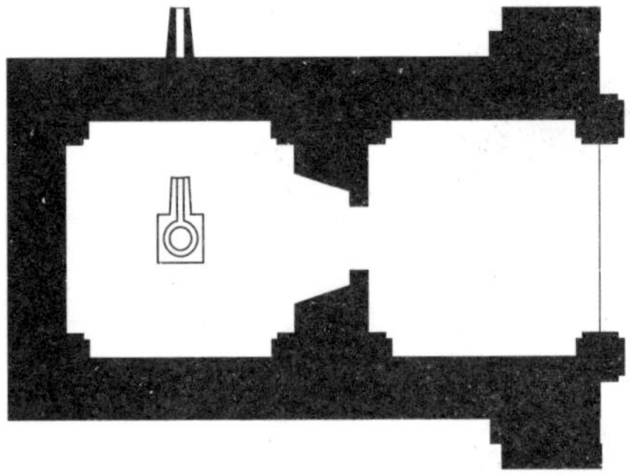

Figure 66: Īśvara Dvikūṭa Temple *vimāna* element

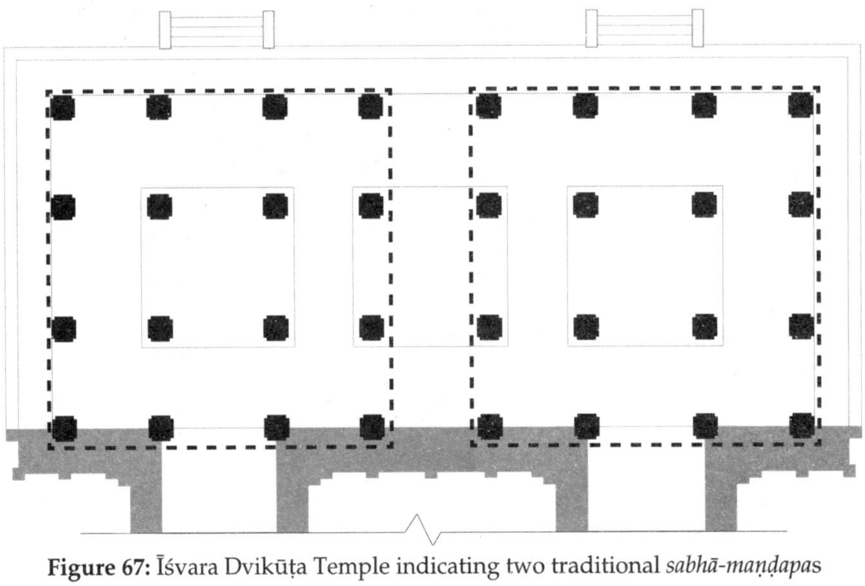

Figure 67: Īśvara Dvikūṭa Temple indicating two traditional *sabhā-maṇḍapa*s

101 Redrawn using PageMaker 6.0 from KMS II, p. 433, description on pp. 205-06. See also **Preface**.

Plate 86: Īśvara Dvikūṭa Temple plan

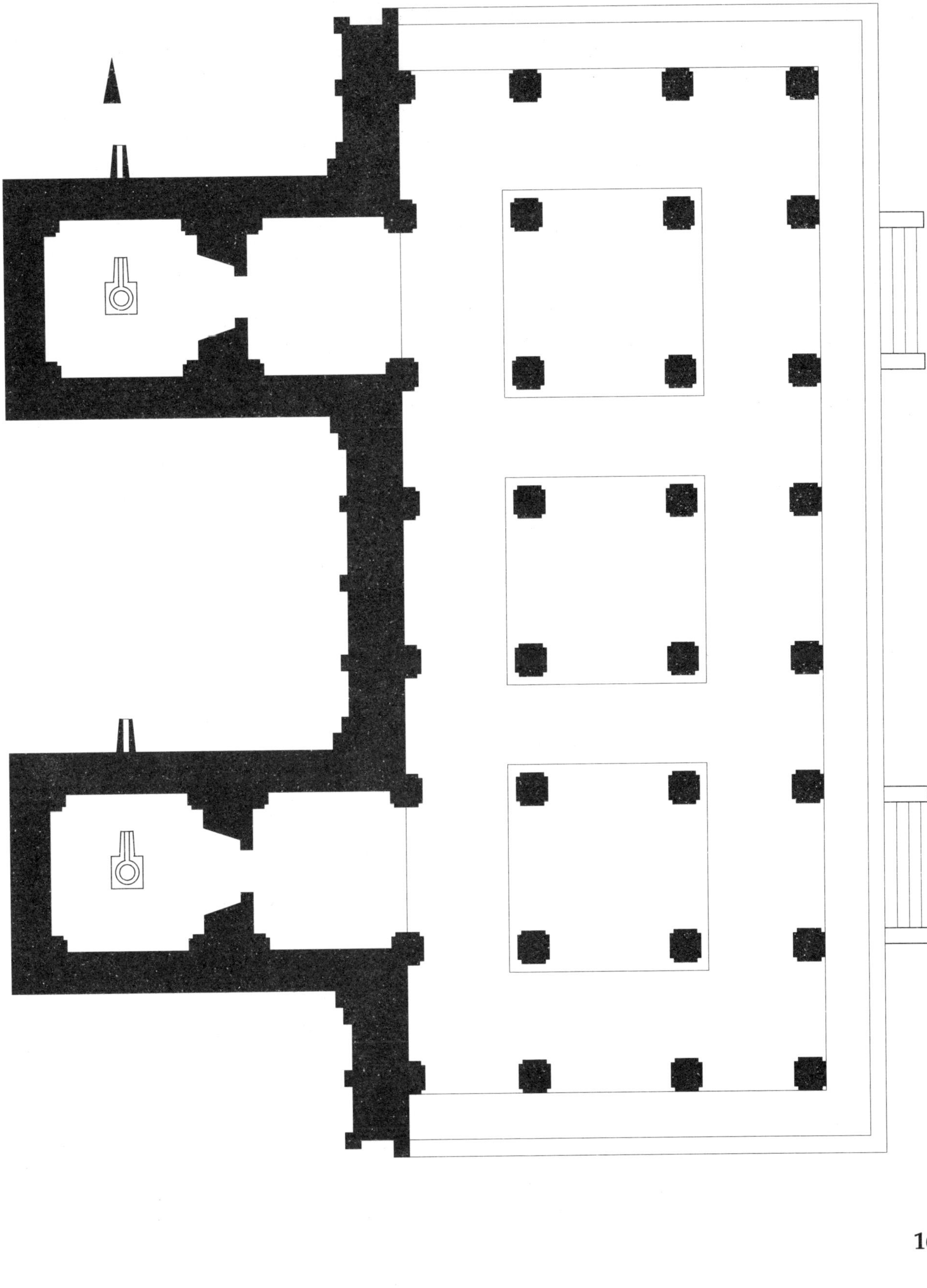

Lakṣmī-Narasiṁha Trikūṭa Temple, Bhadravatī, Karnataka (a. CE 1225)

Dedicated to the Vaiṣṇava deity, the Lord Viṣṇu with his consort Lakṣmī on his lap — i.e. Lakṣmī-Narasiṁha — the Lakṣmī-Narasiṁha Trikūṭa Temple[102] ranks just below the famed Keśava Trikūṭa Temple, of Somnāthpur, in the development of its plan. Like the Somnathpur monument, this temple exhibits an **A**-type *trikūṭa* plan.

The Lakṣmī-Narasiṁha Trikūṭa Temple is made up of the principle western *vimāna* which enshrines an image of Lakṣmī-Narasiṁha. The layout of the outer wall of the *garbhagṛha* is stellar, *en plan* — i.e. consisting of a sixteen-point star (**Plate 88**). The northern sanctum, dedicated to Lord Viṣṇu as Puruṣottama, and southern sanctum which enshrines Veṇugopāla are, likewise, stellar, *en plan*, however with a slight variation (**Plate 89**) in the stellate form. However, the three *garbhagṛhas* are square and appended to square *antarāla* which are attached to a common, square *sabhā-maṇḍapa*. The *sabhā-maṇḍapa* is enclosed and the exterior walls present a complicated surface. On either side of the entrance into the principle *vimāna* are two deep niches. The *sabhā-maṇḍapa* is supported by sixteen pillars in the traditional arrangement — i.e. four free-standing columns in the centre raised on a square platform and twelve engaged columns, four of which are quarter, corner columns — which form nine *aṅkanas*. A wide passageway, the width of the intercolumnar space, leads from the *sabhā-maṇḍapa* to a small, square, enclosed space, a *gūḍha-maṇḍapa*. Both the *sabhā-maṇḍapa* and the *gūḍha-maṇḍapa* are without windows creating an extremely dark interior. From this space a doorway leads to the open *mukha-maṇḍapa* with two free-standing columns on its easternmost side.

[102] Redrawn using PageMaker 6.0 from KMS II, p. 466, description on pp. 255-56. See also **Preface**.

Plate 87: Lakṣmī-Narasiṁha Trikūṭa Temple plan

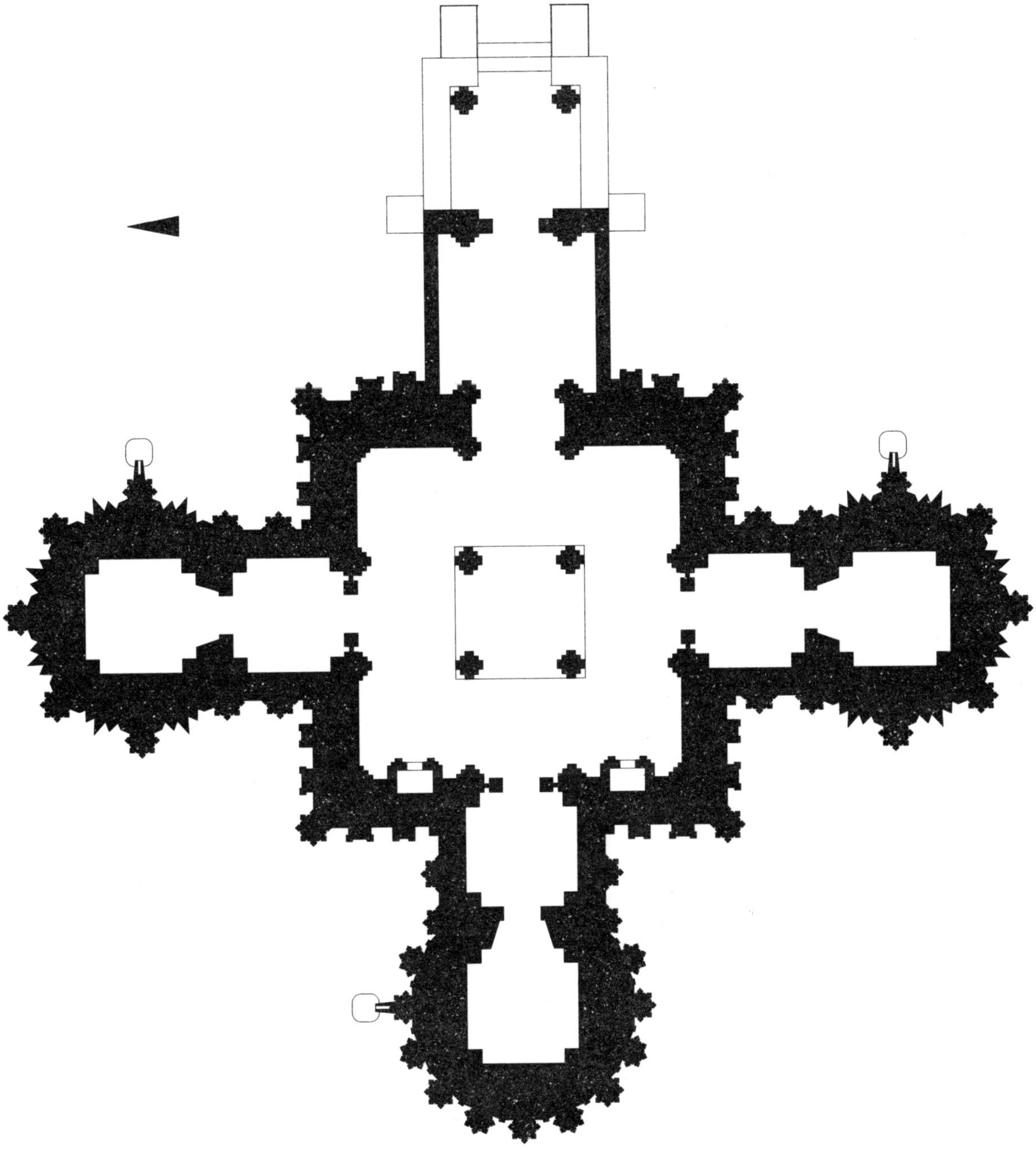

Plate 88: Lakṣmī-Narasiṁha Trikūṭa Temple western *vimāna* with a sixteen-point star

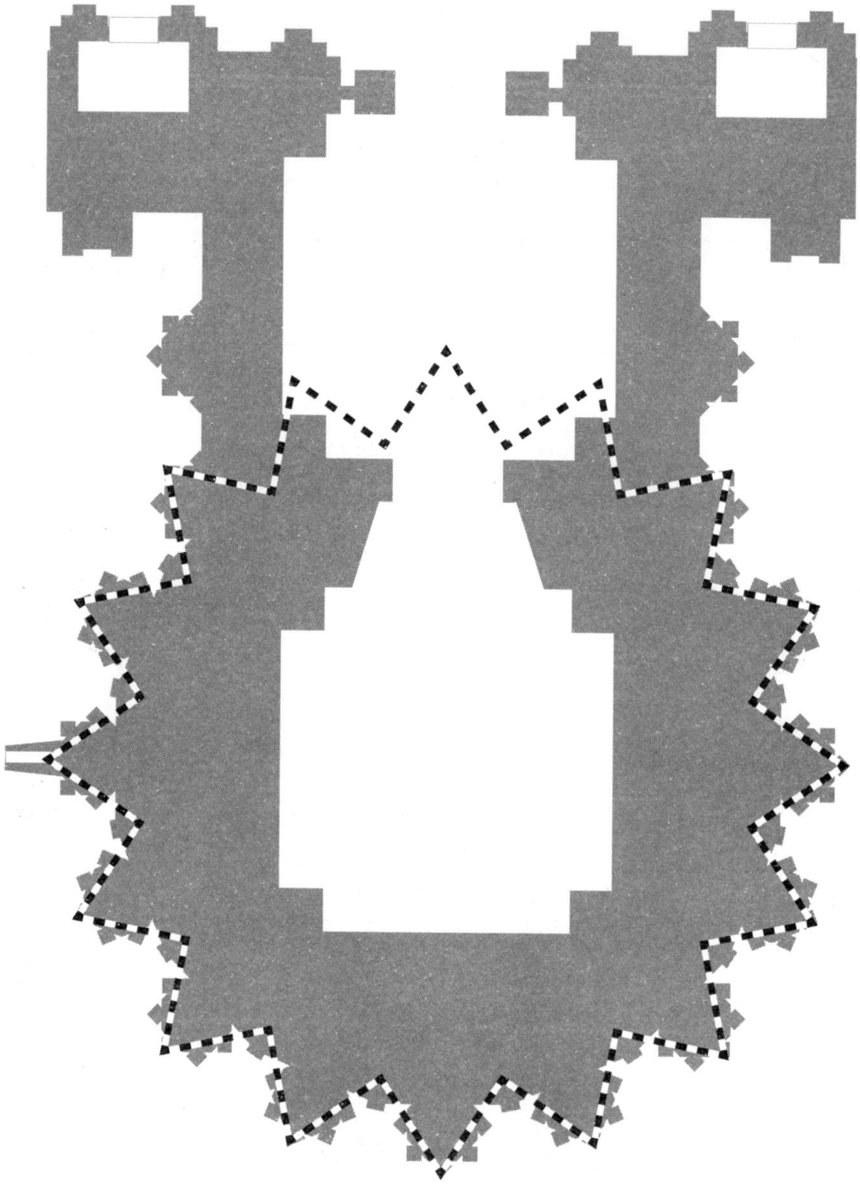

Plate 89: Lakṣmī-Narasiṁha Trikūṭa Temple northern and southern *vimānas'* element with a sixteen-point star

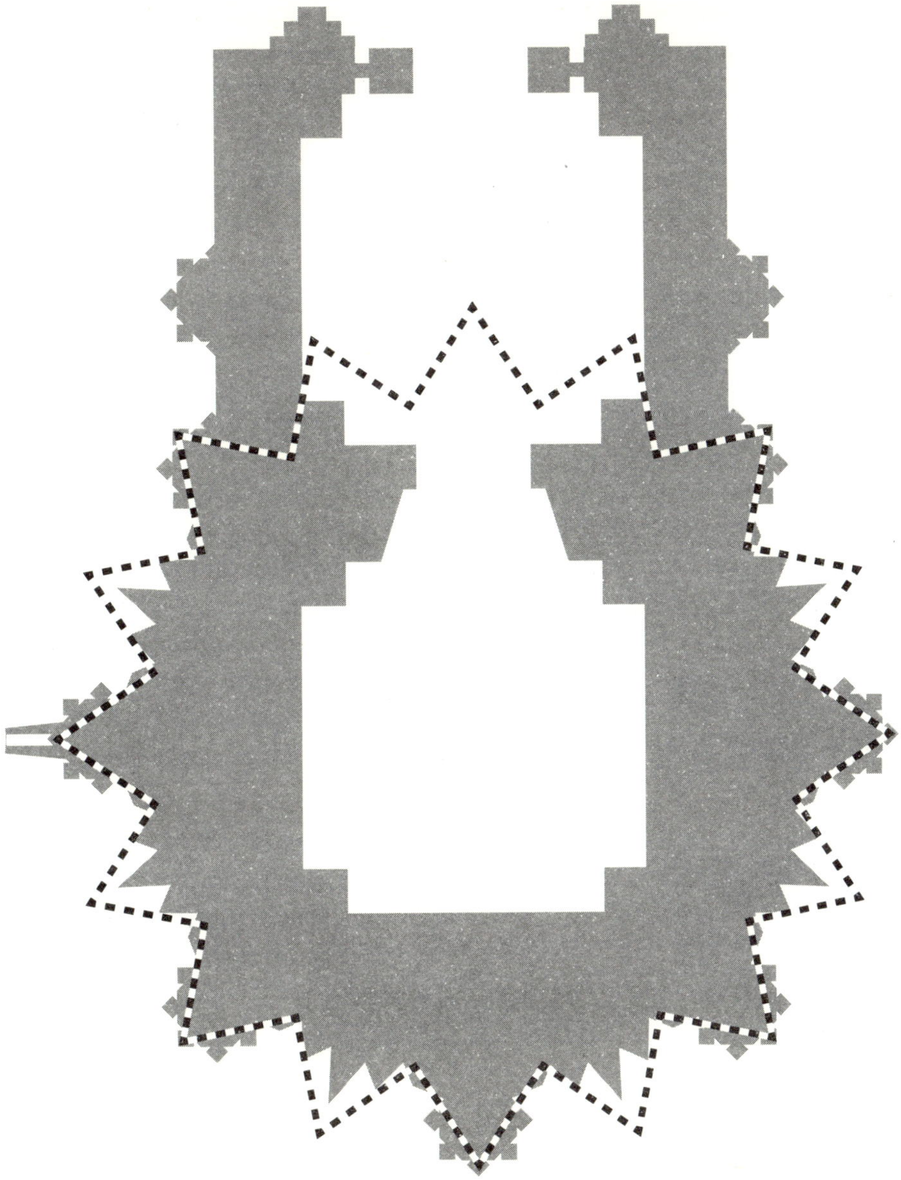

Pañcaliṅgeśvara Pañcakūṭa Temple, Govindanahaḷḷi, Karnataka (*c*. CE 1230)

The Pañcaliṅgeśvara Pañcakūṭa Temple[103] at Govindanahaḷḷi, is a **C**-type *pañcakūṭa* plan (**Figure 5**). It was constructed during the co-reigns of the Hoysaḷa monarchs, Narasiṁha II (r. CE 1220-38) with Someśvara (r. CE 1233-67).

The temple is made up of five identical *vimānas* set side by side, north to south and facing east (**Figure 68**). Each of the *vimānas* is *pañcaratha* with square *garbhagṛha* and all *vimānas* hold a Śivaliṅga. To the east of the *garbhagṛhas* are square *antarālas* which open onto a common, rectangular *sabhā-maṇḍapa*. However, there is an anomaly in the spacing of these five *vimānas* and *sabhā-maṇḍapa* — i.e. the northern two elements are spaced closer together giving the whole an unbalanced appearance. The *sabhā-maṇḍapa* is enclosed on the north, south and west, and open on the east side. It holds eighty columns, sixteen in front of each *vimāna* in the traditional arrangement (**Figure 68**) — i.e. four free-standing columns in the centre raised on a square platform surrounded by eight free-standing columns and four engaged columns; or at the ends there are four free-standing columns in the centre raised on a square platform with five free-standing columns and seven engaged. Added to the eighty columns of the *sabhā-maṇḍapa*, there are an additional twenty columns just to the east of the eighty. These twenty act as part of the façade of the Pañcaliṅgeśvara Pañcakūṭa Temple and contain *jalandhara* between each of them to allow a small amount of light and some breeze into the interior. In front of the third and fourth *vimānas* — i.e. from the north — are *mukha-maṇḍapas* which consist of a platform with four free-standing and two engaged columns each. To the north and to the south of each of the two *mukha-maṇḍapas* are flights of stairs that lead down to ground level (**Figure 69**).

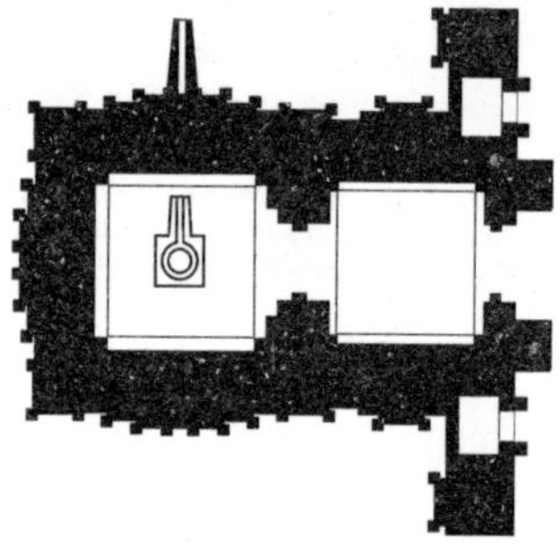

Figure 68: Pañcaliṅgeśvara Pañcakūṭa Temple *vimāna* element

The application of a *paramaśāyika maṇḍala* is seen to conform to both the *garbhagṛha* and the *sabhā-maṇḍapa* (**Plate 91**). A grid, based upon an *āsana maṇḍala* seems most applicable to the whole (**Plate 92**).

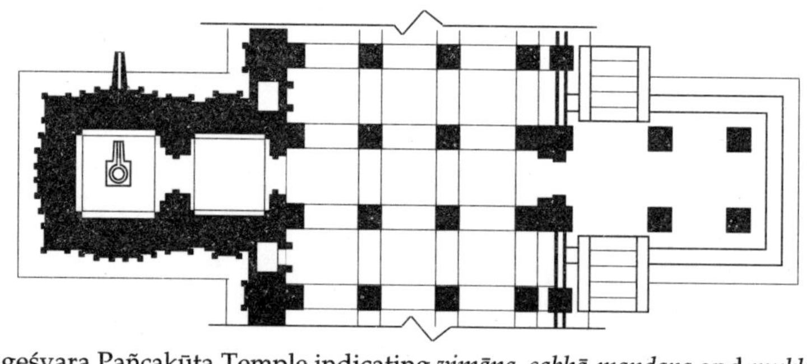

Figure 69: Pañcaliṅgeśvara Pañcakūṭa Temple indicating *vimāna*, *sabhā-maṇḍapa* and *mukha-maṇḍapa* elements

103 Redrawn using PageMaker 6.0 from KMS II, on p. 488, description on pp. 277-78. See also **Preface**.

Plate 90: Pañcaliṅgeśvara Pañcakūṭa Temple plan

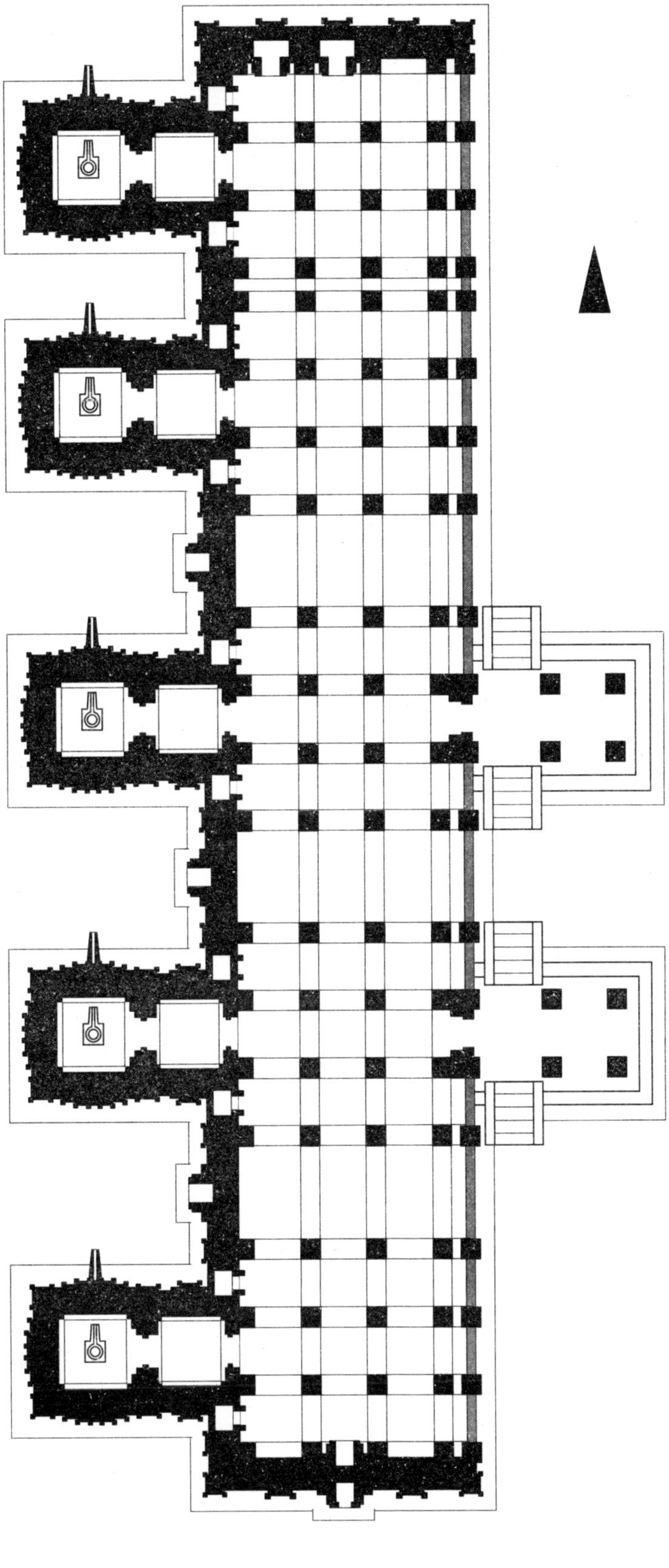

Plate 91: Pañcaliṅgeśvara Pañcakūṭa Temple with *paramaśāyika maṇḍala* over *garbhagṛha* and *sabhā-maṇḍapa*

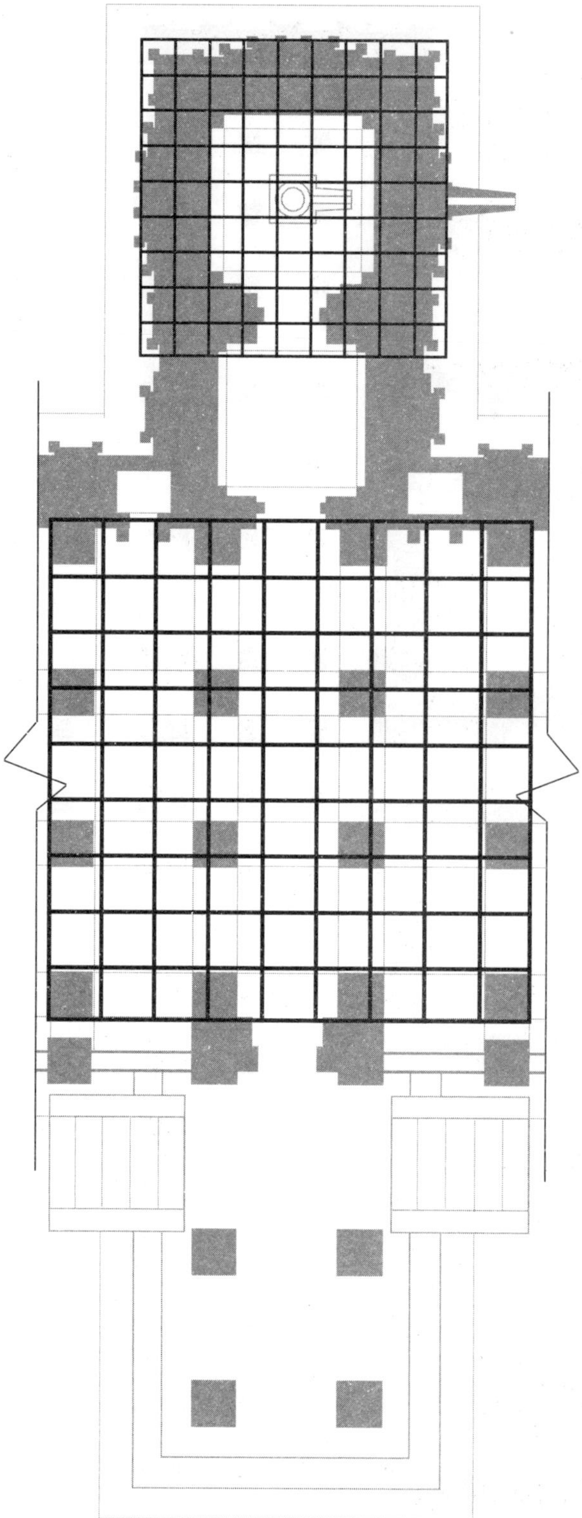

Plate 92: Pañcaliṅgeśvara Pañcakūṭa Temple with grid based on *āsana maṇḍala*

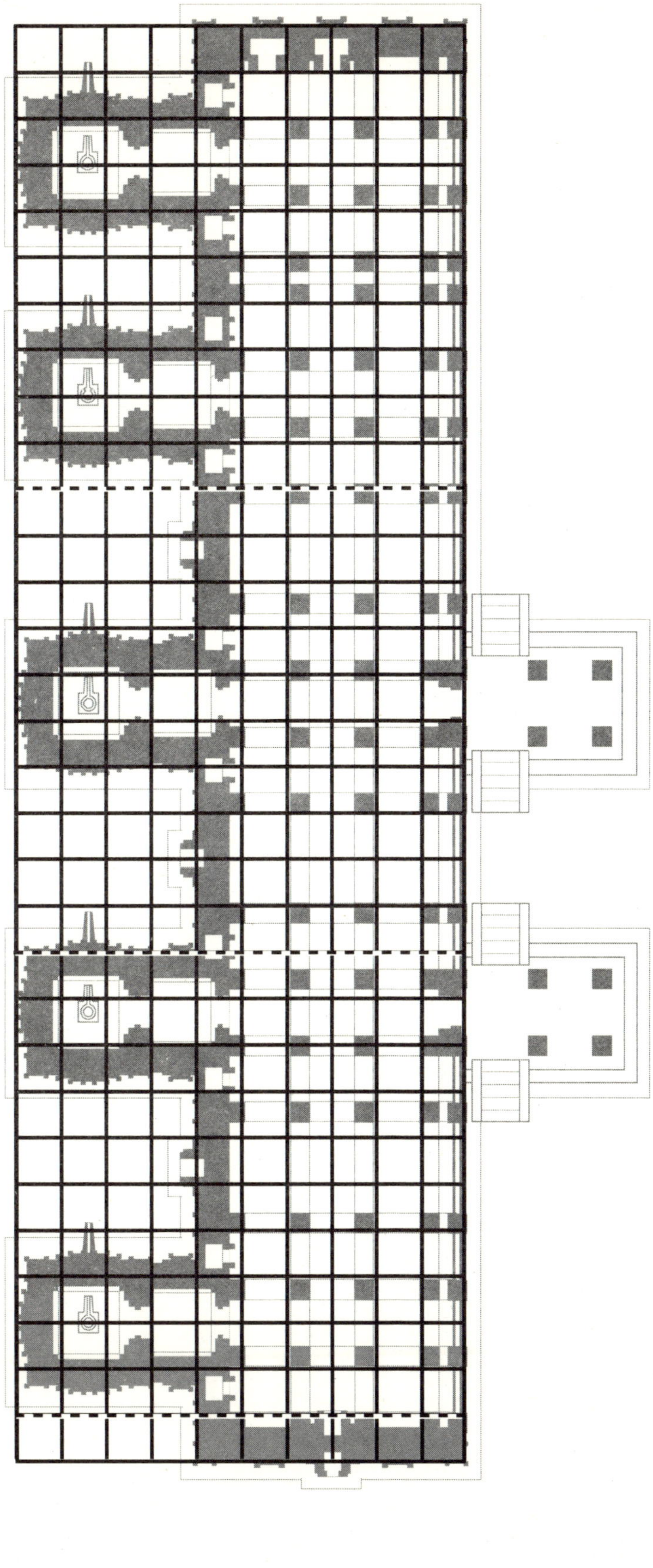

Mallikārjuna Trikūṭa Temple, Basaralu, Karnataka (CE 1234)

Unlike the Mallikārjuna Trikūṭa Temple of Devaranavadagi (**Plate 61**) which finds the monument, *en toto*, dedicated to Lord Śiva, the Mallikārjuna Trikūṭa Temple[104] at Basaralu is dedicated to Lord Śiva in the form of a Śivaliṅga, the Lord Viṣṇu in the form of Keśava and the deity Sūrya. It was conceived and constructed during the reigns of the Hoysaḷa king Narasiṁha II (r. CE 1220-38) who co-reigned with King Someśvara (r. CE 1233-67). The Mallikārjuna Trikūṭa Temple is an **A**-type *trikūṭa* plan (**Figure 3**).

The temple consists of a principle, square *garbhagr̥ha* facing east holding a Śivaliṅga and attached to a square *antarāla*. The *antarāla* opens via a narrow door onto the common *sabhā-maṇḍapa*. Two other *garbhagr̥has*, one to the north dedicated to Keśava and the southern *garbhagr̥ha* assigned to Sūrya, are both without *antarāla* and are virtually identical (**Figure 69**). The square *sabhā-maṇḍapa* is open just beyond the northern and southern *vimānas*. It consists of the traditional sixteen columns — i.e. four free-standing columns in the centre raised on a square platform, four free-standing to the east and eight engaged columns, two of which are quarter, corner columns — which form nine *aṅkanas*. In the north-west and south-west corners of the *mukha-maṇḍapa* are four shrines — i.e. two each in the corners (**Figure 70**). The *mukha-maṇḍapa* extends eastward and is composed of four free-standing columns, two of which are shared with those of the *sabhā-maṇḍapa*. A short distance from the doorway into the *mukha-maṇḍapa* are four free-standing columns supporting the roof of the *nandī-maṇḍapa*. Between the *mukha-maṇḍapa* and the *nandī-maṇḍapa* of the Mallikārjuna Trikūṭa Temple are two staircases, one leading towards the north and the other towards the south. They descend to a wide terrace surrounding the whole which serves as an external *pradakṣiṇāpatha*.

The application of a *maṇḍala* to the Mallikārjuna Trikūṭa Temple presents some problems. The placing of a *paramaśāyika maṇḍala* over the temple and centred on the *sabhā-maṇḍapa* does present certain interesting conjunctions (**Plate 94**). But, it does not include all the temple — i.e. a portion of the *nandī-maṇḍapa* is outside the *padas*. Similarly the application of a *vāstu-puruṣa maṇḍala* also creates certain problems (**Plate 95**).

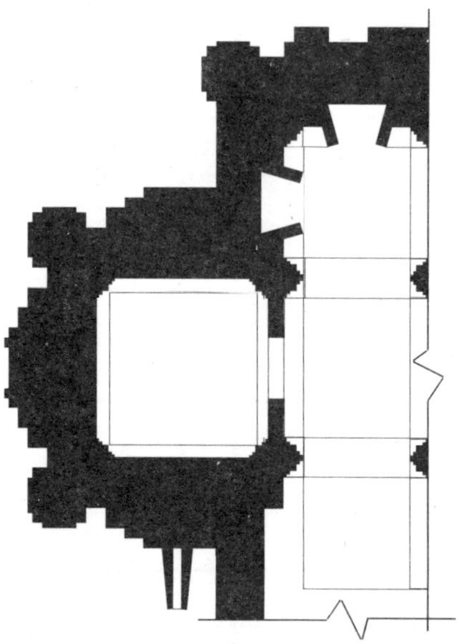

Figure 70: Mallikārjuna Trikūṭa Temple northern and southern *vimāna* elements and corner shrines

[104] Redrawn using PageMaker 6.0 from KMS II, p. 460, description on pp. 239-41. See also **Preface**.

Plate 93: Mallikārjuna Trikūṭa Temple plan

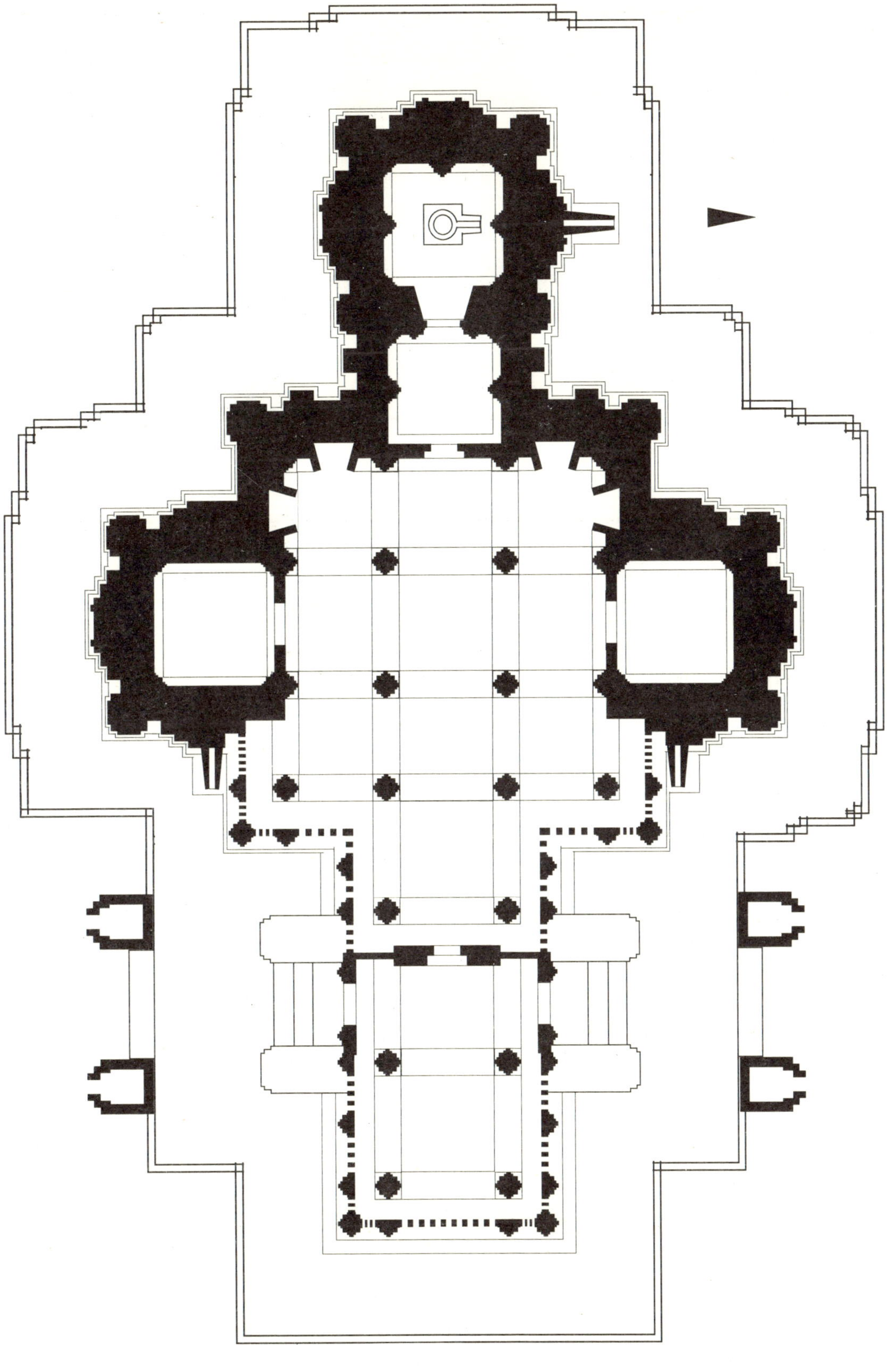

Plate 94: Mallikārjuna Trikūṭa Temple with *paramaśāyika maṇḍala*

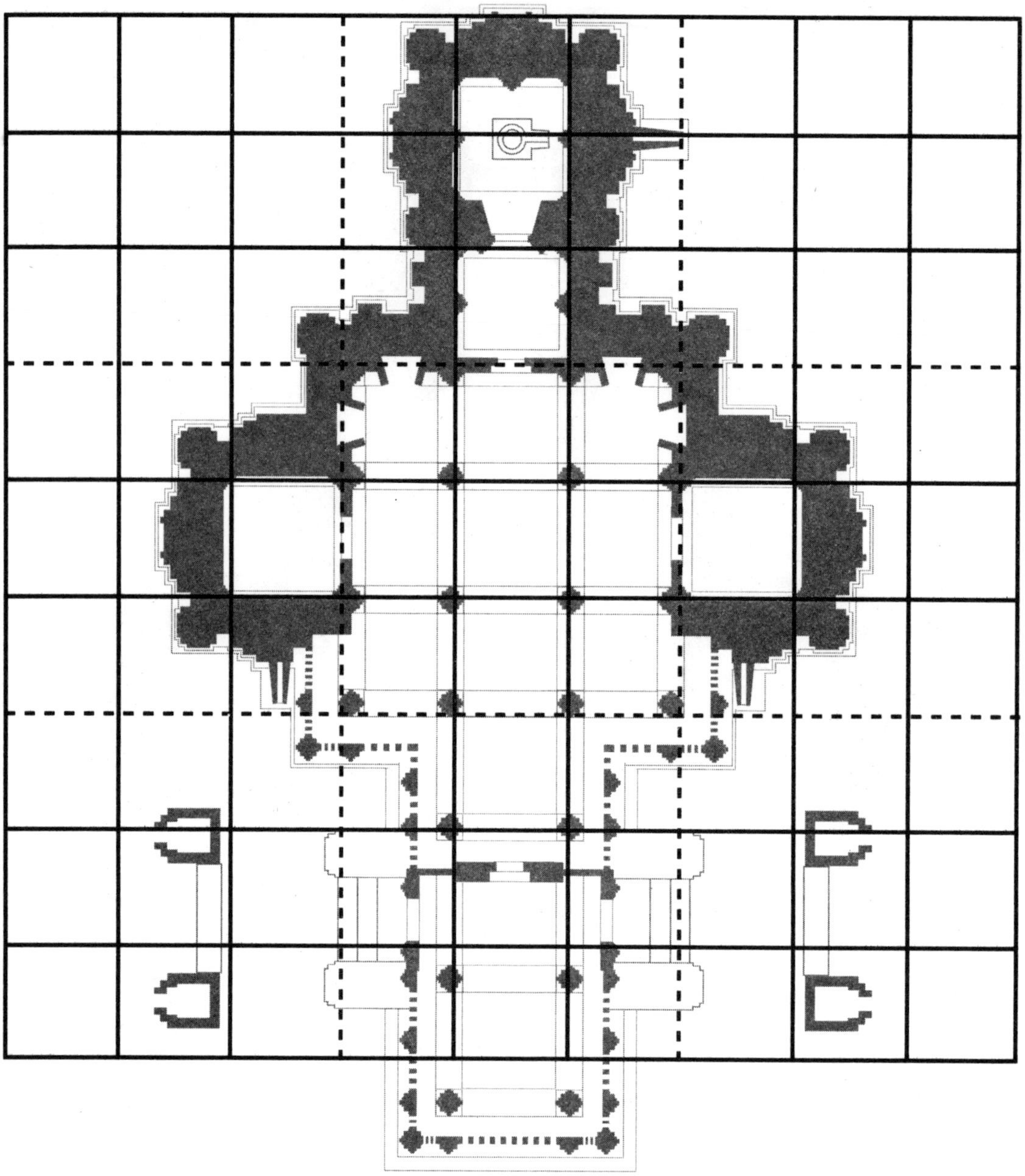

Plate 95: Mallikārjuna Trikūṭa Temple with circular *vāstu-puruṣa maṇḍala*

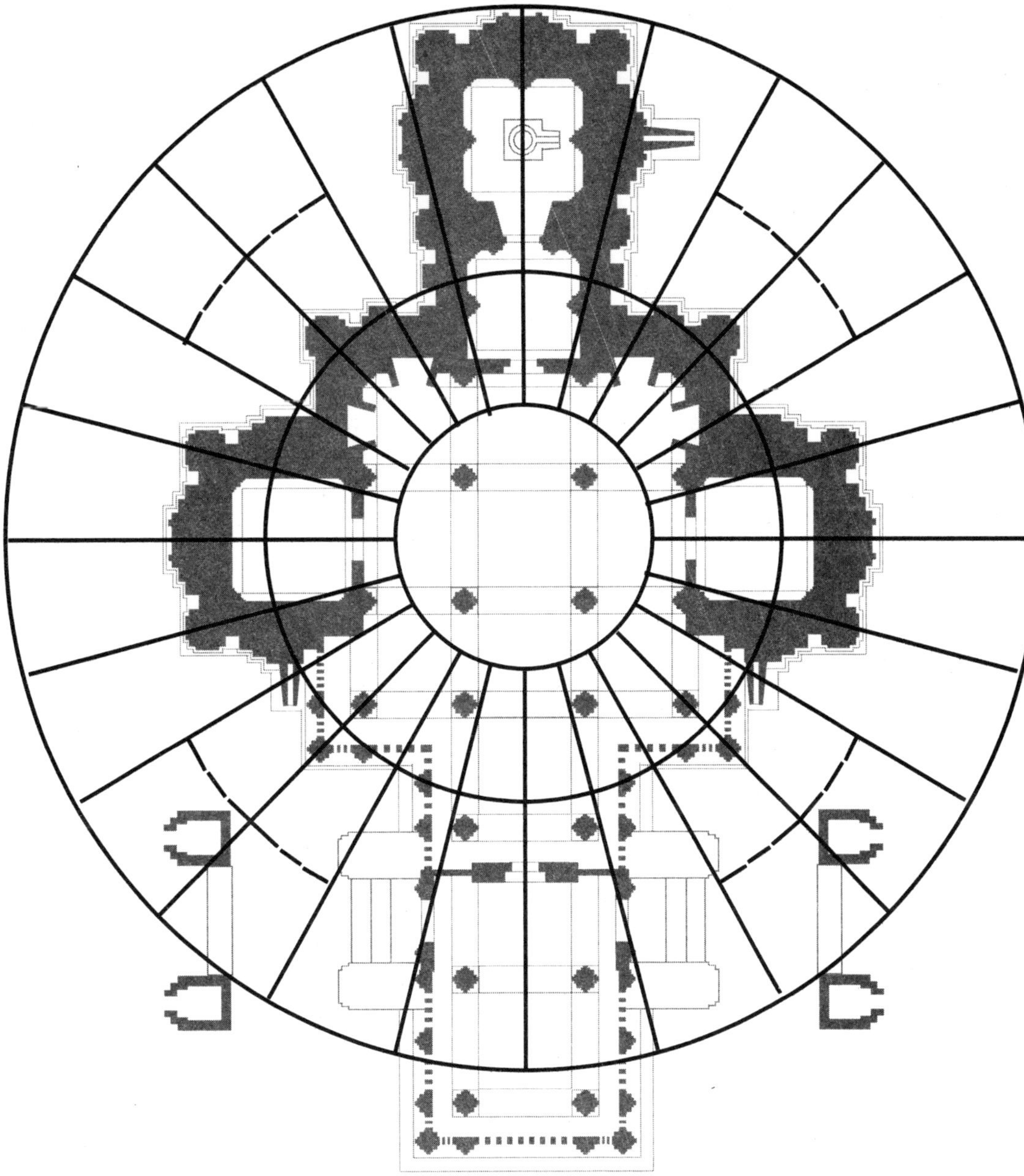

Sūrya Temple, Koṇārka, Orissa (CE 1240)

Constructed during the reign of the Gaṅga monarch, King Narasiṁhadeva I (r. CE 1238-64) (**Appendix D**), the Sūrya Temple[105] at Koṇārka is one of the most famous Hindu temples in India. Although, it generally considered to have been an *ekakūṭa* plan, there are elements which seem to indicate other considerations. Certainly, it was one of the most colossal temples — i.e. the *jagamohana* is one of the largest unencumbered spaces in the history of Hindu temple architecture.

Off the central element, over which the towering *śikhara* stood, are three attached elements. Normally they are shown, *en plan*, as solid forms. However, there are those who see it differently. This "variation" is indicated in **Plate 96**. Although, there has never been a concerted assertion that these three planal forms were shrines, there is a question of their *raison d'être*. It is quite probable that these three elements were, indeed, shrines and may have been connected with the interior of the *vimāna*/ sanctum. The supposition that these may have been solid decorative forms is untenable, unless, however, they were constructed as buttress elements for the soaring, nearly 68 m high, *śikhara*. But if that were the case — i.e. buttresses for the *śikhara* — they would have had to be more closely linked to perform their task.

[105] Redrawn using PageMaker 6.0 from HS II, p. 123; the Internet site www.art-and-archaeology.com/India/konarak/konarakplan.jpg which presented a plan with the three elements off the main, ruined section, attributed to *Monuments of India*, vol. 1.

Plate 96: Sūrya Temple plan

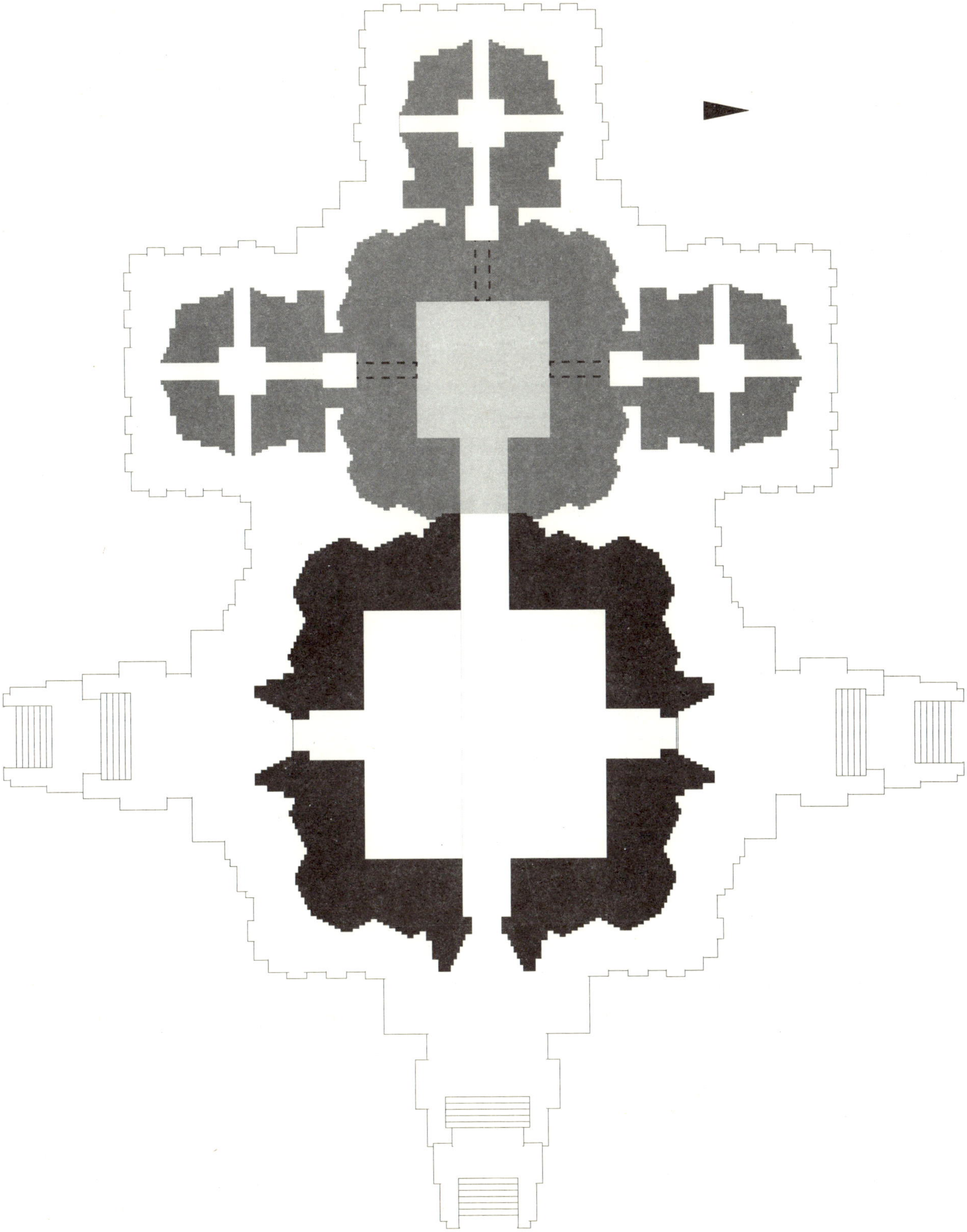

Keśava Trikūṭa Temple, Somanāthapur, Karnataka (*c.* CE 1268)

"The plan of the Keśava Temple may be said to mark a consummation of the development of medieval Indian architecture."[106] Conceived and constructed by the Hoysaḷa general Somanātha during the reign of the King Narasiṁha III (r. CE 1254-92), the Keśava Trikūṭa Temple[107] at Somanāthapur is one of the more famous temple complexes in India. Raised at a time when the Hoysaḷa kingdom was in a ṣtate of flux, between the zenith of the kingdom under King Ballāla II (Vīraballāla) (r. CE 1173–1220) and the politically expedient Suzerainty to the Delhi sultanate by the last great monarch, King Ballāla III (r. CE 1291–1342), the temple presents the grand coda of the great temple complexes of the Hoysaḷas. The Keśava Trikūṭa Temple is an **A**-type *trikūṭa* plan (**Figure 3**).

This intricate, axial complex is made up of an elaborate entrance gate in the east, a girdle wall (*prākāra*) against which are situated sixty-four shrines and a colonnaded court. From the level of the colonnaded court four stairways lead down to the courtyard — i.e. one on an axis with the main entrance, one centred in the north with a corresponding one centred in the south, and a set of stairs found between the fourth and fifth columns from the south in the western colonnade. Within this court rests the temple proper. The Keśava Trikūṭa Temple consists of three identical *vimāna*s (**Figure 71**). The western *garbhagṛha* is dedicated to the Lord Viṣṇu as Nārāyaṇa with Lakṣmī on his knee — i.e. Lakṣmī-Nārāyaṇa; the southern sanctum holds Lord Viṣṇu as Veṇugopāla; and the northern *garbhagṛha* enshrines the Lord Viṣṇu as Janārdana. The square *garbhagṛha*s are surrounded by a stellate wall based upon a sixteen-point star (**Figure 72**). The *garbhagṛha*s are attached to square *antarāla*s each of which opens onto a common *sabhā-maṇḍapa*. The *sabhā-maṇḍapa* is enclosed in its western precincts while that part beyond the northern and southern *vimāna*s is enclosed with columns and *jalandhara*. Thirty-six columns support the roof of the *sabhā-maṇḍapa*, of those sixteen are free-standing and twenty are engaged. The *mukha-maṇḍapa*, like the *sabhā-maṇḍapa* is enclosed on three sides by columns and *jalandhara* and a short flight of stairs leads down to a broad platform. This basal platform mimics the shape of the temple, including the stellar *vimāna*s and serves as a broad, exterior *pradakṣiṇāpatha*. In fact, the Keśava Trikūṭa Temple possesses three possible *pradakṣiṇāpatha*s — i.e. (1) that which is within the colonnaded *prākāra*, (2) the lower courtyard separating the *prākāra* from the temple, and (3) the raised platform surrounding the temple.

In the application of a *maṇḍala*, there are several possibilities and all have their points of applicability (**Plates 98-99**). In the use of both the *paramaśāyika* and / or the circular *vāstu-puruṣa maṇḍala*s, they seem to apply to the temple and its elaborate platform more comfortably.

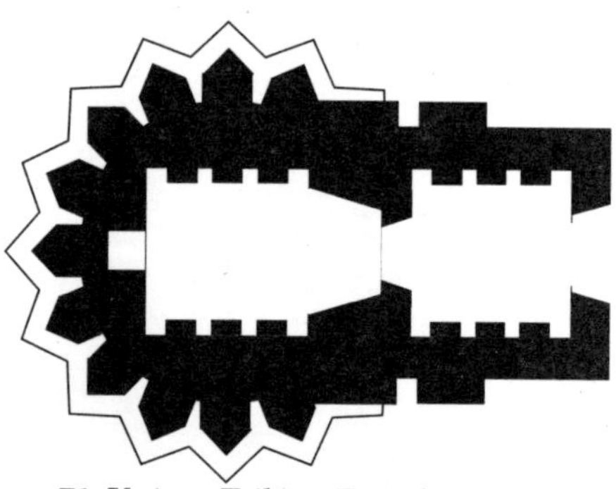

Figure 71: Keśava Trikūṭa Temple *vimāna* element

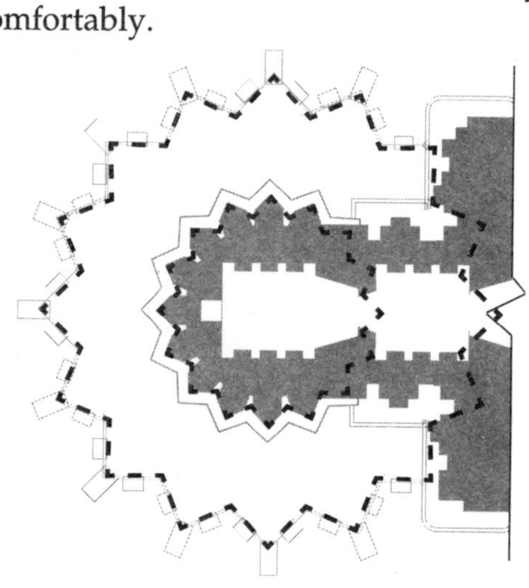

Figure 72: Keśava Trikūṭa Temple with a sixteen-point star

[106] HS II, p. 176.

[107] Redrawn using PageMaker 6.0 from HS II, p. 182.

Plate 97: Keśava Trikūṭa Temple plan

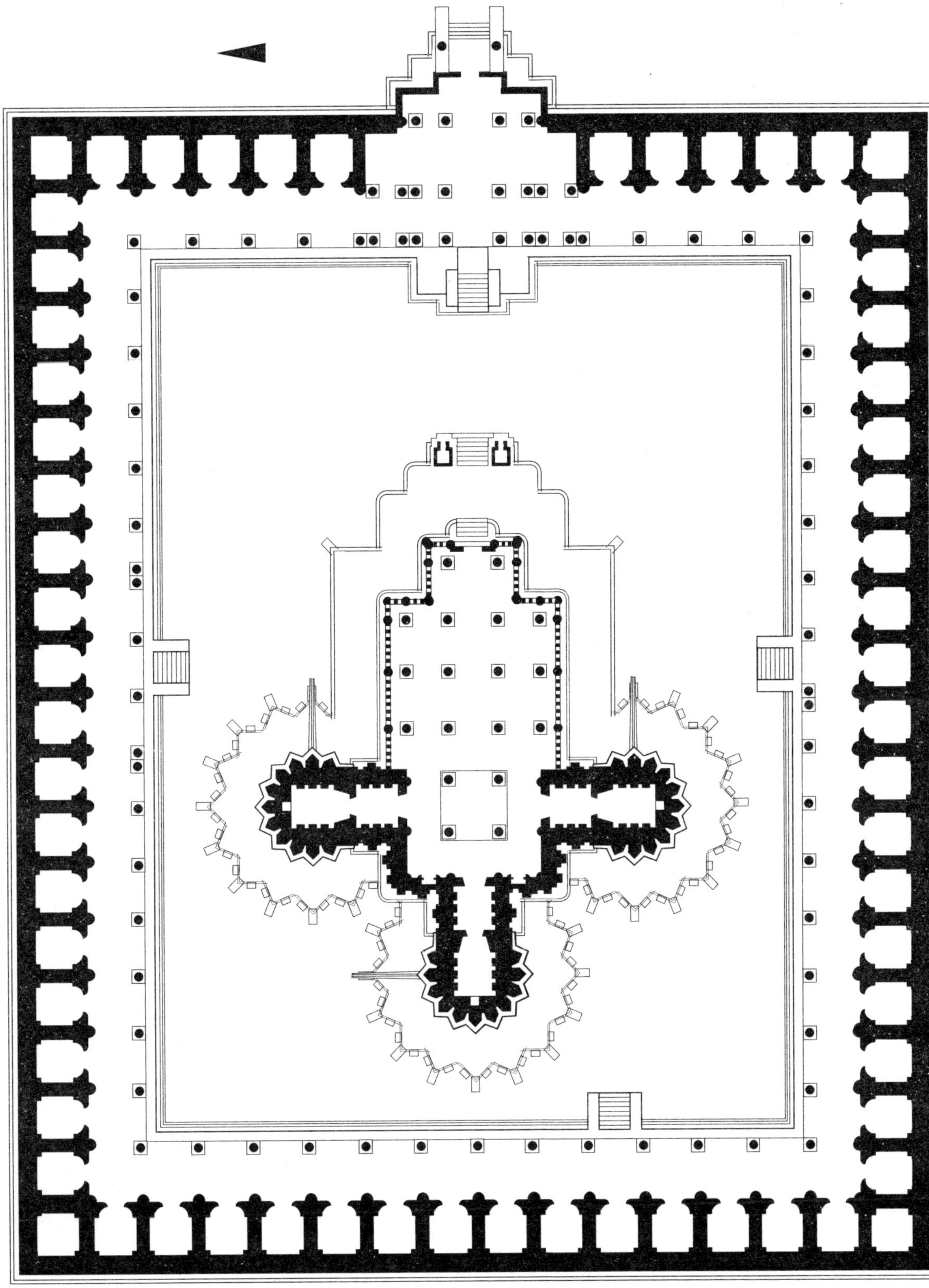

Plate 98: Keśava Trikūṭa Temple detail with *paramaśāyika maṇḍala*

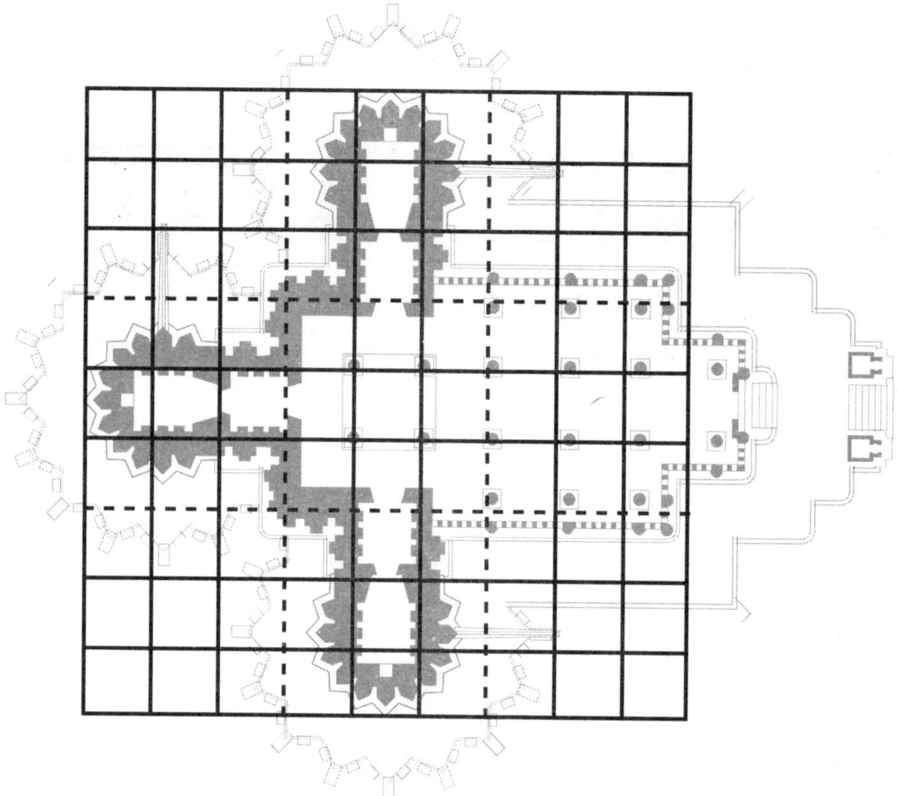

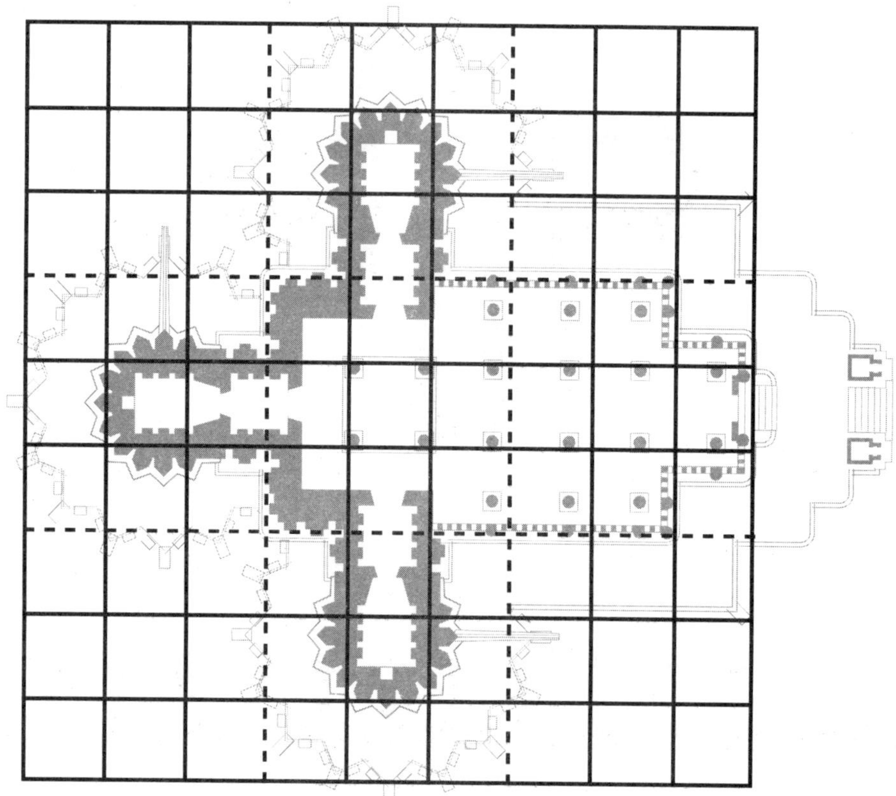

Plate 99: Keśava Trikūṭa Temple detail with circular *vāstu-puruṣa maṇḍala*

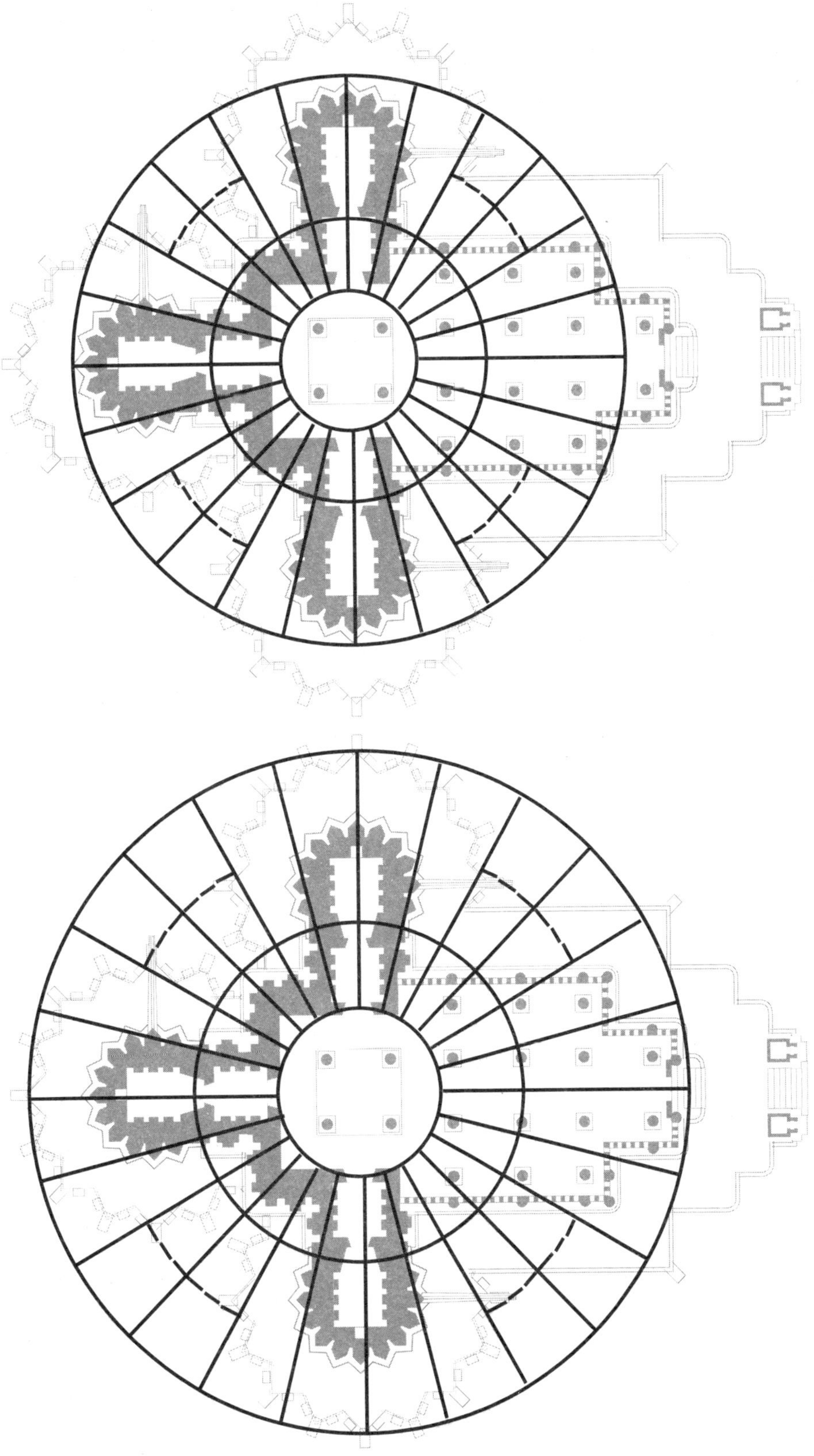

Śaiva Dvikūṭa Temple, Hampī, Karnataka (a. CE 1325)

Between the Virūpākṣa Temple Complex and the Kṛṣṇa Temple Complex in the Sacred Centre of Vijayanagara is found the Hemakūṭa Hill (**Appendix C, Plate 138**). Early in the history surroundings Hampī, this hill was seen as a sacred place and many small temples and shrines were constructed here. The Śaiva Dvikūṭa Temple[108] preceded the brilliant Vijayanagara Empire. The temple may have been connected through Kampilideva (Kampilarasadeva) (r. CE 1300-26), the second and last king of the Kummatadurga or Kampili kingdom, and Harihara I (r. CE 1336-56) the first king of Vijayanagara who was said to have been married to a daughter of the Kampili king. The Śaiva Dvikūṭa Temple is a **D**-type *dvikūṭa* plan (**Figure 2**).

The Śaiva Dvikūṭa Temple consists of two, nearly identical *garbhagṛhas* with square *antarālas* and *sabhā-maṇḍapas* placed side to side. It is apparent that the southern component was constructed first. When the addition of the northern component was achieved is not known. The *antarālas* are square as are the *garbhagṛhas*. The *garbhagṛhas* are nearly identical, however, there is a greater shift, *en plan*, in the *antarālas*. The first, the southern *sabhā-maṇḍapa* contains sixteen columns in the traditional arrangement — i.e. four free-standing columns in the centre raised on a square platform, four free-standing columns in the corners and eight engaged columns — which form nine *aṅkanas*. The northern *sabhā-maṇḍapa* is not square but exhibits twelve free-standing columns and, *en plan*, it seems to be interlocking with the southern *sabhā-maṇḍapa* (**Figure 73**). To the east and the south of the southern *sabhā-maṇḍapa* are two identical *mukha-maṇḍapas* supported by two columns and a short flight of steps that lead down to a broad, irregular terrace which acts as an external *pradakṣiṇāpatha*. The twin *mukha-maṇḍapas* causes one to suspect that a third may have originally existed to the north of the southern *sabhā-maṇḍapa*.

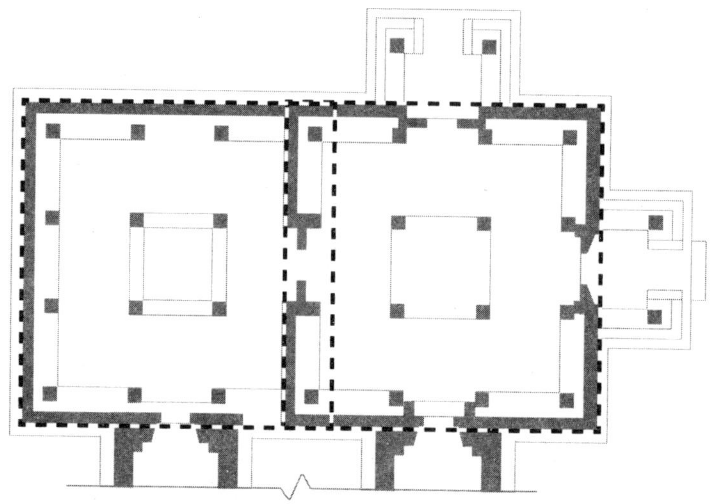

Figure 73: Śaiva Dvikūṭa Temple with indicating interlocking *sabhā-maṇḍapas*

108 Redrawn using PageMaker 6.0 from KMS, p. 142, description on pp. 64-66, and KMS II, p. 436, description on pp. 208-09. See also **Preface**.

Plate 100: Śaiva Dvikūṭa Temple plan

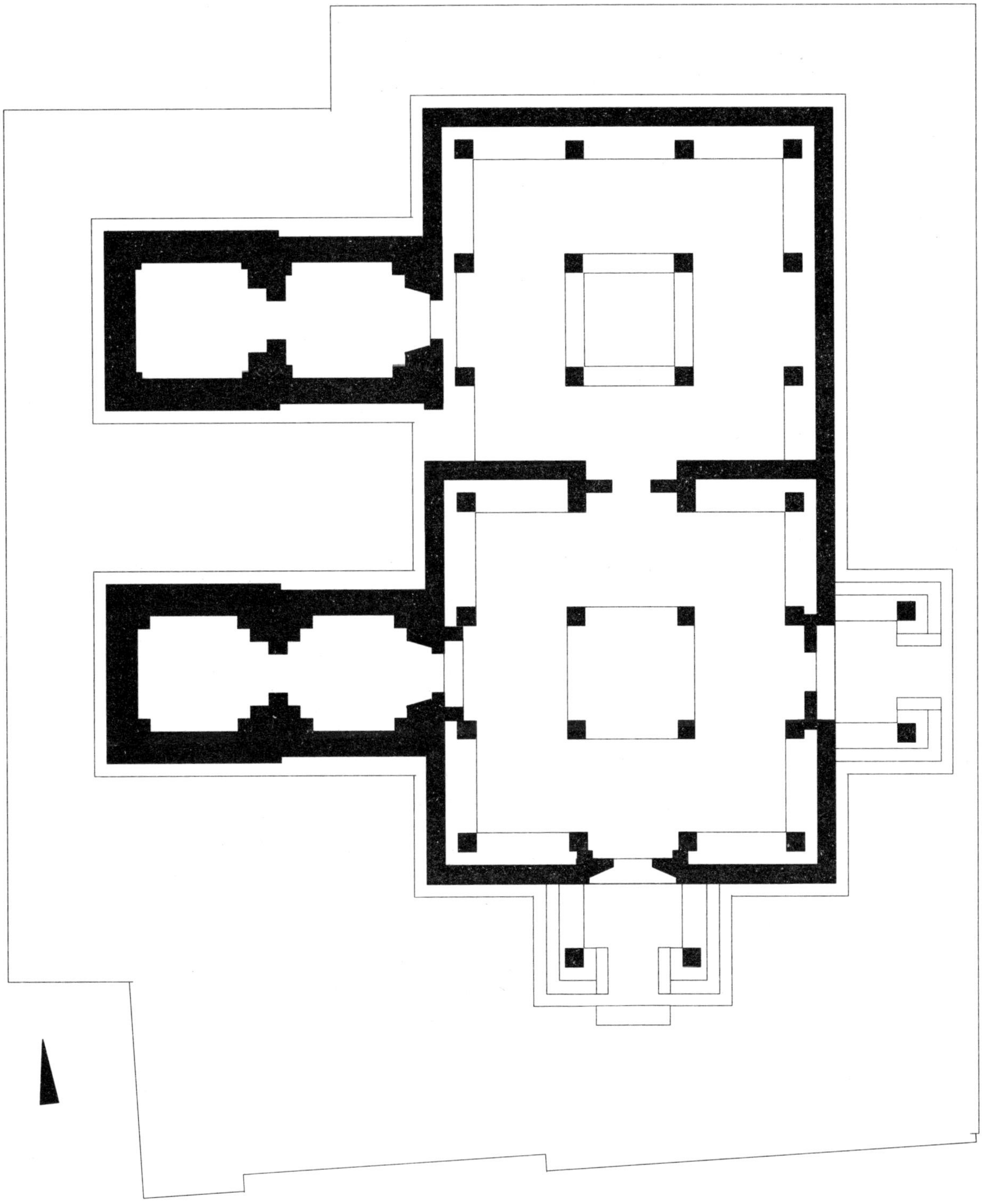

Kampilarāya Trikūṭa Temple (No. 1), Hampī, Karnataka (a. CE 1325)

The Śaiva Kampilarāya Trikūṭa Temple (No. 1)[109] is associated with King Kampilideva (Kampilarasadeva) (r. CE 1300-26), the second and last king of the brief Kummatadurga or Kampili kingdom (**Appendix D**). It, along with a small number of temples/shrines, were constructed on the Hemakūṭa Hill (**Appendix C, Plate 138**) by the short-lived Kummatadurga Dynasty. It is an A-type *trikūṭa* plan (**Figure 2**).

The Kampilarāya Trikūṭa Temple (No. 1) consists of three identical *vimānas*, *en plan* (**Figure 74**). They are made up of square *garbhagṛhas* attached to square *antarālas*, all of which share a common *sabhā-maṇḍapa*. The principle *vimāna* is in the south, facing north and is matched on the east and west by the other two *vimānas*. Six shallow niches are created by the *garbhagṛha* elements in the thick walls of the *sabhā-maṇḍapa*. The common *sabhā-maṇḍapa* is enclosed on three sides and open to the north. It consists of sixteen columns disposed in the usual manner — i.e. four free-standing columns in the centre raised on a square platform, two free-standing columns to the north and ten engaged columns, two of which are quarter, corner columns — which form nine *aṅkanas*. North of the *sabhā-maṇḍapa* is a *mukha-maṇḍapa* with two free-standing columns and sharing two columns of the *sabhā-maṇḍapa*. This plan with one side of the *sabhā-maṇḍapa* open is encountered in the Īśvara Trikūṭa Temple of Basarakoḍu (**Plate 32**), the Basavaṇṇa (Traipuruṣa) Trikūṭa Temple of Malghana (**Plate 33**) and the Sūrya-Nārāyaṇa Trikūṭa Temple at Magala (**Plate 85**), among others.

The application of a *maṇḍala* over the whole presents interesting conjunctions. Either a *paramaśāyika maṇḍala* (**Plate 102**) or a circular *vāstu-puruṣa maṇḍala* (**Plate 103**) seems applicable.

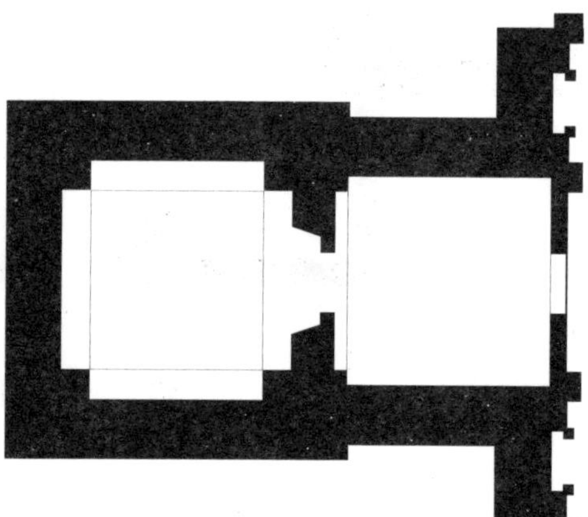

Figure 74: Kampilarāya Trikūṭa Temple (No. 1) *vimāna* element

[109] Redrawn using PageMaker 6.0 from JF, p. 18; KMS, p. 143, description on pp. 66-68; and KMS II, p. 474, description on pp. 262-63. See also **Preface**.

Plate 101: Kampilarāya Trikūṭa Temple (No. 1) plan

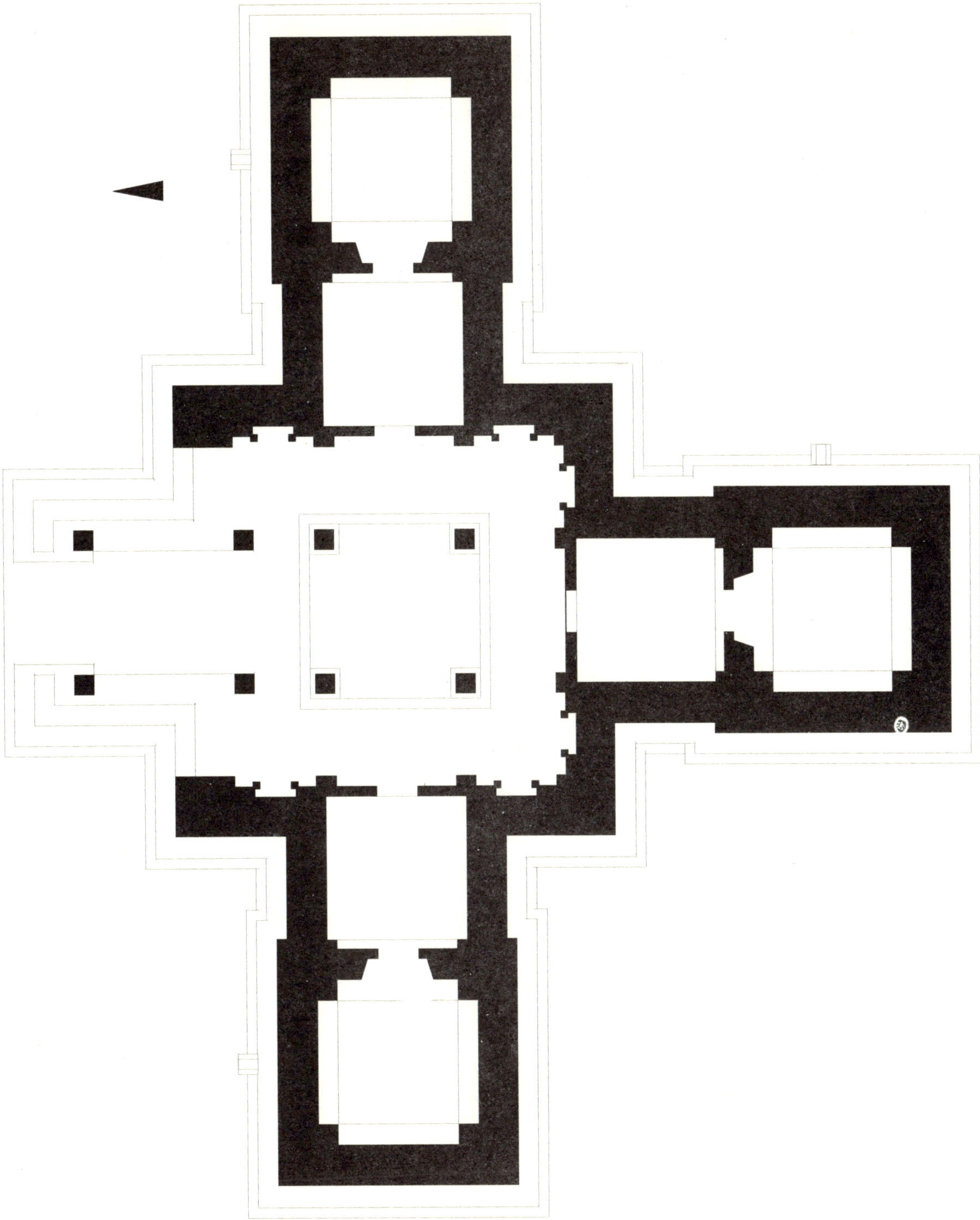

Plate 102: Kampilarāya Trikūṭa Temple (No. 1) with *paramaśāyika maṇḍala*

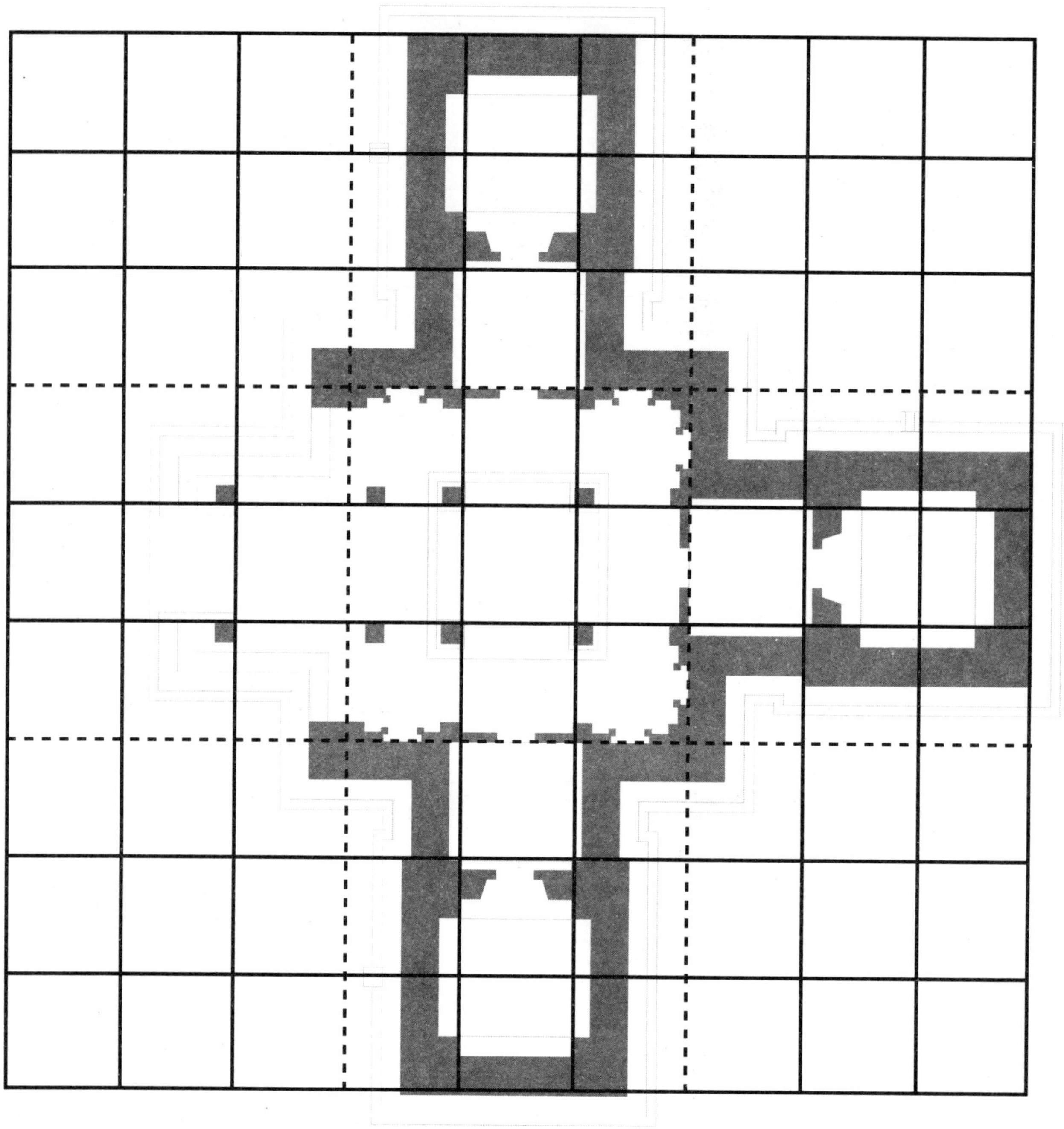

Plate 103: Kampilarāya Trikūṭa Temple (No. 1) with circular *vāstu-puruṣa maṇḍala*

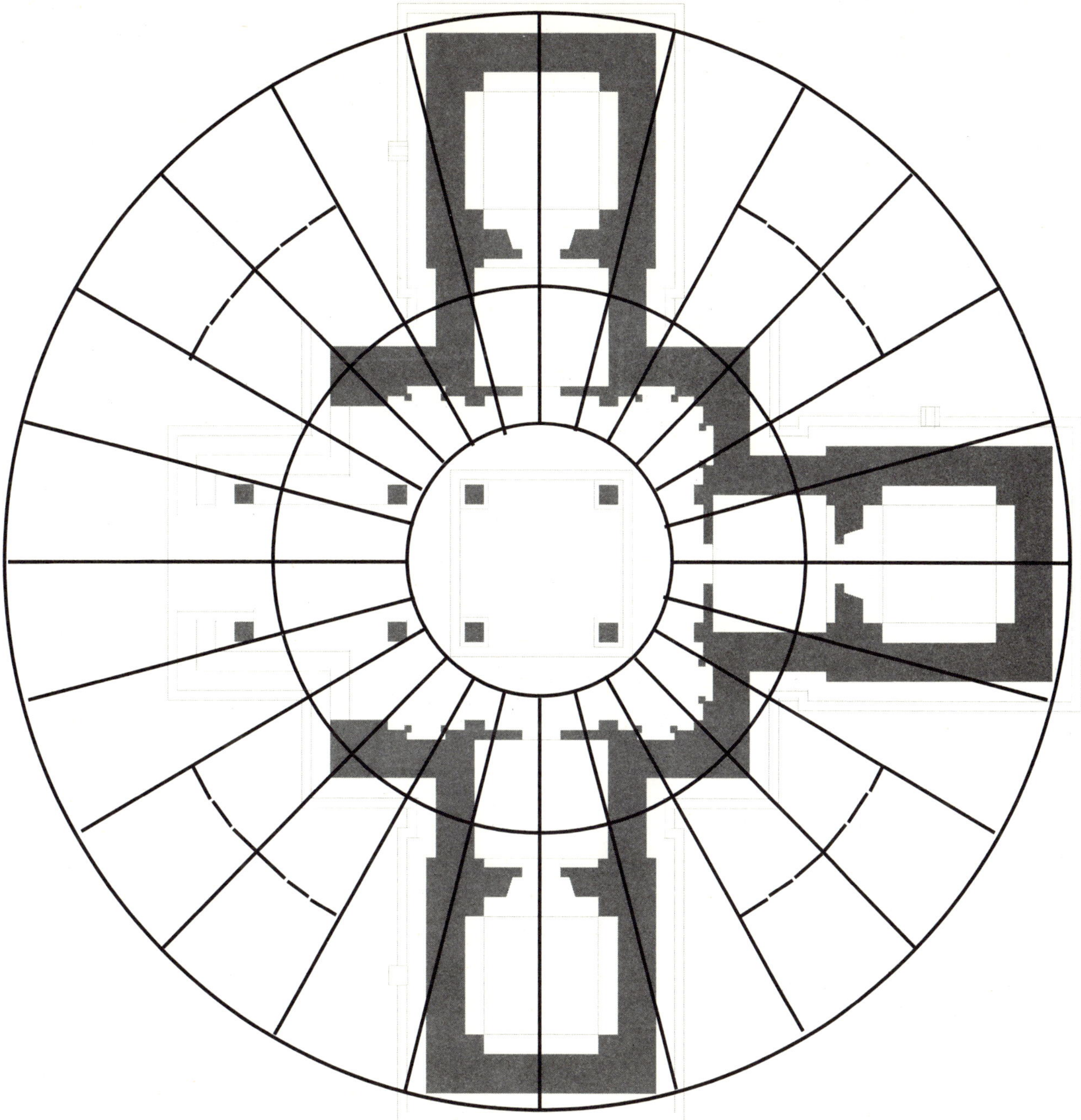

Kampilarāya Trikūṭa Temple (No. 3), Hampī, Karnataka (*c.* CE 1300-26)

The third of the temples constructed during the short-lived Kummatadurga kingdom is the Śaiva Kampilarāya Trikūṭa Temple (No. 3)[110] also found on the Hemakūṭa Hill. Inscriptions clearly establish that the temple was constructed during the reign of King Kampilideva (Kampilarasadeva) (r. CE 1300-26) (**Appendix D**).

The Kampilarāya Trikūṭa Temple (No. 3) is nearly a carbon copy of the Kampilarāya Trikūṭa Temple (No. 1) (**Plate 101**) except that this temple is aligned towards the east, rather than the north and the exterior walls are more elaborate. It consists of three identical *vimānas*, *en plan* (**Figure 75**). They are made up of square *garbhagṛhas* attached to square *antarālas*, all of which share a common *sabhā-maṇḍapa*. The principle *vimāna* is in the west, facing north and is matched on the north and south by the other two *vimānas*. The common *sabhā-maṇḍapa* is enclosed whereas that of Kampilarāya Trikūṭa Temple (No. 1) is open on one side. The *sabhā-maṇḍapa* consists of sixteen columns disposed in the usual manner — i.e. four free-standing columns in the centre raised on a square platform and twelve engaged columns, four of which are quarter, corner columns — which form nine *aṅkanas*. East of the *sabhā-maṇḍapa* is a *mukha-maṇḍapa* with twelve free-standing columns, eight mimic the size of those found in the *sabhā-maṇḍapa* and four are smaller.

As with the Kampilarāya Trikūṭa Temple (No. 1), the application of a *maṇḍala* over the Kampilarāya Trikūṭa Temple (No. 3) presents interesting conjunctions. Either a *paramaśāyika maṇḍala* (**Plate 105**) or a circular *vāstu-puruṣa maṇḍala* (**Plate 106**) seems applicable.

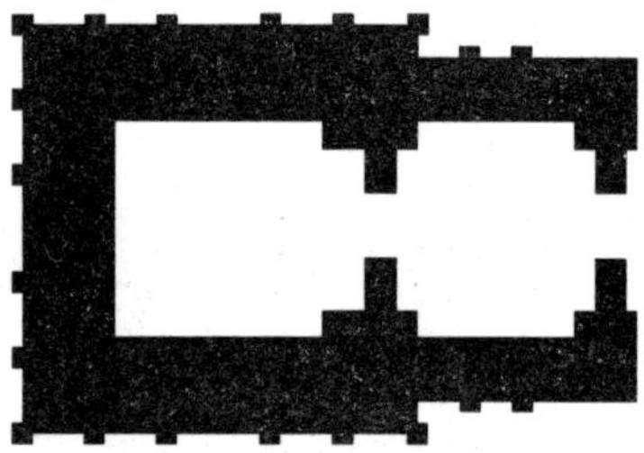

Figure 75: Kampilarāya Trikūṭa Temple (No. 3) *vimāna* element

[110] Redrawn using PageMaker 6.0 from KMS, p. 144, description on pp. 70-71; and KMS II, p. 475, description on pp. 263-64. See also **Preface**.

Plate 104: Kampilarāya Trikūṭa Temple (No. 3) plan

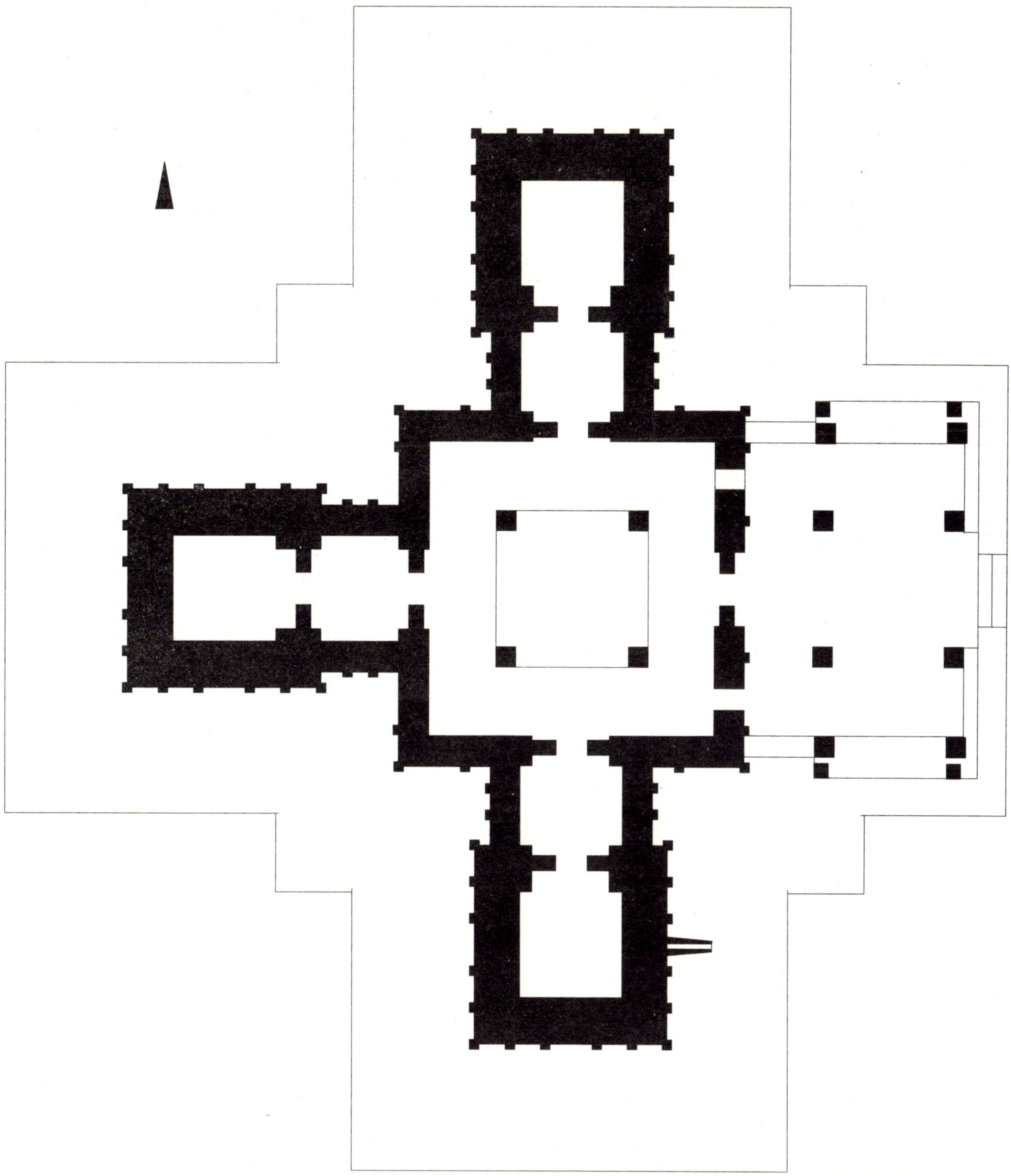

Plate 105: Kampilarāya Trikūṭa Temple (No. 3) with *paramaśāyika maṇḍala*

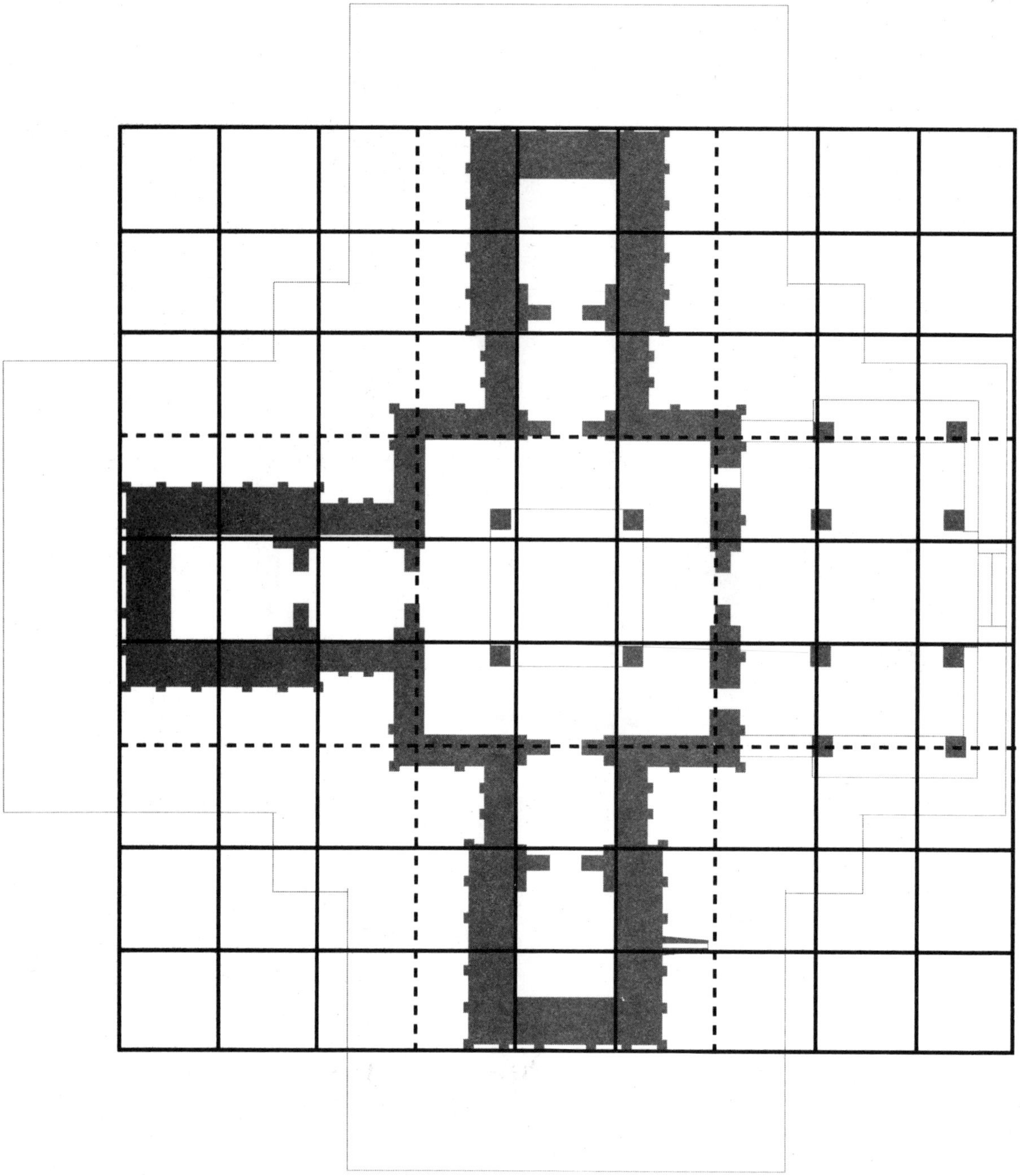

Plate 106: Kampilarāya Trikūṭa Temple (No. 3) with circular *vāstu-puruṣa maṇḍala*

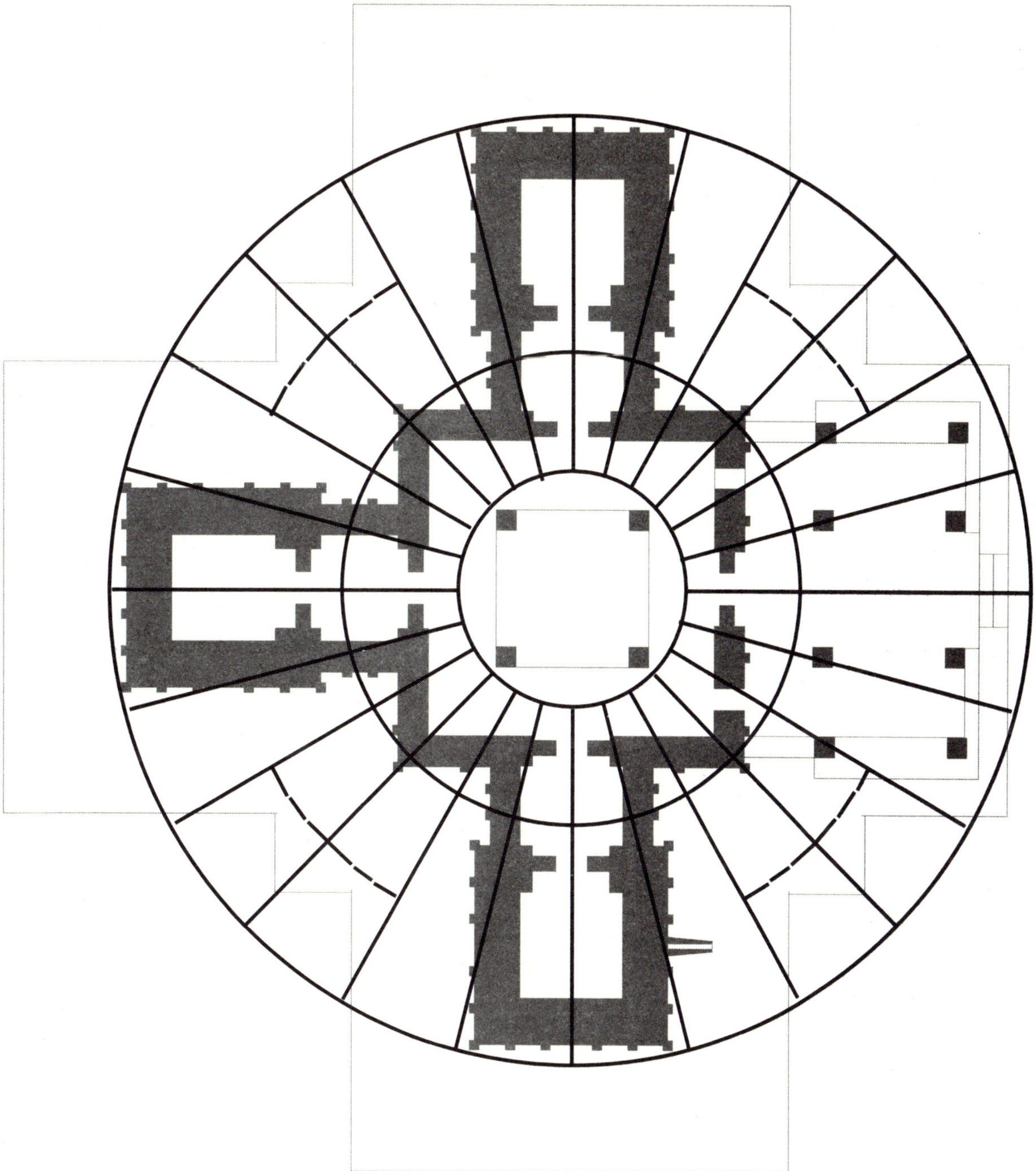

Minor Dvikūṭa Shrine (Amman), Vijayanagara (a. CE 1350)

The Rāmacandra Temple at Vijayanagara is the *chapelle royale* of the emperors of Vijayanagara. It consists of a complex in which is seen a large, free-standing temple, a small free-standing temple and several shrines attached to the girdle wall. The whole is asymmetrical, but rectilinear (**Appendix C, Plate 139**). The deity Amman or Mariamman is an important and powerful goddess, particularly in south India where she is seen as a powerful mother goddess as well as the goddess of disease, particularly small pox, and rain.

To the north and a bit to the west of the main temple is a small, free-standing Minor Dvikūṭa Shrine (Amman) of which the presiding deity is not shown.[111] The Minor Dvikūṭa Shrine (Amman)[112] is asymmetrical and is seen as a **C**-type *dvikūṭa* temple (**Figure 2**). This *dvikūṭa* **C**-type temple may be seen as one of the earlier exemplars of this design type. Generally, the *dvikūṭa* temples that predate the Minor Dvikūṭa Shrine are either of the **A**-type plan — e.g. the Kallappa-Mallappa (Harihara) Dvikūṭa Temple of Devaragennur (**Plate 25**), or the Kāśīviśveśvara Dvikūṭa Temple at Lakkuṇḍī (**Plate 28**) — or the **D**-type *dvikūṭa* temple — e.g. the Hoysaḷeśvara Dvikūṭa Temple of Halebiḍ (**Plate 49**) or the Bastī or Kalla-Guḍi Dvikūṭa Temple at Degamve (**Plate 81**).

The Minor Dvikūṭa Shrine (Amman) is aligned towards the east. The predominant *garbhagṛha* — i.e. in the west — is rectangular, *en plan*, and attached to a rectangular *antarāla*. From the northern edge of this *antarāla*, a common space, extends the second *garbhagṛha*, which is square, *en plan*. A simple, *maṇḍapa* extends towards the east and is open to the east. The interior exhibits six columns which support the roof and six engaged columns. A narrow flight of stairs leads down to ground level. The exterior of the two *garbhagṛha*s and the *antarāla* are highly developed with small, centred shrines and seem to mirror the elaborate exterior of the main temple's *garbhagṛha*s and *antarāla*.

The rectangular *garbhagṛha*, seen here, is not unique, but is not commonly encountered either. They are, from time to time, found in temples where the presiding deity is often portrayed in a reclining position — e.g. the Anantasayana Trikūṭa Temple, Navali (**Plate 48**) which is dedicated to the recumbent form of Lord Viṣṇu.

111 AD, pp. 37-39. However, KMS, p. 50, list the "Hazāra Rāma" temple as one of a number of Vijayanagara temple complexes that include an "Amman or Devī shrine" within their precincts.

112 The plan is redrawn using Adobe PageMaker 6.0, from AD, p. 47.

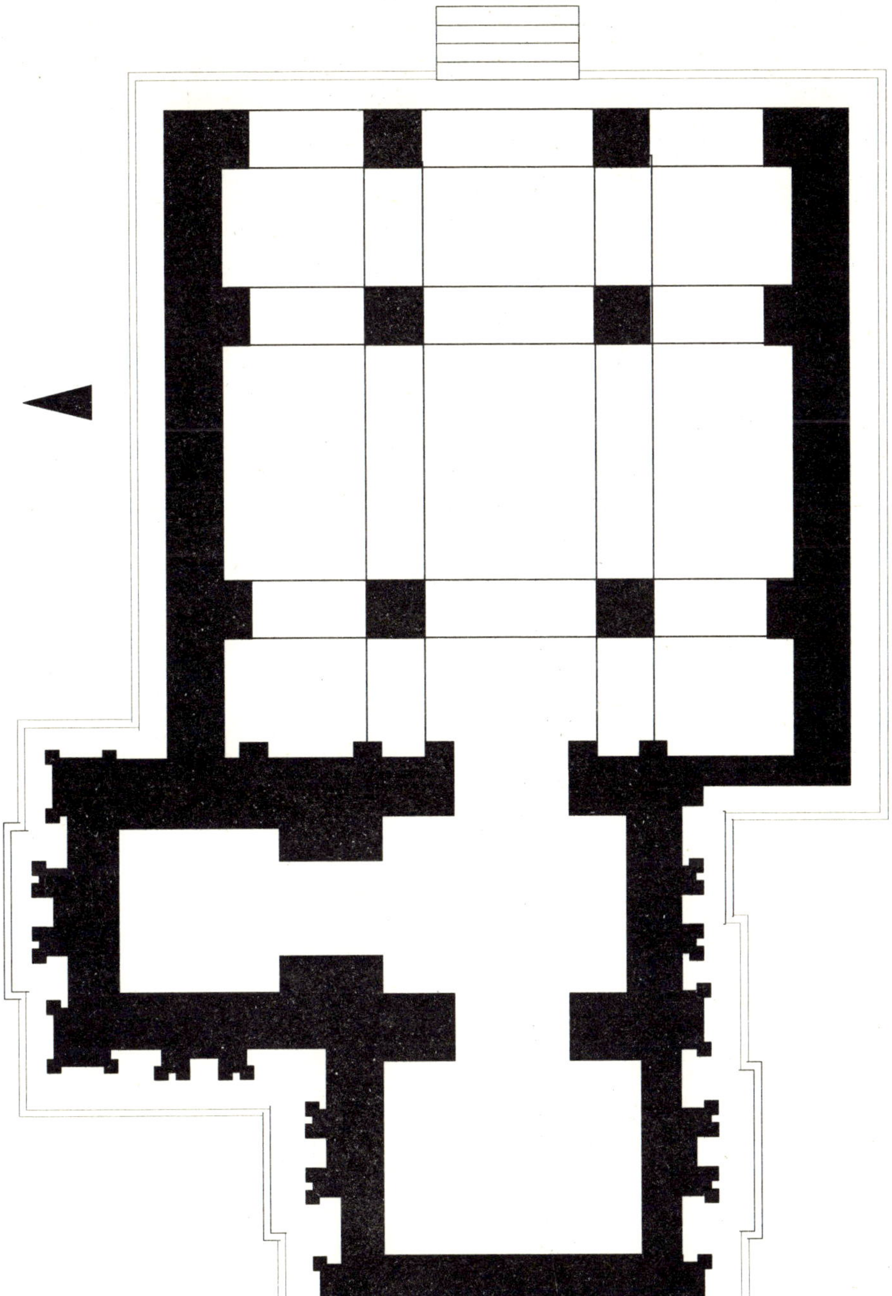

Plate 107: Minor Dvikūṭa Shrine (Amman) plan

Kunthu Jinanātha Dvikūṭa Jinālaya, Kamalapura, Karnataka (a. CE 1375)

One of a number of **C**-type *dvikūṭa* (**Figure 2**) plan temples that are found in the region, the Kunthu Jinanātha Dvikūṭa Jinālaya[113] is dedicated to the Jaina *tīrthaṅkara* Kunthanātha. Built during the reign of Harihara II (r. CE 1377–1404) of Vijayanagara (**Appendix D**). As with a number of smaller Jaina sanctuaries, the exterior is quite plain and the interior architectural detail is also held at a minimum.

The Kunthu Jinanātha Dvikūṭa Jinālaya consists of a main sanctuary in the south. The *garbhagṛha* is square and leads to an *antarāla* which is rectangular. The *antarāla* leads directly into a rectangular *sabhā-maṇḍapa* with two small niches flanking the entrance to the sanctum. Like many *sabhā-maṇḍapa*s, the one here, in the Kunthu Jinanātha Dvikūṭa Jinālaya consists of sixteen columns — i.e. four free-standing columns in the centre and twelve engaged columns, four of which are quarter, corner columns — which form nine *aṅkanas*. To the north is a second square *sabhā-maṇḍapa* also with sixteen columns in the traditional arrangement — i.e. four free-standing columns in the centre raised on a square platform and twelve engaged columns, four of which are quarter, corner columns — which, again, form nine *aṅkanas*. To the west of this *sabhā-maṇḍapa* is the second *garbhagṛha* which is square, *en plan*. It is thought that an image of *tīrthaṅkara* had been enshrined herein. Unlike the principle *vimāna*, this sanctum is without an *antarāla*. The second *sabhā-maṇḍapa* possesses entrances to the north and the east. On either side of the four doorways of this *sabhā-maṇḍapa* are deep niches — i.e. two each on the north, south, east and west. To the north of the second *sabhā-maṇḍapa* is a large *mukha-maṇḍapa* supported by eight columns, four of which are free-standing. To the east of the same *sabhā-maṇḍapa* is a smaller *mukha-maṇḍapa* supported by four columns, two of which are free-standing.

113 Redrawn using PageMaker 6.0 from KMS II, p. 437, description on pp. 209-10. See also **Preface**.

Plate 108: Kunthu Jinanātha Dvikūṭa Jinālaya plan

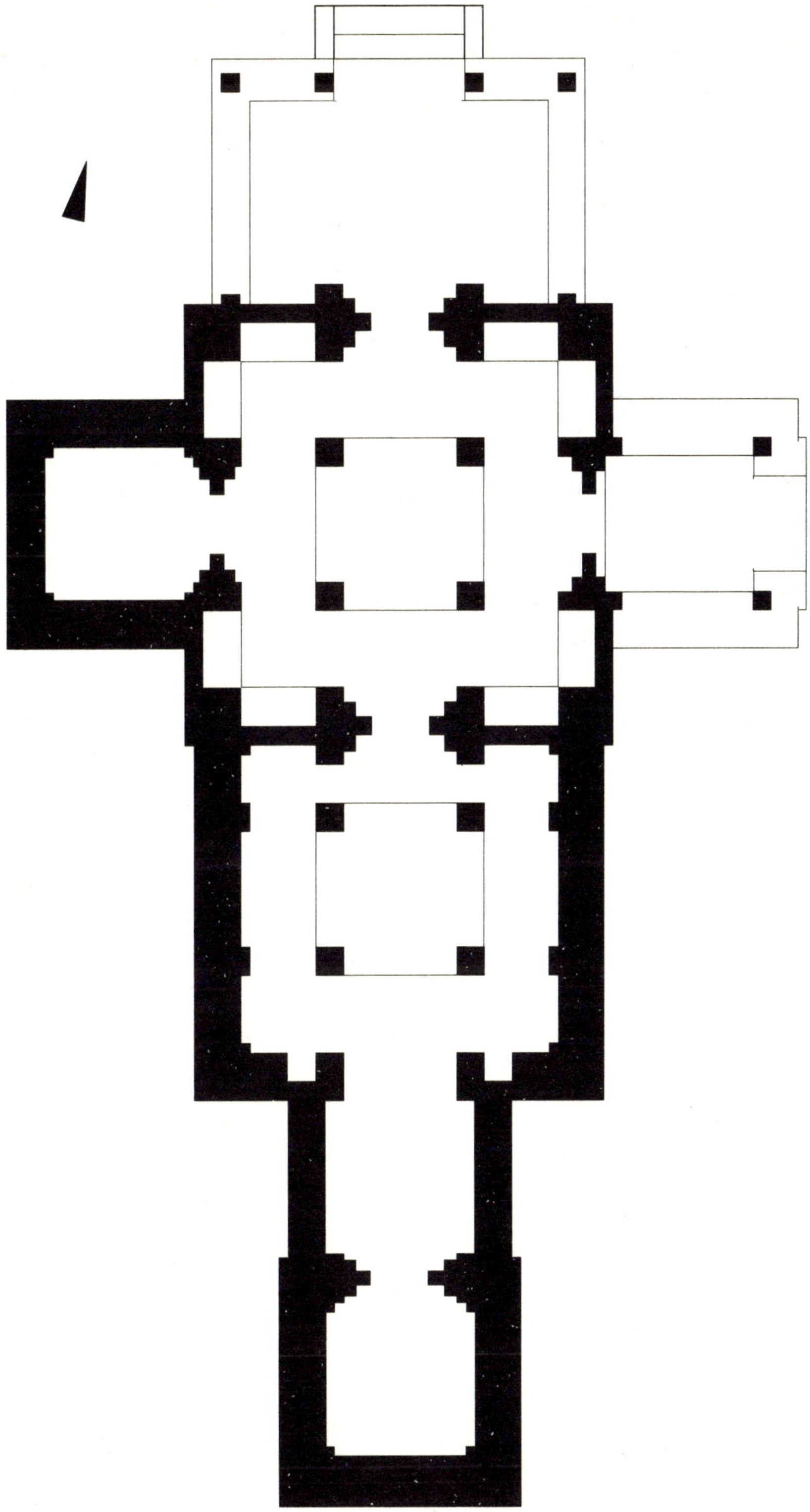

Pārśvanātha Dvikūṭa Jinālaya, Hampī, Karnataka (CE 1426)

Built during the reign of the Vijayanagara king Devarāya II (r. CE 1422-46) (**Appendix D**), the Pārśvanātha Dvikūṭa Jinālaya[114] is a **C**-type *dvikūṭa* temple. It is similar in design to the Kunthu Jinanātha Dvikūṭa Jinālaya of Kamalapura (**Plate 108**).

The Pārśvanātha Dvikūṭa Jinālaya consists of a principle *vimāna* in the south in which stood an image of the Jaina *tīrthaṅkara* Pārśvanātha. The *garbhagṛha* is square and leads to a shallow, rectangular *antarāla* both within thick walls. The *antarāla* leads directly into a rectangular *sabhā-maṇḍapa*. This *sabhā-maṇḍapa*, like many of the others cited in this study, consists of sixteen columns — i.e. four free-standing columns in the centre raised on a platform and twelve engaged columns, four of which are quarter, corner columns — which form nine *aṅkanas*. To the north is a larger, square *sabhā-maṇḍapa* with sixteen columns in the traditional arrangement — i.e. four free-standing columns in the centre raised on a square platform and twelve engaged columns, four of which are quarter, corner columns — which also forms nine *aṅkanas*. To the west is a second *garbhagṛha* which is without an *antarāla*, and which may have enshrined a Jaina *tīrthaṅkara*. The walls of this *garbhagṛha* are not as thick as those found in the southern *vimāna*. To the north of this *sabhā-maṇḍapa* is a wide *mukha-maṇḍapa* supported by eight columns, four of which are free-standing; while to the east of the northern *sabhā-maṇḍapa* is a smaller *mukha-maṇḍapa* supported by four columns, two of which are engaged to the wall of the *sabhā-maṇḍapa*.

[114] Redrawn using PageMaker 6.0 from KMS II, p. 438, description on pp. 210-11. See also **Preface**.

Plate 109: Pārśvanātha Dvikūṭa Jinālaya plan

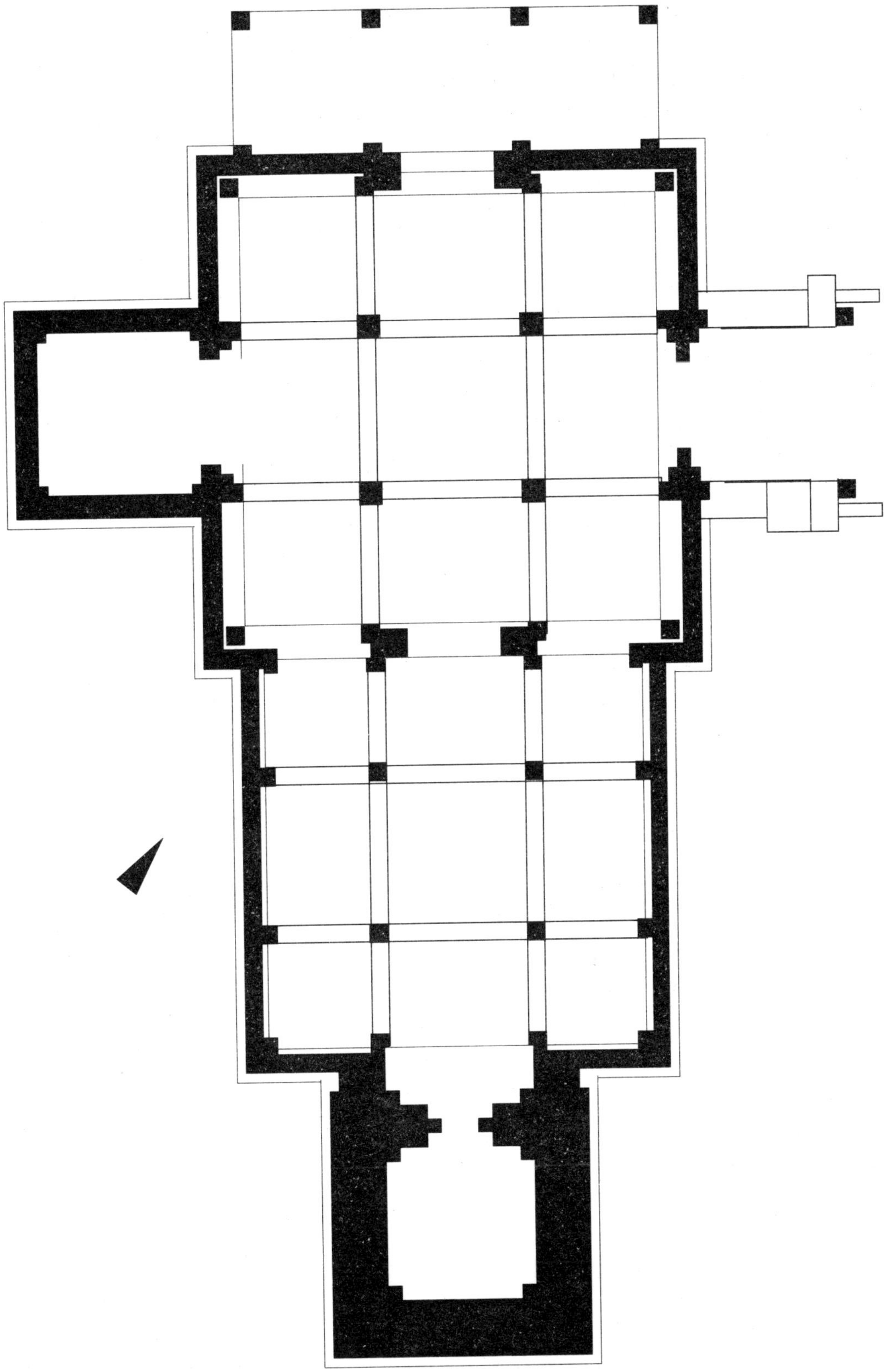

Amman Dvikūṭa Temple, Malayavanta Raghunātha Temple Complex, Kamalapura, Karnataka (fifteenth century CE)

The Malayavanta Raghunātha Temple Complex at Kamalapura is dedicated to Rāma, a form of Lord Viṣṇu. In that complex the Amman Dvikūṭa Temple[115] is a short distance to the north-west of the principal temple of the complex. Amman, also known as Mariamman,[116] is a goddess who in the south of India, particularly Tamil Nadu, has gained considerable popularity. Her origins are considered by some to be pre-Vedic and she is seen as the sister of Lord Viṣṇu. Numerous Amman temples are often found as part of a larger complex and a few appear as an independent temple. As with many of the temples dedicated to this deity, the Amman Dvikūṭa Temple presents a **D**-type *dvikūṭa* plan.

The temple consists of a principal *vimāna* with a square *garbhagṛha* and rectangular *antarāla*. The *antarāla*'s eastern doorway gives way to a square *sabhā-maṇḍapa* with sixteen columns disposed in the usual manner — i.e. four free-standing columns in the centre raised on a square platform and twelve engaged columns, four of which are quarter, corner columns — which form nine *aṅkanas*. To the north of the *sabhā-maṇḍapa* is a second, square *garbhagṛha*, but without *antarāla*. The main entrance to the temple is in the east. A flight of stairs leads down to the large *mukha-maṇḍapa* which is composed of twenty free-standing columns, two of which bracket the eastern extremity of the *sabhā-maṇḍapa*. In the eastern, centre of the *mukha-maṇḍapa* is another flight of steps which leads down to the ground level.

---

115 Redrawn using PageMaker 6.0 from KMS, pp. 161, 163, description pp. 88-90; KMS II, p. 416, description on pp. 186-87-212. See also **Preface**.

116 See: FWB IV, pp. 346-47.

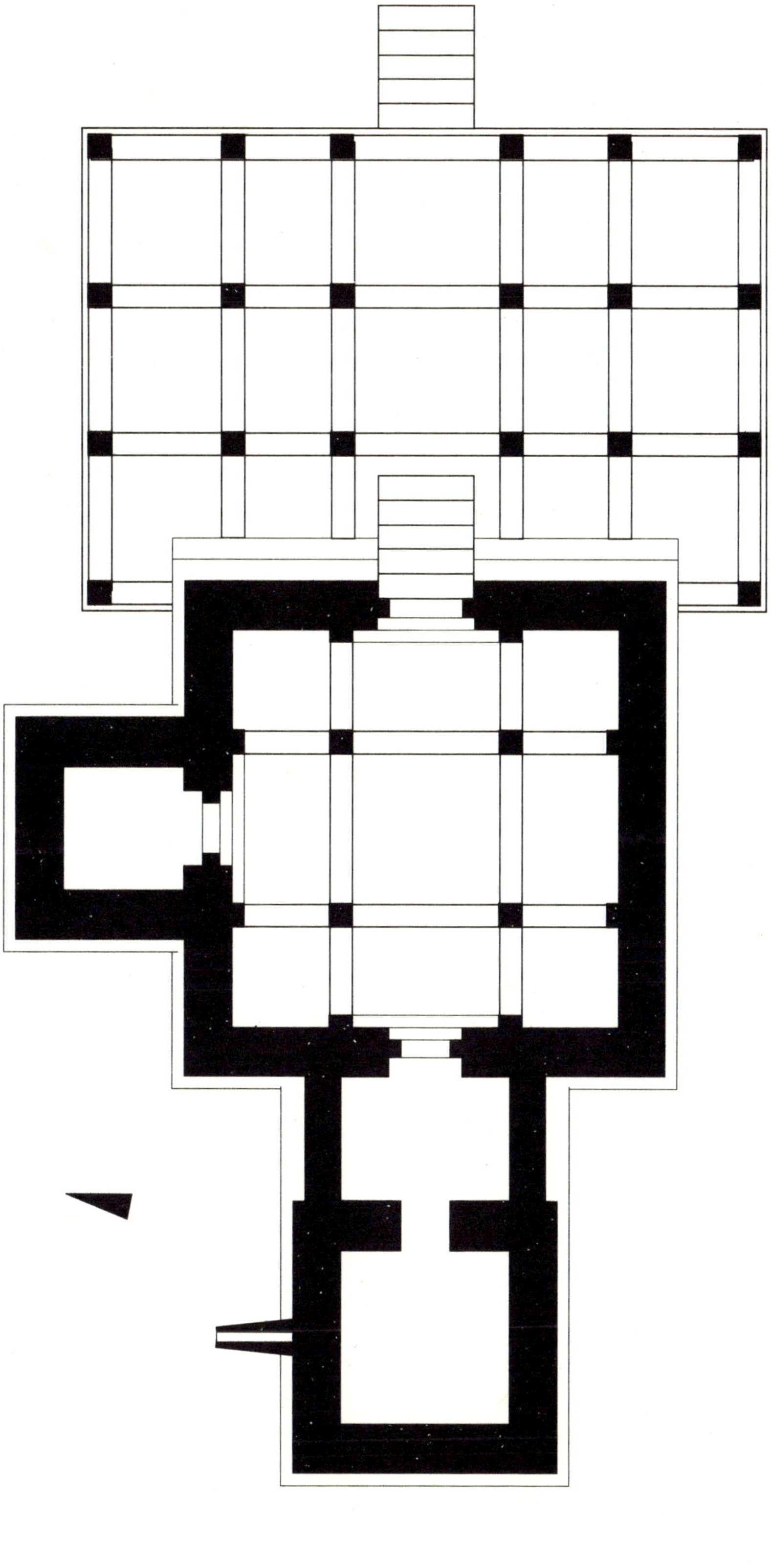

Amman Dvikūṭa Shrine, Viṭṭhala Temple Complex, Hampī, Karnataka (*c.* CE 1500)

Situated to the north-east of the Royal Centre of Vijayanagara (**Appendix C, Plate 138**), the Viṭṭhala Temple complex (**Appendix C, Plate 140**) epitomizes exuberance with restraint. The complex is dedicated to Lord Viṣṇu's incarnation as Viṭṭhala, a minor *avatāra*. Some see Viṭṭhala as an incarnation of Kr̥ṣṇa.[117] The temple complex was essentially constructed by the Emperor Kr̥ṣṇadevarāya (r. CE 1509-30) (**Appendix D**). To the north-west of the main temple in the complex is the Amman Dvikūṭa Shrine,[118] which displays a **C**-type *dvikūṭa* plan.

The *vimāna* is elongated, consisting of a square *garbhagr̥ha* to which is attached an *antarāla*. A small, enclosed *mukha-maṇḍapa* or *ardha-maṇḍapa* which is of the same dimension as the preceding two spaces. This opens onto a *sabhā-maṇḍapa* of sixteen traditionally arranged columns — i.e. four free-standing columns in the centre raised on a square platform and twelve engaged columns, four of which are quarter, corner columns — which forms nine *aṅkanas*. Centred in the northern wall of the *sabhā-maṇḍapa* is a second, square *garbhagr̥ha*, but without *antarāla*. On the east is an open *mukha-maṇḍapa* made up of sixteen columns, four of which are engaged to the eastern wall of the *sabhā-maṇḍapa*.

The most interesting feature of the Amman Dvikūṭa Shrine is not its **C**-type *dvikūṭa* plan, but the elongation of the *vimāna* which normally includes a *garbhagr̥ha* and *antarāla*. However here a third space is added before the *sabhā-maṇḍapa*. It is, at times, referred to as an *ardha-maṇḍapa* (half hall) since it is an entry to the sanctum. This form is repeated in other temples of the region.

117 FWB IV, p. 660.

118 Redrawn using PageMaker 6.0 from HS II, p. 196; KMS, p. 166, description on pp. 93-94. In addition, KMS, p. 93, states that the temple is dedicated to Rukmiṇī who is the consort of Viṭṭhala.

Plate 111: Amman Dvikūṭa Shrine plan

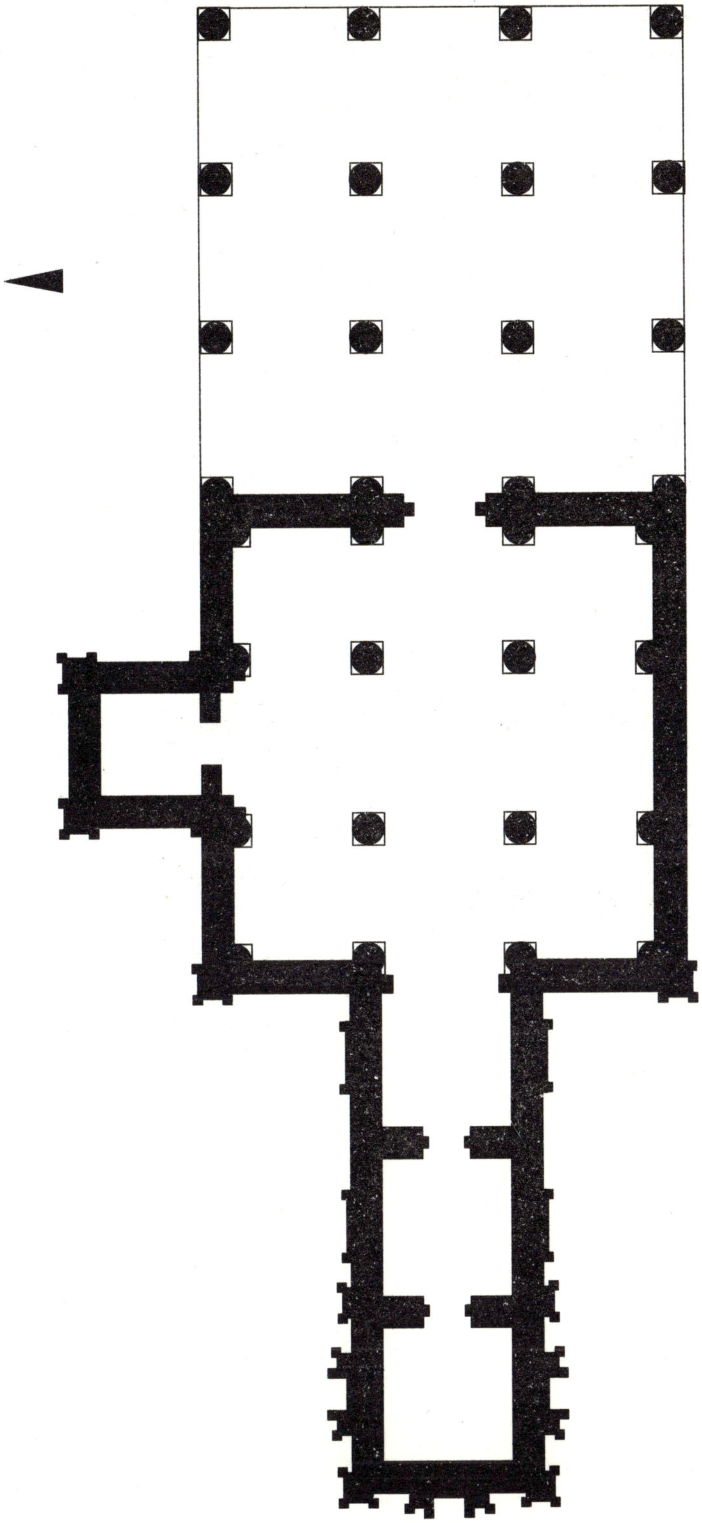

Candraśekhara Dvikūṭa Temple, Hampī, Karnataka (a. CE 1425)

Related to the Amman Dvikūṭa Shrine of the Viṭṭhala Temple Complex (**Plate 111**), the Candraśekhara Dvikūṭa Temple[119] is a Śaiva temple of the **B**-type *dvikūṭa* plan. It is found near the Square Water Pavilion (**Appendix C, Plate 138**) to the south-east of the Ceremonial Centre.[120]

The temple is similar to the Amman Dvikūṭa Shrine of the Viṭṭhala Temple Complex in the elongation of the *vimānas*. The temple exhibits the principal sanctum in the west, facing east. It is identical to the second *vimāna* towards the north facing south (**Figure 76**), being made up of a square *garbhagṛha* with a square *antarāla* and a square *ardha-maṇḍapa* that opens directly onto a common *sabhā-maṇḍapa*. The *sabhā-maṇḍapa* is square and enclosed. As with a majority of *sabhā-maṇḍapas* in the region, it exhibits sixteen traditionally arranged columns — i.e. four free-standing columns in the centre raised on a square platform and twelve engaged columns, four of which are quarter, corner columns — which forms nine *aṅkanas*. To the east is a large *mukha-maṇḍapa* consisting of twenty free-standing, evenly spaced columns.[121] At the easternmost edge is a flight of steps leading to the ground. In addition the Candraśekhara Dvikūṭa Temple possesses a second entrance to the *sabhā-maṇḍapa*. This is a simple flight of steps, centred in the southern wall of the *sabhā-maṇḍapa*.

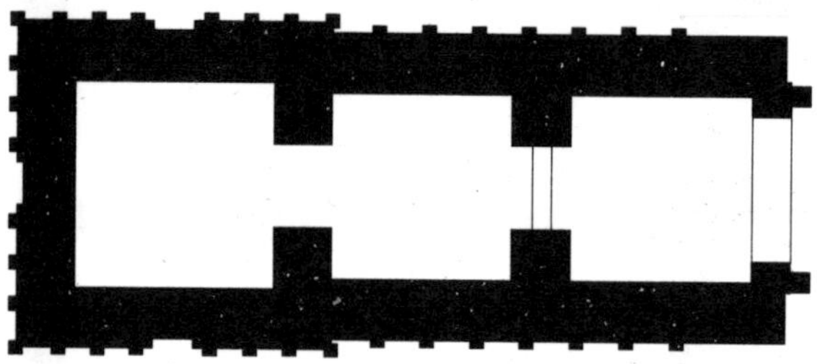

Figure 76: Candraśekhara Dvikūṭa Temple *vimāna* element

119 Redrawn using PageMaker 6.0 from KMS, on p. 156, description on pp. 83-84. See also **Preface**.

120 KMS, p. 83, identifies the Square Water Pavilion as the "Queen's Bath". This name is frequently employed, erroneously. See: JF.

121 KMS, p. 84, states: "The *mukha-maṇḍapa* is open and stands on eight pillars". "Plan 13: Candraśekhara temple plan, Hampī", p. 156 and the section on the following page, clearly indicates twenty columns made up of three ranks of six columns each and two columns bracketing the *sabhā-maṇḍapa*'s eastern most façade.

Plate 112: Candraśekhara Dvikūṭa Temple plan

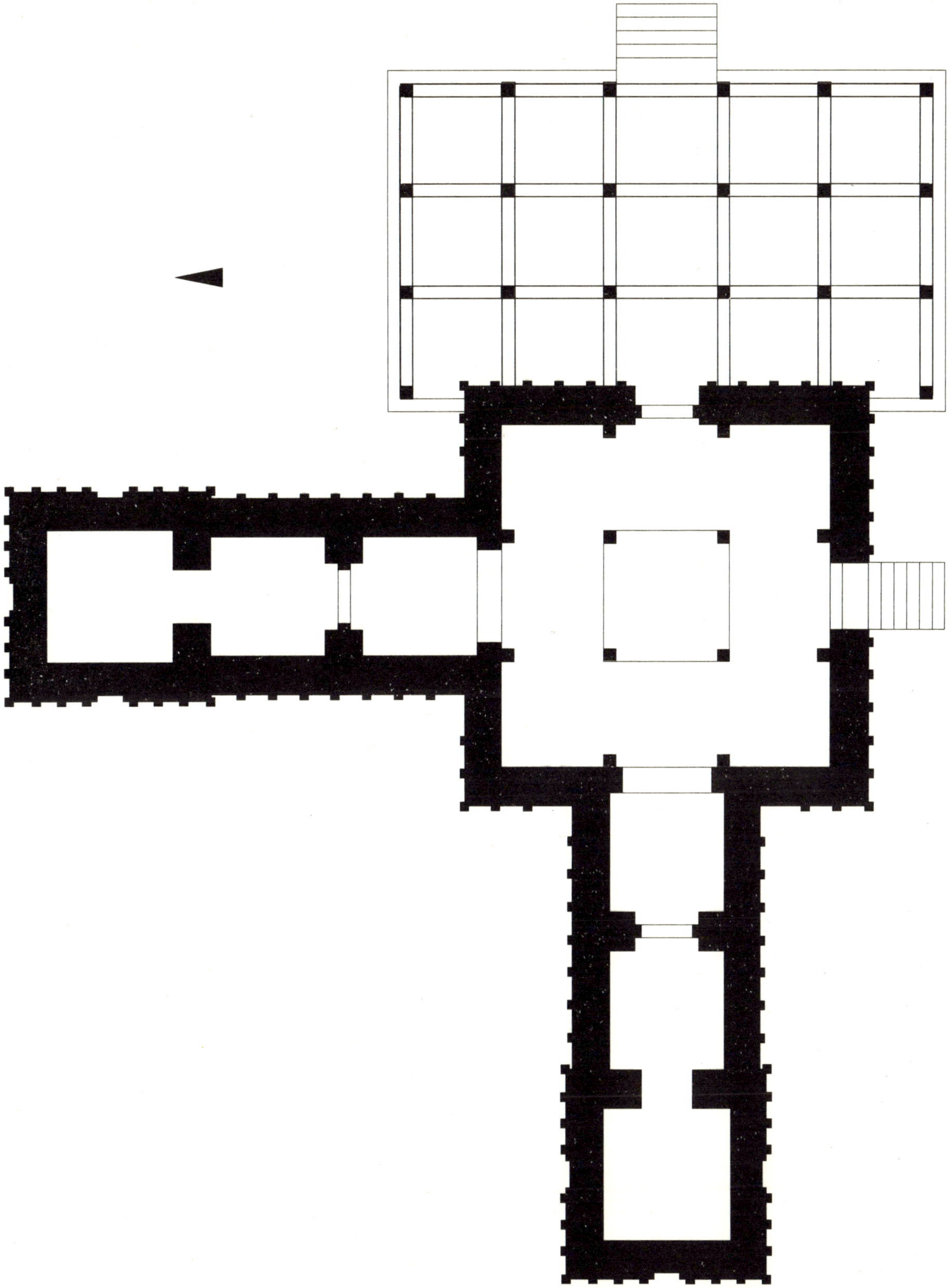

Amman Dvikūṭa Shrine, Acyutarāya Temple Complex, Hampī, Karnataka (a. CE 1530)

The Vijayanagara Empire had grown in both size and brilliance by the time the Emperor Acyutadevarāya (r. CE 1530-42) (**Appendix D**) sat on the *gaddī*. However, it was not to remain in its powerful position for long. Soon after assuming power he oversaw the construction of the Acyutarāya Temple Complex at Hampī (**Appendix C, Plate 141**). The complex was dedicated to Lord Viṣṇu as Veṅkaṭeśvara, locally referred to as Tiruveṅgaḷanātha. Part of that complex was the **C**-type *dvikūṭa* (**Figure 2**) Amman Dvikūṭa Shrine.[122]

This small shrine lies to the south-west of the main temple, and is oriented towards the north. It consists of a square *garbhagṛha* with a square *antarāla* opening onto a common, three-quarters enclosed *sabhā-maṇḍapa*. A second *garbhagṛha* is found on the west side of the *sabhā-maṇḍapa*. The *sabhā-maṇḍapa* is square, three-quarters enclosed — i.e. open towards the north — and consists of sixteen columns traditionally arranged — i.e. four free-standing columns in the centre raised on a square platform, two free-standing columns in the north and ten engaged columns, two of which are quarter, corner columns — which form nine *aṅkanas*. A short flight of stairs leads down to the ground level.

The location of this Amman Shrine adjacent to the main temple of the complex, and in the same general alignment seems to indicate some iconographic relationship — e.g. Minor Dvikūṭa Shrine (Amman) (**Plate 107**; also **Appendix C, Plate 139**), and the Amman Dvikūṭa Shrine, Viṭṭhala Temple Complex (**Plate 111**; also **Appendix C, Plate 140**). As one faces the main temple of the complex, the Amman Shrines are to the right and either roughly parallel with the *garbhagṛha* or farther back as seen in **Appendix C, Plates 139-141**.

122 Redrawn using PageMaker 6.0 from KMS, p. 167, description on pp. 95-96. See also **Preface**.

Plate 113: Amman Dvikūṭa Shrine plan

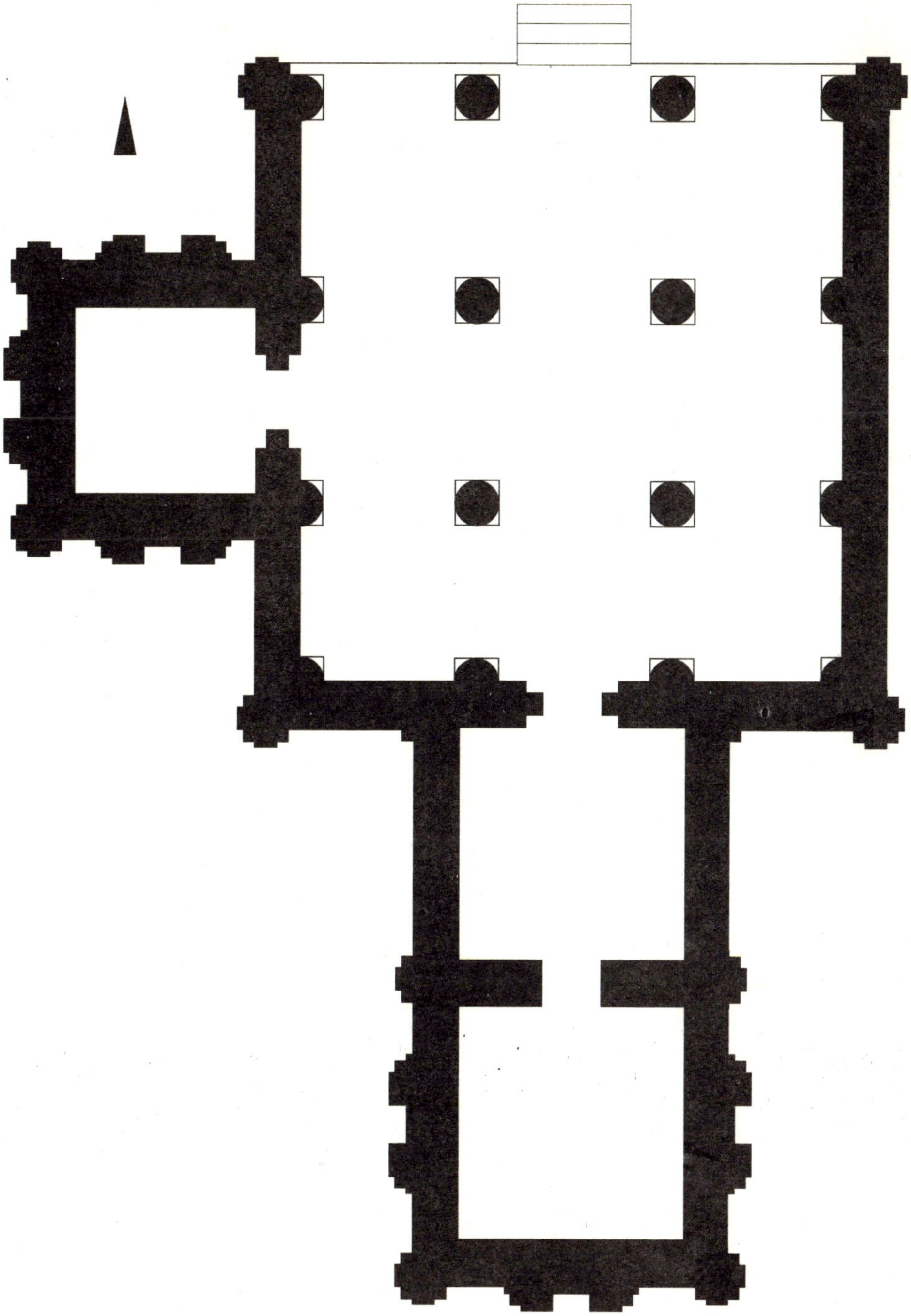

Trikūṭeśvara (Śiva) Temple, Timmalapur, Karnataka (*c*. CE 1539)

Towards the end of the reign of Acyutadevarāya of the Tuluva Dynasty (**Appendix D**), in Timmalapur, a temple was constructed by a wealthy functionary of the Imperial Court. The Trikūṭeśvara (Śiva) Temple[123] is of the **A**-type *trikūṭa* plan (**Figure 2**) and aligned towards the north.

The Trikūṭeśvara (Śiva) Temple is made up of the principal, square *garbhagṛha* to which is attached a square *antarāla*. From the *antarāla* extends a rectangular *ardha-maṇḍapa* which opens onto a common, enclosed *sabhā-maṇḍapa*. The width of these three elements — i.e. the *garbhagṛha*, *antarāla* and *ardha-maṇḍapa* — are successively narrower as they approach the *sabhā-maṇḍapa*, making for a pleasing design, *en plan*, and one that is rarely encountered. Attached to the *sabhā-maṇḍapa*, to the east and to the west, are two additional *vimāna*s of identical design (**Figure 77**). Each of the *garbhagṛha*s exhibits a shallow niche in its exposed façade. The enclosed *sabhā-maṇḍapa* is square and exhibits sixteen columns in the usual arrangement — i.e. four free-standing columns in the centre raised on a square platform and twelve engaged columns, four of which are quarter, corner columns — which form nine *aṅkana*s. Centred in the northern façade is the entrance which gives way to a large, dramatic, rectangular *mukha-maṇḍapa*.[124] The *mukha-maṇḍapa* consists of twenty columns in six files — i.e. four each in the outer two files and three each in the inner four files. To the north of the *mukha-maṇḍapa* is a short flight of steps to ground level. The whole is set within a *prākāra* with a gate to the north-west.

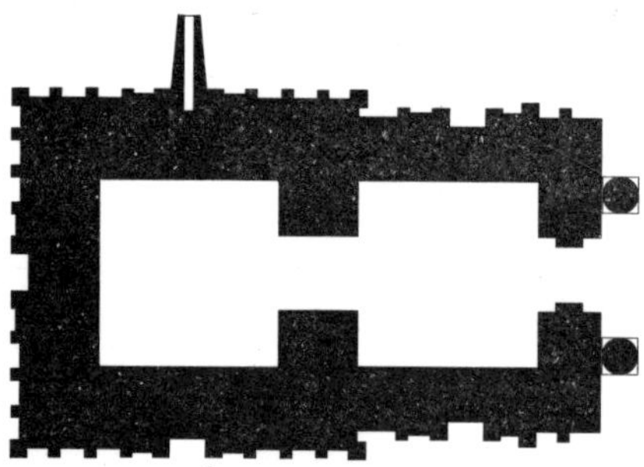

Figure 77: Trikūṭeśvara (Śiva) Temple east–west *vimāna* element

123 Redrawn using PageMaker 6.0 from KMS, p. 174, description on pp. 112-13. See also **Preface**.

124 KMS, p. 112, states: "The *mukha-maṇḍapa* is square and contains twenty-four pillars in six rows." The "Plan 26", on p. 174, is one of the few plans in this publication that is presented to scale. The *mukha-maṇḍapa* is clearly rectangular and indicates twenty columns, four of which may be said to be lost within the northern wall of the *sabhā-maṇḍapa*.

Plate 114: Trikūṭeśvara (Śiva) Temple plan

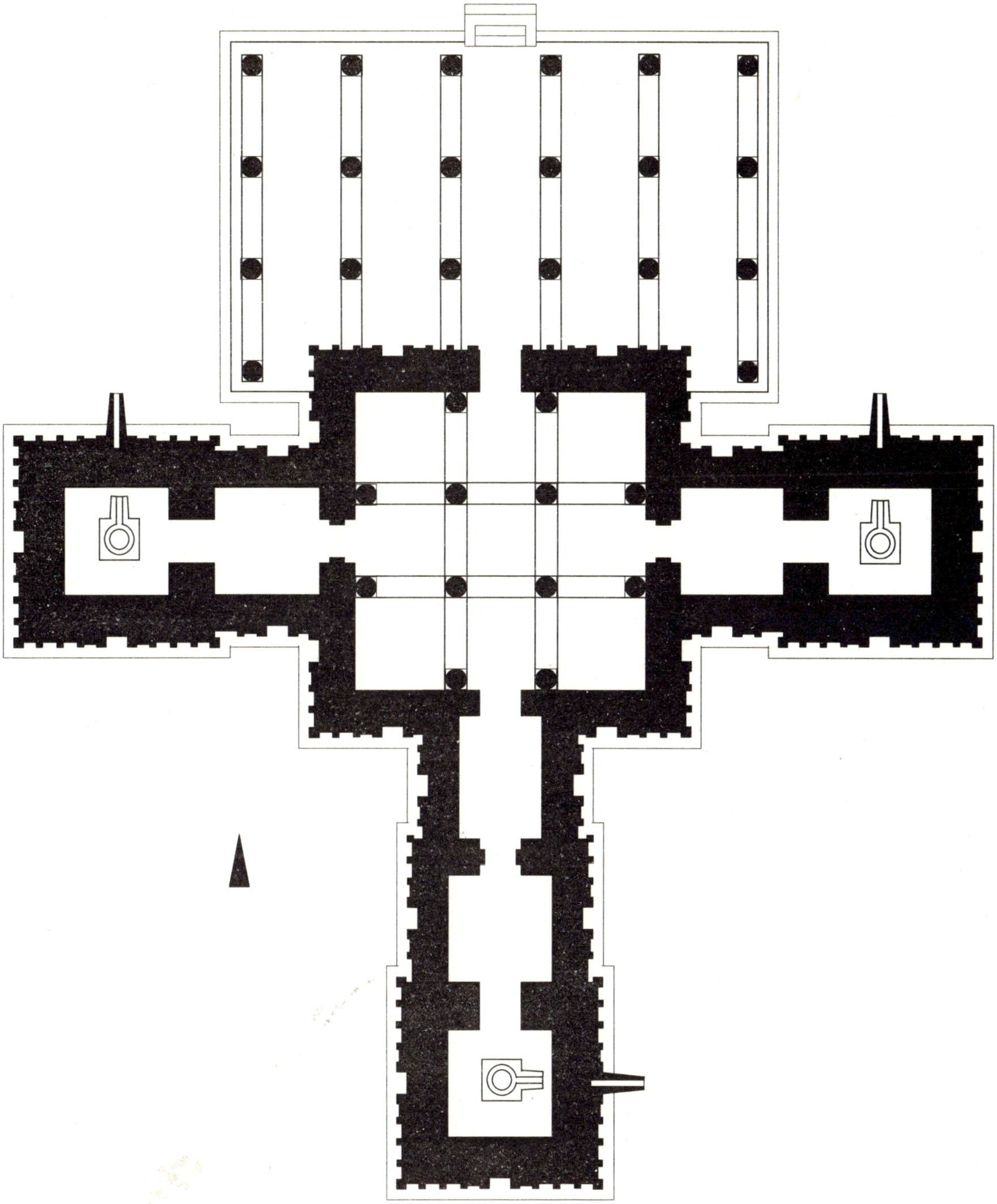

Observations and Conclusions

Temple Types

A number of "temple types" were identified in the Introduction. This is illustrated by the table in which the various temples are categorized, accordingly (pp. 197-98). In studying this table a number of simple conclusions can be drawn. There are twenty-five *dvikūṭa* temples within the selected temples of this study. Of these twenty-five, nine are **A**-type, four are **B**-type, seven are **C**-type and five are **D**-type. There are thirty-eight *trikūṭa* temples within the selected temples of this study. Of these, twenty-nine are **A**-type, four are **B**-type, two are **C**-type and three are **D**-type. There are two *catuṣkūṭa* temples within the selected temples of this study and both are **B**-type. The *pañcakūṭa*, *saptakūṭa*, *navakūṭa* and *cauṅsaṭha* temples may be considered as being either rare or not generally utilized. **A**-type temples, especially *dvikūṭa* and *trikūṭa*, tend to predominate. **A**-type far exceeds other types of *trikūṭa* temples in number and may be seen as the preferred type within the purview of this study. Of interest, within a specified time-frame is the appearance of **C**-type *dvikūṭa* temples, particularly as associated with the rise of Vijayanagara and their particular aesthetic.

In-line Temple Plans

It would seem that the design of a *dvikūṭa* or *trikūṭa* or *pañcakūṭa* temple, in-line type — i.e. **D**-type, **D**-type and **C**-type, respectively, would all be essentially similar, i.e. formulating an *ekakūṭa* plan and replicating it the required number of times as was done in the Pañcaliṅgeśvara Temple (**Plate 90**). But for some reason the *sthapati* of the Śaiva Dvikūṭa Temple (**Plate 7**) and the Īśvara Dvikūṭa Temple (**Plate 86**) certainly lined up their elements correctly for this type, but the individual elements were remarkably bland, undeveloped. The solution is simple enough as seen in the Paya-Thon-Zu of Pagan (a. CE 1250) (**Appendix C, Plate 129**). One might assert that the reason for these overly simple solutions was because the temples/shrines were of a minor importance to the whole or they were patronized by someone of limited means (**Plates 12** or **86**).

The in-line design, *en plan*, of a *dvikūṭa* temple, **D**-type, finds examples in the Śaiva Dvikūṭa Temple (**Plate 12**), the Hoysaḷeśvara Dvikūṭa Temple (**Plate 49**), the Bastī or Kala-Guḍi Dvikūṭa Temple (**Plate 81**) and the Īśvara Dvikūṭa Temple (**Plate 86**). With the exception of the large, developed Hoysaḷeśvara Dvikūṭa Temple and the Bastī or Kala-Guḍi Dvikūṭa Temple, the solutions found in the other two of this type are less than satisfactory.

Pañcakūṭa temple, **C**-type, finds a singular example in Pañcaliṅgeśvara Temple (**Plate 90**). Here, one encounters the replication of a fairly developed *vimāna* and an elaborate *sabhā-maṇḍapa*.

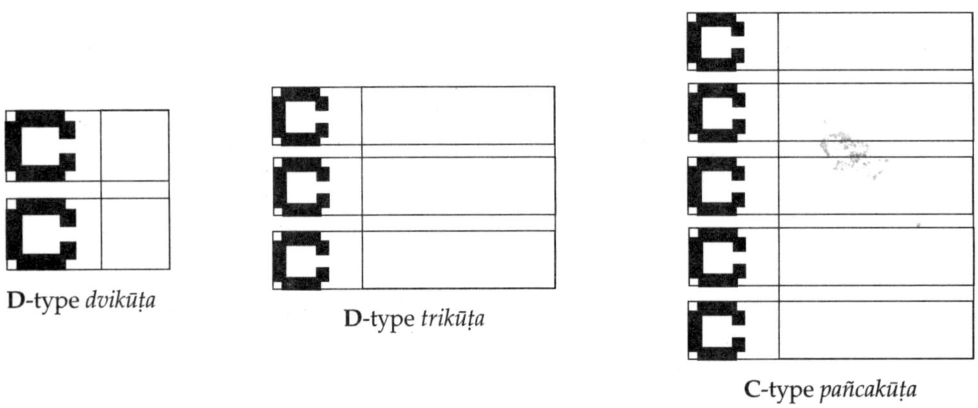

Figure 78: In-line plan types

Temple	*Dvikūṭa*				*Trikūṭa*				*Catus kūṭa*			*Other*
	A	B	C	D	A	B	C	D	A	B	C	
Amman Dvikūṭa Shrine, Acyutarāya Temple Complex, Hampī			■									
Amman Dvikūṭa Shrine, Kamalapur												
Amman Dvikūṭa Shrine, Viṭṭhala Temple Complex, Hampī			■					■				Variation
Anantaśayana Trikūṭa Temple, Navali					■							
Basavaṇṇa (Traipuruṣa) Trikūṭa Temple, Malghana									■			
Bastī or Kalla-Guḍi Dvikūṭa Temple, Degamve										■		
Bhīmeśvara Catuṣkūṭa Temple, Nīlaguṇḍa	■											
Buceśvara Dvikūṭa Temple, Koravangala												
Candramaulīśvara Temple, Unkal								■				Multi sanctum
Candragupta Trikūṭa Basadi, Śravaṇabeḷagoḷa		■										
Candraśekhara Dvikūṭa Temple, Hampī												
Causaṭh Yoginī Mandir and Gaurī-Śaṅkara Temple,												Circular, eighty-one shrine
Cauṅsaṭh Yoginī Sanctuary, Khajurāho												Rectangular, sixty-seven shrines
Cauṅsaṭh Yoginī Temple, Hīrāpur												Circular, sixty-four shrines
Cennakeśava Temple, Beḷūr	■											Variation
Gaṅgādhareśvara Dvikūṭa Temple, Ḍoḍḍaiśvara				■								
Hoysaḷeśvara Dvikūṭa Temple, Halebiḍ				■								
Īśvara Dvikūṭa Temple, Arsikere					■							
Īśvara Trikūṭa Temple, Basarakoḍu					■							
Jaina Basadī No. 15, Deogaṛh					■							
Jaina Tīrthaṅkara Trikūṭa Basadī, Arasibedi					■							
Jambuliṅgeśvara Trikūṭa Shrine, Bādāmī												
Kailāsanātha Temple, Kāñcīpuram		■										
Kalideva Dvikūṭa Temple, Kummsi	■											Seven to nine shrines
Kallappa-Mallappa (Harihara) Dvikūṭa Temple, Devaragennur		■										
Kalleśvara Dvikūṭa Temple, Bagali												
Kalleśvara Saptakūṭa Temple, Bennikallu												
Kampilarāya Trikūṭa Temple (No. 1), Hampī												Seven shrines
Kampilarāya Trikūṭa Temple (No. 3), Hampī					■							
Kāśīviśveśvara Dvikūṭa Temple, Lakkuṇḍī					■							
Kedāreśvara Trikūṭa Temple, Balagamve	■											
Keśava Trikūṭa Temple, Somanāthapur					■							
Koṭe Śaṅkaraliṅga Dvikūṭa Temple, Nimbal	■				■							
Kunthu Jinanātha Dvikūṭa Jinālaya, Kamalapura			■									
Kunthunātha Dvikūṭa Temple, Kamalapura												
Lakṣmī-Devī Catuṣkūṭa Temple, Doḍḍa Gaḍḍuvalli										■		
Lakṣmī-Narasiṁha Trikūṭa Temple, Bhadravatī					■							
Mahādeva Trikūṭa Temple, Benakoṭagī					■							
Mallikārjuna Trikūṭa Temple, Basaralu						■						
Mallikārjuna Trikūṭa Temple, Hirebevinuru						■						
Mallikārjuna Trikūṭa Temple, Hospeṭ					■							
Mallikārjuna Trikūṭa Temple, Katnahaḷḷi					■							
Minor Dvikūṭa Shrine, Rāmacandra Temple Complex, Vijayanagara			■									Variation

Temple	*Dvikūṭa*				*Trikūṭa*				*Catus kūṭa*			*Other*
	A	B	C	D	A	B	C	D	A	B	C	
Nārāyaṇa Trikūṭa Temple, Anekannambadi						■						
Nārāyaṇa Trikūṭa Temple, Iṅgaleśvara					■							
Navaliṅgeśvara Navakūṭa Temple, Kukkanur												Nine shrines, irregular
Pañcaliṅgeśvara Pañcakūṭa Temple, Govindanahaḷḷi												Five shrines, C-type
Parmānanda Trikūṭa Temple, Konnur					■							
Pārśvanātha Dvikūṭa Jinālaya, Hampī			■									
Rachiguḍi Trikūṭa Temple, Aihoḷe					■							
Rāmaliṅga Dvikūṭa Temple, Horti	■											
Rāmaliṅga Dvikūṭa Temple, Sirur	■											
Rāmaliṅga Trikūṭa Temple, Iṭigi					■							
Rāmaliṅgeśvara Trikūṭa Temple, Kundaragi					■							
Rāmeśvara Dvikūṭa Temple, Yaragal	■											
Rāmeśvara Trikūṭa Shrine, Kurugod					■							Suggested
Rāmeśvara Trikūṭa Shrine, Yaragal					■							
Śambhuliṅga Dvikūṭa Temple, Kakkalameli	■											
Saṅgameśvara Trikūṭa Temple, Bevura					■							
Saṅgameśvara Trikūṭa Temple, Babaleśvara					■							
Śaṅkaraliṅga Trikūṭa Temple, Dhulakheḍa						■						
Śaṅkaraliṅga Dvikūṭa Temple, Kalakere		■										
Siddhaliṅgeśvara Pañcakūṭa Temple, Siruvala												Five shrines, A-type
Siddheśvara Dvikūṭa Temple, Algoḍu				■								
Śaiva Dvikūṭa Temple, Chauḍadampur				■								
Śaiva Dvikūṭa Temple, Hampī				■								
Someśvara Trikūṭa Temple, Haralhaḷḷi					■							
Someśvara Trikūṭa Temple, Iṅgaleśvara					■							
Someśvara Trikūṭa Shrine, Kabali							■					
Sūrya-Nārāyaṇa Trikūṭa Temple, Magala					■							
Sūrya Temple, Koṇārka					■							
Trikūṭeśvara Temple, Gaḍag							■					
Trikūṭeśvara Trikūṭa Temple, Gorur					■							
Trikūṭeśvara Trikūṭa Temple, Timmalapur					■							
Vaidyanātheśvara Dvikūṭa Temple, Vaidyanāthapura			■									
Vīranārāyaṇa Trikūṭa Temple, Belvadi					■							Variation

Sabhā-maṇḍapa

ARRANGEMENT OF COLUMNS

Many of the *sabhā-maṇḍapa*s share the common feature of sixteen columns supporting the roof. These, by sheer dint of the number of examples, become a traditional arrangement — i.e. four free-standing columns in the centre and twelve engaged columns, four of which are quarter, corner columns — forming nine *aṅkana*s (**Figure 79**). Two numbers appear in this arrangement — sixteen and nine. Sixteen which refers to the number of columns, *en toto*, is "a feminine number, is a number whose √ is 4. This integer also signifies completeness and its formation is propitious (1 + 3 + 5 + 7 = 16, 4 + 4 + 4 + 4 = 16, 4 x 4 = 16, 8 + 8 = 16 or 2 x 8 = 16). Sixteen also signifies balance being made up of opposites — the Sun and Venus. It denotes divine destruction, the fall of man and the visible world."[1] It would appear that the numeral nine — i.e. the *aṅkana*s — has special significance in this arrangement. "Nine is a perfect number whose √ is 3 as well a number possessing an imposing formation (3 + 3 + 3 = 9, 3 x 3 = 9 or 1 + 3 + 5 = 9). It is called perfect since it is formed from three and nine and always reproduces itself when multiplied with any number (9 x 9 = 81 = 9, 9 x 18 = 162 = 9). It is a magnification of that most sacred number, and by association and as a derivation from three, nine also becomes one of the most sacred numbers. It is the last whole number before the commencement of the compound numbers. Nine denotes completion, perfection, force, wisdom, silence and when associated with three it connotes space."[2] As with anything that seems to become standard, there are always exceptions. Notable are the thirty-six columns in the *sabhā-maṇḍapa* of the Śaṅkaraliṅga Trikūṭa Temple of Kalakere (**Plate 72**) or the twelve columns of the Śaṅkaraliṅga Trikūṭa Temple at Dhūlakheḍa (**Plate 54**). However, the vast majority of *sabhā-maṇḍapas* indicate the predilection for the employment of sixteen columns.

THREE-QUARTER

There seems to be a tendency in the southern subcontinent to attach a *sabhā-maṇḍapa* (a hall of gathering) directly to the entrance of the *antarāla*. Often in the north when a gathering hall becomes part of a temple, it encloses the *vimāna*, creating an internal *pradakṣiṇāpatha* (**Appendix C, Plates 126, 136-137**). Numerous temples of Kerala do not employ a *sabhā-maṇḍapa*, rather they construct an open *namaskāra-maṇḍapa* which serves the same purpose — i.e. a place of gathering (**Appendix A, Glossary**, p. 222).

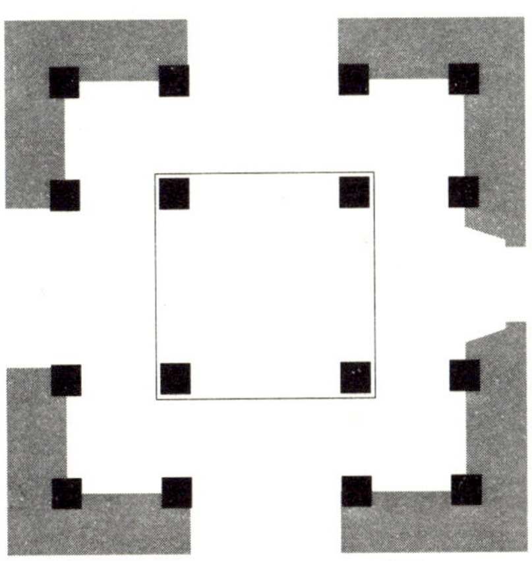

Figure 79: Traditional arrangement of sixteen columns in a *sabhā-maṇḍapa*

Generally, the tendency in the south-western region of the subcontinent is to design a *sabhā-maṇḍapa* which is enclosed, i.e. enclosed by four walls, which opens into the sanctum(s) as well as providing a means of ingress and egress from the temple. However, there are a number of temples within this consideration which exhibit *sabhā-maṇḍapas* that are enclosed on three sides and open on the fourth side (**Figures 81-89**) —

[1] FWB II, p. 70.

[2] Ibid., p. 47.

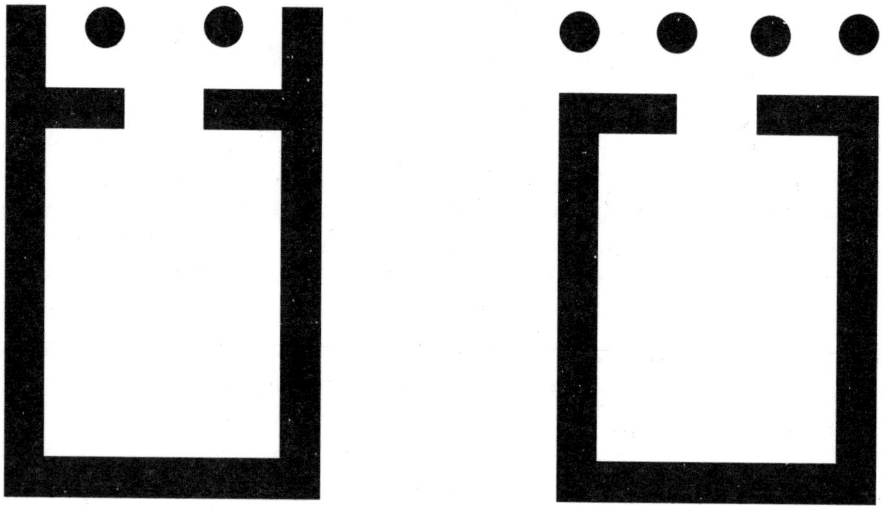

Figure 80: Greek in *antis* plan (left) and *prostyle* plan (right)

i.e. three-quarters enclosed. In most instances this development mimics the *in antis* rather than the *prostyle* solution seen in early Greek temples (**Figure 80**). The reason for this solution may be purely for aesthetic reasons, however, the removal of the fourth, solid wall and the retention of the columns, does allow for an abundance of ambient light to infuse the columned *sabhā-maṇḍapa* and a smaller amount to filter into the otherwise dark recesses of the *garbhagṛha*. It is also of interest to note that this particular solution appears to have found more favour in the south of the subcontinent where the sunlight is more prevalent and higher in the sky than in the north. On the other hand, the light that occurs within the *garbhagṛha* is that artificial, holy light generated by sacred lamps.

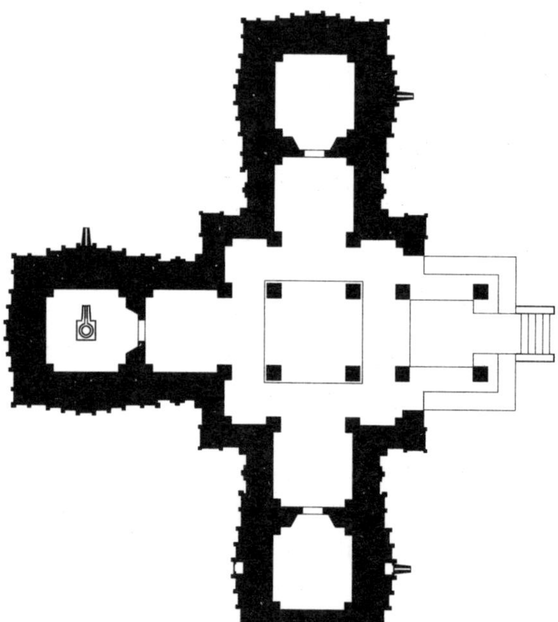

Figure 81: Īśvara Trikūṭa Temple, Basarakoḍu (a. 1100)

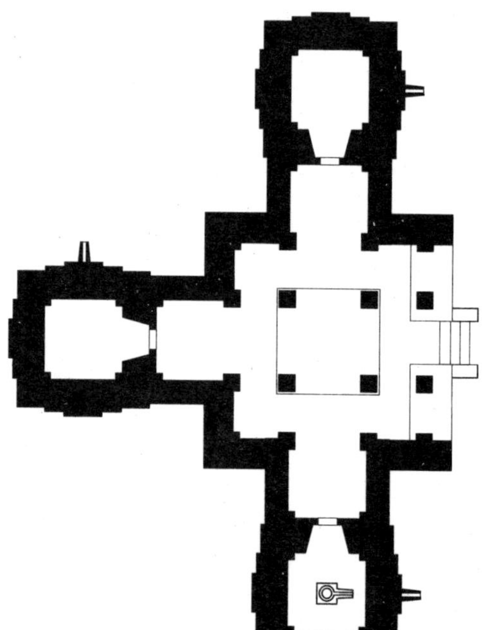

Figure 82: Basavaṇṇa (Traipuruṣa) Trikūṭa Temple, Malghana (a. 1100)

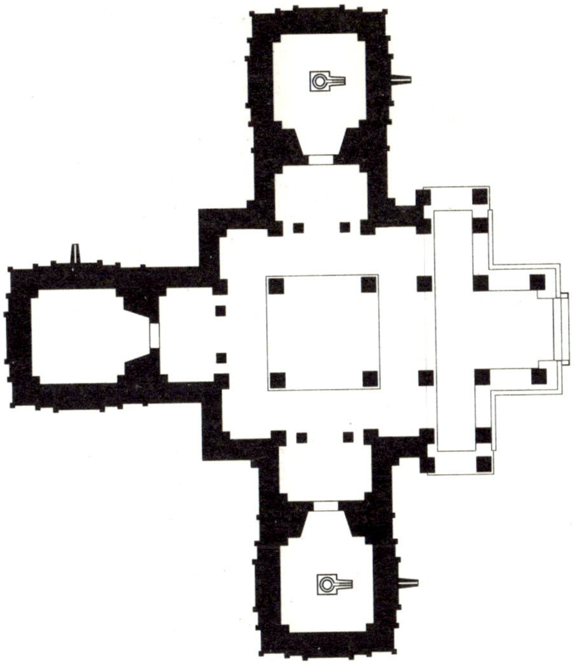

Figure 83: Nārāyaṇa Trikūṭa Temple, Iṅgaleśvara (*c.* 1150)

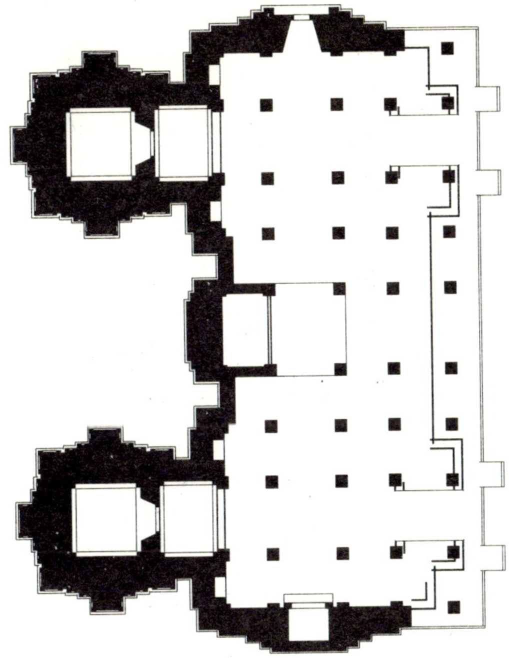

Figure 84: Bastī or Kalla-Guḍi Dvikūṭa Temple, Degamve (*c.* 1175)

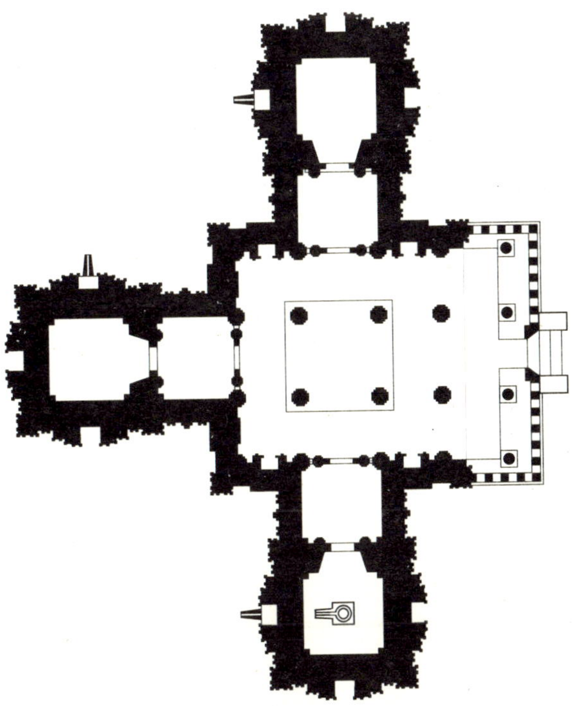

Figure 85: Sūrya-Nārāyaṇa Trikūṭa Temple, Magala (a. 1209)

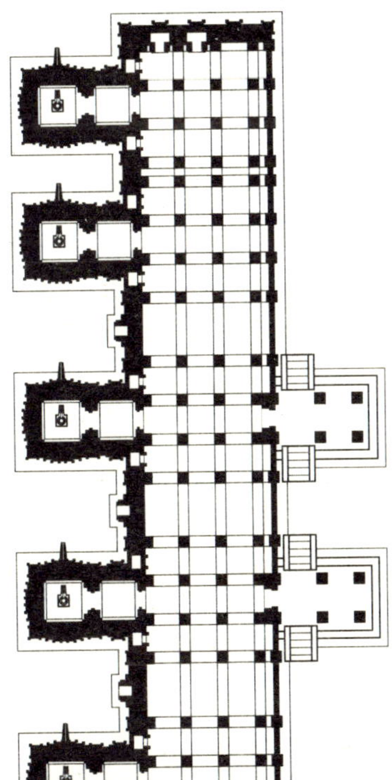

Figure 86: Pañcaliṅgeśvara Temple, Govindanahaḷḷi (*c.* 1230)

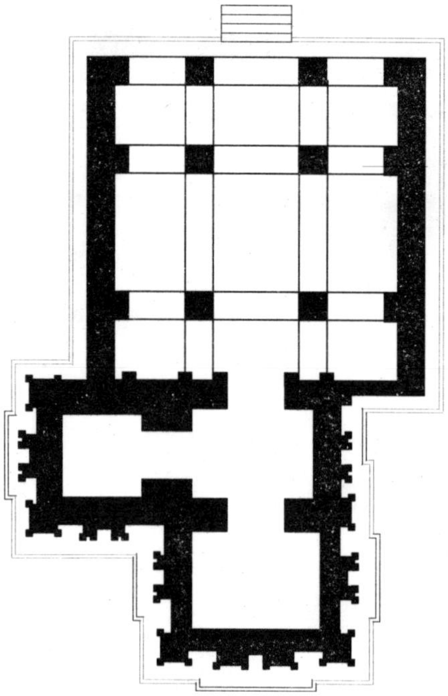

Figure 87: Minor Dvikūṭa Shrine, Rāmacandra Temple Complex (a. 1350)

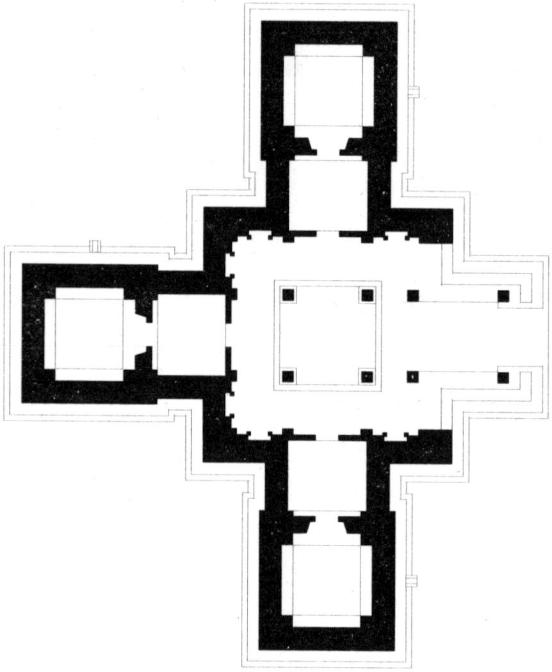

Figure 88: Kampilarāya Trikūṭa Temple (No. 1), Hampī (a. 1525)

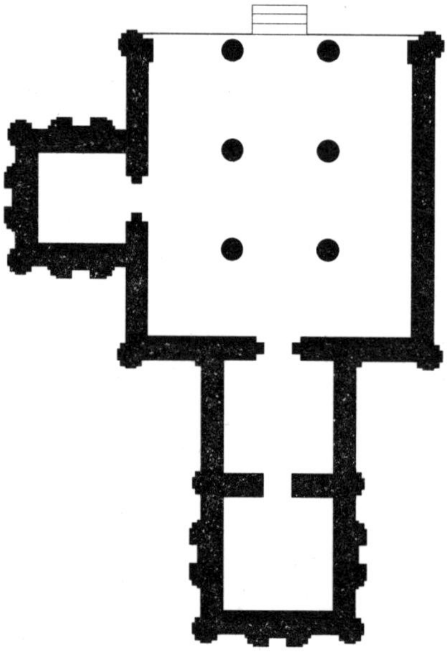

Figure 89: Amman Dvikūṭa Shrine, Acyutarāya Temple Complex, Hampī (a. 1530)

THREE-QUARTER VARIATION

Another variation, the second, on the normally encountered closed *sabhā-maṇḍapa*, is seen in temples in which the fourth wall is open, however, the normal fourth rank of columns are not present (**Figures 90-92**). In this variation the usual four free-standing columns in the centre raised on a square platform are present. But, the twelve engaged columns are reduced to eight and the four quarter, corner columns now are only two. Finally, rather than nine *aṅkanas* being formed by the traditional number are in this "three-quarter variation", reduced to six. The Rāmaliṅga Trikūṭa Temple at Iṭigi indicates a further variation (**Figure 92**). Here the fourth rank is present, free-standing and doubles as part of the *mukha-maṇḍapa*.

Both the three-quarter and three-quarter variation to the *sabhā-maṇḍapa* have one intrinsic value. They allow light into a space that in the enclosed *sabhā-maṇḍapa* is severely restricted. Even in the tropical and subtropical climes, where the sun is often directly overhead, an enclosed *sabhā-maṇḍapa* causes the interior of structures to be unduly dark. Of course, one has to take into account the flywheel effect that thick masonry and stone structures have upon the resultant heat. Considering the mystique of "miracle, mystery and authority" — i.e. a paradigm established by F. Dostoyevsky in *Brothers Karamazov* — a darkened *garbhagṛha* may be preferable.

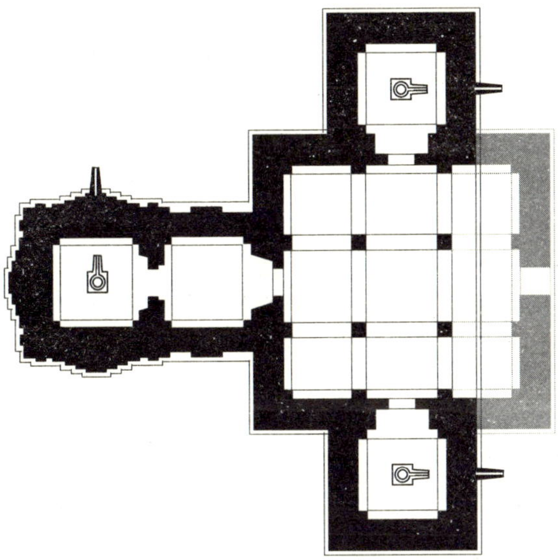

Figure 90: Śaṅkaraliṅga Trikūṭa Temple, Dhūlakheḍa (a. 1125)

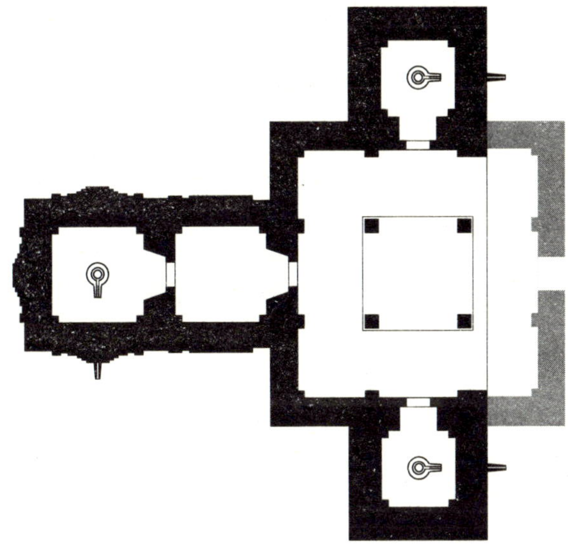

Figure 91: Śaṅkaraliṅga Trikūṭa Temple I, Dhūlakheḍa (a. 1150)

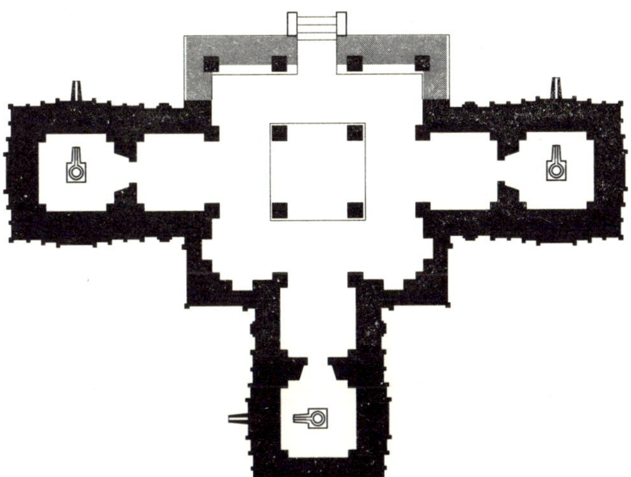

Figure 92: Rāmaliṅga Trikūṭa Temple, Iṭigi (*c.* 1150)

Amman Temples/Shrines

Amman or Devī or Rukmiṇī — which is it to be?

Amman or Mariyamman (aka Ammaniamma, Ammann, Devī, Maarimman, Mahāmāyā, Mari, Mariamman, Marika, Mariyammā, Śītalādevī) is a deity who "is popular with the Draviḍians of south India and amongst the Malaysian Hindus. She is a mother goddess, the goddess of smallpox as well as the goddess of rain. Generally, a village deity who is associated with the Śaivas and the Śakti cults. As a village deity she evolved from local nature, animistic deities who had been amalgamated into the Vedic/Hindu pantheon. A story is told of her purity, miraculous powers and faithfulness to her husband. One day, while walking afar she sees two *gandharvas* making love, she envies them and looses her power. Her husband realizing her failing, although not her faithfulness, commands his son to sever her head. She is later restored to life with the head of a brāhmaṇa and the body of an untouchable".[3] Some say that Mariamman is the sister of Lord Viṣṇu as Śrīraṅganāthar where she is referred to as Mahāmāyā.

Kuresh states: "The Amman or Devī shrines within the temple complex are the characteristics (*sic*) features and the contribution of Vijayanagara artists. The Amman shrine is generally built to the left side of the principal temple, ..."[4] It would seem that this is not only an astute observation, but one which is most probable since a number of complexes are identified with Amman temples/shrines — e.g. the Minor Dvikūṭa Shrine (Amman) within the "Haẓāra Rāmacandra Swamy Temple Complex"[5] in Vijayanagara (**Plate 107**), the Amman Dvikūṭa Shrine within the Mālyavanta Ragunātha Complex at Kamalapura (**Plate 110**), the Amman Dvikūṭa Shrine within the Viṭṭhala Temple Complex in Hampī (**Plate 111**) and the Amman Dvikūṭa Shrine within the Acyutarāya Temple Complex in Hampī (**Plate 113**). The identification of Amman with the Rāmacandra Temple Complex is not universally accepted[6] although, by dint of the evidence of numbers, it would seem quite possible. In addition, near the Karnataka town of Udipi, famed for its Udipi Kr̥ṣṇa Temple, or Kr̥ṣṇa Muṭṭ, is an important temple dedicated to Mariamman at Kaup.

In describing the Viṭṭhala Temple Complex at Hampī, Suresh states: "Towards the north-western corner of the complex is constructed a (*sic*) Amman shrine, which is meant for the Goddess Rukmiṇī, the consort of Viṭṭhala".[7] Rukmiṇī is a goddess who is associated with the Vaiṣṇavas. Rukmiṇī (aka Devī) is a "goddess, a form or manifestation of the deity Devī and related to the Vaiṣṇavas (the worship to Lord Visṇu). One of the eight notable consorts of Kr̥ṣṇa *avatāra* (Śrī Kr̥ṣṇa)."[8] Viṭṭhala (aka Kr̥ṣṇa, Paṇḍharinātha, Viṣṇu, Viṭhobā, Viṭṭhala) is "considered by some to be a minor *avatāra* of Lord Viṣṇu. This deity is popular in southern India, particularly in Vijayanagara where a major complex was raised in the deity's honour. Viṭṭhala is seen as an incarnation of Kr̥ṣṇa who is an *avatāra*

---

3 FWB IV, p. 346.

4 KMS, p. 50.

5 Ibid., p. 82, identifies this shrine as "the Amman shrine". However, on p. 153, where the Rāmacandra Temple Complex is shown in its entirety, it is identified by the letter "F" and \, below further identified as "subsidiary temple".

6 AD. pp. 37-39.

7 KMS, p. 93.

8 FWB IV, p. 454.

of Lord Viṣṇu".[9] Rukmiṇī is related to Amman only as a form of Devī. Rukmiṇī is not considered as a "mother" goddess. Amman is generally more closely associated with the Śaivas than the Vaiṣṇavas and is never considered as a consort of Lord Viṣṇu or Kṛṣṇāvatāra, although, she is seen by some to be the sister of Lord Viṣṇu.

Therefore, the question is, "Should these temples/shrines which are always associated with Vaiṣṇava complexes be identified as Amman temples/shrines?" Or, as Suresh hints, "Should they be identified as Rukmiṇī temples/shrines?"

Occurrences of Sanctums by Sect

Temples within the range of this study which are wholly or partially dedicated to Lord Viṣṇu, number sixteen (**Sect of Considered Temples**, pp. 207-08). On the other hand, those temples or shrines which are either exclusively or partially dedicated to Lord Śiva account for fifty-five, nearly three-and-a-half times more than to Lord Viṣṇu. The popularity for the Śaiva in the south of India accounts for this large number. Śakti temples account for thirteen, Jaina *basadī* see five designations and those which hold Sūrya sanctums number six. Of passing interest is that the Emperors of Vijayanagara seemed to have a predilection for Vaiṣṇava temples.

Reoccurring Deity-forms

There appears time and time again particular forms of both Lord Viṣṇu and Lord Śiva throughout the purview of the temples considered herein. Keśava, a form of Lord Viṣṇu, appears again and again — e.g. the Basavaṇṇa (Traipuruṣa) Trikūṭa Temple (**Plate 33**), the Someśvara Trikūṭa Temple (**Plate 37**), the Lakṣmī-Devī Catuṣkūṭa Temple (**Plate 42**), the Cennakeśava Temple (**Plate 45**) the Nārāyaṇa Trikūṭa Temple (**Plate 56**), the Mallikārjuna Trikūṭa Temple (**Plate 93**) and the Keśava Trikūṭa Temple (**Plate 97**). Likewise, Mallikārjuna, a form of Lord Śiva, is also prominent — e.g. the Mallikārjuna Trikūṭa Temple (**Plate 52**), the Mallikārjuna Trikūṭa Temple (**Plate 61**), the Mallikārjuna Trikūṭa Temple (**Plate 62**), the Rāmeśvara Trikūṭa Temple (**Plate 80**) and the Mallikārjuna Trikūṭa Temple (**Plate 93**). And, the deity Sūrya appears a number of times — e.g. the Basavaṇṇa (Traipuruṣa) Trikūṭa Temple (**Plate 33**), the Someśvara Trikūṭa Shrine (**Plate 37**), the Buceśvara Dvikūṭa Temple (**Plate 77**), the Sūrya-Nārāyaṇa Trikūṭa Temple (**Plate 85**), the Mallikārjuna Trikūṭa Temple (**Plate 93**) and the Sūrya Temple (**Plate 96**).

Multiple Dedications

There are a number of temples found within the purview of this study which are dedicated to deities of either Vaiṣṇava deities and Śaiva deities, or Vaiṣṇava, Śaiva and Śākta deities. A small number of temples are dedicated to two deities. These would include the Kallappa-Mallappa (Harihara) Dvikūṭa Temple (**Plate 25**) which is dedicated to both Lord Viṣṇu and Lord Śiva. Its design seems to indicate that these two deities were given equal status. The Buceśvara Dvikūṭa Temple (**Plate 77**) is dedicated to Lord Śiva and the deity Sūrya. The Kāśīviśveśvara Dvikūṭa Temple (**Plate 28**) sees the main *vimāna* with a Śivaliṅga and the eastern *vimāna* dedicated to Sūrya-Nārāyaṇa. And, the Siddheśvara Dvikūṭa Temple (**Plate 7**) sees the image of Siddheśvara (Śiva) in the west and the Śakti image in the smaller eastern sanctum.

[9] FWB IV, p. 660.

There appears, within the range of this study, a large number of temples dedicated to three deities. The Basavaṇṇa (Traipuruṣa) Trikūṭa Temple is dedicated to Lord Viṣṇu as Keśava, Lord Śiva and Sūrya (**Plate 33**), where the middle *vimāna* is the realm of Keśava. Whereas the Someśvara Trikūṭa Temple finds Lord Viṣṇu as Keśava, Lord Śiva and Sūrya within the three *garbhagṛhas* (**Plate 37**), the sanctum dedicated to Lord Śiva seems to predominate. The Mallikārjuna Trikūṭa Temple (**Plate 93**) is consecrated to Lord Śiva, Lord Viṣṇu as Keśava and to the deity Sūrya. The *garbhagṛha* holding the Śivaliṅga has pride of place in this temple. Nārāyaṇa Trikūṭa Temple (**Plate 75**) places the Viṣṇu image in the principal, the middle *garbhagṛha* and the Śivaliṅga and Śākta image in the flanking eastern and western *vimānas*. The Saṅgameśvara Trikūṭa Temple (**Plate 63**) finds the image of Lord Viṣṇu as Keśava in the principal or central *vimāna* with Sūrya in the flanking eastern and Śivaliṅga in the corresponding west. Originally, the Someśvara Trikūṭa Temple (**Plate 82**) is consecrated to Lord Śiva in the form of a Śivaliṅga, Lord Viṣṇu as Nārāyaṇa and to Śakti. In the original configuration the Nārāyaṇa image occupied the principal *garbhagṛha* while the other two deities flanked this image. And the Sūrya-Nārāyaṇa Trikūṭa Temple (**Plate 85**) is dedicated to Lord Viṣṇu as Keśava, the Śivaliṅga and the deity Sūrya. Again, the image of Keśava is flanked by the other two deities.

One temple is unique within the range considered here, and that is the Lakṣmī-Devī Catuṣkūṭa Temple (**Plate 42**) which is dedicated to Lakṣmī, Lord Viṣṇu as Keśava, the Śivaliṅga and the deity Kālī. In this temple the principal sanctum is occupied by Keśava with Lakṣmī flanking on the east and the Śivaliṅga on the west. The Goddess Kālī occupies the northern *vimāna*, opposite that of Keśava. Is there any significance to this arrangement? Looking on Lakṣmī as the consort of Lord Viṣṇu, and Kālī as the consort of Lord Śiva, then we find that the Vaiṣṇava occupying the south and east, with the Śaiva in the north and west. On the other hand, it may be viewed as the Vaiṣṇava occupying the south, the Śaiva the west and the Śakti the north and east. Still further, by the alignment of the temple — i.e. south to north — the *vimāna* of Keśava with the flanking sanctums occupies pride of place. But, opposite and slightly separated in this **B**-type *catuṣkūṭa* plan is Kālī.

A second *catuṣkūṭa* temple warrants interest as well — i.e. Bhīmeśvara Catuṣkūṭa Temple (**Plate 16**). The western *vimāna* enshrines a Śivaliṅga, the northern *garbhagṛha* is dedicated to Keśava, and the southern to Lord Brahmā which is unusual. The separate eastern *garbhagṛha* enshrines Sūrya. The inclusion of a *vimāna* dedicated to Lord Brahmā is most rare. Frequently, in *pañcāyatana* temples a minor shrine may be dedicated to this deity, but in a temple, a *garbhagṛha* enshrining Lord Brahmā is extraordinary.

It is interesting to see the "balance" in these dedications. The incorporation of deities from the three major sects within a single temple does not, of course, indicate a wild rush towards ecumenism within the Hindu faith. Rather, it seems to indicate the particular and/or peculiar bent of an individual patron. All of them, eventually, point to *Brahman*, the Absolute.

Sect of Considered Temples

Temple	*Viṣṇu*	*Śiva*	*Śakti*	*Jaina*	*Other*
Amman Dvikūṭa Shrine, Acyutarāya Temple Complex, Hampī			■		
Amman Dvikūṭa Shrine, Kamalapura			■		
Amman Dvikūṭa Shrine, Viṭṭhala Temple Complex, Hampī			■		
Anantaśayana Trikūṭa Temple, Navali	■				
Basavaṇṇa (Traipuruṣa) Trikūṭa Temple, Malghana	■	■			Sūrya ■
Bastī or Kalla-Guḍi Dvikūṭa Temple, Degamve			■		
Bhīmeśvara Catuṣkūṭa Temple, Nīlaguṇḍa	■	■			Sūrya and Brahmā ■
Buceśvara Dvikūṭa Temple, Koravaṅgala		■			
Candramaulīśvara Temple, Unkal		■			
Candragupta Trikūṭa Basadī, Śravaṇabeḷagoḷa				■	
Candraśekhara Dvikūṭa Temple, Hampī		■			
Causaṭh Yoginī Mandir and Gaurī-Śaṅkara Temple, Bherāghāṭ			■		
Cauṅsaṭh Yoginī Sanctuary, Khajurāho			■		
Cauṅsaṭh Yoginī Temple, Hīrāpur			■		
Cennakeśava Temple, Beḷūr	■				
Gaṅgādhareśvara Dvikūṭa Temple, Ḍoḍḍaiśvara		■			
Hoysaḷeśvara Dvikūṭa Temple, Halebiḍ		■			
Īśvara Dvikūṭa Temple, Arsikere		■			
Īśvara Trikūṭa Temple, Basarakoḍu		■			
Jaina Basadī No. 15, Deogaṛh				■	
Jaina Tīrthaṅkara Trikūṭa Basadī, Arasibedi				■	
Jambuliṅgeśvara Trikūṭa Shrine, Bādāmī		■			
Kailāsanātha Temple, Kāñcīpuram		■			
Kalideva Dvikūṭa Temple, Kummsi		■			
Kallappa-Mallappa (Harihara) Dvikūṭa Temple, Devaragennur	■	■			
Kalleśvara Dvikūṭa Temple, Bagali		■			
Kampilarāya Trikūṭa Temple (No. 1), Hampī		■			
Kampilarāya Trikūṭa Temple (No. 3), Hampī		■			
Kāśīviśveśvara Dvikūṭa Temple, Lakkuṇḍī	■	■			
Kedāreśvara Trikūṭa Temple, Balagamve		■			
Keśava Trikūṭa Temple, Somanāthapur	■				
Koṭe Śaṅkaraliṅga Dvikūṭa Temple, Nimbal		■			
Kunthu Jinanātha Dvikūṭa Jinālaya, Kamalapura				■	
Lakṣmī-Devī Catuṣkūṭa Temple, Doḍḍa Gaḍḍuvalli	■	■	■		
Lakṣmī-Narasiṁha Trikūṭa Temple, Bhadravatī	■				
Mahādeva Trikūṭa Temple, Benakoṭagī		■			
Mallikārjuna Trikūṭa Temple, Basaralu	■	■			Sūrya ■
Mallikārjuna Trikūṭa Temple, Devaranavadagi		■			
Mallikārjuna Trikūṭa Temple, Hirebevinuru		■			
Mallikārjuna Trikūṭa Temple, Hospeṭ		■			
Mallikārjuna Trikūṭa Temple, Katnahaḷḷi		■			
Minor Dvikūṭa Shrine, Rāmacandra Temple Complex, Vijayanagara			■		
Nārāyaṇa Trikūṭa Temple, Anekannambadi	■				
Nārāyaṇa Trikūṭa Temple, Iṅgaleśvara	■	■	■		

Sect of Considered Temples (Continued)

Temple	*Viṣṇu*	*Śiva*	*Śakti*	*Jaina*	*Other*
Navaliṅgeśvara Navakūṭa Temple, Kukkanur		■			
Pañcaliṅgeśvara Pañcakūṭa Temple, Govindanahaḷḷi		■			
Paramānanda Trikūṭa Temple, Konnur		■			
Pārśvanātha Dvikūṭa Jinālaya, Hampī				■	
Rachi-Guḍi Trikūṭa Temple, Aihoḷe		■			
Rāmaliṅga Dvikūṭa Temple, Horti		■			
Rāmaliṅga Dvikūṭa Temple, Sirur		■			
Rāmaliṅga Trikūṭa Temple, Iṭigi		■			
Rāmaliṅgeśvara Trikūṭa Temple, Kundaragi		■			
Rāmeśvara Dvikūṭa Temple, Yaragaḷ		■			
Rāmeśvara Trikūṭa Shrine, Kurugod		■			
Rāmeśvara Trikūṭa Shrine, Yaragal		■			
Śambuliṅga Dvikūṭa Temple, Kakkalameli		■			
Saṅgameśvara Trikūṭa Temple, Bevura	■	■			
Saṅgameśvara Trikūṭa Temple, Babaleśvara		■			
Śaṅkaraliṅga Trikūṭa Temple, Dhūlakheḍa		■			
Śaṅkaraliṅga Dvikūṭa Temple, Kalakere		■			
Siddhaliṅgeśvara Pañcakūṭa Temple, Siruvala		■			
Siddheśvara Dvikūṭa Temple, Aḷgoḍu		■	■		
Śaiva Dvikūṭa Temple, Chauḍadampur		■			
Śaiva Dvikūṭa Temple, Hampī		■			
Someśvara Trikūṭa Temple, Haralhaḷḷi		■			
Someśvara Trikūṭa Temple, Iṅgaleśvara	■	■	■		
Someśvara Trikūṭa Temple, Kabali	■	■			Sūrya
Sūrya-Nārāyaṇa Trikūṭa Temple, Magala	■	■			Sūrya
Sūrya Temple, Koṇārka					Sūrya
Trikūṭeśvara Temple, Gaḍag		■			
Trikūṭeśvara Trikūṭa Temple, Gorur		■			
Trikūṭeśvara (Śiva) Temple, Timmalapur		■			
Vaidyanātheśvara Dvikūṭa Temple, Vaidyanāthapura		■			
Vīranārāyaṇa Trikūṭa Temple, Belvadi	■				

Appendix A

Glossary and Application of Terms

Glossary

abhiṣeka-maṇḍapa (Indic): The term refers to a hall for ritual bathing.

additive architectural process: As opposed to the subtractive architectural process (monolithic), it refers to structures which are composed or individual structural elements — i.e. bricks, stone blocks and/or wooden members — which are assembled to enclose space or form a structure.

ādhāraśilā (Indic): The term refers to a base stone under the shrine upon which are placed various propitious items, such as *nidhikumbha, padma, kūrma* and *yoganala*.

adhiṣṭhāna (Indic): It refers to the base or podium of a temple or other structure made up of succeeding layers of moulding. It appears directly beneath the *vedikā*.

alinda (Indic): The term refers to an aisle and related to *pradakṣiṇāpatha*.

alpa-vimāna (Indic): It refers to a single-storey temple or *vimāna*.

āmalaka (Indic): The term refers to the finials of a *śikhara* or *chattrāvalī* which is characterized as resembling a lotus bud.

aṇḍa (Indic: aka *dhātu-garbha, garbha, gaeba*): The term refers to an egg-shape, more specifically to the hemispherical form of a *stūpa*. It is also referred to as *garbha* and *gaeba*.

andhārika (Indic): It refers to an enclosed ambulatory or *pradakṣiṇāpatha*.

aṅkanas (Indic): A bay bordered by four columns in the corners.

antara-bhittī (Indic): The term refers to the wall of a sanctum particularly when the temple is of the *sandhāra* type.

antarāla (Indic): A narrow passageway or vestibule connecting the *garbhagr̥ha* and/or the *ardha-maṇḍapa* with the maṇḍapa or a space in front of the door leading to the sanctum.

arcana-maṇḍapa (Indic: aka *namaskāra-maṇḍapa*): Another term for *namaskāra-maṇḍapa*. (See **Application of Terms**.)

ardha-maṇḍapa (Indic: aka *antarāla, mukha-maṇḍapa, śukanāsī*): The term refers to a transitional element, a wide passageway between the *garbhagr̥ha* and *maṇḍapa*. It is frequently utilized as a storage area for the various accouterments needed during worship. (See **Application of Terms**.)

anardha-ratha (Indic): It refers to the second and fourth *ratha*s in a *pañcaratha* plan. (See **Application of Terms**.)

antaryāmin (Indic): The term refers to the divine image (literally "the indwelling Lord") of a temple found in the *garbhagr̥ha*.

ardha-mantapa (Indic: aka *artha-maṇḍapa*): The term refers to a porch or entrance space, frequently open. It is also a term which refers to either an enclosed space, often attached to an *antarāla*, or a porch adjacent to the *maṇḍapa*. (See **Application of Terms**.)

artha-mantapa (Indic: aka *ardha-maṇḍapa*): A variant spelling for the term *ardha-maṇḍapa*.

astasra (Indic): The term refers to a temple plan that is octagonal or stellar in form.

axiality: The symmetrical arrangement of the elements of a plan along a given axis. If that axis is the east–west axis, then the northern half is a duplicate of the southern half.

ayatasra: It refers to a temple plan that is rectangular in form.

bāgh (Arab.): The term refers to a garden, usually square or made up of square components. It may also refer to a pleasure palace.

bāhya-bhittī (Indic): It refers to the outer wall, generally of a *vimāna*.

balikkal-maṇḍapa (Indic): A columned hall raised above the principal *balipīṭha*, opposite the main entrance of a temple. (See *namaskāra-maṇḍapa*.)

base/basis: The term base or basis is used by a number of scholars — e.g. Anagarika Govinda — to refer to an architectural base or basis, generally consisting of one or more low platforms which serve as a transition from the ground to and/or upon which a major structure, itself consisting of a number of standardized elements — e.g. the basis of a *stūpa* or a temple — is placed.

bhadra (Indic): It refers to an offset or central projection in a wall and related to a *ratha*. (See

Application of Terms.)

bhadraratha (Indic): The term refers to a central offset or wall division and related to a *ratha*. (See **Application of Terms**.)

bhadrāvalokana (Indic): It refers to an opening in a *bhadra* or *bhadraratha*.

bhittī (Indic): The term refers to a wall.

bhoga-maṇḍapa (Indic): A Orissan hall of offering.

bhūmi (Indic): The term refers to "strata", more specifically to the decreasing donut-shaped forms that make up the spire of a *stūpa*. See *chattrāvalī*.

brahmakānta (Indic): A tetragonal column associated with south India.

Brahmaśilā (Indic: aka *napuṁsakaśilā*): The term refers to a stone slab that is placed upon the *yoganāla*.

brahma-sthāna (Indic): It refers to the panel in the centre of a *maṇḍala*.

caitya (Indic: aka *cetiya, stūpa*): Another term for *stūpa*. As in a *caitya* hall, the *stūpa* tends to be carved from solid rock as a memorial. See *dhammacetiya, dhātucetiya, paribhogacetiya, stūpa, uddeśikacetiya*.

caityagṛha (Indic): A place or hall of worship.

caitya hall (Indic): The term refers to a sacred temple, generally Buddhist, frequently carved from solid rock. It consists of a colonnaded hall, generally apsidal with a *caitya* at the centre point of the arc.

chandi (Indon.: aka *caṇḍī*): A temple or temple complex in Indonesia — e.g. *Chandi Sewu*. It may be derived from or refered to: *cedi*, or Caṇḍī (goddess of death).

candraśilā (Indic): The lowest step of a staircase that is half moon or half-circular shaped.

cakravartin (Indic: aka *cakkavatī*): The term refers to the concept of a universal monarch. One who possesses all the qualities of a great leader as exemplified in the Emperor Aśoka, who was considered to be a *cakravartin*.

chapakara (Indic): An apsidal form.

chatramukha (Indic: aka *sarvatobhadra*): Another term for *sarvatobhadra*.

chatrī (Indic): A kiosk with a dome usually supported by four or eight pillars.

chatta (Pāli: aka *chattra, hti*): A variant term for *chattra*. See *chattra*.

chattra (Indic: aka *chāttā*): The term refers to an umbrella or a parasol. It applies to a finials ornament in the form of a parasol, usually placed over a *chattrāvalī* or over shrines.

chattrāvalī (Indic: aka *hti, koṭa, kūṭa*): The term refers to the area of a *stūpa* above the *aṇḍa* and/or *harmikā*, which consists of a series of circular mouldings, descending in size as it raises. In some cases the *chattrāvalī* is massive and in other cases it is quite slender.

caturasra (Indic): The term refers to a temple plan that is square in form.

caturasra koṣṭha (Indic: aka *catussurakoṣṭha, harmikā, hataraes koṭuva*): A variant term for *harmikā*. See *harmikā*.

catuṣkūṭi (Indic): The term refers to a temple that has four sanctums.

catuṣki (Indic): The term refers to a bay bounded by four pillars or columns.

catuṣsurakoṣṭha (Indic: aka *caturasra koṣṭha, harmikā, hataraes koṭuva*): A variant term for *harmikā*. See *harmikā*.

chedi (Thai: aka *caitya, dagobā, pagoḍā, stūpa, zeidi*): The term refers to the Thai equivalent of a *stūpa*. Its form is often greatly elongated into a tall thin form and may contain holy relics, ashes of monarchs, saints or other meritorious persons. In the later periods it loses its circular shape and becomes more angular, but still retains the basic elements.

cetiya (Pāli: aka *caitya*): See *caitya*.

cetiyāgāra (Pāli): A roofed circular structure enclosing a smaller *stūpa* prevalent in Sri Lanka.

cross-axiality: The symmetrical arrangement of the elements of a plan along both axes, precisely duplicating each quadrant. This term is not applied to rectangular plans. The north–south and east–west axes divide the form. The north-west quadrant is a duplicate of the north-east, south-west and south-east quadrants. This quadrant can either be mirrored in any of the other three, or rotated 90°, 180°, and 270° to achieve the whole.

dagabā (Javanese: aka *dagobā, dhātu-garbha, pagoḍā,*

stūpa): The term refers to a *stūpa*, as in the *dagabā* of Borobudur. See *stūpa*.

dagobā (Indic: aka *dagabā, pagoḍā*): A variant spelling for the term *dagabā*. See *dagabā*.

devagṛha (Indic): It refers to a shrine or temple; literally "house of the divinity".

devakoṣṭha (Indic): The term refers to a niche enshrining a deity.

devakula (Indic): It refers to a shrine.

devālaya (Indic: aka *prāsāda, vimāna, tīrtha*): A place of worship — i.e. a temple or a shrine. It means "the house of god". (See **Application of Terms**.)

devatā koṭuva (Sinhalese): The term refers to a cylindrical transition between the *chattrāvalī* and the *harmikā*, and means "the enclosure of the gods".

dhātu (Indic): It refers to relic(s).

dhātu-garbha (Indic: *dagabā, dagobā, pagoḍā*): The term means "relic womb" and early it was referred to the *harmikā*, then it became associated with the *aṇḍa*. See *dagabā*.

Draviḍa (Indic): A style of architecture or temple type prevalent in the south of India where the Draviḍians are located, particularly in Kerala and Tamil Nadu. (See **Application of Terms**.)

dvāra (Indic): A door. (See **Application of Terms**.)

dvāra-mukha-sopāna (Indic): The term refers to a flight of stairs at the main entrance.

dvikūṭa (Indic): A temple with two sanctums.

engaged column (pillar): A column which has part of the shaft attached to a wall as opposed to a freestanding column. (See **Application of Terms**.)

file: The term refers to a linear element of objects. Specifically, *file* refers to the vertical line from front to back. It is directionally perpendicular to a *rank*.

free-standing column (pillar): The term as used herein refers to a pillar or column that is not engaged. (See **Application of Terms**.)

gaddī: It refers to a cushioned seat upon which a ruler used to sit. It has come to refer to "a throne" proper within the Hindu/Indian context. It may also refer to "the throne" of a particular state.

gaeba (Sinhalese: aka *garbha, aṇḍa*): A variant term for *aṇḍa*. See *aṇḍa*.

galā (Indic: aka *grīvā*): A variant term for *grīvā*. See *grīvā*.

gandal(s) (Indic: aka *pilimages*): A temple or chapel structure reserved for a large Buddha image.

garbha (Indic: aka *aṇḍa, gaeba*): A variant term for *aṇḍa*. See *aṇḍa*.

garbhagṛha (Indic: aka *khapphathat, ruanthat*): It refers to the *sanctum-sanctorum*, specifically of a Hindu temple. It is the place where the image of the main deity is housed and the access to it is limited to the priesthood. It is the holiest area of a temple and the term refers to the womb — i.e. "womb chamber" — found in the sanctum. (See **Application of Terms**.)

gedige(s) (Indic): A rectangular as opposed to a square temple structure , generally in Sri Lanka, usually constructed of bricks. Later the term is applied to rectangular, roofed stone structures.

ghana-dvāra (Indic): The term refers to a false door often found in a *bhadra* other than the opening to the *garbhagṛha*. (See **Application of Terms**.)

ghaṭa (Indic): A vase or pitcher and the term is often used to describe the shape of a temple.

ghaṭa-prāsāda (Indic): It refers to a vase-shaped temple, usually consisting of a circular sanctum and an extended *kapilī*.

gopura(m) (Indic: aka *sum pratu*): An elaborate, crowned gateway to a temple compound.

granite: A very hard, igneous rock suitable for permanent construction. It is difficult to work, but most permanent.

grīvā (Indic: aka *galā*): The term refers to a transitional element of a *śikhara* between the *āmalaka* and the *śukanāsikā*.

gūḍha-maṇḍapa (Indic): The term refers to an enclosed or closed hall within a temple. (See *maṇḍapa* and **Application of Terms**.)

harmikā (Indic: aka *catuṣsurakoṣṭha, caturasra koṣṭha, hataraes koṭuva*): A rectilinear form, traditionally a casket containing treasures, used as a transitional form between the *aṇḍa* and the *chattrāvalī* of a *stūpa*. It as an altar-like structure and is also referred to as *catuṣsurakoṣṭha, caturasra koṣṭha* and *hataraes koṭuva*.

hataraes koṭuva (Sinhalese: aka *catuṣsurakoṣṭha, caturasra koṣṭha, hamikā*): A variant term for *harmikā*. See *harmikā*.

hti (Burman: aka *chattra, koṭa, kūṭa*): The term refers to a parasol form used as a finials. See *chattra*.

hypaethral: A temple without a roof.

jālī (Arab./Indic): A thin, stone screen with a perforated design. (See **Application of Terms**.)

jagamohana (Indic: aka *maṇḍapa, mukhaśālā, navaraṅga*): The term refers to the assembly hall, or *maṇḍapa*, of a Nāgara temple. (See **Application of Terms**.)

jagatī (Indic): A plinth.

jalandhara (Indic): A window of stone in which square openings are evenly spaced vertically and horizontally. They are thicker and heavier in design than *jālī*. (See **Application of Terms**.)

jaṅghā (Indic): The term refers to "shank" and is the base part of a *śikhara*. It also may refer to a wall, either exterior or interior.

kaeraella (Indic): The term refers to a spherical form used as a finials to a *stūpa* spire in certain cultures. It is related to *kalaśa*.

kakṣāsana (Indic): It is a "seat-back" or railing. The area above is open and may have columns either partially engaged or resting on the top surface.

kalaśa (Indic): A vessel or vase, and is applied to a form of similar shape used as a decorative element frequently at the corners of terraces or roofs in Pagan.

kalyāṇa-maṇḍapa (Indic): An open, pillared hall where the wedding (*kalyāṇa*) festivals of the gods are celebrated. (See **Application of Terms**.)

kapilī (Indic): A vestibule or porch usually extending from the entrance of a sanctum. (See **Application of Terms**.)

karṇas (Indic): An angle, a corner projection or a corner wall division.

khakāra (Indic): A rectangular plan.

koṇārka-ratha (Indic): The term refers to the first and fifth *rathas* in a *pañcaratha* plan. (See **Application of Terms**.)

koṭa (Sinhalese: aka *chattrāvalī, hti, kūṭa*): It refers to a spire. See *chattrāvalī*.

kuḍyastambha (Indic): It is an engaged pier or pilaster. (See **Application of Terms**.)

kuṇḍa (Indic): A reservoir, a tank.

kūṭa (Indic: aka *chattrāvalī, hti, koṭa*): The term refers to a spire. See *chattrāvalī*.

laterite: A type of clay-like top soil which is easily cut into blocks. When protected and dried the material is quite hard and relatively stable. It is often employed as a core building material and, if properly treated — i.e. covered by a more permanent or waterproof material such as stucco —and maintained, it may last for centuries. Many of the temples of Angkor have laterite cores.

liṅgam (Indic): It refers to the abstract form, often phallic, which represents Lord Śiva.

mahal (Indic) (aka *mandira*): Originally, the term referred to any hall or ceremonial room, pavilion or apartment within a palace or other notable structure. See *bhavana*. By extension it is now commonly applied to a palace — e.g. Gagan Mahal of Bījāpur, the Rāja Mahal of Tirupati, or the Rāja Mahal of Amber. See *gaṛh mahal*.

mahāmaṇḍapa (Indic): A large columned hall between the *antarāla* and *maṇḍapa*. (See *maṇḍapa* and **Application of Terms**.)

mañca (Indic): The term refers to an elevated platform or a dais.

maṇḍala (Indic): A sacred, cosmic geometric form or drawing. In the Hindu tradition it is generally square, the centre of which is the locus of a major deity. The construction of which offers spiritual and cosmic production. It is also conceived as being three-dimensional. In the Buddhist tradition the *maṇḍala* tends to be circular.

maṇḍapa (Indic: aka *jagamohana, kalyāṇa-maṇḍapa, mandira, mantapa, mukhaśālā, navaraṅga, nṛtta-maṇḍapa, sabhā-maṇḍapa*): The term is generic and refers to a covered structure, a hypostyle hall of a Hindu temple which serves as an assembly hall for the devotees. Generally, the *maṇḍapa* holds a series of columns. (See also *mukha-maṇḍapa, gūḍha-maṇḍapa, mahāmaṇḍapa* and **Application of Terms**.)

mandira (Indic): A *maṇḍapa* of a northern Nāgara

style temple.

maṇḍūka-maṇḍala (Indic): It refers to a sacred *maṇḍala* composed of sixty-four *pada*s, and employed in the plan of a temple.

mantapa (Indic): A variant of *maṇḍapa*. See *maṇḍapa*.

marble: A hard, metamorphic rock that is often used in construction. It is easier to work than granite, and is considerably more permanent than laterite.

marmas (Indic): Points of intersection of *pada*s which are not to be touched by the walls of the temple.

maṭha (Indic): A monastery.

medhi (Indic): An area either between the *vedikā* and the base of a *stūpa*, or the area between the base of the *stūpa* and the *aṇḍa* which is used for *pradakṣiṇā*.

mirror cross-axiality: The symmetrical arrangement of the elements of a plan along both axis, mirroring each quadrant. This term is applied to rectangular plans. The north–south and east–west axes divide the form. The north-west quadrant is a mirror duplicate of the north-east, south-west and south-east quadrants. This quadrant can be mirrored in any of the other three. It cannot be rotated to achieve the whole as can be seen in the cross-axial plan.

mukhacatuṣki (Indic): It is an entry porch supported by four columns. (See **Application of Terms**.)

mukha-maṇḍapa (Indic): The term refers to a pillared hall in line with the sanctum. It is also seen as the first hall in front of the sanctum when there are more than one and generally without columns. It also refers to an entrance porch or vestibule in smaller temples or shrines that are enclosed within a larger form. See *ardha-maṇḍapa*. (See **Application of Terms**.)

mukhamantapa (Indic): A variant of *mukha-maṇḍapa*. See *mukha-maṇḍapa*.

mukhaśālā (Indic): The term refers to an assembly hall. A variant of the term *jagamohana*. See *jagamohana* and **Application of Terms**.)

mūlaprāsāda (Indic): It refers to the main hall or block of a temple. See *vimāna*.

Nāgara (Indic): A style of architecture or temple type prevalent in the north of India. (See **Application of Terms**.)

nālambalam (Indic): It is a cloister or colonnaded passage around an open court which encloses a temples.

namaskāra-maṇḍapa (Indic: aka *arcana-maṇḍapa*): The term refers to a separate hall, usually in front of a a shrine or temple which may have a *maṇḍapa*. This *maṇḍapa* is used for worship (*namaskāra* = prayer) and protects the devotees from the sun as well as the rain. (See **Application of Terms**.)

Nandī-maṇḍapa (Indic): An open *śālā* or pavilion dedicated to Nandī, the bull.

napuṁsakaśilā (Indic: aka *brahmaśilā*): A variant of the term *brahmaśilā*. See *brahmaśilā*.

nāsikā (Indic): The term refers to "nose". Architecturally, it refers to any ornament that is nose-like in form or profile.

naṭa-mandira (Indic): An Orissan hall for dance.

nāṭya-śālā (Indic): It is a pavilion or hall for musical dance performances.

navaraṅga: (Indic: aka *maṇḍapa*) A variant term for *maṇḍapa*. See *maṇḍapa* and **Application of Terms**.)

nidhikumbha (Indic): It refers to a pot laid atop the *ādhāraśilā* in the foundation beneath the *garbhagṛha*.

nirandhara (Indic): A structure without an enclosed ambulatory or *pradakṣiṇāpatha*.

nṛtta-maṇḍapa (Indic: aka *maṇḍapa, navaraṅga*): A variant term for *maṇḍapa*. See *maṇḍapa*.

nṛtta-mantapa (Indic): A variant spelling for *nṛtta-maṇḍapa*. See *maṇḍapa*.

pada (Indic): The term refers to foot, more specifically to the individual squares which make up a *maṇḍala*.

padakkhina (Pāli: aka *pradakṣiṇā*): The Pāli equivalent for *pradakṣiṇā*.

padmagarbhamaṇḍala (Indic): A *maṇḍala* popular in south India. The *maṇḍala* consisting of 256 *pada*s.

padma-prāsāda (Indic): The term refers to a circular temple type.

pagoḍā (Burman: aka *dagabā, dagobā, dhātu-garbha*): A variant term for *dagabā*. See *dagabā*.

pañca-prākāra (Indic): Five successive enclosures.

pañcaratha (Indic): The term refers to two separate extensions, generally in the middle portion of the surface of a wall, creating five surfaces per face. (See *ratha* and *triratha* and**Application of Terms.**)

pañcāyatana (Indic): An ensemble with five shrines, a quincunx arrangement.

paramaśāyika maṇḍala (Indic): A *maṇḍala* with eighty-one *padas*.

parivāra (Indic): It refers to figures which are attendant upon a deity-image. Frequently these figures are found in the ambulatories (*pradakṣiṇāpathas*) or may encircle the deity proper.

pendentive: An inverted triangle which is the transition from a square space to a dome. See squinch.

pilimage(s) (Indic: aka *gaṇḍals*): The term which generally refers to *gandals* in Sri Lanka. See *gandals*.

pita-deul: A meeting hall or a structure for the performance of dance in a temple.

pīṭha (Indic): The term refers to a pedestal, plinth or platform.

pradakṣiṇā (Indic: aka *prathaksin, padakkhina*): The term refers to the act of merit known as circumambulation, or procession around a shrine in a clockwise direction.

pradakṣiṇāpatha (Indic; Malayalam: *cuttu-nadi*): The term refers to the hallway within a shrine, or area reserved for circumambulation. It is relatively synonymous with the ambulatory of Romanesque and Gothic churches of the West. (See **Application of Terms.**)

prākāra (Indic): A walled enclosure, or an enclosure wall, or the girdle wall of a temple.

prāsāda (Indic: aka *vimāna, devālaya, tīrtha*; Pāli; Thai: *prasad, prasat*): It refers to a temple plan and is related to a palace in make-up. It may also refer to a mansion or palace.

prathaksin (Thai: aka *pradakṣiṇā*): The Thai equivalent for *pradakṣiṇā*.

pratibhadra (Indic): It refers to *bhadras* which are offset and/or flanking each other.

pratiratha (Indic): The term refers to wall offsets which flank *bhadras*.

pseudo-sarvatobhadra (Indic): A *vimāna* which has a portal and three *ghana-dvāra* or false doors at the other cardinal points. (See *sarvatobhadra* and **Application of Terms.**)

pūjā (Indic): The term refers to an act of worship or prayer in which supplications are made to the deity, often accompanied by some type of offering, or any other act of merit such as *pradakṣiṇā*.

puṣpaka (Indic: aka *ratha*): It refers to a cosmic, magical chariot. It is often a term applied to a temple

quincunx: It is an arrangement in which a structure is surrounded by four subsidiary structures, usually at the cardinal or intercardinal points. See *pañcāyatana*.

raha-ratha (Indic): The third *ratha* in a *pañcaratha* plan. (See **Application of Terms.**)

raṅga-maṇḍapa (Indic): An open pillared hall (*maṇḍapa*). (See **Application of Terms.**)

rank (Eng.): The term as used refers to a horizontal line of objects in a row. Specifically, rank refers to the horizontal line from one side to another. It is directionally perpendicular to a file.

ratha (Indic: aka *puṣpaka, bhadra*): It is an extension of a wall surface, generally on all four sides. If there is a single extension, the form is called *triratha* — creating three surfaces per face. If there are two extensions, the form is called *pañcaratha* — creating five surfaces per face. It also refers to a chariot, and, therefore, a temple type. See *pañcaratha* and *triratha*. Also, a variant of the term *puṣpaka*. (See *puṣpaka* and **Application of Terms.**)

rotating axiality: An arrangement of the elements of a plan along a single axis in which half the plan is rotated 180°. This term is applied to rectangular plans. For example, in the case of the house of Rājā Bīrbal, the north–south axis divides the form and that half-plan is rotated 180° arriving at the complete plan.

sabhā-maṇḍapa (Indic): The term refers to a pillared hall or a large hall for assembly. Frequently it is seen enclosed, although it may be open. (See **Application of Terms.**)

śālā: (Thai) A roofed structure without walls, a pavilion raised on a plinth and generally found within a *wat*. It shelters one from the sun and rain. In Hindu architecture it refers to a rectangular space.

sanctum: The term is used herein to refer to the most sacred area of a temple normally including the *garbhagṛha* and its enclosing walls. In certain temples — e.g. apsidal temples — it may also include the vestibule. (See **Application of Terms.**)

sandhāra (Indic): It is a structure with an enclosed ambulatory or *pradakṣiṇāpatha*.

sarvatobhadra (Indic: aka *chatramukha*): The term refers to a temple type, square or round, with four openings or doors, or false doors at the cardinal points. (See **Application of Terms**.)

śikhara (Indic): It is a tower-like superstructure over the *garbhagṛha* of a temple or any part thereof. It is made up of various sculptural devices and its form can vary.

śilpa-śāstras (Indic): The term refers to ancient treatises of design — e.g. the *Mānasāra, Mayamatam* and *Arthaśāstra*.

siṁhāsana (Indic): It refers to a lion (*siṁha*) throne (*āsana*).

sopāna (Indic): Steps or a flight of steps.

sopāna-maṇḍapa (Indic): It is a subsidiary *maṇḍapa* usually accessed by a flight of stairs.

śrī-kovil (Indic): The term refers to the main shrine in Kerala temples.

stambha (Indic): A sacred, free-standing pillar.

sthaṇḍilamaṇḍala (Indic): It is a *maṇḍala* plan composed of 49 *padas* which is preferred in the south of India.

sthapati (Indic): An architect-builder, who in the Indian Hindu tradition was what the "master builder" was to the European Medieval tradition.

stūpa (Indic: *cedi, caitya, cetiya, dagabā, dagobā, dhātu-garbha, pagoḍā, sotoba, zeidi*): The term refers to a Buddhist architectural form consisting of a square or circular base upon which rests a hemispherical form (*aṇḍa*). The *aṇḍa* may vary in shape from a hemisphere to bell-shape, to the form of an inverted pot or may be more angular and attenuated. Upon the *aṇḍa* rests a square or cylindrical altar-like form (*harmikā*) from which a spire (*chattrāvalī*) rises. Its origin is from a burial tumulus and was frequently employed as a vehicle for various relics.

stūpikā (Indic): The small *stūpa*-like forms which are used as subsidiary forms or as finials.

subtractive architectural process: As opposed to the additive architectural process, it refers to a monolithic structure which is formed by removing extraneous material to create a space. The caves of Ajantā, or the *rathas* of Mahābalipuram would be considered as an example of the subtractive architectural process.

śukanāsī (Indic: aka *ardha-maṇḍapa, mukha-maṇḍapa*): A variant term referring to the *ardha-maṇḍapa* and refers to a porch. (See *ardha-maṇḍapa* and **Application of Terms**.)

surru-maṇḍapa (Indic): It refers to a hall enclosing the front part of a Kerala temple. (See **Application of Terms**.)

cuttu-nadi (Malayalam; Indic: *pradakṣiṇāpatha*): The term refers to a *pradakṣiṇāpatha*.

Tipitaka: (Indic: aka *Tripiṭaka*) A variant term for *Tripiṭaka*. See *Tripiṭaka*.

tīrtha (Indic): A temple as a means of crossing the ocean of transmigratory existence. See *vimāna*.

toraṇa (Indic): An ornamental gate, generally associated with shrines and temples.

trikūṭa (Indic: aka *trikūṭaśālā*): A temple that has three sanctums, one in line with the *maṇḍapa* and two set on an axis 90° to the main axis.

trikūṭaśālā: (Indic: aka *trikūṭa*): A variant of *trikūṭa*. See *trikūṭa*.

trimālā (Indic: aka *tunmal pesava*): A base, sometimes, as in the case of modern *dagobās*, octagonal in form which elevates the *stūpa* form (threefold base, *aṇḍa, harmikā* and *kūṭa*) above the ground.

Tripiṭaka (Pāli): The sacred Buddhist canons of the Therevāda sect. Literally it means "three baskets".

triratha (Indic): The term to a single extension, generally in the middle portion of the surface of a wall, creating three surfaces per face. (See *ratha* and *pañcaratha*, and **Application of Terms**.)

tritala (Indic): A three-storeyed temple.

tunmal pesava (Indic: aka *trimālā*): Another term for *trimālā*.

utsava-maṇḍapa (Indic): A hall dedicated to the worship of the *utsava-mūrtis* of the gods.

vāma (Indic): The left or left hand.

vāmācāra (Indic): A Tāntric cult worship which is often associated to the Śakti cult — i.e. the "cult of the left hand".

vatadage (Sinhalese): The term refers to a domelike structure or a roofed structure in which is housed a *dagobā*. It is referred to as a "relic house".

vedikā (Indic): A stone fence which traditionally surrounds a *stūpa*. It also refers to that member between the *adhiṣṭhana* and the wall (*bhittī*) of the temple proper.

vesara (Indic): A style of architecture or temple type which is seen as a combination of the Nāgara and Draviḍa styles.

vihāra (Indic): The term refers to a monastery and particularly refers to the rectilinear, subtractive monasteries as those found at Ajantā. It also refers to a monastery with a sanctum or shrine included. See *wat*.

vimāna (Indic: aka *prāsāda, devālaya, mūlaprāsāda, tīrtha*): The term *vimāna* may refer to the tower-like structure or the main structure of a temple complex in the south of India which contains the sanctum, the *garbhagṛha* and frequently a *pradakṣiṇāpatha*. It also refers to a vehicle upon which a deity sits and is transported. It also refers to a temple which becomes a vehicle (*vimāna*) carrying the faithful. See *mūlaprāsāda*.

vṛṣa (Indic): A circle or circular plan.

vṛtta (Indic): A temple plan that is circular in form.

vṛttayata (Indic): A temple plan that is elliptical in form.

vyākaraṇa-maṇḍapa (Indic): A hall for religious education and festivals and is found within a temple complex.

yoganāla (Indic): A conical tube, constructed of copper, is placed just under the *brahmaśilā* in the dedicatory foundation of the *garbhagṛha*.

zenānā (Indic): The private area for women, particularly in a Muslim palace, as opposed to the men's area — the *mardānā*.

Glossary — Application of Terms

There are numerous terms which apply to the temples of India and their various components. These terms vary considerably from locale to locale — e.g. the term for an enclosed or open gathering hall that is often connected to the *vimāna* is known variously as: *gūḍha-maṇḍapa, jagamohana, mahāmaṇḍapa, maṇḍapa, mukhaśālā, navaraṅga, nṛtta-mantapa* or *sabhā-maṇḍapa*. The following illustrations indicate, as much as possible, those variations.

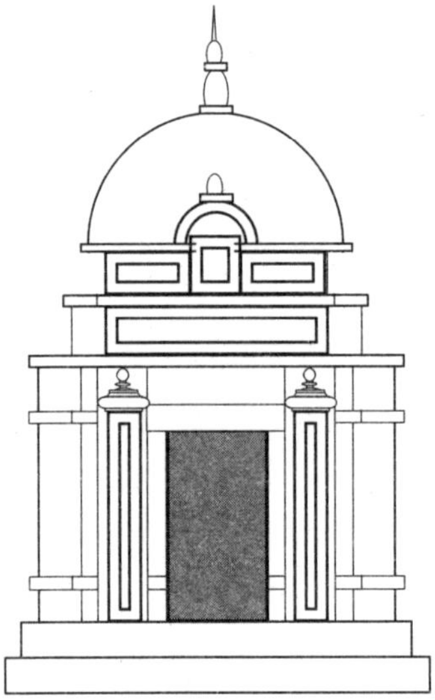

Draviḍa

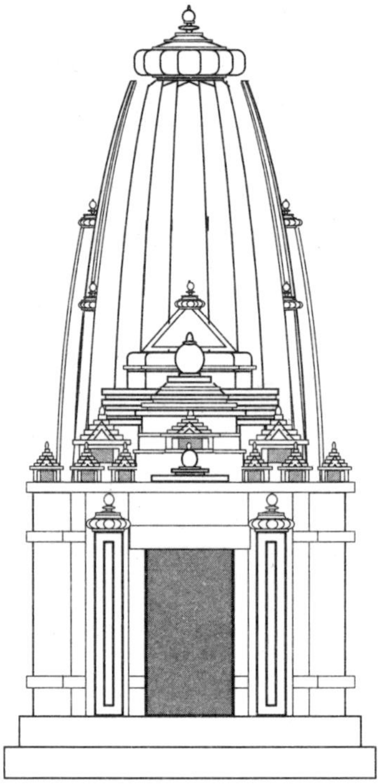

Nāgara

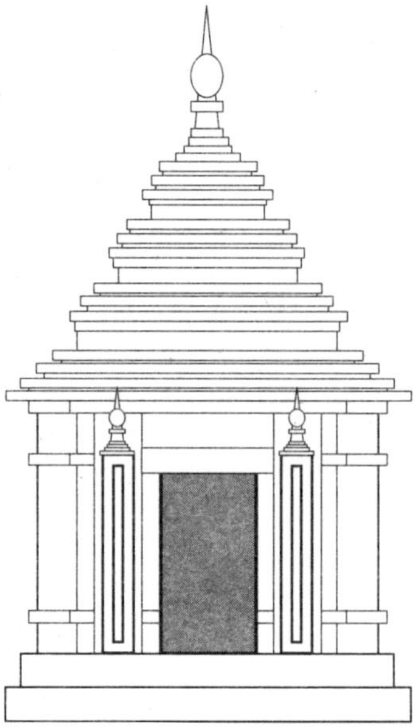

Vesara

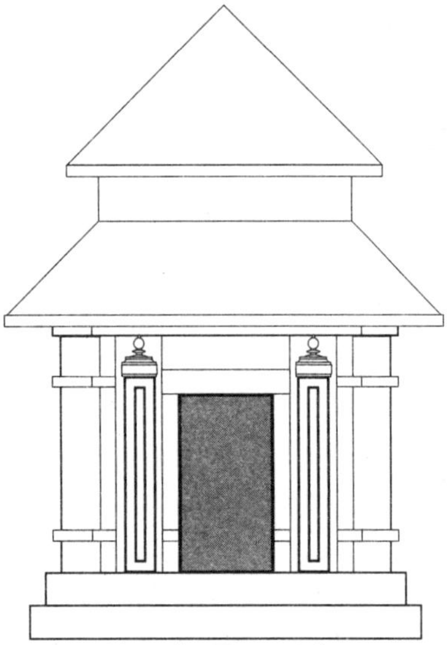

Kerala Draviḍa

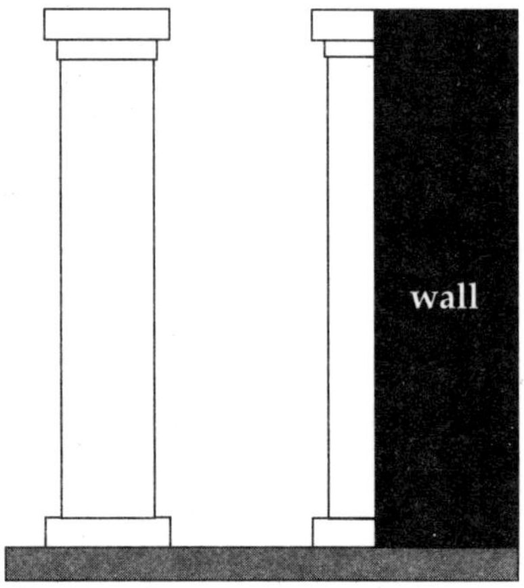

free-standing engaged

Column Types

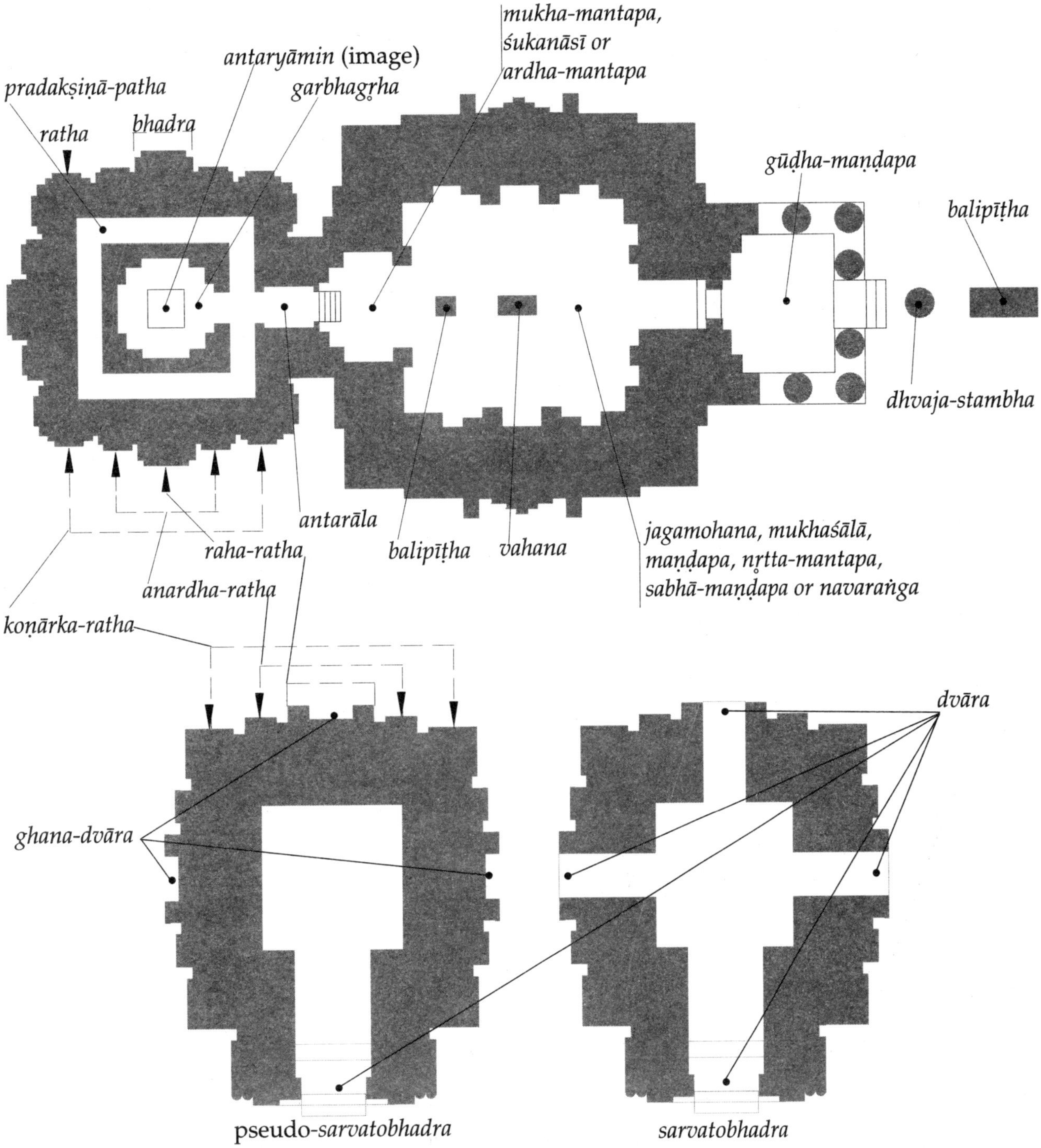
mukha-mantapa,
śukanāsī or
ardha-mantapa
antaryāmin (image)
pradakṣiṇā-patha
garbhagṛha
ratha
bhadra
gūḍha-maṇḍapa
balipīṭha
dhvaja-stambha
antarāla
raha-ratha
balipīṭha
vahana
jagamohana, mukhaśālā,
maṇḍapa, nṛtta-mantapa,
sabhā-maṇḍapa or navaraṅga
anardha-ratha
koṇārka-ratha
dvāra
ghana-dvāra
pseudo-sarvatobhadra
sarvatobhadra

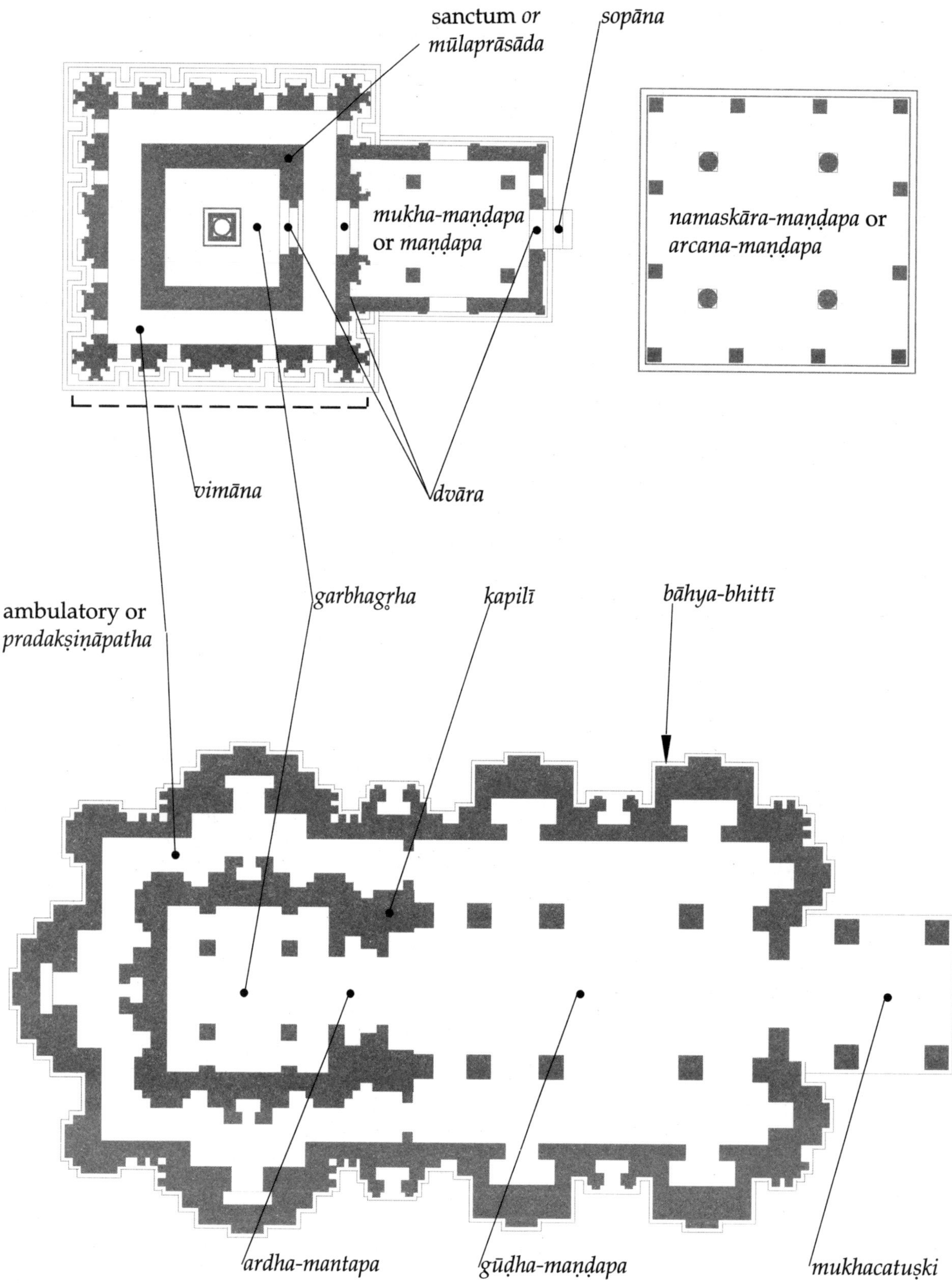
sanctum *or* *mūlaprāsāda*
sopāna
namaskāra-maṇḍapa or *arcana-maṇḍapa*
mukha-maṇḍapa or *maṇḍapa*
vimāna
dvāra
ambulatory or *pradakṣiṇāpatha*
garbhagṛha
kapilī
bāhya-bhittī
ardha-mantapa
gūḍha-maṇḍapa
mukhacatuṣki

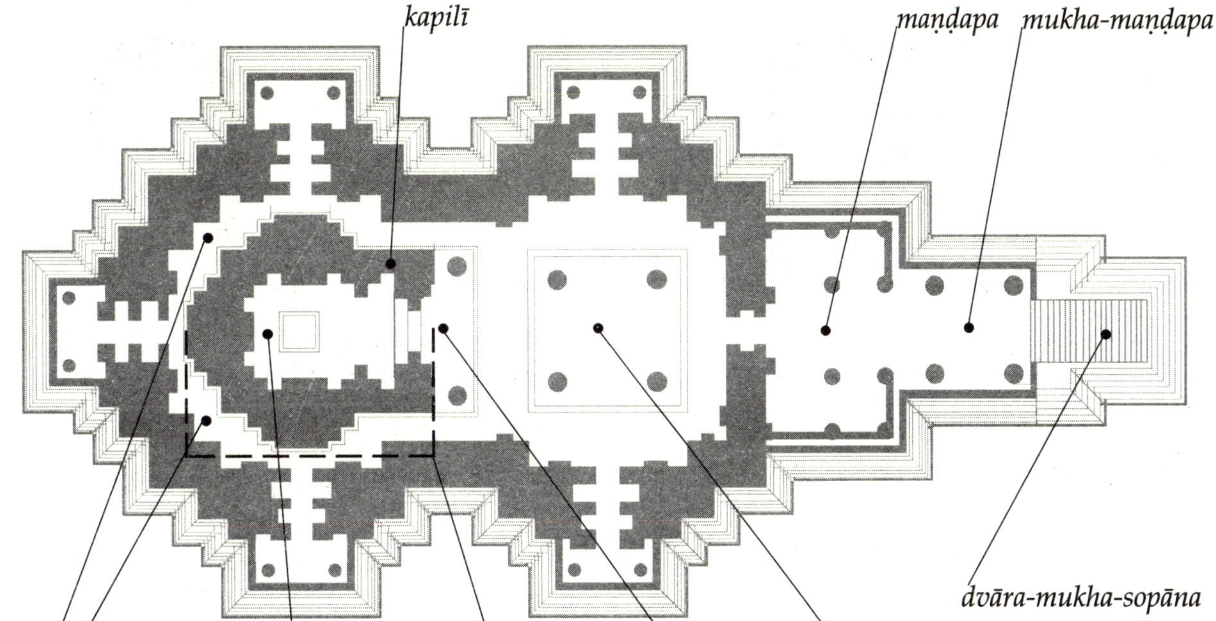
kapilī
maṇḍapa
mukha-maṇḍapa
dvāra-mukha-sopāna
ambulatory or
pradakṣiṇāpatha
garbhagṛha
sanctum
mūlaprāsāda
or vimāna
antarāla
mahāmaṇḍapa,
gūḍha-maṇḍapa

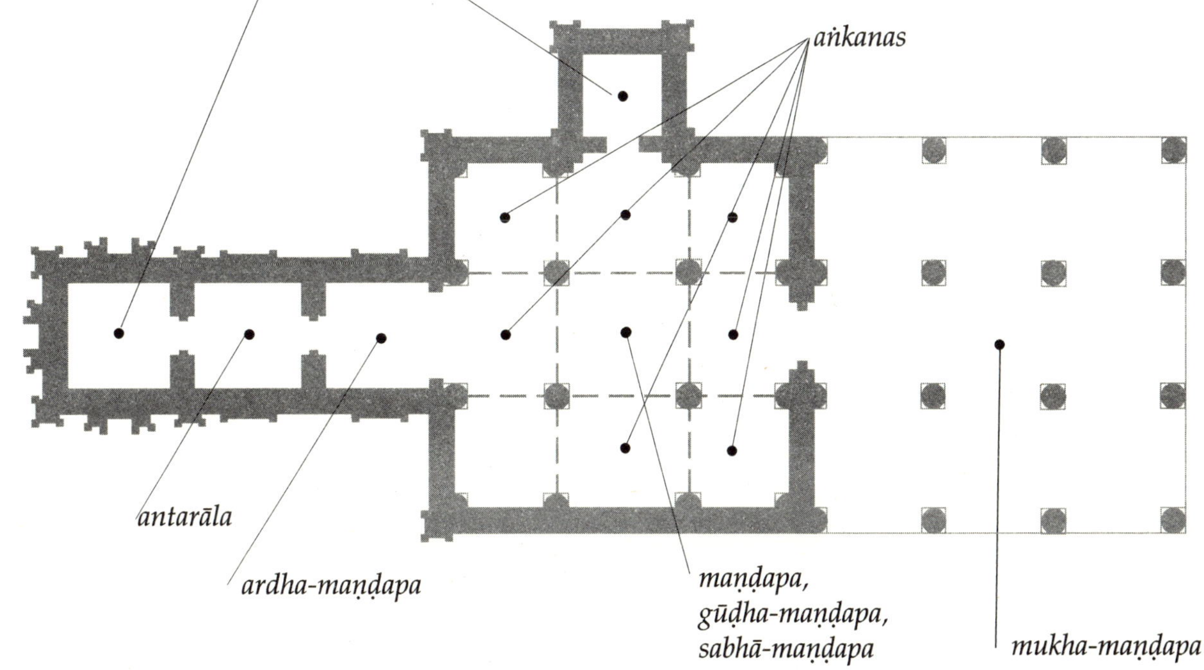
aṅkanas
antarāla
ardha-maṇḍapa
maṇḍapa,
gūḍha-maṇḍapa,
sabhā-maṇḍapa
mukha-maṇḍapa

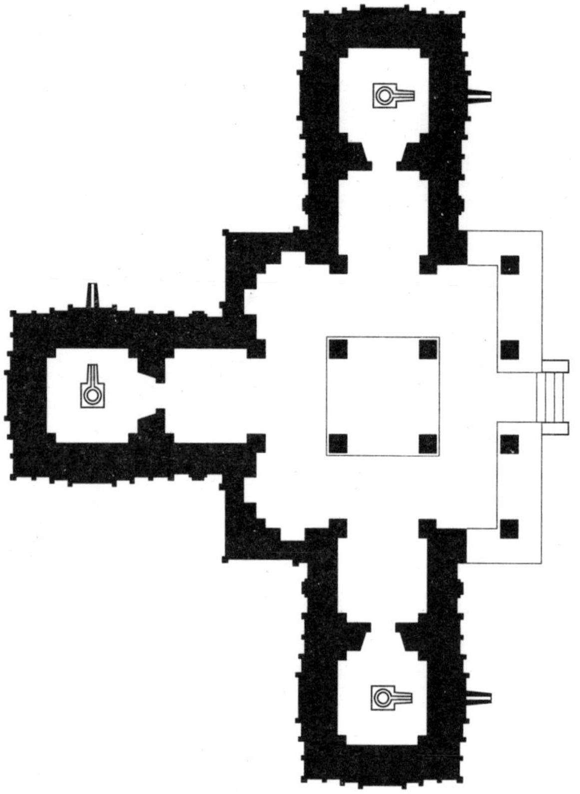

three-quarter enclosed *sabhā-maṇḍapa*

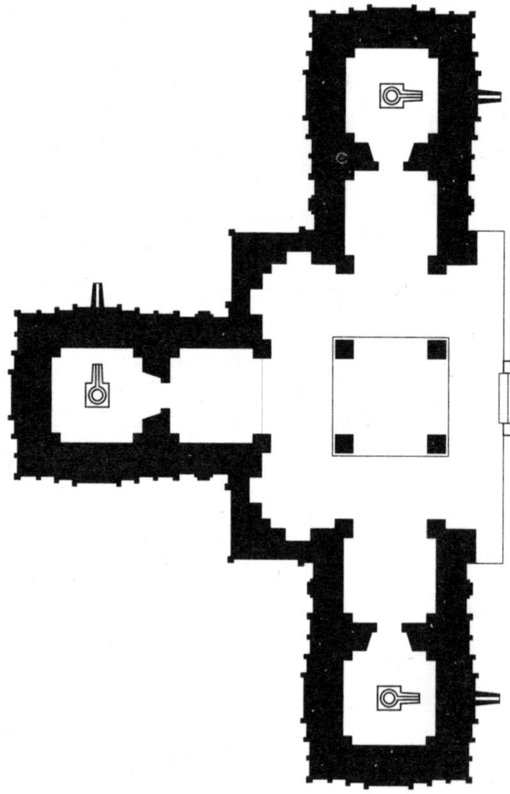

three-quarter *sabhā-maṇḍapa*

Appendix B

List of Dvikūṭa, Trikūṭa, Catuṣkūṭa, Pañcakūṭa, Saptakūṭa, Navakūṭa and Cauṅsaṭh Temples

Dvikūṭa, Trikūṭa, Catuṣkūṭa, Pañcakūṭa, Saptakūṭa, Navakūṭa and Cauṅsaṭh Temples

Dvikūṭa Temples

Amman Dvikūṭa Shrine, Kamalapura, Karnataka
Basavaṇṇa Dvikūṭa Temple, Harvi, Karnataka
Bastī or Kalla-Guḍi Dvikūṭa Temple, Degamve, Karnataka
Buceśvara Dvikūṭa Temple, Koravaṅgala, Karnataka
Candraśekhara Dvikūṭa Temple, Hampī, Karnataka
Ciñcoli Basavaṇṇa Dvikūṭa Temple, Gabbur, Karnataka
Dvikūṭa Temple, Chauḍadampur, Karnataka
Elubavi Basavaṇṇa Dvikūṭa Temple, Gabbur, Karnataka
Gaṅgeśvara-Brahmeśvara Dvikūṭa Temple, Asandi, Karnataka
Gaṅgādhareśvara Dvikūṭa Temple, Ḍoḍḍīśivara, Karnataka
Hoysaḷeśvara Dvikūṭa Temple, Halebiḍ, Karnataka
Īśvara Dvikūṭa Temple, Arsikere, Karnataka
Kalleśvara Dvikūṭa Temple, Bagali, Karnataka[1]
Kalideva Dvikūṭa Temple, Kummsi, Karnataka
Kallappa-Mallappa (Harihara) Dvikūṭa Temple, Devaragennur, Karnataka
Kappe Cannigarāya Dvikūṭa Temple, Beluru, Karnataka
Kappe Cannigarāya Dvikūṭa Temple, Somanāthapur, Karnataka
Kāśīviśveśvara Dvikūṭa Temple, Lakkuṇḍī, Karnataka
Keśaveśvara Dvikūṭa Temple, Agrahāra-Belaguli, Karnataka
Koṭe Śaṅkaraliṅga Dvikūṭa Temple, Nimbal, Karnataka
Kunthunātha Dvikūṭa Temple, Kamalapura, Karnataka
Kunthu Jinanātha Jinālaya Dvikūṭa Temple, Kamalapura, Karnataka
Lakṣmī-Nārāyaṇa Dvikūṭa Temple, Muttati, Karnataka
Mallikārjuna Dvikūṭa Temple, Muḍhol, Karnataka
Narasiṁha Dvikūṭa Temple, Raṅgapur, Karnataka
Pārśvanātha Dvikūṭa Temple, Hampī, Karnataka
Rāmaliṅga Dvikūṭa Temple, Horti, Karnataka
Rāmaliṅga Dvikūṭa Temple, Sirūr, Karnataka
Rāmaliṅgeśvara Dvikūṭa Temple, Taḷikoṭe, Karnataka
Rāmeśvara Dvikūṭa Temple, Yaragaḷ, Karnataka
Siddheśvara Dvikūṭa Temple, Algoḍu, Karnataka
Siddheśvara Dvikūṭa Temple, Hosura, Karnataka
Śaṁbhuliṅga Dvikūṭa Temple, Kakkalameli, Karnataka
Śaṅkaraliṅga Dvikūṭa Temple, Kalakeri, Karnataka
Śiva Dvikūṭa Temple, Hampī, Karnataka
Tripurāntakeśvara Dvikūṭa Temple, Balagamve, Karnataka
Twin Dvikūṭa Temple, Hampī, Karnataka
Vaidyanātheśvara Dvikūṭa Temple, Vaidyanathapur, Karnataka
Veṅkateśvara Dvikūṭa Temple, Gabbur, Karnataka

Trikūṭa Temples

Anantaśayana Trikūṭa Basadī, Navali, Karnataka
Basavaṇṇa (Traipuruṣa) Trikūṭa Temple, Malghana, Karnataka
Cāmuṇḍeśvari Trikūṭa Basadī, Undiganal, Karnataka
Candragupta Trikūṭa Basadī, Śravaṇabeḷagoḷa, Karnataka
Candramaulīśvara Trikūṭa Temple, Unkal, Karnataka
Chatteśvara Trikūṭa Temple, Chattachatanahaḷḷi, Karnataka
Gaṅgādhara Trikūṭa Temple, Kolur, Karnataka
Harihareśvara Trikūṭa Temple, Hariharapur, Karnataka
Īśvara Trikūṭa Temple, Basarkodu, Karnataka
Īśvara Trikūṭa Temple, Kadlevada, Karnataka
Jaina Trikūṭa Temple No. 15, Deogaṛh, Rajasthan
Jaina Trikūṭa Temple, Harasur
Jambuliṅgeśvara Trikūṭa Temple, Bādāmī, Karnataka
Kalleśvara Trikūṭa Temple, Angoor, Karnataka
Kalleśvara Trikūṭa Temple, Halavagalu, Karnataka
Kampilarāya Trikūṭa Temple (No. 1), Hampī, Karnataka
Kampilarāya Trikūṭa Temple (No. 3), Hampī, Karnataka
Kedāreśvara Trikūṭa Temple, Balagamve, Karnataka
Kedāreśvara Trikūṭa Temple, Halebiḍ, Karnataka
Keśava Trikūṭa Temple, Somanāthapur, Karnataka
Kumāraswāmy Trikūṭa Temple, Kudatini, Karnataka
Lakṣmī-Narasiṁha Trikūṭa Temple, Adaguru, Karnataka
Lakṣmī-Narasiṁha Trikūṭa Temple, Bhadravatī, Karnataka
Lakṣmī-Narasiṁha Trikūṭa Temple, Haranahaḷḷi, Karnataka

---

1 KMS II lists this temple in the section designated as "Trikūṭa Temples", however as he notes it is composed of two sanctums in one unit with "a detached Sūrya temple" to the east and illustrates the same in vol. II, pp. 214 and 442.

Lakṣmī-Narasiṁha Trikūṭa Temple, Hosaholalu, Karnataka
Lakṣmī-Narasiṁha Trikūṭa Temple, Javagallu, Karnataka
Lakṣmī-Narasiṁha Trikūṭa Temple, Nuggihaḷḷi, Karnataka
Lakṣmī-Narasiṁha Trikūṭa Temple, Vignasante, Karnataka
Mādhavarāya Trikūṭa Temple, Belluru, Karnataka
Mallesvara Trikūṭa Temple, Aghalya, Karnataka
Mahādeva Trikūṭa Temple, Benagotagi, Karnataka
Mahāliṅgeśvara Trikūṭa Temple, Raṅgapura, Karnataka
Mallikārjuna Trikūṭa Temple, Basaralu, Karnataka
Mallikārjuna Trikūṭa Temple, Devaranavadagi, Karnataka
Mallikārjuna Trikūṭa Temple, Hirebevinuru, Karnataka
Mallikārjuna Trikūṭa Temple, Hirenalluru, Karnataka
Mallikārjuna Trikūṭa Temple, Katnahaḷḷi, Karnataka
Murukallumaṭha Trikūṭa Temple, Kottur, Karnataka
Nārāyaṇa Trikūṭa Temple, Anekannambadi, Karnataka
Nārāyaṇa Trikūṭa Temple, Iṅgaleśvara, Karnataka
Nelaguḍi Trikūṭa Temple, Bagalavada, Karnataka
Paramānanda Trikūṭa Temple, Konnur, Karnataka
Rachi Trikūṭa Temple, Aihoḷe, Karnataka
Rāmaliṅga Trikūṭa Temple, Iṭigi, Karnataka
Rāmaliṅgeśvara Trikūṭa Temple, Kundaragi, Karnataka
Rāmeśvara Trikūṭa Temple, Gurugod, Karnataka
Rāmeśvara Trikūṭa Temple, Yargaḷ, Karnataka
Sadaśiva Trikūṭa Temple, Kondaparti
Saṁbhuliṅgeśvara Trikūṭa Temple, Keresante, Karnataka
Saṅgameśvara Trikūṭa Temple, Babaleśvara, Karnataka
Saṅgameśvara Trikūṭa Temple, Bevura, Karnataka
Saumyakeśvara Trikūṭa Temple, Nagamangala, Orissa
Śaṅkaraliṅga Trikūṭa Temple, Dhulakheḍa, Karnataka
Someśvara Trikūṭa Temple, Haralhaḷḷi, Karnataka
Someśvara Trikūṭa Temple, Hottul
Someśvara Trikūṭa Temple, Iṅgaleśvara, Karnataka
Someśvara Trikūṭa Temple, Kabbali, Karnataka
Sūrya Trikūṭa Temple, Koṇārka, Orissa
Sūrya-Nārāyaṇa Trikūṭa Temple, Magala, Orissa
Trayambakeśvara Trikūṭa Temple, Kavital, Karnataka
Trikūṭa Basadī (Jaina), Arasibidi, Karnataka
Trikūṭa Shrine, Kaṭākṣapura, Andhra Pradesh
Śrī Keśavanātha Pañcamukha Liṅgeśvara Trikūṭa Temple, Raikal
Trikūṭa Śiva Temple, Upparapaḷḷi, Andhra Pradesh
Śrī Kātyāyanī Sahita Rāmaliṅgeśvara Swāmy Temple, Trikūṭa Temple, Vaddeman
Trikūṭa (Three Mast Heads / or Three Shrine) Temple, Chamarājanagar
Trikūṭa Temple, Chatchatnahaḷḷi
Trikūṭa Temple, Nidigonda
Trikūṭa Temple, Halebiḍ
Trikūṭa Temple, Ballisavi
Trikūṭa Temple, Kothali, Karnataka
Trikūṭa Temple, Kuṣmañci, Andhra Pradesh
Trikūṭa Temple, Methi
Trikūṭa Temple I, Nagalapadu
Trikūṭa Temple II, Nagalapadu
Trikūṭa Temple, Pālampeṭ, Andhra Pradesh
Trikūṭa Temple I, Pālampeṭ
Trikūṭa Temple II, Pālampeṭ
Trikūṭa Temple III, Pālampeṭ
Trikūṭa Temple, Kondaparti, Andhra Pradesh
Trikūṭa Temple, Kulgi
Trikūṭa Śivālayam Temple, Nagalapadu
Trikūṭeśvara Temple, Gaḍag, Karnataka
Trikūṭeśvara Temple, Gorur, Karnataka
Triliṅgeśvara Temple, Muḍhol, Karnataka
Śiva Trikūṭa Temple, Timmalapur, Karnataka
Vīranārāyaṇa Trikūṭa Temple, Belvadi, Karnataka
Yoga-Mādhava Trikūṭa Temple, Sattikere, Karnataka

Catuṣkūṭa Temples

Bhīmeśvara Catuṣkūṭa Temple, Nīlaguṇḍa, Karnataka
Lakṣmīdevī Temple, Doḍḍa Gaḍḍuvalli, Karnataka

Pañcakūṭa Temples

Cauvuṇḍarāya Pañcakūṭa Basadī, Śravaṇabeḷagoḷa, Karnataka
Harihara Pañcakūṭa Basadī, Gabbur, Karnataka
Mallikārjuna Pañcakūṭa Temple, Ujjini, Karnataka
Marula Siddheśvara Pañcakūṭa Temple, Mallat, Karnataka
Pañcaliṅgeśvara Pañcakūṭa Temple, Govindanahaḷḷi, Karnataka
Pañcaliṅgeśvara Pañcakūṭa Temple, Somanāthapura, Karnataka
Pañcakūṭa Basadī (Jaina), Humcha, Karnataka

Pañcakūṭa Basadī (Jaina), Kambadahaḷḷi, Karnataka
Pañcakūṭa Basadī (Jaina), Nagamangoḷa, Karnataka
Pañcakūṭa Basadī (Jaina), Sirval, Karnataka
Pārśvanātha Pañcakūṭa Basadī (Jaina), Koppal, Karnataka
Siddhaliṅgeśvara Pañcakūṭa Basadī, Siruval, Karnataka
Sūryanārāyaṇa Pañcakūṭa Basadī, Koḷūr, Karnataka

Saptakūṭa Temples

Kalleśvara Saptakūṭa Temple, Bennikaḷḷūr, Karnataka

Navakūṭa Temple

Navaliṅga Navakūṭa Temple, Kukkanur, Karnataka

Cauṅsaṭh Temples

Cauṅsaṭh Yoginī Mandir and Gaurī Śaṅkara Temple, Bherāghāṭ, Madhya Pradesh
Cauṅsaṭh Yoginī Pīṭha, Rānīpur-Jharial, Orissa
Cauṅsaṭh Yoginī Sanctuary, Khajurāho, Madhya Pradesh
Cauṅsaṭh Yoginī Temple, Hīrāpur, Orissa
Ekottaso Mahādeva Mandir (Cauṅsaṭh Yoginī [Liṅga] Mandir), Mitāoli, Madhya Pradesh

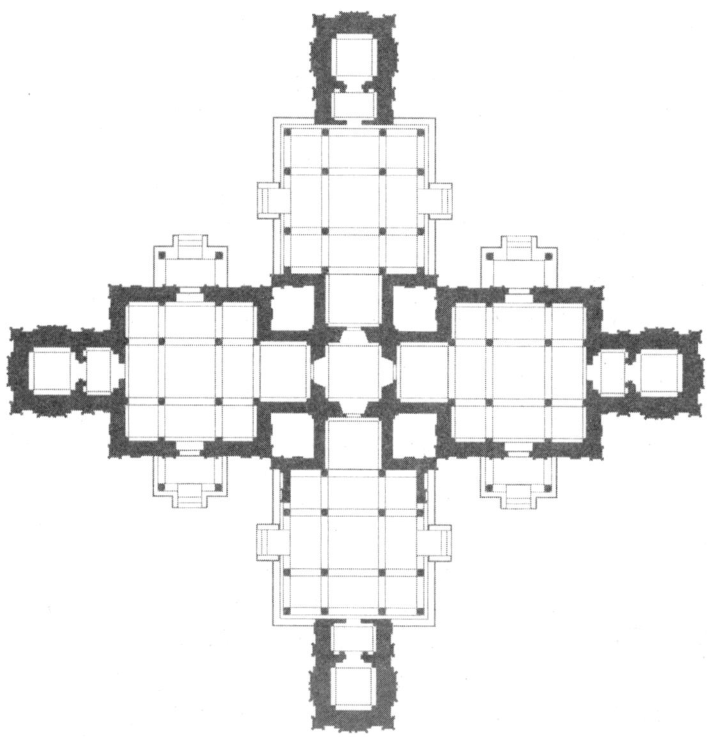

Appendix C

Miscellaneous Plans and Elevations

Plate 115: Pantheon, Rome (a. CE 118)

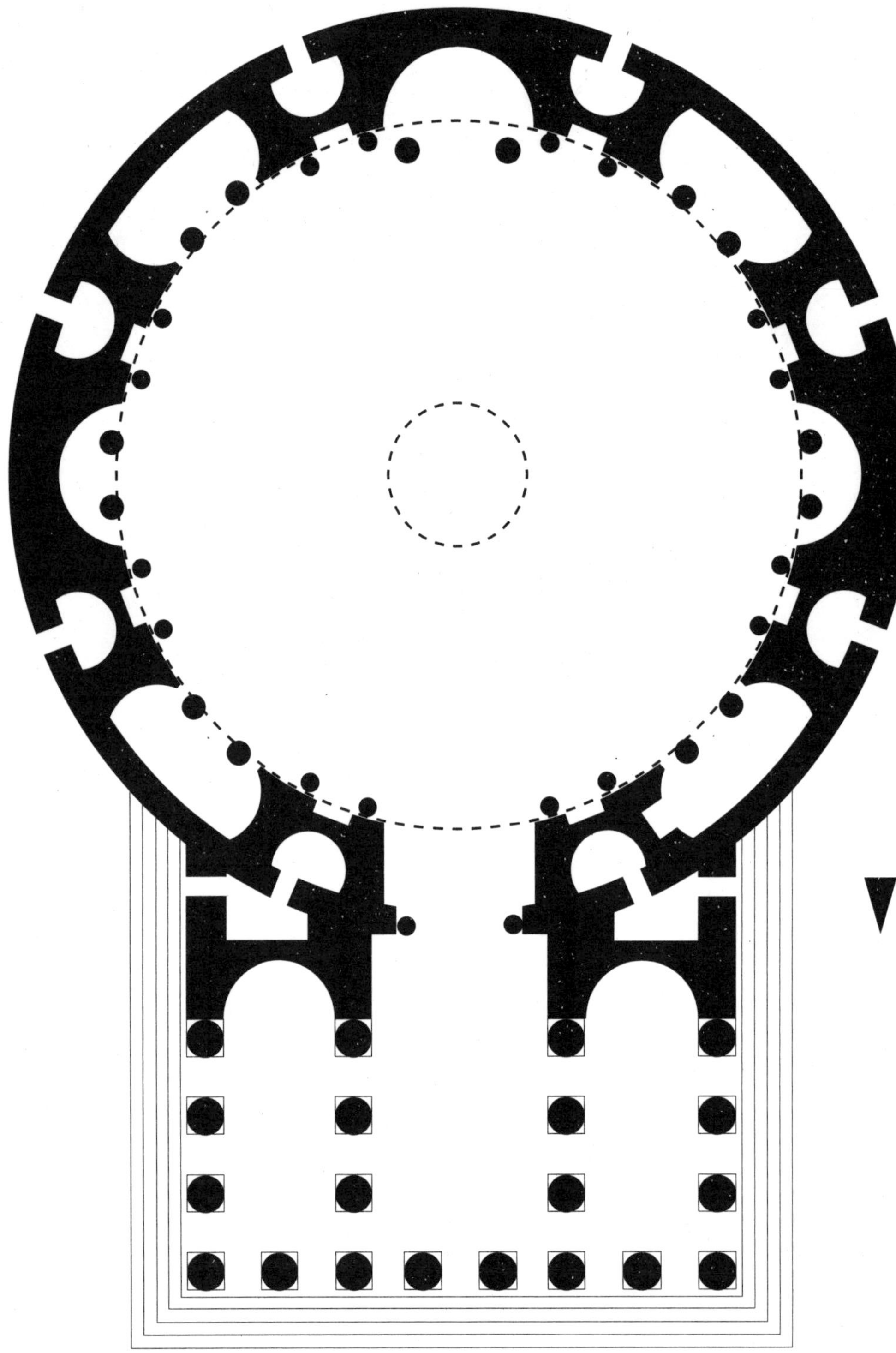

Plate 116: Santa Costanza, Rome (*c.* CE 350)

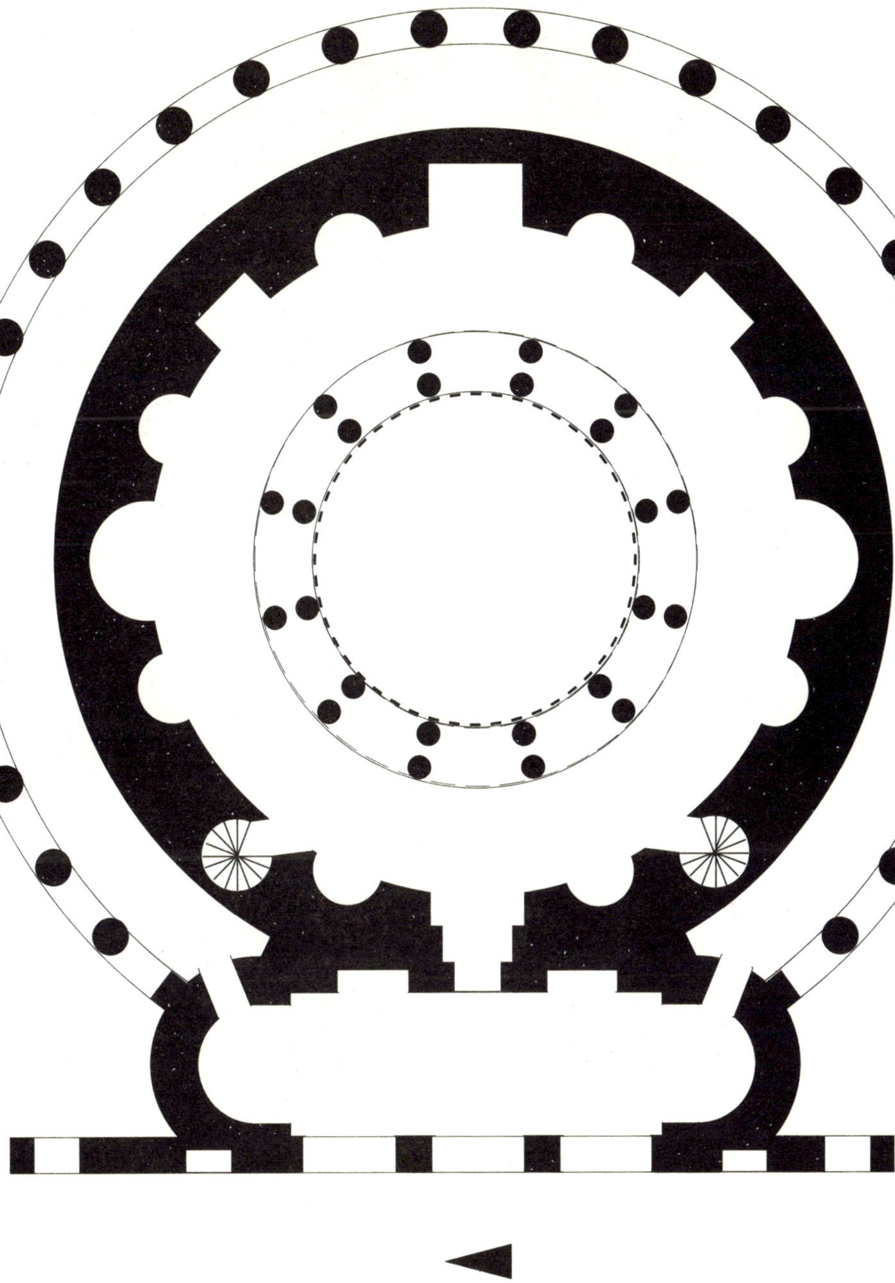

Plate 117: Brunelleschi, Santa Maria degli Angeli, Florence (CE 1434-37)

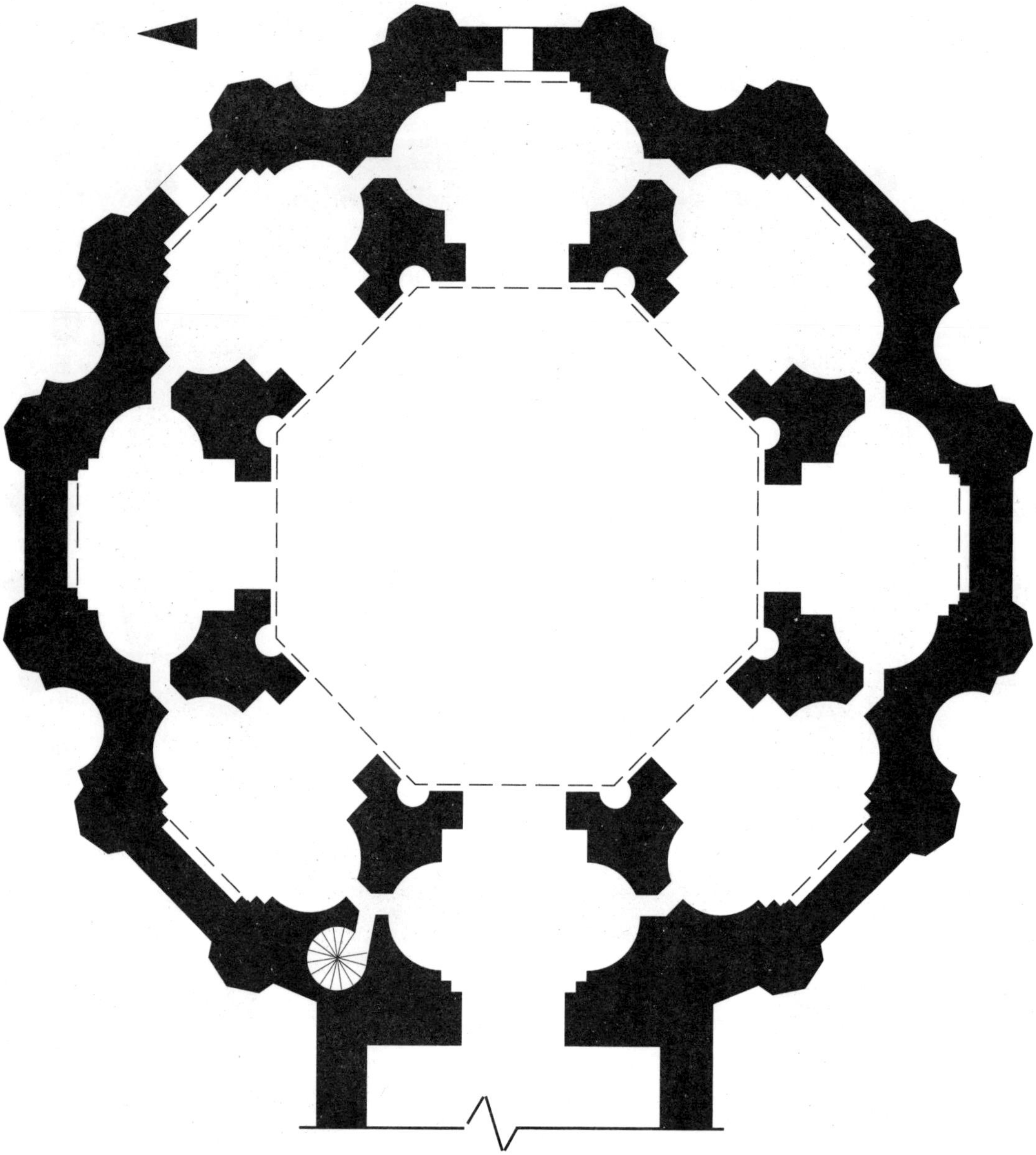

Plate 118: Bramante, Tempietto, San Pietro in Montorio, Rome (CE 1504)

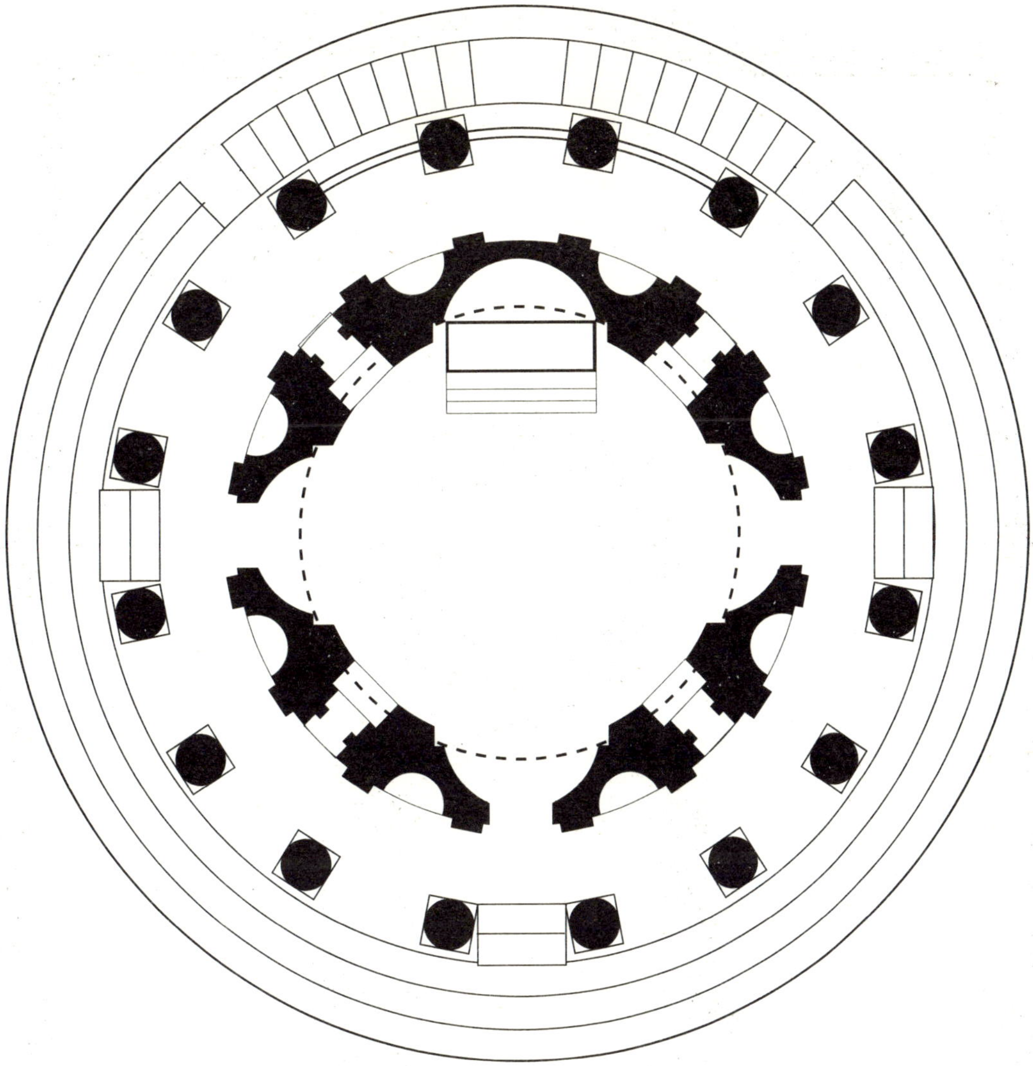

Plate 119: Brahmeśvara Temple, *pañcāyatana* plan

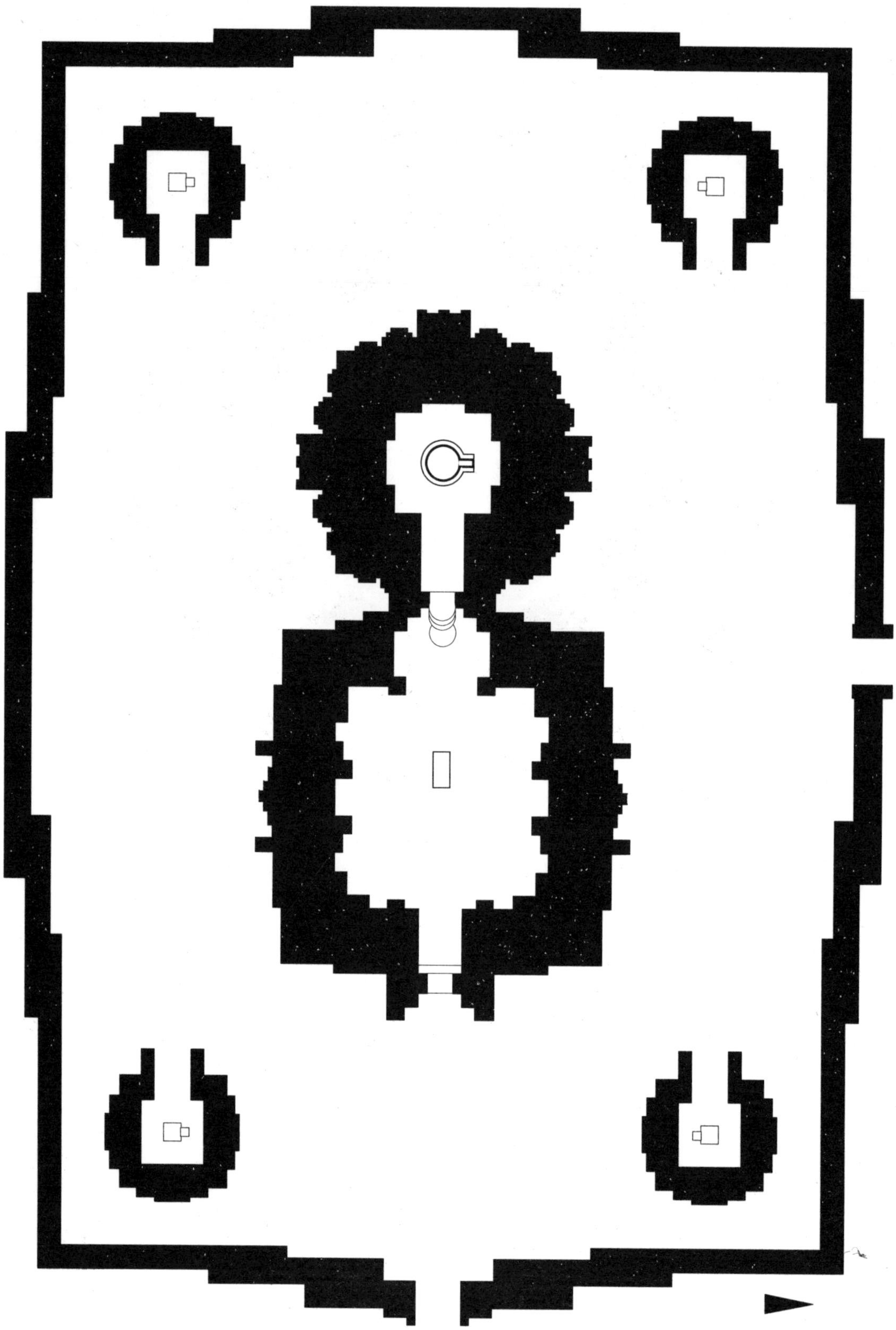

Plate 120: Gupta Temple, Deogaṛh (*c.* CE 500-25)

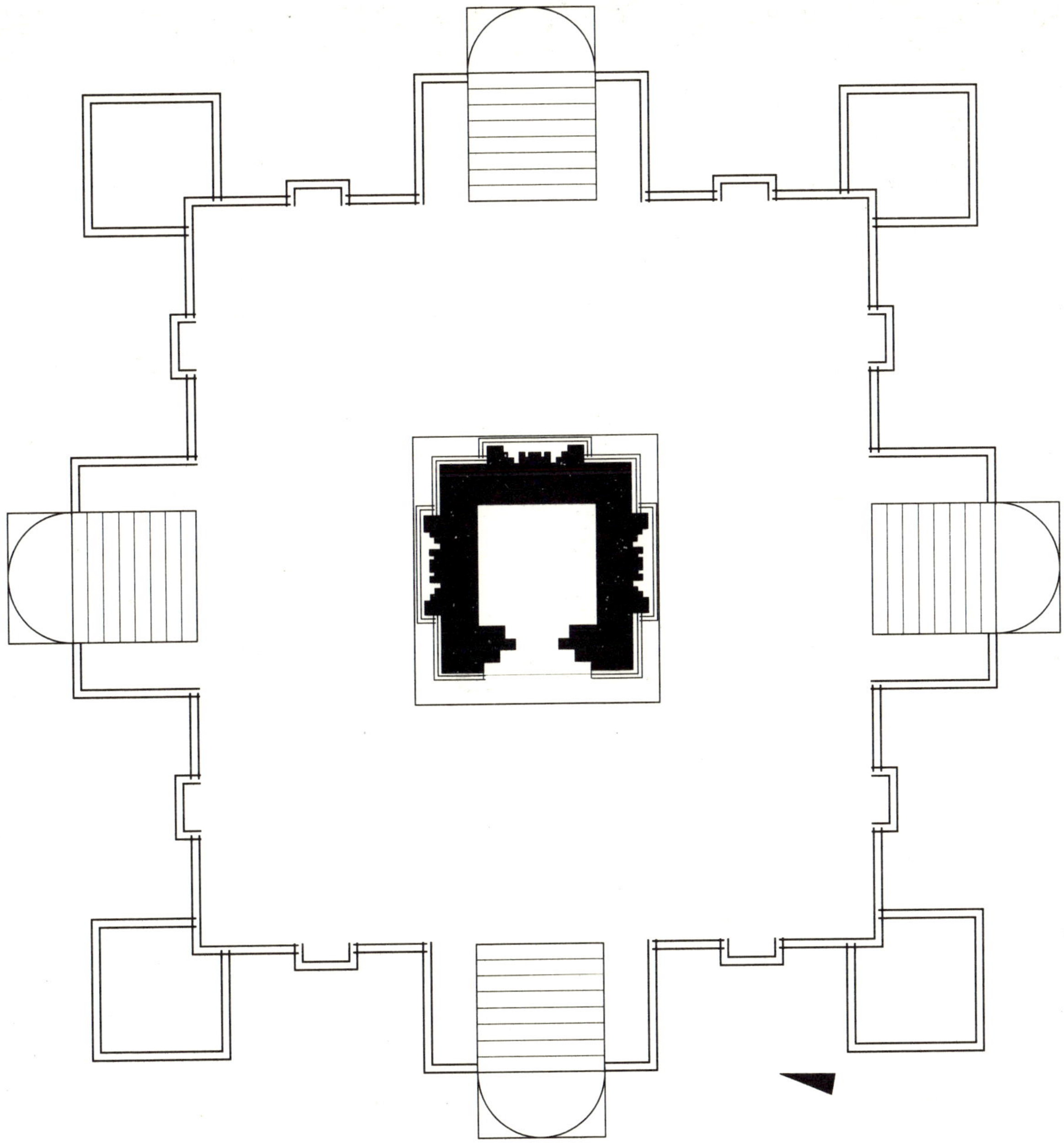

Plate 121: Avantisvāmi Temple, Avantipur (*c*. CE 850-60)

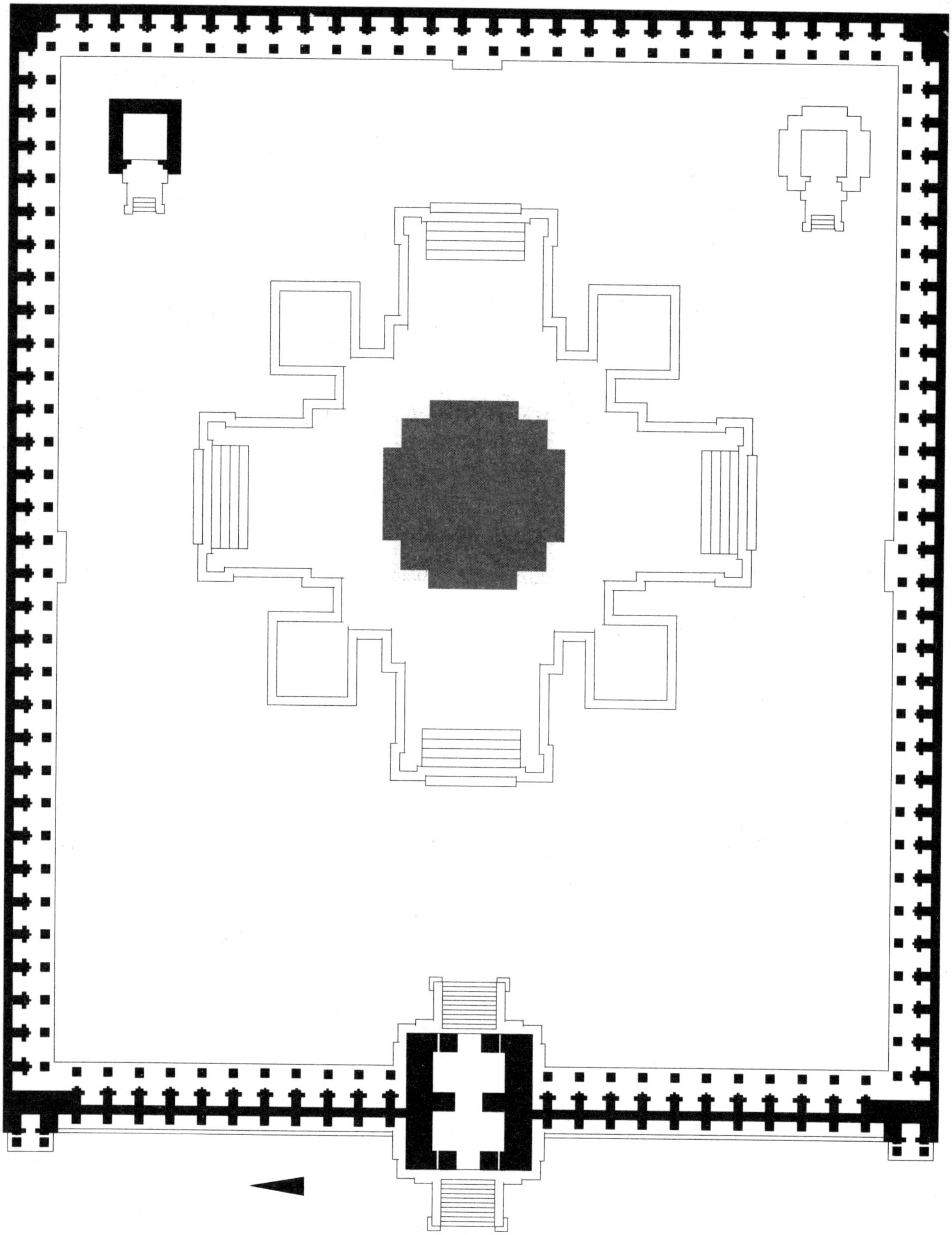

Plate 122: Bakheng Ensemble, Angkor

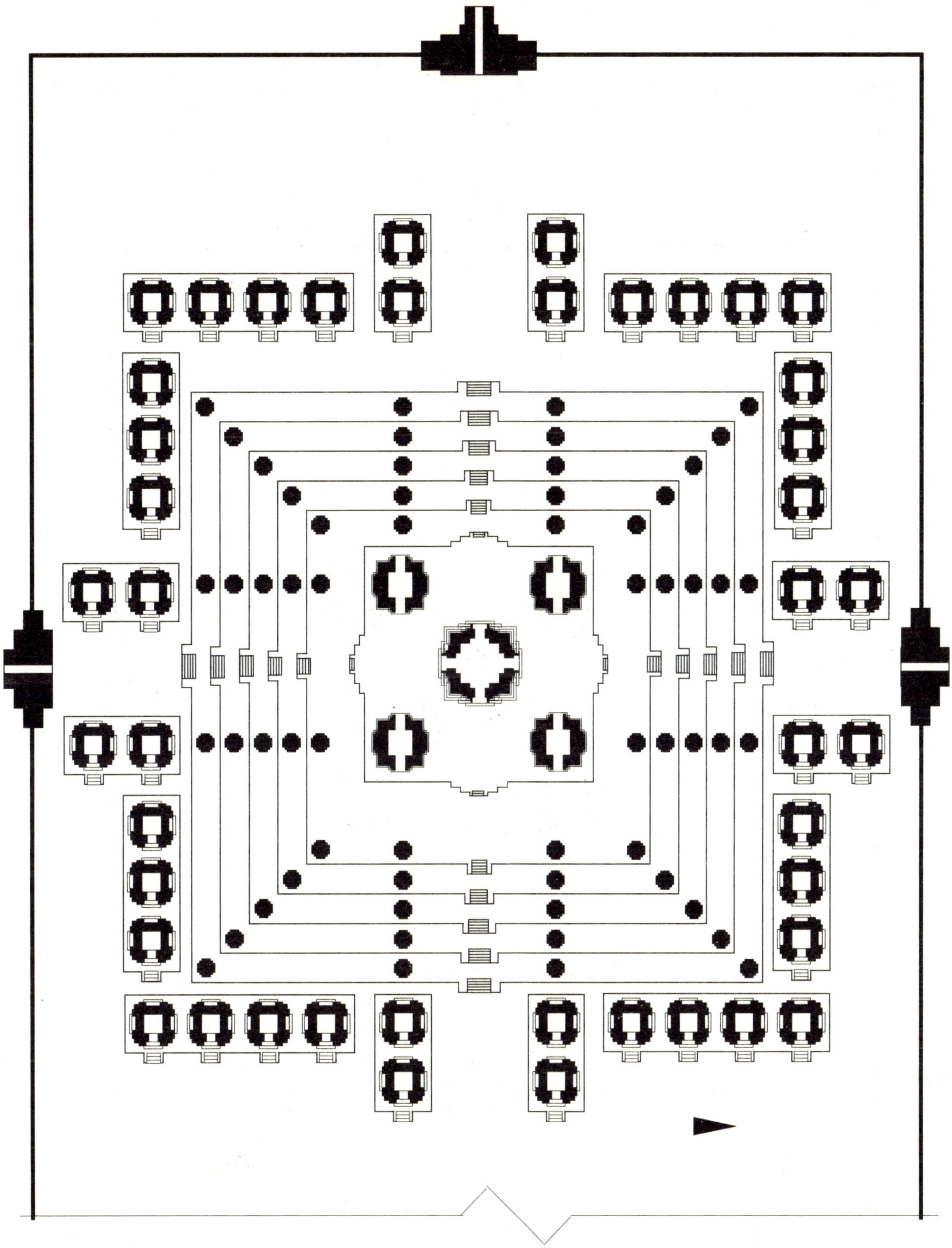

Plate 123: Ta Keo, Angkor

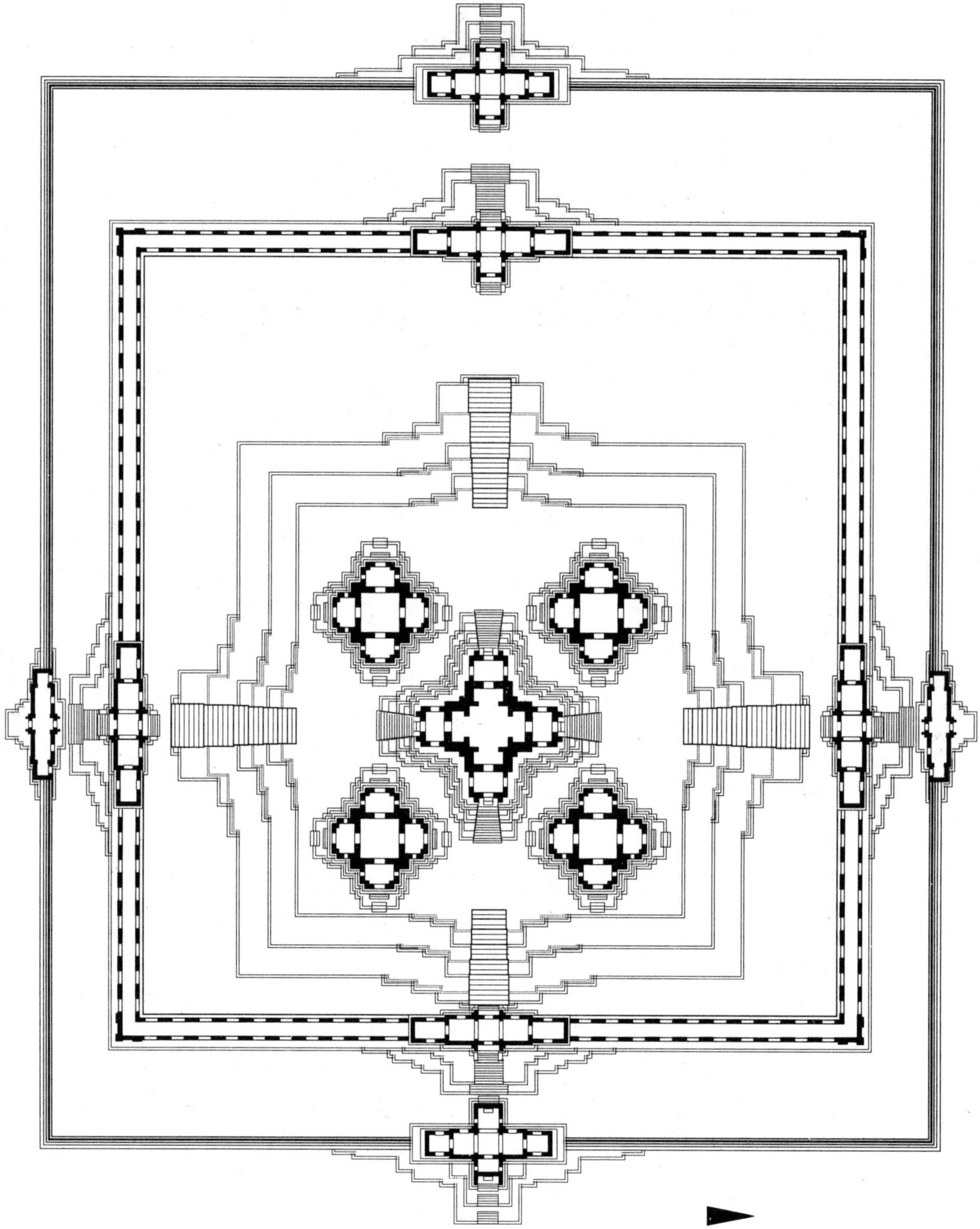

Plate 124: Chandi Panataran Sanctuary, Blitar, Java (CE 1320-70)

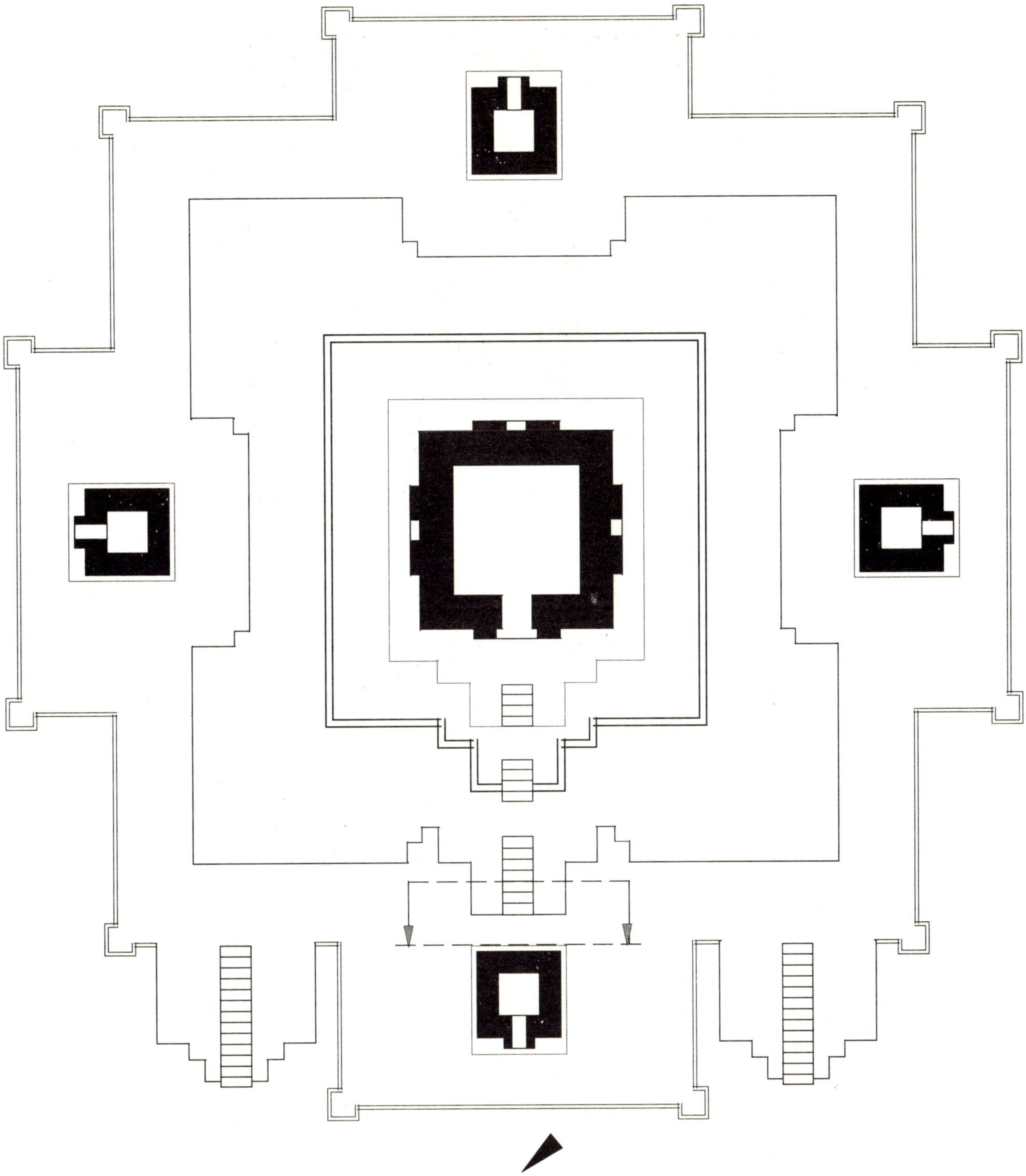

Plate 125: Madhukeśvara Temple Complex, Mukhaliṅgam (*c.* CE 800-25)

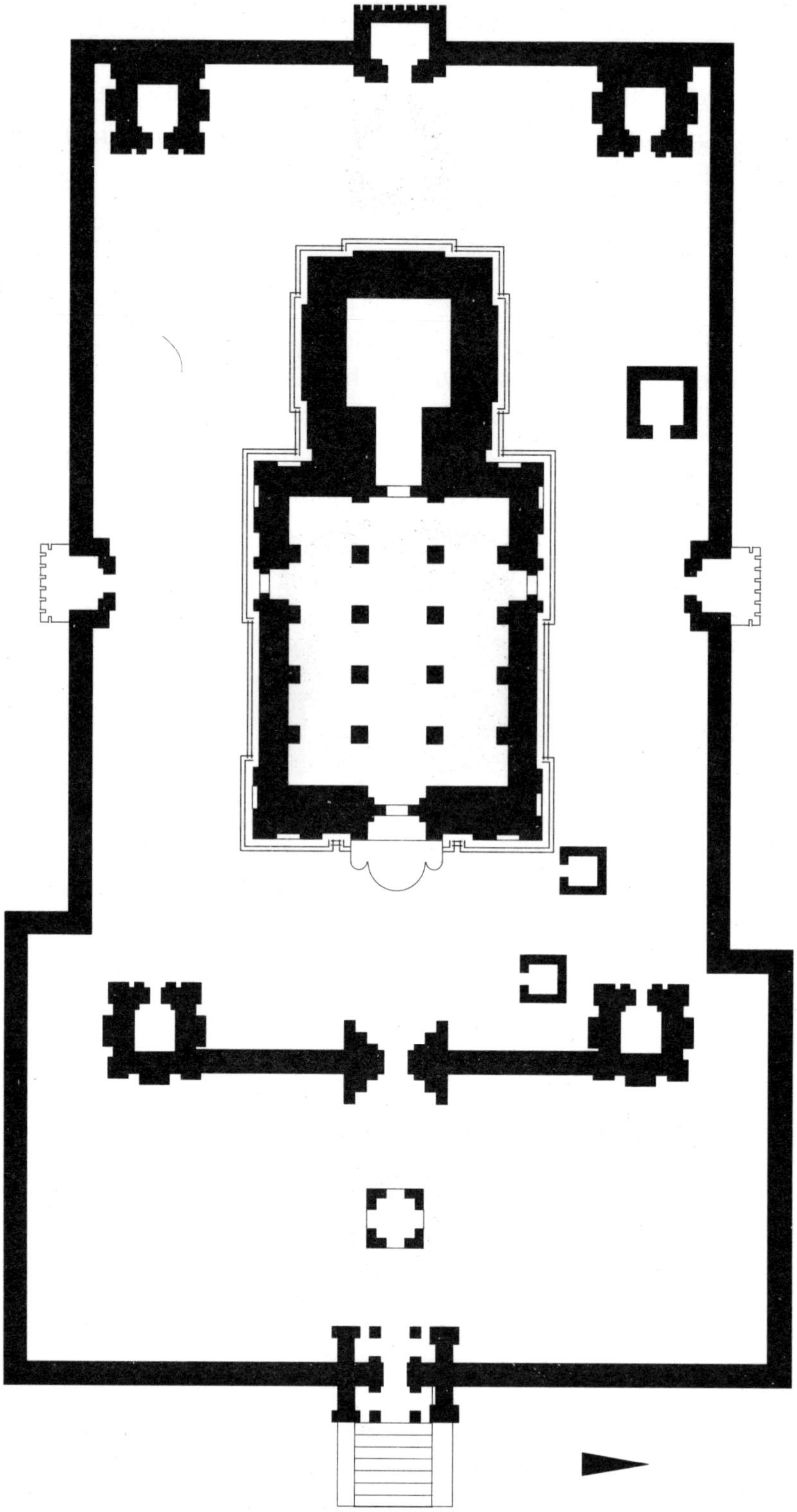

Plate 126: Lakṣmaṇa Temple Ensemble, Khajurāho (a. CE 954)

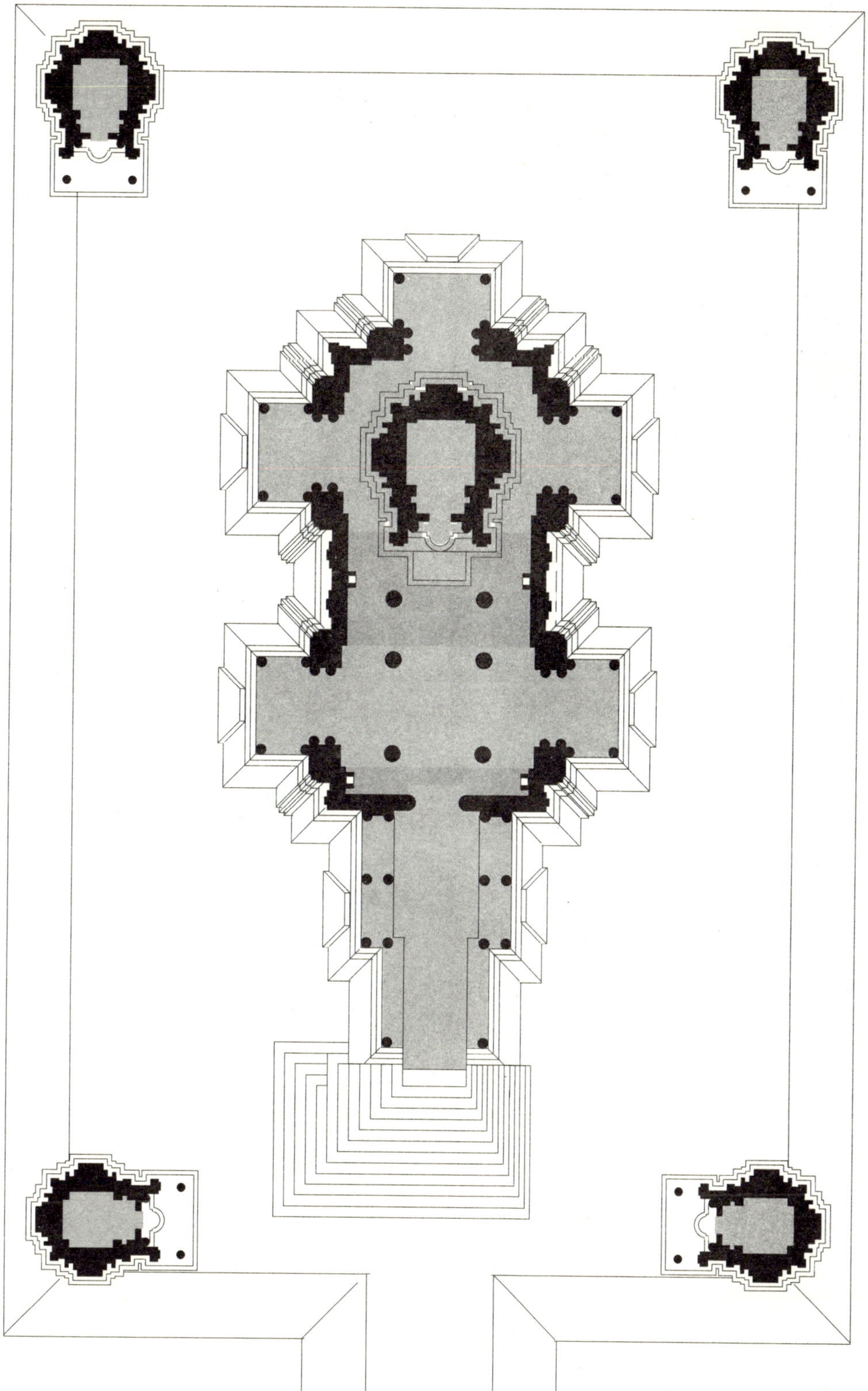

Plate 127: Dhamma-Yazika, Pagan

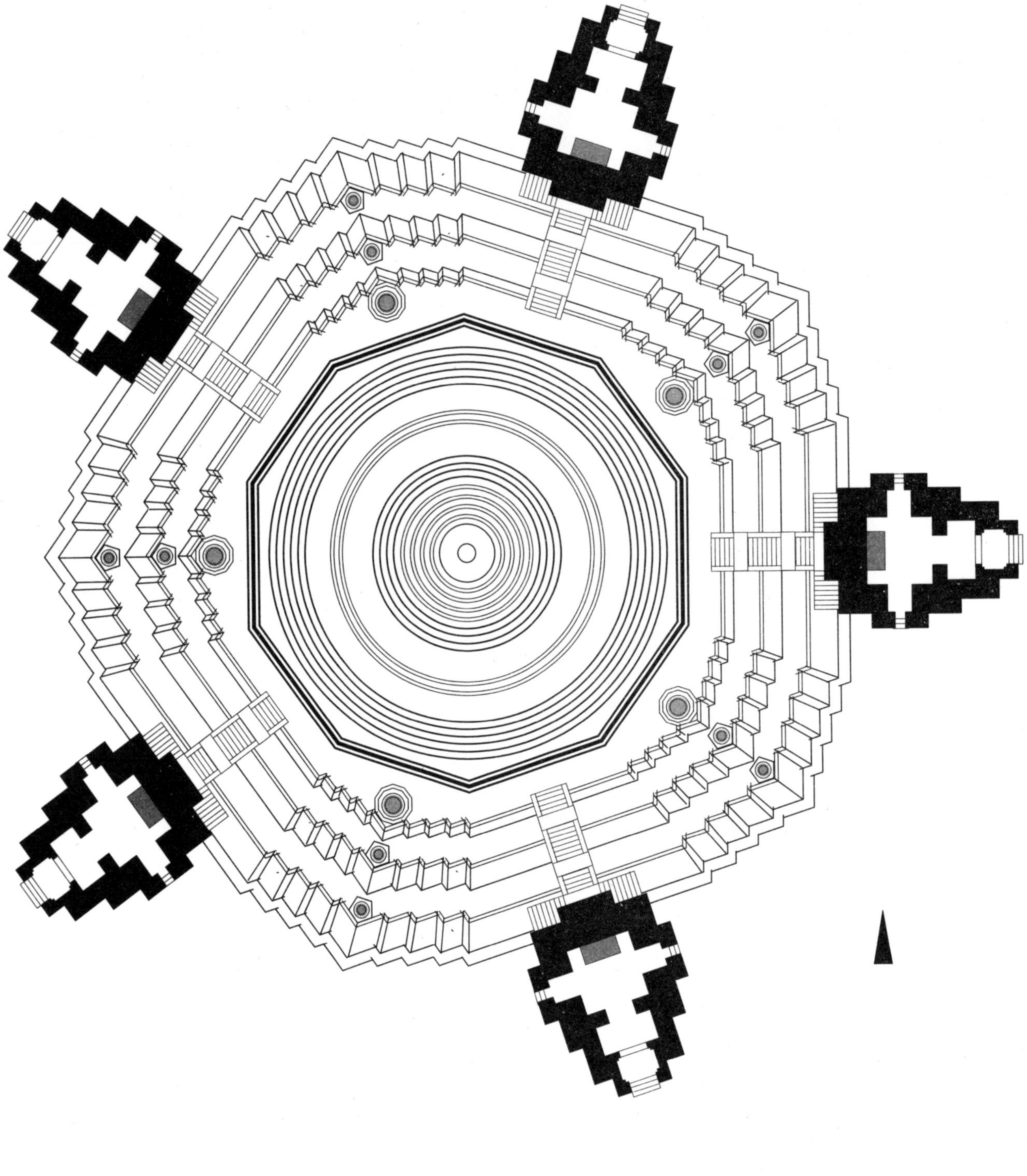

Plate 128: Pentagonal Temple (Pañca-Buddhas), Pagan (a. CE 1175)

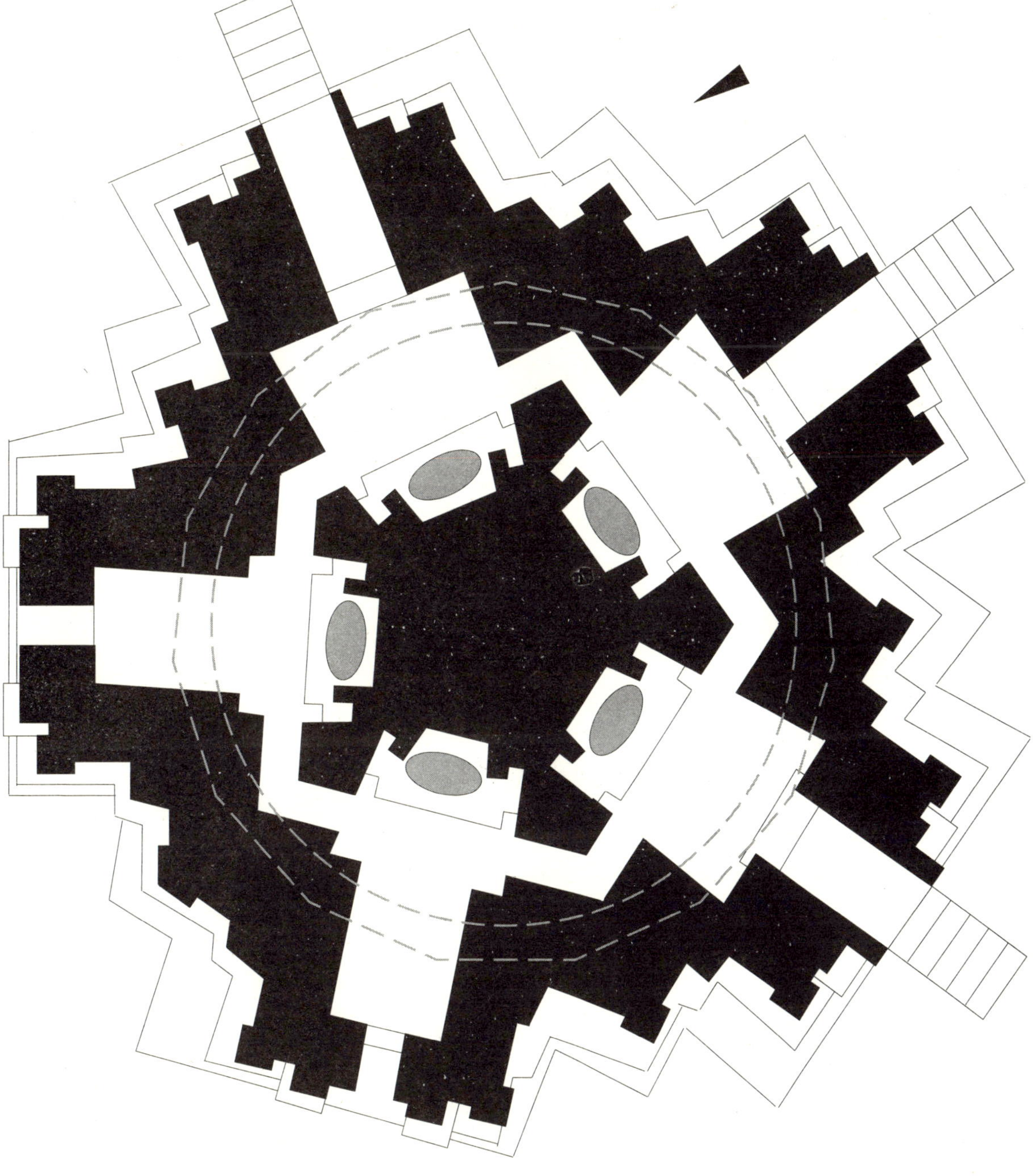

Plate 129: Paya-Thon-Zu, Pagan (a. CE 1250)

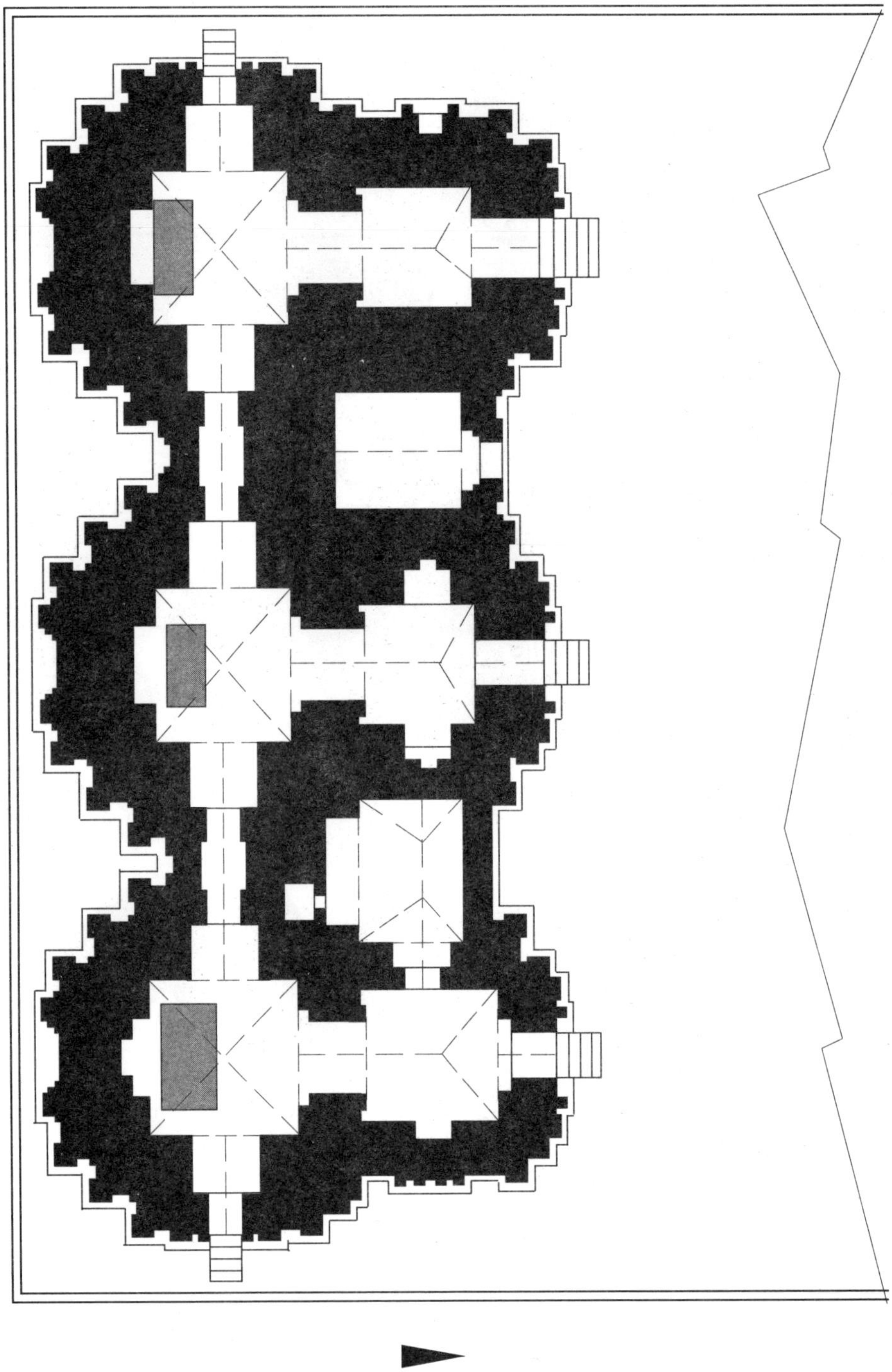

Plate 130: Telī-kā-mandir Temple, Gwalior (*c.* CE 750)

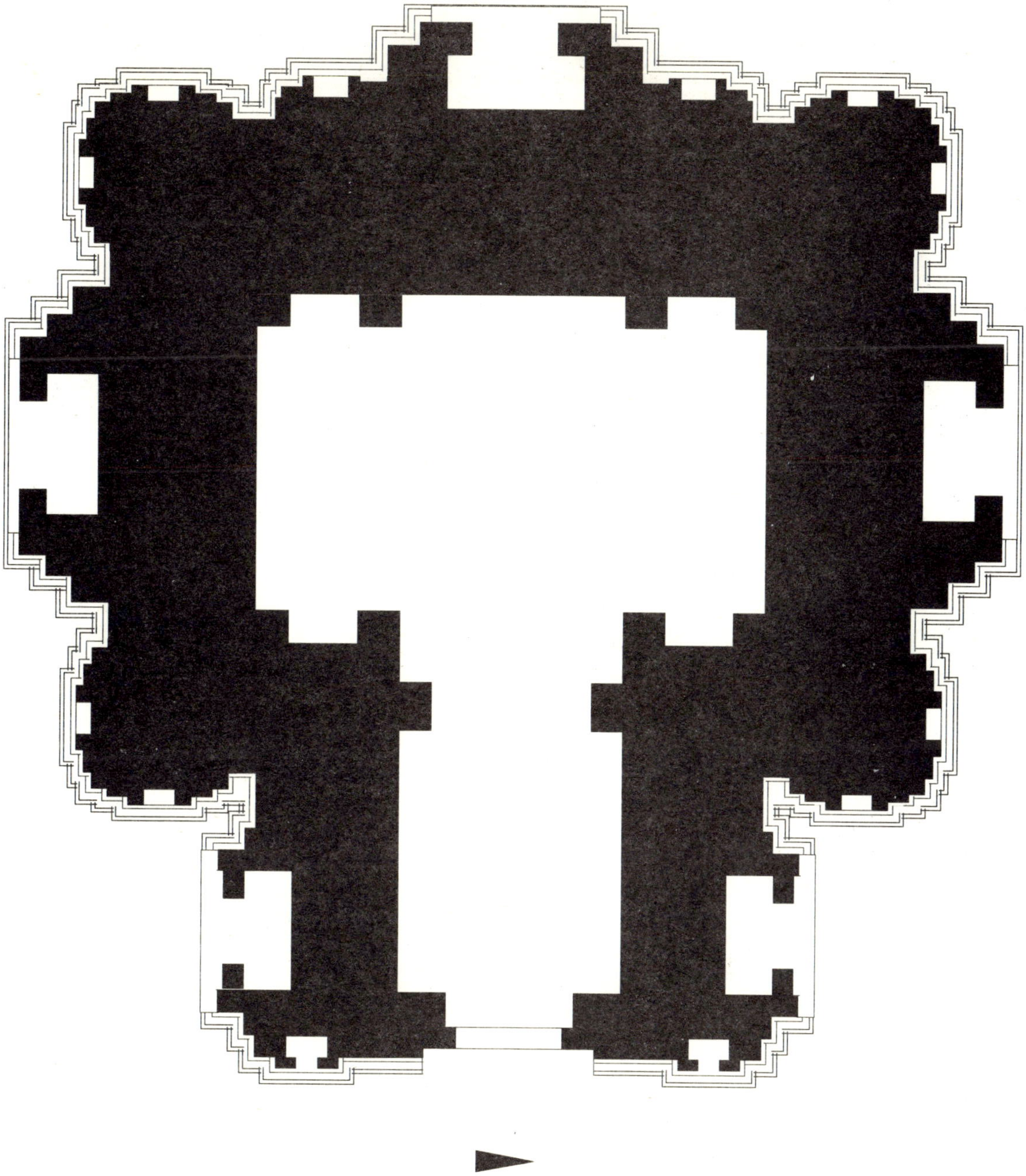

Plate 131: Cauṅsaṭh Yoginī Temple, Rānīpur-Jharial, Orissa (a. CE 700)

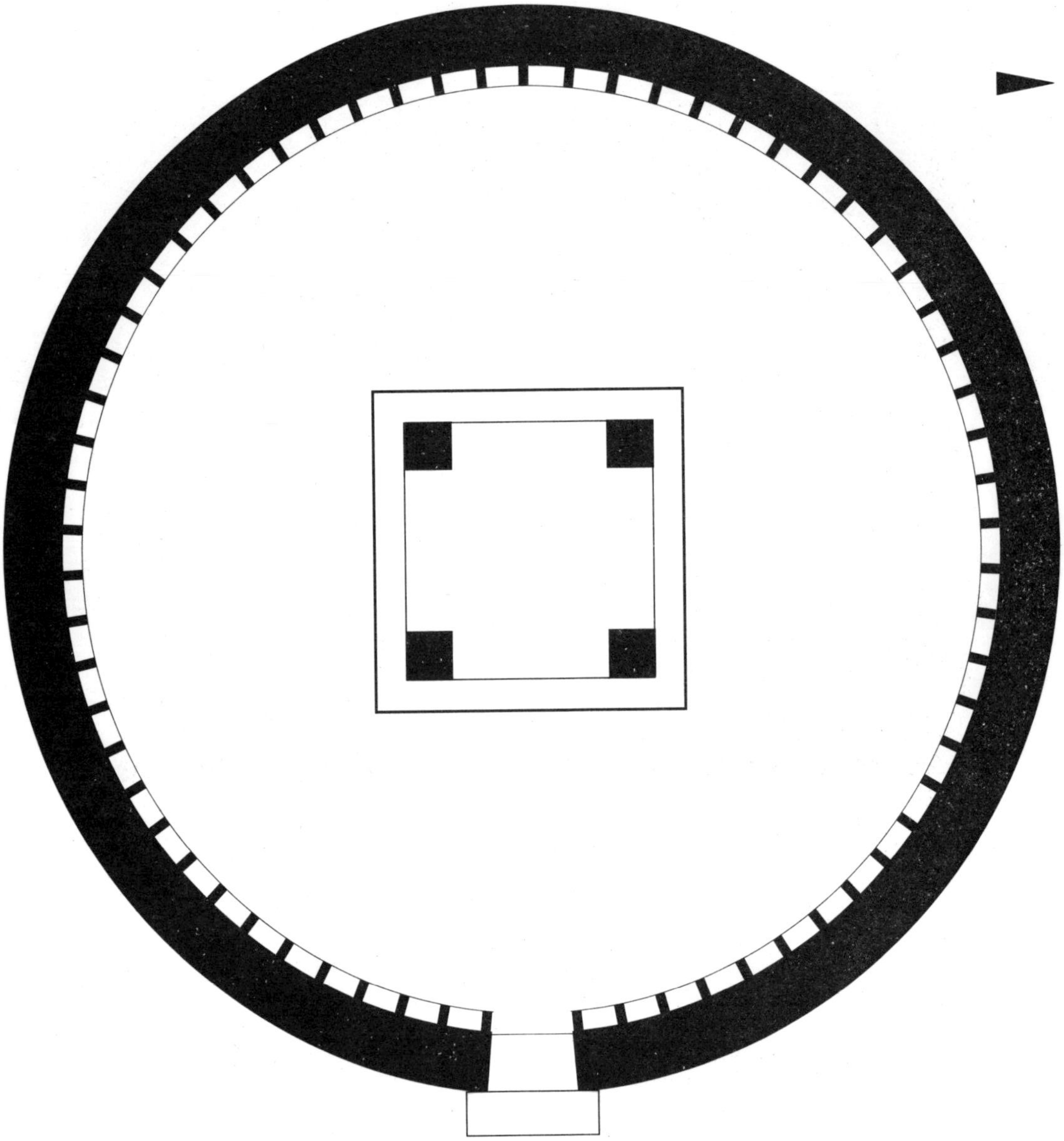

Plate 132: Ekottaso Mahādeva Mandir (Cauṅsaṭh [Liṅga] Mandir), Mitāoli, Madhya Pradesh

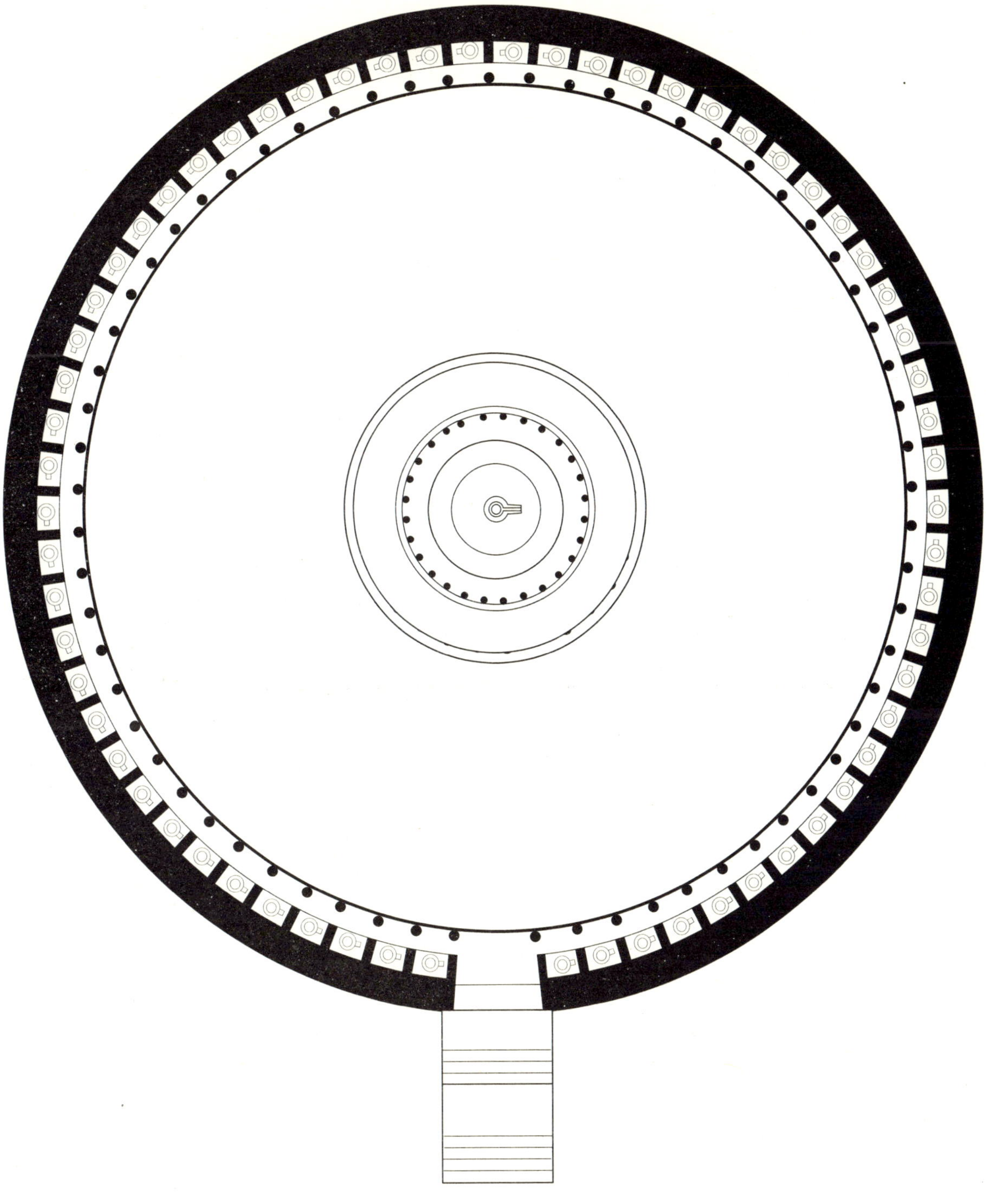

Plate 133: Siddaliṅgeśvara Pañcakūṭa Temple (left) and Mahā-vihāra Dharmapāla, Sanctuary (right)

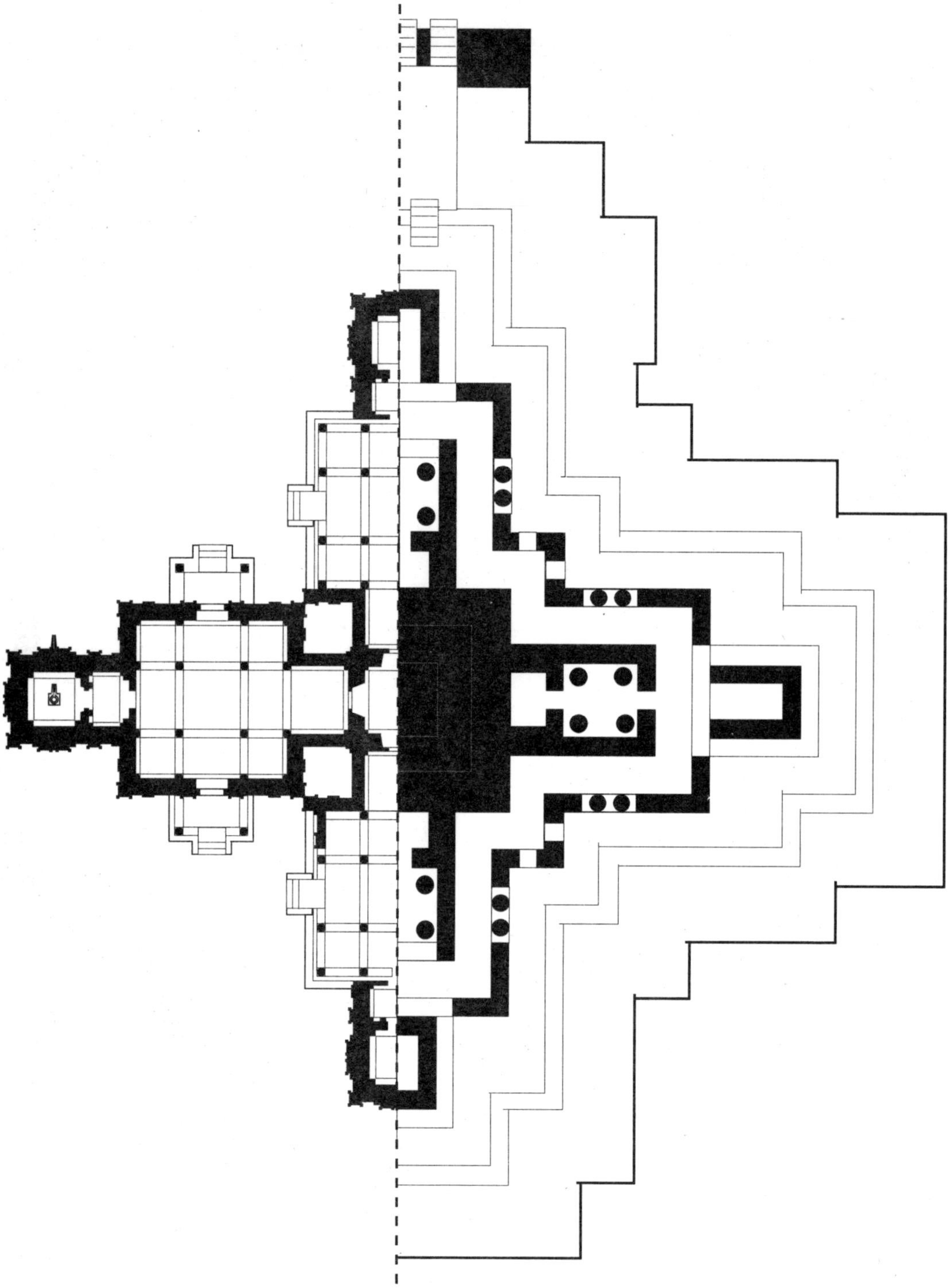

Plate 134: Paramaśāyika maṇḍala indicating ninefold division

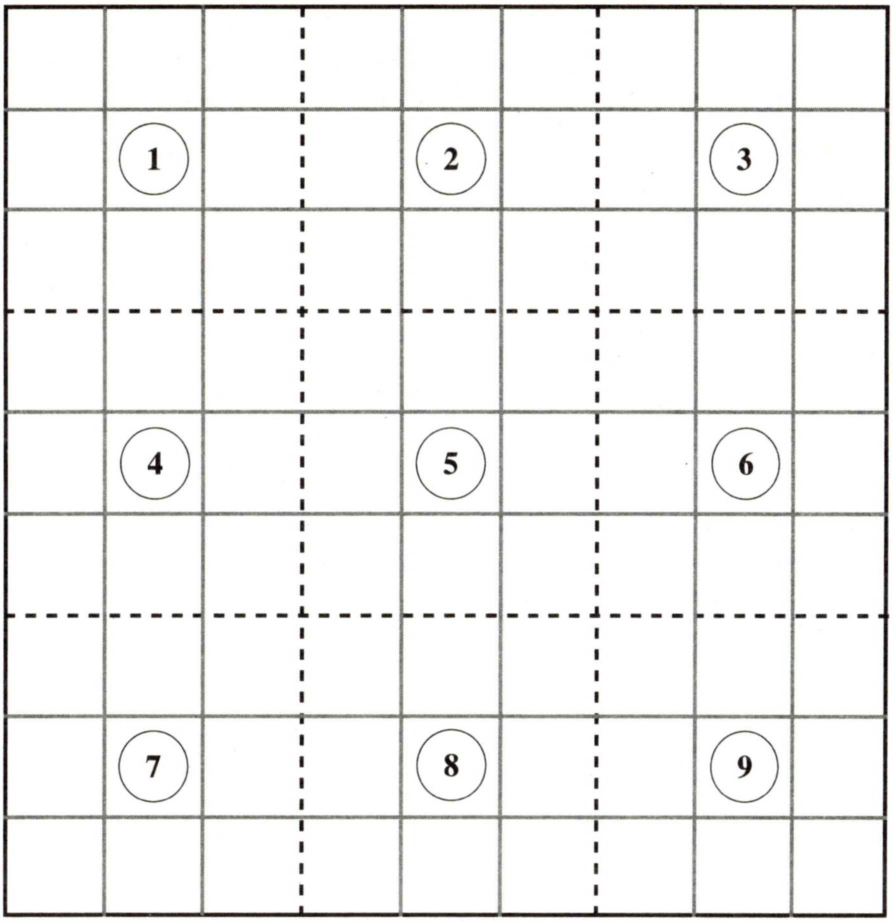

Plate 135: Segments of a circular *vāstu-puruṣa maṇḍala*

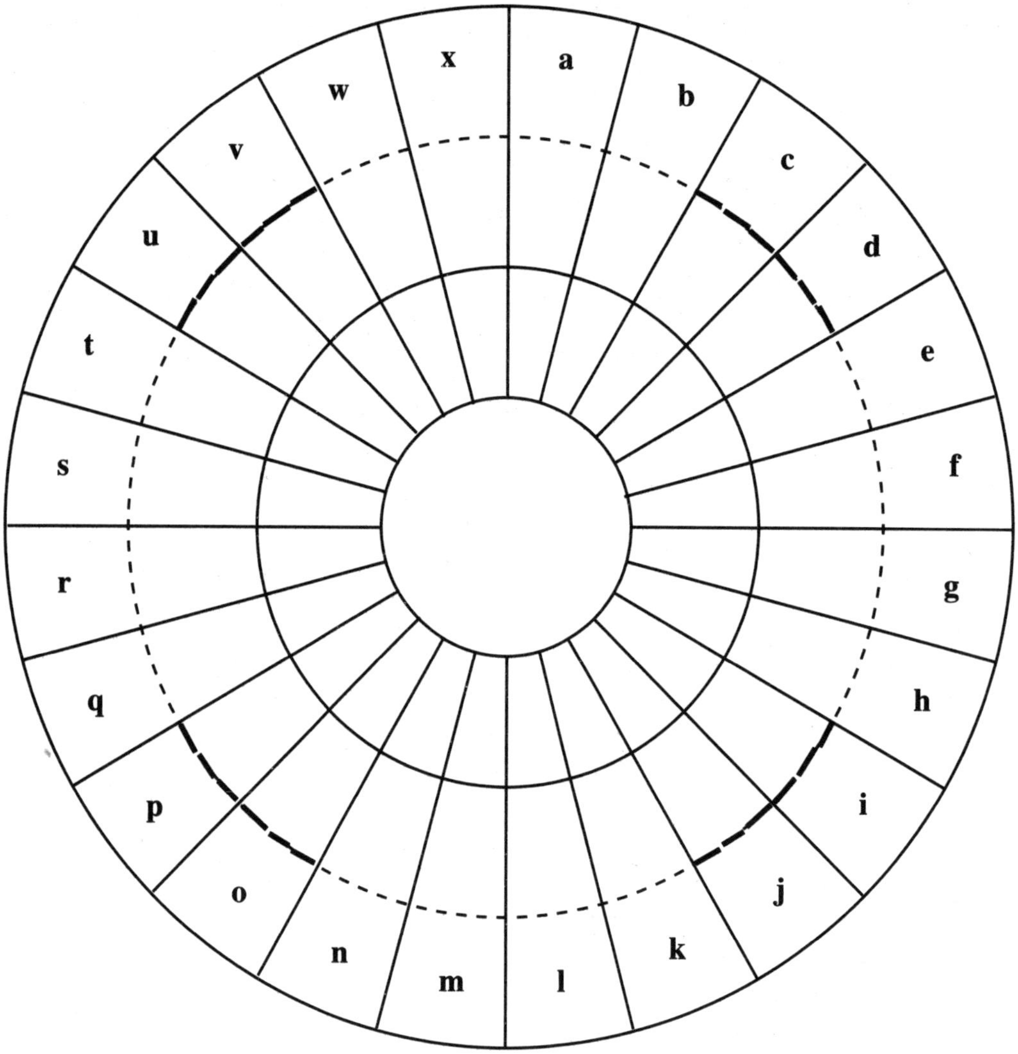

Plate 136: Svarga-Brahma Temple, Ālampur, Andhra Pradesh (*c.* CE 681-96)

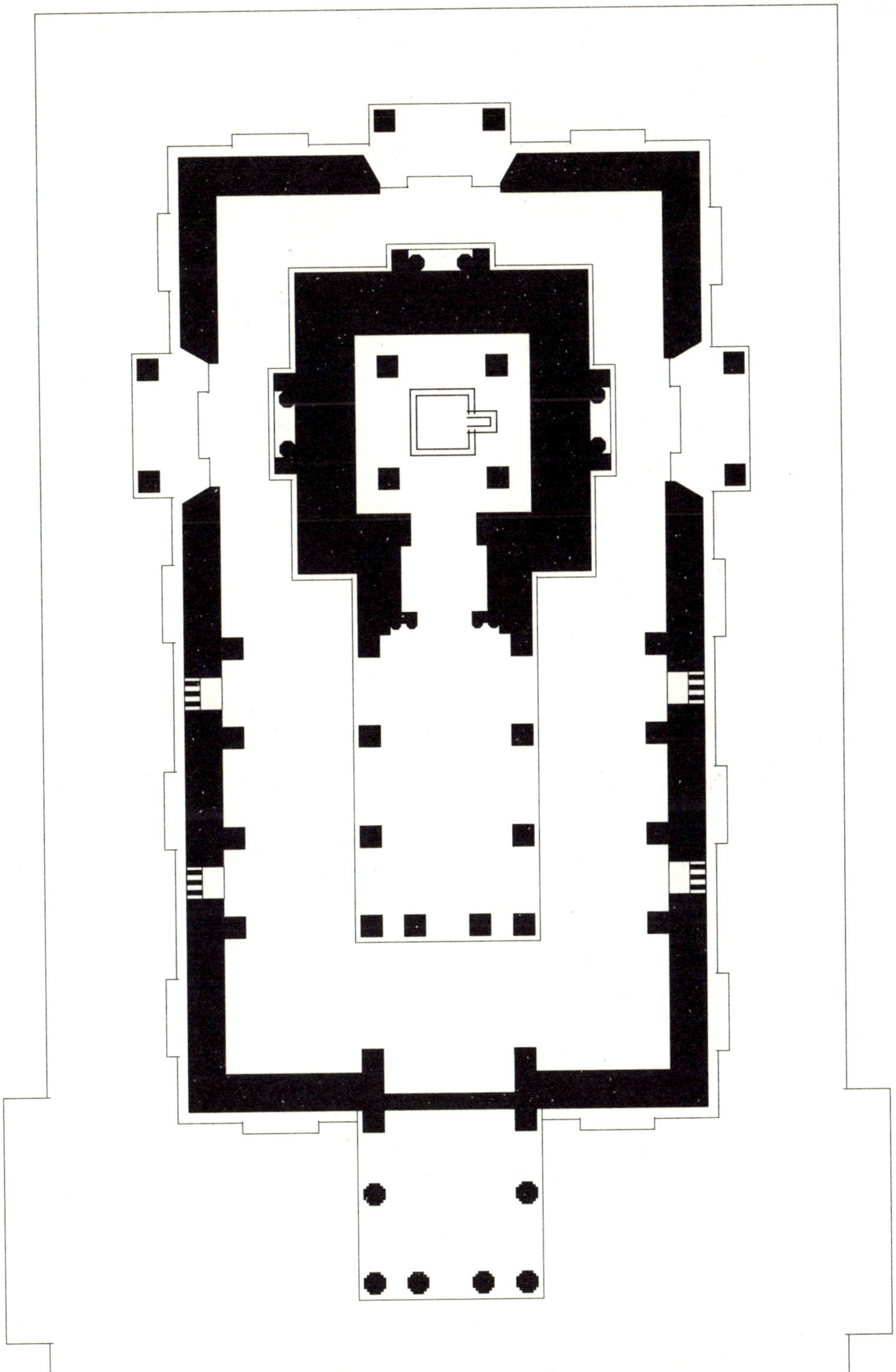

Plate 137: Kandarīya Mahādeva, Khajurāho, Madhya Pradesh (*c.* CE 1017-29)

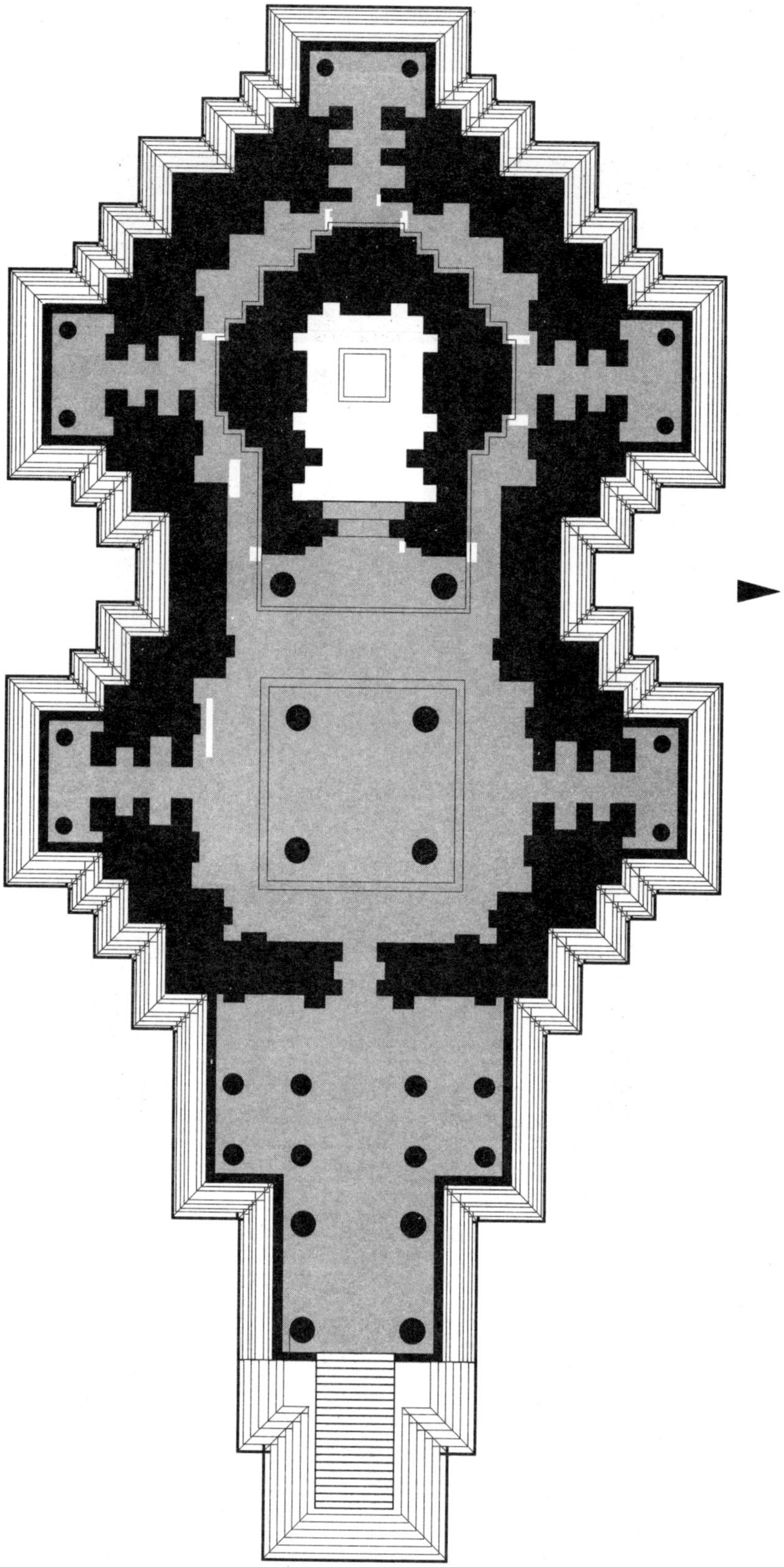

Plate 138: Imperial Vijayanagara

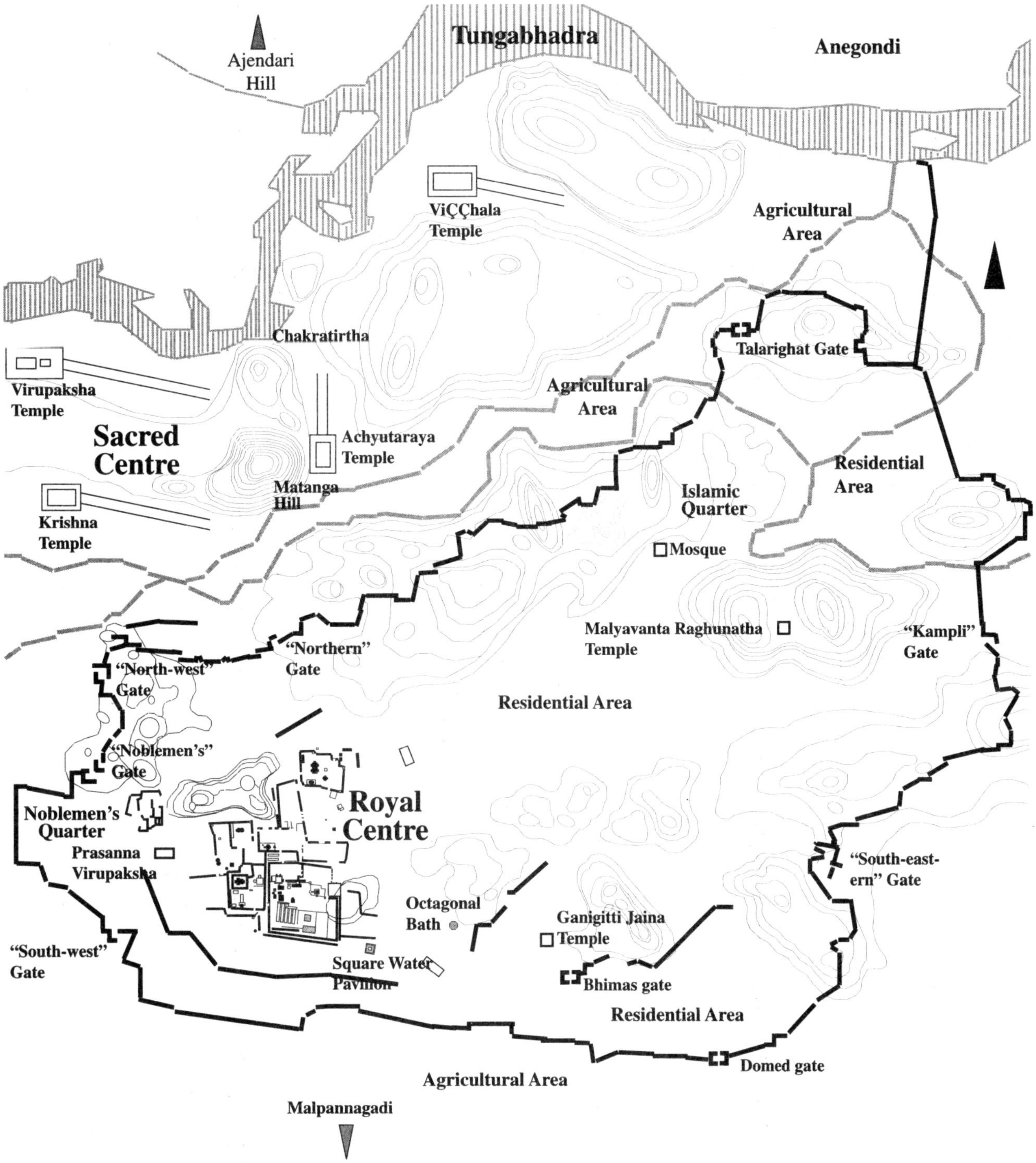

Plate 139: Rāmacandra Temple Complex, Vijayanagara

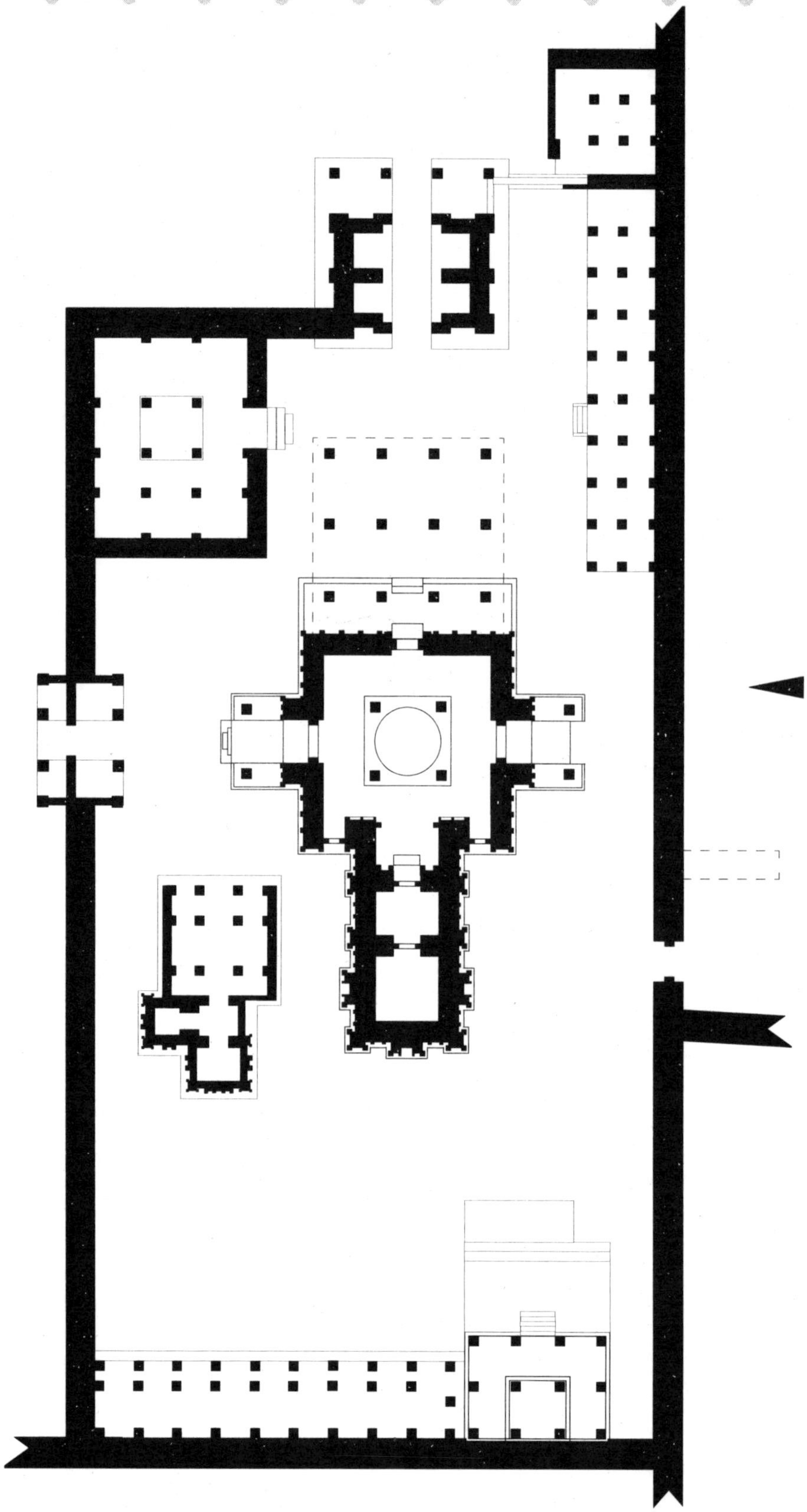

Plate 140: Viṭṭhala Temple Complex, Hampī

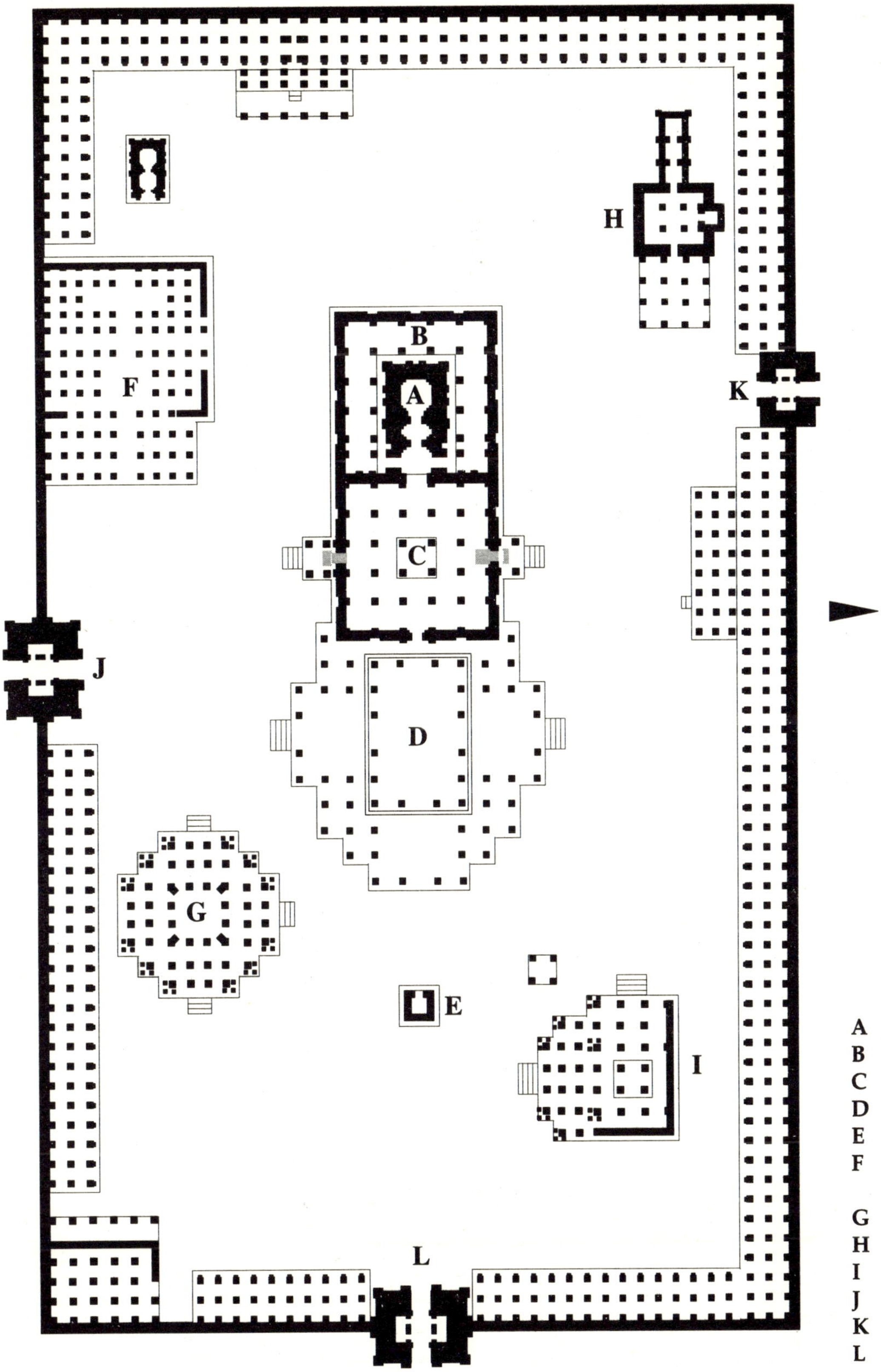

A *garbhagṛha*
B *pradakṣiṇāpatha*
C *ardha-maṇḍapa*
D *mahāmaṇḍapa*
E *garuḍa-maṇḍapa*
F hundred-pillared *maṇḍapa*
G *kalyāṇa-maṇḍapa*
H Amman Temple
I *utsava-maṇḍapa*
J south *gopuram*
K north *gopuram*
L east *gopuram*

Plate 141: Acyutarāya (Tiruveṅgalanātha) Temple Complex, Hampī

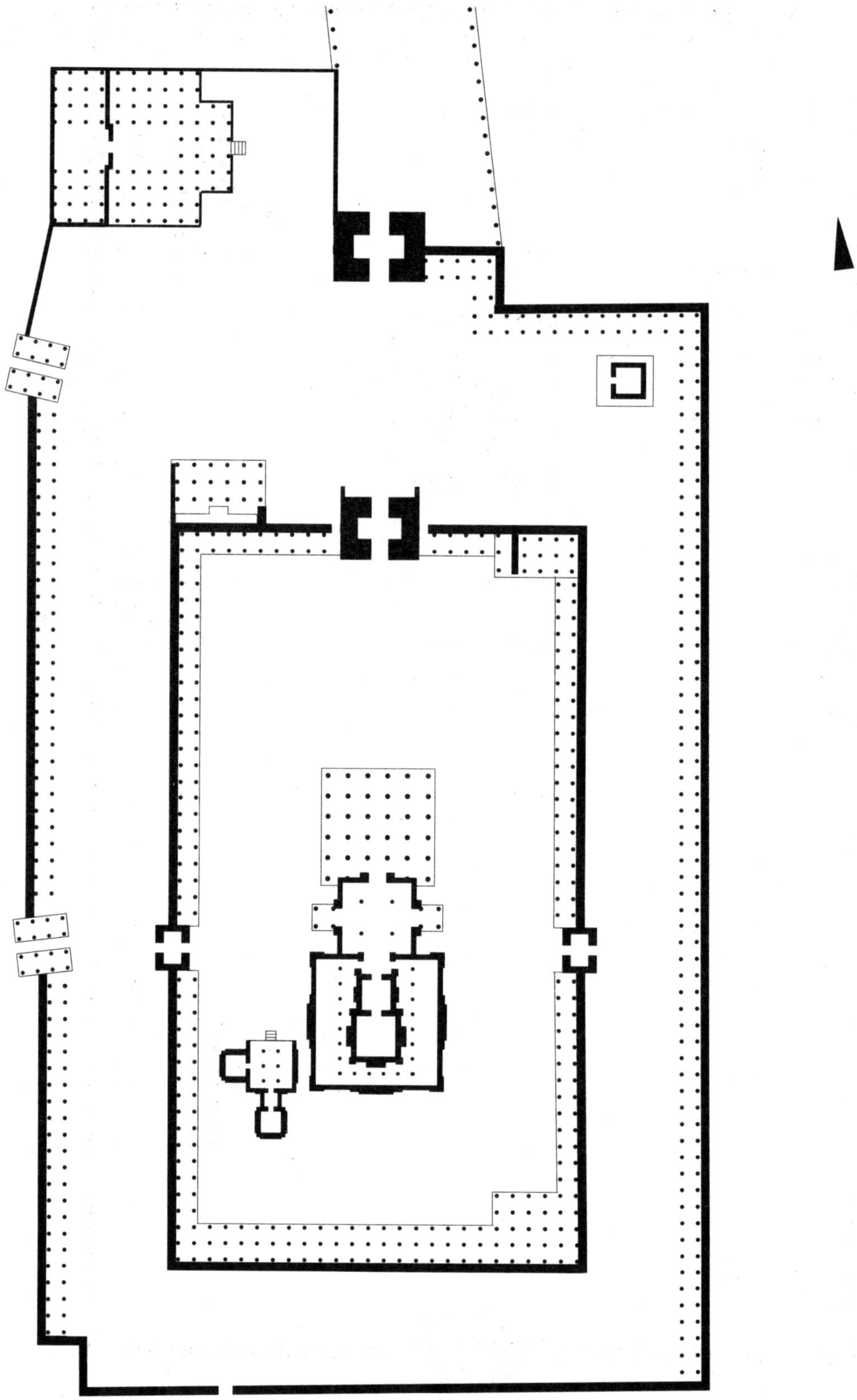

Appendix D

Relevant Ruling Dynasties

GUPTA

Gupta Dynasty (North)

(CE 275–600)

Gupta	*c*. CE 275–300
Ghaṭotkaca	*c*. 300-20
Candragupta I	*c*. 329-50
Samudragupta	*c*. 350-70
Rāmagupta	*c*. 370-76
Candragupta II	*c*. 376–415
Kumāragupta I	*c*. 415-55
Skandagupta	*c*. 455-67
Kumāragupta II	*c*. 467-77
Budhagupta	*c*. 477-95
Candragupta III	*c*. 495–500
Vainyagupta	*c*. 500-10
Narasiṁhagupta	*c*. 510-40
Kumāragupta III	*c*. 540-50
Viṣṇugupta	*c*. 550-?

– – – – –

PALLAVA

Pallava Dynasty (South Central)

(*c*. CE 315–912)

Siṁhavarman I	*c*. CE 315-345
Skandavarman I	*c*. 345-355 with
Viṣṇugopa	*c*. 350- 55
Kumāraviṣṇu I	*c*. 355- 70
Skandavarman II	*c*. 370- 85
Vīravarman	*c*. 385–400
Skandavarman III	*c*. 400-38
Siṁhavarman II	*c*. 438-60
Skandavarman IV	*c*. 460-80
Nandivarman I	*c*. 480–500
Kumāraviṣṇu II	*c*. 500-20
Buddhavarman	*c*. 520-40
Kumāraviṣṇu III	*c*. 540-50
Siṁhavarman III	*c*. 550-74
Siṁhaviṣṇu	*c*. 574–600
Mahendravarman I	*c*. 600-30
Narasiṁhavarman I	630-68
Mahendravarman II	668-70
Parameśvaravarman I	670-80
Narasiṁhavarman II	680–720
Parameśvaravarman II	720-31
Nandivarman II	731-95
Dantivarman	795–845 with
Nandivarman III	844-66 with
Nṛpatuṅgavarman	855-96 with

Aparājita	879-97
Kampavarman	899–912

– – – – –

MYSORE
Gaṅga (Western) Dynasty
(CE 350–1000)

Koṅgunivarman Mādhava I	*c.* 350-70
Mādhava II	370-90
Harivarman	390–410
Viṣṇugopa	410-30
Mādhava III Tandaṅgala	430-69
Avinīta	469–529
Durvinīta	529-79
Karnataka dominance	
Mushkara	579–604
Polavīra	604-29
Śrī Vikrama	629-54
Bhūvikrama	654-79
Śivamāra I	679–726
Śrī Puruṣa	726-88
Śivamāra II	788–816
Rājamalla I	816-43
Nītimārga I Eregaṅga	843-70
Rājamalla II	870–907
Nītimārga II Eregaṅga	907-21
Narasiṁha	921-33
Rājamalla III	933-38
Butuga II	938-61
Marulagaṅga Nītimārga	961-63
Mārasiṁha II Satyavākya	963-75
Rājamalla IV Satyavākya	975-86
Rājamalla V Rakkasagaṅga	986-99
Nītimārga Permanadi	999
to Coḷa	

– – – – –

ORISSA/KALIṄGA
Gaṅga (Eastern) Dynasty
(*c.* CE 496–1435)

Indravarman I	*c.* 496–535
Hastivarman Rājasinha	*c.* 535-50
Indravarman II	*c.* 550-90
Indravarman III	*c.* 590–625
Dānārṇava	*c.* 625
Indravarman IV	*c.* 625-50
Devendravarman I	fl. *c.* 679

Anantavarman I	fl. *c.* 700
Nandavarman	fl. *c.* 717
Devendravarman II	fl. *c.* 747
Rājendravarman I	fl. *c.* 760
Anantavarman II	*c.* 780–803
Devendravarman III	*c.* 803-09
Rājendravarman II	*c.* 809-40
Devendravarman IV	*c.* 840
Satyavarman	fl. *c.* 847/9
Vajrahasta I	fl. *c.* 856
Madhu Kāmārṇava I	?
Vajrahasta II	?
Devendravarman V	?
Vīrasinha	?
Kāmārṇava I	?
Dānārṇava	?
Guṇārṇava I	? -869
Kāmārṇava II	?
Rānārṇava	?
Vajrahasta III	869–913
(Kāmārṇava III)	?
(Guṇārṇava II)	?
(Potaṅkuśa)	*c.* 921-36
(Kaligalaṅkuśa)	*c.* 936-46
Guṇḍama I	*c.* 946-53
Kāmārṇava IV	*c.* 953-78
Vinayāditya	*c.* 978-80
Vajrahasta IV	*c.* 980–1015
Kāmārṇava V	1015
Guṇḍama II	1015-
Madhu Kāmārṇava II	1019-38
Vajrahasta VI	1038-70
Rājarājadeva I	1070-78
Ānandavarman Choḍagaṅga	1078–1147
(Anaṅgabhīmadeva I)	*c.* 1148
Kāmārṇava VI	*c.* 1148-57
Rāghava	*c.* 1157-71
Rājarāja II	*c.* 1171–1205
Rājarāja III	*c.* 1205-16
Anaṅgabhīmadeva III	*c.* 1216-38
Narasiṁhadeva I	1238-64
Bhānudeva I	1264-78
Narasiṁhadeva II	1278–1306
Bhānudeva II	1306-28
Narasiṁhadeva III	1328-52
Bhānudeva III	1352-78
Narasiṁhadeva IV	1378–1414
Bhānudeva IV	1414-35

– – – – –

CĀḶUKYA
Early Cāḷukya Dynasty (Bādāmī)
(CE 543–757)

Pulakeśin I	CE 543-66
Kīrttivarman I	566-97
Maṅgaleśa	597–610
Pulakeśin II	610-42
interregnum Pallava ascendency (642-54)	
Vikramāditya I	654-81
Vinayāditya	681-96
Vijayāditya	696–733
Vikramāditya II	733-44
Kīrttivarman II	744-52

– – – – –

CĀḶUKYA
Eastern Cāḷukya Dynasty (Veṅgī)
(CE 543–1070)

Pulakeśin I	CE 543-66
Kīrttivarman I	566-97
Maṅgaleśa	597–610
Pulakeśin II	610-42
interregnum	
Kubja Viṣṇuvardhana I	624-41
Jayasiṁha I	641-73
Indra Bhaṭṭāraka	673
Viṣṇuvardhana II	673-82
Maṅgi Yuvarāja	682–706
Jayasiṁha II	706-18
Kokkilli	719
Viṣṇuvardhana III	719-55
Vijayāditya I	755-72
Viṣṇuvardhana IV	772–808
Vijayāditya II	808-47
Viṣṇuvardhana V	847-49
Gunaga Vijayāditya III	849-92
Cāḷukya Bhīma I	892–921
Vijayāditya IV	921
Amma I	921-27
Tala	927
Beta Vijayāditya	927
Vikramāditya II	927-28
Bhīma II	928
Yuddhamalla II	928-35
Cāḷukya Bhīma II	935-47
Amma II	947-70
Dānārṇava	970-71
interregnum	

Śaktivarman I	1000-11
Vimalāditya	1011-18
Rājarāja Narendra	1019-61
Rājendra (Kulottuṅga)	

- - - - -

RĀṢṬRAKŪṬA

Rāṣṭrakūṭa Dynasty (West Central)

(CE 543–982)

?	?
Durgarāja	CE 570-90
?	?
Dantidurga	735-56
Kṛṣṇa I	756-80
Govinda III	780–815
Amoghavarṣa	815-80
Kṛṣṇa II	880–914
Indra III	914-20
Amoghavarṣa II	929-30
Govinda IV	930-35
Amoghavarṣa III	935-39
Kṛṣṇa III	939-67
Amoghavarṣa Khottiga	967-72
Karka (Kakka) Amoghavarṣa IV	972-73
Indra II	973-82

- - - - -

PRATIHĀRA

Pratihāra Dynasty (Gujarat)

(*c.* CE 730–1019)

Nāgabhaṭṭa I	*c.* CE 730-60
Kakkuka	760-?
Devarāja	?-772
Vatsarāja	*c.* 772-94
Nāgabhaṭṭa II	*c.* 794–833
Rāmbhadra	*c.* 833-36
Mihir-Bhoja (Bhoja I) Ādivarāha	*c.* 836-92
Mahendrapāla I	*c.* 892–912
Mahipāla (Kṣitipāla)	*c.* 912-42
Bhoja II	*c.* 942-?
Vināyakapāla	?-*c.* 946
Mahendrapāla II	*c.* 946-48
Devapāla	*c.* 948-60
Vijayapāla	*c.* 960-?
Rājyapāla	?-1019
Trilocanpāla	*c.* 1019-30

Jasapāla	c. 1030-36

– – – – –

BHAUMAKARA
Bhaumakara Dynasty (Orissa)
(*c.* CE 736–949)

Ksemaṅkaradeva	*c.* CE 736-86
Śivakaradeva I (Unmatasiṁha)	*c.* 786-90
Śubhakaradeva I	*c.* 790–809
Śivakaradeva II	*c.* 809-29
Śāntikaradeva I (Lalitahara)	*c.* 829-36
Śubhakaradeva II	*c.* 836-39
Śubhakaradeva III	*c.* 839-46
Tribhuvanamahādevī I	*c.* 846-?
Śāntikaradeva II (Lonabhara)	?-81
Śubhakaradeva IV (Kusumahara II)	*c.* 881-85
Śivakaradeva III	*c.* 885-94
Tribhuvanamahadevī II (Mahādevī)	*c.* 894-?
Śāntikaradeva III	?
Śubhakaradeva V	?
Gaurīmahādevī	?-*c.* 916
Daṇḍīmahādevī	916-23
Vakulamahādevī	923-40
Dharmamahādevī	940-49

– – – – –

NORTHERN KAḶACURI
Kaḷacuri/Cedi or Haihaya Dynasty
(Tripurī/Tewar)
(*c.* CE 750–12th century)

Śaṅkaragaṇa I	*c.* CE 750-75
?	
Lakṣmaṇarāja I	825-50
Kokalla I	850-90
Śaṅkragaṇa II	890-?
Bālaharṣa	?-915
Yuvarājadeva I Keyūravarṣa	915-45
Lakṣmaṇarāja II	945-70
?	?
Yuvarāja II	?-980
Kokalla II	980–1015
Gāṅgeyadeva Vikramāditya	1015-41
Lakṣmī-Karṇa	1041-73
Yaśaḥkarṇa	1073–1120
?	?
Gayākarṇa	1123-53
Narasiṁha	1153-63

Jayasiṁha	1163-?

SOUTHERN KAḶACURI

Kaḷacuri Dynasty (Uchita)
(11th century – CE 1184)
feudatories of Cāḷukya

Uchita	?
Asaga	?
Kannam	?
Kiriasaga	?
Bijjala I	?
Kannama	?
Jogama	?
Permardi	?
Bijjala II	1130-67
declared independence in 1162	
Sovideva (Someśvara)	1167-76
Mallugi	1176
Saṅkama (Saṅkamavarmādeva)	1176-80
Āhavamalla	1180-83
Siṅghana	1183-84
to Cāḷukyas	

– – – – –

SOMAVAṀŚĪ

Somavaṁśī Dynasty (Orissa)
(*c*. 800–1110)

Śivagupta	?-*c*. CE 882
Janamejaya Mahābhavagupta I	*c*. 882–922
Yayāti Mahāśivagupta I	*c*. 922-55
Bhīmaratha Mahābhavagupta II	*c*. 955-80
Dharmaratha Mahāśivgagupta II	*c*. 980-?
Nahuṣa Mahābhavagupta III	*c*. 1005-21
Indraratha	1021-25
Caṇḍīhara Yayāti Mahāśivagupta III	*c*. 1025-40
Uddyotakeśarī Mahābhavagupta IV	*c*. 1040-*c*. 1060 with
Karṇakeśarī	*c*. 1040-65
Janamejaya Mahāśivagupta IV	*c*. 1065-85
Purañjaya Mahābhavagupta V	1085–1100
Karṇadeva Mahāśivagupta V	1100-10

– – – – –

CERAS /KULAŚEKHARA

Ceras /Kulaśekhara Dynasty (South-west)
(CE 800–1106)

Kulaśekharavarman	CE 800-20

Rājeśekharavarman	820-44
Sthānu Ravivarman	844-85
Rāmavarman Kulaśekhara	885–917
Kodai Ravivarman	917-47
Indu Kodaivarman	947-62
Bhāskara Ravivarman I	962–1020
Bhāskara Ravivarman II	978–1025
Ravi Rāmavarman	1025-35
Bhāskara Ravivarman II	1035-90
Rāmavarman Kulaśekhara	1090–1106
Śrīvalarāma	1090–1100

– – – – –

CANDELLA

Candella Dynasty (Khajurāho)

(*c.* CE 831–1202)

Candravarman (Nannuka)	*c.* CE 831-45
Vākpati	845-65
Jaya Śakti (Jejja) co-ruled	865-85
Vijai Śakti	865-85
Rahila Deva	885–905
Harṣadeva	905-25
Yaśovarman (Lakṣavarman)	925-50
Dhaṅga	950-99
Gaṇḍa	999–1003
Vidyādhara Candella	1003-35
Vijayapāla	1035-50
Devavarman	1050-60
Kīrtivarman	1060–1100
Sallakṣavarman	1100-10
Jayavarman	1110-20
Pṛthvīvarman	1120-28
Madanavarman	1129-65
Paramardideva (Parmal)	1165–1203
Trailokyavarman	1203-45
Vīravarman	1245-85
Bhojavarman	1285-88
Hammīravarman	1288–1308

– – – – –

COḶA

Vijayālaya Dynasty (Tañjāvur Coḷa)

(CE 850–1071)

Vijayālaya	CE 850-71
Āditya-rāja I	*c.* 871–907
Parāntaka I	907-55
Gaṇḍarāditya	950-57

Ariñjaya	956-57
Parāntaka II Sundara Coḷa	956
Āditya II Karikala	956-69
Madurānkaka Uttama Coḷa	973-85
Rājarāja I Coḷa	985–1014
Rājendra I Coḷa	1012-44
Rājādhirāja I	1018-54
Rājendra II	1052-60
Rāmamahendra	1060-63
Vīra Rājendra	1063-70
Adhi Rājendra	1070-71
Rājendra III (Kulottuṅga)	1070–1120

– – – – –

CĀḶUKYA
Cāḷukya (Solaṅkī) Dynasty (Gujarat)
(*c.* CE 950–1304)

Mūlarāja I	*c.* CE 950-95
Cāmuṇḍarāja	995–1009
Vallabharāja	1009
Durlabharajā	1009-21
Bhīmadeva I	1023-63
Karṇadeva I	1063-93
Siddharāja Jayasiṁha	1093–1125
Kumārapāla	1125-71
Ajayapāla	1171-76
Mūlarāja II?	1176-78
Bhīmadeva II	1178–1242
Tribhuvanapāla	1242-44
Vāghela Branch	
Viśāla Vāghela	*c.* CE 1244-62
Arjuna	1262-75
Sāraṅgadeva (Karan Ghelo)	1275-97
Karṇadeva II Vāghela	1297–1304
to Delhi	

– – – – –

CĀḶUKYA
Western Cāḷukya Dynasty (Kalyāṇa)
(CE 975–1200)

Taila Āhavamalla or Tailapa II	CE 973-95
Satyāśraya Irivabedaṅga	995–1008
Daśavarman	1008
Vikramāditya I (V)	1008-14
Ayyana	1014-15
Jayasiṁha I Jagadekamalla	1015-43
Someśvara I (Trailokyamalla or Āhavamalladeva)	1043-68

Someśvara II	1068-76
Vikramāditya II (VI)	1076–1127
Someśvara III	1127-35
Jagadekamalla II	1135-51
Taila III	1151-56

Kaḷacuri dominance

Cāḷukya Dynasty

Someśvara IV	1183–1200

– – – – –

GOA
Kadamba Dynasty
(CE 1000–1334)

Guhulladeva I	980-1005
Ṣaṣṭhadeva I	?
Jayakeśi I	1050-75
Ṣaṣṭhadeva II	*c.* 1075
Guhulladeva II	1075–1100
Vijayāditya	1100-04
Jayakeśi II	1104-47
Śivacittavīrapermadideva	1147-87
Viṣṇucitta	1187-88
Jayakeśi III	1188–1212
to Devīgiri	
Ṣaṣṭhadeva III(?)	1224-?
Kāmadeva(?)	?-1277
to Devīgiri	
?	1313-?
?	?-1334
to Delhi	

– – – – –

HOYSAḶA
Hoysaḷa Dynasty (South Deccan and Mysore)
(CE 1022–1346)

Nṛpakāma	CE 1022-47
Vinayādita	1047-98 with
Ereyaṅga	1063–1100
Ballāla I	1100-10
Biṭṭiga Viṣṇuvardhana	1110-52
Narasiṁha I	1152-73
Ballāla II (Vīraballāla)	1173–1220
Narasiṁha II	1220-38 with
Someśvara	1233-67 with
Narasiṁha III	1254-92 with
Ballāla III	1291–1342

Virūpākṣa Ballāla IV	1342-46

- - - - -

COḶA
Cāḷukya Dynasty (Coḷa)
(CE 1120–1279)

Vikrama Coḷa	CE 1120-35
Kulottuṅga II	1133-50 with
Rājarāja II	1146-63
Rājādhirāja II	1163-66 and 1179-82
Kulottuṅga III	1178–1217/1218
Rājarāja III	1216-46
Rājendra IV	1246-79

- - - - -

CERAS/VENAD
Ceras/Venad Dynasty (South-west)
(CE 1125–1678)

Śrī Vīra Kerala Varmā I Rājā of Venad	CE 1125-45
Śrī Kodai Kerala Varmā	1145-61
Śrī Vīra Ravi Varmā	1161-64
Śrī Vīra Kerala Varmā II	1164-67
Śrī Vīra Udaya Mārtaṇḍa	1167-73
Śrī Devadarman Kerala Varmā III	1173-96
Śrī Vīra Rāma Varmā Tiruvadi	1196–1209
Śrī Vīra Raman Kerala Varmā	1209-14
?	?
Śrī Vīra Ravi Kerala Varman Tiruvadi	1235-52
Śrī Vīra Padmanābha Mārtaṇḍa Varmā Tiruvadi	1252–1305
Śrī Āditya Varmā	1305-16
Śrī Vīra Udaya Mārtaṇḍa Varmā	1316-33
Śrī Āditya Varmā	1333-36
Śrī Vīra Rāma Udaya Mārtaṇḍa Varmā Tiruvadi	1336-42
Śrī Vīra Kerala Varmā Tiruvadi	1342-63
Śrī Vīra Mārtaṇḍa Varmā III	1363-66
Śrī Vīra Udaya Mārtaṇḍa Varmā	1366-82
Śrī Kerala Varmā Kulaśekhara Perumāḷ	1382-83
Śrī Vīra Ravi Varmā	1383
Śrī Chera Udaya Mārtaṇḍa Varmā	1383–1444
Venad Mootha Rājā	1444-58
Śrī Vīra Mārtaṇḍa Varmā	1458-71
Āditya Varmā	1471-78
Ravi Varmā	1478–1504
Śrī Vīra Ravi Varmā	1504-28
Mārtaṇḍa Varmā	1528-37
Udaya Mārtaṇḍa Varmā	1537-50
Kerala Varmā	1550-53

Āditya Varmā	1553-67
Udaya Mārtaṇḍa Varmā	1567-94
Śrī Vīra Ravi Varmā Kulaśekhara Perumāḷ	1594–1604
Śrī Vīra Varmā	1604-06
Ravi Varmā	1606-19
Unni Kerala Varmā	1619-25
Ravi Varmā	1625-31
Unni Kerala Varmā	1631-61
Āditya Varmā	1661-78

becomes Kulaśekhara Rājās of Travancore

– – – – –

KUMMATADURGA/KAMPILĪ

Siṅgeya Dynasty
(CE 1280–1326)

Siṅgeya Nāyaka III	CE 1280–1300
Kampilideva (Kampilarasadeva)	1300-26

to Delhi Sultanate

– – – – –

SAṄGAMA

Saṅgama Dynasty (Vijayanagara)
(CE 1336–1485)

Harihara I	CE 1336-56
Bukka Rāya I	1366-77
Harihara II	1377–1404
Virūpākṣa I	1404-05
Bukka Rāya II	1405-06
Devarāya I	1406-22
Rāmacandra	1422-30
Devarāya II	1422-46
Vijaya II	1446-47
Mallikārjuna	1446-65
Virūpākṣa II	1465-85

– – – – –

SALUVA

Saluva Dynasty (Vijayanagara)
(CE 1485–1505)

Narasiṁha Saluva	CE 1485-90
Timma	1490-91
Immadi Narasiṁha Rao	1491–1505

– – – – –

NĀYAKAS

Nāyakas Dynasty (Gingee)
(CE 1490–1750)

Nāyaka Tubāki Kr̥ṣṇappā	1490–1521
?	1521-29
Viśvanātha	1529-64
Kr̥ṣṇappā I	1564-72
Vīrappā	1572-95
Kr̥ṣṇappā II	1595–1601
Muttu Kr̥ṣṇappā	1601-09
Muttu Vīrappā I	1609-23
Tirumalla	1623-59
Muttu Vīrappā II	1659-82

to Marāṭhā Confederation 1676
to Mughals 1691

Rajā Sarūp Singh	1691–1714
Desingh	1714

to Nawāb of Ārcoṭ 1714
to France 1750
to England 1761

Nāyakas Dynasty (Madurai)
(CE 1529–1736)

Viśvanātha	CE 1529-64
Kr̥ṣṇappā I	1564-72
Vīrappā	1572-95
Kr̥ṣṇappā II	1595–1601
Muttu Kr̥ṣṇappā	1601-09
Muttu Vīrappā I	1609-23
Tirumalla	1623-59
Muttu Vīrappā II	1659-82
Cokkanātha	1659-78
Muttu Liṅga	1678-82
Muttu Vīrappā III	1682-89
Maṅgammal	1689–1706
Vijayaraṅga Cokkanātha	1706-32
Mīnākṣī	1732-36

to France 1736-63
to England 1763–1948
to India 1948

Nāyaka Dynasty (Thañjāvur)
(CE 1549–1673)

Sevappā	CE 1549-72
Acyutappā	1572–1614
Raghunātha	1614-?
Vijaya Rāghava	?-1673

Musunuri Nāyak Dynasty
(CE 1326-70)

Musunuri Prolayanayyak (Prolaaseedu)	1326-?
Kaapayanayyak (Kaapsneedu)	?-1370

to Delhi

– – – – –

TULUVA
Tuluva Dynasty (Vijayanagara)
(CE 1505-76)

Vīra Narasiṁha (Naresh Tuluva)	CE 1505-09
Kṛṣṇadevarāya	1509-30
Acyutadevarāya	1530-42
Veṅkaṭa	1542
Sadāśivarāya	1542-76

capital moved to **Penukoṇḍa** (1565)

– – – – –

ARAVIḌU
Araviḍu Dynasty (Vijayanagara)
(CE 1569–1664)

Tirumala I	CE 1569-72
Śrī Raṅgarāya (Kṛṣṇadeva Raṅga II)	1572-85
Veṅkaṭa (Venkattapatti Rāyalu)	1586–1614
capital moved to **Chandragiri** (*c.* 1601)	
Raṅga III (Chikka Rāya)	CE 1614
Raṅga IV	1614-?
Rāmarāya	1629-34
Pedda Veṅkaṭa II	1634-*c.* 1642
Raṅga (V) (Śrī Raṅgarāya)	1642-64

to the Mughal Empire

– – – – –

KULAŚEKHARA
Kulaśekhara Dynasty (Travancore)
(*c.* CE 1678–1948)

Ravi Varmā	CE 1678–1704
Unni Kerala Varmā III	1704-18
Āditya Varmā	1718-24
Rajā Rāma Varmā I	1724-29
Mārtaṇḍa Varmā III	1729-58
Rāma Varmā II	1758-98
Bala Rama Varmā I	1798–1810

Rāma Varmā III (q.v.)	1810-?
Mārtaṇḍa Varmā IV (q.v.)	?-1815
Rānī Ghaurī Pārvatī Bāī (regent)	1815-29
Rāma Varmā III	1892-46
Mārtaṇḍa Varmā IV	1846-60
Mahārājā Rāma Varmā IV (q.v.)	1860-?
Rāma Varmā V (q.v.)	?
Rāma Varmā IV	1860-80
Rāma Varmā V	1880-85
Bala Rāma Varmā II	1885–1924
Bala Rāma Varmā III	1924-48

to India 1948

– – – – –

SINSINI JĀṬ

Sinsini Jāṭ Dynasty (Bharatpur/Deeg)

(Mahārājā of Bharatpur/Deeg)

(CE 1722–1948)

Ṭhākur Badan Singh	1722-33
Mahārājā Sūraj Mal	1733-67
Jawāhar Singh	1767-68
Ratan Singh	1768-69
Keśarī Singh	1769-71
Newal Singh	1771-76
Ranjit Singh	1776–1806
Randhīr Singh	1805-23
Baldeo Singh	1823 -25
Balwant Singh	1825 -53
Jaswant Singh	1853 -93
Rām Singh	1893–1900 (exiled)
Girrāj Kaur (regent)	1900-18
Vrijendra Sawai Kishan Singh	1900-28 (exiled)
Vrijendra Singh	1929-47

to India 1948

– – – – –

Bibliography

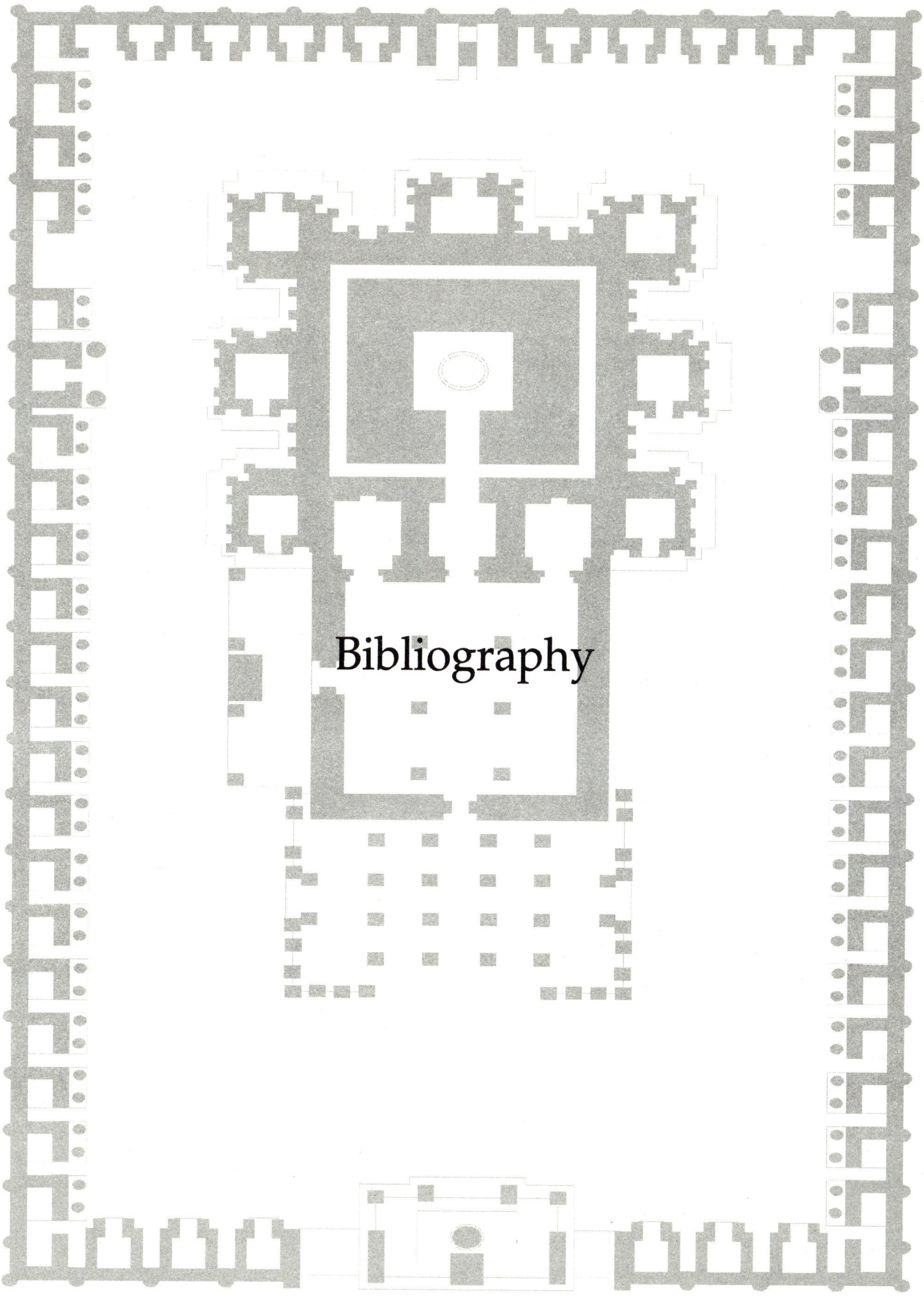

Bibliography

Acharya, P.K., *An Encyclopaedia of Hindu Architecture*, London: 1927-46.

———, *Architecture of Manasara, translated from the Original Sanskrit*, London: 1932.

Banerje, Jitendranath N., *The Development of Hindu Iconography*, 2nd edn. , Calcutta: 1956.

Bary, Theodore de, *Sources of Indian Tradition*, vol. I, New York: 1958.

Brown, Percy, *Indian Architecture* (*Buddhist and Hindu Periods*), Bombay: n.d.

Bunce, Fredrick W., *An Encyclopaedia of Hindu Deities, Demi-Gods, Godlings, Demons and Heroes: With Special Focus on Iconographic Attributes*, 3 vols., New Delhi: 2000.

———, *The Iconography of Architectural Plans: A Study of the Influence of Buddhism and Hinduism on Architectural Plans of South and South-east Asia*, New Delhi: 2002.

———, *Royal Palaces, Residences and Pavilions of India: 13th through 18th Centuries — An Iconographic Consideration*, New Delhi: 2006.

———, *Numbers: Their Iconographic Consideration in Buddhist and Hindu Practices*, New Delhi: 2002.

———, *Monuments of India and the Indianized States*, New Delhi: 2007.

Bussagli, Mario, John Shepley, trs., *Oriental Architecture/1: India, Indonesia, Indochina*, New York: 1989.

Chandra, Pramod, ed., *Studies in Indian Temple Architecture*, Benares: 1975.

Chopra, P.N., T.K. Ravindran and N. Subrahmanian, *History of South India*, 3 vols., New Delhi: 1979.

Cousens, Henry, *The Chalukyan Architecture of the Kanarese Districts* (Archeological Survey of India, vol. XLII, Imperial Series), repr., New Delhi: 1996 (1926).

———, *Bijapur and Its Architectural Remains: With an Historical Outline of the Adil Shahi Dynasty* (Archeological Survey of India, vol. XXXVIII, Imperial Series), repr. Delhi: 1996 (1916).

Dagens, Bruno, ed. and tr., *Mayamata, Traite Sanskrit d'architecture, Premiere Partie*, Paris (?): 1970.

———, *Mayamata, Traite Sanskrit d'architecture, Deuxeme Partie*. Paris (?): 1970.

———, *Mayamatam, Treatise of Housing, Architecture & Iconography*, 2 vols., New Delhi: 1994.

Dallapiccola, Anna et al., *The Ramachandra Temple at Vijayanagara*, New Delhi: 1992.

Danielou, Alain, *Hindu Polytheism*, New York: 1964.

Desai, Devangana, *Khajuraho: Monumental Legacy*, New Delhi: 2000.

Deva, Krishna, *Temples of India*, 2 vols., New Delhi: 1995.

Edwardes, M., *Indian Temples and Palaces*, London: 1959.

Foekema, Gerard, *A Complete Guide to Hoysala Temples*, New Delhi: 1996.

Fritz, J.M., G. Michell and M.S. Nagaraja Rao, *Where Kings and Gods Met: The Royal Centre at Vijayanagara*, Tucson: 1983.

Fritz, J.M. et al., *New Light on Hampi: Recent Research at Vijayanagara*, Mumbai: 2001.

Gollings, J., J.M. Fritz and G. Muchell, *Vijayanagara: City of Victory, a South Indian Hindu Capital*, New York: 1991.

Gopinatha Rao, T.A., *Elements of Hindu Iconography*, 4 vols., Madras: 1914-16; repr., Delhi: 1993.

Grover, Satish, *Masterpieces of Traditional Indian Architecture*, New Delhi: 2004.

Harle, J.C., *Temple Gateways in South India*, Oxford: 1963.

Hardy, Adam, *Indian Temple Architecture: Form and Transformation*, New Delhi: 1995.

Hari Rao, V.N., *The Srirangam Temple: Art and Architecture*, Tirupati: 1967.

Havell, E.B., *Encyclopaedia of Architecture in the Indian Subcontinent*, repr., New Delhi: 2000.

Jung, C.G., *Mandala Symbolism*, tr. R.F.C. Hull, Princeton: 1973.

Kramrisch, S., *The Hindu Temple*, Calcutta: 1946.
Mahapatra, Sthapaka Miranjana, *Silpararnakosa: A Glossary of Orissan Temple Architecture*, New Delhi: 1994.
Michell, George, *The Penguin Guide to the Monuments of India*, Volume I: *Buddhist, Jaina, Hindu*, New York: 1990.
Nilakanta Sastri, *South India Influences in the Far East*. s.l. : 1949.
Rowland, Benjamin, *The Art and Architecture of India: Hindu, Buddhist, Jaina*, Baltimore: 1967.
Sachdev, Vibhuti and Giles Tillotson, *Building Jaipur: The Making of an Indian City*, New Delhi: 2002.
Sarkar, H., *Some Contributions of India to the Ancient Civilization of Indonesia and Malaysia*, Calcutta: 1970.
———, *An Architectural Survey of Temples of Kerala*, New Delhi: 1978.
Sharma, B.N., *Iconographic Parallelism in India and Nepal*, Hyderabad: 1975.
Sherring, M.A., *Banaras: The Sacred City of the Hindus*, London: 1868, repr., Delhi: 1990.
Sivaramamurti, C., *The Art of India*, New York: 1977.
Stierlin, Henri, ed., *Architecture of the World: India*, Lausanne: n.d.
———, *Hindu India: From Khajuraho to the Temple City of Madurai*, Köln: 2002.
Suresh, K.M., *Temples of Hampi: and Its Environs*, Delhi: 2003.
———, *Temples of Karnataka: Ground Plans and Elevations*, Delhi: 2003.
Tadgell, Christopher, *The History of Architecture in India*, London: 1990.
Tewari, S.P., *Hindu Iconography*, New Delhi: 1979.
Thapar, Bindia, *Introduction to Indian Architecture*, Singapore: 2004.
Vatsyayan, Kapila, *The Square and the Circle of the Indian Arts*, New Delhi: 1983.

Internet Sources

www.art-and-archaeology.com/India/konarak/konarakplan.jpg
www.indiantemples.com
www.indiantemples.com/tamilnadu.html
www.sacredsites.com/asia/india/india/html
www.sacredsites.com/asia/India/tiruvanamalai.html
www.srirangam.org
www.sacredsites.com/asia/tamilelibrary.org/teli/temples.html
www.tamilnation.org/culture/architecture/srirangam.html
www.templenet.com/Tamilnadu/df001.html
www.vijayanagara.org/HTML/Sacred.html

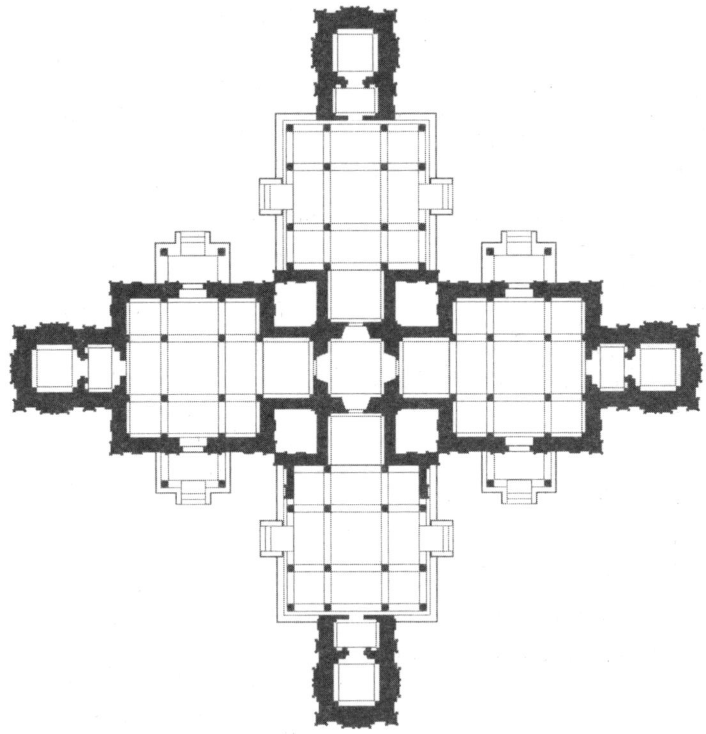